Anonymus

Registrar General of Marriages, Births and Deaths in Ireland

Twenty-eighth annual report, 1891

Anonymus

Registrar General of Marriages, Births and Deaths in Ireland
Twenty-eighth annual report, 1891

ISBN/EAN: 9783742811103

Manufactured in Europe, USA, Canada, Australia, Japa

Cover: Foto ©Suzi / pixelio.de

Manufactured and distributed by brebook publishing software
(www.brebook.com)

Anonymus

Registrar General of Marriages, Births and Deaths in Ireland

TWENTY-EIGHTH

DETAILED

ANNUAL REPORT

OF THE

REGISTRAR-GENERAL (IRELAND):

CONTAINING

A GENERAL ABSTRACT OF THE NUMBERS

OF

MARRIAGES, BIRTHS, AND DEATHS

REGISTERED IN IRELAND

DURING THE YEAR

1891,

TRANSMITTED PURSUANT TO THE PROVISIONS OF THE 7 & 8 VIC., CAP. 81, S. 64;
26 VIC., CAP. 11; AND 26 & 27 VIC., CAP. 90.

GENERAL SUMMARY.

POPULATION. MARRIAGES, THEIR NUMBER AND THEIR RELATION TO POPULATION, RELIGIOUS DENOMINATIONS, AGES, AND CIVIL CONDITION. BIRTHS, THEIR NUMBER AND THEIR RELATION TO POPULATION. DEATHS, THEIR NUMBER AND THEIR RELATION TO POPULATION, AGES, AND CAUSES. EMIGRATION; WEATHER.

Presented to both Houses of Parliament by Command of Her Majesty.

DUBLIN:
PRINTED FOR HER MAJESTY'S STATIONERY OFFICE,
BY ALEXANDER THOM & CO. (LIMITED).

And to be purchased, either directly or through any Bookseller, from
HODGES, FIGGIS, and CO. (Limited), 104, Grafton-street, Dublin; or
EYRE and SPOTTISWOODE, East Harding-street, Fleet-street, E.C.; or
JOHN MENZIES and Co., 12, Hanover-street, Edinburgh, and 90, West Nile-street, Glasgow.

CONTENTS.

REPORT

TO

HIS EXCELLENCY ROBERT OFFLEY ASHBURTON, BARON HOUGHTON,

&c., &c., &c.

LORD LIEUTENANT-GENERAL AND GENERAL GOVERNOR OF IRELAND.

MAY IT PLEASE YOUR EXCELLENCY,—

I have the honour to submit, for your Excellency's consideration, the Twenty-eighth Annual Report on Marriages, Births, and Deaths in Ireland. The tables comprise all the usual details connected with the subject for the year 1891.

GENERAL SUMMARY.

The Marriages registered in Ireland during the year 1891 number 21,475; the Births 108,116; and the Deaths 84,999. The marriage and death rates were slightly above, and the birth-rate slightly below the average for the preceding ten years.

The recorded natural increase of population, or excess of births over deaths, was 23,117: the loss by emigration amounted to 59,623; there would thus appear to have been a decrease of 37,506 in the population during the year, but against a portion of this decrease there is a set-off in immigration, of which no official record has been obtained. The estimated population in the middle of the year (founded on the Census of 1891, and the returns of Births, Deaths, and Emigration for the second quarter of the year) was 4,681,248.

TABLE I.—Showing for each of the years 1881–91, the estimated Population; the number of Marriages, Births, and Deaths registered, and the number of Emigrants enumerated, with the rates per 1,000 of the estimated Population represented thereby; and the averages for the ten years 1881–90.

Years.	*Estimated Population in the middle of each year.	Numbers Registered.			Number of Emigrants as returned by the Enumerators.	Rate per 1,000 of Estimated Population.			
		Marriages.	Births.	Deaths.		Marriages.	Births.	Deaths.	Emigrants.
1881,	[illegible]	[illegible]	[illegible]	[illegible]	[illegible]	[illegible]	[illegible]	[illegible]	[illegible]
1882,	[illegible]	[illegible]	[illegible]	[illegible]	[illegible]	[illegible]	[illegible]	[illegible]	[illegible]
1883,	[illegible]	[illegible]	[illegible]	[illegible]	[illegible]	[illegible]	[illegible]	[illegible]	[illegible]
1884,	[illegible]	[illegible]	[illegible]	[illegible]	[illegible]	[illegible]	[illegible]	[illegible]	[illegible]
1885,	[illegible]	[illegible]	[illegible]	[illegible]	[illegible]	[illegible]	[illegible]	[illegible]	[illegible]
1886,	[illegible]	[illegible]	116,977	[illegible]	[illegible]	[illegible]	[illegible]	[illegible]	[illegible]
1887,	[illegible]	[illegible]	[illegible]	[illegible]	[illegible]	[illegible]	[illegible]	[illegible]	[illegible]
1888,	[illegible]	[illegible]	[illegible]	[illegible]	[illegible]	[illegible]	[illegible]	[illegible]	[illegible]
1889,	[illegible]	[illegible]	[illegible]	[illegible]	[illegible]	[illegible]	[illegible]	[illegible]	[illegible]
1890,	[illegible]	[illegible]	[illegible]	[illegible]	[illegible]	[illegible]	[illegible]	[illegible]	[illegible]
Yearly Average, 1881–90,	[illegible]	[illegible]	[illegible]	[illegible]	[illegible]	[illegible]	[illegible]	[illegible]	[illegible]
1891,	[illegible]	21,476	108,116	[illegible]	[illegible]	[illegible]	[illegible]	[illegible]	[illegible]

There are 2,814 Local Registration Officers holding office directly under the Department or who have entered into bonds with the Registrar-General for the due discharge of their duties. During the year 1891, 520 cases of vacancies or appointments were dealt with.

* See page 163.

A

I append a table showing the number of Searches, &c., since the commencement of the Acts for the Registration of Births and Deaths and of Roman Catholic Marriages in 1864. It will be observed that the steady increase in the number of searches and in the number of certified copies issued noted in recent years was maintained in 1891.

TABLE II.—NUMBER of SEARCHES made; number of CERTIFICATES issued, and AMOUNT received as FEES for SEARCHES, &c., at the GENERAL REGISTER OFFICE, DUBLIN, during the 28 years 1864–91.

YEARS.	Annual Number of Searches in the Registers.	Annual Number of Certificates.	Amount received as Fees for Searches, &c., and paid into Her Majesty's Exchequer.	YEARS.	Annual Number of Searches in the Registers.	Annual Number of Certificates.	Amount received as Fees for Searches, &c., and paid into Her Majesty's Exchequer.
			£ s. d.				£ s. d.
1864, . .	17	8	9 13 6	1878, . .	[illegible]	[illegible]	[illegible]
1865, . .	41	[illegible]	4 17 3	1879, . .	[illegible]	[illegible]	[illegible]
1866, . .	[illegible]	34	[illegible]	1880, . .	[illegible]	[illegible]	[illegible]
1867, . .	[illegible]	[illegible]	11 5 9	1881, . .	[illegible]	[illegible]	[illegible]
1868, . .	[illegible]	47	[illegible]	1882, . .	[illegible]	[illegible]	[illegible]
1869, . .	[illegible]	[illegible]	[illegible]	1883, . .	[illegible]	[illegible]	[illegible]
1870, . .	[illegible]	[illegible]	[illegible]	1884, . .	[illegible]	[illegible]	[illegible]
1871, . .	111	47	[illegible]	1885, . .	[illegible]	[illegible]	[illegible]
1872, . .	[illegible]	[illegible]	[illegible]	1886, . .	[illegible]	[illegible]	[illegible]
1873, . .	[illegible]	[illegible]	[illegible]	1887, . .	[illegible]	[illegible]	[illegible]
1874, . .	[illegible]	[illegible]	[illegible]	1888, . .	[illegible]	[illegible]	[illegible]
1875, . .	[illegible]	[illegible]	[illegible]	1889, . .	[illegible]	[illegible]	[illegible]
1876, . .	[illegible]	[illegible]	[illegible]	1890, . .	[illegible]	[illegible]	[illegible]
1877, . .	[illegible]	[illegible]	[illegible]	1891, . .	[illegible]	[illegible]	[illegible]

During the financial year ended 31st March last 434 cases were reported of offences against the Acts administered by this Department. On careful inquiry into the circumstances, in 164 cases prosecutions were ordered to be instituted against the offenders. In 69 of these the parties were convicted and punished; in 92 the proceedings were abandoned, the parties (in most instances) paying the costs of court and complying with the law; and in 3 cases the summonses were dismissed.

The cases dealt with included the following offences:—Neglect to register Births, neglect to register Deaths, neglect to furnish Certificate of Marriage, failure of Coroner to furnish Certificate of Inquest; giving false information as to age at death, as to cause of death, and as to duration of illness previous to death; giving false information as to Births, viz.—registering illegitimate children as legitimate, and misrepresenting date of birth; omitting to send notification of burial to the Registrar, &c.

The administration of the legal work of the office is, as mentioned in my Reports for 1888 and 1890, entrusted to Mr. Matheson, whose detailed statement of the business transacted will be found at page 169.

One of the cases cited by Mr. Matheson affords another illustration of the methods adopted by unscrupulous persons to secure some small pecuniary advantage by a falsification of the registers, to which I made reference in my last Report. In this instance:—

> C. P. was prosecuted at the Metropolitan Police Court for wilfully giving false information to the Registrar of South City No. 1 District, as to the age of her child, when registering its death, with the view of obtaining, from certain Societies, moneys in excess of the amount prescribed by the Friendly Societies' Acts. She was convicted, and fined £3 or six weeks' imprisonment.

Another of the cases supplies an example of the difficulties experienced by the Registrars in carrying out the provisions of the Burial Sections of the Public Health and Registration Acts. Thus:—

> M. D. was prosecuted at Emyvale Petty Sessions, as Caretaker of a Burial Ground, for neglecting to furnish to the Registrar of Glaslough District the notification of a burial required by sec. 17 of the 43 and 44 Vic., cap. 13. She was convicted and fined with costs.

TABLE III.—Showing, for each PROVINCE and COUNTY in IRELAND, the RATE per 1,000 of the POPULATION, represented by the NUMBER of MARRIAGES, BIRTHS, and DEATHS Registered during the Year 1891.

PROVINCES AND COUNTIES.	Annual Rate per 1,000 of the Population, represented by		
	Marriages.	Births.	Deaths.
IRELAND,	[illegible]	[illegible]	[illegible]
PROVINCES.			
I. LEINSTER,	[illegible]	[illegible]	[illegible]
II. MUNSTER,	[illegible]	[illegible]	[illegible]
III. ULSTER,	[illegible]	[illegible]	[illegible]
IV. CONNAUGHT,	[illegible]	[illegible]	[illegible]
I. LEINSTER.			
Carlow,	[illegible]	[illegible]	[illegible]
Dublin,	[illegible]	[illegible]	[illegible]
Kildare,	[illegible]	[illegible]	[illegible]
Kilkenny,	[illegible]	[illegible]	[illegible]
King's,	[illegible]	[illegible]	[illegible]
Longford,	[illegible]	[illegible]	[illegible]
Louth and Co. of Town of Drogheda,	[illegible]	[illegible]	[illegible]
Meath,	[illegible]	[illegible]	[illegible]
Queen's,	[illegible]	[illegible]	[illegible]
Westmeath,	[illegible]	[illegible]	[illegible]
Wexford,	[illegible]	[illegible]	[illegible]
Wicklow,	[illegible]	[illegible]	[illegible]

PROVINCES AND COUNTIES.	Annual Rate per 1,000 of the Population, represented by		
	Marriages.	Births.	Deaths.
II. MUNSTER.			
Clare,	[illegible]	[illegible]	[illegible]
Cork,	[illegible]	[illegible]	[illegible]
Kerry,	[illegible]	[illegible]	[illegible]
Limerick,	[illegible]	[illegible]	[illegible]
Tipperary,	[illegible]	[illegible]	[illegible]
Waterford,	[illegible]	[illegible]	[illegible]
III. ULSTER.			
Antrim,	[illegible]	[illegible]	[illegible]
Armagh,	[illegible]	[illegible]	[illegible]
Cavan,	[illegible]	[illegible]	[illegible]
Donegal,	[illegible]	[illegible]	[illegible]
Down,	[illegible]	[illegible]	[illegible]
Fermanagh,	[illegible]	[illegible]	[illegible]
Londonderry,	[illegible]	[illegible]	[illegible]
Monaghan,	[illegible]	[illegible]	[illegible]
Tyrone,	[illegible]	[illegible]	[illegible]
IV. CONNAUGHT.			
Galway,	[illegible]	[illegible]	[illegible]
Leitrim,	[illegible]	[illegible]	[illegible]
Mayo,	[illegible]	[illegible]	[illegible]
Roscommon,	[illegible]	[illegible]	[illegible]
Sligo,	[illegible]	[illegible]	[illegible]

MARRIAGES.

I regret to state that in 19 cases returns relating to a portion of the year 1891 have not yet been furnished by the clergy of the Church of Ireland, and in 5 instances by the Presbyterian clergy connected with the General Assembly. The number of marriages celebrated in the majority of these churches is known to have been small, and would not appreciably affect the general statistical results for Ireland, but nevertheless it is unsatisfactory to have to notice even any omissions to comply with Sec. 65 of 7 & 8 Vic., cap. 81, under which these returns are required from the clergy.

The number of Marriages registered during the year is 21,475, being equal to 1 in every 218, or 4·59 per 1,000, of the estimated population,* a rate which is ·14 over that for the previous year, and ·26 above the average for the ten years 1881–90.

Of the 21,475 Marriages registered during the year 1891, 14,697 were between Roman Catholics, 3,570 were celebrated according to the rites and ceremonies of the Church of Ireland; 2,353 were in Presbyterian Meeting-houses; 442 in "Registered Buildings" belonging to various religious denominations; only 399 by civil contract in the Registrars' offices; 4 were according to the usages of the Society of Friends; and 10 according to the Jewish rites.

Of the 3,570 Marriages according to the rites of the Church of Ireland, 38 were by special license, 3,013 by license, 480 after the publication of banns, 8 on Registrar's certificate, and in 31 instances there was no information afforded as to which of these methods was adopted.

TABLE IV.—Marriages registered in Ireland in 1891 and each of the previous ten years, according to the modes of celebration; with the rate per 1,000 of the people thus represented:—

Years.	Marriages registered under 7 and 8 Vic., cap. 81. According to the Rites of the Church of Ireland.	In Registered Presbyterian Meeting-houses.	In Registered Buildings.	In the Registrars' Offices.	Society of Friends.	Jews.	Total.	Roman Catholic Marriages.	Total Marriages Registered.	Rate per 1,000 of estimated corresponding Population represented by Marriages under 7 and 8 Vic., cap. 81.	Roman Catholic Marriages.	Total Marriages.
1881,	[illegible]	[illegible]	[illegible]	[illegible]	[illegible]	[illegible]	[illegible]	[illegible]	[illegible]	[illegible]	[illegible]	[illegible]
1882,	[illegible]	[illegible]	[illegible]	[illegible]	[illegible]	[illegible]	[illegible]	[illegible]	[illegible]	[illegible]	[illegible]	[illegible]
1883,	[illegible]	[illegible]	[illegible]	[illegible]	[illegible]	[illegible]	[illegible]	[illegible]	[illegible]	[illegible]	[illegible]	[illegible]
1884,	[illegible]	[illegible]	[illegible]	[illegible]	[illegible]	[illegible]	[illegible]	[illegible]	[illegible]	[illegible]	[illegible]	[illegible]
1885,	[illegible]	[illegible]	[illegible]	[illegible]	[illegible]	[illegible]	[illegible]	[illegible]	[illegible]	[illegible]	[illegible]	[illegible]
1886,	[illegible]	[illegible]	[illegible]	[illegible]	[illegible]	[illegible]	[illegible]	[illegible]	[illegible]	[illegible]	[illegible]	[illegible]
1887,	[illegible]	[illegible]	[illegible]	[illegible]	[illegible]	[illegible]	[illegible]	[illegible]	[illegible]	[illegible]	[illegible]	[illegible]
1888,	[illegible]	[illegible]	[illegible]	[illegible]	[illegible]	[illegible]	[illegible]	[illegible]	[illegible]	[illegible]	[illegible]	[illegible]
1889,	[illegible]	[illegible]	[illegible]	[illegible]	[illegible]	[illegible]	[illegible]	[illegible]	[illegible]	[illegible]	[illegible]	[illegible]
1890,	[illegible]	[illegible]	[illegible]	[illegible]	[illegible]	[illegible]	[illegible]	[illegible]	[illegible]	[illegible]	[illegible]	[illegible]
Average 1881–90,	[illegible]	[illegible]	373	[illegible]	[illegible]	[illegible]	[illegible]	[illegible]	[illegible]	[illegible]	[illegible]	[illegible]
1891,	[illegible]	[illegible]	[illegible]	[illegible]	[illegible]	[illegible]	[illegible]	[illegible]	[illegible]	[illegible]	[illegible]	[illegible]

During the year 1891 there were issued by the Registrars 738 Licences for Marriage in Registered Buildings and in the Registrars' offices.

The number of Marriage Licences issued by the licensing Ministers of the several Presbyterian bodies is given in the following summary:—

Presbytery or Synod.	Number of Licensing Ministers on 31st December, 1891.	Number of Registered Meeting-houses on 31st December, 1891.	Number of Licences issued.
1. General Assembly of the Presbyterian Church in Ireland,	[illegible]	587	[illegible]
2. Remonstrant Synod of Ulster,	7	10	[illegible]
3. Presbytery of Antrim,	[illegible]	[illegible]	[illegible]
4. United Presbytery or Synod of Munster,	[illegible]	[illegible]	[illegible]
5. Northern Presbytery of Antrim,	[illegible]	[illegible]	[illegible]
Total,	[illegible]	601	[illegible]

There being no civil restrictions as to the time or place for celebrating marriages between Roman Catholics in Ireland, a registration of the churches and chapels of the Roman Catholic Church is not necessary for the purposes of this office; but with reference to other religious bodies, a record is kept of the places of Divine worship in which marriages may lawfully be solemnized without special licence, and from this it appears that, on the 31st December, 1891, there were 1,193 churches and chapels of the Church of Ireland, 601 registered Presbyterian Meeting-houses, and 359 "Registered Buildings" belonging to various religious denominations. Compared with the previous year, these numbers show a decrease of 2 as regards the Church of Ireland, an increase of 1 in the number of Presbyterian Meeting-houses, and an increase of 4 "Registered Buildings."

The following statement shows the several religious bodies having "Registered Buildings" in 1891:—

Denomination.	No. of Places of Worship.	Denomination.	No. of Places of Worship.	Denomination.	No. of Places of Worship.
Methodists,	214	Salvation Army,	7	United Original Seceders,	1
Reformed Presbyterians,	39	Christian Brethren,	8	"Protestant Dissenters,"	1
Independents,	25	Evangelical Union,	3	Non-Subscribing Christians,	1
Baptists,	20	Non-Subscribing Unitarians,	1	"The Catholic Apostolic Church,"	2
Seceders,	10	Jews,	3	Independent Protestants,	1
United Presbyterians,	8	Unitarians,	1		
Methodists, New Connexion,	7	Covenanters,	1	Total,	359
Moravians, or United Brethren,	7				

As more than a moiety of the annual number of Roman Catholic marriages in the provinces of Munster and Connaught are celebrated between Christmas and Shrovetide, the marriages registered in Ireland during the first quarter of the year always largely outnumber those in any of the other quarters. In 1891, the numbers recorded were—in the first quarter 6,353; in the second, 4,990; in the third, 4,311; and in the last, 4,821.

The marriages of bachelors and spinsters constitute 86·5 per cent. of the total; those of widowers and spinsters 8·6 per cent.; of bachelors and widows 2·7 per cent.; and of widowers and widows 2·2 per cent. Thus, 11 in every 100 of the men married were widowers, and 4·9 per cent. of the women were widows; and in 14 instances in every 100 marriages one or both of the contracting parties had been in the married state before.

TABLE V.—Showing by QUARTERLY PERIODS, the number of MARRIAGES registered in Ireland in each of the eleven years 1881–91, and the average number for the ten years 1881–90, distinguishing the number of Roman Catholic marriages registered under the 26 & 27 Vic., cap. 90, and of Protestant and other marriages under the 7 & 8 Vic., cap. 81:—

YEAR.	MARRIAGES.														
	Roman Catholic.					Others.					Total.				
	Quarter ending the last day of				Total.	Quarter ending the last day of				Total.	Quarter ending the last day of				Total.
	Mar.	June.	Sep.	Dec.		Mar.	June.	Sep.	Dec.		Mar.	June.	Sep.	Dec.	
1881, . . .	[illegible]	[illegible]	[illegible]	[illegible]	[illegible]	[illegible]	[illegible]	[illegible]	[illegible]	[illegible]	[illegible]	[illegible]	[illegible]	[illegible]	[illegible]
1882, . . .	[illegible]	[illegible]	[illegible]	[illegible]	[illegible]	[illegible]	[illegible]	[illegible]	[illegible]	[illegible]	[illegible]	[illegible]	[illegible]	[illegible]	[illegible]
1883, . . .	[illegible]	[illegible]	[illegible]	[illegible]	[illegible]	[illegible]	[illegible]	[illegible]	[illegible]	[illegible]	[illegible]	[illegible]	[illegible]	[illegible]	[illegible]
1884, . . .	[illegible]	[illegible]	[illegible]	[illegible]	[illegible]	[illegible]	[illegible]	[illegible]	[illegible]	[illegible]	[illegible]	[illegible]	[illegible]	[illegible]	[illegible]
1885, . . .	[illegible]	[illegible]	[illegible]	[illegible]	[illegible]	[illegible]	[illegible]	[illegible]	[illegible]	[illegible]	[illegible]	[illegible]	[illegible]	[illegible]	[illegible]
1886, . . .	[illegible]	[illegible]	[illegible]	[illegible]	[illegible]	[illegible]	[illegible]	[illegible]	[illegible]	[illegible]	[illegible]	[illegible]	[illegible]	[illegible]	[illegible]
1887, . . .	[illegible]	[illegible]	[illegible]	[illegible]	[illegible]	[illegible]	[illegible]	[illegible]	[illegible]	[illegible]	[illegible]	[illegible]	[illegible]	[illegible]	[illegible]
1888, . . .	[illegible]	[illegible]	[illegible]	[illegible]	[illegible]	[illegible]	[illegible]	[illegible]	[illegible]	[illegible]	[illegible]	[illegible]	[illegible]	[illegible]	[illegible]
1889, . . .	[illegible]	[illegible]	[illegible]	[illegible]	[illegible]	[illegible]	[illegible]	[illegible]	[illegible]	[illegible]	[illegible]	[illegible]	[illegible]	[illegible]	[illegible]
1890, . . .	[illegible]	[illegible]	[illegible]	[illegible]	[illegible]	[illegible]	[illegible]	[illegible]	[illegible]	[illegible]	[illegible]	[illegible]	[illegible]	[illegible]	[illegible]
Average for ten years, 1881–90,	[illegible]	[illegible]	[illegible]	[illegible]	[illegible]	[illegible]	[illegible]	[illegible]	[illegible]	[illegible]	[illegible]	[illegible]	[illegible]	[illegible]	[illegible]
1891, . . .	[illegible]	[illegible]	[illegible]	[illegible]	[illegible]	[illegible]	[illegible]	[illegible]	[illegible]	[illegible]	[illegible]	[illegible]	[illegible]	[illegible]	[illegible]
Equivalent Annual Rate per 1,000 living in—															
Average, 1881–90,	[illegible]	[illegible]	[illegible]	[illegible]	[illegible]	[illegible]	[illegible]	[illegible]	[illegible]	[illegible]	[illegible]	[illegible]	[illegible]	[illegible]	[illegible]
1891, . . .	[illegible]	[illegible]	[illegible]	[illegible]	[illegible]	[illegible]	[illegible]	[illegible]	[illegible]	[illegible]	[illegible]	[illegible]	[illegible]	[illegible]	[illegible]

A complete registry of the exact ages of the persons married would be valuable from many points of view; hence it is matter for regret that in the great majority of instances the ages are not recorded. The requirements of the law are technically complied with by the entry in the age column of "minor" or of "full age," as the case may be, and there seems to be a general and increasing inclination to take advantage of this circumstance, as in 1891 the ages of both parties were specified in only 4,568 instances, being little more than one-fifth of the total number of marriages. In the year 1865, when 30,802 marriages were registered, the ages of both parties were given in 13,910 instances.

Of 21,475 men married during the year, 424, or 1·97 per cent., were minors; and of the women married, 1,892, or 8·81 per cent., were under age. These proportions are considerably below the averages for the preceding ten years.

The highest proportion of husbands (2·49 per cent.) married under age in 1891, was in the province of Ulster, and in that province there was also the highest per-centage of wives (9·72), not of full age.

It may be added that the per-centage of persons married in Ireland who were under age is very far below the corresponding rates in England and Scotland.

The signatures of the contracting parties in the marriage registers or certificates afford a rough test of the progress of elementary education. In the year 1891, 17,318, or 80·6 per cent., of the husbands, and 17,303, or 80·6 per cent., of the wives, wrote their names, and the remainder signed by marks.

These figures, though still leaving much to be desired, contrast hopefully with the corresponding results eleven years since, the per-centage of persons married in 1881 who wrote their names being—men 78·9, and women 69·3.

The per-centages for the several provinces last year range, *for men*, from 73 in Connaught to 84 in Leinster, and, for women, from 77 in Ulster to 84 in Leinster.

In 2,170 instances, both of the parties married signed the register by "mark," and in 3,994 cases the register was thus signed by either the husband or the wife, so that in 6,164 instances, or 28·7 per cent. of the total number of marriages, one or both of the parties signed by mark; and in 15,311 instances, or 71·3 per cent., *both* parties wrote their names.

The number of marriages registered in each of the eleven years 1881–91; the proportion per cent. of persons married who wrote their names in the registers; of minors, of widowers, and of widows are given in the following Table for Ireland, and for each of the four provinces.

TABLE VI.—Showing as regards the Marriages in Ireland and in each of the Four Provinces during the years 1881–91, the proportion per cent. of Persons who signed their Names, of Persons not of Full Age, and of Re-marriages. The figures for the years 1881–84 refer to Registration Provinces; those for 1885–91 to the Provinces Proper.

Provinces.	Year	Signed their Names in the Register: Of 100 Men Married	Signed their Names in the Register: Of 100 Women Married	Persons not of Full Age: Of 100 Men Married	Persons not of Full Age: Of 100 Women Married	Re-marriages: Widowers: Of 100 Men Married	Re-marriages: Widows: Of 100 Women Married
IRELAND.	1881	[illegible]	[illegible]	[illegible]	[illegible]	[illegible]	[illegible]
	1882	[illegible]	[illegible]	[illegible]	[illegible]	[illegible]	[illegible]
	1883	[illegible]	[illegible]	[illegible]	[illegible]	[illegible]	[illegible]
	1884	[illegible]	[illegible]	[illegible]	[illegible]	[illegible]	[illegible]
	1885	[illegible]	[illegible]	[illegible]	[illegible]	[illegible]	[illegible]
	1886	[illegible]	[illegible]	[illegible]	[illegible]	[illegible]	[illegible]
	1887	[illegible]	[illegible]	[illegible]	[illegible]	[illegible]	[illegible]
	1888	[illegible]	[illegible]	[illegible]	[illegible]	[illegible]	[illegible]
	1889	[illegible]	[illegible]	[illegible]	[illegible]	[illegible]	[illegible]
	1890	[illegible]	[illegible]	[illegible]	[illegible]	[illegible]	[illegible]
	1891	[illegible]	[illegible]	[illegible]	[illegible]	[illegible]	[illegible]
LEINSTER.	1881	[illegible]	[illegible]	[illegible]	[illegible]	[illegible]	[illegible]
	1882	[illegible]	[illegible]	[illegible]	[illegible]	[illegible]	[illegible]
	1883	[illegible]	[illegible]	[illegible]	[illegible]	[illegible]	[illegible]
	1884	[illegible]	[illegible]	[illegible]	[illegible]	[illegible]	[illegible]
	1885	[illegible]	[illegible]	[illegible]	[illegible]	[illegible]	[illegible]
	1886	[illegible]	[illegible]	[illegible]	[illegible]	[illegible]	[illegible]
	1887	[illegible]	[illegible]	[illegible]	[illegible]	[illegible]	[illegible]
	1888	[illegible]	[illegible]	[illegible]	[illegible]	[illegible]	[illegible]
	1889	[illegible]	[illegible]	[illegible]	[illegible]	[illegible]	[illegible]
	1890	[illegible]	[illegible]	[illegible]	[illegible]	[illegible]	[illegible]
	1891	[illegible]	[illegible]	[illegible]	[illegible]	[illegible]	[illegible]
MUNSTER.	1881	[illegible]	[illegible]	[illegible]	[illegible]	[illegible]	[illegible]
	1882	[illegible]	[illegible]	[illegible]	[illegible]	[illegible]	[illegible]
	1883	[illegible]	[illegible]	[illegible]	[illegible]	[illegible]	[illegible]
	1884	[illegible]	[illegible]	[illegible]	[illegible]	[illegible]	[illegible]
	1885	[illegible]	[illegible]	[illegible]	[illegible]	[illegible]	[illegible]
MUNSTER—continued.	1886	[illegible]	[illegible]	[illegible]	[illegible]	[illegible]	[illegible]
	1887	[illegible]	[illegible]	[illegible]	[illegible]	[illegible]	[illegible]
	1888	[illegible]	[illegible]	[illegible]	[illegible]	[illegible]	[illegible]
	1889	[illegible]	[illegible]	[illegible]	[illegible]	[illegible]	[illegible]
	1890	[illegible]	[illegible]	[illegible]	[illegible]	[illegible]	[illegible]
	1891	[illegible]	[illegible]	[illegible]	[illegible]	[illegible]	[illegible]
ULSTER.	1881	[illegible]	[illegible]	[illegible]	[illegible]	[illegible]	[illegible]
	1882	[illegible]	[illegible]	[illegible]	[illegible]	[illegible]	[illegible]
	1883	[illegible]	[illegible]	[illegible]	[illegible]	[illegible]	[illegible]
	1884	[illegible]	[illegible]	[illegible]	[illegible]	[illegible]	[illegible]
	1885	[illegible]	[illegible]	[illegible]	[illegible]	[illegible]	[illegible]
	1886	[illegible]	[illegible]	[illegible]	[illegible]	[illegible]	[illegible]
	1887	[illegible]	[illegible]	[illegible]	[illegible]	[illegible]	[illegible]
	1888	[illegible]	[illegible]	[illegible]	[illegible]	[illegible]	[illegible]
	1889	[illegible]	[illegible]	[illegible]	[illegible]	[illegible]	[illegible]
	1890	[illegible]	[illegible]	[illegible]	[illegible]	[illegible]	[illegible]
	1891	[illegible]	[illegible]	[illegible]	[illegible]	[illegible]	[illegible]
CONNAUGHT.	1881	[illegible]	[illegible]	[illegible]	[illegible]	[illegible]	[illegible]
	1882	[illegible]	[illegible]	[illegible]	[illegible]	[illegible]	[illegible]
	1883	[illegible]	[illegible]	[illegible]	[illegible]	[illegible]	[illegible]
	1884	[illegible]	[illegible]	[illegible]	[illegible]	[illegible]	[illegible]
	1885	[illegible]	[illegible]	[illegible]	[illegible]	[illegible]	[illegible]
	1886	[illegible]	[illegible]	[illegible]	[illegible]	[illegible]	[illegible]
	1887	[illegible]	[illegible]	[illegible]	[illegible]	[illegible]	[illegible]
	1888	[illegible]	[illegible]	[illegible]	[illegible]	[illegible]	[illegible]
	1889	[illegible]	[illegible]	[illegible]	[illegible]	[illegible]	[illegible]
	1890	[illegible]	[illegible]	[illegible]	[illegible]	[illegible]	[illegible]
	1891	[illegible]	[illegible]	[illegible]	[illegible]	[illegible]	[illegible]

In proportion to the estimated population at all ages, the registered marriages were most numerous in the province of Ulster, in which, however, the rate was only 5·2 per 1,000 of the population in 1891; Leinster comes next, with 5·0 per 1,000; Munster third, with 4·0 per 1,000; and Connaught last, the rate being 3·3 per 1,000.

The highest rate for any county was 7·6 per 1,000 of the population in 1891, which was the marriage rate for Antrim; and the lowest 3·0 per 1,000, for Galway. Between these, the most favourable were 7·0 for Dublin, and 5·2 for Down; and the least so 3·1 for Meath, and 3·2 for Mayo and Sligo.

BIRTHS.

The number of births registered during the year 1891 was 108,116—55,476 boys and 52,640 girls, or 105·4 of the former to every 100 of the latter—the rate afforded in proportion to the estimated population being 1 in 43·3, or 23·1 per thousand, which is 0·3 under the low average rate for the ten years, 1881–90.

Of the 108,116 children whose births were registered in Ireland during the year 1891, 105,216, or 97·3 per cent. were legitimate, and 2,900, or 2·7 per cent., were illegitimate: these were also the average per-centages for the preceding 10 years. It is unnecessary to say that these results compare very favourably with the returns for most other countries.

Of the children born in wedlock during the year, 54,002 were males, and 51,214 females, being 105·4 of the former to every 100 of the latter, and of the illegitimate children 1,474 were males, and 1,426 females, or 103·4 boys to 100 girls.

Comparing the provinces, we find that the per-centage of children born in Ulster, who were illegitimate, was 4·0; in Leinster, 2·4; in Munster, 2·2; and in Connaught, 0·7.

TABLE VII.—The Per-centage of Legitimate and of Illegitimate Births registered in Ireland during the years 1887–91, by Provinces.

Provinces.	Proportion per cent. of Legitimate Births.					Proportion per cent. of Illegitimate Births.				
	1887.	1888.	1889.	1890.	1891.	1887.	1888.	1889.	1890.	1891.
IRELAND, . . .	[illegible]	[illegible]	[illegible]	[illegible]	[illegible]	[illegible]	[illegible]	[illegible]	[illegible]	[illegible]
LEINSTER, . . .	[illegible]	[illegible]	[illegible]	[illegible]	[illegible]	[illegible]	[illegible]	[illegible]	[illegible]	[illegible]
MUNSTER, . . .	[illegible]	[illegible]	[illegible]	[illegible]	[illegible]	[illegible]	[illegible]	[illegible]	[illegible]	[illegible]
ULSTER, . . .	[illegible]	[illegible]	[illegible]	[illegible]	[illegible]	[illegible]	[illegible]	[illegible]	[illegible]	[illegible]
CONNAUGHT, . . .	[illegible]	[illegible]	[illegible]	[illegible]	[illegible]	[illegible]	[illegible]	[illegible]	[illegible]	[illegible]

The respective total birth-rates for the provinces in 1891 were—Leinster, 23·0 per 1,000 of the population in 1891; Munster, 22·9; Ulster, 24·0; and Connaught, 22·0.

The four counties having the highest rates are Antrim, 29·1 per 1,000 of the population in 1891; Dublin, 27·4; Down, 26·2; and Armagh, 23·7. Those with the lowest rates are—Monaghan, 18·5; Fermanagh, 18·8; Meath, 19·1; and Cavan, 19·2.

Of the total births, 53·2 per cent. were registered in the first six months of the year (181 days), and 46·8 per cent. in the second half of the year (184 days).

The number registered in the first quarter was 28,442; in the second, 29,101; in the third, 25,879; and in the fourth, 24,701.

DEATHS.

The deaths registered during the year amount to 85,999, being equal to 1 in 54·4 or 18·4 per 1,000 of the estimated population. The deaths of males number 42,090, and those of females 43,909, the former being equal to 18·2 in every 1,000 males living, and the latter representing 18·5 per 1,000 females.

As already stated the death-rate (18·4) was somewhat over the average rate for the preceding ten years, which was 17·9 per 1,000.

As usual, very many of the Registrars furnished at the close of each quarter valuable notes on the sanitary condition of their respective districts. These notes were embodied in the Quarterly Returns issued from this department, and emanating as they did, from gentlemen qualified to speak decisively on the subject, it is to be hoped that they received the serious attention of the various Local Authorities intrusted with the administration of the Public Health Acts.

With respect to the death-rates for the four provinces, the rate for Connaught is only 13·2; that for Munster is 17·2; for Ulster, 19·3, and for Leinster, 19·8 per 1,000 of the population in 1891.

Of the thirty-two counties, the four having the lowest registered mortality are—Kerry, 14·0 per 1,000; Sligo, 14·2; Clare, 11·9; and Roscommon, 13·0.

Those in which the rate was highest are—Dublin, 24·6; Antrim, 22·4; Armagh, 20·4; and Down, 20·2.

The deaths registered in the first half of the year generally outnumber those in the second. In 1891, 55·3 per cent. of the total deaths were registered in the six months, January to June inclusive, and only 44·7 per cent. in the remaining six months of the year.

The annual rates represented by the deaths registered in each quarter are as follow:—First quarter, 21·4 per 1,000 of the population; second, 19·2; third, 14·6; and fourth, 18·3.

From the Table on pp. 168–177 it will be seen that, of the 85,999 deaths registered during the year, 2,132 took place in Infirmaries and General and Special Hospitals; 888 in Public Lunatic Asylums; 10,176 in Workhouses and Workhouse Hospitals; and 72,803 were of persons who died "At their Own Homes, &c." As in former Reports a Table (see pages 178–9) is given showing like information for those Registrars' Districts in which the principal Urban Sanitary Districts in Ireland are situated.

The deaths in "Infirmaries and General and Special Hospitals" constitute 9·6 per cent. of the total number, the per-centages for the four provinces varying from 0·3 in Connaught to 6·1 in Leinster. Twelve per cent. of the deaths registered occurred in Workhouses or Workhouse Hospitals, the respective per-centages for the provinces being—Leinster, 13·7; Munster, 16·1; Ulster, 7·4; and Connaught, 9·9.

TABLE VIII.—Showing, by Quarterly Periods, the number of Births and Deaths registered in Ireland in each of the eleven years, 1881–91, and the average number for the ten years, 1881–90.

Year.	Births.					Deaths.				
	Quarter ending the last day of				Total.	Quarter ending the last day of				Total.
	March.	June.	Sept.	Dec.		March.	June.	Sept.	Dec.	
1881,	[illegible]	[illegible]	[illegible]	[illegible]	[illegible]	[illegible]	[illegible]	[illegible]	[illegible]	[illegible]
1882,	[illegible]	[illegible]	[illegible]	[illegible]	[illegible]	[illegible]	[illegible]	[illegible]	[illegible]	[illegible]
1883,	[illegible]	[illegible]	[illegible]	[illegible]	[illegible]	[illegible]	[illegible]	[illegible]	[illegible]	[illegible]
1884,	[illegible]	[illegible]	[illegible]	[illegible]	[illegible]	[illegible]	[illegible]	[illegible]	[illegible]	[illegible]
1885,	[illegible]	[illegible]	[illegible]	[illegible]	[illegible]	[illegible]	[illegible]	[illegible]	[illegible]	[illegible]
1886,	[illegible]	[illegible]	[illegible]	[illegible]	[illegible]	[illegible]	[illegible]	[illegible]	[illegible]	[illegible]
1887,	[illegible]	[illegible]	[illegible]	[illegible]	[illegible]	[illegible]	[illegible]	[illegible]	[illegible]	[illegible]
1888,	[illegible]	[illegible]	[illegible]	[illegible]	[illegible]	[illegible]	[illegible]	[illegible]	[illegible]	[illegible]
1889,	[illegible]	[illegible]	[illegible]	[illegible]	[illegible]	[illegible]	[illegible]	[illegible]	[illegible]	[illegible]
1890,	[illegible]	[illegible]	[illegible]	[illegible]	[illegible]	[illegible]	[illegible]	[illegible]	[illegible]	[illegible]
Average for 10 years, 1881–90,	[illegible]	[illegible]	[illegible]	[illegible]	[illegible]	[illegible]	[illegible]	[illegible]	[illegible]	[illegible]
1891,	[illegible]	[illegible]	[illegible]	[illegible]	[illegible]	[illegible]	[illegible]	[illegible]	[illegible]	[illegible]
Equivalent Annual Rate per 1,000 living:—										
Average, 1881–90,	[illegible]	[illegible]	[illegible]	[illegible]	[illegible]	[illegible]	[illegible]	[illegible]	[illegible]	[illegible]
1891,	[illegible]	[illegible]	[illegible]	[illegible]	[illegible]	[illegible]	[illegible]	[illegible]	[illegible]	[illegible]

CAUSES OF

The following TABLE (IX.) shows (1) the Number of Deaths from All Causes and from present Classification of Causes of Death was adopted, and (2) the respective

YEARS	Total Number of Deaths.	CAUSES OF DEATH.											
		SPECIFIC FEBRILE OR ZYMOTIC DISEASES.											
		Small-pox.	Measles.	Scarlet Fever.	Typhus.	Whooping-cough.	Diphtheria.	Simple continued and ill-defined Fever.	Enteric Fever.	Simple Cholera.	Diarrhoea and Dysentery.	Puerperal Fever.	Other Zymotic Diseases.
(1.) NUMBER													
[illegible]	[illegible]	7	[illegible]	[illegible]	[illegible]	[illegible]	[illegible]	[illegible]	[illegible]	[illegible]	[illegible]	[illegible]	[illegible]
[illegible]	[illegible]	—	[illegible]	[illegible]	[illegible]	[illegible]	[illegible]	[illegible]	[illegible]	[illegible]	[illegible]	[illegible]	[illegible]
[illegible]	[illegible]	—	[illegible]	[illegible]	[illegible]	[illegible]	[illegible]	[illegible]	[illegible]	[illegible]	[illegible]	[illegible]	[illegible]
[illegible]	[illegible]	[illegible]	[illegible]	[illegible]	[illegible]	[illegible]	[illegible]	[illegible]	[illegible]	[illegible]	[illegible]	[illegible]	[illegible]
[illegible]	[illegible]	[illegible]	[illegible]	[illegible]	[illegible]	[illegible]	[illegible]	[illegible]	[illegible]	[illegible]	[illegible]	[illegible]	[illegible]
[illegible]	[illegible]	[illegible]	[illegible]	[illegible]	[illegible]	[illegible]	[illegible]	[illegible]	[illegible]	[illegible]	[illegible]	[illegible]	[illegible]
[illegible]	[illegible]	[illegible]	[illegible]	[illegible]	[illegible]	[illegible]	[illegible]	[illegible]	[illegible]	[illegible]	[illegible]	[illegible]	[illegible]
[illegible]	[illegible]	1	[illegible]	[illegible]	[illegible]	[illegible]	[illegible]	[illegible]	[illegible]	[illegible]	[illegible]	[illegible]	[illegible]
[illegible]	[illegible]	[illegible]	[illegible]	[illegible]	[illegible]	[illegible]	[illegible]	[illegible]	[illegible]	[illegible]	[illegible]	[illegible]	[illegible]
[illegible]	[illegible]	[illegible]	[illegible]	[illegible]	[illegible]	[illegible]	[illegible]	[illegible]	[illegible]	[illegible]	[illegible]	[illegible]	[illegible]
[illegible]	[illegible]	[illegible]	[illegible]	[illegible]	[illegible]	[illegible]	[illegible]	[illegible]	[illegible]	[illegible]	[illegible]	[illegible]	[illegible]
(2.) RATES PER 100,000 OF													
[illegible]	[illegible]	[illegible]	[illegible]	[illegible]	[illegible]	[illegible]	[illegible]	[illegible]	[illegible]	[illegible]	[illegible]	[illegible]	[illegible]
[illegible]	[illegible]	—	[illegible]	[illegible]	[illegible]	[illegible]	[illegible]	[illegible]	[illegible]	[illegible]	[illegible]	[illegible]	[illegible]
[illegible]	[illegible]	—	[illegible]	[illegible]	[illegible]	[illegible]	[illegible]	[illegible]	[illegible]	[illegible]	[illegible]	[illegible]	[illegible]
[illegible]	[illegible]	[illegible]	[illegible]	[illegible]	[illegible]	[illegible]	[illegible]	[illegible]	[illegible]	[illegible]	[illegible]	[illegible]	[illegible]
[illegible]	[illegible]	[illegible]	[illegible]	[illegible]	[illegible]	[illegible]	[illegible]	[illegible]	[illegible]	[illegible]	[illegible]	[illegible]	[illegible]
[illegible]	[illegible]	—	[illegible]	[illegible]	[illegible]	[illegible]	[illegible]	[illegible]	[illegible]	[illegible]	[illegible]	[illegible]	[illegible]
[illegible]	[illegible]	[illegible]	[illegible]	[illegible]	[illegible]	[illegible]	[illegible]	[illegible]	[illegible]	[illegible]	[illegible]	[illegible]	[illegible]
[illegible]	[illegible]	—	[illegible]	[illegible]	[illegible]	[illegible]	[illegible]	[illegible]	[illegible]	[illegible]	[illegible]	[illegible]	[illegible]
[illegible]	[illegible]	[illegible]	[illegible]	[illegible]	[illegible]	[illegible]	[illegible]	[illegible]	[illegible]	[illegible]	[illegible]	[illegible]	[illegible]
[illegible]	[illegible]	[illegible]	[illegible]	[illegible]	[illegible]	[illegible]	[illegible]	[illegible]	[illegible]	[illegible]	[illegible]	[illegible]	[illegible]
[illegible]	[illegible]	[illegible]	[illegible]	[illegible]	[illegible]	[illegible]	[illegible]	[illegible]	[illegible]	[illegible]	[illegible]	[illegible]	[illegible]

I.—SPECIFIC FEBRILE OR ZYMOTIC DISEASES.

The number of deaths from Specific Febrile or Zymotic diseases registered during the year 1891 was 6,415, or 137 in every 100,000 of the estimated population, being 1,477, or 19 per cent. under the number for the preceding year, much below the average for the ten years, 1881-90, and lower than the number for any of those years.

Of the 6,415 deaths from zymotic diseases 3,285, or 51·2 per cent., were amongst children under 10 years of age.

DEATH.

each of the Principal Causes registered in Ireland during each year since 1881, when the Rates per 100,000 of the estimated Population represented by these numbers.

	Causes of Death.																
	Constitutional Diseases.					Local Diseases. Diseases of							Violence.				All other Causes.
	Cancer.	Tabes Mesenterica.	Tubercular Meningitis.	Phthisis.	Other Constitutional Diseases.	Nervous System.	Circulatory System.	Respiratory System.	Digestive System.	Urinary System.	Parturition.	Other Local Diseases.	Accidental.	Homicidal.	Suicidal.	Execution.	
of Deaths.																	
	[illegible]	[illegible]	[illegible]	[illegible]	[illegible]	[illegible]	[illegible]	[illegible]	[illegible]	[illegible]	[illegible]	[illegible]	[illegible]	[illegible]	[illegible]	[illegible]	[illegible]
	[illegible]	[illegible]	[illegible]	[illegible]	[illegible]	[illegible]	[illegible]	[illegible]	[illegible]	[illegible]	[illegible]	[illegible]	[illegible]	[illegible]	[illegible]	—	[illegible]
	[illegible]	[illegible]	[illegible]	[illegible]	[illegible]	[illegible]	[illegible]	[illegible]	[illegible]	[illegible]	[illegible]	[illegible]	[illegible]	[illegible]	[illegible]	[illegible]	[illegible]
	[illegible]	[illegible]	[illegible]	[illegible]	[illegible]	[illegible]	[illegible]	[illegible]	[illegible]	[illegible]	[illegible]	[illegible]	[illegible]	[illegible]	[illegible]	[illegible]	[illegible]
	[illegible]	[illegible]	[illegible]	[illegible]	[illegible]	[illegible]	[illegible]	[illegible]	[illegible]	[illegible]	[illegible]	[illegible]	[illegible]	[illegible]	[illegible]	—	[illegible]
	[illegible]	[illegible]	[illegible]	[illegible]	[illegible]	[illegible]	[illegible]	[illegible]	[illegible]	[illegible]	[illegible]	[illegible]	[illegible]	[illegible]	[illegible]	[illegible]	[illegible]
	[illegible]	[illegible]	[illegible]	[illegible]	[illegible]	[illegible]	[illegible]	[illegible]	[illegible]	[illegible]	[illegible]	[illegible]	[illegible]	[illegible]	[illegible]	[illegible]	[illegible]
	[illegible]	[illegible]	[illegible]	[illegible]	[illegible]	[illegible]	[illegible]	[illegible]	[illegible]	[illegible]	[illegible]	[illegible]	[illegible]	[illegible]	[illegible]	[illegible]	[illegible]
	[illegible]	[illegible]	[illegible]	[illegible]	[illegible]	[illegible]	[illegible]	[illegible]	[illegible]	[illegible]	[illegible]	[illegible]	[illegible]	[illegible]	[illegible]	[illegible]	[illegible]
	[illegible]	[illegible]	[illegible]	[illegible]	[illegible]	[illegible]	[illegible]	[illegible]	[illegible]	[illegible]	[illegible]	[illegible]	[illegible]	[illegible]	[illegible]	[illegible]	[illegible]
	[illegible]	[illegible]	[illegible]	[illegible]	[illegible]	[illegible]	[illegible]	[illegible]	[illegible]	[illegible]	[illegible]	[illegible]	[illegible]	[illegible]	[illegible]	—	[illegible]
the Estimated Population.																	
	[illegible]	[illegible]	[illegible]	[illegible]	[illegible]	[illegible]	[illegible]	[illegible]	[illegible]	[illegible]	[illegible]	[illegible]	[illegible]	[illegible]	[illegible]	—	[illegible]
	[illegible]	[illegible]	[illegible]	[illegible]	[illegible]	[illegible]	[illegible]	[illegible]	[illegible]	[illegible]	[illegible]	[illegible]	[illegible]	[illegible]	[illegible]	—	[illegible]
	[illegible]	[illegible]	[illegible]	[illegible]	[illegible]	[illegible]	[illegible]	[illegible]	[illegible]	[illegible]	[illegible]	[illegible]	[illegible]	[illegible]	[illegible]	[illegible]	[illegible]
	[illegible]	[illegible]	[illegible]	[illegible]	[illegible]	[illegible]	[illegible]	[illegible]	[illegible]	[illegible]	[illegible]	[illegible]	[illegible]	[illegible]	[illegible]	[illegible]	[illegible]
	[illegible]	[illegible]	[illegible]	[illegible]	[illegible]	[illegible]	[illegible]	[illegible]	[illegible]	[illegible]	[illegible]	[illegible]	[illegible]	[illegible]	[illegible]	—	[illegible]
	[illegible]	[illegible]	[illegible]	[illegible]	[illegible]	[illegible]	[illegible]	[illegible]	[illegible]	[illegible]	[illegible]	[illegible]	[illegible]	[illegible]	[illegible]	—	[illegible]
	[illegible]	[illegible]	[illegible]	[illegible]	[illegible]	[illegible]	[illegible]	[illegible]	[illegible]	[illegible]	[illegible]	[illegible]	[illegible]	[illegible]	[illegible]	—	[illegible]
	[illegible]	[illegible]	[illegible]	[illegible]	[illegible]	[illegible]	[illegible]	[illegible]	[illegible]	[illegible]	[illegible]	[illegible]	[illegible]	[illegible]	[illegible]	—	[illegible]
	[illegible]	[illegible]	[illegible]	[illegible]	[illegible]	[illegible]	[illegible]	[illegible]	[illegible]	[illegible]	[illegible]	[illegible]	[illegible]	[illegible]	[illegible]	[illegible]	[illegible]
	[illegible]	[illegible]	[illegible]	[illegible]	[illegible]	[illegible]	[illegible]	[illegible]	[illegible]	[illegible]	[illegible]	[illegible]	[illegible]	[illegible]	[illegible]	[illegible]	[illegible]
	[illegible]	[illegible]	[illegible]	[illegible]	[illegible]	[illegible]	[illegible]	[illegible]	[illegible]	[illegible]	[illegible]	[illegible]	[illegible]	[illegible]	[illegible]	—	[illegible]

The deaths from the eight principal symotic diseases* registered during 1891 form 5·6 per cent. of the deaths from all causes, and are equal to 108 in every 100,000 persons living; the average annual mortality from the same diseases in the preceding 10 years represented 6·0 per cent. of the average number of deaths from all causes, and was equal to 144 deaths in every 100,000 of the estimated mean population.

TABLE X.—Showing the Number of Deaths from the Principal Febrile or Zymotic Diseases registered in Ireland during the year 1891, and the Average Annual Number for the ten years 1881–90; with the Number registered in the several Provinces during each of the seven years 1885–91; and the Rates per 100,000 of the Population.*

Years, &c.			Small-Pox.	Measles.	Scarlet Fever (Scarlatina).	Diphtheria.	Whooping-Cough.	Fever.	Erysipelas.	Influenza.	Diarrhoea and Dysentery.	[illegible]
IRELAND.	No. of Deaths.	Average 1881–90.	[illegible]	[illegible]	[illegible]	[illegible]	[illegible]	[illegible]	[illegible]	[illegible]	[illegible]	[illegible]
		1891.	7	[illegible]	[illegible]	[illegible]	[illegible]	[illegible]	[illegible]	[illegible]	[illegible]	[illegible]
	Rate per 100,000 Inhabitants.*	Average 1881–90.	[illegible]	[illegible]	[illegible]	[illegible]	[illegible]	[illegible]	[illegible]	[illegible]	[illegible]	[illegible]
		1891.	[illegible]	[illegible]	[illegible]	[illegible]	[illegible]	[illegible]	[illegible]	[illegible]	[illegible]	[illegible]
PROVINCES. No. of Deaths.	Leinster.	1885.	[illegible]	[illegible]	[illegible]	[illegible]	[illegible]	[illegible]	[illegible]	[illegible]	[illegible]	[illegible]
		1886.	[illegible]	[illegible]	[illegible]	[illegible]	[illegible]	[illegible]	[illegible]	[illegible]	[illegible]	[illegible]
		1887.	[illegible]	[illegible]	[illegible]	[illegible]	[illegible]	[illegible]	[illegible]	[illegible]	[illegible]	[illegible]
		1888.	[illegible]	[illegible]	[illegible]	[illegible]	[illegible]	[illegible]	[illegible]	[illegible]	[illegible]	[illegible]
		1889.	...	[illegible]	[illegible]	[illegible]	[illegible]	[illegible]	[illegible]	[illegible]	[illegible]	[illegible]
		1890.	...	[illegible]	[illegible]	[illegible]	[illegible]	[illegible]	[illegible]	[illegible]	[illegible]	[illegible]
		1891.	...	[illegible]	[illegible]	[illegible]	[illegible]	[illegible]	[illegible]	[illegible]	[illegible]	[illegible]
	Munster.	1885.	...	[illegible]	[illegible]	[illegible]	[illegible]	[illegible]	[illegible]	[illegible]	[illegible]	[illegible]
		1886.	...	[illegible]	[illegible]	[illegible]	[illegible]	[illegible]	[illegible]	[illegible]	[illegible]	[illegible]
		1887.	...	[illegible]	[illegible]	[illegible]	[illegible]	[illegible]	[illegible]	[illegible]	[illegible]	[illegible]
		1888.	...	[illegible]	[illegible]	[illegible]	[illegible]	[illegible]	[illegible]	[illegible]	[illegible]	[illegible]
		1889.	...	[illegible]	[illegible]	[illegible]	[illegible]	[illegible]	[illegible]	[illegible]	[illegible]	[illegible]
		1890.	...	[illegible]	[illegible]	[illegible]	[illegible]	[illegible]	[illegible]	[illegible]	[illegible]	[illegible]
		1891.	...	[illegible]	[illegible]	[illegible]	[illegible]	[illegible]	[illegible]	[illegible]	[illegible]	[illegible]
	Ulster.	1885.	[illegible]	[illegible]	[illegible]	[illegible]	[illegible]	[illegible]	[illegible]	[illegible]	[illegible]	[illegible]
		1886.	[illegible]	[illegible]	[illegible]	[illegible]	[illegible]	[illegible]	[illegible]	[illegible]	[illegible]	[illegible]
		1887.	[illegible]	[illegible]	[illegible]	[illegible]	[illegible]	[illegible]	[illegible]	[illegible]	[illegible]	[illegible]
		1888.	[illegible]	[illegible]	[illegible]	[illegible]	[illegible]	[illegible]	[illegible]	[illegible]	[illegible]	[illegible]
		1889.	...	[illegible]	[illegible]	[illegible]	[illegible]	[illegible]	[illegible]	[illegible]	[illegible]	[illegible]
		1890.	...	[illegible]	[illegible]	[illegible]	[illegible]	[illegible]	[illegible]	[illegible]	[illegible]	[illegible]
		1891.	6	[illegible]	[illegible]	[illegible]	[illegible]	[illegible]	[illegible]	[illegible]	[illegible]	[illegible]
	Connaught.	1885.	...	[illegible]	[illegible]	[illegible]	[illegible]	[illegible]	[illegible]	[illegible]	[illegible]	[illegible]
		1886.	...	[illegible]	[illegible]	[illegible]	[illegible]	[illegible]	[illegible]	[illegible]	[illegible]	[illegible]
		1887.	...	[illegible]	[illegible]	[illegible]	[illegible]	[illegible]	[illegible]	[illegible]	[illegible]	[illegible]
		1888.	...	[illegible]	[illegible]	[illegible]	[illegible]	[illegible]	[illegible]	[illegible]	[illegible]	[illegible]
		1889.	...	[illegible]	[illegible]	[illegible]	[illegible]	[illegible]	[illegible]	[illegible]	[illegible]	[illegible]
		1890.	...	[illegible]	[illegible]	[illegible]	[illegible]	[illegible]	[illegible]	[illegible]	[illegible]	[illegible]
		1891.	1	[illegible]	[illegible]	[illegible]	[illegible]	[illegible]	[illegible]	[illegible]	[illegible]	[illegible]
PROVINCES. Rate per 100,000 of Population.*	Leinster.	1885.	[illegible]	[illegible]	[illegible]	[illegible]	[illegible]	[illegible]	[illegible]	[illegible]	[illegible]	[illegible]
		1886.	[illegible]	[illegible]	[illegible]	[illegible]	[illegible]	[illegible]	[illegible]	[illegible]	[illegible]	[illegible]
		1887.	[illegible]	[illegible]	[illegible]	[illegible]	[illegible]	[illegible]	[illegible]	[illegible]	[illegible]	[illegible]
		1888.	[illegible]	[illegible]	[illegible]	[illegible]	[illegible]	[illegible]	[illegible]	[illegible]	[illegible]	[illegible]
		1889.	...	[illegible]	[illegible]	[illegible]	[illegible]	[illegible]	[illegible]	[illegible]	[illegible]	[illegible]
		1890.	...	[illegible]	[illegible]	[illegible]	[illegible]	[illegible]	[illegible]	[illegible]	[illegible]	[illegible]
		1891.	...	[illegible]	[illegible]	[illegible]	[illegible]	[illegible]	[illegible]	[illegible]	[illegible]	[illegible]
	Munster.	1885.	...	[illegible]	[illegible]	[illegible]	[illegible]	[illegible]	[illegible]	[illegible]	[illegible]	[illegible]
		1886.	...	[illegible]	[illegible]	[illegible]	[illegible]	[illegible]	[illegible]	[illegible]	[illegible]	[illegible]
		1887.	...	[illegible]	[illegible]	[illegible]	[illegible]	[illegible]	[illegible]	[illegible]	[illegible]	[illegible]
		1888.	...	[illegible]	[illegible]	[illegible]	[illegible]	[illegible]	[illegible]	[illegible]	[illegible]	[illegible]
		1889.	...	[illegible]	[illegible]	[illegible]	[illegible]	[illegible]	[illegible]	[illegible]	[illegible]	[illegible]
		1890.	...	[illegible]	[illegible]	[illegible]	[illegible]	[illegible]	[illegible]	[illegible]	[illegible]	[illegible]
		1891.	...	[illegible]	[illegible]	[illegible]	[illegible]	[illegible]	[illegible]	[illegible]	[illegible]	[illegible]
	Ulster.	1885.	[illegible]	[illegible]	[illegible]	[illegible]	[illegible]	[illegible]	[illegible]	[illegible]	[illegible]	[illegible]
		1886.	[illegible]	[illegible]	[illegible]	[illegible]	[illegible]	[illegible]	[illegible]	[illegible]	[illegible]	[illegible]
		1887.	[illegible]	[illegible]	[illegible]	[illegible]	[illegible]	[illegible]	[illegible]	[illegible]	[illegible]	[illegible]
		1888.	[illegible]	[illegible]	[illegible]	[illegible]	[illegible]	[illegible]	[illegible]	[illegible]	[illegible]	[illegible]
		1889.	...	[illegible]	[illegible]	[illegible]	[illegible]	[illegible]	[illegible]	[illegible]	[illegible]	[illegible]
		1890.	...	[illegible]	[illegible]	[illegible]	[illegible]	[illegible]	[illegible]	[illegible]	[illegible]	[illegible]
		1891.	[illegible]	[illegible]	[illegible]	[illegible]	[illegible]	[illegible]	[illegible]	[illegible]	[illegible]	[illegible]
	Connaught.	1885.	...	[illegible]	[illegible]	[illegible]	[illegible]	[illegible]	[illegible]	[illegible]	[illegible]	[illegible]
		1886.	...	[illegible]	[illegible]	[illegible]	[illegible]	[illegible]	[illegible]	[illegible]	[illegible]	[illegible]
		1887.	...	[illegible]	[illegible]	[illegible]	[illegible]	[illegible]	[illegible]	[illegible]	[illegible]	[illegible]
		1888.	...	[illegible]	[illegible]	[illegible]	[illegible]	[illegible]	[illegible]	[illegible]	[illegible]	[illegible]
		1889.	...	[illegible]	[illegible]	[illegible]	[illegible]	[illegible]	[illegible]	[illegible]	[illegible]	[illegible]
		1890.	...	[illegible]	[illegible]	[illegible]	[illegible]	[illegible]	[illegible]	[illegible]	[illegible]	[illegible]
		1891.	[illegible]	[illegible]	[illegible]	[illegible]	[illegible]	[illegible]	[illegible]	[illegible]	[illegible]	[illegible]

Small-pox.—Seven deaths from small-pox were registered during the year, 6 of which occurred in Ulster and 1 in Connaught. In the two years preceding no fatal cases of the disease were recorded; the average annual number for the ten years 1881–90, was 24 only; and of the total number (241) registered during that period 201 occurred during the first two years, so that in late years deaths from Small-pox have been of very rare occurrence in Ireland.

Measles.—There were but 240 deaths from Measles registered, being 486 under the number for the preceding year; 703 below the average for the ten years, 1881–90, and the lowest number in any year since registration was established in 1864. More than one half of the total number occurred in the province of Connaught, where there were 131 deaths from this cause, (50 of which, equal to 1·8 per 1000 of the population at all ages, occurred in Claremorris Union). In Leinster there were only 11, in Munster 23, and in Ulster 76.

Scarlet Fever.—The mortality for Scarlet Fever also, was lower than in any previous year since the introduction of registration, the number of deaths being 308 only, being 923, or 70 per cent. below the average for the ten years 1881–90, and 11 under the low number for the last year of that period. Of the 308 deaths registered last year, 19 occurred in Leinster, 36 in Munster, 180 in Ulster, and 73 in Connaught, the last number including 21 in Roscommon union.

Diphtheria.—There were only 281 deaths from diphtheria registered, being 65 under the number for the preceding year, and 68 under the average for the ten years 1881–90. The 281 deaths consist of 58 in Leinster (including 19 in the South Dublin union), 48 in Munster (14 of which were in Cork union, and 11 in Kilmallock union), 145 in Ulster (including 34 in Belfast union, 12 in Lurgan union, and 12 in Magherafelt union), and 30 in Connaught. In Ulster the rate represented by deaths from diphtheria was 9·0 per 100,000 of the population, and in Connaught, 4·1.

Whooping-cough.—Deaths from this disease, which had risen from 1,259 in 1888 to 1,481 in 1889, and to 1,493 in 1890, fell last year to 1,280, or 27·3 per 100,000 of the population, being 1·8 under the average rate for the ten years 1881–90. The 1,280 deaths in 1891 were distributed as follows:—337 in Leinster (including 76 in the North, and 88 in the South Dublin union), 341 in Munster (including 60 in Cork union, and 46 in Waterford union), 554 in Ulster (of which 178 were in Belfast union, where during the year 1890 the disease caused 314 deaths, and 44 in *Lurgan* Union), and 48 in Connaught. The respective rates for the four provinces were—Leinster, 28·4 per 100,000 of the population; Munster, 29·1; Ulster, 34·2; and Connaught, 6·6.

Fever.—The total number of deaths from the several forms of continued fever was 1,308, being 169 under the number for the preceding year, and 499 below the average for the ten years 1881–90. The rate represented by the deaths for last year was 27·9 per 100,000 of the population, against an average of 36·7 for the preceding ten years, showing a diminution in the mortality rate equivalent to a decrease of 24 per cent. The deaths from "fever" in Leinster were equal to 32·4 per 100,000 of the population; in Munster the rate was 28·0 per 100,000; in Ulster, 26·9; and in Connaught, 25·1.

The 1,308 deaths from "fever" consist of 266 from typhus (being 123 under the number for 1890, and far below the average for the ten years 1881–90), 859 from enteric fever being 4 over the number for 1890, and somewhat above the average), and 183 from simple continued and ill-defined fever. Enteric fever was again prevalent in Belfast and Dublin, in the former it was less fatal than either of the two years preceding, but in Dublin the mortality although not so heavy as in the year 1889, was somewhat greater than that for the year 1890. The respective numbers for Belfast union were 236 deaths in 1889, 190 in 1890, and 156 in 1891, and for the two unions of Dublin North and Dublin South 231 in 1889, 183 in 1890, and 185 in 1891.

In proportion to the living at the same age, "fever" was most fatal at the age-periods 20 and under 25 years and 25 and under 35, for the former of which the rate was 39·37 per 100,000 and for the latter 34·61, and least so amongst persons aged 75 and upwards, the rate being 10·97 per 100,000.

TABLE XI.—Showing for the year 1891 the Deaths from the several forms of Fever at each Age-Period, with the proportion to the number of the living at each Age represented thereby.

Age-Periods.	Deaths from Fever.												
	Typhus.			Typhoid or Enteric.			Simple Continued.			Total.			No. of Deaths in 100,000 of the Living at each age.
	M.	F.	Total.	M.	F.	Total.	M.	F.	Total.	M.	F.	Total.	
Under 5 years old,	[illegible]	[illegible]	[illegible]	[illegible]	[illegible]	[illegible]	[illegible]	[illegible]	[illegible]	[illegible]	[illegible]	[illegible]	[illegible]
5 and under 10,	[illegible]	[illegible]	[illegible]	[illegible]	[illegible]	[illegible]	[illegible]	[illegible]	[illegible]	[illegible]	[illegible]	[illegible]	[illegible]
10 " 15,	[illegible]	[illegible]	[illegible]	[illegible]	[illegible]	[illegible]	[illegible]	[illegible]	[illegible]	[illegible]	[illegible]	[illegible]	[illegible]
15 " 20,	[illegible]	[illegible]	[illegible]	[illegible]	[illegible]	[illegible]	[illegible]	[illegible]	[illegible]	[illegible]	[illegible]	[illegible]	[illegible]
20 " 25,	[illegible]	[illegible]	[illegible]	[illegible]	[illegible]	[illegible]	[illegible]	[illegible]	[illegible]	[illegible]	[illegible]	[illegible]	[illegible]
25 " 35,	[illegible]	[illegible]	[illegible]	[illegible]	[illegible]	[illegible]	[illegible]	[illegible]	[illegible]	[illegible]	[illegible]	[illegible]	[illegible]
35 " 45,	[illegible]	[illegible]	[illegible]	[illegible]	[illegible]	[illegible]	[illegible]	[illegible]	[illegible]	[illegible]	[illegible]	[illegible]	[illegible]
45 " 55,	[illegible]	[illegible]	[illegible]	[illegible]	[illegible]	[illegible]	[illegible]	[illegible]	[illegible]	[illegible]	[illegible]	[illegible]	[illegible]
55 " 65,	[illegible]	[illegible]	[illegible]	[illegible]	[illegible]	[illegible]	[illegible]	[illegible]	[illegible]	[illegible]	[illegible]	[illegible]	[illegible]
65 " 75,	[illegible]	[illegible]	[illegible]	[illegible]	[illegible]	[illegible]	[illegible]	[illegible]	[illegible]	[illegible]	[illegible]	[illegible]	[illegible]
75 and upwards,	[illegible]	[illegible]	[illegible]	[illegible]	[illegible]	[illegible]	[illegible]	[illegible]	[illegible]	[illegible]	[illegible]	[illegible]	[illegible]
Total,	[illegible]	[illegible]	[illegible]	[illegible]	[illegible]	[illegible]	[illegible]	[illegible]	[illegible]	[illegible]	[illegible]	[illegible]	[illegible]

Erysipelas.—The number of deaths from erysipelas was 170, being 14 over the number for the preceding year, but 72 under the average for the ten years 1881–90.

Puerperal Fever.—There were only 236 deaths from this disease registered, being 89 below the average for the preceding ten years, and 16 under the number for the year 1890.

Influenza.—This disease, which, ordinarily, causes but few deaths in Ireland, proved fatal in 1,712 cases in the year 1890, and caused 891 deaths (386 males and 505 females) in 1891. The 891 deaths in 1891 comprise 130 of children under 10 years of age, and 468 of persons aged 55 years and upwards. In the province of Leinster the influenza death-rate in 1891 was 1·0 per 10,000 of the population; in Munster, 1·5; in Ulster, 3·3; and in Connaught, 0·9. The county rates range from 0·3 per 10,000 in Westmeath to 5·2 in Down.

The Table (XII.) on the opposite page shows, by Sexes and Age-Periods, the distribution of the deaths from influenza through the several counties.

Carlow County	Males,	[illegible]	[illegible]
	Females,	[illegible]	
Dublin	Males,	[illegible]	[illegible]
	Females,	[illegible]	[illegible]
Kildare	Males,	[illegible]	
	Females,	[illegible]	[illegible]
Kilkenny	Males,	[illegible]	[illegible]
	Females,	[illegible]	[illegible]
King's	Males,	[illegible]	
	Females,	[illegible]	[illegible]
Longford	Males,	[illegible]	[illegible]
	Females,	[illegible]	
Louth County and County of the Town of Drogheda	Males,	[illegible]	[illegible]
	Females,	[illegible]	[illegible]
Meath County	Males,	[illegible]	
	Females,	[illegible]	
Queen's	Males,	[illegible]	[illegible]
	Females,	[illegible]	
Westmeath	Males,	[illegible]	
	Females,	[illegible]	
Wexford	Males,	[illegible]	
	Females,	[illegible]	
Wicklow	Males,	[illegible]	
	Females,	[illegible]	[illegible]
Total,	Males,	[illegible]	[illegible]
	Females,	[illegible]	[illegible]
[illegible] Province:			
Clare County	Males,	[illegible]	[illegible]
	Females,	[illegible]	[illegible]
Cork	Males,	[illegible]	[illegible]
	Females,	[illegible]	[illegible]
Kerry	Males,	[illegible]	[illegible]
	Females,	[illegible]	
Limerick	Males,	[illegible]	[illegible]
	Females,	[illegible]	[illegible]
Tipperary	Males,	[illegible]	[illegible]
	Females,	[illegible]	[illegible]
Waterford	Males,	[illegible]	[illegible]
	Females,	[illegible]	[illegible]
Total,	Males,	[illegible]	[illegible]
	Females,	[illegible]	[illegible]
[illegible] Province:			
Antrim County,	Males,	[illegible]	[illegible]
	Females,	[illegible]	[illegible]
Armagh	Males,	[illegible]	[illegible]
	Females,	[illegible]	[illegible]
Cavan	Males,	[illegible]	[illegible]
	Females,	[illegible]	[illegible]
Donegal	Males,	[illegible]	[illegible]
	Females,	[illegible]	[illegible]
Down	Males,	[illegible]	[illegible]
	Females,	[illegible]	[illegible]
Fermanagh	Males,	[illegible]	
	Females,	[illegible]	[illegible]
Londonderry	Males,	[illegible]	[illegible]
	Females,	[illegible]	[illegible]
Monaghan	Males,	[illegible]	
	Females,	[illegible]	
Tyrone	Males,	[illegible]	[illegible]
	Females,	[illegible]	[illegible]
Total.	Males,	[illegible]	[illegible]
	Females,	[illegible]	[illegible]

Diarrhœa and Dysentery.—The mortality from these diseases, although not so low as in the year 1890, was below the average, the number of deaths being 1,308, or 27·8 per 100,000 living, against an average of 1,448, or of 29·3 per 100,000 for the ten years 1881-90.

The rate for Leinster in 1891 was 30·9 per 100,000 of the population; for Munster, 24·2; for Ulster, 33·2; and for Connaught, 15·9. Of the 367 deaths from diarrhœa and dysentery in the province of Leinster, 214 occurred in one or other of the two unions of Dublin North, and Dublin South; and of the 537 deaths in Ulster, 267 were registered in Belfast union.

Simple Cholera.—Seventy deaths were ascribed to this disease, viz.:—18 in Leinster, 17 in Munster, 34 in Ulster, and 1 in Connaught.

Five males and 1 female died from *Hydrophobia*.

II.—Parasitic Diseases.

There were only 60 deaths from diseases of this class.

III.—Dietetic Diseases.

The deaths from dietetic diseases number 142; they comprise 131 from intemperance, 35 of which (34 males and 1 female) were caused by delirium tremens, and 96 (78 males and 18 females) come under the head of chronic alcoholism. The number of deaths from intemperance registered in the preceding year was 143.

IV.—Constitutional Diseases.

From diseases termed "constitutional" there resulted 16,123 deaths (7,669 males and 8,454 females), affording a rate of 1 in 5·3 of all the deaths, and equal to 344 in every 100,000 of the population.

Phthisis or Pulmonary Consumption caused 10,038 deaths (4,654 males and 5,384 females) being equal to 214·4 in every 100,000 persons, against an average annual rate of 209·8 per 100,000 for the previous ten years.

As heretofore, Leinster and Ulster yield the highest rates, and Connaught the lowest. The rates for the four provinces are as follow:—Leinster, 240 per 100,000 of the population: Ulster, 228: Munster, 199: and Connaught, 158.

Of the 3,701 deaths from phthisis in Ulster, 1,133 occurred in Belfast union, the number being equal to 391 per 100,000 of the population, and the 2,854 fatal cases of the disease in Leinster comprise 1,241, or 355 per 100,000 of the population, registered in the unions of Dublin North and Dublin South.

Of the total number of deaths from phthisis in Ireland, 7,397, or 74 per cent., were of persons aged 15 and under 45 years of age.

Mesenteric Disease.—The deaths from mesenteric disease number 950—473 males and 477 females.

Gout.—Only 32 deaths from gout were registered (19 males and 13 females).

TABLE XIII.—DEATHS FROM CANCER.

Part Affected.		Ages at Death. Under 5 years.	5 and under 15.	15 and under 20.	20-	25-	35-	45-	55-	65-	75-	85-	95 and upwards.	Total.
Year 1891.														
Head,	Males,	[illegible]	[illegible]	[illegible]	[illegible]	[illegible]	[illegible]	[illegible]	[illegible]	[illegible]	[illegible]	[illegible]	[illegible]	[illegible]
	Females,	[illegible]	[illegible]	[illegible]	[illegible]	[illegible]	[illegible]	[illegible]	[illegible]	[illegible]	[illegible]	[illegible]	[illegible]	[illegible]
	Total,	[illegible]	[illegible]	[illegible]	[illegible]	[illegible]	[illegible]	[illegible]	[illegible]	[illegible]	[illegible]	[illegible]	[illegible]	[illegible]
Face,	Males,	[illegible]	[illegible]	[illegible]	[illegible]	[illegible]	[illegible]	[illegible]	[illegible]	[illegible]	[illegible]	[illegible]	[illegible]	[illegible]
	Females,	[illegible]	[illegible]	[illegible]	[illegible]	[illegible]	[illegible]	[illegible]	[illegible]	[illegible]	[illegible]	[illegible]	[illegible]	[illegible]
	Total,	[illegible]	[illegible]	[illegible]	[illegible]	[illegible]	[illegible]	[illegible]	[illegible]	[illegible]	[illegible]	[illegible]	[illegible]	[illegible]
Eye,	Males,	[illegible]	[illegible]	[illegible]	[illegible]	[illegible]	[illegible]	[illegible]	[illegible]	[illegible]	[illegible]	[illegible]	[illegible]	[illegible]
	Females,	[illegible]	[illegible]	[illegible]	[illegible]	[illegible]	[illegible]	[illegible]	[illegible]	[illegible]	[illegible]	[illegible]	[illegible]	[illegible]
	Total,	[illegible]	[illegible]	[illegible]	[illegible]	[illegible]	[illegible]	[illegible]	[illegible]	[illegible]	[illegible]	[illegible]	[illegible]	[illegible]
Ear,	Males,	[illegible]	[illegible]	[illegible]	[illegible]	[illegible]	[illegible]	[illegible]	[illegible]	[illegible]	[illegible]	[illegible]	[illegible]	[illegible]
	Females,	[illegible]	[illegible]	[illegible]	[illegible]	[illegible]	[illegible]	[illegible]	[illegible]	[illegible]	[illegible]	[illegible]	[illegible]	[illegible]
	Total,	[illegible]	[illegible]	[illegible]	[illegible]	[illegible]	[illegible]	[illegible]	[illegible]	[illegible]	[illegible]	[illegible]	[illegible]	[illegible]
Jaw,	Males,	[illegible]	[illegible]	[illegible]	[illegible]	[illegible]	[illegible]	[illegible]	[illegible]	[illegible]	[illegible]	[illegible]	[illegible]	[illegible]
	Females,	[illegible]	[illegible]	[illegible]	[illegible]	[illegible]	[illegible]	[illegible]	[illegible]	[illegible]	[illegible]	[illegible]	[illegible]	[illegible]
	Total,	[illegible]	[illegible]	[illegible]	[illegible]	[illegible]	[illegible]	[illegible]	[illegible]	[illegible]	[illegible]	[illegible]	[illegible]	[illegible]
Tongue,	Males,	[illegible]	[illegible]	[illegible]	[illegible]	[illegible]	[illegible]	[illegible]	[illegible]	[illegible]	[illegible]	[illegible]	[illegible]	[illegible]
	Females,	[illegible]	[illegible]	[illegible]	[illegible]	[illegible]	[illegible]	[illegible]	[illegible]	[illegible]	[illegible]	[illegible]	[illegible]	[illegible]
	Total,	[illegible]	[illegible]	[illegible]	[illegible]	[illegible]	[illegible]	[illegible]	[illegible]	[illegible]	[illegible]	[illegible]	[illegible]	[illegible]
Lips,	Males,	[illegible]	[illegible]	[illegible]	[illegible]	[illegible]	[illegible]	[illegible]	[illegible]	[illegible]	[illegible]	[illegible]	[illegible]	[illegible]
	Females,	[illegible]	[illegible]	[illegible]	[illegible]	[illegible]	[illegible]	[illegible]	[illegible]	[illegible]	[illegible]	[illegible]	[illegible]	[illegible]
	Total,	[illegible]	[illegible]	[illegible]	[illegible]	[illegible]	[illegible]	[illegible]	[illegible]	[illegible]	[illegible]	[illegible]	[illegible]	[illegible]
Neck,	Males,	[illegible]	[illegible]	[illegible]	[illegible]	[illegible]	[illegible]	[illegible]	[illegible]	[illegible]	[illegible]	[illegible]	[illegible]	[illegible]
	Females,	[illegible]	[illegible]	[illegible]	[illegible]	[illegible]	[illegible]	[illegible]	[illegible]	[illegible]	[illegible]	[illegible]	[illegible]	[illegible]
	Total,	[illegible]	[illegible]	[illegible]	[illegible]	[illegible]	[illegible]	[illegible]	[illegible]	[illegible]	[illegible]	[illegible]	[illegible]	[illegible]
Throat,	Males,	[illegible]	[illegible]	[illegible]	[illegible]	[illegible]	[illegible]	[illegible]	[illegible]	[illegible]	[illegible]	[illegible]	[illegible]	[illegible]
	Females,	[illegible]	[illegible]	[illegible]	[illegible]	[illegible]	[illegible]	[illegible]	[illegible]	[illegible]	[illegible]	[illegible]	[illegible]	[illegible]
	Total,	[illegible]	[illegible]	[illegible]	[illegible]	[illegible]	[illegible]	[illegible]	[illegible]	[illegible]	[illegible]	[illegible]	[illegible]	[illegible]
Lungs,	Males,	[illegible]	[illegible]	[illegible]	[illegible]	[illegible]	[illegible]	[illegible]	[illegible]	[illegible]	[illegible]	[illegible]	[illegible]	[illegible]
	Females,	[illegible]	[illegible]	[illegible]	[illegible]	[illegible]	[illegible]	[illegible]	[illegible]	[illegible]	[illegible]	[illegible]	[illegible]	[illegible]
	Total,	[illegible]	[illegible]	[illegible]	[illegible]	[illegible]	[illegible]	[illegible]	[illegible]	[illegible]	[illegible]	[illegible]	[illegible]	[illegible]
Œsophagus,	Males,	[illegible]	[illegible]	[illegible]	[illegible]	[illegible]	[illegible]	[illegible]	[illegible]	[illegible]	[illegible]	[illegible]	[illegible]	[illegible]
	Females,	[illegible]	[illegible]	[illegible]	[illegible]	[illegible]	[illegible]	[illegible]	[illegible]	[illegible]	[illegible]	[illegible]	[illegible]	[illegible]
	Total,	[illegible]	[illegible]	[illegible]	[illegible]	[illegible]	[illegible]	[illegible]	[illegible]	[illegible]	[illegible]	[illegible]	[illegible]	[illegible]
Breast,	Males,	[illegible]	[illegible]	[illegible]	[illegible]	[illegible]	[illegible]	[illegible]	[illegible]	[illegible]	[illegible]	[illegible]	[illegible]	[illegible]
	Females,	[illegible]	[illegible]	[illegible]	[illegible]	[illegible]	[illegible]	[illegible]	[illegible]	[illegible]	[illegible]	[illegible]	[illegible]	[illegible]
	Total,	[illegible]	[illegible]	[illegible]	[illegible]	[illegible]	[illegible]	[illegible]	[illegible]	[illegible]	[illegible]	[illegible]	[illegible]	[illegible]
Axilla,	Males,	[illegible]	[illegible]	[illegible]	[illegible]	[illegible]	[illegible]	[illegible]	[illegible]	[illegible]	[illegible]	[illegible]	[illegible]	[illegible]
	Females,	[illegible]	[illegible]	[illegible]	[illegible]	[illegible]	[illegible]	[illegible]	[illegible]	[illegible]	[illegible]	[illegible]	[illegible]	[illegible]
	Total,	[illegible]	[illegible]	[illegible]	[illegible]	[illegible]	[illegible]	[illegible]	[illegible]	[illegible]	[illegible]	[illegible]	[illegible]	[illegible]
Arm,	Males,	[illegible]	[illegible]	[illegible]	[illegible]	[illegible]	[illegible]	[illegible]	[illegible]	[illegible]	[illegible]	[illegible]	[illegible]	[illegible]
	Females,	[illegible]	[illegible]	[illegible]	[illegible]	[illegible]	[illegible]	[illegible]	[illegible]	[illegible]	[illegible]	[illegible]	[illegible]	[illegible]
	Total,	[illegible]	[illegible]	[illegible]	[illegible]	[illegible]	[illegible]	[illegible]	[illegible]	[illegible]	[illegible]	[illegible]	[illegible]	[illegible]
Hand,	Males,	[illegible]	[illegible]	[illegible]	[illegible]	[illegible]	[illegible]	[illegible]	[illegible]	[illegible]	[illegible]	[illegible]	[illegible]	[illegible]
	Females,	[illegible]	[illegible]	[illegible]	[illegible]	[illegible]	[illegible]	[illegible]	[illegible]	[illegible]	[illegible]	[illegible]	[illegible]	[illegible]
	Total,	[illegible]	[illegible]	[illegible]	[illegible]	[illegible]	[illegible]	[illegible]	[illegible]	[illegible]	[illegible]	[illegible]	[illegible]	[illegible]
Stomach,	Males,	[illegible]	[illegible]	[illegible]	[illegible]	[illegible]	[illegible]	[illegible]	[illegible]	[illegible]	[illegible]	[illegible]	[illegible]	[illegible]
	Females,	[illegible]	[illegible]	[illegible]	[illegible]	[illegible]	[illegible]	[illegible]	[illegible]	[illegible]	[illegible]	[illegible]	[illegible]	[illegible]
	Total,	[illegible]	[illegible]	[illegible]	[illegible]	[illegible]	[illegible]	[illegible]	[illegible]	[illegible]	[illegible]	[illegible]	[illegible]	[illegible]
Liver,	Males,	[illegible]	[illegible]	[illegible]	[illegible]	[illegible]	[illegible]	[illegible]	[illegible]	[illegible]	[illegible]	[illegible]	[illegible]	[illegible]
	Females,	[illegible]	[illegible]	[illegible]	[illegible]	[illegible]	[illegible]	[illegible]	[illegible]	[illegible]	[illegible]	[illegible]	[illegible]	[illegible]
	Total,	[illegible]	[illegible]	[illegible]	[illegible]	[illegible]	[illegible]	[illegible]	[illegible]	[illegible]	[illegible]	[illegible]	[illegible]	[illegible]
Peritoneum,	Males,	[illegible]	[illegible]	[illegible]	[illegible]	[illegible]	[illegible]	[illegible]	[illegible]	[illegible]	[illegible]	[illegible]	[illegible]	[illegible]
	Females,	[illegible]	[illegible]	[illegible]	[illegible]	[illegible]	[illegible]	[illegible]	[illegible]	[illegible]	[illegible]	[illegible]	[illegible]	[illegible]
	Total,	[illegible]	[illegible]	[illegible]	[illegible]	[illegible]	[illegible]	[illegible]	[illegible]	[illegible]	[illegible]	[illegible]	[illegible]	[illegible]
"Intestines,"	Males,	[illegible]	[illegible]	[illegible]	[illegible]	[illegible]	[illegible]	[illegible]	[illegible]	[illegible]	[illegible]	[illegible]	[illegible]	[illegible]
	Females,	[illegible]	[illegible]	[illegible]	[illegible]	[illegible]	[illegible]	[illegible]	[illegible]	[illegible]	[illegible]	[illegible]	[illegible]	[illegible]
	Total,	[illegible]	[illegible]	[illegible]	[illegible]	[illegible]	[illegible]	[illegible]	[illegible]	[illegible]	[illegible]	[illegible]	[illegible]	[illegible]

DEATHS FROM CANCER—*continued.*

PART AFFECTED.		AGE AT DEATH.												Total.
		Under 5 years.	5 and under 10.	10 and under 15.	15-	25-	35-	45-	55-	65-	75-	85-	95 and upwards.	
YEAR 1865—*continued.*														
Pylorus,	Males,	-	-	-	-	9	8	8	6	11	-	-	-	34
	Females,	-	-	-	-	-	-	5	5	1	2	-	-	14
	Total,	-	-	-	-	5	2	8	10	12	2	-	-	48
Vagina,	Males,	-	-	-	-	-	-	-	-	-	-	-	-	-
	Females,	-	-	-	-	-	-	1	1	1	3	-	-	6
	Total,	-	-	-	-	-	-	1	1	1	3	-	-	6
Uterus,	Males,	-	-	-	-	-	-	-	-	-	-	-	-	-
	Females,	-	-	-	-	7	29	53	43	29	3	-	-	164
	Total,	-	-	-	-	7	29	53	43	29	3	-	-	164
Rectum,	Males,	-	-	-	-	3	2	16	7	8	4	-	-	40
	Females,	-	-	-	-	1	1	6	10	4	5	-	-	27
	Total,	-	-	-	-	4	3	22	17	12	9	-	-	67
Penis,	Males,	-	-	-	-	1	1	2	3	2	3	1	-	13
	Females,	-	-	-	-	-	-	-	-	-	-	-	-	-
	Total,	-	-	-	-	1	1	2	3	2	3	1	-	13
Bladder,	Males,	-	-	-	-	-	-	2	2	3	-	-	-	7
	Females,	-	-	-	-	-	1	-	-	1	-	-	-	2
	Total,	-	-	-	-	-	1	2	2	4	-	-	-	9
Testicle,	Males,	-	1	-	-	2	-	2	1	1	-	-	-	7
	Females,	-	-	-	-	-	-	-	-	-	-	-	-	-
	Total,	-	1	-	-	2	-	2	1	1	-	-	-	7
Groin,	Males,	-	-	-	-	-	-	1	-	-	-	-	-	1
	Females,	-	-	-	-	-	-	2	2	2	-	-	-	6
	Total,	-	-	-	-	-	-	3	2	2	-	-	-	7
Prostate,	Males,	-	-	-	-	-	-	-	1	1	1	-	-	3
	Females,	-	-	-	-	-	-	-	-	-	-	-	-	-
	Total,	-	-	-	-	-	-	-	1	1	1	-	-	3
Leg,	Males,	-	-	-	2	-	1	6	3	4	5	1	-	23
	Females,	-	-	1	2	-	3	2	2	4	2	-	-	16
	Total,	-	-	1	4	-	4	8	5	8	7	1	-	39
Foot,	Males,	-	1	-	-	1	-	-	3	2	2	1	-	10
	Females,	-	-	-	-	-	-	-	1	2	2	-	-	4
	Total,	-	1	-	-	1	-	-	4	4	4	1	-	14
Other specified parts,	Males,	-	-	-	-	-	-	8	5	3	1	-	-	18
	Females,	-	-	-	-	3	1	7	5	3	1	3	-	23
	Total,	-	-	-	-	3	1	15	7	6	2	3	-	41
Part unspecified,	Males,	-	-	-	2	-	-	3	2	3	12	1	1	41
	Females,	2	3	-	-	16	3	18	10	10	17	3	-	97
	Total,	2	3	-	2	16	3	21	12	13	29	4	1	138
Total year 1865,	Males,	2	4	-	2	31	74	104	173	204	158	17	3	965
	Females,	3	3	3	6	25	161	341	337	226	168	27	1	1,171
	M. & F.,	5	7	3	13	56	235	445	510	430	326	44	4	2,136
Ratio per 1,000,000 (M. & F.) living at the same Age,		[illegible]	[illegible]	[illegible]	[illegible]	[illegible]	[illegible]	[illegible]	[illegible]	[illegible]	[illegible]			[illegible]
Total number year 1864,		2	3	3	16	48	221	444	488	440	330	49	4	2,143
" " " 1863,		2	2	11	1	53	193	446	488	449	341	46	4	2,134
" " " 1862,		1	4	3	8	44	203	457	459	467	286	40	3	[illegible]
" " " 1861,		3	5	10	11	35	217	432	418	429	300	32	3	2,037
" " " 1860,		5	3	4	13	37	202	379	373	437	271	31	4	[illegible]
" " " 1859,		3	3	3	11	57	186	315	416	443	267	38	1	[illegible]
" " " 1858,		3	4	4	9	37	180	470	419	448	264	27	3	[illegible]
" " " 1857,		7	3	13	11	42	183	413	414	404	275	30	3	[illegible]
" " " 1856,		3	10	5	13	53	220	403	470	438	254	34	3	[illegible]
" " " 1855,		4	6	16	8	49	188	400	413	467	264	31	4	[illegible]

V.—Developmental Diseases.

The deaths in this class amount to 18,106, of which 17,641 (7,956 males and 9,685 females), or 20·5 per cent. of the deaths from all causes, were ascribed to "old age." Of the remaining 465 deaths, 373 are tabulated under the head of "premature birth"; 15 were caused by atelectasis, 15 by cyanosis, 35 by spina bifida; &c.

VI.—Local Diseases.

The number of deaths from "local diseases" registered amounted to 37,453 (18,962 males and 18,491 females), or 48·8 per cent. of the deaths from all causes.

Diseases of the Nervous System.—From this group of diseases there resulted 7,908 deaths—4,104 males and 3,804 females. They include 2,396 from convulsions (nearly all children), 1,689 tabulated under the head of "hemiplegia, brain paralysis"; 1,250 from apoplexy; 671 from inflammation of the brain or its membranes, 329 from epilepsy, 438 from insanity (general paralysis of the insane), 5 (all females) from chorea or St. Vitus's dance, 235 from softening of the brain, &c.

Diseases of the Circulatory System.—Diseases of the circulatory system caused 6,375 deaths—3,201 males and 3,174 females.

Diseases of the Respiratory System.—The deaths from these diseases last year amount to 16,194, 8,122 males and 8,072 females—or 345·9 in every 100,000 of the population, against an average of 15,328 or 311·4 per 100,000 of the estimated mean population for the ten years, 1881-90, and higher than the rate for any of those years. The respective rates for the Provinces, in 1891, are Leinster, 355·0 per 100,000 persons; Munster, 338·7; Ulster, 370·3; and Connaught, 285·3.

Of the 16,194 deaths from these causes 10,771 (5,001 males and 5,770 females), resulted from bronchitis, against 9,567 from that disease in the preceding year; 3,481 (2,095 males and 1,386 females) were from pneumonia or inflammation of the lungs; 638 from croup; 509 from asthma and emphysema; 189 from pleurisy; 101 from laryngitis, &c.

Diseases of the Digestive System.—These diseases caused 4,303 deaths (2,169 males and 2,134 females), including 401 from enteritis or inflammation of the bowels; 371 from peritonitis or inflammation of the covering of the bowels; 406 from ileus or obstruction of the bowels; 126 from hernia; 12 (10 males and 2 females) from fistula; 246—163 males and 83 females—from cirrhosis of liver; &c.

Diseases of the Urinary System.—To the various affections of this order of diseases 1,491 deaths (1,026 males and 465 females) were ascribed. Of these deaths, 619 (380 males and 239 females) were from Bright's disease, 176 from acute nephritis or inflammation of the kidneys; 31 from ischuria or suppression of urine; 20 from stone in the bladder; 45 from uræmia, &c.

The remaining deaths from Local Diseases comprise 69 from *Diseases of the Lymphatic System and of Ductless Glands*; 603 from Diseases of the *Reproductive System* (including 182 from diseases of the Organs of Generation, and 421 from the Accidents of Childbirth), 229 from *Diseases* of the *Locomotive System*; and 235 from *Diseases of the Integumentary System*.

VII.—Violent Deaths.

The number of violent deaths registered during the year is 1,897 (1,281 males and 616 females), or 40·5 in every 100,000 of the population, being slightly over the average rate for the ten years 1881-90. Accidents or negligence caused 1,698 of these deaths (including 184 from burns or scalds and 350 from drowning); there were 90 cases of homicide (murder and manslaughter), and 110 of suicide, and one man was executed. By agreement with the Registrar-General for England a modification of the classification of deaths from accidents or negligence was made in 1891, and the tables relating to the subject appended to this Report have been compiled according to the new arrangement.

Inquests.—There were 2,111 inquests reported to the Registrars during the year 1891, being 1 inquest to every 41 deaths registered.

AGES.

Deaths of infants under 1 year old numbered 10,252, being equal to 9·5 per cent. of the number of births registered.

Amongst children under 5 years of age 16,330 deaths occurred—a mortality equal to 34·7 in every 1,000 of the estimated number of the living at that age. Of these, 8,782 were boys and 7,548 girls; the former number representing 36·8 in every 1,000 boys, and the latter 32·6 in every 1,000 girls under 5 years old.

The deaths of persons aged 65 years and upwards are equivalent to 10·5 per cent. of the living at that age.

Among the deaths registered are 725 of persons stated to have been aged 95 years or upwards—344 males and 381 females; of these 176 (88 males and 88 females) were returned as having been 100 years or upwards. In the absence of public records for remote periods, absolute verification of the ages of very old persons is not obtainable, but secondary inquiries having been made as regards persons returned during the year 1890 as centenarians, it was found, in almost every instance, that so far as the Registrars could ascertain the age was correctly stated.

EMIGRATION.

According to the Returns obtained by the Royal Irish Constabulary and the Metropolitan Police, who acted as enumerators at the several Irish seaports, the number of emigrants who left Ireland during the year 1891 amounted to 59,623; of these 30,046 were males and 29,577 were females. Of the whole number, 9,276 were from the Province of Leinster; 24,678 from Munster; 13,264 from Ulster; and 12,405 from Connaught.

Of the total emigrants from Ireland in 1891, 9·5 per cent. were under 15 years of age; 82·6 per cent. were between 15 and 35 years old; 7·9 per cent. were 35 or upwards; and in 2 instances, the ages were not specified.

PRICES OF PROVISIONS, AND PAUPERISM.

The average price of the 4 lb. loaf in Dublin was 6¾d.* Oatmeal (1st quality) averaged 15s. 6d. per cwt. in Dublin, being 2d. over average price for 1890; the average prices of potatoes in Dublin ranged from 3s. 6d. to 4s. 2d. per cwt., against 2s. 7d. to 5s. 3d. in 1890; and those of beef from 49s. 6d. to 61s. 6d. per cwt., against 50s. 6d. to 62s. in 1890.

TABLE XIV.—AVERAGE PRICES in DUBLIN of BREAD, OATMEAL, POTATOES, and BEEF, during the years 1881–91, and the AVERAGE NUMBER of PERSONS in IRELAND receiving IN-DOOR and OUT-DOOR RELIEF on Saturdays in those years; also the AVERAGE PRICES of PROVISIONS and the AVERAGE NUMBER of PERSONS in RECEIPT of RELIEF during each quarter of the year 1891.

Year.	Average Prices of Provisions.				Pauperism.	
	Bread, (4-lb. Loaf)*	Oatmeal (Corn Exchange) per Cwt. (1st quality)	Potatoes (at Pillar Market) per Cwt.	Beef (at the Dublin Cattle Market) per Cwt.	Average Number of Paupers relieved: In-door.	Out-door.
	d.	s. d.	s. d. s. d.	s. d. s. d.		
[illegible]	[illegible]	[illegible]	[illegible]	[illegible]	[illegible]	[illegible]
[illegible]	[illegible]	[illegible]	[illegible]	[illegible]	[illegible]	[illegible]
[illegible]	7	[illegible]	[illegible]	[illegible]	[illegible]	[illegible]
[illegible]	[illegible]	[illegible]	[illegible]	[illegible]	[illegible]	[illegible]
[illegible]	[illegible]	[illegible]	[illegible]	[illegible]	[illegible]	[illegible]
[illegible]	[illegible]	[illegible]	[illegible]	[illegible]	[illegible]	[illegible]
[illegible]	[illegible]	[illegible]	[illegible]	[illegible]	[illegible]	[illegible]
[illegible]	[illegible]	[illegible]	[illegible]	[illegible]	[illegible]	[illegible]
[illegible]	[illegible]	[illegible]	[illegible]	[illegible]	[illegible]	[illegible]
[illegible]	[illegible]	[illegible]	[illegible]	[illegible]	[illegible]	[illegible]
[illegible]	[illegible]	[illegible]	[illegible]	[illegible]	[illegible]	[illegible]
1st Quarter, [illegible]	[illegible]	[illegible]	[illegible]	[illegible]	[illegible]	[illegible]
2nd	7	[illegible]	[illegible]	[illegible]	[illegible]	[illegible]
3rd	[illegible]	[illegible]	[illegible]	[illegible]	[illegible]	[illegible]
4th	7	[illegible]	[illegible]	[illegible]	[illegible]	[illegible]

* Prices for the years [illegible] [illegible] were derived from Returns [illegible] & Co., [illegible] for the third and fourth quarters of [illegible] and for the years [illegible], from Returns [illegible] Limited," and Messrs. Johnston & Co. (or Johnston, Mooney, and O'Brien, Limited)—the prices quoted [illegible]

Surveying the period covered by the several Tables in this Report, *i.e.*, 1891, and the ten years preceding, it is found that beef was lowest in the year 1887, when the average prices ranged from 44*s.* to 53*s.* 6*d.* per cwt.; oatmeal was cheapest in 1889, when the average price was 18*s.* 7*d.* per cwt.; and potatoes, in 1888, when the average range of prices was from 2*s.* 2*d.* to 2*s.* 9*d.* per cwt. The highest average price of oatmeal was 17*s.* 6*d.* in 1884 and 1885; the highest range for potatoes, 3*s.* 9*d.* to 4*s.* 10*d.* per cwt. in 1883, and for beef, 66*s.* 6*d.* to 77*s.* per cwt. in 1883.

From Returns, for which I am indebted to the Local Government Board, it appears that the average number of workhouse inmates in Ireland on Saturdays during the year 1891 was 41,744, being 1,265 under the average for the preceding year; and that the average number of persons receiving out-door relief was 62,328, or 447 over the corresponding number for 1890.

THE WEATHER.

The following particulars and those given on pages 22–42, which are inserted by the kind permission of the Editor of the Dublin Journal of Medical Science, have been derived from Returns of Meteorological Observations taken in Dublin City during the years 1871–91, by J. W. Moore, Esq., M.D., F.R.C.P.I., F.R. MET. SOC., and published in the Journal during the years 1891–92. The Tables on pages 180–182 also, are founded on Dr. Moore's observations.

The mean Atmospherical Pressure has been obtained from daily readings of the barometer at 9 A.M. and 9 P.M., corrected and reduced to 32° Fahrenheit at the mean sea level. The Mean Temperature values have been deduced from the maximal and minimal readings of the thermometer in the shade. The Rainfall is that measured daily at 9 A.M. A rainy day is one on which at least one-hundredth (·01) of an inch of rain falls within the twenty-four hours from 9 A.M. to 9 A.M.

The *Mean Height of the Barometer* during the year 1891 was 29·909 inches. The highest observed reading was 30·675 inches at 9 P.M. on January 14th. The lowest observed reading was 28·251 inches, at 9·30 P.M. on October 13th. The extreme range of atmospherical pressure was 2·424 inches compared with 3·051 inches in 1890.

The *Mean Temperature* of the year, deduced from the arithmetical mean of the maximal and minimal readings of the thermometer in the shade was 49·3°. The highest reading was 75·6° on September 10th; the lowest reading was 23·9° on January 7th. The average mean temperature for the years 1871–90 calculated in the same way, was 49·6°. The mean temperature deduced from the daily readings of the dry bulb thermometer at 9 A.M. and 9 P.M. was 48·5°.

Rain fell on 184 days, including snow or sleet on 14 days, and hail on 23 days. The average number of rainy days in the years 1871–90 was 190·0. The total rainfall measured 27·820 inches compared with an average of 28·382 inches in the twenty years 1871–90. During the first half of 1891 (January to June, inclusive) the rainfall was 8·748 inches on 77 days; during the second half (July to December, inclusive) 19·072 inches fell on 107 days.

As regards the *Direction of the Wind*, 730 observations were made during the year, with this result—N., 49; N.E., 54; E., 53; S.E., 55; S., 84; S.W., 125; W., 178; N.W., 86; Calms, 46.

I have the honour to be

Your Excellency's faithful servant,

THOS. W. GRIMSHAW,

Registrar-General.

GENERAL REGISTER OFFICE,
CHARLEMONT HOUSE,
Dublin, 20th December, 1892.

Twenty-eighth Annual Report of the Registrar-General of

METEOROLOGICAL OBSERVATIONS

FOR EACH MONTH OF THE YEAR 1891.

By J. W. MOORE, Esq., M.D., F.R.C.P.I., F.R. MET. SOC.

(Extracted from the *Dublin Journal of Medical Science*.)

Although temperature was not so low as in previous weeks, the weather of the period ending Saturday the 17th was wintry and inclement on the whole. The most striking feature of the week was the existence of a great anticyclone over Ireland and the Atlantic to the westward of this country from Tuesday to Thursday, inclusive, at a time when a deep depression, with readings of the barometer as low as 29·00 inches, was passing southeastwards across the Scandinavian Peninsula and the Baltic. This anticyclone attained its fullest proportions on Wednesday evening, when the barometer read 30·97 inches at Belmullet, 30·94 inches at Valentia Island, 30·93 inches at Mullaghmore, 30·88 inches at Parsonstown and in Dublin. At Valentia Island the absolute maximal pressure recorded was 30·967 inches at 10·35 a.m. on the 14th. These were the highest pressure-readings recorded in Ireland since January 18, 1882, when the barometer rose to 30·935 inches at 10·30 p.m. in Dublin. A strong, mild S.W. wind blew on Sunday, but the upper current (cirrus cloud) was northerly. Temperature became very changeable after this, and rather low temperatures occurred at night. Very raw, damp, showery weather prevailed from Thursday to the end; but bitter cold again set in over the Continent generally on Friday. In Dublin the mean height of the barometer was 30·606 inches, pressure ranging from 30·873 inches at 9 p.m. of Wednesday (wind, N.), to 30·261 inches about 3 p.m. of Friday (wind, N.N.W.) The corrected mean temperature was 40·3°. The mean dry bulb temperature at 9 a.m. and 9 p.m. was 39·0°. The rainfall was ·136 inch on three days. Hail fell on Saturday the 17th.

Although intense cold prevailed very generally at the beginning of the period ending Saturday the 24th, a considerable recovery of temperature took place as the week wore on, and for the first time since November, 1890, the usual winter cyclonic distribution of pressure was fully established over the Atlantic off the West and North-west of Europe. On Sunday and Monday very severe frost held over England, as well as over central and southern Europe—at 8 a.m. of Sunday, the 18th, the thermometer read 11° at York, 14° at Loughborough, and 15° at Oxford; even in Dublin, where a fresh southerly wind was blowing, frost prevailed and the air was unusually dry and searching, relative humidity being only 53 per cent. Next morning the readings of the thermometer were 6° at Loughborough, 12° at Oxford, 16° at Cambridge, and 18° at York. A great change now set in, having been heralded by much cirriform cloud and solar and lunar halos on Sunday and Monday. At 8 a.m. of Tuesday a depression had its centre (28·95 inches) near the Shetlands, and was causing moderate or fresh gales from S.W. to W. in many parts of the British Islands. On Friday a still deeper depression (28·79 inches) advanced to the same region from S.W. These disturbances threw the weather into a very unsettled state, and frequent showers, with squalls and shifting temperature, were reported from most British stations. In Dublin the mean height of the barometer was 29·715 inches, or ·891 inches below the corresponding value for the previous week—30·606 inches. Pressure ranged between 30·417 inches at 9 a.m. of Sunday (wind S. by E.), and 29·337 inches, at 9 a.m. of Friday (wind, W. by N.) The corrected mean temperature was 38·8°—the mean of the dry bulb readings at 9 a.m. and 9 p.m. being 38·3°. The screened thermometers rose to 53·6° on Friday. Rain was measured on five days—the total quantity being ·307 inch, of which ·151 inch was registered on Tuesday—the maximal daily fall for the month.

The south-westerly type of weather persisted through the last week (25th–31st) all over the North-west of Europe—that is, successive deep depressions travelled north-eastwards along the western coasts of Ireland, Scotland, and Norway, while numerous secondary depressions passed in the same direction across the British Islands and North Sea. Hence, temperature was unstable but usually high for the time of year, strong S.W. and W. winds prevailed, and rain fell frequently. In the East of Europe, on the contrary, conditions were anticyclonic, and very cold weather was reported, the thermometer reading—15° at Moscow on the mornings of Tuesday and Wednesday. On the night of Friday, the 30th, a depression rapidly approached Ireland from S.W., causing a violent gale from S. to W.S.W. during the early morning hours of Saturday, the 31st. The storm was accompanied by heavy showers at times. Rain fell abundantly in the South of England during the week. In Dublin the mean height of the barometer was 29·740 inches. The corrected mean temperature was 40·0°. The mean dry bulb temperature at 9 a.m. and 9 p.m. was 45·3°. The screened thermometers rose to 55·7° on Monday and also on Wednesday, having fallen to 36·8° on Sunday. The rainfall amounted to ·188 inch on three days. The prevailing wind was S.W.

In Dublin, the rainfall up to January, 31, 1891, has amounted ·672 inches on 14 days, compared with a twenty-five years' (1865–1889) average of 2·200 inches on 173 days.

At Knockdolian, Greystones, Co. Wicklow, 1·575 inches of rain fell in January, on 13 days. The heaviest falls in 24 hours were ·360 inch on the 20th, ·150 on the 28th, and ·160 inch on the 30th.

February.—February, 1891, proved a record month for drought, mildness, calm, and fogginess combined. Day after day and week after week an anticyclone lay over Central Europe and the southern half of the British Islands, whereas conditions were cyclonic both in Northern Europe and in the Mediterranean Basin. Calms and fog, or light variable winds prevailed in the anticyclonic area, where also the weather was almost rainless from beginning to end of the month. The S.W. wind on the western edge of the high pressure system raised the temperature in Ireland, but it was low in the S.E. of England owing to calm and fog. Towards the close the diurnal range of temperature in Central England became extraordinary, in consequence of the dispersal of the fog, the dryness of the air, and the absence of cloud by day and night.

In Dublin the mean temperature (44·7°) was 1·9° above the average (42·8°); the mean dry bulb readings at 9 a.m. and 9 p.m. were 43·6°. In the twenty-five years ending with 1889, February was coldest in 1873 (M. T. = 37·9°), and warmest in 1869 (M. T. = 46·7°). In 1886 the M. T. was 39·7°. In the year 1879 (the cold year) it was 40·1°. In 1888 it was as low as 38·6°, in 1889 it was 40·3°, and in 1890 it was 41·5°.

The mean height of the barometer was 30·398 inches, or 0·543 inch above the average value for February—namely, 29·855 inches. The mercury rose to 30·725 inches at 9 a.m. of the 5th, and fell to 29·824 inches at 3 p.m. of the 24th. The observed range of atmospherical pressure was, therefore, 0·901 inch—that is, a little over nine-tenths of an inch.

The mean temperature deduced from daily readings of the dry bulb thermometer at 9 a.m. and 9 p.m. was 43·6°, or 4·1° above the value for January, 1891. Using the formula *Mean Temp.* = *min.* + (*max.*—*min.* × ·50), the M.T. becomes 44·7°, compared with a twenty-five years' average of 42·6°. On the 23rd the thermometer in the screen rose to 61·3°—wind, S.; on the 9th the temperature fell to 30·1°—wind, W.S.W. The minimum on the grass was 25·5° on the 9th.

The rainfall was only ·042 inch, distributed over 2 days. The average rainfall for February in the twenty-five years, 1865–89, inclusive, was 2·150 inches, and the average number of rainy days was 17·2. The rainfall and the rainy days, therefore, were both considerably below the average. In 1883 the rainfall in February was large—3·735 inches on 17 days; in 1879, also, 3·706 inches fell on 23 days. On the other hand, in 1873, only ·923 of an inch was measured on but 8 days; in 1890, only ·808 of an inch fell on but 7 days; and in 1887, only ·341 of an inch fell on 11 days. The rainfall in 1887 was much the smallest recorded in February for very many years. But the present record is probably unparalleled—·042 inch on 2 days. The nearest approach to this drought was in September, 1865, when only ·056 of an inch of rain was measured on but 3 days. There was no snow, sleet, or hail in Dublin.

The atmosphere was foggy on as many as 16 days, namely—the 4th, 5th, 8th, 9th, 13th, 14th, 15th, 16th, 18th, 20th, 23rd, 24th, 25th, 26th, 27th, and 28th. Notwithstanding the prevalence of fog, the amount of cloud—55·3 per cent.—fell far short of the average—66 per cent. High winds were noted on 8 days, reaching the force of a gale on only one day—the 11th.

The temperature exceeded 50° in the screen on as many as 16 days, compared with only 8 days in January, and with only 2 days in February, 1890; while it fell to or below 32° in the screen on only 2 days, compared with 7 days in January, and with 5 in February, 1890. The minima on the grass were 32°, or less, on 17 nights, compared with 21 nights in January, and 18 nights in February, 1890. On no day did the thermometer fail to rise above 40° in the screen.

Very open, favourable weather prevailed throughout the first week (1st–7th) especially in the east of Ireland. After Sunday, the 1st, an anticyclone, with barometrical readings as high as 30·70 inches or upwards, was found lying over France, St. George's and the English Channels. As the sky was densely clouded within the central area of this high pressure system, radiation was checked, and hence little or no frost was felt at the majority of British and Irish stations—the exceptions were in the extreme S.E. of England on Monday morning and central Ireland on Thursday morning. On Monday and Tuesday the S.W. winds blew strongly at times, but later on there was a calm, accompanied by some fog, and finally light to moderate S.W. winds prevailed, with very cloudy skies and open, but dry weather. In Dublin the mean height of the barometer was 30·542 inches, or as much as ·802 inch above the mean pressure during the preceding week, and the pressure reached 30·725 inches at 9 a.m. of Thursday (wind, W. by N.). The mean temperature was 46·2°; the mean dry bulb temperature at 9 a.m. and 9 p.m. was 46·1°. There was practically no measurable rainfall only ·002 inch being caught in the gauge as the result of a slight shower early on the morning of the 5th. The prevailing direction of the wind was S.W.

An area of high pressure was found lying over Ireland, England, France, and Western Germany throughout the second week, while depressions of great depth travelled eastwards across the North of Europe, and more shallow depressions existed over Southern Europe and the Mediterranean. Consequently, the weather was favourable in Ireland, rough and unsettled in Scandinavia, changeable in the Mediterranean Basin. On Wednesday, the 11th, the wind freshened to gale force from W. even in the east of Ireland, but otherwise light winds and calms prevailed. At 8 a.m. of Thursday the barometer was as low as 28·76 inches at Stockholm, which station was then close to the centre of a very perfect cyclone. Ireland lay quite outside the influence of this disturbance, the N.W. gales of which brought intense cold to the Swedish stations, the temperature recorded at 8 a.m. of Friday being −12° at Haparanda, +6° at Stockholm, and +10° at Hernösand. In Dublin the mean height of the barometer during the week was 30·400 inches. The corrected mean temperature was 42·4°. The mean dry bulb temperature at 9 a.m. and 9 p.m. was 41·2°. The screened thermometers fell to 30·1° on Monday, the 9th. The rainfall amounted to ·027 inch only, of which ·024 inch was measured on Friday, the 13th.

During the third week conditions remained anticyclonic in our neighbourhood until Saturday, when evidence of the approach of a low pressure system to the S.W. of Ireland manifested itself in a steady fall of the barometer, the overcasting of the sky with cirriform cloud, and a freshening S.S.E. wind. Throughout the week a large area of high pressure (anticyclone) spread across Central Europe from Ireland to Poland, Hungary, and the south of Russia. Within the sphere of its influence, quiet, cold, foggy weather prevailed, and it was almost rainless. Across northern Europe, however, some large depressions travelled eastwards and conditions were unsettled. Over the Mediterranean, also, areas of relatively low pressure existed, keeping the weather more or less disturbed. Very dense fogs prevailed on Wednesday and Thursday in England and Holland, and on the former day also, in the E. and N.E. of Ireland. So great was the influence of the fog on the temperature in London that the maximum on Thursday was only 27°, whereas the thermometer rose to 59° at Nairn in the north of Scotland. In Dublin the mean height of the barometer was 30·475 inches. The corrected mean temperature was 42·5°. The mean dry bulb temperature at 9 a.m. and 9 p.m. was 40·8°. The prevailing winds were light from southerly points—between S.W. and S.E. The sun had considerable power by day. Rain fell on the early morning of Sunday, the 22nd, to the amount of ·010 inch.

The weather of the fourth week was remarkable in many respects—in England for the prevalence of dense fogs, and an extraordinarily large diurnal range of temperature—at Loughborough the thermometer ranged from 20° to 57° in the 24 hours ending at 8 a.m. of Thursday, and at Cambridge the thermometer fell from 67° on Friday to 23° during the ensuing night—a range of 44° F.; in Ireland for a wave of extreme warmth and dryness of the atmosphere on Monday, and for the passage of a barometrical depression across the country on Wednesday and Thursday without one drop of rain, except at Belmullet. An anticyclonic system hung over Germany throughout the week, and a warm southerly wind skirting the western edge of this system in tangent fashion produced an extraordinary rise of temperature in parts of Ireland on Monday and Tuesday. In Dublin on Monday evening, the 23rd, puffs of warm air were felt from time to time, which raised the temperature to 61·9° at 7.15 p.m. So desiccated was the air at the same time that the wet bulb thermometer read only 47·9°, and the relative humidity fell to 40 per cent. At Mullaghmore, Co. Sligo, the temperature reached 62° next day, while the maximum in London (where dense fog prevailed) was only 39°. At Nairn, in the N.E. of Scotland, the thermometer rose to 64° on this day (Tuesday). On Saturday a strong S.W. to W. wind sprang up, and light showers fell towards evening. In Dublin the mean pressure was 30·166 inches—the barometer falling to 29·834 inches at 3 p.m. of Thursday (wind S.E., light). The corrected mean temperature was 47·8°; the mean dry bulb temperature at 9 a.m. and 9 p.m. was 46·2°. The screened thermometers rose to 61·9° on Monday and fell to 33·8° on Saturday. Rain fell on this last-named day to the amount of only ·003 inch. The wind was either calm, or southerly (S.E. to S.W.).

In Dublin, the rainfall up to February 28, 1891, has amounted to ·714 inch on 16 days, compared with a twenty-five years' (1865–1889) average of 4·350 inches on 34·3 days.

At Knockdolian, Greystones, Co. Wicklow, 1·275 inches of rain fell in January, on 15 days; and only ·120 inch in February on *only one day*, the 21st. At Cloneevin, Killiney, Co. Dublin, only ·470 inch fell on 11 days in January and only ·030 inch on 2 days in February.

March.—Opening with a long-continued westerly gale, March, 1891, proved very severe, cold and showery. The night temperatures were particularly low at most inland stations. The most remarkable features of the month were the destructive "blizzard" of the 9th and 10th in the English Channel, and the fact that the mean temperature in Dublin was no less than 3° below that of February.

In Dublin the arithmetical mean temperature (41·7°) was considerably below the average (43·1°); the mean dry bulb readings at 9 a.m. and 9 p.m. were 40·8°. In the twenty-six years ending with 1890, March was coldest in 1867 and 1883 (M. T. = 39·0°), and warmest in 1868 (M. T. = 47·3°). In 1878 the M. T. was 41·1°, in 1879 (the cold year) it was 42·5°, in 1883 it was as low as 40·8°, and in 1889 it was 44·0°, and in 1890 it was as high as 45·1°. As a general rule, February in Dublin is only a shade colder than March. This is due to the fact that the Continental anticyclone usually embraces the British Isles and Scandinavia in March, causing easterly winds. In the present year, however, February was actually 3·0° warmer than March.

The mean height of the barometer was 29·838 inches, or 0·078 inch lower the corrected average value for March—namely, 29·916 inches. The mercury rose to 30·470 inches at 7 p.m. of the 3rd, and fell to 29·032 inches at 3 p.m. of the 13th. The observed range of atmospherical pressure was, therefore, 1·418 inches—that is, nearly an inch and a half.

The mean temperature deduced from daily readings of the dry bulb thermometer at 9 a.m. and 9 p.m. was 40·8°, or 3·0° below the value for February, 1891. Using the formula, *Mean Temp.* = *Min.* + (*max.*—*min.* × ·481), the M. T. becomes 41·5°. The arithmetical mean of the maximal and minimal readings was 41·7°, compared with a twenty-five years' average of 43·1°. On the 1st the thermometer in the screen rose to 57·9°—wind, W.S.W.; on the 12th the temperature fell to 27·1°—wind, W. The minimum on the grass was 21·6° also on the 12th.

The rainfall was only 1·026 inch, distributed, however, over 16 days. The average rainfall for March in the twenty-five years, 1865–89, inclusive, was 2·061 inches, and the average number of rainy days was 16·5. The rainfall, therefore, was much below the average, while the rainy days were slightly below it. In 1867 the rainfall in March was very large—4·972 inches on 22 days; in 1888, 3·783 inches fell on 18 days; in 1880 also 3·629 inches fell on 21 days. On the other hand, in 1871, only ·815 inch was measured on 12 days; and in 1874 only ·953 inch fell, also on 13 days. In 1887 (the "dry year"), 1·185 inches of rain fell on 13 days; in 1889 1·070 inches fell on, however, as many as 17 days; and in 1890 the fall was as much as 3·039 inches on 17 days.

The atmosphere was foggy on the 12th, 13th, 14th, and 21st. High winds were noted on 14 days, reaching the force of a gale on 5 days, the 3rd, 4th, 5th, 6th, and 25th. *Snow* or *sleet* occurred on the 7th, 8th, 10th, 12th, 23rd, 26th, and 27th; and hail fell on the 2nd, 7th, 8th, 10th, 11th, 13th, 16th, 28th, and 30th. The temperature exceeded 50° in the screen on only 9 days, compared with as many as 14 days in February, and 13 days in March, 1890; while it fell to or below 32° in the screen on as many as 10 days, compared with only 2 days in February and only 4 days in March, 1890. The minima on the grass were 32°, or less, on 20 nights, compared with 17 nights in February and 10 nights in March, 1890. On 3 days the thermometer did not rise to 40° in the screen.

The chief feature of the period ending on Saturday, the 7th, was a singularly persistent westerly gale, which depended upon the passage eastwards across Northern Europe of a series of very deep atmospherical depressions, while an anticyclone held over the Bay of Biscay and France. In Dublin the wind blew freshly from points between W.S.W. and W.N.W. almost continuously until the afternoon of Friday, the 6th, when it moderated, and a copious rainfall occurred, yielding ·130 inch. A great "chill" passed south-eastwards over Western Europe on Friday and Saturday. On Monday evening there was a sharp squall of rain and hail, and on the following day also passing showers fell at intervals. During the week barometrical gradients were often very decided and steep over Western Europe—for example, at 8 a.m. of Monday, the 2nd, the barometer varied from 28·31 inches at Bodö (in the N.W. of Norway) to 30·33 inches in Brittany and 30·28 inches at Biarritz (in the S.W. of France). The mean pressure at 8 a.m. for the week was—at Bodö, 28·861 inches, but at Valentia Island, in Kerry, 30·286 inches. This fact will convey a good idea of the steepness of the baric gradients and the resulting force of the westerly wind. In Dublin the mean height of the barometer was 30·067 inches, pressure ranging from 30·470 inches at 7 p.m. of Tuesday (wind W.N.W.) to 29·658 at 9 p.m. of Saturday (wind W.). The corrected mean temperature was 46·3°. The mean dry bulb temperature at 9 a.m. and 9 p.m. was 46·3°. The shade thermometer rose to 57·9° on Sunday, the 1st. The rainfall amounted to ·160 inch on three days. The prevailing wind was westerly. Snow fell on the Dublin mountains on Saturday afternoon.

The second was a very severe week—in Dublin as cold as the coldest of the whole winter, but otherwise fine; in southern England notable for one of the greatest snow storms and tempests on record, caused by the passage up the English Channel of a complex depression, with two minima, in the interval between Sunday, the 8th, and Wednesday, the 11th. This system produced violent E. to N.E. gales and heavy falls of snow all over the S.W., S., and S.E. of England—the bad weather culminating in a disastrous and fatal "blizzard" on the night of Monday, the 9th. At this time the sky became overcast in Ireland with a canopy of cirriform cloud moving rapidly in an upper current from S.W., while the wind freshened somewhat from E., but the disturbance passed by harmlessly, and only a few snow and hail showers fell from time to time. Very severe frosts were, however, felt at night—the minima at Fassaroe being 21°, 23°, 23°, 18°, 19°, 19°, and 21°. In France warmer weather was experienced, the wind blowing freshly from S. and S.W., and heavy rains falling generally. In Dublin the mean height of the barometer was 29·757 inches. The corrected mean temperature was 35·4°, or exactly the same as that of the week ending January 10th 1891. The mean dry bulb temperature at 9 a.m. and 9 p.m. was 34·8°, or 11·2° below the corresponding value in the previous week. The screened thermometers rose to 46·0° on Saturday having fallen to 27·1° on Thursday; until Wednesday the temperature in the shade did not reach 40°. The prevailing wind was north-easterly. Rainfall was measured on three days, the total amount being ·260 inch, of which ·036 inch fell as snow and hail on Sunday, the 8th, and ·220 inch as rain in the early morning hours of Sunday, the 15th.

Although still cold and changeable, the weather of the week ended Saturday, the 21st, showed a distinct improvement upon that of the previous week. During the first three days conditions were specially unsettled owing to the passage of a deep atmospherical depression south-wards across Ireland to the Bay of Biscay and the Peninsula. At 8 a.m. of Sunday, the 15th, the barometer read only 29·01 inches at Malin Head, and 12 hours later it sank to 28·88 inches at Mullaghmore, Co. Sligo. Rain fell heavily at this time in many parts of the British Islands, and the wind shifted from S.W. to N.E. and E. as the centre of the depression travelled southward. After Sunday winds from polar quarters (E., N.E., and N. to N.W.), held throughout the week. The nights were often clear and frosty: the days were chiefly dry and cool, with clouds at times and cold showers in places. This was particularly so on Friday, when a V-shaped depression, subsidiary to a large system of low pressure over Northern Europe, passed southwards over Great Britain. In Dublin the mean height of the barometer was 29·730 inches, pressure ranging between 29·452 inches at 3 p.m. of Sunday (wind, S.) and 30·061 inches at 9 a.m. of Saturday (wind N.). The corrected mean temperature was 41·6°. The mean dry bulb temperature at 9 a.m. and 9 p.m. was 41·5°. The rainfall equalled ·189 inch, on four days. The prevailing winds were N.E. and N.

The record of the fourth week, ending Saturday, the 28th, is again one of unsettled, generally cold, weather—the prevailing "set" of wind and cloud over North-western Europe being from points between W. and N. Only on Tuesday, the 24th, and in the earlier part of Wednesday, the 25th, was the weather at all mild, and even then the wind blew strongly from S.W. and W. Indeed, on the latter day a fresh or strong westerly gale was felt over the greater part of Ireland. Towards night temperature fell fast, and falls of sleet and snow occurred, accompanied in places by thunder and lightning. Conditions remained very rough and inclement until the afternoon of Good Friday, when the weather moderated and became finer and drier. Saturday, although still harsh, was fine and chiefly sunny. The depression, which caused Wednesday's gale, was of great size and considerable depth—the barometer falling below 28·9 inches near the centre of the system. In Dublin the mean height of the barometer during the week was 29·789 inches. The corrected mean temperature was 42·4°. The mean dry bulb temperature at 9 a.m. and 9 p.m. was 41·8°. The rainfall, which was chiefly in the form of snow or sleet, amounted to ·303 inch, on four days.

Fresh N.W. winds blew on Easter Day, the 29th, and also on Easter Monday. These were followed by a very sharp frost on the morning of the 31st, the thermometer falling to 27·9° in the screen and to 22·7° on the grass.

The rainfall in Dublin during the three months ending March 31st has amounted to only 1·650 inches on only 32 days, compared with 7·470 inches on 48 days during the same period in 1890, 5·738 inches, on 53 days in 1889, 6·097 inches on 41 days in 1888, and a twenty-five years' average of 6·411 inches on 51·0 days (1865–1889, inclusive).

At Knockdolian, Greystones, Co. Wicklow, 1·410 inches of rain fell on 14 days during March; and the total rainfall since January 1, 1891, equals 2·603 inches on 30 days. At Cloneevin, Killiney, Co. Dublin, the rainfall in March was ·740 inch, on 13 days; while the total fall since January 1 has been 1·340 inches, on 25 days, compared with a six years' average (1885–1890, inclusive) of 6·060 inches, on 44 days, for the first quarter of the year.

APRIL.—April, 1891, was a cold, rather dry and March-like month. The mean temperature, rainfall, and rainy days were all below the average. On only one day, the 30th, did the thermometer rise above 60° in the shade.

In Dublin the arithmetical mean temperature (45·7°) was 2·0° below the average (47·7°); the

and 9 p.m. were 45·4°. In the twenty-five years
year), (M. T. = 44·5°), and warmest in 1868 and 1
1887 it was as low as 43·1°, in 1868 it was (
1890 it was 47·8°.
ster was 29·864 inches, or 0·114 inch above the
e mercury rose to 30·313 inches at 9 p.m. of th
, and 9 p.m. of the 28th. The observed range

Saturday, the 25th. Throughout the period an anticyclone, or area of high barometrical pressure, was found over Scotland; whereas pressure was relatively low over Spain, France, and the Bay of Biscay. Hence, fresh to strong easterly or north-easterly winds were prevalent in the British Islands, and on Wednesday and Thursday they reached the force of a moderate gale at many exposed seaboard stations. The rainfall during the week was on the whole trifling, but a considerable fall of cold rain spread westwards from the N.E. of England to the S. and S.E. of Ireland in the interval between Tuesday morning and Thursday morning. On this latter day, also, considerable downpours of rain occurred over the greater part of France. On Friday the northern anticyclone moved southwards, and decreased in intensity. In Dublin the mean height of the barometer was 30·224 inches. The corrected mean temperature was 43·6°, or 1° below that of the previous week. The mean dry bulb temperature at 9 a.m. and 9 p.m. was 43·7°. Rain fell in measurable quantity on only one day—Tuesday—to the amount of ·060 inch. The wind was constantly E. to N.E. The mean temperature was 0·4° below that of the last week of January, 1·0° below that of the last week of February, and 0·9° below that of the first week of March.

In the closing period of the month—26th to the 30th, inclusive—at first of an easterly type, cold and hazy, the weather afterwards became warmer and softer, with fresh S.W. winds and frequent showers. In general, therefore, conditions were favourable and much more genial than for many weeks back. At the beginning of the period an anticyclone stretched from the east of Ireland across England and the North Sea to Holland and Belgium; it was accompanied by fine, cold, hazy weather. On Monday depressions arrived off the N.W. of Scotland and also the W. of France, and by Wednesday gradients for S.W. winds were fully established over Western Europe. A considerable, but short-lived, rise of temperature followed, the thermometer in the shade rising on Thursday, the 30th, to 67° at Cambridge, 66° in Dublin, 65° at Loughborough, 64° in London, and 63° at Parsonstown and Yarmouth. The thermometer in the screen fell to 30·1° on Sunday, and rose to 65·7° on Thursday. The rainfall was ·071 inch on three days. The prevailing winds were S.W. and N.W.

The rainfall in Dublin during the four months ending April 30th has amounted to only 3·203 inches on 40 days, compared with 9·043 inches on 69 days during the same period in 1890, 3·345 inches on 74 days in 1889, 8·090 inches on 34 days in 1888, and a 25 years' average of 8·466 inches on 66·2 days.

At Knockdolian, Greystones, Co. Wicklow, the rainfall during April, 1891, amounted to 2·950 inches, distributed over 13 days; ·930 inch falling on the 1st, and ·720 inch on the 3rd. The total fall since January 1st, 1891, equals 5·735 inches on 43 days.

At Cloneevin, Killiney, Co. Dublin, the rainfall in April was 1·100 inches on 12 days. The total fall since January 1st has been only 2·430 inches on 38 days—the averages of the six previous years for the same four months being 7·748 inches, on 58 days.

May.—May, 1891, was cold for the most part, showery, and unsettled, with an overwhelming prevalence of "polar" winds and frequent falls of hail. On the 16th and 17th, snow, sleet, and hail fell in most parts of the British Islands. Only in the period from the 10th to the 13th inclusive was there anything like summer heat.

In Dublin the arithmetical mean temperature (49·6°) was decidedly below the average (53·0°); the mean dry bulb readings at 9 a.m. and 9 p.m. were 48·5°. In the twenty-six years ending with 1890, May was coldest in 1869 (M. T. = 48·2°), in 1885 (M. T. = 48·7°), and in 1879 (the "cold year") (M. T. = 48·5°). It was warmest in 1868 (the "warm year") (M. T. = 55·8°) and 1875 (M. T. = 54·9°). In 1886, the M. T. was 50·5°, in 1887 it was 51·8°, in 1888 it was 52·3°, in 1889 it was 54·6°, and in 1890 it was 53·2°.

The mean height of the barometer was 29·709 inches, or 0·180 inch below the corrected average value for May—namely, 29·889 inches. The mercury rose to 30·393 inches at 9 a.m. of the 12th, and fell to 29·237 inches at 9 a.m. of the 1st. The observed range of atmospherical pressure was, therefore, 1·056 inches—that is, a little less than an inch and one-tenth.

The mean temperature deduced from daily readings of the dry bulb thermometer at 9 a.m. and 9 p.m. was 49·5°, or 4·1° above the value for April, 1891. Using the formula, *Mean Temp.* = min. + (max.—min. × ·47), the value was 49·3°, or 2·4° above the average mean temperature for May, calculated in the same way, in the twenty-five years, 1865–89, inclusive (51·6°). The arithmetical mean of the maximal and minimal readings was 49·6°, compared with a twenty-five years' average of 52·0°. On the 12th, the thermometer in the screen rose to 67·8°—wind E.N.E.; on the 18th the temperature fell to 32·6°—wind, N.E. The minimum on the grass was 27·3°, on the 18th.

The rainfall amounted to 2·703 inches, distributed over 17 days. The average rainfall for May in the twenty-five years, 1865–89, inclusive, was 2·050 inches, and the average number of rainy days was 15·4. The rainfall and the rainy days, therefore, were above the average. In 1886 the rainfall in May was very large—5·473 inches on 21 days; in 1869 also 5·414 inches fell on 19 days. On the other hand, in 1871, only ·375 of an inch was measured on 9 days; in 1876 only ·798 of an inch fell on 6 days; in 1887 only ·635 of an inch fell on 10 days; and in 1863 only ·978 of an inch on 11 days. In 1890, 2·438 inches fell on 17 days. May was the first month in 1891 in which the rainfall exceeded the average.

A solar halo was seen on the 8th, and a lunar halo on the 17th. High winds were noted on as many as 6 days, attaining the force of a gale, however, on not one occasion. Snow or sleet fell on the 16th and 17th. Hail occurred on the 1st, 2nd, 3rd, 15th, 16th, 17th, 19th, and 20th. Thunder was heard on the 23rd.

During the month the thermometer in the screen did not fall below 32°, but on six nights a temperature of 35° or less recorded on the grass. The mean minimal temperature on the grass was 37·7°, compared with 42·2° in May, 1890, 42·9° in May, 1889, 37·8° in 1888, and 37·0° in 1887.

On Friday, the 1st, heavy showers of rain and hail fell at many stations, and the wind veered from S.W. to N.W. at night, with a rapid fall of temperature. The resulting rainfall in Dublin was ·232 inch. On Saturday, the 2nd, hail also fell.

Changeable, but generally favourable weather prevailed during the week ended Saturday, the 9th. In Ireland the rainfall was heavy, and the amount of sunshine was small; yet the moisture was needed and proved beneficial; and the clouds, which shut out the sunshine by day, checked radiation at night and so prevented the occurrence of those spring-frosts, which are so harmful to vegetation. At first, westerly winds prevailed, with showers of rain and hail. On Monday, the 4th, a southerly current set in over Ireland, lasting until Thursday and bringing clouds and genial rain. On Friday a complex series of low pressure systems was found over the British Islands, the wind shifted to N.E. in Ireland and the weather became bright and bracing as the disturbances travelled away southeastwards. Saturday was again fine—cloudy and dull in the forenoon, fair in the afternoon. In Dublin the mean height of the barometer was 29·890 inches. The corrected mean temperature was 50·1°. The mean dry bulb reading at 9 a.m. and 9 p.m. was 50·7°. The rainfall amounted to ·471 inch on four days, the maximal record in 24 hours being ·310 inch on Thursday. Hail fell on Sunday, the 3rd.

Summer and winter met in the week ended Saturday, the 16th. The first four days were beautiful—bright, sunny, warm days being followed by cool, refreshing nights. Atmospherical pressure was uniformly high, and the type of its distribution was anticyclonic, except in the S.E. of England, where shallow depressions were found on Sunday and Monday, causing dull, cold, and rather rainy weather in that district. In Dublin the prevailing wind was N.E. until Wednesday, and then N.W. to the end of the week. This latter wind was part of the circulation round a succession of depressions, which travelled southeastwards across Scandinavia and the North Sea on and after Wednesday, the 13th. It brought back winter to the British Islands—squalls, hail-storms (accompanied in many places by thunder on Friday), and showers of sleet and snow prevailing on Friday and Saturday. In contrast to this, on Tuesday the thermometer had risen to 81° in the shade at Loughborough, and to 78° in London, while even on Wednesday the maxima were as high as 76° at Oxford and York, 77° at Hurst Castle, 78° in London, and 80° at Cambridge. In Ireland the highest reading was 75° at Parsonstown on Tuesday on which day the maximum in Dublin was 67·8°. In this city the mean pressure was 30·107 inches—highest, 30·293 inches at 9 a.m. of Tuesday (wind, E.N.E.) The corrected mean temperature was 52·1°. The mean dry bulb temperature at 9 a.m. and 9 p.m. was 51·4°. On Tuesday the screened thermometers rose to 67·8°, and on Saturday they fell to 37·7°. The rainfall was ·115 inch, on three days, the maximal fall in 24 hours being ·058 inch on Friday. On Saturday the maximal shade temperature was only 47·0°.

Many years have passed since the third week in May has proved as inclement as that of 1891. Sunday, the 17th, was like a day in midwinter—frequent heavy showers of hail, sleet, and cold rain keeping the temperature so low that the maximum in the screen was only 45·7°. At night a sharp frost occurred on the grass, and the sheltered thermometer fell to 32·5° in the city. The minimum at York during this night was 26°, and snow fell heavily in some of the English midlands. Whitsun Monday proved fair and bright on the east coast of Ireland; but very cold, wet weather prevailed over the South of England, to which district a complex system of low pressure had advanced from the westward. Indeed, all through the week, conditions were cyclonic over Western Europe, and a succession of areas of low pressure passed up the English Channel; then turning northwards, they disappeared off the west coast of Norway. On Saturday a depression advanced more directly over Ireland, where the weather once more became cold and raw, squally and wet. On this day as many as four separate depressions were shown on the weather chart. Thunder and hail showers were a common occurrence during this cold period, which might aptly be called a "relapse into winter." In Dublin the mean height of the barometer was 29·901 inches. The corrected mean temperature was only 45·0°, or 7·1° below that of the previous week (52·1°). The mean dry bulb temperature at 9 a.m. and 9 p.m. was 46·1°. The screened thermometers fell to 32·8° on Monday morning and rose to 56·7° on Friday. The rainfall was ·603 inch, on four days, ·373 inch being measured on Saturday. The prevailing winds were N.W. and N.E.

Very broken, showery weather held throughout the week ended Saturday, the 30th. There was, however, a decided advance in temperature, which became more accentuated towards the close, with the setting in of a southerly air-current. During the greater part of the period the weather in the British Islands was determined by an atmospherical depression, which followed a very erratic course. On Sunday morning the centre of this system lay over St. George's Channel, whence it travelled eastwards across England, causing a prolonged thunderstorm and heavy rainfall in London during the afternoon. On Monday the centre was found off the Wash, where it remained nearly motionless for 24 hours. The system then began to travel slowly westwards, accompanied by thunder and hail showers, reaching Ireland on Thursday morning. On this day six-tenths of an inch of rain fell in Dublin, and thunder was heard at 9 and 11 a.m. With the coming of the S.W. winds of the depression the weather improved on Friday, when the disturbance passed off from the coast of Donegal in a northwesterly direction. In Dublin the mean height of the barometer was 29·677 inches, pressure ranging between 29·924 inches at 9 a.m. of Monday (wind, N.N.E.), and 29·436 inches at 9 p.m. of Thursday (wind, S.E.). The screened mean temperature was 49·0°, or 4·0° above that of the previous week. The mean dry bulb temperature at 9 a.m. and 9 p.m. was 49·8°. The thermometers in the screen rose to 63·6° on Saturday, having fallen to 41·2° on both Monday and Tuesday. The rainfall was ·923 inch on four days—·600 inch being measured on Thursday. Hail fell on Tuesday and thunder was heard on Thursday.

Sunday, the 31st, was squally and for the most part, wet.

The rainfall in Dublin during the five months ended May 31st has amounted to 8·993 inches on 68 days, compared with 11·183 inches on 76 days during the same period in 1890, 10·476 inches on 91 days in 1889, 9·063 inches on 69 days in 1888, 8·489 inches on 62 days in 1887, and a 25 years' average of 10·466 inches on 81·8 days.

At Knockdolian, Greystones, Co. Wicklow, the rainfall in May, 1891, was 3·616 inches, distributed over 16 days. Of this quantity ·840 inch fell on the 7th, ·790 inch on the 23rd, and ·620 inch on the 31st. The total fall since January 1st, 1891, equals 9·310 inches on 39 days.

At Cloneevin, Killiney, Co. Dublin, the rainfall in May was 2·19 inches on 15 days. The total fall since January 1 has been only 4·68 inches on 58 days—the averages of the six previous years for the same five months being 9·38 inches, on 93 days.

June.—A generally favourable month, of high mean temperature and atmospherical pressure, showing a marked preponderance of north-easterly and easterly winds, in marked contrast to June, 1890, when the prevalent winds were S.W. and W. The rainfall was above the average, while the rainy days were just equal to it.

In Dublin the arithmetical mean temperature (59·0°) was slightly above the average (57·8°); the mean dry bulb readings at 9 a.m. and 9 p.m. were 58·0°. In the twenty-six years ending with 1890, June was coldest in 1882 (M. T. = 53·5°), and in 1879 (the "cold year") (M. T. = 53·9°). It was warmest in 1887 (M. T. = 62·3°), in 1865 (M. T. = 61·0°), and in 1868 (the "warm year") (M. T. = 60·3°). In 1886 the M. T. was 57·4°, in 1888 it was 56·2°, in 1889 it was 59·5°, and in 1890 it was 58·1°.

The mean height of the barometer was 30·014 inches, or 0·097 inch above the corrected average value for June—namely, 29·917 inches. The mercury rose to 30·407 inches at 9 a.m. of the 12th, and fell to 29·457 inches at 9 p.m. of the 29th. The observed range of atmospherical pressure was, therefore, 0·950 inches—that is, almost an inch.

The mean temperature deduced from daily readings of the dry bulb thermometer at 9 a.m. and 9 p.m. was 58·0°, or 8·3° above the value for May, 1891. Using the formula, *Mean Temp.* = *Min.* + (*max.* − *Min.* × ·465), the value was 58·5°, or 1·4° above the average mean temperature for June, calculated in the same way, in the twenty-five years, 1865–89, inclusive (57·1°). The arithmetical mean of the maximal and minimal readings was 59·0°, compared with a twenty-five years' average of 57·8°. On the 23rd, the thermometer in the screen rose to 73·8°—wind, N.E.; on the 10th the temperature fell to 43·8°—wind, N.N.E. The minimum on the grass was 38·6°, also on the 10th.

The rainfall amounted to 2·733 inches, distributed over 14 days. The average rainfall for June in the twenty-five years, 1865–89, inclusive, was 1·817 inches, and the average number of rainy days was 13·6. The rainfall was, therefore, much above the average. In 1878 the rainfall in June was very large—5·058 inches on 19 days; in 1879 also 4·046 inches fell on 24 days. On the other hand, in 1889, only ·100 of an inch was measured on 6 days; in 1887, the rainfall was only ·232 of an inch, distributed over only 3 days; in 1874 only ·405 of an inch was measured on 9 days; and in 1868 only ·677 of an inch fell on but 6 days. In 1888 the rainfall was as much as 3·045 inches distributed over as many as 18 days. In 1890 it was 1·290 inches on 18 days.

High winds were noted on only 7 days, and attaining the force of a gale on but one occasion—the 30th. Temperature reached or exceeded 70° in the screen on 5 days, as compared with 17 days in 1887, only 1 day in 1888, 10 days in 1889, and only 2 days in 1890. Thunder was heard on the 13th and 24th, and hail fell on the 15th.

In the first week, ending Saturday, the 6th, the weather remained in a very unsettled, dull, and rainy condition. An anticyclone was found throughout over Scandinavia and the Norwegian Sea, while areas of low pressure advanced towards the British Islands from the southward, throwing off troughs of low pressure which from time to time spread eastwards across Germany. Under these circumstances, dry, fine weather and low temperatures ruled over Northern Europe, but heavy rains and thunderstorms were prevalent over the British Islands, France, and Germany. On Monday morning, the 1st, an easterly breeze and sea-fog caused a remarkable chill in the east of Scotland and north-east of England—at 8 a.m. the thermometer read 46° at Wick and Aberdeen, and only 44° at Shields; at the same hour it read 64° at Holyhead and 67° at Fanö in Denmark—both insular stations. Dublin escaped any electrical disturbances, but the rains were heavy and persistent, and temperature was very low for the time of year. The screened thermometers rose to 62·7° on Wednesday, the 3rd, and fell to 48·2° on Saturday, the 6th—the range of temperature, therefore, was not large. The rainfall was 1·228 inches on five days, ·574 inch falling on Wednesday, and ·391 inch on Thursday. The prevailing winds were S.E. and E.

Very favourable weather, from both a sanitary and an agricultural point of view, held during the week ended Saturday, the 13th. Between Sunday and Wednesday a depression was travelling slowly in an irregular path north-eastwards across France, Belgium, Holland, and Schleswig-Holstein to the Baltic. Heavy rains fell over the Continent in connection with this system of disturbance, but in England it merely caused strong N.E. winds, clouds, and low temperature. Ireland and Scotland were at this time under the influence of an anticyclone, and the weather was chiefly fine and quiet. In Dublin the first two days were rather cloudy and cold, but then came a very fine period, lasting until Friday inclusive, with westerly land breezes or calms and low temperature by night, easterly sea breezes and hot sunshine by day. After Wednesday, England also came under the influence of the high pressure area, which drifted slowly south-eastwards. A slight depression on Saturday morning caused a grateful rainfall in parts of Ireland. The week closed with fair promise of summerlike weather. In Dublin the mean height of the barometer was 30·180 inches, pressure rising to 30·407 inches at 9 a.m. of Friday (wind, E.). The corrected mean temperature was 54·3°, or 2·9° below the average. The mean dry bulb reading at 9 a.m. and 9 p.m. was also 54·3°. The screened thermometers rose to 66·0° on Saturday, having fallen to 43·9° on Wednesday. Rain fell in appreciable amount on only one day—Friday (or rather Saturday morning). The total fall was ·044 inch.

On the week ended Saturday, the 20th, changeable, cool, and showery at first, the weather became settled and in all respects summerlike after Monday, except in the far North of Scotland, where rain continued to fall daily, though not in large quantities. There were some atmospherical depressions in the North at the beginning of the week, and, in connection with these, sharp thunder and hail showers occurred on Monday in both England and Ireland. An anticyclone then spread northwards from France, finally covering the British Islands. At first the wind was S.W. and temperature rose fast; afterwards calms and easterly winds were experienced, the weather remaining fair and warm owing to the powerful sunshine by day. In Dublin the mean height of the barometer was 30·213 inches. The mean temperature (corrected) was 61·8°, or no less than 7·8° higher than that of the previous week. The mean dry bulb temperature at 9 a.m. and 9 p.m. was 61·5°. The screened thermometers rose to 72·5° on Thursday, having fallen to 48·4 on Sunday. Rain fell on two days to the amount of ·269 inch. Of this quantity ·171 inch was the result of the thunder and hail showers of Monday. On Tuesday night the minimal temperature was 60·9°. On Friday the thermometer rose to 78° in the shade at Parsonstown.

Two very different types of weather were witnessed during the week ended Saturday, the 27th. Up to and including Tuesday conditions were anticyclonic and the weather was bright and warm. The centre of high pressure was found over Scandinavia, whence a ridge stretched south-westwards to Scotland and Ireland. Meanwhile, a shallow "thunderstorm" depression travelled slowly northwards across France and finally north-westwards to the south of Ireland, bringing with it violent thunderstorms and downpours of rain. In Dublin a heavy thundershower occurred at 3.15 p.m. of Wednesday, followed by a severe thunderstorm half-an-hour later. Next day there were storms of great intensity over the greater part of England, the accompanying rainfall amounting to 3·04 inches at Liverpool and 2·24 inches at Loughborough. On Friday gradients for southerly winds became steep over Ireland, squally and heavy showers being the result. Saturday was also showery, but the wind drew into S.W. and the barometer rose. Intense heat was felt in Sweden and Norway on and after Monday, the 22nd—readings above 80° being recorded at several stations, the highest of all being 85° at Hernösand (Lat. 62½° N.) on Wednesday. In Scotland also the weather remained quite fine until Friday. Some dense fogs occurred on the North Sea, the Irish Sea, and the English Channel Coasts during the week. In Dublin, the mean height of the barometer was 29·963. The corrected mean temperature was 61·6°. The mean dry bulb temperature at 9 a.m. and 9 p.m. was 61·1°. The screened thermometers rose to 73·6° on Tuesday and fell to 53·1° on Monday. The rainfall was 1·059 inches on four days. Of this quantity ·604 inch fell on Wednesday.

Sunday, the 28th, proved for the most part fine, but a brisk fall of the barometer took place as a depression, which was deep for the time of year, advanced over the kingdom from S.W. On the 29th, heavy showers of rain occurred, and on the 30th the wind blew a moderate gale at times from S.W.

The rainfall in Dublin during the six months ending June 30th has amounted to 6·718 inches on 77 days, compared with 13·413 inches on 94 days during the same period in 1890, 10·576 inches on 97 days in 1889, 10·313 inches on 87 days in 1888, 6·711 inches on 67 days in 1887, and a 25 years' average of 12·913 inches on 93·6 days.

At Knockdolian, Greystones, Co. Wicklow, the rainfall in June, 1891, was 2·615 inches, distributed over 11 days. Of this quantity ·880 inch fell on the 15th, ·370 inch on the 24th, and ·350 inch on the 26th. The total fall since January 1 has been 11·935 inches, on 70 days.

At Cloneevin, Killiney, Co. Dublin, the rainfall in June was 2·07 inches on 14 days. The total fall since January 1 has been only 6·69 inches on 67 days—the averages of the six previous years for the same six months being 11·12 inches, on 84 days.

JULY.—A changeable, squally, showery month, of average temperature and rainfall, with a great preponderance of north-westerly winds—a very common state of things in an Irish July.

In Dublin the arithmetical mean temperature (58·0°) was decidedly below the average (60·6°); the mean dry bulb readings at 9 a.m. and 9 p.m. were 58·3°. In the twenty-six years ending with 1890, July was coldest in 1879 (the "cold year") (M. T. = 57·3°). It was warmest in 1887 (M. T. = 63·7°), and in 1868 (the "warm year") (M. T. 63·5°). In 1886 the M. T. was 61·0°; in 1888 it was as low as 57·8°; in 1889 it was 58·7, and in 1890 it was 58·1°. From this, 1887 proves to have been the warmest since the present records commenced, whilst July, 1888, was almost the coldest.

The mean height of the barometer was 29·936 inches, or 0·021 inch above the corrected average value for July—namely, 29·915 inches. The mercury marked 30·365 inches at 9 a.m. of the 14th, and fell to 29·434 inches at 4.20 p.m. of the 6th. The observed range of atmospherical pressure was, therefore, 0·931 inches—that is, a little less than an inch.

The mean temperature deduced from daily readings of the dry bulb thermometer at 9 a.m. and 9 p.m. was 58·3°, or 0·3° above the value for June, 1891. Using the formula, *Mean Temp.* = min. + (max.—min. × ·465), the value was 58·6°, or 1·8° below the average mean temperature for July, calculated in the same way, in the twenty-five years, 1865–89, inclusive (60·2°). The arithmetical mean of the maximal and minimal readings was 50·0°, compared with a twenty-five years' average of 60·0°. On the 16th, the thermometer in the screen rose to 72·5°—wind, S.W.; on the 10th the temperature fell to 46·8°—wind, N.N.W. The minimum on the grass was 43·0° on this same date.

The rainfall was 2·167 inches, distributed over 15 days. The average rainfall for July in the twenty-five years, 1865–89, inclusive, was 2·420 inches, and the average number of rainy days was 17·2. The rainfall, therefore, was somewhat below the average, while the rainy days were also below it. In 1880 the rainfall in July was very large—6·087 inches on 24 days; in 1871 also

4·391 inches fell on 23 days. On the other hand, in 1870, only ·539 of an inch was measured on 8 days; in 1869, the fall was only ·789 of an inch on 9 days, and in 1868, only ·741 of an inch fell on but 5 days.

High winds were noted on 10 days, and attained the force of a fresh or moderate gale on two occasions—viz., the 6th and 8th. Temperature reached or exceeded 70° in the screen on only 3 days. In July, 1887, temperature reached or exceeded 70° in the screen on no fewer than 17 days. In July, 1888, the maximum was 68·7°. Thunderstorms occurred on the 3rd and 20th.

Cyclonic conditions held over the W. and N.W. of Europe throughout the period ending Saturday, the 4th, and the weather was, therefore, very changeable and showery, with fresh south-westerly winds (at first, S., then veering to W. and N.W.). Frequent and heavy showers occurred. These were accompanied by thunder and lightning on Friday. In London a heavy fall of rain took place on Wednesday, the 1st, and again on Friday, the 3rd, when thunderstorms occurred at Aberdeen, Leith, and Cambridge, as well as in Dublin. On the last-named day, the wind drew round to N.W. and a general though temporary improvement in the weather occurred. In Dublin the thermometer in the screen fell to 50·2° on Friday. Rain fell to the amount of ·803 inch, ·401 inch being the result of Friday's thunderstorm.

During the earlier part of the week ended Saturday, the 11th, the weather was very unsettled, stormy, cold, and rainy. An improvement set in after Wednesday, the 8th; but to the close, it was very cloudy and dull, except for a few hours on Thursday afternoon, when pleasant sunshine was enjoyed. The bad weather, which was general, was brought about by the passage eastwards across the British Islands of a rather deep and complex depression which first appeared over Ireland early on the morning of Sunday, the 5th. This system at first spread out northwards, but then travelled across the North of Ireland and South of Scotland to the North Sea, where it was found on Tuesday morning. It then changed its course, moving southeastwards and finally eastwards, disappearing over the southern part of the Baltic on Friday. Meanwhile an area of high barometer came in over Ireland, causing some improvement in the weather. On Monday and Wednesday the wind reached gale-force in and about Dublin. In England heavy falls of rain and hail occurred, accompanied by much thunder and lightning. In Dublin the mean height of the barometer was 29·887 inches, pressure ranging from 29·434 inches at 4.30 p.m. of Monday (wind, S.W.), to 30·211 inches at 9 p.m. of Thursday (wind, N.N.W.). The corrected mean temperature was 55·0°. The mean of the dry bulb readings at 9 a.m. and 9 p.m. was 55·1°. The screened thermometers fell to 46·5° on Friday. The rainfall was ·494 inch on three rainy days. Of this quantity ·232 inch fell on Monday.

A very great improvement was noticed in the weather of the week ended Saturday, the 18th except in Scotland, where it became rainy after Wednesday, when a depression approached Great Britain from Germany. Atmospherical pressure was high, but of unstable equilibrium, during the first part of the week. On Tuesday morning a depression formed over Germany, whence it began to travel slowly northwestwards, its centre reaching Berlin on Wednesday morning, the middle of the North Sea on Thursday, and the Hebrides on Friday. It caused heavy rains at first in Germany, Denmark, and Holland, then in the N.E. of England and the E. and N. of Scotland. On Friday, a secondary low pressure system moved northwestwards from the Bay of Biscay towards Ireland, where it caused a heavy fall of warm rain during the ensuing night. The S.W. winds in the rear of these disturbances brought a great increase of temperature to the British Islands. On the whole, fair summerlike weather prevailed throughout the week. In Dublin the mean height of the barometer was 30·024 inches, pressure rising to 30·364 inches, at 9 a.m. of Tuesday (wind, N.E.). The corrected mean temperature was 61·2°, or 6·2° above the value for the previous week. The mean dry bulb temperature at 9 a.m. and 9 p.m. was 61·1°. The thermometers in the screen rose to 72·8° on Thursday. The rainfall was ·213 inch on two days, ·122 inch being referred to Saturday.

In the British Islands the weather of the week ended Saturday, the 25th, was distinctly of a changeable and very broken character. Thunderstorms occurred in England on Sunday, Tuesday, and Wednesday—in Dublin on the evening of Monday, the 20th; while heavy rains fell in Scotland, and frequent heavy showers with strong winds—first from S.W., and afterwards from N.W.—were experienced in Ireland. As was to be expected under these circumstances, temperature ruled rather low throughout at all British and Irish stations. Until Tuesday evening, the barometer was low to the N.W. of the British Islands, relatively high over the Peninsula, France, and Germany—hence the fresh S.W. winds of the earlier part of the week. On Wednesday morning the lowest pressure was found off the E. of Scotland and N.E. of England, so that northerly to westerly winds prevailed. This state of things continued until Friday, when the barometer rose, except in the N. of Scotland, and the weather became dry while continuing cool and rather cloudy. In Dublin the mean height of the barometer was 29·908 inches. The corrected mean temperature was 56·4° compared with 61·2° in the previous week. The mean dry bulb temperature at 9 a.m. and 9 p.m. was 55·6°. The rainfall amounted to ·684 inch in four days, of which ·250 inch fell on Sunday. The prevailing winds were S.W. to N.W.

Although changeable and rather cold, with strong north-westerly and northerly winds, the weather was favourable in Ireland compared with Great Britain, where large quantities of rain fell, accompanied by thunder and lightning in many instances. Throughout the period the barometer was highest over Ireland, and between Monday, the 27th, and Friday, the 31st, gradients for N.W. and N. winds were steep, owing to the appearance of successive depressions over the North Sea and its various coasts. Hence the bad weather felt in Great Britain and the comparative immunity from the same enjoyed in Ireland. In Dublin Sunday was cloudy and drizzling at first, then summerlike. In the evening turreted cumulus was seen to S., and next day severe thunderstorms occurred in the South of England. Two fine days followed; but on Tuesday night rain fell heavily for a time. The weather then became cold and dusty, but dry—so remaining until the end of the month.

The rainfall in Dublin during the seven months ending July 31st has amounted to 10·935 inches on 92 days, compared with 15·587 inches on 116 days during the same period in 1890, 13·146 inches on 112 days in 1889, 15·994 inches on 109 days in 1888, 7·935 inches on 80 days in 1887, and a twenty-five years' average of 14·723 inches on 112·6 days.

At Knockdolian, Greystones, Co. Wicklow, the rainfall in July was 1·825 inches on 18 days, compared with 1·469 inches, distributed over 18 days in 1890. Of this quantity ·255 inch fell on the 16th, and ·220 inch on the 5th. The total fall since January 1 has been 13·220 inches on 88 days.

At Clonsevin, Killiney, Co. Dublin, the rainfall in July was 1·26 inches on 17 days. Maximum, equal to ·18 inch on 3rd. The total fall since January 1 has been 8·05 inches on 84 days, compared with a six years' average of 12·996 inches on 89·40 days.

August.—An exceedingly unsettled, cool, rainy, and even stormy month—a constant succession of extensive and often deep atmospherical depressions crossing the British Islands from W. or S.W. at short intervals. The centres of these systems usually traversed the more northern districts, but on the 20th and 21st a cyclone, in which the barometer was as low as 29·15 inches, passed directly over the South of England, causing an excessive fall of rain in that district. On the 25th-26th, a depression was observed in which the barometer sunk to 28·61 inches in the North of Scotland.

The present is the third consecutive year in which August has proved an unfavourable and an rainstorms, accompanied by thunder and lightning, occurred in many places—the showers in Dublin on Sunday and Monday being particularly heavy—·663 of an inch of rain being measured at this station on Sunday alone. Tuesday proved warm, and in most respects summerlike, but next day the wind rose to a moderate gale from W., and this was followed by another considerable downpour of rain. Fresh breezes and light showers characterised the remainder of the week. In London a dry period occurred between Monday evening and Saturday morning. In Dublin the mean height of the barometer was 29·873 inches. The corrected mean temperature was 60·4°, the mean dry bulb readings at 9 a.m. and 9 p.m. being 1·3° lower, namely, 59·1°. The thermometers in the screen rose to 69·3° on Tuesday, the 11th. The rainfall was 1·035 inches on four days—·663 inch being measured on Sunday, when thunder occurred. The prevailing winds were W. and W.N.W.

As for the week ended Saturday, the 22nd, except on Sunday, which was fine and bright at first, although cloudy and threatening in the evening, the weather was eminently unsettled, cloudy, cold, rainy, and at times blustering—quite unlike the middle of August. On Sunday long fan-like sprays of cirriform cloud spread across the sky from the westward, heralding the approach of an extensive depression to our North-west Coasts. Under the influence of this system, the wind freshened from southerly (S.E., S., and S.W.) points, and rain fell generally and in places in large quantities from day to day. The centre of lowest pressure remained off the W. and N.W. of Ireland until Thursday afternoon, shallow secondary depressions developing meanwhile from time to time over Great Britain so as to cause the rainy, unsettled weather to spread to that country also. On Thursday, the weather improved greatly in Ireland as a new depression of rapidly increasing intensity appeared off the S.W. of England, subsequently crossing that country in an east-north-easterly direction. This system caused downpours of rain over all the more southern parts of England, and the North of France—the largest measurements at 8 a.m. of Friday being 1·6 inches at Hurst Castle, 1·5 inches at Cambridge, and 1·4 inches in London. On this day frequent thunder-showers occurred in the neighbourhood of Dublin, where Saturday also proved dull, very wet, and inclement for the most part until 8 p.m., when the sky cleared. In Dublin the mean height of the barometer was 29·699 inches. The corrected mean temperature was 57·3°. The mean dry bulb readings at 9 a.m. and 9 p.m. were 56·8°. Rain was measured every day, the total amount being 1·171 inches, of which ·451 inch was referred to Monday. Thunder occurred frequently on Friday.

As regards the week ended Saturday, the 29th, the record is once more one of very unseasonable broken weather—high winds, low temperatures, and frequent rainfalls being the leading features of the period. This week will be memorable in particular for the passage across the British Islands of what will probably be found to be the deepest atmospherical depression ever observed in August. It is true that deep cyclonic systems pass almost periodically across North-western Europe during the last week of August, but none so deep as that which swept over the British Islands on Tuesday night had appeared during the previous 30 years at least. On the 31st of August, 1876, the barometer sank to 28·920 inches at Shields; on the 28th in 1879, it fell to 29·111 inches in Dublin, and to 28·740 inches at Mullaghmore, Co. Sligo; on the 23th, in 1881, it fell to 29·014 inches in Dublin, and to 28·830 inches at Leith. But on Tuesday night, the 25th, 1891, it sank by 9 p.m. to 28·940 inches in Dublin, and at 8 a.m. next morning it read only 28·61 inches at Sumburgh Head in the Shetlands. The accompanying gales were violent in the extreme—in Dublin almost a tempest blew from S.W. between midnight and 3 a.m. of Wednesday, the 26th. The week generally was inclement, but on Wednesday and Saturday conditions improved for the time being. In Dublin the mean height of the barometer was 29·579 inches, pressure varying between 28·940 inches at 9 p.m. on Tuesday (wind, S.S.W.), and 30·040 inches at 9 p.m. of Saturday (wind, W.N.W.). The corrected mean temperature was 55·8°. The mean dry bulb temperature at 9 a.m. and 9 p.m. was 55·6°. Rain fell on seven days to the total amount of ·889 inch, of which ·333 inch was referred to Monday and ·273 inch to Tuesday. The prevailing winds were S.W. and N.W.

Sunday, the 30th, was at first fine and bright, but cold, the thermometer falling in the shade during the early morning to 32° at Nairn, 35° at Stornoway and Wick, 38° at Aberdeen, and 39° at Loughborough. In Dublin the minimum was 43·6°, at Parsonstown it was 42°. In the afternoon, the sky became overcast, and rain again set in. On Monday, the 31st, there was a moderate or fresh S.W. gale, with heavy showers, but a high temperature in Dublin.

The rainfall in Dublin during the eight months ending August 31st has amounted to 15·848 inches on 117 days, compared with 9·455 inches on 96 days during the same period in 1887, 17·904 inches on 131 days in 1888, 16·820 inches on 134 days in 1889, 18·030 inches on 137 days in 1890, and a 25 years' average of 17·358 inches on 128·1 days.

At Knockdolian, Greystones, Co. Wicklow, the rainfall in August, 1891, was 4·335 inches, distributed over 24 days. Of this quantity 1·250 inches fell on the 17th, and ·475 inch on the 16th.

September.—In the three preceding years, September proved a fine month. In the present year, it was a fine month compared with August; but both at the opening and close the weather was particularly unsettled, showery, and squally. A period of beautiful, summer-like weather accompanied an anticyclone which spread out north-westwards from the Continent over the British Islands in the week ending Saturday, the 12th. This month was remarkable for the frequency of auroral displays, particularly in the far north; for a high mean temperature, and an overwhelming prevalence of south-westerly winds.

In Dublin the arithmetical mean temperature (57·6°) was decidedly above the average (55·8°); the mean dry bulb readings at 9 a.m. and 9 p.m. were 56·4°. In the twenty-six years ending with 1890, September was coldest in 1886 and in 1882 (M. T. = 53·0°), and warmest in 1865 (M. T. = 61·4°). In 1880, the M. T. was as high as 58·6°; in the year 1879 (the "cold year"), it was 54·8°; in 1887, it was 54·0°; in 1888, it was 54·4°; in 1889, 55·5°, or exactly the average; and in 1890, it was as high as 59·6°. So warm a September as that of 1890 had not occurred for a quarter of a century.

The mean height of the barometer was 29·902 inches, or 0·009 inch below the corrected average value for September—namely, 29·910 inches. The mercury rose to 30·271 inches at 9 p.m. of the 15th, and fell to 29·076 inches at 9 a.m. of the 1st. The observed range of atmospherical pressure was, therefore, 1·193 inches—that is, a little less than one inch and two-tenths.

The mean temperature deduced from daily readings of the dry bulb thermometer at 9 a.m. and 9 p.m. was 56·4°, or only 0·8° below the value for August, 1891. Using the formula, *Mean Temp. = min. + (max. − min. × ·476)*, the mean temperature was 57·3°, or 1·8° above the average mean temperature for September, calculated in the same way, in the twenty-five years, 1865–89, inclusive (55·5°). The arithmetical mean of the maximal and minimal readings was 57·6°, compared with a twenty-five years' average of 55·9°. On the 10th, the thermometer in the screen rose to 75·6°—wind, S.; on the 7th the temperature fell to 41·8—wind, W. The minimum on the grass was 35·7° on the 7th.

The rainfall was 2·132 inches, distributed over 19 days—the rainfall was somewhat below and the rainy days were somewhat above the average. The average rainfall for September in the twenty-five years, 1865–89, inclusive, was 2·476 inches, and the average number of rainy days was 15·7. In 1871, the rainfall in September was very large—4·043 inches on, however, only 13 days. On the other hand, in 1865, only ·058 inch was measured on but 3 days. In 1888, the rainfall was only ·728 inch on 10 days; in 1889, 1·043 inches fell on 18 days; and in 1890, 2·439 inches fell on 11 days.

High winds were noted on as many as 14 days, but attained the force of a gale on only four occasions—the 1st, 21st, 26th, and 30th. A solar halo appeared on the 10th, lunar halos on the nights of the 15th and 16th. Thunder and lightning occurred on the 13th. Auroræ were observed on the 2nd, 9th, and 11th. There was a fog on the 10th.

At 8 a.m. of Tuesday, the 1st, the barometer was down to 28·35 inches at Stornoway in the Hebrides. Strong gales from points between S. and W. blew in most parts of the British Islands, and the accompanying rains were very heavy in many places. After Wednesday, the 2nd, gradients became less steep, so that the wind moderated, but showers continued to fall daily in most districts. On Saturday, the weather again broke up in Ireland. On Wednesday evening faint aurora was seen near Dublin, and the following night aurora was reported from Wick and Aberdeen. In Dublin the barometer ranged between 29·076 inches at 9 a.m. of Tuesday (wind W.N.W., fresh gale), and 30·057 inches at 9 a.m. of Saturday (wind, S.W.). Rain fell daily during the 5 first days to the total amount of ·667 inch, of which ·244 inch was credited to Tuesday, and ·334 inch to Saturday.

The week ended Saturday, the 12th, witnessed a remarkable and gratifying change from storm and rain and cold to calm, bright sunshine and midsummer heat. This most acceptable transformation was brought about by the gradual extension westwards and north-westwards of an anticyclone, or area of high atmospherical pressure, which already at the beginning of the week was found over France and Germany. Early on Sunday morning and again on Monday night rain fell freely in Dublin, but from Tuesday onwards the weather was very fine. The last three days were summer-like in the extreme—the screened thermometers rising to 73·6°, 73·5°, and 69·5° respectively. Thursday's maximum was the highest marked in Dublin during 1891, and is to be compared with maxima of 73·5° in June, 72·8° in July, and only 69·4° in August. On this same day (Thursday) the thermometer rose to 80° at York, 82° in London, and 88° at Loughborough and Cambridge. The Loughborough maximum on Friday was 86°. The change to fair weather extended westwards only slowly, for rain fell in Munster and Connaught daily up to Thursday—the measurement at Valentia Island, in Kerry, was as much as 2·52 inches. Aurora borealis was seen on the evenings of Wednesday and Friday. On Tuesday and Thursday evenings also displays of it were reported from different parts of north-western Europe. In Dublin the mean height of the barometer was 29·998 inches, pressure increasing intermittently from 29·707 inches at 9 a.m. of Sunday (wind W.) to 30·122 inches at 9 p.m. of Thursday (wind calm). The corrected mean temperature was 60·2°, or 4·0° above that of the previous week. The mean dry bulb temperature at 9 a.m. and 9 p.m. was 59·3°. The thermometers in the screen rose to 73·6° on Thursday, having fallen to 44·3° on Monday. Rain fell to the amount of ·110 inch on Monday night.

Although changeable, and cloudy and squally at times, the weather of the period ended Saturday, the 19th, was on the whole favourable to both health and agriculture. At the beginning a V-shaped depression came in over Ireland from the south-westward, subsequently travelling in a north-easterly direction across this country on Sunday, Great Britain on Monday, and Norway on Tuesday. In front of the "trough" of low pressure the wind was southerly, temperature was high, and rain prevailed accompanied by a good deal of thunder and lightning. In Dublin distant thunder was heard on Sunday afternoon and frequent lightning was seen towards N.W. after dark. The rainfall attending this system was not heavy in Ireland or England, but in Scotland and Norway it was considerable. As the "trough" passed away, the wind shifted to N.W., with a fall of temperature, clearing sky, and bracing air. During the rest of the week, fresh W. and S.W. winds, clouds, and showers were prevalent, an anticyclone over France and Germany causing rather steep gradients for such winds in Ireland and Great Britain. In Dublin the mean height of the barometer was 29·970 inches, pressure ranging from a minimum of 29·717 inches at 9 p.m. of Sunday (wind S.) to a maximum of 30·271 inches at 9 p.m. of Tuesday (wind W.). The corrected mean temperature was 59·1°. The mean dry bulb temperature at 9 a.m. and 9 p.m. was 58·1°. The thermometers in the screen rose to 67·7° on Sunday and fell to 52·1° on Saturday. The rainfall measured ·762 inch on three days. Of this quantity, ·167 inch fell on Sunday, the 13th, and no less than ·583 inch on Saturday night and the early morning of Sunday, the 20th. Lunar halos were seen on the evenings of Wednesday and Friday, a solar halo on Saturday forenoon. The prevailing wind was westerly.

During the week ended Saturday, the 26th, cyclonic conditions and unsettled weather held over the British Islands except on Thursday and Friday, when an anticyclone spread north-westwards over England from the Continent. But the beginning and close of the week showed a remarkable contrast as regards the area and distribution of the bad weather. In the interval between the evenings of Saturday, the 19th, and of Tuesday, the 22nd, a serious depression travelled north-eastwards across England to the North Sea, which it reached on Monday morning, and then southwards down the East coast of England, finally disappearing over the East of France on Wednesday, the 23rd. This disturbance caused northerly gales and torrents of rain in Scotland (3·6 inches at Aberdeen), Wales, and West of England, smaller quantities elsewhere, and thunderstorms at many British Stations. As the wind died down and the sky cleared, temperature fell fast at night, so that on Wednesday morning a minimum of 32° was recorded at Nairn, in Scotland. At this time, a new series of depressions began to travel north-eastwards across Ireland, where the weather became warmer, but unsettled and rainy. This renewal of cyclonic conditions reached its climax on Saturday, when a fresh gale from W.S.W. prevailed, with showers of rain. In Dublin the mean atmospherical pressure was 29·916 inches, the barometer ranging between 30·108 inches at 9 p.m. of Thursday (wind S.W.), and 29·587 inches at 9 a.m. of Saturday (wind W.S.W.). The corrected mean temperature was 54·4°. The mean dry bulb temperature at 9 a.m. and 9 p.m. was 53·6°. The thermometers in the screen rose to 64·9° on Thursday, having fallen to 45·9° on Wednesday. The rainfall was ·313 inch, of which ·106 inch was measured on Wednesday and ·188 inch on Friday. The prevailing winds were—first, northerly; afterwards, south-westerly.

The last four days—27th–30th, inclusive—were characterised by changeable, showery weather, with fresh to strong and squally winds from points between W.N.W. and S.S.W. Rain fell daily, but not in large amount, the measurement being only ·080 inch.

The rainfall in Dublin during the nine months ending September 30th has amounted to 16·020 inches on 135 days, compared with 10·968 inches on 119 days during the same period in 1887, 17·092 inches on 160 days in 1888, 19·238 inches on 147 days in 1889, 20·655 inches on 161 days in 1890, and a twenty-five years' average of 19·734 inches on 142·8 days.

At Knockdolian, Greystones, County Wicklow, the rainfall in September, 1891, was 1·957 inches, distributed over 14 days. Of this quantity ·360 inch fell on the 19th, and ·330 inch on the 23rd.

October.—October, 1891, may well be described as a month of contrasts. At the beginning some fine, warm autumnal days were experienced, interrupted indeed by a gale and heavy rain on the 5th. From the 8th to the 14th was a period of violent gales and heavy rains, with brief intervals of fine weather and very unsteady temperature. Then followed a week of low barometer, but fair weather and low temperature in Ireland, heavy rains and gales in England. The closing period, from the 25th to the 31st, was fine and quiet, with ground frosts and local fogs at night, bright and warm sunshine by day, with easterly winds.

In Dublin the arithmetical mean temperature (49·5°) was slightly below the average (49·7°); the mean dry bulb readings at 9 a.m. and 9 p.m. were 48·2°. In the twenty-six years ending with 1890 October was coldest in 1880 (M. T. = 45·4°), and in 1885 (M. T. = 45·6°), and warmest in 1876 (M. T. = 53·1°). In 1886, the M. T. was as high as 53·0°; in the year 1879 (the "cold year"), it was 49·7°. In 1887, it was as low as 47·3°; in 1888, it was 49·1°; in 1889 it was only 48·1°; and in 1890, it was 51·7°.

The mean height of the barometer was 29·626 inches, or 0·214 inch below the corrected average value for October—namely, 29·840 inches. The mercury rose to 30·647 inches at 9 a.m. of the 31st, and fell to 28·251 inches at 2.30 p.m. of the 13th. This was the lowest reading recorded in Dublin since the memorable 8th of December, 1886, when the barometer sank to 27·758 inches at 2.30 p.m. The observed range of atmospherical pressure was, therefore, not less than 2·396 inches—that is, a little less than two inches and four-tenths.

The mean temperature deduced from daily readings of the dry bulb thermometer at 9 a.m. and 9 p.m. was 48·2°, or 8·3° below the value for September, and 9·0° below that for August, 1891. The arithmetical mean of the maximal and minimal readings was 49·5°, compared with a twenty-five years' average of 49·7°. Using the formula, *Mean Temp. = Min. +* (max.—min. × ·460), the value was 49·3°, or 0·2° below the average mean temperature for October, calculated in the same way, in the twenty-five years, 1865–89, inclusive, (49·5°). On the 4th, the thermometer in the screen rose to 62·7°—wind, S.S.W.; on the 25th the temperature fell to 33·0°—wind, W.N.W. The minimum on the grass was 25·0° also on the 25th; on six nights the thermometer sank to or below 32° on the grass.

The rainfall was as much as 8·390 inches, distributed over only 13 days—the rainfall was above, while the rainy days were largely below, the average. The average rainfall for October in the twenty-five years, 1865–89, inclusive, was 3·106 inches, and the average number of rainy days was 17·6. In 1880 the rainfall in October was very large—7·358 inches on 18 days. In 1875, also, 7·049 inches fell on 26 days. On the other hand, in 1890 only ·633 inch fell on but 11 days, in 1884 only ·844 inch was measured on but 14 days, and in 1868 only ·836 inch on 15 days. In 1888, the rainfall was 1·227 inch on 16 days, and in 1889 no less than 4·833 inches fell on 22 days. From these figures, it will be seen that October, 1891, proved the wettest on record for more than a quarter of a century at least.

Solar halos were seen on the 2nd, 7th, and 23rd. High winds were noted on 12 days, and attained the force of a gale on as many as eight occasions—the 5th, 8th, 11th, 13th, 14th, 16th, 18th, and 27th. The atmosphere was more or less foggy in Dublin on the 15th, 22nd, 23rd, 29th, and 30th. Lightning was seen on the evenings of the 1st, 6th, and 20th. Hail fell on the 17th.

Favourable weather held in Dublin during the first three days.

Strong southerly and south-westerly winds, rising to the force of a gale in different parts of

Western Europe at different times, and heavy rains, were the leading features of the weather of the week ended Saturday, the 10th. Dublin escaped the bad weather to a great and even a singular extent. Throughout the period, a large anticyclone was found over Central Russia, where the barometer stood persistently as high as 30·4 to 30·6 inches. At the same time a succession of large and deep depressions passed northwards or north-eastwards along the Atlantic seaboard of Western Europe, causing the high winds and heavy rains already mentioned. From time to time the main system of low pressure threw off secondary depressions, which travelled across England and the North Sea, so that broken weather spread to those districts also. In fact, the weather in England was much worse than that experienced in Dublin, where many fair intervals were enjoyed. On Tuesday evening lightning was seen, and thunder and lightning occurred in the S. and S.E. of England on Wednesday afternoon and night. In Dublin the mean barometrical pressure was only 29·493 inches. The barometer fell from 30·038 inches at 9 a.m. of Sunday (wind, S.S.W.), to 28·990 inches at 9 a.m. of Tuesday (wind, S.W.). The corrected mean temperature was 54·3°. The mean dry bulb temperature at 9 a.m. and 9 p.m. was 53·2°. The screened thermometers rose to 63·7° on Sunday, the 4th. There were gales on Monday and Thursday. Lightning was seen on Tuesday evening. A solar halo appeared next morning. The rainfall was ·907 inch on four days, the maximal fall in 24 hours being ·639 inch on Monday. The prevailing winds were S. and S.W.

A most tempestuous, cold, and rainy period—such is the record of the week ended Saturday, the 17th. No less than three barometrical depressions of the first importance travelled across the British Islands and the adjoining seas during the week, while numerous secondary depressions of less intensity were observed from time to time. The first of the prime disturbances lay to the N.W. of Ireland on Sunday morning, when the barometer was as low as 28·3 inches at Belmullet. Fresh gales from S. to S.W. and heavy rain accompanied this disturbance. Monday, the 12th, was fine but not settled, and in the evening heavy showers fell. On Tuesday the most intense of the three primary depressions mentioned above passed right over Ireland. The centre of the cyclone crossed the Co. Antrim in the evening, and the barometer fell to about 28 inches—at 6 p.m. the reading at Malin Head was 28·02 inches, and it was blowing a whole gale from E.N.E. At the same hour the barometer read 28·13 inches at Donaghadee, where there was a fresh gale from W.S.W. Thunder and lightning occurred in many places, and torrents of rain fell—particularly in Dublin (1·103 inches in 5 hours on Tuesday). The third great depression was found right over the North of Ireland at 8 a.m. of Friday, the 16th, the barometer being down to 28·87 inches near the centre. It caused sudden and violent gales with heavy falls of rain. On Saturday, the wind at last veered to N.W. and the weather moderated and brightened. In Dublin the mean height of the barometer was only 29·253 inches—pressure ranging between 28·231 inches at 2.30 p.m. of Tuesday (wind, S.W.) and 29·694 inches at 9 p.m. of Saturday (wind, W.N.W.). The corrected mean temperature was 48·6°, the mean dry bulb readings at 9 a.m. and 9 p.m. being still lower—viz., 47·3°. The thermometers in the screen rose to 57·9° on Tuesday, having fallen to 38·2° during the preceding night. Rain fell daily to the total amount of 2·437 inches. Of this quantity, 1·176 inches fell on Tuesday. Hail was noted on Saturday. The prevailing winds were S. and S.W.

As regards the week ended Saturday, the 24th, until Wednesday the weather remained in a very disturbed state in all parts of the United Kingdom. After that day, however, a marked improvement took place in Ireland and Scotland, while it remained wet and tempestuous in England until Friday. On Sunday an extensive depression passed over Ireland towards N.N.E. "surging" eastwards at the same time. A downpour of rain and violent southerly gales accompanied this disturbance, the high spring tides increasing the damage done by it along the coasts. This system had scarcely passed away when a new and still more serious depression arrived off the west coast of Ireland, where the barometer fell below 28·80 inches on Wednesday morning. And now a curious thing happened—the barometer began to rise over Ireland while it continued to fall over England. The result was that in the former country the wind moderated and the sky cleared, while strong gales and continuous rain were reported from England. The last four days were really beautifully fine on the east coast of Ireland. Winter set in with great severity in the North of Europe during this week—the 8 a.m. temperatures at Archangel were 19°, 15°, 6°, 6°, 14°, and 15°, up to Friday. In Dublin the mean height of the barometer was 29·336 inches—pressure ranging between 29·917 inches at 9 a.m. of Sunday (wind, S.S.W.) and 28·904 inches at 9 a.m. of Wednesday (wind, S.). The corrected mean temperature was 47·5°. The highest shade temperature was 56·6° on Tuesday; the lowest was 39·0° on Saturday. The mean dry bulb temperature at 9 a.m. and 9 p.m. was 45·7°. Rain fell in measurable amount on two days, the total fall being ·244 inch, of which ·200 inch was referred to Sunday. The prevailing winds were—first, S., afterwards W. Lightning was seen on Tuesday evening.

A remarkable and most acceptable improvement in the weather was observed during the week ended Saturday, the 31st, more particularly in Ireland and Scotland. Already on Sunday an anticyclone, or area of high atmospherical pressure, was in course of formation over Scandinavia and the Norwegian Sea. This system moved gradually southwards and at the same time increased in intensity, until towards the close of the week it covered the British Islands and adjacent districts with central readings of the barometer as high as 30·74 inches. Exceptionally fine, quiet, bright weather held in Ireland after Tuesday. But up to and including that day strong easterly or north-easterly winds and much cloud prevailed, owing to the advance across the Peninsula and France of a succession of low pressure systems. These caused gloomy, wet, and stormy weather in the South of England, and heavy rainfalls in Spain and France. After Tuesday, conditions became tranquil and the sky cleared, so that sharp frosts and fogs occurred at night, while the days were sunny, dry, and bracing. At the end of the week depressions were again appearing over Northern Europe, where with a consequent shift of wind to S.W. a sudden rise of temperature took place, amounting at Haparanda, on the Gulf of Bothnia, to 33°. At that station the thermometer read —1° F. at 8 a.m. of Thursday, but—32° F. at the same hour on Friday. In Dublin the mean height of the barometer was 30·290 inches, pressure steadily increasing from 30·003 inches at 9 a.m. of Sunday (wind, W.N.W.) to 30·047 inches at 9 a.m. of Saturday (wind, E.S.E.). The corrected mean temperature was 45·4°. The mean dry bulb temperature at 9 a.m. and 9 p.m. was 45·1°. The thermometers in the screen rose to 51·7° on Monday, having fallen to 33·0 on Sunday. Very light showers fell on Sunday and Tuesday, but yielded only ·003 inch of rain. There was an easterly gale on Tuesday afternoon. The prevalent winds during the week were N.E. and E.

The rainfall in Dublin during the ten months ending October 31st has amounted to 21·810 inches on 148 days, compared with 17·320 inches on 153 days during the same period in 1887, 19·219 inches on 147 days in 1888, 23·759 inches on 160 days in 1889, 21·491 inches on 162 days in 1890, and a twenty-five years' average of 22·840 inches on 160·4 days.

At Knockdolian, Greystones, Co. Wicklow, the rainfall was as much as 8·129 inches on 14 days. Of this amount 1·180 inches fell on the 5th, ·750 inch on the 13th, ·751 inch on the 10th, and ·650 inch on the 16th. The rainfall in October, 1890, was only ·600 inch, distributed over 13 days. Of this quantity ·160 inch fell on the 6th, and ·120 inch on the 14th. The rainfall at Greystones in October, 1880, was no less than 6·935 inches on 22 days, or more than eleven times as great as the fall in October, 1890.

From January 1st, 1891, up to October 31st, rain fell at Knockdolian, Greystones, on 140 days, to the total amount of 34·744 inches.

the mean height of the barometer was 1·317 inches below that of the former week, temperature was low and unsteady, violent gales alternated with calm and fog, and rain fell in vast quantities all over the British Islands. Gradients for S.W. winds were already established at the beginning of the week, and squalls and rain were reported from time to time. On Tuesday night a very deep depression approached the British Islands from S.W., rapidly growing deeper as it advanced. In its centre the barometer fell to 28·90 inches or lower, with the result that one of the most disastrous storms of modern times swept across England. In Dublin the force of the wind was not great, but rain fell in torrents. On Thursday evening another equally deep depression arrived off the S.W. of Ireland, whence it passed off in a northerly direction. It was accompanied by strong gales and heavy rain in Ireland. Saturday was calm, damp, and foggy, and a most inclement week drew to a close with a slowly rising barometer. In Dublin the mean pressure was 29·201 inches, the barometer ranging between 29·930 inches at 9 a.m. of Sunday (wind, S.S.W.) and 28·334 inches at 7·30 a.m. of Wednesday, (wind, N.N.W.). The mean temperature was 43·6°, the mean dry bulb temperature at 9 a.m. and 9 p.m. was 42·7°. The thermometer in the screen ranged between 35·0° on Saturday and 50° on Thursday. Rain fell on every day, the total measurement being 2·933 inches, of which 1·129 inches were registered on Tuesday.

Dull, showery, and unsettled weather prevailed at the beginning of the week ended Saturday, the 21st, except in parts of Scotland and in the north-west of Ireland, where the weather was fine and the sky clear. These conditions were brought about by the advance up the English Channel of a complex atmospherical depression during the night of Saturday, the 14th, and in the course of Sunday, the 15th. Unfortunately, this state of things led to the complete obscuration by clouds of the total eclipse of the moon, which took place on the night of Sunday; in the north-west of Ireland, however, the eclipse was seen in a clear sky. On and after Tuesday the lowest barometrical readings were again found in the north-west, so that the wind became south-westerly and temperature rose fast, with cloudy, showery weather. Gradients were not very steep, and so no gales were felt except at a few exposed coast stations. On Wednesday temperature rose to 57·8° in Dublin, and to 57° in London and at Cambridge. On Friday the low pressure area passed on to Scandinavia, and the wind drew into N.W. or N. in the British Isles with a reduction of temperature, which became still more decided on Saturday. In Dublin the mean height of the barometer was 29·730 inches—pressure ranging between 29·252 inches at 9 a.m. of Sunday (wind, N.W. to N.) and 29·951 inches at 9 p.m. of Saturday (wind, N.W.). The mean temperature was 44·6°; the mean of the dry bulb readings at 9 a.m. and 9 p.m. was 44·1°. The thermometers in the screen rose to 57·8° on Wednesday (the highest reading recorded since October 13), and fell to 36·1° on Saturday. The rainfall was ·333 inch on four days—of this quantity, ·211 inch fell on Sunday, which was chiefly dull and wet on the east coast of Ireland.

During the week ended Saturday, the 28th, quiet, cold, but changeable weather held until Saturday, when a moderate southerly gale and heavy rain occurred in the morning. Over Western Europe in general the distribution of atmospherical pressure at first was for the most part irregular, and without steep gradients. As the amount of cloud was slight, temperature became and continued low, sharp night frosts being reported from most stations. On Wednesday a depression was found off the N.W. of Scotland, and cold showers of rain, sleet, and hail fell over Ireland, Wales, and parts of England and Scotland. The rainfall was not heavy except at Holyhead, where ·96 inch fell in 48 hours ending 8 a.m. of Thursday. In the wake of the depression just mentioned several shallow secondary systems passed across the British Islands. On Friday afternoon the only serious depression of the week approached Ireland from the Atlantic. It caused heavy rain and a southerly gale on Saturday morning, but the wind soon veered towards W. with a clearing sky. In front of this disturbance a considerable, but transitory, rise of temperature took place. In Dublin the mean height of the barometer was 29·722 inches, pressure ranging between 29·920 inches at 9 a.m. of Sunday (wind, N.W.) and 29·249 inches at 9 a.m. of Saturday (wind, S.S.E.). The mean temperature was 38·7°. The mean dry bulb temperature at 9 a.m. and 9 p.m. was 37·7°. The thermometers in the screen rose to 51·8° on Saturday, having fallen to 31·4° on Tuesday. Rain fell on three days to the total amount of ·359 inch—of this quantity ·260 inch was referred to Friday.

Sunday, the 29th, was a fair, bright, calm day. Monday, the 30th, was changeable.

The rainfall in Dublin during the eleven months ending November 30th has amounted to 24·321 inches on 163 days, compared with 15·378 inches on 141 days during the same period in 1887, 25·768 inches on 173 days in 1888, 23·718 inches on 178 days in 1889, 25·706 inches on 169 days in 1890, and a twenty-five years' average of 25·202 inches on 177·4 days.

At Knockdolian, Greystones, Co. Wicklow, the rainfall in November, 1891, was no less than 5·336 inches, distributed over 15 days. Of this quantity 2·330 inches fell on the 10th, and ·530 of an inch on the 18th.

From January 1st, 1891, up to November 30th, rain fell at Knockdolian, Greystones, on 153 days, and to the total amount of 30·269 inches.

December.—The leading features of the weather were—a preponderance of south-westerly winds, frequent gales, heavy rains, and unsteady, but often high temperature. From the 16th to the 25th, however, an anticyclone lay over England, France, and Germany, and within its central area severe cold and dense fogs with calms prevailed. Even at this time the S.W. wind and mild temperature continued on the Atlantic coasts of Ireland, Scotland, and Norway.

In Dublin the arithmetical mean temperature (43·0°) was decidedly above the average (41·3°); the mean dry bulb readings at 9 a.m. and 9 p.m. were 42·3°. In the twenty-six years ending with 1890, December was coldest in 1878 (M. T. = 32·5°), and in 1874 (M. T. = 30·8°), and warmest in 1865 (M. T. = 46·2°). In 1886 the M. T. was as low as 37·9°; in the year 1879 (the "cold year") it was also 37·9°. In 1887 the M. T. was 39·0°; in 1888 it was 43·6°; in 1889 it was 43·8°; and in 1890 it was 39·1°.

The mean height of the barometer was 29·816 inches, or 0·057 inch below the corrected average value for December—namely, 29·873 inches. The mercury rose to 30·010 inches at 9 a.m. of the 21st and fell to 27·814 inches at 4 p.m. of the 10th. The observed range of atmospherical pressure was therefore, 1·796 inches—that is, a little more than one inch and three-quarters.

The mean temperature deduced from daily readings of the dry bulb thermometer at 9 a.m. and 9 p.m. was 42·3°, or only 0·5° below the value for November, and 5·9° below that for October, 1891. Using the formula, *Mean Temp.* = *Min.* + (max.—min. × ·52), the value was 43·3°, or 1·7° above the average mean temperature for December, calculated in the same way, in the twenty-five years, 1865-89, inclusive (41·6°). The arithmetical mean of the maximal and minimal readings was 43·6°, compared with a twenty-five years' average of 41·8°. On the 3rd the thermometer in the screen rose to 55·0°—wind, S.W.; on the 22nd the temperature fell to 25·3° (wind, S). The minimum on the grass was 19·2° also on the 22nd. There were 6 days of frost in the screen and 15 days of frost on the grass.

The rainfall was 3·209 inches, distributed over 21 days. The average rainfall for December in the twenty-five years, 1865-89, inclusive, was 2·401 inches, and the average number of rainy days was 16·7. The rainfall, therefore, and the rainy days were decidedly above the average. In 1876 the rainfall in December was very large—7·566 inches on 22 days. In 1872, 5·632 inches fell on as many as 24 days; and in 1868 (which was otherwise a fine and dry year), 4·740 inches fell on as many as 27 days. On the other hand, in 1867, only ·771 of an inch was measured on 13 days; and in 1871 the December rainfall was only ·797 of an inch on 14 days. In 1885, only ·742 of an inch of rain was measured on but 10 days, but in 1886 the rainfall was 3·348 inches, distributed over as many as 21 days. In 1887 (the "dry year"), the rainfall was 1·223 inches on 19 days; in 1888, it was 2·911 inches on 17 days; in 1889, 1·634 inches fell on 15 days; and in 1890, it was 1·350 inches on 11 days.

A lunar halo appeared on the 11th, and a lunar rainbow on the 15th. Solar halos were observed on the 5th, 9th, 13th, and 14th. High winds were noted on 14 days, and attained the force of a gale on as many as 8 occasions—the 3rd, 5th, 7th, 9th, 10th, 12th, 15th, and 28th. The atmosphere was more or less foggy in Dublin on the 7th, 18th, 19th, 20th, 21st, 22nd, 23rd, 24th, and 30th. Snow or sleet fell on the 11th. Hail fell on the 10th.

During the period ended Saturday, the 5th, the weather fell into a rough and rainy state, with squally S.W. winds and high but unstable temperature. On Tuesday, the 1st, and again on Thursday, deep depression skirted the western coasts of Ireland and Scotland, with the result that southerly to westerly gales prevailed, with rainy or showery weather in all parts of the country. On Tuesday night a subsidiary disturbance crossed England, where rain fell heavily. At 8 a.m. of Thursday, the barometer was down to 29·01 inches at Stornoway in the Hebrides. During the following night thunder and lightning occurred in the N.W. and N. of Ireland. Another depression passed by on Saturday, when rain fell heavily at times. One of the most striking features of the week was the high temperature experienced on Thursday, when the thermometer rose to 56° at Oxford, Cambridge, and Loughborough; to 57° in London, at Parsonstown, Shields, Leith, and as far north as Nairn; to 58° in Dublin, and to 59° at York. In Dublin the height of the barometer varied between 29·231 inches at 9 a.m. of Thursday (wind, S.S.W.) and 29·898 inches at 9 p.m. of Friday (wind, S.S.W.). Temperature in the screen rose to 58·0° on Thursday. The rainfall was ·258 inches in three days, ·105 inch being measured on Saturday. The wind was chiefly S.S.W.

Very unsettled, rough, wet weather prevailed in all districts during the week ended Saturday, the 12th. Sunday was the only thoroughly fine day, but before night cirrifilum cloud had overspread the sky from the westward, ushering in a deep depression, the centre of which had reached the portion of St. George's Channel between Wexford and Pembroke by 8 a.m. on Monday. A very perfect circulation of strong winds and gales round the cyclonic system was observed. The depression travelled across England and the North Sea to Northern Germany at a great rate. The accompanying rainfall was very heavy in and about Dublin, and at Shields. On Tuesday another depression advanced to the North of Scotland, but this was soon over-shadowed by a much more serious disturbance, over the centre of which the barometer fell to 27·93 inches at 8 a.m. of Thursday, the 10th, at Sumburgh Head in the Shetland Islands. At this time the barometer stood at 30·03 inches at Lisbon, and 30·14 inches at Biarritz. Large quantities of rain or sleet and hail fell, and storms prevailed not only all over the British Islands, but in France, Germany, and Scandinavia also. Thunder and lightning occurred in many parts of Ireland and in the South of England. After a few hours of fair weather on Friday afternoon the weather again became wet and stormy on Saturday. In Dublin the mean pressure was 29·350 inches, the barometer ranging between 28·814 inches at 4 p.m. of Thursday (wind, W.S.W.) and 30·037 inches at 9 p.m. of Friday (wind, W.). The corrected mean temperature was 44·3°. The mean dry bulb temperature at 9 a.m. and 9 p.m. was 43·3°. The screened thermometers rose to 54·2° on Thursday and fell to 33·5° on Saturday. Rain fell daily, the total amount being 2·818 inches, and ·747 inch being credited to Sunday, ·612 inch to Wednesday, and ·717 inch to Saturday. The prevailing wind was westerly.

In the course of the week ended Saturday, the 19th, the weather underwent a complete change over Western Europe. Until Wednesday, the 16th, the distribution of atmospherical pressure was cyclonic, and the weather was for the most part rough, mild, and rainy; except in the North of Scandinavia, where severe cold prevailed, the thermometer reading—13° on Sunday and—14° on Tuesday at Haparanda on the Gulf of Bothnia. In the rear of a depression, which lay over Denmark and the North Sea on Wednesday morning, the barometer rose with great rapidity, so that by 8 a.m. of Thursday a tongue of high pressure, with readings above 30·4 inches, stretched across Norway, the North Sea, England, and the English Channel, to Normandy in France. Within this area temperature fell fast, so that sharp frost began to be felt at the inland English stations. In Ireland and Scotland, however, southerly winds prevailed and temperature remained steady or even rose. On Thursday night the thermometer fell to 23° at York and Loughborough, and to 25° at Oxford. The anticyclone continued to develop until Saturday, when the barometer exceeded 30·73 inches in Holland and Belgium. In Dublin the mean atmospherical pressure was 30·629 inches, the range being from 29·911 inches at 9 a.m. of Sunday (wind, W.N.W.) to 30·497 inches at 9 a.m. of Saturday (wind, S.S.E.). The corrected mean temperature was 44·2°. The mean dry bulb temperature at 9 a.m. and 9 p.m. was 43·6°. The screened thermometers rose to 51·6° on Tuesday and fell to 37·0° on Saturday. The rainfall was ·206 inch on four days, ·100 inch being referred to Monday. The prevailing winds were W.N.W. and S.S.E.

In the fourth week (20th–26th inclusive), very intense cold, with dense fogs, prevailed over the greater part of England until Saturday. In the East of Ireland also the cold was of considerable intensity until Christmas Day, when a thaw occurred, followed by rain and moderate to fresh S.W. winds on Saturday. Over the greater part of Norway and of Scotland and on the west coast of Ireland, there was an almost complete absence of frost during the week, owing to the prevalence of a southerly to westerly air-current in those localities. The cold in England was due to an anticyclone, which first formed on Thursday, the 17th, and persisted until Friday, the 25th. One of the most striking features accompanying the calm of the anticyclone was the density and persistence of the fog in the London district. For more than 70 hours the metropolis was wrapped in Cimmerian darkness by day as well as by night. In Dublin the fog was thick at times, but much pleasant sunshine was enjoyed at intervals. The mean height of the barometer was 30·226 inches, pressure decreasing from 30·610 inches at 9 a.m. of Monday (wind, calm) to 29·341 inches at 4 p.m. of Saturday (wind, S.W.). The corrected mean temperature was 36·1°. The mean dry bulb temperature at 9 a.m. and 9 p.m. was 34·5°. The screened thermometers fell to 25·2° on Tuesday and rose to 54·7° on Saturday. Rain was measured on two days, the total quantity being ·047 inch, of which ·035 inch fell on Saturday. The prevailing winds were S.S.E. and S. The rise of temperature towards the close of the week spread from Spain across France to the British Islands.

As compared with the previous week, the closing period (27th–31st inclusive) was much milder; but the weather was in an unsettled, showery condition for the most part. The barometer was lowest over the Norwegian Sea, highest over the Peninsula. Temperature was generally above the average for the time of year over the greater part of Europe—the excess of warmth on the Continent on Wednesday and Thursday being particularly noticeable. Rain fell frequently, sleet and hail in Scotland, with a thunderstorm at Stornoway on Tuesday evening. In Dublin the rainfall was not very heavy, but the five days all yielded an appreciable measurement. The screened thermometers rose to 52·3° on Tuesday. The prevailing winds were S.W. and W., set in on the evening of the 31st.

The rainfall in Dublin during the year ending December 31st has amounted to 27·820 inches on 184 days, compared with 27·502 inches on 200 days in 1890, 27·371 inches on 183 days in 1889, 26·679 inches on 186 days in 1888, 16·601 inches on 160 days in 1887, and a twenty-five years' average of 27·696 inches on 191·3 days.

At Knockdolian, Greystones, Co. Wicklow, the rainfall in December, 1891, was 4·630 inches, distributed over 23 days. Of this quantity 1·160 inches fell on the 6th, and ·940 of an inch on the 12th.

From January 1st to December 31st, 1891, rain fell at Knockdolian, Greystones, on 178 days, and to the total amount of 34·949 inches.

Rainfall in 1891,

At 40, Fitzwilliam-square, West, Dublin.

Rain Gauge:—Diameter of funnel, 8 in. Height of top—Above ground, 3 ft. 2 in.; above sea level, 50 ft.

Month	Total Depth.	Greatest Fall in 24 hours.		Number of Days on which ·01 or more fell.	Month.	Total Depth.	Greatest Fall in 24 hours.		Number of Days on which ·01 or more fell.
	Inches.	Depth.	Date.			Inches.	Depth.	Date.	
January,	[illegible]	·141	[illegible]	14	August,	[illegible]	[illegible]	15th	22
February,	[illegible]	·214	[illegible]	9	September,	[illegible]	[illegible]	[illegible]	14
March,	[illegible]	·224	[illegible]	[illegible]	October,	[illegible]	1·214	[illegible]	13
April,	[illegible]	·141	[illegible]	14	November,	[illegible]	1·730	[illegible]	15
May,	[illegible]	[illegible]	[illegible]	17	December,	[illegible]	·747	[illegible]	21
June,	[illegible]	[illegible]	[illegible]	[illegible]					
July,	[illegible]	[illegible]	[illegible]	[illegible]	Total,	27·820	–	–	184

The rainfall was only ·124 of an inch in excess of the average annual measurement of the twenty-five years, 1865–89, inclusive—viz., 27·696 inches.

It will be remembered that the rainfall in 1887 was very exceptionally small—16·601 inches, the only approach to this measurement in Dublin being in 1870, when only 20·859 inches fell, and in 1884 when the measurement was 20·467 inches. In seven of the twenty-five years in question the rainfall was less than 25 inches, and in 1885 it was 22·614 inches.

The scanty rainfall in 1887 was in marked contrast to the abundant downpour in 1886, when 31·904 inches—or as nearly as possible double the fall of 1887—fell on 220 days. Only twice since these records commenced has the rainfall in Dublin exceeded that of 1886—namely, in 1872, when 31·348 inches fell on 220 days, and in 1880, when 34·312 inches were measured on, however, only 188 days.

In 1891 there were 186 rainy days, or days upon which not less than ·01 inch of rain (one hundredth of an inch) was measured. This was in defect of the average number of rainy days, which was 194·3 in the twenty-five years, 1865–89, inclusive. In 1868—the warm dry year of recent times—as well as in 1887, the rainy days were only 160, and in 1870 they were only 145. In 1868, however, the rainfall amounted to 24·935 inches, or more than 8 inches above the measurement in 1887, and even in 1870, 20·859 inches were recorded.

The rainfall in 24 hours from 9 a.m. to 9 a.m. exceeded one inch on two occasions, viz.—October 13th (1·176 inches), and November 10th (1·229 inches). On August 8th, also, nearly an inch fell (·985 inch).

Included in the 186 rainy days in 1891, are 12 on which snow or sleet fell, and 25 on which there was hail. In January hail was observed on 2 days, in March on 9 days, in April on 2 days, and in May on 8 days. Hail also fell once in June, August, October, and December. Snow or sleet fell on 3 days in January, on 7 days in March, on 2 days in May, and on 1 day in September, November, and December. Thunder occurred on nine occasions during the year—once in May and September, twice in June and July, and three times in August. Lightning was also seen on one occasion in each of the following months—viz., August and September, and three times in October.

The rainfall was distributed as follows:—1·880 inches fell on 33 days in the first quarter, 7·098 inches on 45 days in the second, 9·272 inches on 55 days in the third, and 9·800 inches on 49 days in the fourth and last quarter.

The rainfall in the first six months was only 8·748 inches, on 77 days—that is, not one-third of the year's record. In August, as much as 4·085 inches fell on 23 days.

Of the 9·800 inches which fell in the fourth quarter of the year, 3·490 inches were measured in October on, however, only 13 days, and 3·220 inches in December on 21 days.

Abstract of Meteorological Observations taken at Dublin (83, Fitzwilliam-square, West), during the Year 1891.

Month.	Ab. Max.	Date.	Ab. Min.	Date.	Mean Temp. Max.	Mean Temp. Min.	Amount.	Rainy Days.	Mean Height of Barometer reduced to Sea Level.	Highest Pressure.	Date.	Lowest Pressure.	Date.	Prevalent Winds.
	°		°		°	°	Inch		Ins.	Ins.		Ins.		
January,	[illegible]	[illegible]	[illegible]	[illegible]	[illegible]	[illegible]	[illegible]	[illegible]	[illegible]	[illegible]	[illegible]	[illegible]	[illegible]	S.W., W.
February,	[illegible]	[illegible]	[illegible]	[illegible]	[illegible]	[illegible]	[illegible]	[illegible]	[illegible]	[illegible]	[illegible]	[illegible]	[illegible]	W., S.W.
March,	[illegible]	[illegible]	[illegible]	[illegible]	[illegible]	[illegible]	[illegible]	[illegible]	[illegible]	[illegible]	[illegible]	[illegible]	[illegible]	Calm, W., S.W., [illegible]
April,	[illegible]	[illegible]	[illegible]	[illegible]	[illegible]	[illegible]	[illegible]	[illegible]	[illegible]	[illegible]	[illegible]	[illegible]	[illegible]	[illegible]
May,	[illegible]	[illegible]	[illegible]	[illegible]	[illegible]	[illegible]	[illegible]	[illegible]	[illegible]	[illegible]	[illegible]	[illegible]	[illegible]	N.W., N.E.
June,	[illegible]	[illegible]	[illegible]	[illegible]	[illegible]	[illegible]	[illegible]	[illegible]	[illegible]	[illegible]	[illegible]	[illegible]	[illegible]	N.E., E.
July,	[illegible]	[illegible]	[illegible]	[illegible]	[illegible]	[illegible]	[illegible]	[illegible]	[illegible]	[illegible]	[illegible]	[illegible]	[illegible]	N.W., S.W.
August,	[illegible]	[illegible]	[illegible]	[illegible]	[illegible]	[illegible]	[illegible]	[illegible]	[illegible]	[illegible]	[illegible]	[illegible]	[illegible]	W., S.W.
September,	[illegible]	[illegible]	[illegible]	[illegible]	[illegible]	[illegible]	[illegible]	[illegible]	[illegible]	[illegible]	[illegible]	[illegible]	[illegible]	[illegible]
October,	[illegible]	[illegible]	[illegible]	[illegible]	[illegible]	[illegible]	[illegible]	[illegible]	[illegible]	[illegible]	[illegible]	[illegible]	[illegible]	[illegible]
November,	[illegible]	[illegible]	[illegible]	[illegible]	[illegible]	[illegible]	[illegible]	[illegible]	[illegible]	[illegible]	[illegible]	[illegible]	[illegible]	S.W., W.
December,	[illegible]	[illegible]	[illegible]	[illegible]	[illegible]	[illegible]	[illegible]	[illegible]	[illegible]	[illegible]	[illegible]	[illegible]	[illegible]	[illegible]
Extremes, Totals, and Means	[illegible]	[illegible]	[illegible]	[illegible]	[illegible]	[illegible]	[illegible]	[illegible]	[illegible]	[illegible]	[illegible]	[illegible]	[illegible]	W., S.W.

ANNUAL ABSTRACTS

OF

MARRIAGES, BIRTHS, AND DEATHS.

1801.

ABSTRACT OF MARRIAGES.—Marriages registered in Ireland, pursuant to the

No.	PROVINCES AND COUNTIES.	Area in Statute Acres, exclusive of the larger Rivers, Lakes, and Tideways.	Population, 1861.	TOTAL MARRIAGES.	MARRIAGES — Registered under the Act 7 & 8 Vict., c. 81. — According to the Rites of the Church of Ireland: Special Licence.	Licence.	Banns.	Registrar's Certificate.	Not stated by which of the foregoing Forms.	Total.	In Registered Presbyterian Meeting Houses.	In Registered Buildings.	In the Registrar's Office.	Society of Friends.	Jews.	TOTAL Registered under the Act 7 & 8 Vict., c. 81.	Roman Catholic Marriages Registered under the 26 & 27 Vict., c. 90.
	IRELAND,	[illegible]	[illegible]	[illegible]	[illegible]	[illegible]	[illegible]	[illegible]	[illegible]	[illegible]	[illegible]	[illegible]	[illegible]	[illegible]	[illegible]	[illegible]	[illegible]
No.	PROVINCES.																
I.	LEINSTER,	[illegible]	[illegible]	[illegible]	[illegible]	[illegible]	[illegible]	[illegible]	[illegible]	[illegible]	[illegible]	[illegible]	[illegible]	[illegible]	[illegible]	[illegible]	[illegible]
II.	MUNSTER,	[illegible]	[illegible]	[illegible]	[illegible]	[illegible]	[illegible]	[illegible]	[illegible]	[illegible]	[illegible]	[illegible]	[illegible]	.	[illegible]	[illegible]	[illegible]
III.	ULSTER,	[illegible]	[illegible]	[illegible]	[illegible]	[illegible]	[illegible]	-	[illegible]	[illegible]	[illegible]	[illegible]	[illegible]	[illegible]	.	[illegible]	[illegible]
IV.	CONNAUGHT,	[illegible]	[illegible]	[illegible]	-	[illegible]	[illegible]	[illegible]	.	[illegible]	[illegible]	[illegible]	[illegible]	-	.	[illegible]	[illegible]
	I.—PROVINCE OF LEINSTER.—																
1	Carlow,	[illegible]	[illegible]	[illegible]	.	[illegible]	[illegible]	.	.	[illegible]	-	.	-	.	.	[illegible]	[illegible]
2	Dublin,	[illegible]	[illegible]	[illegible]	[illegible]	[illegible]	[illegible]	[illegible]	[illegible]	[illegible]	[illegible]	[illegible]	[illegible]	[illegible]	[illegible]	[illegible]	[illegible]
3	Kildare,	[illegible]	[illegible]	[illegible]	.	[illegible]	[illegible]	.	[illegible]	[illegible]	[illegible]	[illegible]	[illegible]	.	.	[illegible]	[illegible]
4	Kilkenny,	[illegible]	[illegible]	[illegible]	.	[illegible]	[illegible]	.	.	[illegible]	.	-	-	.	.	[illegible]	[illegible]
5	King's,	[illegible]	[illegible]	[illegible]	.	[illegible]	.	.	[illegible]	[illegible]	[illegible]	.	[illegible]	.	.	[illegible]	[illegible]
6	Longford,	[illegible]	[illegible]	[illegible]	.	[illegible]	.	.	.	[illegible]	[illegible]	-	[illegible]	.	.	[illegible]	[illegible]
7	Louth, and Co. of the Town of Drogheda,	[illegible]	[illegible]	[illegible]	.	[illegible]	.	.	[illegible]	[illegible]	[illegible]	[illegible]	[illegible]	.	.	[illegible]	[illegible]
8	Meath,	[illegible]	[illegible]	[illegible]	.	[illegible]	-	.	.	[illegible]	[illegible]	-	.	.	.	[illegible]	[illegible]
9	Queen's,	[illegible]	[illegible]	[illegible]	.	[illegible]	.	.	[illegible]	[illegible]	.	[illegible]	[illegible]	.	.	[illegible]	[illegible]
10	Westmeath,	[illegible]	[illegible]	[illegible]	.	[illegible]	[illegible]	.	.	[illegible]	.	-	[illegible]	.	.	[illegible]	[illegible]
11	Wexford,	[illegible]	[illegible]	[illegible]	.	[illegible]	.	.	[illegible]	[illegible]	[illegible]	[illegible]	[illegible]	.	.	[illegible]	[illegible]
12	Wicklow,	[illegible]	[illegible]	[illegible]	.	[illegible]	.	.	[illegible]	[illegible]	[illegible]	[illegible]	-	.	.	[illegible]	[illegible]
	II.—PROVINCE OF MUNSTER.—																
13	Clare,	[illegible]	[illegible]	[illegible]	[illegible]	[illegible]	[illegible]	-	.	[illegible]	.	[illegible]	[illegible]	.	.	[illegible]	[illegible]
14	Cork,	[illegible]	[illegible]	[illegible]	[illegible]	[illegible]	[illegible]	[illegible]	[illegible]	[illegible]	[illegible]	[illegible]	[illegible]	.	[illegible]	[illegible]	[illegible]
15	Kerry,	[illegible]	[illegible]	[illegible]	.	[illegible]	[illegible]	.	.	[illegible]	-	.	[illegible]	.	.	[illegible]	[illegible]
16	Limerick,	[illegible]	[illegible]	[illegible]	.	[illegible]	[illegible]	.	[illegible]	[illegible]	.	[illegible]	[illegible]	.	.	[illegible]	[illegible]
17	Tipperary,	[illegible]	[illegible]	[illegible]	.	[illegible]	[illegible]	.	.	[illegible]	.	[illegible]	.	.	.	[illegible]	[illegible]
18	Waterford,	[illegible]	[illegible]	[illegible]	.	[illegible]	.	.	[illegible]	[illegible]	.	[illegible]	-	.	.	[illegible]	[illegible]
	III.—PROVINCE OF ULSTER.—																
19	Antrim,	[illegible]	[illegible]	[illegible]	[illegible]	[illegible]	[illegible]	-	[illegible]	[illegible]	[illegible]	[illegible]	[illegible]	[illegible]	.	[illegible]	[illegible]
20	Armagh,	[illegible]	[illegible]	[illegible]	[illegible]	[illegible]	-	.	[illegible]	[illegible]	[illegible]	[illegible]	[illegible]	.	.	[illegible]	[illegible]
21	Cavan,	[illegible]	[illegible]	[illegible]	.	[illegible]	-	.	[illegible]	[illegible]	[illegible]	[illegible]	-	.	.	[illegible]	[illegible]
22	Donegal,	[illegible]	[illegible]	[illegible]	.	[illegible]	[illegible]	.	[illegible]	[illegible]	[illegible]	[illegible]	[illegible]	.	.	[illegible]	[illegible]
23	Down,	[illegible]	[illegible]	[illegible]	.	[illegible]	[illegible]	.	[illegible]	[illegible]	[illegible]	[illegible]	[illegible]	-	.	[illegible]	[illegible]
24	Fermanagh,	[illegible]	[illegible]	[illegible]	[illegible]	[illegible]	.	.	[illegible]	[illegible]	[illegible]	[illegible]	[illegible]	.	.	[illegible]	[illegible]
25	Londonderry,	[illegible]	[illegible]	[illegible]	.	[illegible]	[illegible]	.	-	[illegible]	[illegible]	[illegible]	[illegible]	.	.	[illegible]	[illegible]
26	Monaghan,	[illegible]	[illegible]	[illegible]	[illegible]	[illegible]	-	.	.	[illegible]	[illegible]	[illegible]	[illegible]	.	-	[illegible]	[illegible]
27	Tyrone,	[illegible]	[illegible]	[illegible]	[illegible]	[illegible]	.	.	[illegible]	[illegible]	[illegible]	[illegible]	[illegible]	.	.	[illegible]	[illegible]
	IV.—PROVINCE OF CONNAUGHT.—																
28	Galway,	[illegible]	[illegible]	[illegible]	-	[illegible]	[illegible]	.	-	[illegible]	[illegible]	.	[illegible]	.	.	[illegible]	[illegible]
29	Leitrim,	[illegible]	[illegible]	[illegible]	.	[illegible]	.	.	.	[illegible]	[illegible]	[illegible]	.	.	.	[illegible]	[illegible]
30	Mayo,	[illegible]	[illegible]	[illegible]	.	[illegible]	.	.	.	[illegible]	[illegible]	[illegible]	[illegible]	.	.	[illegible]	[illegible]
31	Roscommon,	[illegible]	[illegible]	[illegible]	.	[illegible]	.	[illegible]	-	[illegible]	[illegible]	.	.	.	.	[illegible]	[illegible]
32	Sligo,	[illegible]	[illegible]	[illegible]	.	[illegible]	[illegible]	.	-	[illegible]	[illegible]	[illegible]	[illegible]	.	.	[illegible]	[illegible]

Abstract of Marriages, 1891.

Acts 7 & 8 Vic., c. 81, and 26 & 27 Vic., c. 90, in the year ending 31st December, 1891.

Marriages: Registered in the Quarters ending the last day of: March	June	September	December	Contracted between: Bachelors and Spinsters	Bachelors and Widows	Widowers and Spinsters	Widowers and Widows	Of: Widowers	Widows	Of Persons not of full Age: Men	Women	Signed the Marriage Register with Marks: Men	Women	Cases in which: Both signed	One signed	PROVINCES and COUNTIES.
[illegible]	[illegible]	[illegible]	[illegible]	[illegible]	[illegible]	[illegible]	[illegible]	[illegible]	[illegible]	[illegible]	[illegible]	[illegible]	[illegible]	[illegible]	[illegible]	IRELAND.
																PROVINCES.
[illegible]	[illegible]	[illegible]	[illegible]	[illegible]	[illegible]	[illegible]	[illegible]	[illegible]	[illegible]	[illegible]	[illegible]	[illegible]	[illegible]	[illegible]	[illegible]	LEINSTER.
[illegible]	[illegible]	[illegible]	[illegible]	[illegible]	[illegible]	[illegible]	[illegible]	[illegible]	[illegible]	[illegible]	[illegible]	[illegible]	[illegible]	[illegible]	[illegible]	MUNSTER.
[illegible]	[illegible]	[illegible]	[illegible]	[illegible]	[illegible]	[illegible]	[illegible]	[illegible]	[illegible]	[illegible]	[illegible]	[illegible]	[illegible]	[illegible]	[illegible]	ULSTER.
[illegible]	[illegible]	[illegible]	[illegible]	[illegible]	[illegible]	[illegible]	[illegible]	[illegible]	[illegible]	[illegible]	[illegible]	[illegible]	[illegible]	[illegible]	[illegible]	CONNAUGHT.

MARRIAGES in the Year 1891—in Counties.

[illegible]	[illegible]	[illegible]	[illegible]	[illegible]	-	[illegible]	[illegible]	[illegible]	[illegible]	[illegible]	[illegible]	[illegible]	[illegible]	[illegible]	[illegible]	Carlow.
[illegible]	[illegible]	[illegible]	[illegible]	[illegible]	[illegible]	[illegible]	[illegible]	[illegible]	[illegible]	[illegible]	[illegible]	[illegible]	[illegible]	[illegible]	[illegible]	Dublin.
[illegible]	[illegible]	[illegible]	[illegible]	[illegible]	[illegible]	[illegible]	[illegible]	[illegible]	[illegible]	[illegible]	[illegible]	[illegible]	[illegible]	[illegible]	[illegible]	Kildare.
[illegible]	[illegible]	[illegible]	[illegible]	[illegible]	[illegible]	[illegible]	[illegible]	[illegible]	[illegible]	[illegible]	[illegible]	[illegible]	[illegible]	[illegible]	[illegible]	Kilkenny.
[illegible]	[illegible]	[illegible]	[illegible]	[illegible]	[illegible]	[illegible]	[illegible]	[illegible]	[illegible]	[illegible]	[illegible]	[illegible]	[illegible]	[illegible]	[illegible]	King's.
[illegible]	[illegible]	[illegible]	[illegible]	[illegible]	[illegible]	[illegible]	[illegible]	[illegible]	[illegible]	[illegible]	[illegible]	[illegible]	[illegible]	[illegible]	[illegible]	Longford.
[illegible]	[illegible]	[illegible]	[illegible]	[illegible]	[illegible]	[illegible]	[illegible]	[illegible]	[illegible]	[illegible]	[illegible]	[illegible]	[illegible]	[illegible]	[illegible]	Louth, and Co. Town of Drogheda.
[illegible]	[illegible]	[illegible]	[illegible]	[illegible]	[illegible]	[illegible]	[illegible]	[illegible]	[illegible]	[illegible]	[illegible]	[illegible]	[illegible]	[illegible]	[illegible]	Meath.
[illegible]	[illegible]	[illegible]	[illegible]	[illegible]	[illegible]	[illegible]	[illegible]	[illegible]	[illegible]	[illegible]	[illegible]	[illegible]	[illegible]	[illegible]	[illegible]	Queen's.
[illegible]	[illegible]	[illegible]	[illegible]	[illegible]	[illegible]	[illegible]	[illegible]	[illegible]	[illegible]	[illegible]	[illegible]	[illegible]	[illegible]	[illegible]	[illegible]	Westmeath.
[illegible]	[illegible]	[illegible]	[illegible]	[illegible]	[illegible]	[illegible]	[illegible]	[illegible]	[illegible]	[illegible]	[illegible]	[illegible]	[illegible]	[illegible]	[illegible]	Wexford.
[illegible]	[illegible]	[illegible]	[illegible]	[illegible]	[illegible]	[illegible]	[illegible]	[illegible]	[illegible]	[illegible]	[illegible]	[illegible]	[illegible]	[illegible]	[illegible]	Wicklow.

ABSTRACT OF MARRIAGES.—Marriages registered in Ireland, pursuant to the

I.—PROVINCE OF LEINSTER.—

No.	SUPERINTENDENT REGISTRARS' DISTRICTS.	Area in Statute Acres, exclusive of the larger Rivers, Lakes, and Tideways.	Population, 1861.	TOTAL MARRIAGES.	Special Licence.	Licence.	Banns.	Registrar's Certificate.	Not stated by whom, or by what authority.	Total.	In Registered Presbyterian Meeting Houses.	In Registered Buildings.	In the Registrar's Office.	Society of Friends.	Jews.	TOTAL Registered under the Act 7 & 8 Vic., c. 81.	Roman Catholic Marriages registered under the Act 26 Vic., c. 27.
	1. Carlow Co.																
1	Baltinglass, part of,	[illegible]	[illegible]	[illegible]	[illegible]	[illegible]	[illegible]	[illegible]	[illegible]	[illegible]	[illegible]	[illegible]	[illegible]	[illegible]	[illegible]	[illegible]	[illegible]
2	Carlow, do.	[illegible]	[illegible]	[illegible]	[illegible]	[illegible]	[illegible]	[illegible]	[illegible]	[illegible]	[illegible]	[illegible]	[illegible]	[illegible]	[illegible]	[illegible]	[illegible]
3	Enniscorthy, do.	[illegible]	[illegible]	[illegible]	[illegible]	[illegible]	[illegible]	[illegible]	[illegible]	[illegible]	[illegible]	[illegible]	[illegible]	[illegible]	[illegible]	[illegible]	[illegible]
4	New Ross, do.	[illegible]	[illegible]	[illegible]	[illegible]	[illegible]	[illegible]	[illegible]	[illegible]	[illegible]	[illegible]	[illegible]	[illegible]	[illegible]	[illegible]	[illegible]	[illegible]
5	Shillelagh, do.	[illegible]	[illegible]	[illegible]	[illegible]	[illegible]	[illegible]	[illegible]	[illegible]	[illegible]	[illegible]	[illegible]	[illegible]	[illegible]	[illegible]	[illegible]	[illegible]
	2. Dublin Co.																
6	Balrothery,	[illegible]	[illegible]	[illegible]	[illegible]	[illegible]	[illegible]	[illegible]	[illegible]	[illegible]	[illegible]	[illegible]	[illegible]	[illegible]	[illegible]	[illegible]	[illegible]
7	Celbridge, part of,	[illegible]	[illegible]	[illegible]	[illegible]	[illegible]	[illegible]	[illegible]	[illegible]	[illegible]	[illegible]	[illegible]	[illegible]	[illegible]	[illegible]	[illegible]	[illegible]
8	Dublin, North,	[illegible]	[illegible]	[illegible]	[illegible]	[illegible]	[illegible]	[illegible]	[illegible]	[illegible]	[illegible]	[illegible]	[illegible]	[illegible]	[illegible]	[illegible]	[illegible]
9	Dublin, South,	[illegible]	[illegible]	[illegible]	[illegible]	[illegible]	[illegible]	[illegible]	[illegible]	[illegible]	[illegible]	[illegible]	[illegible]	[illegible]	[illegible]	[illegible]	[illegible]
10	[illegible], part of,	[illegible]	[illegible]	[illegible]	[illegible]	[illegible]	[illegible]	[illegible]	[illegible]	[illegible]	[illegible]	[illegible]	[illegible]	[illegible]	[illegible]	[illegible]	[illegible]
11	Rathdown, do.	[illegible]	[illegible]	[illegible]	[illegible]	[illegible]	[illegible]	[illegible]	[illegible]	[illegible]	[illegible]	[illegible]	[illegible]	[illegible]	[illegible]	[illegible]	[illegible]
	3. Kildare Co.																
12	Athy, part of,	[illegible]	[illegible]	[illegible]	[illegible]	[illegible]	[illegible]	[illegible]	[illegible]	[illegible]	[illegible]	[illegible]	[illegible]	[illegible]	[illegible]	[illegible]	[illegible]
13	Baltinglass, do.	[illegible]	[illegible]	[illegible]	[illegible]	[illegible]	[illegible]	[illegible]	[illegible]	[illegible]	[illegible]	[illegible]	[illegible]	[illegible]	[illegible]	[illegible]	[illegible]
14	Celbridge, do.	[illegible]	[illegible]	[illegible]	[illegible]	[illegible]	[illegible]	[illegible]	[illegible]	[illegible]	[illegible]	[illegible]	[illegible]	[illegible]	[illegible]	[illegible]	[illegible]
15	Edenderry, do.	[illegible]	[illegible]	[illegible]	[illegible]	[illegible]	[illegible]	[illegible]	[illegible]	[illegible]	[illegible]	[illegible]	[illegible]	[illegible]	[illegible]	[illegible]	[illegible]
16	Naas, do.	[illegible]	[illegible]	[illegible]	[illegible]	[illegible]	[illegible]	[illegible]	[illegible]	[illegible]	[illegible]	[illegible]	[illegible]	[illegible]	[illegible]	[illegible]	[illegible]
	4. Kilkenny Co.																
17	Callan, part of,	[illegible]	[illegible]	[illegible]	[illegible]	[illegible]	[illegible]	[illegible]	[illegible]	[illegible]	[illegible]	[illegible]	[illegible]	[illegible]	[illegible]	[illegible]	[illegible]
18	Castlecomer, do.	[illegible]	[illegible]	[illegible]	[illegible]	[illegible]	[illegible]	[illegible]	[illegible]	[illegible]	[illegible]	[illegible]	[illegible]	[illegible]	[illegible]	[illegible]	[illegible]
19	[illegible],	[illegible]	[illegible]	[illegible]	[illegible]	[illegible]	[illegible]	[illegible]	[illegible]	[illegible]	[illegible]	[illegible]	[illegible]	[illegible]	[illegible]	[illegible]	[illegible]
20	Kilkenny,	[illegible]	[illegible]	[illegible]	[illegible]	[illegible]	[illegible]	[illegible]	[illegible]	[illegible]	[illegible]	[illegible]	[illegible]	[illegible]	[illegible]	[illegible]	[illegible]
21	New Ross, part of,	[illegible]	[illegible]	[illegible]	[illegible]	[illegible]	[illegible]	[illegible]	[illegible]	[illegible]	[illegible]	[illegible]	[illegible]	[illegible]	[illegible]	[illegible]	[illegible]
22	Thomastown,	[illegible]	[illegible]	[illegible]	[illegible]	[illegible]	[illegible]	[illegible]	[illegible]	[illegible]	[illegible]	[illegible]	[illegible]	[illegible]	[illegible]	[illegible]	[illegible]
23	Urlingford, part of,	[illegible]	[illegible]	[illegible]	[illegible]	[illegible]	[illegible]	[illegible]	[illegible]	[illegible]	[illegible]	[illegible]	[illegible]	[illegible]	[illegible]	[illegible]	[illegible]
24	Waterford, do.	[illegible]	[illegible]	[illegible]	[illegible]	[illegible]	[illegible]	[illegible]	[illegible]	[illegible]	[illegible]	[illegible]	[illegible]	[illegible]	[illegible]	[illegible]	[illegible]
	5. King's Co.																
25	Edenderry, part of,	[illegible]	[illegible]	[illegible]	[illegible]	[illegible]	[illegible]	[illegible]	[illegible]	[illegible]	[illegible]	[illegible]	[illegible]	[illegible]	[illegible]	[illegible]	[illegible]
26	Mountmellick, do.	[illegible]	[illegible]	[illegible]	[illegible]	[illegible]	[illegible]	[illegible]	[illegible]	[illegible]	[illegible]	[illegible]	[illegible]	[illegible]	[illegible]	[illegible]	[illegible]
27	Parsonstown, do.	[illegible]	[illegible]	[illegible]	[illegible]	[illegible]	[illegible]	[illegible]	[illegible]	[illegible]	[illegible]	[illegible]	[illegible]	[illegible]	[illegible]	[illegible]	[illegible]
28	Roscrea, do.	[illegible]	[illegible]	[illegible]	[illegible]	[illegible]	[illegible]	[illegible]	[illegible]	[illegible]	[illegible]	[illegible]	[illegible]	[illegible]	[illegible]	[illegible]	[illegible]
29	Tullamore, do.	[illegible]	[illegible]	[illegible]	[illegible]	[illegible]	[illegible]	[illegible]	[illegible]	[illegible]	[illegible]	[illegible]	[illegible]	[illegible]	[illegible]	[illegible]	[illegible]
	6. Longford Co.																
30	Ballymahon, part of,	[illegible]	[illegible]	[illegible]	[illegible]	[illegible]	[illegible]	[illegible]	[illegible]	[illegible]	[illegible]	[illegible]	[illegible]	[illegible]	[illegible]	[illegible]	[illegible]
31	Granard, do.	[illegible]	[illegible]	[illegible]	[illegible]	[illegible]	[illegible]	[illegible]	[illegible]	[illegible]	[illegible]	[illegible]	[illegible]	[illegible]	[illegible]	[illegible]	[illegible]
32	Longford,	[illegible]	[illegible]	[illegible]	[illegible]	[illegible]	[illegible]	[illegible]	[illegible]	[illegible]	[illegible]	[illegible]	[illegible]	[illegible]	[illegible]	[illegible]	[illegible]
	7. Louth and Co. of Town of Drogheda.																
33	Ardee, part of,	[illegible]	[illegible]	[illegible]	[illegible]	[illegible]	[illegible]	[illegible]	[illegible]	[illegible]	[illegible]	[illegible]	[illegible]	[illegible]	[illegible]	[illegible]	[illegible]
34	Dundalk, do.	[illegible]	[illegible]	[illegible]	[illegible]	[illegible]	[illegible]	[illegible]	[illegible]	[illegible]	[illegible]	[illegible]	[illegible]	[illegible]	[illegible]	[illegible]	[illegible]
35	Drogheda, do.	[illegible]	[illegible]	[illegible]	[illegible]	[illegible]	[illegible]	[illegible]	[illegible]	[illegible]	[illegible]	[illegible]	[illegible]	[illegible]	[illegible]	[illegible]	[illegible]

Acts 7 & 8 Vict., c. 81, and 26 & 27 Vic., c. 90, in the year ending 31st December, 1891.

MARRIAGES in the Year 1891—in SUPERINTENDENT REGISTRARS' DISTRICTS.

Registered in the Quarter ending the last day of: March	June	September	December	Contracted between: Bachelors and Spinsters	Bachelors and Widows	Widowers and Spinsters	Widowers and Widows	Of: [illegible]	[illegible]	Of Persons not of Full Age: Men	Women	Signed the Marriage Register with Marks: Men	Women	Cases in which: [illegible]	[illegible]	SUPERINTENDENT REGISTRARS' DISTRICTS.
																1. Carlow Co.
1	[illegible]	[illegible]	-	[illegible]	-	-	-	-	-	-	[illegible]	[illegible]	[illegible]	[illegible]	-	Baltinglass, part of.
[illegible]	[illegible]	[illegible]	[illegible]	[illegible]	-	[illegible]	[illegible]	[illegible]	[illegible]	-	[illegible]	[illegible]	[illegible]	[illegible]	[illegible]	Carlow, do.
-	-	-	-	-	-	-	-	-	-	-	-	-	-	-	-	Enniscorthy, do.
[illegible]	[illegible]	[illegible]	1	[illegible]	-	[illegible]	-	[illegible]	-	-	-	[illegible]	[illegible]	[illegible]	-	New Ross, do.
[illegible]	[illegible]	[illegible]	7	[illegible]	-	[illegible]	[illegible]	[illegible]	[illegible]	1	-	[illegible]	[illegible]	1	[illegible]	Shillelagh, do.
																2. Dublin Co.
[illegible]	[illegible]	[illegible]	[illegible]	[illegible]	[illegible]	[illegible]	[illegible]	[illegible]	[illegible]	[illegible]	[illegible]	[illegible]	[illegible]	[illegible]	[illegible]	Balrothery.
[illegible]	[illegible]	[illegible]	-	[illegible]	-	[illegible]	-	[illegible]	-	-	-	-	[illegible]	-	[illegible]	Celbridge, part of.
[illegible]	[illegible]	[illegible]	[illegible]	[illegible]	[illegible]	[illegible]	[illegible]	[illegible]	[illegible]	[illegible]	[illegible]	[illegible]	[illegible]	[illegible]	[illegible]	Dublin, North.
[illegible]	[illegible]	[illegible]	[illegible]	[illegible]	[illegible]	[illegible]	[illegible]	[illegible]	[illegible]	[illegible]	[illegible]	[illegible]	[illegible]	[illegible]	[illegible]	Dublin, South.
-	-	-	[illegible]	[illegible]	-	-	-	-	-	-	-	[illegible]	-	-	[illegible]	Dunshaughlin, part of.
[illegible]	[illegible]	[illegible]	[illegible]	[illegible]	[illegible]	[illegible]	[illegible]	[illegible]	[illegible]	[illegible]	[illegible]	[illegible]	[illegible]	[illegible]	[illegible]	Rathdown do.
																3. Kildare Co.
[illegible]	[illegible]	[illegible]	[illegible]	[illegible]	[illegible]	[illegible]	[illegible]	[illegible]	[illegible]	[illegible]	[illegible]	[illegible]	[illegible]	[illegible]	[illegible]	Athy, part of.
[illegible]	-	[illegible]	[illegible]	[illegible]		-	-	-	-	-	[illegible]	[illegible]	-	-	[illegible]	Baltinglass, do.
[illegible]	[illegible]	[illegible]	[illegible]	[illegible]	[illegible]	[illegible]	-	[illegible]	[illegible]	[illegible]	[illegible]	[illegible]	-	-	[illegible]	Celbridge, do.
[illegible]	[illegible]	[illegible]	[illegible]	[illegible]	[illegible]	[illegible]	-	[illegible]	[illegible]	[illegible]	[illegible]	[illegible]	[illegible]	-	[illegible]	Edenderry, do.
[illegible]	[illegible]	[illegible]	[illegible]	[illegible]	[illegible]	[illegible]	[illegible]	[illegible]	[illegible]	[illegible]	[illegible]	[illegible]	[illegible]	[illegible]	[illegible]	Naas, do.
																4. Kilkenny Co.
[illegible]	[illegible]	[illegible]	[illegible]	[illegible]	-	[illegible]	-	[illegible]	-	-	[illegible]	[illegible]	[illegible]	[illegible]	[illegible]	Callan, part of
[illegible]	[illegible]	[illegible]	[illegible]	[illegible]	-	-	-	-	-	-	-	[illegible]	[illegible]	[illegible]	-	Carrick-on-Suir, do.
[illegible]	[illegible]	[illegible]	[illegible]	[illegible]	[illegible]	[illegible]	[illegible]	[illegible]	[illegible]	-	[illegible]	[illegible]	[illegible]	[illegible]	[illegible]	Castlecomer.
[illegible]	[illegible]	[illegible]	[illegible]	[illegible]	[illegible]	[illegible]	[illegible]	[illegible]	[illegible]	[illegible]	[illegible]	[illegible]	[illegible]	[illegible]	[illegible]	Kilkenny.
[illegible]	[illegible]	[illegible]	[illegible]	[illegible]	-	-	[illegible]	[illegible]	[illegible]	-	[illegible]	[illegible]	[illegible]	-	[illegible]	New Ross, part of.
[illegible]	[illegible]	[illegible]	[illegible]	[illegible]	-	[illegible]	-	[illegible]	-	-	[illegible]	[illegible]	[illegible]	[illegible]	[illegible]	Thomastown.
[illegible]	[illegible]	[illegible]	[illegible]	[illegible]	[illegible]	1	[illegible]	[illegible]	[illegible]	-	[illegible]	[illegible]	[illegible]	[illegible]	[illegible]	Urlingford, part of.
[illegible]	[illegible]	[illegible]	[illegible]	[illegible]	[illegible]	[illegible]	[illegible]	[illegible]	[illegible]		1	[illegible]	[illegible]	[illegible]	[illegible]	Waterford, do.
																5. King's Co.
[illegible]	[illegible]	[illegible]	[illegible]	[illegible]	[illegible]	[illegible]	-	[illegible]	[illegible]	-	[illegible]	[illegible]	[illegible]	[illegible]	[illegible]	Edenderry, part of.
[illegible]	[illegible]	[illegible]	[illegible]	[illegible]	[illegible]	[illegible]	-	[illegible]	[illegible]	-		[illegible]	[illegible]	[illegible]	[illegible]	Mountmellick, do.
[illegible]	[illegible]	[illegible]	[illegible]	[illegible]	[illegible]	[illegible]	[illegible]	[illegible]	[illegible]	[illegible]	[illegible]	[illegible]	[illegible]	[illegible]	[illegible]	Parsonstown, do.
[illegible]	[illegible]	[illegible]	[illegible]	[illegible]	[illegible]	[illegible]	[illegible]	[illegible]	[illegible]	-	[illegible]	[illegible]	[illegible]	[illegible]	[illegible]	Roscrea, do.
[illegible]	[illegible]	[illegible]	[illegible]	[illegible]	-	[illegible]	-	[illegible]	-	[illegible]	[illegible]	[illegible]	[illegible]	[illegible]	[illegible]	Tullamore, do.
																6. Longford Co.
[illegible]	[illegible]	[illegible]	[illegible]	[illegible]	[illegible]	[illegible]	-	[illegible]	[illegible]	-	-	[illegible]	[illegible]	[illegible]	[illegible]	Ballymahon, part of.
[illegible]	[illegible]	[illegible]	[illegible]	[illegible]	[illegible]	[illegible]	[illegible]	[illegible]	[illegible]	[illegible]	[illegible]	[illegible]	[illegible]	[illegible]	[illegible]	Granard, do.
[illegible]	[illegible]	[illegible]	[illegible]	[illegible]	[illegible]	[illegible]	-	[illegible]	[illegible]	[illegible]	[illegible]	[illegible]	[illegible]	[illegible]	[illegible]	Longford.
																7. Louth and Co. of Town of Drogheda.
[illegible]	[illegible]	[illegible]	[illegible]	[illegible]	-	[illegible]	[illegible]	[illegible]	[illegible]	-	[illegible]	[illegible]	[illegible]	[illegible]	[illegible]	Ardee, part of
[illegible]	[illegible]	[illegible]	[illegible]	[illegible]	[illegible]	[illegible]	-	[illegible]	[illegible]	[illegible]	[illegible]	[illegible]	[illegible]	[illegible]	[illegible]	Dundalk, do.
[illegible]	[illegible]	[illegible]	[illegible]	[illegible]	[illegible]	[illegible]	[illegible]	[illegible]	[illegible]	[illegible]	[illegible]	[illegible]	[illegible]	[illegible]	[illegible]	Drogheda, do.

I.—PROVINCE OF LEINSTER—*continued.*

No.	SUPERINTENDENT REGISTRARS' DISTRICTS.	Area in Statute Acres, exclusive of the larger Rivers, Lakes, and Tideways.	Population, 1861.	TOTAL MARRIAGES.	Special Licence.	Licence.	Banns.	Registrar's Certificate.	Fiat [illegible]	Total.	[illegible] Presbyterian [illegible]	In Registered Buildings.	In the Registrar's Office.	Society of Friends.	Jews.	[illegible]
	8. [illegible] Co.															
[illegible]	[illegible], part of	[illegible]	[illegible]	[illegible]	[illegible]	[illegible]	[illegible]	[illegible]	[illegible]	[illegible]	[illegible]	[illegible]	[illegible]	[illegible]	[illegible]	[illegible]
37	[illegible], do.	[illegible]	[illegible]	.	[illegible]	[illegible]	[illegible]	[illegible]	[illegible]	[illegible]	[illegible]	[illegible]	[illegible]	[illegible]	[illegible]	[illegible]
[illegible]	[illegible], do.	[illegible]	[illegible]	[illegible]	[illegible]	[illegible]	[illegible]	[illegible]	[illegible]	[illegible]	[illegible]	[illegible]	[illegible]	[illegible]	[illegible]	[illegible]
[illegible]	[illegible], do.	[illegible]	[illegible]	[illegible]	[illegible]	[illegible]	[illegible]	[illegible]	[illegible]	[illegible]	[illegible]	[illegible]	[illegible]	[illegible]	[illegible]	[illegible]
[illegible]	[illegible], do.	[illegible]	[illegible]	[illegible]	[illegible]	[illegible]	[illegible]	[illegible]	[illegible]	[illegible]	[illegible]	[illegible]	[illegible]	[illegible]	[illegible]	[illegible]
[illegible]	[illegible], do.	[illegible]	[illegible]	[illegible]	[illegible]	[illegible]	[illegible]	[illegible]	[illegible]	[illegible]	[illegible]	[illegible]	[illegible]	[illegible]	[illegible]	[illegible]
[illegible]	[illegible]	[illegible]	[illegible]	[illegible]	[illegible]	[illegible]	[illegible]	[illegible]	[illegible]	[illegible]	[illegible]	[illegible]	[illegible]	[illegible]	[illegible]	[illegible]
43	[illegible], part of	[illegible]	[illegible]	[illegible]	[illegible]	[illegible]	[illegible]	[illegible]	[illegible]	[illegible]	[illegible]	[illegible]	[illegible]	[illegible]	[illegible]	[illegible]
[illegible]	[illegible]	[illegible]	[illegible]	[illegible]	[illegible]	[illegible]	[illegible]	[illegible]	[illegible]	[illegible]	[illegible]	[illegible]	[illegible]	[illegible]	[illegible]	[illegible]
	9. Queen's Co.															
45	[illegible]	[illegible]	[illegible]	[illegible]	[illegible]	[illegible]	[illegible]	[illegible]	[illegible]	[illegible]	[illegible]	[illegible]	[illegible]	[illegible]	[illegible]	[illegible]
[illegible]	[illegible], part of	[illegible]	[illegible]	[illegible]	[illegible]	[illegible]	[illegible]	[illegible]	[illegible]	[illegible]	[illegible]	[illegible]	[illegible]	[illegible]	[illegible]	[illegible]
47	[illegible], do.	[illegible]	[illegible]	[illegible]	[illegible]	[illegible]	[illegible]	[illegible]	[illegible]	[illegible]	[illegible]	[illegible]	[illegible]	[illegible]	[illegible]	[illegible]
[illegible]	[illegible], do.	[illegible]	[illegible]	[illegible]	[illegible]	[illegible]	[illegible]	[illegible]	[illegible]	[illegible]	[illegible]	[illegible]	[illegible]	[illegible]	[illegible]	[illegible]
[illegible]	[illegible], do.	[illegible]	[illegible]	[illegible]	[illegible]	[illegible]	[illegible]	[illegible]	[illegible]	[illegible]	[illegible]	[illegible]	[illegible]	[illegible]	[illegible]	[illegible]
[illegible]	[illegible], do.	[illegible]	[illegible]	.	[illegible]	[illegible]	[illegible]	[illegible]	[illegible]	[illegible]	[illegible]	[illegible]	[illegible]	[illegible]	[illegible]	[illegible]
	10. Westmeath Co.															
[illegible]	[illegible], part of	[illegible]	[illegible]	[illegible]	[illegible]	[illegible]	[illegible]	[illegible]	[illegible]	[illegible]	[illegible]	[illegible]	[illegible]	[illegible]	[illegible]	[illegible]
[illegible]	[illegible], do.	[illegible]	[illegible]	[illegible]	[illegible]	[illegible]	[illegible]	[illegible]	[illegible]	[illegible]	[illegible]	[illegible]	[illegible]	[illegible]	[illegible]	[illegible]
[illegible]	[illegible]	[illegible]	[illegible]	[illegible]	[illegible]	[illegible]	[illegible]	[illegible]	[illegible]	[illegible]	[illegible]	[illegible]	[illegible]	[illegible]	[illegible]	[illegible]
[illegible]	[illegible], part of	[illegible]	[illegible]	[illegible]	[illegible]	[illegible]	[illegible]	[illegible]	[illegible]	[illegible]	[illegible]	[illegible]	[illegible]	[illegible]	[illegible]	[illegible]
[illegible]	[illegible]	[illegible]	[illegible]	[illegible]	[illegible]	[illegible]	[illegible]	[illegible]	[illegible]	[illegible]	[illegible]	[illegible]	[illegible]	[illegible]	[illegible]	[illegible]
[illegible]	[illegible], part of	[illegible]	[illegible]	[illegible]	[illegible]	[illegible]	[illegible]	[illegible]	[illegible]	[illegible]	[illegible]	[illegible]	[illegible]	[illegible]	[illegible]	[illegible]
	11. Wexford Co.															
[illegible]	[illegible], part of	[illegible]	[illegible]	[illegible]	[illegible]	[illegible]	[illegible]	[illegible]	[illegible]	[illegible]	[illegible]	[illegible]	[illegible]	[illegible]	[illegible]	[illegible]
[illegible]	[illegible]	[illegible]	[illegible]	[illegible]	[illegible]	[illegible]	[illegible]	[illegible]	[illegible]	[illegible]	[illegible]	[illegible]	[illegible]	[illegible]	[illegible]	[illegible]
[illegible]	[illegible], part of	[illegible]	[illegible]	[illegible]	[illegible]	[illegible]	[illegible]	[illegible]	[illegible]	[illegible]	[illegible]	[illegible]	[illegible]	[illegible]	[illegible]	[illegible]
[illegible]	[illegible], do.	[illegible]	[illegible]	.	[illegible]	[illegible]	[illegible]	[illegible]	[illegible]	[illegible]	[illegible]	[illegible]	[illegible]	[illegible]	[illegible]	[illegible]
[illegible]	[illegible]	[illegible]	[illegible]	[illegible]	[illegible]	[illegible]	[illegible]	[illegible]	[illegible]	[illegible]	[illegible]	[illegible]	[illegible]	[illegible]	[illegible]	[illegible]
	12. Wicklow Co.															
[illegible]	[illegible], part of	[illegible]	[illegible]	[illegible]	[illegible]	[illegible]	[illegible]	[illegible]	[illegible]	[illegible]	[illegible]	[illegible]	[illegible]	[illegible]	[illegible]	[illegible]
[illegible]	[illegible], do.	[illegible]	[illegible]	[illegible]	[illegible]	[illegible]	[illegible]	[illegible]	[illegible]	[illegible]	[illegible]	[illegible]	[illegible]	[illegible]	[illegible]	[illegible]
[illegible]	[illegible], do.	[illegible]	[illegible]	[illegible]	[illegible]	[illegible]	[illegible]	[illegible]	[illegible]	[illegible]	[illegible]	[illegible]	[illegible]	[illegible]	[illegible]	[illegible]
[illegible]	[illegible]	[illegible]	[illegible]	[illegible]	[illegible]	[illegible]	[illegible]	[illegible]	[illegible]	[illegible]	[illegible]	[illegible]	[illegible]	[illegible]	[illegible]	[illegible]
[illegible]	[illegible], part of	[illegible]	[illegible]	[illegible]	[illegible]	[illegible]	[illegible]	[illegible]	[illegible]	[illegible]	[illegible]	[illegible]	[illegible]	[illegible]	[illegible]	[illegible]

[illegible]	[illegible]	[illegible]

II.—PROVINCE OF MUNSTER—*continued.*

MARRIAGES. Registered under the Act 7 & 8 Vic., c. 81.

Column headings: Superintendent Registrars' Districts; Area in Statute Acres, exclusive of the larger Rivers, Lakes, and Tideways; Population, 1861; Total Marriages; According to the Rites of the Church of Ireland: Special Licence, Licence, Banns, Registrar's Certificate, Not stated by which of the foregoing Forms, Total; In Registered Presbyterian Meeting Houses; In Registered Buildings; In the Registrar's Office; Society of Friends; Jews; Total Registered under the Act.

No.	Superintendent Registrars' Districts	Area	Population, 1861	Total Marriages	
	36. Cork Co.				
76	Bandon,	[illegible]	[illegible]	[illegible]	[illegible]
77	Bantry,	[illegible]	[illegible]	[illegible]	[illegible]
78	Castletown,	[illegible]	[illegible]	[illegible]	[illegible]
79	Clonakilty,	[illegible]	[illegible]	[illegible]	[illegible]
80	Cork,	[illegible]	[illegible]	[illegible]	[illegible]
81	Dunmanway,	[illegible]	[illegible]	[illegible]	[illegible]
82	Fermoy,	[illegible]	[illegible]	[illegible]	[illegible]
83	Kanturk,	[illegible]	[illegible]	[illegible]	[illegible]
84	Kilmallock, part of,	[illegible]	[illegible]	[illegible]	[illegible]
85	Kinsale,	[illegible]	[illegible]	[illegible]	[illegible]
86	Macroom,	[illegible]	[illegible]	[illegible]	[illegible]
87	Mallow,	[illegible]	[illegible]	[illegible]	[illegible]
88	Midleton,	[illegible]	[illegible]	[illegible]	[illegible]
89	Millstreet,	[illegible]	[illegible]	[illegible]	[illegible]
90	Mitchelstown, part of,	[illegible]	[illegible]	[illegible]	[illegible]
91	Skibbereen,	[illegible]	[illegible]	[illegible]	[illegible]
92	Skull,	[illegible]	[illegible]	[illegible]	[illegible]
93	Youghal, part of,	[illegible]	[illegible]	[illegible]	[illegible]
	37. Kerry Co.				
94	Cahirciveen,	[illegible]	[illegible]	[illegible]	[illegible]
95	Dingle,	[illegible]	[illegible]	[illegible]	[illegible]
96	Glin, part of,	[illegible]	[illegible]	[illegible]	[illegible]
97	Kenmare,	[illegible]	[illegible]	[illegible]	[illegible]
98	Killarney,	[illegible]	[illegible]	[illegible]	[illegible]
99	Listowel,	[illegible]	[illegible]	[illegible]	[illegible]
100	Tralee,	[illegible]	[illegible]	[illegible]	[illegible]
	38. Limerick Co.				
101	Croom,	[illegible]	[illegible]	[illegible]	[illegible]
102	Glin, part of,	[illegible]	[illegible]	[illegible]	[illegible]
103	Kilmallock, do.	[illegible]	[illegible]	[illegible]	[illegible]
104	Limerick, do.	[illegible]	[illegible]	[illegible]	[illegible]
105	Mitchelstown, do.	[illegible]	[illegible]	[illegible]	[illegible]
106	Newcastle,	[illegible]	[illegible]	[illegible]	[illegible]
107	Rathkeale,	[illegible]	[illegible]	[illegible]	[illegible]
108	Tipperary, part of,	[illegible]	[illegible]	[illegible]	[illegible]
	39. Tipperary Co.				
109	Borrisokane,	[illegible]	[illegible]	[illegible]	[illegible]
110	Callan, part of,	[illegible]	[illegible]	[illegible]	[illegible]
111	Carrick-on-Suir, do.	[illegible]	[illegible]	[illegible]	[illegible]
112	Cashel,	[illegible]	[illegible]	[illegible]	[illegible]
113	Clogheen,	[illegible]	[illegible]	[illegible]	[illegible]
114	Clonmel, part of,	[illegible]	[illegible]	[illegible]	[illegible]
115	Nenagh,	[illegible]	[illegible]	[illegible]	[illegible]
116	Parsonstown, part of,	[illegible]	[illegible]	[illegible]	[illegible]
117	Roscrea, do.	[illegible]	[illegible]	[illegible]	[illegible]
118	Thurles,	[illegible]	[illegible]	[illegible]	[illegible]
119	Tipperary, part of,	[illegible]	[illegible]	[illegible]	[illegible]
120	Urlingford, do.	[illegible]	[illegible]	[illegible]	[illegible]

MARRIAGES in the Year 1891—in SUPERINTENDENT REGISTRARS' DISTRICTS.

Registered in the Quarter ending the last day of: March	June	September	December	Contracted between: Bachelors and Spinsters	Bachelors and Widows	Widowers and Spinsters	Widowers and Widows	Of: Widowers	Widows	Of Persons under Full Age: Men	Women	Signed the Marriage Register with Marks: Men	Women	Cases in which: Both signed	One signed	SUPERINTENDENT REGISTRARS' DISTRICTS
																14. Cork Co.
[illegible]	[illegible]	[illegible]	[illegible]	[illegible]	[illegible]	[illegible]	-	[illegible]	[illegible]	.	[illegible]	[illegible]	[illegible]	[illegible]	[illegible]	Bandon.
[illegible]	[illegible]	[illegible]	[illegible]	[illegible]	-	[illegible]	[illegible]	[illegible]	[illegible]	.	[illegible]	[illegible]	[illegible]	[illegible]	[illegible]	Bantry.
[illegible]	[illegible]	[illegible]	[illegible]	[illegible]	[illegible]	[illegible]	-	[illegible]	[illegible]	.	[illegible]	[illegible]	[illegible]	[illegible]	[illegible]	Castletown.
[illegible]	[illegible]	[illegible]	[illegible]	[illegible]	.	-	[illegible]	[illegible]	[illegible]	-	[illegible]	[illegible]	[illegible]	[illegible]	[illegible]	Clonakilty.
[illegible]	[illegible]	[illegible]	[illegible]	[illegible]	[illegible]	[illegible]	[illegible]	[illegible]	[illegible]	[illegible]	[illegible]	[illegible]	[illegible]	[illegible]	[illegible]	Cork.
[illegible]	[illegible]	[illegible]	[illegible]	[illegible]	-	[illegible]	[illegible]	[illegible]	[illegible]	.	[illegible]	[illegible]	[illegible]	[illegible]	[illegible]	Dunmanway.
[illegible]	[illegible]	[illegible]	[illegible]	[illegible]	[illegible]	[illegible]	[illegible]	[illegible]	[illegible]	.	[illegible]	[illegible]	[illegible]	[illegible]	[illegible]	Fermoy.
[illegible]	[illegible]	[illegible]	[illegible]	[illegible]	[illegible]	[illegible]	[illegible]	[illegible]	[illegible]	.	[illegible]	[illegible]	[illegible]	[illegible]	[illegible]	Kanturk.
[illegible]	[illegible]	[illegible]	[illegible]	[illegible]	-	.	.	.	-	.	[illegible]	[illegible]	[illegible]	[illegible]	.	Kilmallock, part of
[illegible]	[illegible]	[illegible]	[illegible]	[illegible]	[illegible]	[illegible]	[illegible]	[illegible]	[illegible]	[illegible]	[illegible]	[illegible]	[illegible]	[illegible]	[illegible]	Kinsale.
[illegible]	[illegible]	[illegible]	[illegible]	[illegible]	[illegible]	[illegible]	[illegible]	[illegible]	[illegible]	-	[illegible]	[illegible]	[illegible]	[illegible]	[illegible]	Macroom.
[illegible]	[illegible]	[illegible]	[illegible]	[illegible]	[illegible]	.	[illegible]	[illegible]	[illegible]	-	[illegible]	[illegible]	[illegible]	[illegible]	[illegible]	Mallow.
[illegible]	[illegible]	[illegible]	[illegible]	[illegible]	.	[illegible]	[illegible]	[illegible]	[illegible]	-	.	[illegible]	[illegible]	[illegible]	[illegible]	Midleton.
[illegible]	[illegible]	[illegible]	[illegible]	[illegible]	[illegible]	[illegible]	.	[illegible]	[illegible]	.	-	[illegible]	[illegible]	[illegible]	[illegible]	Millstreet.
[illegible]	[illegible]	[illegible]	[illegible]	[illegible]	-	[illegible]	.	[illegible]	-	.	.	[illegible]	[illegible]	[illegible]	[illegible]	Mitchelstown, part of.
[illegible]	[illegible]	[illegible]	[illegible]	[illegible]	[illegible]	[illegible]	[illegible]	[illegible]	[illegible]	.	[illegible]	[illegible]	[illegible]	[illegible]	[illegible]	Skibbereen.
[illegible]	[illegible]	[illegible]	[illegible]	[illegible]	.	[illegible]	.	[illegible]	-	.	[illegible]	[illegible]	[illegible]	[illegible]	[illegible]	Skull.
[illegible]	[illegible]	[illegible]	[illegible]	[illegible]	[illegible]	[illegible]	[illegible]	[illegible]	[illegible]	.	-	[illegible]	[illegible]	[illegible]	[illegible]	Youghal, part of.
																15. Kerry Co.
[illegible]	[illegible]	[illegible]	[illegible]	[illegible]	.	[illegible]	[illegible]	[illegible]	[illegible]	-	[illegible]	[illegible]	[illegible]	[illegible]	[illegible]	Cahersiveen.
[illegible]	[illegible]	[illegible]	[illegible]	[illegible]	[illegible]	[illegible]	[illegible]	[illegible]	[illegible]	.	[illegible]	[illegible]	[illegible]	[illegible]	[illegible]	Dingle.
[illegible]	[illegible]	[illegible]	[illegible]	[illegible]	[illegible]	[illegible]	[illegible]	[illegible]	[illegible]	[illegible]	[illegible]	[illegible]	[illegible]	[illegible]	[illegible]	Glin, part of
[illegible]	[illegible]	[illegible]	[illegible]	[illegible]	[illegible]	[illegible]	[illegible]	[illegible]	[illegible]	[illegible]	[illegible]	[illegible]	[illegible]	[illegible]	[illegible]	Kenmare.
[illegible]	[illegible]	[illegible]	[illegible]	[illegible]	[illegible]	[illegible]	[illegible]	[illegible]	[illegible]	[illegible]	[illegible]	[illegible]	[illegible]	[illegible]	[illegible]	Killarney.
[illegible]	[illegible]	[illegible]	[illegible]	[illegible]	[illegible]	[illegible]	[illegible]	[illegible]	[illegible]	[illegible]	[illegible]	[illegible]	[illegible]	[illegible]	[illegible]	Listowel.
[illegible]	[illegible]	[illegible]	[illegible]	[illegible]	[illegible]	[illegible]	[illegible]	[illegible]	[illegible]	[illegible]	[illegible]	[illegible]	[illegible]	[illegible]	[illegible]	Tralee.
																16. Limerick Co.
[illegible]	[illegible]	[illegible]	[illegible]	[illegible]	[illegible]	[illegible]	[illegible]	[illegible]	[illegible]	[illegible]	[illegible]	[illegible]	[illegible]	[illegible]	[illegible]	Croom.
[illegible]	[illegible]	[illegible]	[illegible]	[illegible]	[illegible]	[illegible]	[illegible]	[illegible]	[illegible]	[illegible]	[illegible]	[illegible]	[illegible]	[illegible]	[illegible]	Glin, part of
[illegible]	[illegible]	[illegible]	[illegible]	[illegible]	[illegible]	[illegible]	[illegible]	[illegible]	[illegible]	[illegible]	[illegible]	[illegible]	[illegible]	[illegible]	[illegible]	Kilmallock, do.
[illegible]	[illegible]	[illegible]	[illegible]	[illegible]	[illegible]	[illegible]	[illegible]	[illegible]	[illegible]	[illegible]	[illegible]	[illegible]	[illegible]	[illegible]	[illegible]	Limerick, do.
[illegible]	[illegible]	[illegible]	[illegible]	[illegible]	[illegible]	[illegible]	[illegible]	[illegible]	[illegible]	[illegible]	[illegible]	[illegible]	[illegible]	[illegible]	[illegible]	Mitchelstown, do.
[illegible]	[illegible]	[illegible]	[illegible]	[illegible]	[illegible]	[illegible]	[illegible]	[illegible]	[illegible]	[illegible]	[illegible]	[illegible]	[illegible]	[illegible]	[illegible]	Newcastle.
[illegible]	[illegible]	[illegible]	[illegible]	[illegible]	[illegible]	[illegible]	[illegible]	[illegible]	[illegible]	[illegible]	[illegible]	[illegible]	[illegible]	[illegible]	[illegible]	Rathkeale.
[illegible]	[illegible]	[illegible]	[illegible]	[illegible]	[illegible]	[illegible]	[illegible]	[illegible]	[illegible]	[illegible]	[illegible]	[illegible]	[illegible]	[illegible]	[illegible]	Tipperary, part of.
																17. Tipperary Co.
[illegible]	[illegible]	[illegible]	[illegible]	[illegible]	[illegible]	[illegible]	[illegible]	[illegible]	[illegible]	[illegible]	[illegible]	[illegible]	[illegible]	[illegible]	[illegible]	Borrisokane.
[illegible]	[illegible]	[illegible]	[illegible]	[illegible]	[illegible]	[illegible]	[illegible]	[illegible]	[illegible]	[illegible]	[illegible]	[illegible]	[illegible]	[illegible]	[illegible]	Callan, part of
[illegible]	[illegible]	[illegible]	[illegible]	[illegible]	[illegible]	[illegible]	[illegible]	[illegible]	[illegible]	[illegible]	[illegible]	[illegible]	[illegible]	[illegible]	[illegible]	Carrick-on-Suir, do.
[illegible]	[illegible]	[illegible]	[illegible]	[illegible]	[illegible]	[illegible]	[illegible]	[illegible]	[illegible]	[illegible]	[illegible]	[illegible]	[illegible]	[illegible]	[illegible]	Cashel.
[illegible]	[illegible]	[illegible]	[illegible]	[illegible]	[illegible]	[illegible]	[illegible]	[illegible]	[illegible]	[illegible]	[illegible]	[illegible]	[illegible]	[illegible]	[illegible]	Clogheen.
[illegible]	[illegible]	[illegible]	[illegible]	[illegible]	[illegible]	[illegible]	[illegible]	[illegible]	[illegible]	[illegible]	[illegible]	[illegible]	[illegible]	[illegible]	[illegible]	Clonmel, part of
[illegible]	[illegible]	[illegible]	[illegible]	[illegible]	[illegible]	[illegible]	[illegible]	[illegible]	[illegible]	[illegible]	[illegible]	[illegible]	[illegible]	[illegible]	[illegible]	Nenagh.
[illegible]	[illegible]	[illegible]	[illegible]	[illegible]	[illegible]	[illegible]	[illegible]	[illegible]	[illegible]	[illegible]	[illegible]	[illegible]	[illegible]	[illegible]	[illegible]	Parsonstown, part of
[illegible]	[illegible]	[illegible]	[illegible]	[illegible]	[illegible]	[illegible]	[illegible]	[illegible]	[illegible]	[illegible]	[illegible]	[illegible]	[illegible]	[illegible]	[illegible]	Roscrea, do.
[illegible]	[illegible]	[illegible]	[illegible]	[illegible]	[illegible]	[illegible]	[illegible]	[illegible]	[illegible]	[illegible]	[illegible]	[illegible]	[illegible]	[illegible]	[illegible]	Thurles.
[illegible]	[illegible]	[illegible]	[illegible]	[illegible]	[illegible]	[illegible]	[illegible]	[illegible]	[illegible]	[illegible]	[illegible]	[illegible]	[illegible]	[illegible]	[illegible]	Tipperary, part of
[illegible]	[illegible]	[illegible]	[illegible]	[illegible]	[illegible]	[illegible]	[illegible]	[illegible]	[illegible]	[illegible]	[illegible]	[illegible]	[illegible]	[illegible]	[illegible]	Urlingford, do.

MARRIAGES in the Year 1891—in Superintendent Registrars' Districts

Registered in the Quarter ending the last day of: March	June	September	December	Contracted between: Bachelors and Spinsters	Bachelors and Widows	Widowers and Spinsters	Widowers and Widows	Of: Widowers	Widows	Of Persons not of full age: Men	Women	Signed the Marriage Register with Marks: Men	Women	Cases in which: Both signed	One signed	SUPERINTENDENT REGISTRARS' DISTRICTS.
																16. Waterford Co.
[illegible]	-	[illegible]	[illegible]	[illegible]	-	[illegible]	-	[illegible]	-	[illegible]	[illegible]	[illegible]	[illegible]	[illegible]	[illegible]	Carrick-on-Suir, part of
[illegible]	-	[illegible]	[illegible]	[illegible]	-	-	-	-	-	-	[illegible]	[illegible]	[illegible]	-	[illegible]	Clonmel, do.
[illegible]	[illegible]	[illegible]	[illegible]	[illegible]	[illegible]	[illegible]	-	[illegible]	[illegible]	[illegible]	[illegible]	[illegible]	[illegible]	[illegible]	[illegible]	Dungarvan.
[illegible]	[illegible]	[illegible]	[illegible]	[illegible]	[illegible]	[illegible]	[illegible]	[illegible]	[illegible]	-	[illegible]	[illegible]	[illegible]	[illegible]	[illegible]	Kilmacthomas.
[illegible]	[illegible]	[illegible]	[illegible]	[illegible]	-	[illegible]	[illegible]	[illegible]	[illegible]	[illegible]	[illegible]	[illegible]	[illegible]	[illegible]	[illegible]	Lismore.
[illegible]	[illegible]	[illegible]	[illegible]	[illegible]	[illegible]	[illegible]	[illegible]	[illegible]	[illegible]	[illegible]	[illegible]	[illegible]	[illegible]	[illegible]	[illegible]	Waterford, part of.
[illegible]	[illegible]	[illegible]	[illegible]	[illegible]	-	[illegible]	[illegible]	[illegible]	[illegible]	[illegible]	[illegible]	[illegible]	[illegible]	[illegible]	[illegible]	Youghal, part of.

MARRIAGES in the Year 1891—in Superintendent Registrars' Districts

Registered in the Quarter ending the last day of: March	June	September	December	Contracted between: Bachelors and Spinsters	Bachelors and Widows	Widowers and Spinsters	Widowers and Widows	Of: Widowers	Widows	Of Persons not of full age: Men	Women	Signed the Marriage Register with Marks: Men	Women	Cases in which: Both signed	One signed	SUPERINTENDENT REGISTRARS' DISTRICTS.
																18. Antrim Co.
[illegible]	[illegible]	[illegible]	[illegible]	[illegible]	[illegible]	[illegible]	[illegible]	[illegible]	[illegible]	[illegible]	[illegible]	[illegible]	[illegible]	[illegible]	[illegible]	Antrim.
[illegible]	[illegible]	[illegible]	[illegible]	[illegible]	[illegible]	[illegible]	[illegible]	[illegible]	[illegible]	[illegible]	[illegible]	[illegible]	[illegible]	[illegible]	[illegible]	Ballycastle.
[illegible]	[illegible]	[illegible]	[illegible]	[illegible]	[illegible]	[illegible]	[illegible]	[illegible]	[illegible]	[illegible]	[illegible]	[illegible]	[illegible]	[illegible]	[illegible]	Ballymena.
[illegible]	[illegible]	[illegible]	[illegible]	[illegible]	[illegible]	11	[illegible]	[illegible]	[illegible]	[illegible]	[illegible]	[illegible]	[illegible]	[illegible]	[illegible]	Ballymoney, part of.
[illegible]	[illegible]	[illegible]	[illegible]	[illegible]	[illegible]	[illegible]	[illegible]	[illegible]	[illegible]	[illegible]	[illegible]	[illegible]	[illegible]	[illegible]	[illegible]	Belfast, do.
[illegible]	[illegible]	[illegible]	[illegible]	[illegible]	-	[illegible]	[illegible]	[illegible]	[illegible]	[illegible]	[illegible]	[illegible]	[illegible]	[illegible]	[illegible]	Coleraine, do.
[illegible]	[illegible]	[illegible]	[illegible]	[illegible]	[illegible]	[illegible]	[illegible]	[illegible]	[illegible]	[illegible]	[illegible]	[illegible]	[illegible]	[illegible]	[illegible]	Larne.
[illegible]	[illegible]	[illegible]	[illegible]	[illegible]	[illegible]	[illegible]	[illegible]	[illegible]	[illegible]	[illegible]	[illegible]	[illegible]	[illegible]	[illegible]	[illegible]	Lisburn, part of.
[illegible]	[illegible]	[illegible]	[illegible]	[illegible]	-	[illegible]	-	[illegible]	-	-	[illegible]	[illegible]	[illegible]	[illegible]	[illegible]	Lurgan, do.
																19. Armagh Co.
[illegible]	[illegible]	[illegible]	[illegible]	[illegible]	[illegible]	[illegible]	[illegible]	[illegible]	[illegible]	[illegible]	[illegible]	[illegible]	[illegible]	[illegible]	[illegible]	Armagh, part of.
[illegible]	[illegible]	[illegible]	[illegible]	[illegible]	[illegible]	[illegible]	[illegible]	[illegible]	[illegible]	[illegible]	[illegible]	[illegible]	[illegible]	[illegible]	[illegible]	Banbridge, do.
[illegible]	[illegible]	[illegible]	[illegible]	[illegible]	[illegible]	[illegible]	[illegible]	[illegible]	[illegible]	-	[illegible]	[illegible]	[illegible]	[illegible]	[illegible]	Castleblayney, do.
-	-	-	-	-	-	-	-	-	-	-	-	-	-	-	-	Dundalk, do.
[illegible]	[illegible]	[illegible]	[illegible]	[illegible]	[illegible]	[illegible]	[illegible]	[illegible]	[illegible]	[illegible]	[illegible]	[illegible]	[illegible]	[illegible]	[illegible]	Lurgan, do.
[illegible]	[illegible]	[illegible]	[illegible]	[illegible]	-	[illegible]	[illegible]	[illegible]	[illegible]	[illegible]	[illegible]	[illegible]	[illegible]	[illegible]	[illegible]	Newry, do.
																21. Cavan Co.
[illegible]	[illegible]	[illegible]	[illegible]	[illegible]	-	[illegible]	[illegible]	[illegible]	[illegible]	[illegible]	[illegible]	[illegible]	[illegible]	[illegible]	[illegible]	Bailieborough.
[illegible]	[illegible]	[illegible]	[illegible]	[illegible]	[illegible]	[illegible]	[illegible]	[illegible]	[illegible]	-	[illegible]	[illegible]	[illegible]	[illegible]	[illegible]	Bawnboy, part of.
[illegible]	[illegible]	[illegible]	[illegible]	[illegible]	[illegible]	[illegible]	[illegible]	[illegible]	[illegible]	[illegible]	[illegible]	[illegible]	[illegible]	[illegible]	[illegible]	Cavan.
[illegible]	[illegible]	[illegible]	[illegible]	[illegible]	[illegible]	[illegible]	[illegible]	[illegible]	[illegible]	[illegible]	[illegible]	[illegible]	[illegible]	[illegible]	[illegible]	Cootehill, part of.
[illegible]	[illegible]	[illegible]	[illegible]	[illegible]	-	[illegible]	-	[illegible]	-	-	[illegible]	[illegible]	[illegible]	[illegible]	[illegible]	Enniskillen, do.
[illegible]	[illegible]	[illegible]	[illegible]	[illegible]	[illegible]	[illegible]	-	[illegible]	[illegible]	-	[illegible]	[illegible]	[illegible]	[illegible]	[illegible]	Granard, do.
[illegible]	[illegible]	[illegible]	[illegible]	[illegible]	[illegible]	-	-	-	[illegible]	-	[illegible]	[illegible]	[illegible]	[illegible]	[illegible]	Kells, do.
[illegible]	[illegible]	[illegible]	[illegible]	[illegible]	[illegible]	-	-	[illegible]	[illegible]	-	[illegible]	[illegible]	-	-	[illegible]	Oldcastle, do.
																22. Donegal Co.
[illegible]	[illegible]	[illegible]	[illegible]	[illegible]	[illegible]	[illegible]	[illegible]	[illegible]	[illegible]	[illegible]	[illegible]	[illegible]	[illegible]	[illegible]	[illegible]	Ballyshannon, part of.
[illegible]	[illegible]	[illegible]	[illegible]	[illegible]	-	[illegible]	-	[illegible]	-	[illegible]	[illegible]	[illegible]	[illegible]	[illegible]	[illegible]	Donegal.
[illegible]	[illegible]	[illegible]	[illegible]	[illegible]	[illegible]	[illegible]	[illegible]	[illegible]	[illegible]	[illegible]	[illegible]	[illegible]	[illegible]	[illegible]	[illegible]	Dunfanaghy.
[illegible]	[illegible]	[illegible]	[illegible]	[illegible]	[illegible]	[illegible]	[illegible]	[illegible]	[illegible]	[illegible]	[illegible]	[illegible]	[illegible]	[illegible]	[illegible]	Glenties.
[illegible]	[illegible]	[illegible]	[illegible]	[illegible]	[illegible]	[illegible]	[illegible]	[illegible]	[illegible]	-	[illegible]	[illegible]	[illegible]	[illegible]	[illegible]	Inishowen.
[illegible]	[illegible]	[illegible]	[illegible]	[illegible]	-	[illegible]	[illegible]	[illegible]	[illegible]	-	[illegible]	[illegible]	[illegible]	[illegible]	[illegible]	Letterkenny.
[illegible]	[illegible]	[illegible]	[illegible]	[illegible]	-	[illegible]	-	[illegible]	[illegible]	-	[illegible]	[illegible]	[illegible]	[illegible]	[illegible]	Londonderry, part of.

III.—PROVINCE OF ULSTER—continued.

MARRIAGES.

No.	63. Down Co.																
[illegible]	[illegible]	[illegible]	[illegible]	[illegible]	[illegible]	[illegible]	[illegible]	[illegible]	[illegible]	[illegible]	[illegible]	[illegible]	[illegible]	[illegible]	[illegible]	[illegible]	[illegible]
[illegible]	[illegible]	[illegible]	[illegible]	[illegible]	[illegible]	[illegible]	[illegible]	[illegible]	[illegible]	[illegible]	[illegible]	[illegible]	[illegible]	[illegible]	[illegible]	[illegible]	[illegible]
[illegible]	[illegible]	[illegible]	[illegible]	[illegible]	[illegible]	[illegible]	[illegible]	[illegible]	[illegible]	[illegible]	[illegible]	[illegible]	[illegible]	[illegible]	[illegible]	[illegible]	[illegible]
[illegible]	[illegible]	[illegible]	[illegible]	[illegible]	[illegible]	[illegible]	[illegible]	[illegible]	[illegible]	[illegible]	[illegible]	[illegible]	[illegible]	[illegible]	[illegible]	[illegible]	[illegible]
[illegible]	[illegible]	[illegible]	[illegible]	[illegible]	[illegible]	[illegible]	[illegible]	[illegible]	[illegible]	[illegible]	[illegible]	[illegible]	[illegible]	[illegible]	[illegible]	[illegible]	[illegible]
[illegible]	[illegible]	[illegible]	[illegible]	[illegible]	[illegible]	[illegible]	[illegible]	[illegible]	[illegible]	[illegible]	[illegible]	[illegible]	[illegible]	[illegible]	[illegible]	[illegible]	[illegible]
[illegible]	[illegible]	[illegible]	[illegible]	[illegible]	[illegible]	[illegible]	[illegible]	[illegible]	[illegible]	[illegible]	[illegible]	[illegible]	[illegible]	[illegible]	[illegible]	[illegible]	[illegible]
[illegible]	[illegible]	[illegible]	[illegible]	[illegible]	[illegible]	[illegible]	[illegible]	[illegible]	[illegible]	[illegible]	[illegible]	[illegible]	[illegible]	[illegible]	[illegible]	[illegible]	[illegible]
	64. Fermanagh Co.																
[illegible]	[illegible]	[illegible]	[illegible]	[illegible]	[illegible]	[illegible]	[illegible]	[illegible]	[illegible]	[illegible]	[illegible]	[illegible]	[illegible]	[illegible]	[illegible]	[illegible]	[illegible]
[illegible]	[illegible]	[illegible]	[illegible]	[illegible]	[illegible]	[illegible]	[illegible]	[illegible]	[illegible]	[illegible]	[illegible]	[illegible]	[illegible]	[illegible]	[illegible]	[illegible]	[illegible]
[illegible]	[illegible]	[illegible]	[illegible]	[illegible]	[illegible]	[illegible]	[illegible]	[illegible]	[illegible]	[illegible]	[illegible]	[illegible]	[illegible]	[illegible]	[illegible]	[illegible]	[illegible]
[illegible]	[illegible]	[illegible]	[illegible]	[illegible]	[illegible]	[illegible]	[illegible]	[illegible]	[illegible]	[illegible]	[illegible]	[illegible]	[illegible]	[illegible]	[illegible]	[illegible]	[illegible]
[illegible]	[illegible]	[illegible]	[illegible]	[illegible]	[illegible]	[illegible]	[illegible]	[illegible]	[illegible]	[illegible]	[illegible]	[illegible]	[illegible]	[illegible]	[illegible]	[illegible]	[illegible]
	65. Londonderry Co.																
[illegible]	[illegible]	[illegible]	[illegible]	[illegible]	[illegible]	[illegible]	[illegible]	[illegible]	[illegible]	[illegible]	[illegible]	[illegible]	[illegible]	[illegible]	[illegible]	[illegible]	[illegible]
[illegible]	[illegible]	[illegible]	[illegible]	[illegible]	[illegible]	[illegible]	[illegible]	[illegible]	[illegible]	[illegible]	[illegible]	[illegible]	[illegible]	[illegible]	[illegible]	[illegible]	[illegible]
[illegible]	[illegible]	[illegible]	[illegible]	[illegible]	[illegible]	[illegible]	[illegible]	[illegible]	[illegible]	[illegible]	[illegible]	[illegible]	[illegible]	[illegible]	[illegible]	[illegible]	[illegible]
[illegible]	[illegible]	[illegible]	[illegible]	[illegible]	[illegible]	[illegible]	[illegible]	[illegible]	[illegible]	[illegible]	[illegible]	[illegible]	[illegible]	[illegible]	[illegible]	[illegible]	[illegible]
[illegible]	[illegible]	[illegible]	[illegible]	[illegible]	[illegible]	[illegible]	[illegible]	[illegible]	[illegible]	[illegible]	[illegible]	[illegible]	[illegible]	[illegible]	[illegible]	[illegible]	[illegible]
	66. Monaghan Co.																
[illegible]	[illegible]	[illegible]	[illegible]	[illegible]	[illegible]	[illegible]	[illegible]	[illegible]	[illegible]	[illegible]	[illegible]	[illegible]	[illegible]	[illegible]	[illegible]	[illegible]	[illegible]
[illegible]	[illegible]	[illegible]	[illegible]	[illegible]	[illegible]	[illegible]	[illegible]	[illegible]	[illegible]	[illegible]	[illegible]	[illegible]	[illegible]	[illegible]	[illegible]	[illegible]	[illegible]
[illegible]	[illegible]	[illegible]	[illegible]	[illegible]	[illegible]	[illegible]	[illegible]	[illegible]	[illegible]	[illegible]	[illegible]	[illegible]	[illegible]	[illegible]	[illegible]	[illegible]	[illegible]
[illegible]	[illegible]	[illegible]	[illegible]	[illegible]	[illegible]	[illegible]	[illegible]	[illegible]	[illegible]	[illegible]	[illegible]	[illegible]	[illegible]	[illegible]	[illegible]	[illegible]	[illegible]
[illegible]	[illegible]	[illegible]	[illegible]	[illegible]	[illegible]	[illegible]	[illegible]	[illegible]	[illegible]	[illegible]	[illegible]	[illegible]	[illegible]	[illegible]	[illegible]	[illegible]	[illegible]
[illegible]	[illegible]	[illegible]	[illegible]	[illegible]	[illegible]	[illegible]	[illegible]	[illegible]	[illegible]	[illegible]	[illegible]	[illegible]	[illegible]	[illegible]	[illegible]	[illegible]	[illegible]
[illegible]	[illegible]	[illegible]	[illegible]	[illegible]	[illegible]	[illegible]	[illegible]	[illegible]	[illegible]	[illegible]	[illegible]	[illegible]	[illegible]	[illegible]	[illegible]	[illegible]	[illegible]
	67. Tyrone Co.																
[illegible]	[illegible]	[illegible]	[illegible]	[illegible]	[illegible]	[illegible]	[illegible]	[illegible]	[illegible]	[illegible]	[illegible]	[illegible]	[illegible]	[illegible]	[illegible]	[illegible]	[illegible]
[illegible]	[illegible]	[illegible]	[illegible]	[illegible]	[illegible]	[illegible]	[illegible]	[illegible]	[illegible]	[illegible]	[illegible]	[illegible]	[illegible]	[illegible]	[illegible]	[illegible]	[illegible]
[illegible]	[illegible]	[illegible]	[illegible]	[illegible]	[illegible]	[illegible]	[illegible]	[illegible]	[illegible]	[illegible]	[illegible]	[illegible]	[illegible]	[illegible]	[illegible]	[illegible]	[illegible]
[illegible]	[illegible]	[illegible]	[illegible]	[illegible]	[illegible]	[illegible]	[illegible]	[illegible]	[illegible]	[illegible]	[illegible]	[illegible]	[illegible]	[illegible]	[illegible]	[illegible]	[illegible]
[illegible]	[illegible]	[illegible]	[illegible]	[illegible]	[illegible]	[illegible]	[illegible]	[illegible]	[illegible]	[illegible]	[illegible]	[illegible]	[illegible]	[illegible]	[illegible]	[illegible]	[illegible]
[illegible]	[illegible]	[illegible]	[illegible]	[illegible]	[illegible]	[illegible]	[illegible]	[illegible]	[illegible]	[illegible]	[illegible]	[illegible]	[illegible]	[illegible]	[illegible]	[illegible]	[illegible]
[illegible]	[illegible]	[illegible]	[illegible]	[illegible]	[illegible]	[illegible]	[illegible]	[illegible]	[illegible]	[illegible]	[illegible]	[illegible]	[illegible]	[illegible]	[illegible]	[illegible]	[illegible]
[illegible]	[illegible]	[illegible]	[illegible]	[illegible]	[illegible]	[illegible]	[illegible]	[illegible]	[illegible]	[illegible]	[illegible]	[illegible]	[illegible]	[illegible]	[illegible]	[illegible]	[illegible]
[illegible]	[illegible]	[illegible]	[illegible]	[illegible]	[illegible]	[illegible]	[illegible]	[illegible]	[illegible]	[illegible]	[illegible]	[illegible]	[illegible]	[illegible]	[illegible]	[illegible]	[illegible]

MARRIAGES in the Year 1891—in SUPERINTENDENT REGISTRARS' DISTRICTS.

MARRIAGES.												Signed the Marriage Register with Marks.		
Registered in the Quarter ending the last day of				Contracted between				Of		Of Persons not of full age.				Cases in which
March.	June.	September.	December.	Bachelors and Spinsters.	Bachelors and Widows.	Widowers and Spinsters.	Widowers and Widows.	Widowers.	Widows.	Men.	Women.	Men.	Women.	Both signed.
[illegible]	[illegible]	[illegible]	[illegible]	[illegible]	[illegible]	[illegible]	[illegible]	[illegible]	[illegible]	[illegible]	[illegible]	[illegible]	[illegible]	[illegible]
[illegible]	[illegible]	[illegible]	[illegible]	[illegible]	[illegible]	[illegible]	[illegible]	[illegible]	[illegible]	[illegible]	[illegible]	[illegible]	[illegible]	[illegible]
[illegible]	[illegible]	[illegible]	[illegible]	[illegible]	[illegible]	[illegible]	[illegible]	[illegible]	[illegible]	[illegible]	[illegible]	[illegible]	[illegible]	[illegible]
[illegible]	[illegible]	[illegible]	[illegible]	[illegible]	[illegible]	[illegible]	[illegible]	[illegible]	[illegible]	[illegible]	[illegible]	[illegible]	[illegible]	[illegible]
[illegible]	[illegible]	[illegible]	[illegible]	[illegible]	.	[illegible]	.	[illegible]	.	.	[illegible]	[illegible]	[illegible]	[illegible]
[illegible]	[illegible]	[illegible]	[illegible]	[illegible]	[illegible]	[illegible]	[illegible]	[illegible]	[illegible]	.	[illegible]	[illegible]	[illegible]	[illegible]
[illegible]	[illegible]	[illegible]	[illegible]	[illegible]	[illegible]	[illegible]	[illegible]	[illegible]	[illegible]	[illegible]	[illegible]	[illegible]	[illegible]	[illegible]
[illegible]	[illegible]	[illegible]	[illegible]	[illegible]	[illegible]	[illegible]	[illegible]	[illegible]	[illegible]	[illegible]	[illegible]	[illegible]	[illegible]	[illegible]
[illegible]	[illegible]	[illegible]	[illegible]	[illegible]	.	[illegible]	.	[illegible]	.	.	[illegible]	.	[illegible]	-
[illegible]	[illegible]	[illegible]	[illegible]	[illegible]	.	[illegible]	.	[illegible]	.	.	[illegible]	[illegible]	[illegible]	[illegible]
[illegible]	[illegible]	[illegible]	[illegible]	[illegible]	[illegible]	[illegible]	[illegible]	[illegible]	[illegible]	[illegible]	[illegible]	[illegible]	[illegible]	[illegible]
[illegible]	[illegible]	[illegible]	[illegible]	[illegible]	[illegible]	[illegible]	[illegible]	[illegible]	[illegible]	.	[illegible]	[illegible]	[illegible]	[illegible]
[illegible]	[illegible]	[illegible]	[illegible]	[illegible]	[illegible]	[illegible]	[illegible]	[illegible]	[illegible]	[illegible]	[illegible]	[illegible]	[illegible]	[illegible]
[illegible]	[illegible]	[illegible]	[illegible]	[illegible]	.	[illegible]	-	[illegible]	-	.	[illegible]	[illegible]	[illegible]	[illegible]
[illegible]	[illegible]	[illegible]	[illegible]	[illegible]	[illegible]	[illegible]	-	[illegible]	[illegible]	[illegible]	[illegible]	[illegible]	[illegible]	[illegible]
[illegible]	[illegible]	[illegible]	[illegible]	[illegible]	[illegible]	[illegible]	[illegible]	[illegible]	[illegible]	[illegible]	[illegible]	[illegible]	[illegible]	[illegible]
[illegible]	[illegible]	[illegible]	[illegible]	[illegible]	[illegible]	[illegible]	[illegible]	[illegible]	[illegible]	[illegible]	[illegible]	[illegible]	[illegible]	[illegible]
[illegible]	[illegible]	[illegible]	[illegible]	[illegible]	[illegible]	[illegible]	[illegible]	[illegible]	[illegible]	[illegible]	[illegible]	[illegible]	[illegible]	[illegible]
[illegible]	[illegible]	[illegible]	[illegible]	[illegible]	[illegible]	[illegible]	-	[illegible]	[illegible]	.	[illegible]	[illegible]	[illegible]	[illegible]
[illegible]	[illegible]	[illegible]	[illegible]	[illegible]	[illegible]	[illegible]	.	[illegible]	[illegible]	[illegible]	[illegible]	[illegible]	[illegible]	[illegible]
-	[illegible]	.	[illegible]	[illegible]	.	.	.	.	.	.	.	[illegible]	[illegible]	.
[illegible]	[illegible]	[illegible]	[illegible]	[illegible]	.	[illegible]	.	[illegible]	.	.	[illegible]	[illegible]	[illegible]	[illegible]
[illegible]	[illegible]	[illegible]	[illegible]	[illegible]	.	[illegible]	.	[illegible]	.	.	[illegible]	[illegible]	[illegible]	.
[illegible]	[illegible]	[illegible]	[illegible]	[illegible]	.	.	.	.	-	.	.	[illegible]	[illegible]	[illegible]
[illegible]	[illegible]	[illegible]	[illegible]	[illegible]	[illegible]	[illegible]	[illegible]	[illegible]	[illegible]	[illegible]	[illegible]	[illegible]	[illegible]	[illegible]
[illegible]	[illegible]	.	[illegible]	[illegible]	.	.	.	.	.	.	[illegible]	[illegible]	[illegible]	[illegible]
[illegible]	[illegible]	[illegible]	[illegible]	[illegible]	[illegible]	[illegible]	[illegible]	[illegible]	[illegible]	[illegible]	[illegible]	[illegible]	[illegible]	[illegible]
[illegible]	[illegible]	[illegible]	[illegible]	[illegible]	[illegible]	[illegible]	.	[illegible]	[illegible]	.	[illegible]	[illegible]	[illegible]	[illegible]
[illegible]	[illegible]	[illegible]	[illegible]	[illegible]	[illegible]	[illegible]	[illegible]	[illegible]	[illegible]	[illegible]	[illegible]	[illegible]	[illegible]	[illegible]
[illegible]	[illegible]	[illegible]	[illegible]	[illegible]	[illegible]	[illegible]	[illegible]	[illegible]	[illegible]	[illegible]	[illegible]	[illegible]	[illegible]	[illegible]
[illegible]	[illegible]	[illegible]	[illegible]	[illegible]	[illegible]	[illegible]	[illegible]	[illegible]	[illegible]	.	.	[illegible]	[illegible]	-
[illegible]	[illegible]	.	.	[illegible]	.	[illegible]	.	[illegible]	.	.	.	[illegible]	[illegible]	[illegible]
[illegible]	[illegible]	[illegible]	[illegible]	[illegible]	[illegible]	[illegible]		[illegible]	[illegible]	[illegible]	[illegible]	[illegible]	[illegible]	[illegible]
[illegible]	[illegible]	[illegible]	[illegible]	[illegible]	[illegible]	[illegible]	[illegible]	[illegible]	[illegible]	[illegible]	[illegible]		[illegible]	[illegible]

IV.—PROVINCE OF CONNAUGHT.—

No.	Superintendent Registrar's Districts.	Area in Statute Acres, exclusive of the larger Rivers, Lakes, and Tideways.	Population, 1861.	Total Marriages.	Marriages: Registered under the Act 7 & 8 Vic., c. 81 (According to the Rites of the Church of Ireland: Special Licence, Licence, Banns, Registrar's Certificate, Not specified …; In Registered Presbyterian Meeting Houses; In Registered Buildings; In the Registrar's Office; Society of Friends; Jews; Total Registered under the …)
	28. Galway Co.				
[illegible]	[illegible], part of,	[illegible]	[illegible]	[illegible]	[illegible]
[illegible]	[illegible], do.	[illegible]	[illegible]	1	[illegible]
[illegible]	[illegible]	[illegible]	[illegible]	[illegible]	[illegible]
[illegible]	[illegible]	[illegible]	[illegible]	[illegible]	[illegible]
[illegible]	[illegible]	[illegible]	[illegible]	41	[illegible]
[illegible]	[illegible]	[illegible]	[illegible]	[illegible]	[illegible]
[illegible]	[illegible]	[illegible]	[illegible]	[illegible]	[illegible]
[illegible]	[illegible]	[illegible]	[illegible]	[illegible]	[illegible]
[illegible]	[illegible]	[illegible]	[illegible]	[illegible]	[illegible]
[illegible]	[illegible]	[illegible]	[illegible]	[illegible]	[illegible]
[illegible]	[illegible], part of,	[illegible]	[illegible]	[illegible]	[illegible]
[illegible]	[illegible], do.	[illegible]	[illegible]	5	[illegible]
[illegible]	[illegible]	[illegible]	[illegible]	[illegible]	[illegible]
	29. Leitrim Co.				
[illegible]	[illegible], part of,	[illegible]	[illegible]	[illegible]	[illegible]
[illegible]	[illegible], do.	[illegible]	[illegible]	[illegible]	[illegible]
[illegible]	[illegible], do.	[illegible]	[illegible]	[illegible]	[illegible]
[illegible]	[illegible]	[illegible]	[illegible]	[illegible]	[illegible]
[illegible]	[illegible]	[illegible]	[illegible]	[illegible]	[illegible]
	30. Mayo Co.				
[illegible]	[illegible], part of,	[illegible]	[illegible]	[illegible]	[illegible]
[illegible]	[illegible], do.	[illegible]	[illegible]	[illegible]	[illegible]
[illegible]	[illegible]	[illegible]	[illegible]	[illegible]	[illegible]
[illegible]	[illegible]	[illegible]	[illegible]	[illegible]	[illegible]
[illegible]	[illegible], part of,	[illegible]	[illegible]	[illegible]	[illegible]
[illegible]	[illegible]	[illegible]	[illegible]	[illegible]	[illegible]
[illegible]	[illegible]	[illegible]	[illegible]	[illegible]	[illegible]
[illegible]	[illegible]	[illegible]	[illegible]	[illegible]	[illegible]
[illegible]	[illegible]	[illegible]	[illegible]	[illegible]	[illegible]
	31. Roscommon Co.				
[illegible]	[illegible], part of,	[illegible]	[illegible]	[illegible]	[illegible]
[illegible]	[illegible], do.	[illegible]	[illegible]	[illegible]	[illegible]
[illegible]	[illegible], do.	[illegible]	[illegible]	[illegible]	[illegible]
[illegible]	[illegible], do.	[illegible]	[illegible]	[illegible]	[illegible]
[illegible]	[illegible], do.	[illegible]	[illegible]	[illegible]	[illegible]
[illegible]	[illegible], do.	[illegible]	[illegible]	[illegible]	[illegible]
[illegible]	[illegible]	[illegible]	[illegible]	[illegible]	[illegible]
	32. Sligo Co.				
[illegible]	[illegible], part of,	[illegible]	[illegible]	1	[illegible]
[illegible]	[illegible], do.	[illegible]	[illegible]	[illegible]	[illegible]
[illegible]	[illegible]	[illegible]	[illegible]	[illegible]	[illegible]
[illegible]	[illegible]	[illegible]	[illegible]	[illegible]	[illegible]
[illegible]	[illegible]	[illegible]	[illegible]	[illegible]	[illegible]

MARRIAGES in the Year 1891—in SUPERINTENDENT REGISTRARS' DISTRICTS.

MARRIAGES. Registered in the Quarter ending the last day of: March	June	September	December	Contracted between: Bachelors and Spinsters	Bachelors and Widows	Widowers and Spinsters	Widowers and Widows	Of: Widowers	Widows	Of Persons not of full Age: Men	Women	Signed the Marriage Register with Marks: Men	Women	Cases in which: Both signed	One signed	SUPERINTENDENT REGISTRARS' DISTRICTS.
																53. Galway Co.
[illegible]	[illegible]	[illegible]	[illegible]	[illegible]	[illegible]	[illegible]	[illegible]	[illegible]	[illegible]	[illegible]	[illegible]	[illegible]	[illegible]	[illegible]	[illegible]	Ballinasloe, part of.
[illegible]	[illegible]	[illegible]	[illegible]	[illegible]	[illegible]	[illegible]	[illegible]	[illegible]	[illegible]	[illegible]	[illegible]	[illegible]	[illegible]	[illegible]	[illegible]	Ballinrobe, do.
[illegible]	[illegible]	[illegible]	[illegible]	[illegible]	[illegible]	[illegible]	[illegible]	[illegible]	[illegible]	[illegible]	[illegible]	[illegible]	[illegible]	[illegible]	[illegible]	Clifden.
[illegible]	[illegible]	[illegible]	[illegible]	[illegible]	[illegible]	[illegible]	[illegible]	[illegible]	[illegible]	[illegible]	[illegible]	[illegible]	[illegible]	[illegible]	[illegible]	Galway.
[illegible]	[illegible]	[illegible]	[illegible]	[illegible]	[illegible]	[illegible]	[illegible]	[illegible]	[illegible]	[illegible]	[illegible]	[illegible]	[illegible]	[illegible]	[illegible]	Glenamaddy.
[illegible]	[illegible]	[illegible]	[illegible]	[illegible]	[illegible]	[illegible]	[illegible]	[illegible]	[illegible]	[illegible]	[illegible]	[illegible]	[illegible]	[illegible]	[illegible]	Gort.
[illegible]	[illegible]	[illegible]	[illegible]	[illegible]	[illegible]	[illegible]	[illegible]	[illegible]	[illegible]	[illegible]	[illegible]	[illegible]	[illegible]	[illegible]	[illegible]	Loughrea.
[illegible]	[illegible]	[illegible]	[illegible]	[illegible]	[illegible]	[illegible]	[illegible]	[illegible]	[illegible]	[illegible]	[illegible]	[illegible]	[illegible]	[illegible]	[illegible]	Mountbellew.
[illegible]	[illegible]	[illegible]	[illegible]	[illegible]	[illegible]	[illegible]	[illegible]	[illegible]	[illegible]	[illegible]	[illegible]	[illegible]	[illegible]	[illegible]	[illegible]	Oughterard.
[illegible]	[illegible]	[illegible]	[illegible]	[illegible]	[illegible]	[illegible]	[illegible]	[illegible]	[illegible]	[illegible]	[illegible]	[illegible]	[illegible]	[illegible]	[illegible]	Portumna.
[illegible]	[illegible]	[illegible]	[illegible]	[illegible]	[illegible]	[illegible]	[illegible]	[illegible]	[illegible]	[illegible]	[illegible]	[illegible]	[illegible]	[illegible]	[illegible]	Roscommon, part of.
[illegible]	[illegible]	[illegible]	[illegible]	[illegible]	[illegible]	[illegible]	[illegible]	[illegible]	[illegible]	[illegible]	[illegible]	[illegible]	[illegible]	[illegible]	[illegible]	Scarriff, do.
[illegible]	[illegible]	[illegible]	[illegible]	[illegible]	[illegible]	[illegible]	[illegible]	[illegible]	[illegible]	[illegible]	[illegible]	[illegible]	[illegible]	[illegible]	[illegible]	Tuam.
																54. Leitrim Co.
[illegible]	[illegible]	[illegible]	[illegible]	[illegible]	[illegible]	[illegible]	[illegible]	[illegible]	[illegible]	[illegible]	[illegible]	[illegible]	[illegible]	[illegible]	[illegible]	Ballyshannon, part of.
[illegible]	[illegible]	[illegible]	[illegible]	[illegible]	[illegible]	[illegible]	[illegible]	[illegible]	[illegible]	[illegible]	[illegible]	[illegible]	[illegible]	[illegible]	[illegible]	Bawnboy, do.
[illegible]	[illegible]	[illegible]	[illegible]	[illegible]	[illegible]	[illegible]	[illegible]	[illegible]	[illegible]	[illegible]	[illegible]	[illegible]	[illegible]	[illegible]	[illegible]	Carrick-on-Shan. do.
[illegible]	[illegible]	[illegible]	[illegible]	[illegible]	[illegible]	[illegible]	[illegible]	[illegible]	[illegible]	[illegible]	[illegible]	[illegible]	[illegible]	[illegible]	[illegible]	Manorhamilton.
[illegible]	[illegible]	[illegible]	[illegible]	[illegible]	[illegible]	[illegible]	[illegible]	[illegible]	[illegible]	[illegible]	[illegible]	[illegible]	[illegible]	[illegible]	[illegible]	Mohill.
																55. Mayo Co.
[illegible]	[illegible]	[illegible]	[illegible]	[illegible]	[illegible]	[illegible]	[illegible]	[illegible]	[illegible]	[illegible]	[illegible]	[illegible]	[illegible]	[illegible]	[illegible]	Ballina, part of.
[illegible]	[illegible]	[illegible]	[illegible]	[illegible]	[illegible]	[illegible]	[illegible]	[illegible]	[illegible]	[illegible]	[illegible]	[illegible]	[illegible]	[illegible]	[illegible]	Ballinrobe, do.
[illegible]	[illegible]	[illegible]	[illegible]	[illegible]	[illegible]	[illegible]	[illegible]	[illegible]	[illegible]	[illegible]	[illegible]	[illegible]	[illegible]	[illegible]	[illegible]	Belmullet.
[illegible]	[illegible]	[illegible]	[illegible]	[illegible]	[illegible]	[illegible]	[illegible]	[illegible]	[illegible]	[illegible]	[illegible]	[illegible]	[illegible]	[illegible]	[illegible]	Castlebar.
[illegible]	[illegible]	[illegible]	[illegible]	[illegible]	[illegible]	[illegible]	[illegible]	[illegible]	[illegible]	[illegible]	[illegible]	[illegible]	[illegible]	[illegible]	[illegible]	Castlerea, part of.
[illegible]	[illegible]	[illegible]	[illegible]	[illegible]	[illegible]	[illegible]	[illegible]	[illegible]	[illegible]	[illegible]	[illegible]	[illegible]	[illegible]	[illegible]	[illegible]	Claremorris.
[illegible]	[illegible]	[illegible]	[illegible]	[illegible]	[illegible]	[illegible]	[illegible]	[illegible]	[illegible]	[illegible]	[illegible]	[illegible]	[illegible]	[illegible]	[illegible]	Killala.
[illegible]	[illegible]	[illegible]	[illegible]	[illegible]	[illegible]	[illegible]	[illegible]	[illegible]	[illegible]	[illegible]	[illegible]	[illegible]	[illegible]	[illegible]	[illegible]	Swinford.
[illegible]	[illegible]	[illegible]	[illegible]	[illegible]	[illegible]	[illegible]	[illegible]	[illegible]	[illegible]	[illegible]	[illegible]	[illegible]	[illegible]	[illegible]	[illegible]	Westport.
																56. Roscommon Co.
[illegible]	[illegible]	[illegible]	[illegible]	[illegible]	[illegible]	[illegible]	[illegible]	[illegible]	[illegible]	[illegible]	[illegible]	[illegible]	[illegible]	[illegible]	[illegible]	Athlone, part of.
[illegible]	[illegible]	[illegible]	[illegible]	[illegible]	[illegible]	[illegible]	[illegible]	[illegible]	[illegible]	[illegible]	[illegible]	[illegible]	[illegible]	[illegible]	[illegible]	Ballinasloe, do.
[illegible]	[illegible]	[illegible]	[illegible]	[illegible]	[illegible]	[illegible]	[illegible]	[illegible]	[illegible]	[illegible]	[illegible]	[illegible]	[illegible]	[illegible]	[illegible]	Boyle, do.
[illegible]	[illegible]	[illegible]	[illegible]	[illegible]	[illegible]	[illegible]	[illegible]	[illegible]	[illegible]	[illegible]	[illegible]	[illegible]	[illegible]	[illegible]	[illegible]	Carrick-on-Shan. do.
[illegible]	[illegible]	[illegible]	[illegible]	[illegible]	[illegible]	[illegible]	[illegible]	[illegible]	[illegible]	[illegible]	[illegible]	[illegible]	[illegible]	[illegible]	[illegible]	Castlerea, do.
[illegible]	[illegible]	[illegible]	[illegible]	[illegible]	[illegible]	[illegible]	[illegible]	[illegible]	[illegible]	[illegible]	[illegible]	[illegible]	[illegible]	[illegible]	[illegible]	Roscommon, do.
[illegible]	[illegible]	[illegible]	[illegible]	[illegible]	[illegible]	[illegible]	[illegible]	[illegible]	[illegible]	[illegible]	[illegible]	[illegible]	[illegible]	[illegible]	[illegible]	Strokestown.
																57. Sligo Co.
[illegible]	[illegible]	[illegible]	[illegible]	[illegible]	[illegible]	[illegible]	[illegible]	[illegible]	[illegible]	[illegible]	[illegible]	[illegible]	[illegible]	[illegible]	[illegible]	Ballina, part of.
[illegible]	[illegible]	[illegible]	[illegible]	[illegible]	[illegible]	[illegible]	[illegible]	[illegible]	[illegible]	[illegible]	[illegible]	[illegible]	[illegible]	[illegible]	[illegible]	Boyle, do.
[illegible]	[illegible]	[illegible]	[illegible]	[illegible]	[illegible]	[illegible]	[illegible]	[illegible]	[illegible]	[illegible]	[illegible]	[illegible]	[illegible]	[illegible]	[illegible]	Dromore West.
[illegible]	[illegible]	[illegible]	[illegible]	[illegible]	[illegible]	[illegible]	[illegible]	[illegible]	[illegible]	[illegible]	[illegible]	[illegible]	[illegible]	[illegible]	[illegible]	Sligo.
[illegible]	[illegible]	[illegible]	[illegible]	[illegible]	[illegible]	[illegible]	[illegible]	[illegible]	[illegible]	[illegible]	[illegible]	[illegible]	[illegible]	[illegible]	[illegible]	Tobercurry.

Ages of 9,132 Persons who were Married in Ireland in the Year 1891.

The Total Number of Marriages registered in Ireland in the Year 1891 was 21,475; the precise Ages of both Parties were specified in 4,566 instances.

Ages of 4,566 Men and 4,566 Women married in Ireland in the Year 1891.

—	[illegible]	[illegible]	[illegible]	[illegible]	[illegible]	[illegible]	[illegible]	[illegible]	[illegible]	[illegible]	[illegible]	[illegible]	[illegible]	[illegible]	[illegible]	[illegible]	[illegible]	[illegible]	[illegible]	Total
Men,	.	.	[illegible]	[illegible]	[illegible]	[illegible]	[illegible]	[illegible]	[illegible]	[illegible]	[illegible]	[illegible]	[illegible]	[illegible]	[illegible]	[illegible]	[illegible]	[illegible]	[illegible]	[illegible]
Women,	.	[illegible]	[illegible]	[illegible]	[illegible]	[illegible]	[illegible]	[illegible]	[illegible]	[illegible]	[illegible]	[illegible]	[illegible]	[illegible]	[illegible]	.	.	.	[illegible]	[illegible]

Ages of 4,133 Bachelors and 4,367 Spinsters married in 1891.

—	[illegible]	[illegible]	[illegible]	[illegible]	[illegible]	[illegible]	[illegible]	[illegible]	[illegible]	[illegible]	[illegible]	[illegible]	[illegible]	[illegible]	[illegible]	[illegible]	[illegible]	[illegible]	[illegible]	Total
Bachelors,	.	.	[illegible]	[illegible]	[illegible]	[illegible]	[illegible]	[illegible]	[illegible]	[illegible]	[illegible]	[illegible]	[illegible]	[illegible]	[illegible]	[illegible]	[illegible]	[illegible]	.	[illegible]
Spinsters,	.	[illegible]	[illegible]	[illegible]	[illegible]	[illegible]	[illegible]	[illegible]	[illegible]	[illegible]	[illegible]	[illegible]	[illegible]	[illegible]	[illegible]	[illegible]	.	.	.	[illegible]

Ages of 433 Widowers and 199 Widows married in 1891.

—	[illegible]	[illegible]	[illegible]	[illegible]	[illegible]	[illegible]	[illegible]	[illegible]	[illegible]	[illegible]	[illegible]	[illegible]	[illegible]	[illegible]	[illegible]	[illegible]	[illegible]	[illegible]	[illegible]	Total
Widowers,	.	.	.	.	.	.	[illegible]	[illegible]	[illegible]	[illegible]	[illegible]	[illegible]	[illegible]	[illegible]	[illegible]	[illegible]	[illegible]	[illegible]	[illegible]	[illegible]
Widows,	.	.	.	.	.	[illegible]	[illegible]	[illegible]	[illegible]	[illegible]	[illegible]	[illegible]	[illegible]	[illegible]	[illegible]	.	.	.	[illegible]	[illegible]

Ages of 4,566 Husbands and their Wives in combination in 1891.

Years	Ages of Wives.																			Total Husbands	
Ages of Husbands	[illegible]	[illegible]	[illegible]	[illegible]	[illegible]	[illegible]	[illegible]	[illegible]	[illegible]	[illegible]	[illegible]	[illegible]	[illegible]	[illegible]	[illegible]	[illegible]	[illegible]	[illegible]	[illegible]	[illegible]	Ages of Husbands
[illegible]	[illegible]	[illegible]	[illegible]	[illegible]	[illegible]	[illegible]	[illegible]	[illegible]	[illegible]	[illegible]	[illegible]	[illegible]	[illegible]	[illegible]	[illegible]	[illegible]	[illegible]	[illegible]	[illegible]	[illegible]	[illegible]
[illegible]	[illegible]	[illegible]	[illegible]	[illegible]	[illegible]	[illegible]	[illegible]	[illegible]	[illegible]	[illegible]	[illegible]	[illegible]	[illegible]	[illegible]	[illegible]	[illegible]	[illegible]	[illegible]	[illegible]	[illegible]	[illegible]
[illegible]	[illegible]	[illegible]	[illegible]	[illegible]	[illegible]	[illegible]	[illegible]	[illegible]	[illegible]	[illegible]	[illegible]	[illegible]	[illegible]	[illegible]	[illegible]	[illegible]	[illegible]	[illegible]	[illegible]	[illegible]	[illegible]
[illegible]	[illegible]	[illegible]	[illegible]	[illegible]	[illegible]	[illegible]	[illegible]	[illegible]	[illegible]	[illegible]	[illegible]	[illegible]	[illegible]	[illegible]	[illegible]	[illegible]	[illegible]	[illegible]	[illegible]	[illegible]	[illegible]
[illegible]	[illegible]	[illegible]	[illegible]	[illegible]	[illegible]	[illegible]	[illegible]	[illegible]	[illegible]	[illegible]	[illegible]	[illegible]	[illegible]	[illegible]	[illegible]	[illegible]	[illegible]	[illegible]	[illegible]	[illegible]	[illegible]
[illegible]	[illegible]	[illegible]	[illegible]	[illegible]	[illegible]	[illegible]	[illegible]	[illegible]	[illegible]	[illegible]	[illegible]	[illegible]	[illegible]	[illegible]	[illegible]	[illegible]	[illegible]	[illegible]	[illegible]	[illegible]	[illegible]
[illegible]	[illegible]	[illegible]	[illegible]	[illegible]	[illegible]	[illegible]	[illegible]	[illegible]	[illegible]	[illegible]	[illegible]	[illegible]	[illegible]	[illegible]	[illegible]	[illegible]	[illegible]	[illegible]	[illegible]	[illegible]	[illegible]
[illegible]	[illegible]	[illegible]	[illegible]	[illegible]	[illegible]	[illegible]	[illegible]	[illegible]	[illegible]	[illegible]	[illegible]	[illegible]	[illegible]	[illegible]	[illegible]	[illegible]	[illegible]	[illegible]	[illegible]	[illegible]	[illegible]
[illegible]	[illegible]	[illegible]	[illegible]	[illegible]	[illegible]	[illegible]	[illegible]	[illegible]	[illegible]	[illegible]	[illegible]	[illegible]	[illegible]	[illegible]	[illegible]	[illegible]	[illegible]	[illegible]	[illegible]	[illegible]	[illegible]
[illegible]	[illegible]	[illegible]	[illegible]	[illegible]	[illegible]	[illegible]	[illegible]	[illegible]	[illegible]	[illegible]	[illegible]	[illegible]	[illegible]	[illegible]	[illegible]	[illegible]	[illegible]	[illegible]	[illegible]	[illegible]	[illegible]
[illegible]	[illegible]	[illegible]	[illegible]	[illegible]	[illegible]	[illegible]	[illegible]	[illegible]	[illegible]	[illegible]	[illegible]	[illegible]	[illegible]	[illegible]	[illegible]	[illegible]	[illegible]	[illegible]	[illegible]	[illegible]	[illegible]
[illegible]	[illegible]	[illegible]	[illegible]	[illegible]	[illegible]	[illegible]	[illegible]	[illegible]	[illegible]	[illegible]	[illegible]	[illegible]	[illegible]	[illegible]	[illegible]	[illegible]	[illegible]	[illegible]	[illegible]	[illegible]	[illegible]
[illegible]	[illegible]	[illegible]	[illegible]	[illegible]	[illegible]	[illegible]	[illegible]	[illegible]	[illegible]	[illegible]	[illegible]	[illegible]	[illegible]	[illegible]	[illegible]	[illegible]	[illegible]	[illegible]	[illegible]	[illegible]	[illegible]
[illegible]	[illegible]	[illegible]	[illegible]	[illegible]	[illegible]	[illegible]	[illegible]	[illegible]	[illegible]	[illegible]	[illegible]	[illegible]	[illegible]	[illegible]	[illegible]	[illegible]	[illegible]	[illegible]	[illegible]	[illegible]	[illegible]
[illegible]	[illegible]	[illegible]	[illegible]	[illegible]	[illegible]	[illegible]	[illegible]	[illegible]	[illegible]	[illegible]	[illegible]	[illegible]	[illegible]	[illegible]	[illegible]	[illegible]	[illegible]	[illegible]	[illegible]	[illegible]	[illegible]
[illegible]	[illegible]	[illegible]	[illegible]	[illegible]	[illegible]	[illegible]	[illegible]	[illegible]	[illegible]	[illegible]	[illegible]	[illegible]	[illegible]	[illegible]	[illegible]	[illegible]	[illegible]	[illegible]	[illegible]	[illegible]	[illegible]
[illegible]	[illegible]	[illegible]	[illegible]	[illegible]	[illegible]	[illegible]	[illegible]	[illegible]	[illegible]	[illegible]	[illegible]	[illegible]	[illegible]	[illegible]	[illegible]	[illegible]	[illegible]	[illegible]	[illegible]	[illegible]	[illegible]
[illegible]	[illegible]	[illegible]	[illegible]	[illegible]	[illegible]	[illegible]	[illegible]	[illegible]	[illegible]	[illegible]	[illegible]	[illegible]	[illegible]	[illegible]	[illegible]	[illegible]	[illegible]	[illegible]	[illegible]	[illegible]	[illegible]
80 & up.	[illegible]	[illegible]	[illegible]	[illegible]	[illegible]	[illegible]	[illegible]	[illegible]	[illegible]	[illegible]	[illegible]	[illegible]	[illegible]	[illegible]	[illegible]	[illegible]	[illegible]	[illegible]	[illegible]	[illegible]	80 & up.
																				[illegible]	[illegible] husbands.
Total Wives.	.	[illegible]	[illegible]	[illegible]	[illegible]	[illegible]	[illegible]	[illegible]	[illegible]	[illegible]	[illegible]	[illegible]	[illegible]	[illegible]	[illegible]	.	.	.	[illegible]	[illegible]	Wives.

[illegible]

Ages of 116 Bachelors and 116 Widows who intermarried in the year 1891.

Years (Ages of Bachelors)	15-	16-	17-	18-	19-	20-	21-	25-	30-	35-	40-	45-	50-	55-	60-	65-	70-	75-	80-	Total Bachelors	
15-	.	.	.	.	.	.	.	.	.	.	.	.	.	.	.	.	.	.	.	.	15-
16-	.	.	.	.	.	.	.	.	.	.	.	.	.	.	.	.	.	.	.	.	16-
17-	.	.	.	.	.	.	.	.	.	.	.	.	.	.	.	.	.	.	.	.	17-
18-	.	.	.	.	.	.	.	.	.	.	.	.	.	.	.	.	.	.	.	.	18-
19-	.	.	.	.	.	.	.	.	.	.	.	.	.	.	.	.	.	.	.	.	19-
20-	.	.	.	.	.	.	.	.	1	.	.	.	.	.	.	.	.	.	.	[illegible]	20-
21-	.	.	.	.	.	.	[illegible]	[illegible]	[illegible]	1	[illegible]	.	.	.	.	.	.	.	.	15	21-
25-	.	.	.	.	.	1	[illegible]	16	14	[illegible]	.	1	.	1	.	.	.	.	.	[illegible]	25-
30-	.	.	.	.	.	.	[illegible]	7	[illegible]	[illegible]	[illegible]	.	1	.	.	.	.	.	.	[illegible]	30-
35-	.	.	.	.	.	.	.	[illegible]	4	6	1	.	.	.	.	.	.	.	.	[illegible]	35-
40-	.	.	.	.	.	.	.	[illegible]	[illegible]	4	[illegible]	[illegible]	[illegible]	.	.	.	.	.	.	[illegible]	40-
45-	.	.	.	.	.	.	[illegible]	.	1	.	[illegible]	.	[illegible]	.	.	.	.	.	.	7	45-
50-	.	.	.	.	.	.	.	.	.	1	.	[illegible]	1	.	.	.	.	.	.	[illegible]	50-
55-	.	.	.	.	.	.	.	.	.	1	.	.	.	.	.	.	.	.	.	1	55-
60-	.	.	.	.	.	.	.	.	.	.	.	.	.	.	.	.	.	.	.	.	60-
65-	.	.	.	.	.	.	.	.	.	.	.	.	.	.	.	.	.	.	.	.	65-
70-	.	.	.	.	.	.	.	.	.	.	.	.	.	.	.	.	.	.	.	.	70-
75-	.	.	.	.	.	.	.	.	.	.	.	.	.	.	.	.	.	.	.	.	75-
80 & up.	.	.	.	.	.	.	.	.	.	.	.	.	.	.	.	.	.	.	.	.	80 & up.
																				116	Bachelors.
Total Widows.	.	.	.	.	.	1	17	[illegible]	[illegible]	[illegible]	16	[illegible]	[illegible]	1	-	.	.	.	.	116	Widows.

Ages of 350 Widowers and 350 Spinsters who intermarried in the year 1891.

Years (Ages of Widowers)	15-	16-	17-	18-	19-	20-	21-	25-	30-	35-	40-	45-	50-	55-	60-	65-	70-	75-	80-	Total Widowers	
15-	.	.	.	.	.	.	.	.	.	.	.	.	.	.	.	.	.	.	.	.	15-
16-	.	.	.	.	.	.	.	.	.	.	.	.	.	.	.	.	.	.	.	.	16-
17-	.	.	.	.	.	.	.	.	.	.	.	.	.	.	.	.	.	.	.	.	17-
18-	.	.	.	.	.	.	.	.	.	.	.	.	.	.	.	.	.	.	.	.	18-
19-	.	.	.	.	.	.	.	.	.	.	.	.	.	.	.	.	.	.	.	.	19-
20-	.	.	.	.	.	.	.	.	.	.	.	.	.	.	.	.	.	.	.	.	20-
21-	.	.	.	.	1	.	[illegible]	1	.	.	.	.	.	.	.	.	.	.	.	6	21-
25-	.	.	.	.	[illegible]	[illegible]	[illegible]	[illegible]	.	.	.	.	.	.	.	.	.	.	.	[illegible]	25-
30-	.	.	.	2	[illegible]	[illegible]	[illegible]	[illegible]	[illegible]	[illegible]	1	.	.	.	.	.	.	.	.	[illegible]	30-
35-	.	.	[illegible]	.	1	.	[illegible]	[illegible]	[illegible]	[illegible]	[illegible]	.	.	.	.	.	.	.	.	[illegible]	35-
40-	.	.	[illegible]	[illegible]	.	1	[illegible]	[illegible]	[illegible]	[illegible]	4	[illegible]	[illegible]	.	.	.	.	.	.	[illegible]	40-
45-	.	.	.	.	.	.	[illegible]	[illegible]	[illegible]	[illegible]	[illegible]	[illegible]	[illegible]	.	.	.	.	.	.	[illegible]	45-
50-	.	.	.	[illegible]	.	.	[illegible]	[illegible]	6	6	[illegible]	[illegible]	[illegible]	.	[illegible]	.	.	.	.	[illegible]	50-
55-	.	.	.	.	.	1	.	[illegible]	.	.	4	[illegible]	1	1	.	.	.	.	.	[illegible]	55-
60-	.	.	.	[illegible]	.	1	1	1	[illegible]	[illegible]	1	[illegible]	[illegible]	.	.	.	.	.	.	11	60-
65-	.	.	.	.	.	.	.	.	.	.	.	.	1	.	.	.	.	.	.	[illegible]	65-
70-	.	.	.	.	.	.	.	.	.	.	.	.	[illegible]	.	1	.	.	.	.	[illegible]	70-
75-	.	.	.	.	.	.	.	.	.	.	.	.	.	.	.	.	.	.	.	.	75-
80 & up.	.	.	.	.	.	.	.	.	.	.	.	.	.	.	.	.	.	.	.	.	80 & up.
																				350	Widowers.
Total Spinsters.	.	.	1	[illegible]	[illegible]	[illegible]	[illegible]	[illegible]	[illegible]	[illegible]	[illegible]	[illegible]	[illegible]	1	[illegible]	-	.	.	-	350	Spinsters.

MARRIAGES, BIRTHS, AND DEATHS in each PROVINCE and COUNTY in IRELAND, registered in the year 1891.

MARRIAGES, BIRTHS and DEATHS registered in the Year 1891.

2.—PROVINCE OF LEINSTER.—MARRIAGES, BIRTHS, AND DEATHS, 1891.

SUPERINTENDENT REGISTRARS' DISTRICTS, ARRANGED BY COUNTIES*

*[illegible]

No.	Superintendent Registrars' Districts.	Area in Statute Acres.	Population, 1881.	Total: Marriages.	Total: Births.	Total: Deaths.	Births: Including Legitimate Births: Males.	Births: Including Legitimate Births: Females.	Births: Illegitimate Births: Males.	Births: Illegitimate Births: Females.	Deaths: Males.	Deaths: Females.	Excess of Births over Deaths.
	1. Carlow Co.*												
1	[illegible], part of	[illegible]	[illegible]	6	[illegible]	[illegible]	[illegible]	[illegible]	.	.	[illegible]	[illegible]	[illegible]
2	Carlow, do.	[illegible]	[illegible]	[illegible]	[illegible]	[illegible]	[illegible]	[illegible]	[illegible]	[illegible]	[illegible]	[illegible]	[illegible]
3	[illegible], do.	[illegible]	[illegible]	.	[illegible]	[illegible]	[illegible]	[illegible]	1	.	7	[illegible]	[illegible]
4	[illegible], do.	[illegible]	[illegible]	[illegible]	[illegible]	[illegible]	[illegible]	[illegible]	.	.	[illegible]	[illegible]	[illegible]
5	[illegible], do.	[illegible]	[illegible]	[illegible]	71	[illegible]	41	[illegible]	.	.	[illegible]	[illegible]	[illegible]
	2. Dublin Co.												
6	[illegible]	[illegible]	[illegible]	[illegible]	[illegible]	[illegible]	[illegible]	[illegible]	.	[illegible]	[illegible]	[illegible]	[illegible]
7	[illegible], part of	[illegible]	[illegible]	[illegible]	[illegible]	[illegible]	[illegible]	[illegible]	.	.	[illegible]	[illegible]	[illegible]
8	[illegible]	[illegible]	[illegible]	[illegible]	[illegible]	[illegible]	[illegible]	[illegible]	[illegible]	[illegible]	[illegible]	[illegible]	[illegible]
9	[illegible]	[illegible]	[illegible]	[illegible]	[illegible]	[illegible]	[illegible]	[illegible]	[illegible]	[illegible]	[illegible]	[illegible]	[illegible]
10	[illegible], part of	[illegible]	[illegible]	1	[illegible]	[illegible]	[illegible]	7	.	.	[illegible]	[illegible]	[illegible]
11	[illegible], do.	[illegible]	[illegible]	[illegible]	[illegible]	[illegible]	[illegible]	[illegible]	[illegible]	[illegible]	[illegible]	[illegible]	[illegible]
	3. Kildare Co.												
12	Athy, part of	[illegible]	[illegible]	[illegible]	[illegible]	[illegible]	[illegible]	[illegible]	[illegible]	[illegible]	[illegible]	[illegible]	[illegible]
13	[illegible], do.	[illegible]	[illegible]	[illegible]	[illegible]	[illegible]	[illegible]	[illegible]	1	[illegible]	[illegible]	[illegible]	[illegible]
14	[illegible], do.	[illegible]	[illegible]	[illegible]	[illegible]	[illegible]	[illegible]	[illegible]	[illegible]	[illegible]	[illegible]	[illegible]	[illegible]
15	[illegible], do.	[illegible]	[illegible]	[illegible]	[illegible]	[illegible]	[illegible]	[illegible]	[illegible]	[illegible]	[illegible]	[illegible]	[illegible]
16	[illegible], do.	[illegible]	[illegible]	[illegible]	[illegible]	[illegible]	[illegible]	[illegible]	[illegible]	[illegible]	[illegible]	[illegible]	[illegible]
	4. Kilkenny Co.												
17	[illegible], part of	[illegible]	[illegible]	[illegible]	[illegible]	[illegible]	[illegible]	[illegible]	[illegible]	[illegible]	[illegible]	[illegible]	[illegible]
18	[illegible], do.	[illegible]	[illegible]	[illegible]	[illegible]	[illegible]	[illegible]	[illegible]	[illegible]	[illegible]	[illegible]	[illegible]	[illegible]
19	[illegible]	[illegible]	[illegible]	[illegible]	[illegible]	[illegible]	[illegible]	[illegible]	[illegible]	[illegible]	[illegible]	[illegible]	[illegible]
20	[illegible]	[illegible]	[illegible]	[illegible]	[illegible]	[illegible]	[illegible]	[illegible]	[illegible]	[illegible]	[illegible]	[illegible]	[illegible]
21	[illegible], part of	[illegible]	[illegible]	[illegible]	[illegible]	[illegible]	[illegible]	[illegible]	.	.	[illegible]	[illegible]	[illegible]
22	[illegible]	[illegible]	[illegible]	[illegible]	[illegible]	[illegible]	[illegible]	[illegible]	[illegible]	[illegible]	[illegible]	[illegible]	[illegible]
23	[illegible], part of	[illegible]	[illegible]	[illegible]	[illegible]	[illegible]	[illegible]	[illegible]	[illegible]	[illegible]	[illegible]	[illegible]	[illegible]
24	[illegible], do.	[illegible]	[illegible]	[illegible]	[illegible]	[illegible]	[illegible]	[illegible]	1	.	[illegible]	[illegible]	[illegible]
	5. King's Co.												
25	[illegible], part of	[illegible]	[illegible]	[illegible]	[illegible]	[illegible]	[illegible]	[illegible]	1	.	[illegible]	[illegible]	[illegible]
26	[illegible], do.	[illegible]	[illegible]	[illegible]	[illegible]	[illegible]	[illegible]	[illegible]	.	[illegible]	[illegible]	[illegible]	[illegible]
27	[illegible], do.	[illegible]	[illegible]	[illegible]	[illegible]	[illegible]	[illegible]	[illegible]	[illegible]	[illegible]	[illegible]	[illegible]	[illegible]
28	[illegible], do.	[illegible]	[illegible]	[illegible]	[illegible]	[illegible]	[illegible]	[illegible]	1	.	[illegible]	[illegible]	[illegible]
29	[illegible], do.	[illegible]	[illegible]	[illegible]	[illegible]	[illegible]	[illegible]	[illegible]	[illegible]	1	[illegible]	[illegible]	[illegible]
	6. Longford Co.												
30	[illegible], part of	[illegible]	[illegible]	[illegible]	[illegible]	[illegible]	[illegible]	[illegible]	[illegible]	.	[illegible]	[illegible]	[illegible]
31	[illegible], do.	[illegible]	[illegible]	[illegible]	[illegible]	[illegible]	[illegible]	[illegible]	.	[illegible]	[illegible]	[illegible]	[illegible]
32	[illegible]	[illegible]	[illegible]	[illegible]	[illegible]	[illegible]	[illegible]	[illegible]	[illegible]	[illegible]	[illegible]	[illegible]	[illegible]
	7. Louth and Co. of Town of Drogheda.												
33	Ardee, part of	[illegible]	[illegible]	[illegible]	[illegible]	[illegible]	[illegible]	[illegible]	1	[illegible]	[illegible]	[illegible]	[illegible]

II. PROVINCE OF LEINSTER.—MARRIAGES, BIRTHS, AND DEATHS, 1891—
SUPERINTENDENT REGISTRARS' DISTRICTS—*continued.*

No.	Superintendent Registrars' Districts.	Area in Statute Acres.	Population, 1881.	Total: Marriages.	Total: Births.	Total: Deaths.	Births: Males.	Births: Females.	[illegible]: Males.	[illegible]: Females.	Deaths: Males.	Deaths: Females.	[illegible]
	[illegible] Co.												
[illegible]	[illegible]	[illegible]	[illegible]	[illegible]	[illegible]	[illegible]	[illegible]	[illegible]	[illegible]	[illegible]	[illegible]	[illegible]	[illegible]
[illegible]	[illegible]	[illegible]	[illegible]	[illegible]	[illegible]	[illegible]	[illegible]	[illegible]	[illegible]	[illegible]	[illegible]	[illegible]	[illegible]
[illegible]	[illegible]	[illegible]	[illegible]	[illegible]	[illegible]	[illegible]	[illegible]	[illegible]	[illegible]	[illegible]	[illegible]	[illegible]	[illegible]
[illegible]	[illegible]	[illegible]	[illegible]	[illegible]	[illegible]	[illegible]	[illegible]	[illegible]	[illegible]	[illegible]	[illegible]	[illegible]	[illegible]
[illegible]	[illegible]	[illegible]	[illegible]	[illegible]	[illegible]	[illegible]	[illegible]	[illegible]	[illegible]	[illegible]	[illegible]	[illegible]	[illegible]
[illegible]	[illegible]	[illegible]	[illegible]	[illegible]	[illegible]	[illegible]	[illegible]	[illegible]	[illegible]	[illegible]	[illegible]	[illegible]	[illegible]
[illegible]	[illegible]	[illegible]	[illegible]	[illegible]	[illegible]	[illegible]	[illegible]	[illegible]	[illegible]	[illegible]	[illegible]	[illegible]	[illegible]
[illegible]	[illegible]	[illegible]	[illegible]	[illegible]	[illegible]	[illegible]	[illegible]	[illegible]	[illegible]	[illegible]	[illegible]	[illegible]	[illegible]
[illegible]	[illegible]	[illegible]	[illegible]	[illegible]	[illegible]	[illegible]	[illegible]	[illegible]	[illegible]	[illegible]	[illegible]	[illegible]	[illegible]
	[illegible] Queen's Co.												
[illegible]	[illegible]	[illegible]	[illegible]	[illegible]	[illegible]	[illegible]	[illegible]	[illegible]	[illegible]	[illegible]	[illegible]	[illegible]	[illegible]
[illegible]	[illegible]	[illegible]	[illegible]	[illegible]	[illegible]	[illegible]	[illegible]	[illegible]	[illegible]	[illegible]	[illegible]	[illegible]	[illegible]
[illegible]	[illegible]	[illegible]	[illegible]	[illegible]	[illegible]	[illegible]	[illegible]	[illegible]	[illegible]	[illegible]	[illegible]	[illegible]	[illegible]
[illegible]	[illegible]	[illegible]	[illegible]	[illegible]	[illegible]	[illegible]	[illegible]	[illegible]	[illegible]	[illegible]	[illegible]	[illegible]	[illegible]
[illegible]	[illegible]	[illegible]	[illegible]	[illegible]	[illegible]	[illegible]	[illegible]	[illegible]	[illegible]	[illegible]	[illegible]	[illegible]	[illegible]
[illegible]	[illegible]	[illegible]	[illegible]	[illegible]	[illegible]	[illegible]	[illegible]	[illegible]	[illegible]	[illegible]	[illegible]	[illegible]	[illegible]
	10. Westmeath Co.												
[illegible]	[illegible]	[illegible]	[illegible]	[illegible]	[illegible]	[illegible]	[illegible]	[illegible]	[illegible]	[illegible]	[illegible]	[illegible]	[illegible]
[illegible]	[illegible]	[illegible]	[illegible]	[illegible]	[illegible]	[illegible]	[illegible]	[illegible]	[illegible]	[illegible]	[illegible]	[illegible]	[illegible]
[illegible]	[illegible]	[illegible]	[illegible]	[illegible]	[illegible]	[illegible]	[illegible]	[illegible]	[illegible]	[illegible]	[illegible]	[illegible]	[illegible]
[illegible]	[illegible]	[illegible]	[illegible]	[illegible]	[illegible]	[illegible]	[illegible]	[illegible]	[illegible]	[illegible]	[illegible]	[illegible]	[illegible]
[illegible]	[illegible]	[illegible]	[illegible]	[illegible]	[illegible]	[illegible]	[illegible]	[illegible]	[illegible]	[illegible]	[illegible]	[illegible]	[illegible]
[illegible]	[illegible]	[illegible]	[illegible]	[illegible]	[illegible]	[illegible]	[illegible]	[illegible]	[illegible]	[illegible]	[illegible]	[illegible]	[illegible]
	11. Wexford Co.												
[illegible]	[illegible]	[illegible]	[illegible]	[illegible]	[illegible]	[illegible]	[illegible]	[illegible]	[illegible]	[illegible]	[illegible]	[illegible]	[illegible]
[illegible]	[illegible]	[illegible]	[illegible]	[illegible]	[illegible]	[illegible]	[illegible]	[illegible]	[illegible]	[illegible]	[illegible]	[illegible]	[illegible]
[illegible]	[illegible]	[illegible]	[illegible]	[illegible]	[illegible]	[illegible]	[illegible]	[illegible]	[illegible]	[illegible]	[illegible]	[illegible]	[illegible]
[illegible]	[illegible]	[illegible]	[illegible]	[illegible]	[illegible]	[illegible]	[illegible]	[illegible]	[illegible]	[illegible]	[illegible]	[illegible]	[illegible]
[illegible]	[illegible]	[illegible]	[illegible]	[illegible]	[illegible]	[illegible]	[illegible]	[illegible]	[illegible]	[illegible]	[illegible]	[illegible]	[illegible]
	12. Wicklow Co.												
[illegible]	[illegible]	[illegible]	[illegible]	[illegible]	[illegible]	[illegible]	[illegible]	[illegible]	[illegible]	[illegible]	[illegible]	[illegible]	[illegible]
[illegible]	[illegible]	[illegible]	[illegible]	[illegible]	[illegible]	[illegible]	[illegible]	[illegible]	[illegible]	[illegible]	[illegible]	[illegible]	[illegible]
[illegible]	[illegible]	[illegible]	[illegible]	[illegible]	[illegible]	[illegible]	[illegible]	[illegible]	[illegible]	[illegible]	[illegible]	[illegible]	[illegible]
[illegible]	[illegible]	[illegible]	[illegible]	[illegible]	[illegible]	[illegible]	[illegible]	[illegible]	[illegible]	[illegible]	[illegible]	[illegible]	[illegible]
[illegible]	[illegible]	[illegible]	[illegible]	[illegible]	[illegible]	[illegible]	[illegible]	[illegible]	[illegible]	[illegible]	[illegible]	[illegible]	[illegible]

III.—PROVINCE OF MUNSTER.—MARRIAGES, BIRTHS, AND DEATHS, 1891—
SUPERINTENDENT REGISTRARS' DISTRICTS.

No.	Superintendent Registrars' Districts.	Area in Statute Acres.	Population, 1881.	Total: Marriages.	Total: Births.	Total: Deaths.	Births: Males.	Births: Females.	[illegible]: Males.	[illegible]: Females.	Deaths: Males.	Deaths: Females.	[illegible]
	13. Clare Co.												
[illegible]	[illegible]	[illegible]	[illegible]	[illegible]	[illegible]	[illegible]	[illegible]	[illegible]	[illegible]	[illegible]	[illegible]	[illegible]	[illegible]
[illegible]	[illegible]	[illegible]	[illegible]	[illegible]	[illegible]	[illegible]	[illegible]	[illegible]	[illegible]	[illegible]	[illegible]	[illegible]	[illegible]
[illegible]	[illegible]	[illegible]	[illegible]	[illegible]	[illegible]	[illegible]	[illegible]	[illegible]	[illegible]	[illegible]	[illegible]	[illegible]	[illegible]
[illegible]	[illegible]	[illegible]	[illegible]	[illegible]	[illegible]	[illegible]	[illegible]	[illegible]	[illegible]	[illegible]	[illegible]	[illegible]	[illegible]
[illegible]	[illegible]	[illegible]	[illegible]	[illegible]	[illegible]	[illegible]	[illegible]	[illegible]	[illegible]	[illegible]	[illegible]	[illegible]	[illegible]
[illegible]	[illegible]	[illegible]	[illegible]	[illegible]	[illegible]	[illegible]	[illegible]	[illegible]	[illegible]	[illegible]	[illegible]	[illegible]	[illegible]
[illegible]	[illegible]	[illegible]	[illegible]	[illegible]	[illegible]	[illegible]	[illegible]	[illegible]	[illegible]	[illegible]	[illegible]	[illegible]	[illegible]
[illegible]	[illegible]	[illegible]	[illegible]	[illegible]	[illegible]	[illegible]	[illegible]	[illegible]	[illegible]	[illegible]	[illegible]	[illegible]	[illegible]
[illegible]	[illegible]	[illegible]	[illegible]	[illegible]	[illegible]	[illegible]	[illegible]	[illegible]	[illegible]	[illegible]	[illegible]	[illegible]	[illegible]

II.—PROVINCE OF [illegible].—MARRIAGES, BIRTHS, AND DEATHS, 1891—
SUPERINTENDENT REGISTRARS' DISTRICTS—*continued.*

No.	SUPERINTENDENT REGISTRARS' DISTRICTS	Area in Statute Acres	Population, 1891	TOTAL: MARRIAGES	TOTAL: BIRTHS	TOTAL: DEATHS	BIRTHS: [illegible] Males	BIRTHS: [illegible] Females	BIRTHS: Illegitimate Males	BIRTHS: Illegitimate Females	DEATHS: Males	DEATHS: Females	[illegible]
	14. Cork Co.												
[illegible]	[illegible]	[illegible]	[illegible]	[illegible]	[illegible]	[illegible]	[illegible]	[illegible]	[illegible]	[illegible]	[illegible]	[illegible]	[illegible]
[illegible]	[illegible]	[illegible]	[illegible]	[illegible]	[illegible]	[illegible]	[illegible]	[illegible]	[illegible]	[illegible]	[illegible]	[illegible]	[illegible]
[illegible]	[illegible]	[illegible]	[illegible]	[illegible]	[illegible]	[illegible]	[illegible]	[illegible]	[illegible]	[illegible]	[illegible]	[illegible]	[illegible]
[illegible]	[illegible]	[illegible]	[illegible]	[illegible]	[illegible]	[illegible]	[illegible]	[illegible]	[illegible]	[illegible]	[illegible]	[illegible]	[illegible]
[illegible]	Cork,	[illegible]	[illegible]	[illegible]	[illegible]	[illegible]	[illegible]	[illegible]	[illegible]	[illegible]	[illegible]	[illegible]	[illegible]
[illegible]	[illegible]	[illegible]	[illegible]	[illegible]	[illegible]	[illegible]	[illegible]	[illegible]	[illegible]	[illegible]	[illegible]	[illegible]	[illegible]
[illegible]	[illegible]	[illegible]	[illegible]	[illegible]	[illegible]	[illegible]	[illegible]	[illegible]	[illegible]	[illegible]	[illegible]	[illegible]	[illegible]
[illegible]	[illegible]	[illegible]	[illegible]	[illegible]	[illegible]	[illegible]	[illegible]	[illegible]	[illegible]	[illegible]	[illegible]	[illegible]	[illegible]
[illegible]	[illegible], part of,	[illegible]	[illegible]	[illegible]	[illegible]	[illegible]	[illegible]	[illegible]	[illegible]	[illegible]	[illegible]	[illegible]	[illegible]
[illegible]	[illegible]	[illegible]	[illegible]	[illegible]	[illegible]	[illegible]	[illegible]	[illegible]	[illegible]	[illegible]	[illegible]	[illegible]	[illegible]
[illegible]	[illegible]	[illegible]	[illegible]	[illegible]	[illegible]	[illegible]	[illegible]	[illegible]	[illegible]	[illegible]	[illegible]	[illegible]	[illegible]
[illegible]	[illegible]	[illegible]	[illegible]	[illegible]	[illegible]	[illegible]	[illegible]	[illegible]	[illegible]	[illegible]	[illegible]	[illegible]	[illegible]
[illegible]	[illegible]	[illegible]	[illegible]	[illegible]	[illegible]	[illegible]	[illegible]	[illegible]	[illegible]	[illegible]	[illegible]	[illegible]	[illegible]
[illegible]	[illegible]	[illegible]	[illegible]	[illegible]	[illegible]	[illegible]	[illegible]	[illegible]	[illegible]	[illegible]	[illegible]	[illegible]	[illegible]
[illegible]	[illegible], part of,	[illegible]	[illegible]	[illegible]	[illegible]	[illegible]	[illegible]	[illegible]	[illegible]	[illegible]	[illegible]	[illegible]	[illegible]
[illegible]	[illegible]	[illegible]	[illegible]	[illegible]	[illegible]	[illegible]	[illegible]	[illegible]	[illegible]	[illegible]	[illegible]	[illegible]	[illegible]
[illegible]	[illegible]	[illegible]	[illegible]	[illegible]	[illegible]	[illegible]	[illegible]	[illegible]	[illegible]	[illegible]	[illegible]	[illegible]	[illegible]
[illegible]	[illegible], part of,	[illegible]	[illegible]	[illegible]	[illegible]	[illegible]	[illegible]	[illegible]	[illegible]	[illegible]	[illegible]	[illegible]	[illegible]
	15. Kerry Co.												
[illegible]	[illegible]	[illegible]	[illegible]	[illegible]	[illegible]	[illegible]	[illegible]	[illegible]	[illegible]	[illegible]	[illegible]	[illegible]	[illegible]
[illegible]	[illegible]	[illegible]	[illegible]	[illegible]	[illegible]	[illegible]	[illegible]	[illegible]	[illegible]	[illegible]	[illegible]	[illegible]	[illegible]
[illegible]	[illegible], part of,	[illegible]	[illegible]	[illegible]	[illegible]	[illegible]	[illegible]	[illegible]	[illegible]	[illegible]	[illegible]	[illegible]	[illegible]
[illegible]	[illegible]	[illegible]	[illegible]	[illegible]	[illegible]	[illegible]	[illegible]	[illegible]	[illegible]	[illegible]	[illegible]	[illegible]	[illegible]
[illegible]	[illegible]	[illegible]	[illegible]	[illegible]	[illegible]	[illegible]	[illegible]	[illegible]	[illegible]	[illegible]	[illegible]	[illegible]	[illegible]
[illegible]	[illegible]	[illegible]	[illegible]	[illegible]	[illegible]	[illegible]	[illegible]	[illegible]	[illegible]	[illegible]	[illegible]	[illegible]	[illegible]
[illegible]	[illegible]	[illegible]	[illegible]	[illegible]	[illegible]	[illegible]	[illegible]	[illegible]	[illegible]	[illegible]	[illegible]	[illegible]	[illegible]
	16. [illegible] Co.												
[illegible]	[illegible]	[illegible]	[illegible]	[illegible]	[illegible]	[illegible]	[illegible]	[illegible]	[illegible]	[illegible]	[illegible]	[illegible]	[illegible]
[illegible]	[illegible], part of,	[illegible]	[illegible]	[illegible]	[illegible]	[illegible]	[illegible]	[illegible]	[illegible]	[illegible]	[illegible]	[illegible]	[illegible]
[illegible]	[illegible], do.	[illegible]	[illegible]	[illegible]	[illegible]	[illegible]	[illegible]	[illegible]	[illegible]	[illegible]	[illegible]	[illegible]	[illegible]
[illegible]	[illegible], do.	[illegible]	[illegible]	[illegible]	[illegible]	[illegible]	[illegible]	[illegible]	[illegible]	[illegible]	[illegible]	[illegible]	[illegible]
[illegible]	[illegible], do.	[illegible]	[illegible]	[illegible]	[illegible]	[illegible]	[illegible]	[illegible]	[illegible]	[illegible]	[illegible]	[illegible]	[illegible]
[illegible]	[illegible]	[illegible]	[illegible]	[illegible]	[illegible]	[illegible]	[illegible]	[illegible]	[illegible]	[illegible]	[illegible]	[illegible]	[illegible]
[illegible]	[illegible]	[illegible]	[illegible]	[illegible]	[illegible]	[illegible]	[illegible]	[illegible]	[illegible]	[illegible]	[illegible]	[illegible]	[illegible]
[illegible]	[illegible], part of,	[illegible]	[illegible]	[illegible]	[illegible]	[illegible]	[illegible]	[illegible]	[illegible]	[illegible]	[illegible]	[illegible]	[illegible]
	17. [illegible] Co.												
[illegible]	[illegible]	[illegible]	[illegible]	[illegible]	[illegible]	[illegible]	[illegible]	[illegible]	[illegible]	[illegible]	[illegible]	[illegible]	[illegible]
[illegible]	[illegible], part of,	[illegible]	[illegible]	[illegible]	[illegible]	[illegible]	[illegible]	[illegible]	[illegible]	[illegible]	[illegible]	[illegible]	[illegible]
[illegible]	[illegible], do.	[illegible]	[illegible]	[illegible]	[illegible]	[illegible]	[illegible]	[illegible]	[illegible]	[illegible]	[illegible]	[illegible]	[illegible]
[illegible]	[illegible]	[illegible]	[illegible]	[illegible]	[illegible]	[illegible]	[illegible]	[illegible]	[illegible]	[illegible]	[illegible]	[illegible]	[illegible]
[illegible]	[illegible]	[illegible]	[illegible]	[illegible]	[illegible]	[illegible]	[illegible]	[illegible]	[illegible]	[illegible]	[illegible]	[illegible]	[illegible]
[illegible]	[illegible], part of,	[illegible]	[illegible]	[illegible]	[illegible]	[illegible]	[illegible]	[illegible]	[illegible]	[illegible]	[illegible]	[illegible]	[illegible]
[illegible]	[illegible]	[illegible]	[illegible]	[illegible]	[illegible]	[illegible]	[illegible]	[illegible]	[illegible]	[illegible]	[illegible]	[illegible]	[illegible]
[illegible]	[illegible], part of,	[illegible]	[illegible]	[illegible]	[illegible]	[illegible]	[illegible]	[illegible]	[illegible]	[illegible]	[illegible]	[illegible]	[illegible]
[illegible]	[illegible], do.	[illegible]	[illegible]	[illegible]	[illegible]	[illegible]	[illegible]	[illegible]	[illegible]	[illegible]	[illegible]	[illegible]	[illegible]
[illegible]	[illegible]	[illegible]	[illegible]	[illegible]	[illegible]	[illegible]	[illegible]	[illegible]	[illegible]	[illegible]	[illegible]	[illegible]	[illegible]
[illegible]	[illegible], part of,	[illegible]	[illegible]	[illegible]	[illegible]	[illegible]	[illegible]	[illegible]	[illegible]	[illegible]	[illegible]	[illegible]	[illegible]
[illegible]	[illegible], do.	[illegible]	[illegible]	[illegible]	[illegible]	[illegible]	[illegible]	[illegible]	[illegible]	[illegible]	[illegible]	[illegible]	[illegible]

II.—PROVINCE OF MUNSTER.—MARRIAGES, BIRTHS, AND DEATHS, 1891—
SUPERINTENDENT REGISTRARS' DISTRICTS—*continued.*

No.	Superintendent Registrars' Districts.	Area in Statute Acres.	Population, 1891.	Total: Marriages.	Total: Births.	Total: Deaths.	Births, including Illegitimate: Males.	Births, including Illegitimate: Females.	Illegitimate Births: Males.	Illegitimate Births: Females.	Deaths: Males.	Deaths: Females.
	XX. Waterford Co.											
[illegible]	Carrick-on-Suir, part of,	[illegible]	[illegible]	[illegible]	[illegible]	[illegible]	[illegible]	[illegible]	[illegible]	[illegible]	[illegible]	[illegible]
[illegible]	Clonmel, do.	[illegible]	[illegible]	[illegible]	[illegible]	[illegible]	[illegible]	[illegible]	.	.	[illegible]	[illegible]
[illegible]	Dungarvan,	[illegible]	[illegible]	[illegible]	[illegible]	[illegible]	[illegible]	[illegible]	[illegible]	[illegible]	[illegible]	[illegible]
[illegible]	Kilmacthomas,	[illegible]	[illegible]	[illegible]	[illegible]	[illegible]	[illegible]	[illegible]	[illegible]	[illegible]	[illegible]	[illegible]
[illegible]	Lismore,	[illegible]	[illegible]	[illegible]	[illegible]	[illegible]	[illegible]	[illegible]	[illegible]	[illegible]	[illegible]	[illegible]
[illegible]	Waterford, part of,	[illegible]	[illegible]	[illegible]	[illegible]	[illegible]	[illegible]	[illegible]	[illegible]	[illegible]	[illegible]	[illegible]
[illegible]	Youghal, do.	[illegible]	[illegible]	[illegible]	[illegible]	[illegible]	[illegible]	[illegible]	[illegible]	[illegible]	[illegible]	[illegible]

III.—PROVINCE OF ULSTER.—MARRIAGES, BIRTHS, AND DEATHS, 1891—
SUPERINTENDENT REGISTRARS' DISTRICTS.

No.	Superintendent Registrars' Districts.	Area in Statute Acres.	Population, 1891.	Total: Marriages.	Total: Births.	Total: Deaths.	Births, including Illegitimate: Males.	Births, including Illegitimate: Females.	Illegitimate Births: Males.	Illegitimate Births: Females.	Deaths: Males.	Deaths: Females.
	XXI. Antrim Co.											
[illegible]	Antrim,	[illegible]	[illegible]	[illegible]	[illegible]	[illegible]	[illegible]	[illegible]	[illegible]	[illegible]	[illegible]	[illegible]
[illegible]	Ballycastle,	[illegible]	[illegible]	[illegible]	[illegible]	[illegible]	[illegible]	[illegible]	[illegible]	[illegible]	[illegible]	[illegible]
[illegible]	Ballymena,	[illegible]	[illegible]	[illegible]	[illegible]	[illegible]	[illegible]	[illegible]	[illegible]	[illegible]	[illegible]	[illegible]
[illegible]	Ballymoney, part of,	[illegible]	[illegible]	[illegible]	[illegible]	[illegible]	[illegible]	[illegible]	[illegible]	[illegible]	[illegible]	[illegible]
[illegible]	Belfast, do.	[illegible]	[illegible]	[illegible]	[illegible]	[illegible]	[illegible]	[illegible]	[illegible]	[illegible]	[illegible]	[illegible]
[illegible]	Coleraine, do.	[illegible]	[illegible]	[illegible]	[illegible]	[illegible]	[illegible]	[illegible]	[illegible]	[illegible]	[illegible]	[illegible]
[illegible]	Larne,	[illegible]	[illegible]	[illegible]	[illegible]	[illegible]	[illegible]	[illegible]	[illegible]	[illegible]	[illegible]	[illegible]
[illegible]	Lisburn, part of,	[illegible]	[illegible]	[illegible]	[illegible]	[illegible]	[illegible]	[illegible]	[illegible]	[illegible]	[illegible]	[illegible]
[illegible]	Lurgan, do.	[illegible]	[illegible]	[illegible]	[illegible]	[illegible]	[illegible]	[illegible]	[illegible]	[illegible]	[illegible]	[illegible]
	XXII. Armagh Co.											
[illegible]	Armagh, part of,	[illegible]	[illegible]	[illegible]	[illegible]	[illegible]	[illegible]	[illegible]	[illegible]	[illegible]	[illegible]	[illegible]
[illegible]	Banbridge, do.	[illegible]	[illegible]	[illegible]	[illegible]	[illegible]	[illegible]	[illegible]	[illegible]	[illegible]	[illegible]	[illegible]
[illegible]	Castleblayney, do.	[illegible]	[illegible]	[illegible]	[illegible]	[illegible]	[illegible]	[illegible]	[illegible]	[illegible]	[illegible]	[illegible]
[illegible]	Dundalk, do.	[illegible]	[illegible]	[illegible]	[illegible]	[illegible]	[illegible]	[illegible]	[illegible]	[illegible]	[illegible]	[illegible]
[illegible]	Lurgan, do.	[illegible]	[illegible]	[illegible]	[illegible]	[illegible]	[illegible]	[illegible]	[illegible]	[illegible]	[illegible]	[illegible]
[illegible]	Newry, do.	[illegible]	[illegible]	[illegible]	[illegible]	[illegible]	[illegible]	[illegible]	[illegible]	[illegible]	[illegible]	[illegible]
	XXIII. Cavan Co.											
[illegible]	Bailieborough,	[illegible]	[illegible]	[illegible]	[illegible]	[illegible]	[illegible]	[illegible]	[illegible]	[illegible]	[illegible]	[illegible]
[illegible]	Bawnboy, part of,	[illegible]	[illegible]	[illegible]	[illegible]	[illegible]	[illegible]	[illegible]	[illegible]	[illegible]	[illegible]	[illegible]
[illegible]	Cavan,	[illegible]	[illegible]	[illegible]	[illegible]	[illegible]	[illegible]	[illegible]	[illegible]	[illegible]	[illegible]	[illegible]
[illegible]	Cootehill, part of,	[illegible]	[illegible]	[illegible]	[illegible]	[illegible]	[illegible]	[illegible]	[illegible]	[illegible]	[illegible]	[illegible]
[illegible]	Enniskillen, do.	[illegible]	[illegible]	[illegible]	[illegible]	[illegible]	[illegible]	[illegible]	[illegible]	[illegible]	[illegible]	[illegible]
[illegible]	Granard, do.	[illegible]	[illegible]	[illegible]	[illegible]	[illegible]	[illegible]	[illegible]	[illegible]	[illegible]	[illegible]	[illegible]
[illegible]	Kells, do.	[illegible]	[illegible]	[illegible]	[illegible]	[illegible]	[illegible]	[illegible]	[illegible]	[illegible]	[illegible]	[illegible]
[illegible]	Oldcastle, do.	[illegible]	[illegible]	[illegible]	[illegible]	[illegible]	[illegible]	[illegible]	[illegible]	[illegible]	[illegible]	[illegible]
	XXIV. Donegal Co.											
[illegible]	Ballyshannon, part of,	[illegible]	[illegible]	[illegible]	[illegible]	[illegible]	[illegible]	[illegible]	[illegible]	[illegible]	[illegible]	[illegible]
[illegible]	Donegal,	[illegible]	[illegible]	[illegible]	[illegible]	[illegible]	[illegible]	[illegible]	[illegible]	[illegible]	[illegible]	[illegible]
[illegible]	Dunfanaghy,	[illegible]	[illegible]	[illegible]	[illegible]	[illegible]	[illegible]	[illegible]	[illegible]	[illegible]	[illegible]	[illegible]
[illegible]	Glenties,	[illegible]	[illegible]	[illegible]	[illegible]	[illegible]	[illegible]	[illegible]	[illegible]	[illegible]	[illegible]	[illegible]
[illegible]	Inishowen,	[illegible]	[illegible]	[illegible]	[illegible]	[illegible]	[illegible]	[illegible]	[illegible]	[illegible]	[illegible]	[illegible]
[illegible]	Letterkenny,	[illegible]	[illegible]	[illegible]	[illegible]	[illegible]	[illegible]	[illegible]	[illegible]	[illegible]	[illegible]	[illegible]
[illegible]	Londonderry, part of,	[illegible]	[illegible]	[illegible]	[illegible]	[illegible]	[illegible]	[illegible]	[illegible]	[illegible]	[illegible]	[illegible]
[illegible]	Milford,	[illegible]	[illegible]	[illegible]	[illegible]	[illegible]	[illegible]	[illegible]	[illegible]	[illegible]	[illegible]	[illegible]
[illegible]	Strabane, part of,	[illegible]	[illegible]	[illegible]	[illegible]	[illegible]	[illegible]	[illegible]	[illegible]	[illegible]	[illegible]	[illegible]
[illegible]	Stranorlar,	[illegible]	[illegible]	[illegible]	[illegible]	[illegible]	[illegible]	[illegible]	[illegible]	[illegible]	[illegible]	[illegible]

III.—PROVINCE OF ULSTER.—MARRIAGES, BIRTHS, AND DEATHS, 1891—
SUPERINTENDENT REGISTRARS' DISTRICTS—*continued.*

No.	SUPERINTENDENT REGISTRARS' DISTRICTS.	Area in Statute Acres.	Population, 1891.	TOTAL. Marriages.	Births.	Deaths.	Births. Including Illegitimate Births. Males.	Females.	Illegitimate Births. Males.	Females.	Deaths. Males.	Females.	Excess of Births over Deaths.
	Down Co.												
[illegible]	[illegible]	[illegible]	[illegible]	[illegible]	[illegible]	[illegible]	[illegible]	[illegible]	[illegible]	[illegible]	[illegible]	[illegible]	[illegible]
[illegible]	[illegible]	[illegible]	[illegible]	[illegible]	[illegible]	[illegible]	[illegible]	[illegible]	[illegible]	[illegible]	[illegible]	[illegible]	[illegible]
[illegible]	[illegible]	[illegible]	[illegible]	[illegible]	[illegible]	[illegible]	[illegible]	[illegible]	[illegible]	[illegible]	[illegible]	[illegible]	[illegible]
[illegible]	[illegible]	[illegible]	[illegible]	[illegible]	[illegible]	[illegible]	[illegible]	[illegible]	[illegible]	[illegible]	[illegible]	[illegible]	[illegible]
[illegible]	[illegible]	[illegible]	[illegible]	[illegible]	[illegible]	[illegible]	[illegible]	[illegible]	[illegible]	[illegible]	[illegible]	[illegible]	[illegible]
[illegible]	[illegible]	[illegible]	[illegible]	[illegible]	[illegible]	[illegible]	[illegible]	[illegible]	[illegible]	[illegible]	[illegible]	[illegible]	[illegible]
[illegible]	[illegible]	[illegible]	[illegible]	[illegible]	[illegible]	[illegible]	[illegible]	[illegible]	[illegible]	[illegible]	[illegible]	[illegible]	[illegible]
[illegible]	[illegible]	[illegible]	[illegible]	[illegible]	[illegible]	[illegible]	[illegible]	[illegible]	[illegible]	[illegible]	[illegible]	[illegible]	[illegible]
	Fermanagh Co.												
[illegible]	[illegible]	[illegible]	[illegible]	[illegible]	[illegible]	[illegible]	[illegible]	[illegible]	[illegible]	[illegible]	[illegible]	[illegible]	[illegible]
[illegible]	[illegible]	[illegible]	[illegible]	[illegible]	[illegible]	[illegible]	[illegible]	[illegible]	[illegible]	[illegible]	[illegible]	[illegible]	[illegible]
[illegible]	[illegible]	[illegible]	[illegible]	[illegible]	[illegible]	[illegible]	[illegible]	[illegible]	[illegible]	[illegible]	[illegible]	[illegible]	[illegible]
[illegible]	[illegible]	[illegible]	[illegible]	[illegible]	[illegible]	[illegible]	[illegible]	[illegible]	[illegible]	[illegible]	[illegible]	[illegible]	[illegible]
[illegible]	[illegible]	[illegible]	[illegible]	[illegible]	[illegible]	[illegible]	[illegible]	[illegible]	[illegible]	[illegible]	[illegible]	[illegible]	[illegible]
	Londonderry Co.												
[illegible]	[illegible]	[illegible]	[illegible]	[illegible]	[illegible]	[illegible]	[illegible]	[illegible]	[illegible]	[illegible]	[illegible]	[illegible]	[illegible]
[illegible]	[illegible]	[illegible]	[illegible]	[illegible]	[illegible]	[illegible]	[illegible]	[illegible]	[illegible]	[illegible]	[illegible]	[illegible]	[illegible]
[illegible]	[illegible]	[illegible]	[illegible]	[illegible]	[illegible]	[illegible]	[illegible]	[illegible]	[illegible]	[illegible]	[illegible]	[illegible]	[illegible]
[illegible]	[illegible]	[illegible]	[illegible]	[illegible]	[illegible]	[illegible]	[illegible]	[illegible]	[illegible]	[illegible]	[illegible]	[illegible]	[illegible]
[illegible]	[illegible]	[illegible]	[illegible]	[illegible]	[illegible]	[illegible]	[illegible]	[illegible]	[illegible]	[illegible]	[illegible]	[illegible]	[illegible]
	Monaghan Co.												
[illegible]	[illegible]	[illegible]	[illegible]	[illegible]	[illegible]	[illegible]	[illegible]	[illegible]	[illegible]	[illegible]	[illegible]	[illegible]	[illegible]
[illegible]	[illegible]	[illegible]	[illegible]	[illegible]	[illegible]	[illegible]	[illegible]	[illegible]	[illegible]	[illegible]	[illegible]	[illegible]	[illegible]
[illegible]	[illegible]	[illegible]	[illegible]	[illegible]	[illegible]	[illegible]	[illegible]	[illegible]	[illegible]	[illegible]	[illegible]	[illegible]	[illegible]
[illegible]	[illegible]	[illegible]	[illegible]	[illegible]	[illegible]	[illegible]	[illegible]	[illegible]	[illegible]	[illegible]	[illegible]	[illegible]	[illegible]
[illegible]	[illegible]	[illegible]	[illegible]	[illegible]	[illegible]	[illegible]	[illegible]	[illegible]	[illegible]	[illegible]	[illegible]	[illegible]	[illegible]
[illegible]	[illegible]	[illegible]	[illegible]	[illegible]	[illegible]	[illegible]	[illegible]	[illegible]	[illegible]	[illegible]	[illegible]	[illegible]	[illegible]
[illegible]	[illegible]	[illegible]	[illegible]	[illegible]	[illegible]	[illegible]	[illegible]	[illegible]	[illegible]	[illegible]	[illegible]	[illegible]	[illegible]
	Tyrone Co.												
[illegible]	[illegible]	[illegible]	[illegible]	[illegible]	[illegible]	[illegible]	[illegible]	[illegible]	[illegible]	[illegible]	[illegible]	[illegible]	[illegible]
[illegible]	[illegible]	[illegible]	[illegible]	[illegible]	[illegible]	[illegible]	[illegible]	[illegible]	[illegible]	[illegible]	[illegible]	[illegible]	[illegible]
[illegible]	[illegible]	[illegible]	[illegible]	[illegible]	[illegible]	[illegible]	[illegible]	[illegible]	[illegible]	[illegible]	[illegible]	[illegible]	[illegible]
[illegible]	[illegible]	[illegible]	[illegible]	[illegible]	[illegible]	[illegible]	[illegible]	[illegible]	[illegible]	[illegible]	[illegible]	[illegible]	[illegible]
[illegible]	[illegible]	[illegible]	[illegible]	[illegible]	[illegible]	[illegible]	[illegible]	[illegible]	[illegible]	[illegible]	[illegible]	[illegible]	[illegible]
[illegible]	[illegible]	[illegible]	[illegible]	[illegible]	[illegible]	[illegible]	[illegible]	[illegible]	[illegible]	[illegible]	[illegible]	[illegible]	[illegible]
[illegible]	[illegible]	[illegible]	[illegible]	[illegible]	[illegible]	[illegible]	[illegible]	[illegible]	[illegible]	[illegible]	[illegible]	[illegible]	[illegible]
[illegible]	[illegible]	[illegible]	[illegible]	[illegible]	[illegible]	[illegible]	[illegible]	[illegible]	[illegible]	[illegible]	[illegible]	[illegible]	[illegible]
[illegible]	[illegible]	[illegible]	[illegible]	[illegible]	[illegible]	[illegible]	[illegible]	[illegible]	[illegible]	[illegible]	[illegible]	[illegible]	[illegible]

IV.—PROVINCE OF CONNAUGHT.—MARRIAGES, BIRTHS, AND DEATHS, 1891—SUPERINTENDENT REGISTRARS' DISTRICTS.

No.	Superintendent Registrars' Districts.	Area in Statute Acres.	Population, 1891.	Total: Marriages.	Total: Births.	Total: Deaths.	Births, including Legitimate: Males.	Births, including Legitimate: Females.	Illegitimate Births: Males.	Illegitimate Births: Females.	Deaths: Males.	Deaths: Females.	[illegible]
	33. Galway Co.												
[illegible]	Ballinasloe, part of,	[illegible]	[illegible]	[illegible]	[illegible]	[illegible]	[illegible]	[illegible]	[illegible]	[illegible]	[illegible]	[illegible]	[illegible]
[illegible]	Ballinrobe, do.	[illegible]	[illegible]	[illegible]	[illegible]	[illegible]	[illegible]	[illegible]	[illegible]	[illegible]	[illegible]	[illegible]	[illegible]
[illegible]	Clifden,	[illegible]	[illegible]	[illegible]	[illegible]	[illegible]	[illegible]	[illegible]	[illegible]	[illegible]	[illegible]	[illegible]	[illegible]
[illegible]	Galway,	[illegible]	[illegible]	[illegible]	[illegible]	[illegible]	[illegible]	[illegible]	[illegible]	[illegible]	[illegible]	[illegible]	[illegible]
[illegible]	Glenamaddy,	[illegible]	[illegible]	[illegible]	[illegible]	[illegible]	[illegible]	[illegible]	[illegible]	[illegible]	[illegible]	[illegible]	[illegible]
[illegible]	Gort,	[illegible]	[illegible]	[illegible]	[illegible]	[illegible]	[illegible]	[illegible]	[illegible]	[illegible]	[illegible]	[illegible]	[illegible]
[illegible]	Loughrea,	[illegible]	[illegible]	[illegible]	[illegible]	[illegible]	[illegible]	[illegible]	[illegible]	[illegible]	[illegible]	[illegible]	[illegible]
[illegible]	Mount Bellew,	[illegible]	[illegible]	[illegible]	[illegible]	[illegible]	[illegible]	[illegible]	[illegible]	[illegible]	[illegible]	[illegible]	[illegible]
[illegible]	Oughterard,	[illegible]	[illegible]	[illegible]	[illegible]	[illegible]	[illegible]	[illegible]	[illegible]	[illegible]	[illegible]	[illegible]	[illegible]
[illegible]	Portumna,	[illegible]	[illegible]	[illegible]	[illegible]	[illegible]	[illegible]	[illegible]	[illegible]	[illegible]	[illegible]	[illegible]	[illegible]
[illegible]	Roscommon, part of,	[illegible]	[illegible]	[illegible]	[illegible]	[illegible]	[illegible]	[illegible]	[illegible]	[illegible]	[illegible]	[illegible]	[illegible]
[illegible]	Scarriff, do.	[illegible]	[illegible]	[illegible]	[illegible]	[illegible]	[illegible]	[illegible]	[illegible]	[illegible]	[illegible]	[illegible]	[illegible]
[illegible]	Tuam,	[illegible]	[illegible]	[illegible]	[illegible]	[illegible]	[illegible]	[illegible]	[illegible]	[illegible]	[illegible]	[illegible]	[illegible]
	39. Leitrim Co.												
[illegible]	Ballyshannon, part of,	[illegible]	[illegible]	[illegible]	[illegible]	[illegible]	[illegible]	[illegible]	[illegible]	[illegible]	[illegible]	[illegible]	[illegible]
[illegible]	Bawboy, do.	[illegible]	[illegible]	[illegible]	[illegible]	[illegible]	[illegible]	[illegible]	[illegible]	[illegible]	[illegible]	[illegible]	[illegible]
[illegible]	Carrick-on-Shan. do.	[illegible]	[illegible]	[illegible]	[illegible]	[illegible]	[illegible]	[illegible]	[illegible]	[illegible]	[illegible]	[illegible]	[illegible]
[illegible]	Manorhamilton,	[illegible]	[illegible]	[illegible]	[illegible]	[illegible]	[illegible]	[illegible]	[illegible]	[illegible]	[illegible]	[illegible]	[illegible]
[illegible]	Mohill,	[illegible]	[illegible]	[illegible]	[illegible]	[illegible]	[illegible]	[illegible]	[illegible]	[illegible]	[illegible]	[illegible]	[illegible]
	40. Mayo Co.												
[illegible]	Ballina, part of,	[illegible]	[illegible]	[illegible]	[illegible]	[illegible]	[illegible]	[illegible]	[illegible]	[illegible]	[illegible]	[illegible]	[illegible]
[illegible]	Ballinrobe, do.	[illegible]	[illegible]	[illegible]	[illegible]	[illegible]	[illegible]	[illegible]	[illegible]	[illegible]	[illegible]	[illegible]	[illegible]
[illegible]	Belmullet,	[illegible]	[illegible]	[illegible]	[illegible]	[illegible]	[illegible]	[illegible]	[illegible]	[illegible]	[illegible]	[illegible]	[illegible]
[illegible]	Castlebar,	[illegible]	[illegible]	[illegible]	[illegible]	[illegible]	[illegible]	[illegible]	[illegible]	[illegible]	[illegible]	[illegible]	[illegible]
[illegible]	Castlereagh, part of,	[illegible]	[illegible]	[illegible]	[illegible]	[illegible]	[illegible]	[illegible]	[illegible]	[illegible]	[illegible]	[illegible]	[illegible]
[illegible]	Claremorris,	[illegible]	[illegible]	[illegible]	[illegible]	[illegible]	[illegible]	[illegible]	[illegible]	[illegible]	[illegible]	[illegible]	[illegible]
[illegible]	Killala,	[illegible]	[illegible]	[illegible]	[illegible]	[illegible]	[illegible]	[illegible]	[illegible]	[illegible]	[illegible]	[illegible]	[illegible]
[illegible]	Swinford,	[illegible]	[illegible]	[illegible]	[illegible]	[illegible]	[illegible]	[illegible]	[illegible]	[illegible]	[illegible]	[illegible]	[illegible]
[illegible]	Westport,	[illegible]	[illegible]	[illegible]	[illegible]	[illegible]	[illegible]	[illegible]	[illegible]	[illegible]	[illegible]	[illegible]	[illegible]
	41. Roscommon Co.												
[illegible]	Athlone, part of,	[illegible]	[illegible]	[illegible]	[illegible]	[illegible]	[illegible]	[illegible]	[illegible]	[illegible]	[illegible]	[illegible]	[illegible]
[illegible]	Ballinasloe, do.	[illegible]	[illegible]	[illegible]	[illegible]	[illegible]	[illegible]	[illegible]	[illegible]	[illegible]	[illegible]	[illegible]	[illegible]
[illegible]	Boyle, do.	[illegible]	[illegible]	[illegible]	[illegible]	[illegible]	[illegible]	[illegible]	[illegible]	[illegible]	[illegible]	[illegible]	[illegible]
[illegible]	Carrick-on-Shan. do.	[illegible]	[illegible]	[illegible]	[illegible]	[illegible]	[illegible]	[illegible]	[illegible]	[illegible]	[illegible]	[illegible]	[illegible]
[illegible]	Castlerea, do.	[illegible]	[illegible]	[illegible]	[illegible]	[illegible]	[illegible]	[illegible]	[illegible]	[illegible]	[illegible]	[illegible]	[illegible]
[illegible]	Roscommon, do.	[illegible]	[illegible]	[illegible]	[illegible]	[illegible]	[illegible]	[illegible]	[illegible]	[illegible]	[illegible]	[illegible]	[illegible]
[illegible]	Strokestown,	[illegible]	[illegible]	[illegible]	[illegible]	[illegible]	[illegible]	[illegible]	[illegible]	[illegible]	[illegible]	[illegible]	[illegible]
	42. Sligo Co.												
[illegible]	Ballina, part of,	[illegible]	[illegible]	[illegible]	[illegible]	[illegible]	[illegible]	[illegible]	[illegible]	[illegible]	[illegible]	[illegible]	[illegible]
[illegible]	Boyle, do.	[illegible]	[illegible]	[illegible]	[illegible]	[illegible]	[illegible]	[illegible]	[illegible]	[illegible]	[illegible]	[illegible]	[illegible]
[illegible]	Dromore West,	[illegible]	[illegible]	[illegible]	[illegible]	[illegible]	[illegible]	[illegible]	[illegible]	[illegible]	[illegible]	[illegible]	[illegible]
[illegible]	Sligo,	[illegible]	[illegible]	[illegible]	[illegible]	[illegible]	[illegible]	[illegible]	[illegible]	[illegible]	[illegible]	[illegible]	[illegible]
[illegible]	Tobercurry,	[illegible]	[illegible]	[illegible]	[illegible]	[illegible]	[illegible]	[illegible]	[illegible]	[illegible]	[illegible]	[illegible]	[illegible]

[illegible]				MARRI.	BIRTHS	DEATHS	Males	Females	Wid.
[illegible]	Abbeyleix,	[illegible]	[illegible]	[illegible]	[illegible]	[illegible]	[illegible]	[illegible]	[illegible]
[illegible]	Antrim,	[illegible]	[illegible]	[illegible]	[illegible]	[illegible]	[illegible]	[illegible]	[illegible]
[illegible]	Ardee,	[illegible]	[illegible]	[illegible]	[illegible]	[illegible]	[illegible]	[illegible]	[illegible]
[illegible]	Armagh,	[illegible]	[illegible]	[illegible]	[illegible]	[illegible]	[illegible]	[illegible]	[illegible]
[illegible]	Athlone,	[illegible]	[illegible]	[illegible]	[illegible]	[illegible]	[illegible]	[illegible]	[illegible]
[illegible]	Athy,	[illegible]	[illegible]	[illegible]	[illegible]	[illegible]	[illegible]	[illegible]	[illegible]
[illegible]	Bailieborough,	[illegible]	[illegible]	[illegible]	[illegible]	[illegible]	[illegible]	[illegible]	[illegible]
[illegible]	Ballina,	[illegible]	[illegible]	[illegible]	[illegible]	[illegible]	[illegible]	[illegible]	[illegible]
[illegible]	Ballinasloe,	[illegible]	[illegible]	[illegible]	[illegible]	[illegible]	[illegible]	[illegible]	[illegible]
[illegible]	Ballinrobe,	[illegible]	[illegible]	[illegible]	[illegible]	[illegible]	[illegible]	[illegible]	[illegible]
[illegible]	Ballycastle,	[illegible]	[illegible]	[illegible]	[illegible]	[illegible]	[illegible]	[illegible]	[illegible]
[illegible]	Ballymahon,	[illegible]	[illegible]	[illegible]	[illegible]	[illegible]	[illegible]	[illegible]	[illegible]
[illegible]	Ballymena,	[illegible]	[illegible]	[illegible]	[illegible]	[illegible]	[illegible]	[illegible]	[illegible]
[illegible]	Ballymoney,	[illegible]	[illegible]	[illegible]	[illegible]	[illegible]	[illegible]	[illegible]	[illegible]
[illegible]	Ballyshannon,	[illegible]	[illegible]	[illegible]	[illegible]	[illegible]	[illegible]	[illegible]	[illegible]
[illegible]	Ballyvaghan,	[illegible]	[illegible]	[illegible]	[illegible]	[illegible]	[illegible]	[illegible]	[illegible]
[illegible]	Balrothery,	[illegible]	[illegible]	[illegible]	[illegible]	[illegible]	[illegible]	[illegible]	[illegible]
[illegible]	Baltinglass,	[illegible]	[illegible]	[illegible]	[illegible]	[illegible]	[illegible]	[illegible]	[illegible]
[illegible]	Banbridge,	[illegible]	[illegible]	[illegible]	[illegible]	[illegible]	[illegible]	[illegible]	[illegible]
[illegible]	Bandon,	[illegible]	[illegible]	[illegible]	[illegible]	[illegible]	[illegible]	[illegible]	[illegible]
[illegible]	Bantry,	[illegible]	[illegible]	[illegible]	[illegible]	[illegible]	[illegible]	[illegible]	[illegible]
[illegible]	Bawnboy,	[illegible]	[illegible]	[illegible]	[illegible]	[illegible]	[illegible]	[illegible]	[illegible]
[illegible]	Belfast,	[illegible]	[illegible]	[illegible]	[illegible]	[illegible]	[illegible]	[illegible]	[illegible]
[illegible]	Belmullet,	[illegible]	[illegible]	[illegible]	[illegible]	[illegible]	[illegible]	[illegible]	[illegible]
[illegible]	Borrisokane,	[illegible]	[illegible]	[illegible]	[illegible]	[illegible]	[illegible]	[illegible]	[illegible]
[illegible]	Boyle,	[illegible]	[illegible]	[illegible]	[illegible]	[illegible]	[illegible]	[illegible]	[illegible]
[illegible]	Cahersiveen,	[illegible]	[illegible]	[illegible]	[illegible]	[illegible]	[illegible]	[illegible]	[illegible]
[illegible]	Callan,	[illegible]	[illegible]	[illegible]	[illegible]	[illegible]	[illegible]	[illegible]	[illegible]
[illegible]	Carlow,	[illegible]	[illegible]	[illegible]	[illegible]	[illegible]	[illegible]	[illegible]	[illegible]
[illegible]	Carrickmacross,	[illegible]	[illegible]	[illegible]	[illegible]	[illegible]	[illegible]	[illegible]	[illegible]
[illegible]	Carrick-on-Shannon,	[illegible]	[illegible]	[illegible]	[illegible]	[illegible]	[illegible]	[illegible]	[illegible]
[illegible]	Carrick-on-Suir,	[illegible]	[illegible]	[illegible]	[illegible]	[illegible]	[illegible]	[illegible]	[illegible]
[illegible]	Cashel,	[illegible]	[illegible]	[illegible]	[illegible]	[illegible]	[illegible]	[illegible]	[illegible]
[illegible]	Castlebar,	[illegible]	[illegible]	[illegible]	[illegible]	[illegible]	[illegible]	[illegible]	[illegible]
[illegible]	Castleblayney,	[illegible]	[illegible]	[illegible]	[illegible]	[illegible]	[illegible]	[illegible]	[illegible]
[illegible]	Castlederg,	[illegible]	[illegible]	[illegible]	[illegible]	[illegible]	[illegible]	[illegible]	[illegible]
[illegible]	Castlerea,	[illegible]	[illegible]	[illegible]	[illegible]	[illegible]	[illegible]	[illegible]	[illegible]
[illegible]	Castlereagh,	[illegible]	[illegible]	[illegible]	[illegible]	[illegible]	[illegible]	[illegible]	[illegible]
[illegible]	Castletown,	[illegible]	[illegible]	[illegible]	[illegible]	[illegible]	[illegible]	[illegible]	[illegible]
[illegible]	Cavan,	[illegible]	[illegible]	[illegible]	[illegible]	[illegible]	[illegible]	[illegible]	[illegible]
[illegible]	Celbridge,	[illegible]	[illegible]	[illegible]	[illegible]	[illegible]	[illegible]	[illegible]	[illegible]
[illegible]	Claremorris,	[illegible]	[illegible]	[illegible]	[illegible]	[illegible]	[illegible]	[illegible]	[illegible]
[illegible]	Clifden,	[illegible]	[illegible]	[illegible]	[illegible]	[illegible]	[illegible]	[illegible]	[illegible]
[illegible]	Clogheen,	[illegible]	[illegible]	[illegible]	[illegible]	[illegible]	[illegible]	[illegible]	[illegible]
[illegible]	Clogher,	[illegible]	[illegible]	[illegible]	[illegible]	[illegible]	[illegible]	[illegible]	[illegible]
[illegible]	Clonakilty,	[illegible]	[illegible]	[illegible]	[illegible]	[illegible]	[illegible]	[illegible]	[illegible]
[illegible]	Clones,	[illegible]	[illegible]	[illegible]	[illegible]	[illegible]	[illegible]	[illegible]	[illegible]
[illegible]	Clonmel,	[illegible]	[illegible]	[illegible]	[illegible]	[illegible]	[illegible]	[illegible]	[illegible]
[illegible]	Coleraine,	[illegible]	[illegible]	[illegible]	[illegible]	[illegible]	[illegible]	[illegible]	[illegible]
[illegible]	Cookstown,	[illegible]	[illegible]	[illegible]	[illegible]	[illegible]	[illegible]	[illegible]	[illegible]
[illegible]	Cootehill,	[illegible]	[illegible]	[illegible]	[illegible]	[illegible]	[illegible]	[illegible]	[illegible]
[illegible]	Cork,	[illegible]	[illegible]	[illegible]	[illegible]	[illegible]	[illegible]	[illegible]	[illegible]
[illegible]	Corofin,	[illegible]	[illegible]	[illegible]	[illegible]	[illegible]	[illegible]	[illegible]	[illegible]

MARRIAGES, BIRTHS, AND DEATHS, REGISTERED IN THE YEAR 1891.

SUPERINTENDENT REGISTRARS' DISTRICTS OR POOR LAW UNIONS, ARRANGED ALPHABETICALLY—*con.*

Number or Position of Union in preceding Abstract.	Superintendent Registrars' Districts or Poor Law Unions.	Area in Statute Acres.	Population 1891.	TOTAL. Marriages.	TOTAL. Births.	TOTAL. Deaths.	BIRTHS. Legitimate Births. Males.	BIRTHS. Legitimate Births. Females.	BIRTHS. Illegitimate Births. Males.	BIRTHS. Illegitimate Births. Females.	DEATHS. Males.	DEATHS. Females.	Excess of Births over Deaths.
[illegible]	Corofin,	[illegible]	[illegible]	[illegible]	[illegible]	[illegible]	[illegible]	[illegible]	[illegible]	[illegible]	[illegible]	[illegible]	[illegible]
[illegible]	Croom,	[illegible]	[illegible]	[illegible]	[illegible]	[illegible]	[illegible]	[illegible]	[illegible]	[illegible]	[illegible]	[illegible]	[illegible]
[illegible]	Dingle,	[illegible]	[illegible]	[illegible]	[illegible]	[illegible]	[illegible]	[illegible]	[illegible]	[illegible]	[illegible]	[illegible]	[illegible]
[illegible]	Donegal,	[illegible]	[illegible]	[illegible]	[illegible]	[illegible]	[illegible]	[illegible]	[illegible]	[illegible]	[illegible]	[illegible]	[illegible]
[illegible]	Downpatrick,	[illegible]	[illegible]	[illegible]	[illegible]	[illegible]	[illegible]	[illegible]	[illegible]	[illegible]	[illegible]	[illegible]	[illegible]
[illegible]	Drogheda,	[illegible]	[illegible]	[illegible]	[illegible]	[illegible]	[illegible]	[illegible]	[illegible]	[illegible]	[illegible]	[illegible]	[illegible]
[illegible]	Dromore West,	[illegible]	[illegible]	[illegible]	[illegible]	[illegible]	[illegible]	[illegible]	[illegible]	[illegible]	[illegible]	[illegible]	[illegible]
[illegible]	Dublin, North,	[illegible]	[illegible]	[illegible]	[illegible]	[illegible]	[illegible]	[illegible]	[illegible]	[illegible]	[illegible]	[illegible]	[illegible]
[illegible]	Dublin, South,	[illegible]	[illegible]	[illegible]	[illegible]	[illegible]	[illegible]	[illegible]	[illegible]	[illegible]	[illegible]	[illegible]	[illegible]
[illegible]	Dundalk,	[illegible]	[illegible]	[illegible]	[illegible]	[illegible]	[illegible]	[illegible]	[illegible]	[illegible]	[illegible]	[illegible]	[illegible]
[illegible]	Dunfanaghy,	[illegible]	[illegible]	[illegible]	[illegible]	[illegible]	[illegible]	[illegible]	[illegible]	[illegible]	[illegible]	[illegible]	[illegible]
[illegible]	Dungannon,	[illegible]	[illegible]	[illegible]	[illegible]	[illegible]	[illegible]	[illegible]	[illegible]	[illegible]	[illegible]	[illegible]	[illegible]
[illegible]	Dungarvan,	[illegible]	[illegible]	[illegible]	[illegible]	[illegible]	[illegible]	[illegible]	[illegible]	[illegible]	[illegible]	[illegible]	[illegible]
[illegible]	Dunmanway,	[illegible]	[illegible]	[illegible]	[illegible]	[illegible]	[illegible]	[illegible]	[illegible]	[illegible]	[illegible]	[illegible]	[illegible]
[illegible]	Dunshaughlin,	[illegible]	[illegible]	[illegible]	[illegible]	[illegible]	[illegible]	[illegible]	[illegible]	[illegible]	[illegible]	[illegible]	[illegible]
[illegible]	Edenderry,	[illegible]	[illegible]	[illegible]	[illegible]	[illegible]	[illegible]	[illegible]	[illegible]	[illegible]	[illegible]	[illegible]	[illegible]
[illegible]	Ennis,	[illegible]	[illegible]	[illegible]	[illegible]	[illegible]	[illegible]	[illegible]	[illegible]	[illegible]	[illegible]	[illegible]	[illegible]
[illegible]	Enniscorthy,	[illegible]	[illegible]	[illegible]	[illegible]	[illegible]	[illegible]	[illegible]	[illegible]	[illegible]	[illegible]	[illegible]	[illegible]
[illegible]	Enniskillen,	[illegible]	[illegible]	[illegible]	[illegible]	[illegible]	[illegible]	[illegible]	[illegible]	[illegible]	[illegible]	[illegible]	[illegible]
[illegible]	Ennistymon,	[illegible]	[illegible]	[illegible]	[illegible]	[illegible]	[illegible]	[illegible]	[illegible]	[illegible]	[illegible]	[illegible]	[illegible]
[illegible]	Fermoy,	[illegible]	[illegible]	[illegible]	[illegible]	[illegible]	[illegible]	[illegible]	[illegible]	[illegible]	[illegible]	[illegible]	[illegible]
[illegible]	Galway,	[illegible]	[illegible]	[illegible]	[illegible]	[illegible]	[illegible]	[illegible]	[illegible]	[illegible]	[illegible]	[illegible]	[illegible]
[illegible]	Glennamaddy,	[illegible]	[illegible]	[illegible]	[illegible]	[illegible]	[illegible]	[illegible]	[illegible]	[illegible]	[illegible]	[illegible]	[illegible]
[illegible]	Glenties,	[illegible]	[illegible]	[illegible]	[illegible]	[illegible]	[illegible]	[illegible]	[illegible]	[illegible]	[illegible]	[illegible]	[illegible]
[illegible]	Glin,	[illegible]	[illegible]	[illegible]	[illegible]	[illegible]	[illegible]	[illegible]	[illegible]	[illegible]	[illegible]	[illegible]	[illegible]
[illegible]	Gorey,	[illegible]	[illegible]	[illegible]	[illegible]	[illegible]	[illegible]	[illegible]	[illegible]	[illegible]	[illegible]	[illegible]	[illegible]
[illegible]	Gort,	[illegible]	[illegible]	[illegible]	[illegible]	[illegible]	[illegible]	[illegible]	[illegible]	[illegible]	[illegible]	[illegible]	[illegible]
[illegible]	Granard,	[illegible]	[illegible]	[illegible]	[illegible]	[illegible]	[illegible]	[illegible]	[illegible]	[illegible]	[illegible]	[illegible]	[illegible]
[illegible]	Inishowen,	[illegible]	[illegible]	[illegible]	[illegible]	[illegible]	[illegible]	[illegible]	[illegible]	[illegible]	[illegible]	[illegible]	[illegible]
[illegible]	Kanturk,	[illegible]	[illegible]	[illegible]	[illegible]	[illegible]	[illegible]	[illegible]	[illegible]	[illegible]	[illegible]	[illegible]	[illegible]
[illegible]	Kells,	[illegible]	[illegible]	[illegible]	[illegible]	[illegible]	[illegible]	[illegible]	[illegible]	[illegible]	[illegible]	[illegible]	[illegible]
[illegible]	Kenmare,	[illegible]	[illegible]	[illegible]	[illegible]	[illegible]	[illegible]	[illegible]	[illegible]	[illegible]	[illegible]	[illegible]	[illegible]
[illegible]	Kilkeel,	[illegible]	[illegible]	[illegible]	[illegible]	[illegible]	[illegible]	[illegible]	[illegible]	[illegible]	[illegible]	[illegible]	[illegible]
[illegible]	Kilkenny,	[illegible]	[illegible]	[illegible]	[illegible]	[illegible]	[illegible]	[illegible]	[illegible]	[illegible]	[illegible]	[illegible]	[illegible]
[illegible]	Killadysert,	[illegible]	[illegible]	[illegible]	[illegible]	[illegible]	[illegible]	[illegible]	[illegible]	[illegible]	[illegible]	[illegible]	[illegible]
[illegible]	Killala,	[illegible]	[illegible]	[illegible]	[illegible]	[illegible]	[illegible]	[illegible]	[illegible]	[illegible]	[illegible]	[illegible]	[illegible]
[illegible]	Killarney,	[illegible]	[illegible]	[illegible]	[illegible]	[illegible]	[illegible]	[illegible]	[illegible]	[illegible]	[illegible]	[illegible]	[illegible]
[illegible]	Kilmacthomas,	[illegible]	[illegible]	[illegible]	[illegible]	[illegible]	[illegible]	[illegible]	[illegible]	[illegible]	[illegible]	[illegible]	[illegible]
[illegible]	Kilmallock,	[illegible]	[illegible]	[illegible]	[illegible]	[illegible]	[illegible]	[illegible]	[illegible]	[illegible]	[illegible]	[illegible]	[illegible]
[illegible]	Kilrush,	[illegible]	[illegible]	[illegible]	[illegible]	[illegible]	[illegible]	[illegible]	[illegible]	[illegible]	[illegible]	[illegible]	[illegible]
[illegible]	Kinsale,	[illegible]	[illegible]	[illegible]	[illegible]	[illegible]	[illegible]	[illegible]	[illegible]	[illegible]	[illegible]	[illegible]	[illegible]
[illegible]	Larne,	[illegible]	[illegible]	[illegible]	[illegible]	[illegible]	[illegible]	[illegible]	[illegible]	[illegible]	[illegible]	[illegible]	[illegible]
[illegible]	Letterkenny,	[illegible]	[illegible]	[illegible]	[illegible]	[illegible]	[illegible]	[illegible]	[illegible]	[illegible]	[illegible]	[illegible]	[illegible]
[illegible]	Limerick,	[illegible]	[illegible]	[illegible]	[illegible]	[illegible]	[illegible]	[illegible]	[illegible]	[illegible]	[illegible]	[illegible]	[illegible]
[illegible]	Lisburn,	[illegible]	[illegible]	[illegible]	[illegible]	[illegible]	[illegible]	[illegible]	[illegible]	[illegible]	[illegible]	[illegible]	[illegible]
[illegible]	Lismore,	[illegible]	[illegible]	[illegible]	[illegible]	[illegible]	[illegible]	[illegible]	[illegible]	[illegible]	[illegible]	[illegible]	[illegible]
[illegible]	Lisnaskea,	[illegible]	[illegible]	[illegible]	[illegible]	[illegible]	[illegible]	[illegible]	[illegible]	[illegible]	[illegible]	[illegible]	[illegible]
[illegible]	Listowel,	[illegible]	[illegible]	[illegible]	[illegible]	[illegible]	[illegible]	[illegible]	[illegible]	[illegible]	[illegible]	[illegible]	[illegible]
[illegible]	Longford,	[illegible]	[illegible]	[illegible]	[illegible]	[illegible]	[illegible]	[illegible]	[illegible]	[illegible]	[illegible]	[illegible]	[illegible]
[illegible]	Londonderry,	[illegible]	[illegible]	[illegible]	[illegible]	[illegible]	[illegible]	[illegible]	[illegible]	[illegible]	[illegible]	[illegible]	[illegible]

MARRIAGES, BIRTHS, AND DEATHS, REGISTERED IN THE YEAR 1891.

SUPERINTENDENT REGISTRARS' DISTRICTS OR POOR LAW UNIONS, ARRANGED ALPHABETICALLY—*con.*

Number of Members of Union in preceding Abstract.	SUPERINTENDENT REGISTRARS' DISTRICTS and POOR LAW UNIONS.	Area in Statute Acres.	Population, 1891.	TOTAL: Marriages	TOTAL: Births	TOTAL: Deaths	BIRTHS: Legitimate: Males	BIRTHS: Legitimate: Females	BIRTHS: Illegitimate: Males	BIRTHS: Illegitimate: Females	DEATHS: Males	DEATHS: Females	[illegible]
[illegible]	Longford,	[illegible]	[illegible]	[illegible]	[illegible]	[illegible]	[illegible]	[illegible]	[illegible]	[illegible]	[illegible]	[illegible]	[illegible]
[illegible]	Loughrea,	[illegible]	[illegible]	[illegible]	[illegible]	[illegible]	[illegible]	[illegible]	[illegible]	[illegible]	[illegible]	[illegible]	[illegible]
[illegible]	Lurgan,	[illegible]	[illegible]	[illegible]	[illegible]	[illegible]	[illegible]	[illegible]	[illegible]	[illegible]	[illegible]	[illegible]	[illegible]
[illegible]	Macroom,	[illegible]	[illegible]	[illegible]	[illegible]	[illegible]	[illegible]	[illegible]	[illegible]	[illegible]	[illegible]	[illegible]	[illegible]
[illegible]	Magherafelt,	[illegible]	[illegible]	[illegible]	[illegible]	[illegible]	[illegible]	[illegible]	[illegible]	[illegible]	[illegible]	[illegible]	[illegible]
[illegible]	Mallow,	[illegible]	[illegible]	[illegible]	[illegible]	[illegible]	[illegible]	[illegible]	[illegible]	[illegible]	[illegible]	[illegible]	[illegible]
[illegible]	Manorhamilton,	[illegible]	[illegible]	[illegible]	[illegible]	[illegible]	[illegible]	[illegible]	[illegible]	[illegible]	[illegible]	[illegible]	[illegible]
[illegible]	Midleton,	[illegible]	[illegible]	[illegible]	[illegible]	[illegible]	[illegible]	[illegible]	[illegible]	[illegible]	[illegible]	[illegible]	[illegible]
[illegible]	Milford,	[illegible]	[illegible]	[illegible]	[illegible]	[illegible]	[illegible]	[illegible]	[illegible]	[illegible]	[illegible]	[illegible]	[illegible]
[illegible]	Millstreet,	[illegible]	[illegible]	[illegible]	[illegible]	[illegible]	[illegible]	[illegible]	[illegible]	[illegible]	[illegible]	[illegible]	[illegible]
[illegible]	Mitchelstown,	[illegible]	[illegible]	[illegible]	[illegible]	[illegible]	[illegible]	[illegible]	[illegible]	[illegible]	[illegible]	[illegible]	[illegible]
[illegible]	Mohill,	[illegible]	[illegible]	[illegible]	[illegible]	[illegible]	[illegible]	[illegible]	[illegible]	[illegible]	[illegible]	[illegible]	[illegible]
[illegible]	Monaghan,	[illegible]	[illegible]	[illegible]	[illegible]	[illegible]	[illegible]	[illegible]	[illegible]	[illegible]	[illegible]	[illegible]	[illegible]
[illegible]	Mountbellew,	[illegible]	[illegible]	[illegible]	[illegible]	[illegible]	[illegible]	[illegible]	[illegible]	[illegible]	[illegible]	[illegible]	[illegible]
[illegible]	Mountmellick,	[illegible]	[illegible]	[illegible]	[illegible]	[illegible]	[illegible]	[illegible]	[illegible]	[illegible]	[illegible]	[illegible]	[illegible]
[illegible]	Mullingar,	[illegible]	[illegible]	[illegible]	[illegible]	[illegible]	[illegible]	[illegible]	[illegible]	[illegible]	[illegible]	[illegible]	[illegible]
[illegible]	Naas,	[illegible]	[illegible]	[illegible]	[illegible]	[illegible]	[illegible]	[illegible]	[illegible]	[illegible]	[illegible]	[illegible]	[illegible]
[illegible]	Navan,	[illegible]	[illegible]	[illegible]	[illegible]	[illegible]	[illegible]	[illegible]	[illegible]	[illegible]	[illegible]	[illegible]	[illegible]
[illegible]	Nenagh,	[illegible]	[illegible]	[illegible]	[illegible]	[illegible]	[illegible]	[illegible]	[illegible]	[illegible]	[illegible]	[illegible]	[illegible]
[illegible]	Newcastle,	[illegible]	[illegible]	[illegible]	[illegible]	[illegible]	[illegible]	[illegible]	[illegible]	[illegible]	[illegible]	[illegible]	[illegible]
[illegible]	New Ross,	[illegible]	[illegible]	[illegible]	[illegible]	[illegible]	[illegible]	[illegible]	[illegible]	[illegible]	[illegible]	[illegible]	[illegible]
[illegible]	Newry,	[illegible]	[illegible]	[illegible]	[illegible]	[illegible]	[illegible]	[illegible]	[illegible]	[illegible]	[illegible]	[illegible]	[illegible]
[illegible]	Newtownards,	[illegible]	[illegible]	[illegible]	[illegible]	[illegible]	[illegible]	[illegible]	[illegible]	[illegible]	[illegible]	[illegible]	[illegible]
[illegible]	Oldcastle,	[illegible]	[illegible]	[illegible]	[illegible]	[illegible]	[illegible]	[illegible]	[illegible]	[illegible]	[illegible]	[illegible]	[illegible]
[illegible]	Omagh,	[illegible]	[illegible]	[illegible]	[illegible]	[illegible]	[illegible]	[illegible]	[illegible]	[illegible]	[illegible]	[illegible]	[illegible]
[illegible]	Oughterard,	[illegible]	[illegible]	[illegible]	[illegible]	[illegible]	[illegible]	[illegible]	[illegible]	[illegible]	[illegible]	[illegible]	[illegible]
[illegible]	Parsonstown,	[illegible]	[illegible]	[illegible]	[illegible]	[illegible]	[illegible]	[illegible]	[illegible]	[illegible]	[illegible]	[illegible]	[illegible]
[illegible]	Portumna,	[illegible]	[illegible]	[illegible]	[illegible]	[illegible]	[illegible]	[illegible]	[illegible]	[illegible]	[illegible]	[illegible]	[illegible]
[illegible]	Rathdown,	[illegible]	[illegible]	[illegible]	[illegible]	[illegible]	[illegible]	[illegible]	[illegible]	[illegible]	[illegible]	[illegible]	[illegible]
[illegible]	Rathdrum,	[illegible]	[illegible]	[illegible]	[illegible]	[illegible]	[illegible]	[illegible]	[illegible]	[illegible]	[illegible]	[illegible]	[illegible]
[illegible]	Rathkeale,	[illegible]	[illegible]	[illegible]	[illegible]	[illegible]	[illegible]	[illegible]	[illegible]	[illegible]	[illegible]	[illegible]	[illegible]
[illegible]	Roscommon,	[illegible]	[illegible]	[illegible]	[illegible]	[illegible]	[illegible]	[illegible]	[illegible]	[illegible]	[illegible]	[illegible]	[illegible]
[illegible]	Roscrea,	[illegible]	[illegible]	[illegible]	[illegible]	[illegible]	[illegible]	[illegible]	[illegible]	[illegible]	[illegible]	[illegible]	[illegible]
[illegible]	Scariff,	[illegible]	[illegible]	[illegible]	[illegible]	[illegible]	[illegible]	[illegible]	[illegible]	[illegible]	[illegible]	[illegible]	[illegible]
[illegible]	Shillelagh,	[illegible]	[illegible]	[illegible]	[illegible]	[illegible]	[illegible]	[illegible]	[illegible]	[illegible]	[illegible]	[illegible]	[illegible]
[illegible]	Skibbereen,	[illegible]	[illegible]	[illegible]	[illegible]	[illegible]	[illegible]	[illegible]	[illegible]	[illegible]	[illegible]	[illegible]	[illegible]
[illegible]	Skull,	[illegible]	[illegible]	[illegible]	[illegible]	[illegible]	[illegible]	[illegible]	[illegible]	[illegible]	[illegible]	[illegible]	[illegible]
[illegible]	Sligo,	[illegible]	[illegible]	[illegible]	[illegible]	[illegible]	[illegible]	[illegible]	[illegible]	[illegible]	[illegible]	[illegible]	[illegible]
[illegible]	Strabane,	[illegible]	[illegible]	[illegible]	[illegible]	[illegible]	[illegible]	[illegible]	[illegible]	[illegible]	[illegible]	[illegible]	[illegible]
[illegible]	Stranorlar,	[illegible]	[illegible]	[illegible]	[illegible]	[illegible]	[illegible]	[illegible]	[illegible]	[illegible]	[illegible]	[illegible]	[illegible]
[illegible]	Strokestown,	[illegible]	[illegible]	[illegible]	[illegible]	[illegible]	[illegible]	[illegible]	[illegible]	[illegible]	[illegible]	[illegible]	[illegible]
[illegible]	Swineford,	[illegible]	[illegible]	[illegible]	[illegible]	[illegible]	[illegible]	[illegible]	[illegible]	[illegible]	[illegible]	[illegible]	[illegible]
[illegible]	Thomastown,	[illegible]	[illegible]	[illegible]	[illegible]	[illegible]	[illegible]	[illegible]	[illegible]	[illegible]	[illegible]	[illegible]	[illegible]
[illegible]	Thurles,	[illegible]	[illegible]	[illegible]	[illegible]	[illegible]	[illegible]	[illegible]	[illegible]	[illegible]	[illegible]	[illegible]	[illegible]
[illegible]	Tipperary,	[illegible]	[illegible]	[illegible]	[illegible]	[illegible]	[illegible]	[illegible]	[illegible]	[illegible]	[illegible]	[illegible]	[illegible]
[illegible]	Tobercurry,	[illegible]	[illegible]	[illegible]	[illegible]	[illegible]	[illegible]	[illegible]	[illegible]	[illegible]	[illegible]	[illegible]	[illegible]
[illegible]	Tralee,	[illegible]	[illegible]	[illegible]	[illegible]	[illegible]	[illegible]	[illegible]	[illegible]	[illegible]	[illegible]	[illegible]	[illegible]
[illegible]	Trim,	[illegible]	[illegible]	[illegible]	[illegible]	[illegible]	[illegible]	[illegible]	[illegible]	[illegible]	[illegible]	[illegible]	[illegible]
[illegible]	Tuam,	[illegible]	[illegible]	[illegible]	[illegible]	[illegible]	[illegible]	[illegible]	[illegible]	[illegible]	[illegible]	[illegible]	[illegible]
[illegible]	Tulla,	[illegible]	[illegible]	[illegible]	[illegible]	[illegible]	[illegible]	[illegible]	[illegible]	[illegible]	[illegible]	[illegible]	[illegible]
[illegible]	Tullamore,	[illegible]	[illegible]	[illegible]	[illegible]	[illegible]	[illegible]	[illegible]	[illegible]	[illegible]	[illegible]	[illegible]	[illegible]
[illegible]	Urlingford,	[illegible]	[illegible]	[illegible]	[illegible]	[illegible]	[illegible]	[illegible]	[illegible]	[illegible]	[illegible]	[illegible]	[illegible]
[illegible]	Waterford,	[illegible]	[illegible]	[illegible]	[illegible]	[illegible]	[illegible]	[illegible]	[illegible]	[illegible]	[illegible]	[illegible]	[illegible]
[illegible]	Westport,	[illegible]	[illegible]	[illegible]	[illegible]	[illegible]	[illegible]	[illegible]	[illegible]	[illegible]	[illegible]	[illegible]	[illegible]
[illegible]	Wexford,	[illegible]	[illegible]	[illegible]	[illegible]	[illegible]	[illegible]	[illegible]	[illegible]	[illegible]	[illegible]	[illegible]	[illegible]
[illegible]	Youghal,	[illegible]	[illegible]	[illegible]	[illegible]	[illegible]	[illegible]	[illegible]	[illegible]	[illegible]	[illegible]	[illegible]	[illegible]

BIRTHS AND DEATHS Registered in the Year 1881—Registrars' Districts, arranged by Counties and Superintendent Registrars' Districts.

For Abstract showing the Total Numbers for each of those Registrars' Districts which extend into more than one County, see page 24.

No.	Registrars' Districts.	Area in Statute Acres.	Population in 1881.	Total Births.	Total Deaths.	Births including Illegitimate Births: Males.	Births including Illegitimate Births: Females.	Illegitimate Births: Males.	Illegitimate Births: Females.	Deaths: Males.	Deaths: Females.	Excess of Births over Deaths.
	II.—PROVINCE OF [illegible].											
	[illegible] Co.											
	1. [illegible], S.R. District, part of.											
1	[illegible], part of,	2,[illegible]	[illegible]	[illegible]	[illegible]	[illegible]	[illegible]	.	.	3	6	.
2	[illegible], &c.,	11,[illegible]	3,[illegible]	[illegible]	[illegible]	[illegible]	[illegible]	.	.	15	[illegible]	11
	2. [illegible], part of.											
1	[illegible],	14,[illegible]	[illegible]	77	41	[illegible]	47	1	3	21	[illegible]	36
2	[illegible],	[illegible]	4,[illegible]	[illegible]	47	[illegible]	[illegible]	2	.	[illegible]	[illegible]	—[illegible]
3	[illegible], part of, W.,	[illegible]	[illegible]	[illegible]	[illegible]	[illegible]	[illegible]	1	7	[illegible]	[illegible]	—[illegible]
4	[illegible],	[illegible]	4,[illegible]	[illegible]	41	[illegible]	[illegible]	.	.	[illegible]	[illegible]	4
5	[illegible],	[illegible]	[illegible]	75	[illegible]	[illegible]	[illegible]	.	.	[illegible]	[illegible]	[illegible]
6	[illegible],	[illegible]	[illegible]	111	[illegible]	[illegible]	51	.	3	[illegible]	[illegible]	[illegible]
	3. [illegible], part of.											
1	[illegible], part of,	[illegible]	1,[illegible]	[illegible]	18	[illegible]	[illegible]	1	.	7	4	3
	4. New Ross, part of.											
1	[illegible],	[illegible]	[illegible]	76	73	[illegible]	[illegible]	.	.	[illegible]	[illegible]	3
	5. [illegible], part of.											
1	[illegible] and [illegible], part of,	4,[illegible]	[illegible]	73	93	[illegible]	[illegible]	.	.	[illegible]	[illegible]	—[illegible]
2	[illegible] & [illegible], &c.,	14,347	2,[illegible]	[illegible]	41	[illegible]	[illegible]	.	.	[illegible]	24	16
	[illegible] Co.											
	6. [illegible].											
1	[illegible],	[illegible]	[illegible]	[illegible]	[illegible]	[illegible]	[illegible]	.	3	[illegible]	37	[illegible]
2	[illegible], W.,	7,772	[illegible]	[illegible]	[illegible]	[illegible]	[illegible]	.	3	[illegible]	[illegible]	—[illegible]
3	[illegible],	16,544	1,[illegible]	[illegible]	21	19	[illegible]	.	.	11	[illegible]	7
4	[illegible],	[illegible]	[illegible]	[illegible]	[illegible]	[illegible]	[illegible]	.	.	[illegible]	[illegible]	13
5	[illegible],	[illegible]	[illegible]	[illegible]	[illegible]	[illegible]	[illegible]	.	.	[illegible]	[illegible]	11
6	[illegible],	[illegible]	[illegible]	[illegible]	[illegible]	[illegible]	[illegible]	.	1	[illegible]	[illegible]	6
	7. [illegible], part of.											
1	[illegible], part of,	[illegible]	2,[illegible]	[illegible]	[illegible]	47	[illegible]	.	.	14	[illegible]	43
2	[illegible],	17,[illegible]	[illegible]	[illegible]	[illegible]	[illegible]	11	.	.	[illegible]	15	—[illegible]
	8. Dublin, North.											
1	[illegible] & [illegible],	[illegible]	7,[illegible]	[illegible]	[illegible]	75	[illegible]	1	.	[illegible]	[illegible]	[illegible]
2	[illegible] and [illegible], No. 1,	[illegible]	4,[illegible]	[illegible]	[illegible]	[illegible]	47	1	.	[illegible]	43	3
3	” ” No. 2,	[illegible]	[illegible]	[illegible]	[illegible]	[illegible]	[illegible]	.	.	[illegible]	[illegible]	[illegible]
4	[illegible] & [illegible], No. 1,	[illegible]	[illegible]	[illegible]	[illegible]	[illegible]	[illegible]	1	.	[illegible]	[illegible]	[illegible]
5	” ” No. 2,	[illegible]	[illegible]	[illegible]	[illegible]	[illegible]	[illegible]	[illegible]	.	7	18	.
6	[illegible] and [illegible],	[illegible]	6,[illegible]	141	[illegible]	79	[illegible]	.	1	[illegible]	[illegible]	[illegible]
7	North City, No. 1, East,	1,[illegible]	16,[illegible]	[illegible]	[illegible]	[illegible]	[illegible]	.	.	[illegible]	[illegible]	177
8	” ” West,		[illegible]	[illegible]	[illegible]	[illegible]	[illegible]	.	1	611	[illegible]	—[illegible]
9	” No. 2,		[illegible]	1,[illegible]	[illegible]	[illegible]	[illegible]	[illegible]	[illegible]	[illegible]	[illegible]	1,[illegible]
10	” No. 3, W.,		25,[illegible]	[illegible]	1,[illegible]	[illegible]	[illegible]	[illegible]	15	[illegible]	[illegible]	—[illegible]
	9. Dublin, South.											
1	[illegible],	[illegible]	[illegible]	[illegible]	[illegible]	[illegible]	[illegible]	.	.	[illegible]	[illegible]	6
2	[illegible],	[illegible]	[illegible]	[illegible]	[illegible]	[illegible]	176	1	.	[illegible]	[illegible]	71
3	[illegible],	[illegible]	[illegible]	[illegible]	[illegible]	[illegible]	134	.	1	[illegible]	[illegible]	[illegible]
4	[illegible],	[illegible]	[illegible]	[illegible]	[illegible]	[illegible]	[illegible]	.	9	[illegible]	[illegible]	[illegible]
5	[illegible],	[illegible]	27,[illegible]	[illegible]	[illegible]	[illegible]	231	1	1	[illegible]	574	—[illegible]
6	South City, No. 1, W.,	1,[illegible]	33,[illegible]	[illegible]	1,[illegible]	[illegible]	[illegible]	[illegible]	[illegible]	[illegible]	[illegible]	—[illegible]
7	” No. 2,		16,[illegible]	[illegible]	[illegible]	[illegible]	211	.	1	193	[illegible]	[illegible]
8	” No. 3,		[illegible]	1,[illegible]	1,[illegible]	711	[illegible]	[illegible]	11	[illegible]	[illegible]	[illegible]
9	” No. 4,		[illegible]	1,[illegible]	[illegible]	[illegible]	[illegible]	[illegible]	[illegible]	[illegible]	[illegible]	817
10	[illegible],	23,[illegible]	[illegible]	[illegible]	[illegible]	[illegible]	[illegible]	.	.	[illegible]	19	[illegible]

[illegible]

BIRTHS AND DEATHS Registered in the Year 1891—Registrars' Districts, arranged by Counties and Superintendent Registrars' Districts—continued.

	Registrars' Districts.	Area in Statute Acres.	Population in 1881.	Total: Births.	Total: Deaths.	Births: Including Illegitimate Births: Males.	Births: Including Illegitimate Births: Females.	Illegitimate Births: Males.	Illegitimate Births: Females.	Deaths: Males.	Deaths: Females.
	I.—Province of Leinster—con.										
	10. Dunshaughlin, part of.										
1	Garristown, part of,	9,7[illegible]	[illegible]	15	22	8	7	.	.	13	6
	11. Rathdown, part of.										
1	Blackrock & Stillorgan, No. 1,	[illegible]	7,[illegible]	[illegible]	[illegible]	[illegible]	71	.	.	[illegible]	[illegible]
2	" No. 2,	[illegible]	[illegible]	79	[illegible]	[illegible]	[illegible]	.	.	[illegible]	[illegible]
3	Bray and Rathmichael, No. 1, part of, W.,	4,[illegible]	[illegible]	77	11[illegible]	[illegible]	[illegible]	[illegible]	4	[illegible]	[illegible]
4	" No. 2, part of,		1,[illegible]	[illegible]	[illegible]	[illegible]	[illegible]	1	.	[illegible]	[illegible]
5	Dundrum & Glencullen, No. 1,	[illegible]	4,4[illegible]	[illegible]	[illegible]	[illegible]	[illegible]	.	.	[illegible]	[illegible]
6	" No. 2,	7,[illegible]	1,[illegible]	47	[illegible]	[illegible]	[illegible]	.	1	[illegible]	[illegible]
7	Killiney,	4,[illegible]	[illegible]	1[illegible]	[illegible]	[illegible]	[illegible]	.	.	[illegible]	[illegible]
8	Kingstown, No. 1,	1,[illegible]	[illegible]	[illegible]	17[illegible]	[illegible]	11[illegible]	1	.	[illegible]	[illegible]
9	" No. 2,		[illegible]	[illegible]	1[illegible]	[illegible]	[illegible]	[illegible]	1	[illegible]	[illegible]
	Kildare Co.										
	12. Athy, part of.										
1	Athy, W.,	[illegible]	[illegible]	[illegible]	1[illegible]	[illegible]	[illegible]	6	[illegible]	[illegible]	[illegible]
2	Castledermot,	[illegible]	1,[illegible]	46	[illegible]	[illegible]	18	[illegible]	.	17	11
3	Fontstown,	[illegible]	[illegible]	[illegible]	[illegible]	[illegible]	[illegible]	[illegible]	.	[illegible]	15
4	[illegible],	[illegible]	[illegible]	12[illegible]	10[illegible]	[illegible]	64	1	[illegible]	47	65
	13. Baltinglass, part of.										
1	[illegible], part of,	[illegible]	1,[illegible]	[illegible]	[illegible]	[illegible]	[illegible]	1	3	11	11
2	[illegible], do.,	[illegible]	[illegible]	[illegible]	[illegible]	3	[illegible]	2	.	7	[illegible]
	14. Celbridge, part of.										
1	Celbridge, W.,	[illegible]	[illegible]	71	[illegible]	[illegible]	[illegible]	[illegible]	[illegible]	[illegible]	[illegible]
2	Kilcock,	[illegible]	[illegible]	79	[illegible]	[illegible]	34	1	.	[illegible]	[illegible]
3	Leixlip, part of,	2,[illegible]	1,[illegible]	[illegible]	14	[illegible]	11	.	.	[illegible]	[illegible]
4	Maynooth, do.,	[illegible]	1,[illegible]	[illegible]	[illegible]	11	14	.	.	[illegible]	[illegible]
	15. Edenderry, part of.										
1	Carbury,	[illegible]	[illegible]	[illegible]	[illegible]	[illegible]	17	1	.	[illegible]	[illegible]
2	Johnstown,	10,[illegible]	1,[illegible]	[illegible]	[illegible]	[illegible]	[illegible]	.	.	[illegible]	[illegible]
3	[illegible], part of,	10,[illegible]	1,[illegible]	[illegible]	[illegible]	[illegible]	[illegible]	.	[illegible]	[illegible]	[illegible]
	16. Naas, part of.										
1	Blessington & Ballymore, pt. of,	[illegible]	1,[illegible]	[illegible]	[illegible]	[illegible]	[illegible]	.	[illegible]	[illegible]	1[illegible]
2	Clane and Timahoe, North,	[illegible]	[illegible]	[illegible]	[illegible]	[illegible]	4[illegible]	.	2	[illegible]	[illegible]
3	Kilcullen,	[illegible]	[illegible]	1[illegible]	[illegible]	[illegible]	[illegible]	1	.	[illegible]	[illegible]
4	Kildare,	[illegible]	[illegible]	[illegible]	[illegible]	[illegible]	[illegible]	1	[illegible]	[illegible]	[illegible]
5	Naas and Curragh, W.,	[illegible]	[illegible]	1[illegible]	1[illegible]	[illegible]	[illegible]	[illegible]	[illegible]	[illegible]	[illegible]
6	Newbridge,	16,27[illegible]	10,[illegible]	[illegible]	[illegible]	[illegible]	[illegible]	[illegible]	.	71	[illegible]
7	Rathmore,	[illegible]	1,[illegible]	[illegible]	[illegible]	[illegible]	4	.	.	1[illegible]	[illegible]
8	Robertstown and Kilmeague,	[illegible]	[illegible]	[illegible]	[illegible]	[illegible]	[illegible]	1	1	[illegible]	[illegible]
	Kilkenny Co.										
	17. Callan, part of.										
1	Callan, W.,	[illegible]	[illegible]	[illegible]	1[illegible]	47	[illegible]	[illegible]	[illegible]	[illegible]	[illegible]
2	[illegible],	[illegible]	[illegible]	[illegible]	[illegible]	[illegible]	[illegible]	1	[illegible]	[illegible]	[illegible]
	18. Carrick-on-Suir, part of.										
1	Piltown,	[illegible]	[illegible]	[illegible]	[illegible]	[illegible]	47	[illegible]	[illegible]	[illegible]	[illegible]
	19. Castlecomer.										
1	Ballyragget,	[illegible]	[illegible]	[illegible]	[illegible]	[illegible]	[illegible]	.	.	[illegible]	[illegible]
2	Castlecomer, W.,	[illegible]	[illegible]	[illegible]	[illegible]	[illegible]	[illegible]	7	2	[illegible]	[illegible]

BIRTHS AND DEATHS Registered in the Year 1891—REGISTRARS' DISTRICTS, arranged by COUNTIES and SUPERINTENDENT REGISTRARS' DISTRICTS—*continued.*

No.	REGISTRARS' DISTRICTS.	Area in Statute Acres.	Population in 1881.	TOTAL. BIRTHS.	TOTAL. DEATHS.	BIRTHS. Legitimate. Males.	BIRTHS. Legitimate. Females.	BIRTHS. Illegitimate. Males.	BIRTHS. Illegitimate. Females.	DEATHS. Males.	DEATHS. Females.	[illegible]
	I.—PROVINCE OF LEINSTER—*con.*											
	70. KILKENNY.											
1	[illegible],	[illegible]	[illegible]	[illegible]	41	[illegible]	71	1	-	[illegible]	[illegible]	
2	Gowran,	[illegible]	[illegible]	[illegible]	[illegible]	[illegible]	[illegible]	1	-	[illegible]	41	
3	Kilkenny, No. 1, W.,	[illegible]	[illegible]	[illegible]	[illegible]	[illegible]	[illegible]	[illegible]	1	111	[illegible]	
4	" 2,	[illegible]	[illegible]	[illegible]	[illegible]	[illegible]	[illegible]	1	1	[illegible]	[illegible]	
5	[illegible],	[illegible]	[illegible]	[illegible]	[illegible]	[illegible]	[illegible]	-	-	[illegible]	[illegible]	
6	Tullaroan,	[illegible]	[illegible]	[illegible]	[illegible]	[illegible]	[illegible]	1	-	[illegible]	[illegible]	
	71. NEW ROSS, part of.											
1	[illegible],	[illegible]	[illegible]	[illegible]	[illegible]	[illegible]	37	-	-	[illegible]	[illegible]	
	72. THOMASTOWN.											
1	[illegible],	[illegible]	[illegible]	[illegible]	[illegible]	[illegible]	41	[illegible]	-	[illegible]	[illegible]	
2	Inistioge,	[illegible]	[illegible]	[illegible]	[illegible]	[illegible]	[illegible]	[illegible]	1	[illegible]	[illegible]	
3	Knocktopher,	[illegible]	[illegible]	[illegible]	[illegible]	[illegible]	[illegible]	1	-	[illegible]	[illegible]	
4	Thomastown, W.	[illegible]	[illegible]	[illegible]	74	[illegible]	47	[illegible]	1	[illegible]	[illegible]	
	73. URLINGFORD, part of.											
1	[illegible],	[illegible]	[illegible]	[illegible]	[illegible]	[illegible]	[illegible]	1	-	[illegible]	11	
2	Johnstown, part of,	[illegible]	[illegible]	[illegible]	[illegible]	[illegible]	[illegible]	1	1	[illegible]	[illegible]	
3	[illegible], part of, W.,	[illegible]	[illegible]	[illegible]	[illegible]	[illegible]	[illegible]	1	[illegible]	[illegible]	[illegible]	
	74. WATERFORD, part of.											
1	[illegible],	[illegible]	[illegible]	[illegible]	77	[illegible]	47	1	-	[illegible]	[illegible]	
2	[illegible],	[illegible]	[illegible]	[illegible]	[illegible]	[illegible]	[illegible]	-	-	[illegible]	[illegible]	
	King's Co.											
	75. EDENDERRY, part of.											
1	Edenderry, W.	[illegible]	[illegible]	[illegible]	[illegible]	[illegible]	[illegible]	-	-	[illegible]	[illegible]	
2	Rathangan, part of,	[illegible]	[illegible]	14	[illegible]	[illegible]	[illegible]	-	-	[illegible]	[illegible]	
3	Rhode,	[illegible]	[illegible]	[illegible]	[illegible]	[illegible]	[illegible]	1	-	[illegible]	[illegible]	
	76. MOUNTMELLICK, part of.											
1	[illegible], part of,	[illegible]	[illegible]	[illegible]	[illegible]	[illegible]	[illegible]	-	[illegible]	[illegible]	[illegible]	
	77. PARSONSTOWN, part of.											
1	Banagher,	[illegible]	[illegible]	[illegible]	[illegible]	[illegible]	[illegible]	[illegible]	-	[illegible]	[illegible]	
2	Ferbane,	[illegible]	[illegible]	[illegible]	[illegible]	[illegible]	[illegible]	-	-	[illegible]	[illegible]	
3	Frankford,	[illegible]	[illegible]	[illegible]	[illegible]	[illegible]	[illegible]	-	-	[illegible]	[illegible]	
4	[illegible],	[illegible]	[illegible]	[illegible]	[illegible]	[illegible]	[illegible]	-	-	[illegible]	[illegible]	
5	Kinnitty,	[illegible]	[illegible]	[illegible]	[illegible]	[illegible]	[illegible]	[illegible]	-	[illegible]	[illegible]	
6	Parsonstown, W.	[illegible]	[illegible]	[illegible]	[illegible]	[illegible]	[illegible]	[illegible]	[illegible]	[illegible]	[illegible]	
	78. ROSCREA, part of.											
1	Roscrea, No. 1, part of,	[illegible]	[illegible]	[illegible]	[illegible]	[illegible]	[illegible]	-	-	[illegible]	[illegible]	
2	" 2,	[illegible]	[illegible]	[illegible]	[illegible]	[illegible]	11	-	-	[illegible]	[illegible]	
3	Shinrone,	[illegible]	[illegible]	[illegible]	[illegible]	[illegible]	[illegible]	1	-	[illegible]	[illegible]	
	79. TULLAMORE, part of.											
1	Clara,	[illegible]	[illegible]	[illegible]	[illegible]	[illegible]	[illegible]	-	-	[illegible]	[illegible]	
2	Kilbeggan, part of,	[illegible]	[illegible]	[illegible]	[illegible]	[illegible]	[illegible]	-	-	[illegible]	[illegible]	
3	[illegible],	[illegible]	[illegible]	[illegible]	[illegible]	[illegible]	[illegible]	-	1	[illegible]	[illegible]	
4	Philipstown,	[illegible]	[illegible]	[illegible]	[illegible]	[illegible]	[illegible]	-	-	[illegible]	[illegible]	
5	Tullamore, W.	[illegible]	[illegible]	[illegible]	[illegible]	[illegible]	[illegible]	[illegible]	-	[illegible]	[illegible]	

	I.—PROVINCE OF ARMAGH.—con.						
	Longford Co.						
	25. Rathcline, part of.						
1	Abbeyshrule,	10,120	1,134	60	46	40	38
2	Ballymahon, W.	13,364	3,109	133	80	38	68
	26. Granard, part of.						
1	Ballinalee,	22,104	4,420	86	36	34	40
2	Granard, W.,	30,433	8,045	130	170	64	56
3	Ardagh, part of,	14,800	3,723	70	36	30	40
4	[illegible] do.,	13,869	2,063	44	41	30	16
	27. Longford.						
1	Drumlish,	33,412	9,876	211	145	104	107
2	Killashee,	10,900	4,045	37	40	82	47
3	Longford, W.,	34,300	10,836	227	101	116	111
	Louth Co., and Co. of Town of Drogheda.						
	28. Ardee, part of.						
1	Ardee, W.,	37,320	5,833	114	127	81	43
2	Castlebellingham,	14,740	2,800	40	30	63	30
3	Collon, part of,	6,969	1,184	18	21	9	7
4	Dunleer,	16,779	3,102	43	40	34	37
	29. Drogheda, part of.						
1	Drogheda, No. 1,	6,215	6,351	133	87	46	38
2	" 2,	4,841	6,637	159	111	78	67
3	Mornington, part of,	11,730	2,803	54	34	19	16
4	St. Mary's, do.,	134	2,164	31	36	43	30
5	Termonfeckin,	20,225	4,436	78	70	40	60
	30. Dundalk, part of.						
1	Ballymascanlon, part of,	13,680	3,477	63	71	30	36
2	Castletown,	19,625	6,147	155	100	75	43
3	Dromiskin,	20,107	3,811	41	43	30	71
4	Dundalk, W.,	17,278	17,275	425	547	210	218
5	Louth, part of,	16,874	3,890	78	62	47	44
6	Ravensdale,	17,958	3,004	64	59	40	23
	Meath Co.						
	31. Ardee, part of.						
1	Collon, part of,	6,480	783	10	8	4	4
2	Drumconrath,	23,911	3,037	64	31	36	23
	32. Castletown, part of.						
1	Kilmainhamwood, part of,	7,300	673	8	6	4	6
	33. Drogheda, part of.						
1	Duleek,	30,234	2,706	37	54	30	30
2	Mornington, part of,	4,882	330	6	6	-	5
3	St. Mary's, part of, W.,	9,477	3,478	86	140	35	30
4	[illegible],	31,434	2,467	41	41	23	23

BIRTHS AND DEATHS Registered in the Year 1891—Registrars' Districts, arranged by Counties and Superintendent Registrars' Districts—*continued.*

Registrars' Districts	Area in Statute Acres	Population in 1891	Total: Births	Total: Deaths	Births (including Illegitimate Births): Males	Births (including Illegitimate Births): Females	Illegitimate Births: Males	Illegitimate Births: Females	Deaths: Males	Deaths: Females
I.—PROVINCE OF LEINSTER—con.										
40. Edenderry, part of.										
1 Ballylaggan,	23,846	2,163	43	34	14	21	.	.	23	19
41. Kells, part of.										
1 Kells, W.,	[illegible]	[illegible]	126	104	[illegible]	46	8	9	37	67
2 Kilskeer,	[illegible]	[illegible]	61	43	[illegible]	26	.	.	26	17
3 Moynalty, part of,	[illegible]	[illegible]	[illegible]	[illegible]	[illegible]	[illegible]	1	1	17	[illegible]
4 Mullagh,	[illegible]	[illegible]	43	33	[illegible]	18	.	1	[illegible]	21
42. Navan.										
1 Castletown,	[illegible]	[illegible]	[illegible]	54	[illegible]	[illegible]	.	.	[illegible]	25
2 Navan, W.,	[illegible]	[illegible]	[illegible]	210	107	[illegible]	[illegible]	.	107	103
3 Painestown,	27,316	[illegible]	[illegible]	43	37	[illegible]	1	1	19	[illegible]
43. Oldcastle, part of.										
1 Crossakeel,	[illegible]	[illegible]	[illegible]	[illegible]	14	[illegible]	.	.	15	15
2 Oldcastle, W.,	[illegible]	[illegible]	71	70	35	[illegible]	1	1	[illegible]	[illegible]
44. Trim.										
1 Athboy,	[illegible]	[illegible]	64	[illegible]	[illegible]	[illegible]	1	1	45	[illegible]
2 Ballivor,	[illegible]	[illegible]	[illegible]	[illegible]	[illegible]	[illegible]	.	.	24	[illegible]
3 Kilmessan,	[illegible]	[illegible]	64	64	35	[illegible]	1	.	[illegible]	[illegible]
4 Trim, W.,	[illegible]	4,323	[illegible]	94	[illegible]	41	.	1	37	57
Queen's Co.										
45. Abbeyleix.										
1 Abbeyleix, W.,	[illegible]	[illegible]	[illegible]	[illegible]	[illegible]	44	[illegible]	4	[illegible]	47
2 Ballinakill,	[illegible]	[illegible]	[illegible]	[illegible]	70	[illegible]	1	.	[illegible]	[illegible]
3 Ballyroan,	[illegible]	[illegible]	64	[illegible]	35	[illegible]	.	.	[illegible]	[illegible]
4 Castletown,	[illegible]	2,460	41	[illegible]	[illegible]	[illegible]	.	.	14	[illegible]
5 Durrow,	[illegible]	[illegible]	[illegible]	47	33	31	.	1	22	[illegible]
6 Rathdowney,	[illegible]	[illegible]	[illegible]	[illegible]	65	[illegible]	1	.	19	[illegible]
46. Athy, part of.										
1 Ballylynan,	[illegible]	[illegible]	44	37	[illegible]	[illegible]	1	.	[illegible]	61
2 Stradbally,	[illegible]	[illegible]	14	[illegible]	[illegible]	[illegible]	.	.	24	14
47. Carlow, part of.										
1 Ballickmoyler and Newtown,	[illegible]	[illegible]	105	81	[illegible]	[illegible]	.	.	[illegible]	47
2 Carlow, part of,	7,464	[illegible]	65	[illegible]	17	[illegible]	.	.	14	15
48. Mountmellick, part of.										
1 Clonaslee,	[illegible]	[illegible]	46	[illegible]	[illegible]	[illegible]	.	.	[illegible]	[illegible]
2 Clonygowan, part of,	[illegible]	[illegible]	[illegible]	19	[illegible]	[illegible]	.	.	9	[illegible]
3 Coolrain,	[illegible]	[illegible]	[illegible]	24	15	[illegible]	.	.	[illegible]	15
4 Kess,	[illegible]	[illegible]	[illegible]	[illegible]	[illegible]	[illegible]	.	3	[illegible]	[illegible]
5 Maryborough,	[illegible]	[illegible]	112	67	[illegible]	[illegible]	1	.	[illegible]	45
6 Mountmellick, W.,	[illegible]	[illegible]	130	133	73	57	[illegible]	6	77	55
7 Mountrath,	[illegible]	[illegible]	[illegible]	[illegible]	48	[illegible]	[illegible]	1	[illegible]	[illegible]
49. Roscrea, part of.										
1 Borris-in-Ossory,	[illegible]	[illegible]	[illegible]	48	[illegible]	[illegible]	1	.	[illegible]	[illegible]
2 Roscrea, No. 2, part of,	[illegible]	[illegible]	[illegible]	5	4	5	.	.	4	1
50. Tullamore, part of.										
1 [illegible], part of,	[illegible]	[illegible]	[illegible]	[illegible]	[illegible]	[illegible]	.	.	1	[illegible]

	I.—PROVINCE OF LEINSTER—con.						
	Westmeath Co.						
	31. Athlone, part of.						
1	Athlone, No. 1, E., .	10,177	4,722	[illegible]	[illegible]	35	[illegible]
2	[illegible], . .	[illegible]	[illegible]	15	33	[illegible]	67
3	[illegible] . .	[illegible]	[illegible]	120	[illegible]	[illegible]	[illegible]
	32. Ballymahon, part of.						
1	Ballymore, .	[illegible]	[illegible]	73	[illegible]	[illegible]	27
	33. Delvin.						
1	Castlepollard, . .	[illegible]	[illegible]	73	47	[illegible]	[illegible]
2	Clonmellon, . .	[illegible]	[illegible]	67	47	[illegible]	[illegible]
3	Delvin, W., . .	[illegible]	[illegible]	[illegible]	34	[illegible]	[illegible]
	34. Granard, part of.						
1	Coole, . . .	11,018	1,244	[illegible]	11	14	3
2	Finnea, part of, .	8,016	1,220	[illegible]	14	6	5
3	Street, do. .	[illegible]	1,[illegible]	[illegible]	[illegible]	10	22
	35. Mullingar.						
1	Ballynacargy, .	[illegible]	4,[illegible]	73	[illegible]	[illegible]	[illegible]
2	Castletown Geoghegan, .	[illegible]	[illegible]	[illegible]	[illegible]	[illegible]	[illegible]
3	Killucan, . .	[illegible]	[illegible]	57	[illegible]	[illegible]	[illegible]
4	[illegible], . .	[illegible]	[illegible]	70	[illegible]	[illegible]	22
5	Mullingar, W., .	[illegible]	[illegible]	[illegible]	[illegible]	[illegible]	[illegible]
6	Multyfarnham, .	22,[illegible]	[illegible]	[illegible]	[illegible]	27	31
7	Tyrrellspass, . .	[illegible]	[illegible]	77	73	[illegible]	34
	36. Tullamore, part of.						
1	Kilbeggan, part of, .	[illegible]	[illegible]	[illegible]	41	[illegible]	67
	Wexford Co.						
	37. Enniscorthy, part of.						
1	Clonroche, . .	[illegible]	4,[illegible]	[illegible]	[illegible]	[illegible]	[illegible]
2	Enniscorthy, No. 1, .	[illegible]	[illegible]	123	[illegible]	77	[illegible]
3	" " 2, U., .	[illegible]	[illegible]	[illegible]	146	[illegible]	[illegible]
4	Ferns, . .	[illegible]	[illegible]	44	[illegible]	11	[illegible]
5	Killane, . .	[illegible]	[illegible]	[illegible]	75	[illegible]	[illegible]
6	Newtownbarry, part of, .	[illegible]	[illegible]	[illegible]	[illegible]	[illegible]	[illegible]
7	Oulart, . .	[illegible]	[illegible]	[illegible]	[illegible]	71	[illegible]

	I.—PROVINCE OF LEINSTER—*con.*						
	41. WEXFORD.						
1	Bannow, . . .	24,265	4,014	77	[illegible]	[illegible]	42
2	Bridgetown, . . .	23,282	5,035	142	84	47	43
3	Broadway, . . .	21,811	4,430	145	84	33	43
4	Crossabeg, . . .	26,571	5,079	43	[illegible]	[illegible]	[illegible]
5	Taghmon and Glynn, . .	24,738	3,391	47	31	29	23
6	Wexford, W., . .	16,313	14,474	[illegible]	[illegible]	187	173
	WICKLOW CO.						
	61. BALTINGLASS, part of						
1	Baltinglass, part of, W., .	17,893	3,[illegible]	49	48	37	33
2	Dunlavin, . . .	42,033	4,364	[illegible]	74	[illegible]	57
3	Kiltegan, part of, . .	43,720	3,720	[illegible]	45	37	44
	62. NAAS, part of.						
1	Blessington & Ballymore, pt. of,	51,887	3,315	[illegible]	[illegible]	[illegible]	39
	64. RATHDOWN, part of.						
1	Bray and Rathmichael, No. 1, part of,	8,5[illegible]	151	8	.	8	1
2	" " 2, do.,		3,[illegible]	[illegible]	46	47	37
3	Delgany, . . .	8,[illegible]	3,[illegible]	61	[illegible]	38	61
4	Powerscourt, . . .	32,435	3,184	30	[illegible]	39	16
	65. RATHDRUM.						
1	Annamoe, . . .	38,[illegible]	3,[illegible]	44	[illegible]	32	61
2	Arklow, . . .	16,798	4,515	134	105	79	79
3	Aughrim, . . .	30,[illegible]	3,[illegible]	51	35	23	6
4	Dunganstown, . . .	32,435	2,[illegible]	44	43	35	33
5	Newbridge, . . .	18,347	3,[illegible]	37	46	36	37
6	Newcastle, . . .	30,[illegible]	3,361	43	41	34	36
7	Rathdrum, W., . .	38,[illegible]	3,141	65	54	33	38
8	Wicklow, . . .	24,784	4,[illegible]	142	61	79	56
	66. SHILLELAGH, part of.						
1	Carnew & Coolattin, pt. of, W.,	28,794	3,[illegible]	61	[illegible]	47	49
2	Coolkenno and Shillelagh, part of,	13,730	2,[illegible]	39	50	11	17
3	Tinahely, . . .	48,[illegible]	4,173	76	56	43	37
	II.—PROVINCE OF MUNSTER.						
	CLARE CO.						
	67. BALLYVAUGHAN.						
1	Ballyvaughan, W., . .	71,[illegible]	4,[illegible]	[illegible]	73	[illegible]	41
	68. CORROFIN.						
1	Corrofin, W., . . .	71,[illegible]	6,[illegible]	[illegible]		46	[illegible]
	69. ENNIS.						
1	Crusheen, . . .	33,730	3,131	[illegible]	43	13	[illegible]
2	Ennis, No. 1, W., . .	7,[illegible]	7,[illegible]	40	207	[illegible]	79
3	" 2, . .	17,[illegible]	3,[illegible]	47	41	37	30
4	Kilmaley, . . .	33,[illegible]	4,[illegible]	61	45	45	40
5	Kilraghtis, . . .	30,131	4,[illegible]	[illegible]	27	[illegible]	[illegible]

[illegible]	[illegible]	176	101
[illegible]	[illegible]	[illegible]	[illegible]
[illegible]	[illegible]	81	[illegible]
[illegible]	[illegible]	[illegible]	[illegible]
[illegible]	[illegible]	[illegible]	[illegible]
[illegible]	[illegible]	[illegible]	[illegible]
[illegible]	[illegible]	174	[illegible]
[illegible]	[illegible]	[illegible]	[illegible]
[illegible]	[illegible]	[illegible]	[illegible]
[illegible]	[illegible]	[illegible]	[illegible]
[illegible]	[illegible]	[illegible]	[illegible]
[illegible]	[illegible]	[illegible]	[illegible]
[illegible]	[illegible]	[illegible]	[illegible]
[illegible]	[illegible]	[illegible]	[illegible]
[illegible]	[illegible]	[illegible]	[illegible]

BIRTHS AND DEATHS Registered in the year 1891—Registrars' Districts, arranged by Counties and Superintendent Registrars' Districts—continued.

No.	Registrars' Districts.	Area in Statute Acres.	Population in 1891.	Total: Births.	Total: Deaths.	Births: Legitimate: Males.	Births: Legitimate: Females.	Births: Illegitimate: Males.	Births: Illegitimate: Females.	Deaths: Males.	Deaths: Females.
	III.—Province of Munster—con.										
	39 Cork.										
1	Ballincollig,	[illegible]	[illegible]	[illegible]	[illegible]	[illegible]	[illegible]	[illegible]	.	[illegible]	[illegible]
2	Ballygarvan,	[illegible]	[illegible]	[illegible]	[illegible]	[illegible]	[illegible]	.	.	[illegible]	[illegible]
3	Blarney,	[illegible]	[illegible]	[illegible]	[illegible]	[illegible]	[illegible]	.	.	[illegible]	[illegible]
4	Carrigaline, No. 1,	[illegible]	[illegible]	[illegible]	[illegible]	[illegible]	[illegible]	.	.	[illegible]	[illegible]
5	" No. 2,	[illegible]	[illegible]	[illegible]	[illegible]	[illegible]	[illegible]	1	.	[illegible]	[illegible]
6	Crookstown, No. 1,	[illegible]	[illegible]	[illegible]	[illegible]	[illegible]	[illegible]	1	.	[illegible]	[illegible]
7	" No. 2,	[illegible]	[illegible]	[illegible]	[illegible]	[illegible]	[illegible]	1	.	[illegible]	[illegible]
8	Cork, No. 1,	[illegible]	[illegible]	[illegible]	[illegible]	[illegible]	[illegible]	.	1	[illegible]	[illegible]
9	" No. 2,		[illegible]	[illegible]	[illegible]	[illegible]	[illegible]	1	1	[illegible]	[illegible]
10	" No. 3,		[illegible]	[illegible]	[illegible]	[illegible]	[illegible]	1	.	[illegible]	[illegible]
11	" No. 4,		[illegible]	[illegible]	[illegible]	[illegible]	[illegible]	.	.	[illegible]	[illegible]
12	" No. 5,	[illegible]	[illegible]	[illegible]	[illegible]	[illegible]	[illegible]	[illegible]	1	[illegible]	[illegible]
13	" No. 6,		[illegible]	[illegible]	[illegible]	[illegible]	[illegible]	1	.	[illegible]	[illegible]
14	" No. 7,		[illegible]	[illegible]	[illegible]	[illegible]	[illegible]	.	.	[illegible]	[illegible]
15	" No. 8, W.,		[illegible]	[illegible]	1,041	[illegible]	[illegible]	[illegible]	[illegible]	[illegible]	[illegible]
16	" No. 9,		[illegible]	[illegible]	[illegible]	[illegible]	[illegible]	.	1	[illegible]	[illegible]
17	Douglas,	[illegible]	[illegible]	[illegible]	[illegible]	[illegible]	[illegible]	.	1	[illegible]	[illegible]
18	Tracton,	[illegible]	[illegible]	[illegible]	[illegible]	[illegible]	[illegible]	.	.	[illegible]	[illegible]
19	Queenstown, No. 1,	[illegible]	[illegible]	[illegible]	[illegible]	61	[illegible]	1	.	[illegible]	[illegible]
20	" No. 2,		[illegible]	[illegible]	[illegible]	[illegible]	[illegible]	.	1	[illegible]	[illegible]
21	Whitechurch,	[illegible]	[illegible]	[illegible]	[illegible]	[illegible]	[illegible]	.	.	[illegible]	[illegible]
	40. Dunmanway.										
1	Ballineen,	[illegible]	[illegible]	[illegible]	[illegible]	[illegible]	[illegible]	.	.	[illegible]	[illegible]
2	Coolmountain,	[illegible]	[illegible]	[illegible]	[illegible]	[illegible]	[illegible]	.	1	[illegible]	[illegible]
3	Dunmanway, W.,	[illegible]	[illegible]	[illegible]	[illegible]	[illegible]	[illegible]	[illegible]	[illegible]	[illegible]	[illegible]
	41. Fermoy.										
1	Ballyhooly,	[illegible]	[illegible]	[illegible]	[illegible]	[illegible]	[illegible]	1	1	[illegible]	[illegible]
2	Ballynoe,	[illegible]	[illegible]	[illegible]	[illegible]	[illegible]	[illegible]	.	.	[illegible]	[illegible]
3	Fermoy, W.,	[illegible]	[illegible]	[illegible]	[illegible]	114	[illegible]	[illegible]	[illegible]	[illegible]	[illegible]
4	Kilworth,	[illegible]	[illegible]	[illegible]	[illegible]	[illegible]	[illegible]	1	1	[illegible]	[illegible]
5	Rathcormack,	[illegible]	[illegible]	[illegible]	[illegible]	[illegible]	[illegible]	.	.	[illegible]	[illegible]
	42. Kanturk.										
1	Boherbue,	[illegible]	[illegible]	[illegible]	[illegible]	[illegible]	[illegible]	.	.	[illegible]	[illegible]
2	Kanturk, W.,	[illegible]	[illegible]	[illegible]	[illegible]	[illegible]	[illegible]	[illegible]	[illegible]	[illegible]	[illegible]
3	Millstreet,	[illegible]	[illegible]	[illegible]	[illegible]	[illegible]	[illegible]	1	.	[illegible]	[illegible]
4	Newmarket,	[illegible]	[illegible]	[illegible]	[illegible]	[illegible]	[illegible]	1	1	[illegible]	[illegible]
	43. Kilmallock, part of.										
1	Charleville, part of,	[illegible]	[illegible]	[illegible]	[illegible]	[illegible]	[illegible]	1	.	[illegible]	[illegible]
	44. Kinsale.										
1	Ballyfeard,	[illegible]	[illegible]	[illegible]	[illegible]	[illegible]	[illegible]	.	.	[illegible]	[illegible]
2	Ballymartle,	[illegible]	[illegible]	[illegible]	[illegible]	[illegible]	[illegible]	1	1	[illegible]	[illegible]
3	Courtmacsherry,	[illegible]	[illegible]	74	[illegible]	[illegible]	[illegible]	1	.	[illegible]	[illegible]
4	Innishannon,	[illegible]	[illegible]	[illegible]	[illegible]	[illegible]	[illegible]	.	1	[illegible]	[illegible]
5	Kinsale, W.,	[illegible]	[illegible]	[illegible]	[illegible]	[illegible]	[illegible]	.	[illegible]	[illegible]	[illegible]
	45. Macroom.										
1	Clondrohid,	[illegible]	[illegible]	[illegible]	[illegible]	[illegible]	[illegible]	.	.	[illegible]	[illegible]
2	Clonmoyle,	[illegible]	[illegible]	[illegible]	74	[illegible]	[illegible]	1	1	[illegible]	[illegible]
3	Inchigeelagh,	[illegible]	[illegible]	[illegible]	[illegible]	[illegible]	[illegible]	.	1	[illegible]	[illegible]
4	Macroom, W.,	[illegible]	[illegible]	[illegible]	[illegible]	[illegible]	[illegible]	.	.	[illegible]	[illegible]
5	Kilnamartery,	[illegible]	[illegible]	[illegible]	[illegible]	[illegible]	[illegible]	.	.	[illegible]	[illegible]

[illegible]	[illegible],	39,[illegible]
4	[illegible],	47,[illegible]
5	[illegible], W.,	[illegible]
6	[illegible],	22,[illegible]

[illegible]

1	[illegible],	11,[illegible]
2	[illegible],	[illegible]
3	[illegible],	[illegible]
4	[illegible], No. 1, W.,	[illegible]
5	„ 2,	17,[illegible]
6	[illegible], East,	[illegible]

[illegible]

1	[illegible],	[illegible]
2	[illegible], W.,	[illegible]

[illegible], part of.

1	[illegible],	[illegible]
2	[illegible], part of, W.,	[illegible]

[illegible]

1	[illegible],	43,[illegible]
2	[illegible], W.,	[illegible]
3	[illegible],	[illegible]
4	[illegible],	27,[illegible]

[illegible]

1	[illegible],	[illegible]
2	[illegible], E.,	34,[illegible]

[illegible], part of.

1	[illegible],	16,[illegible]
2	[illegible], part of,	13,[illegible]
3	[illegible], W.,	4,[illegible]

Kerry Co.

94. [illegible]

1	[illegible], W.,	[illegible]
2	[illegible],	[illegible]
3	[illegible],	[illegible]
4	[illegible],	[illegible]
5	[illegible],	[illegible]

95. [illegible]

1	[illegible],	[illegible]
2	[illegible],	[illegible]
3	Dingle, W.,	[illegible]
4	[illegible],	[illegible]

[illegible], part of.

1	[illegible], No. 1, part of	1[illegible]

BIRTHS AND DEATHS Registered in the Year 18[illegible]1—Registrars' Districts, arranged by Counties and Superintendent Registrars' Districts—*continued.*

No.	Registrars' Districts.	Area in Statute Acres.	Population in 18[illegible]1.	Total: Births.	Total: Deaths.	Births, including Illegitimate Births: Males.	Births, including Illegitimate Births: Females.	Illegitimate Births: Males.	Illegitimate Births: Females.	Deaths: Males.	Deaths: Females.	[illegible]
	XI.—PROVINCE OF MUNSTER—*con.*											
	97. Kenmare.											
1	Kenmare, W.,	91,097	4,330	73	45	[illegible]	39	3	1	25	27	
2	Kilgarvan,	42,185	4,027	74	43	[illegible]	35	.	.	26	17	
3	Sneem,	88,[illegible]	3,[illegible]	114	[illegible]	[illegible]	49	.	1	24	24	
4	Tuosist,	33,777	3,[illegible]	[illegible]	[illegible]	[illegible]	43	.	.	17	14	
	98. Killarney.											
1	[illegible]	77,944	8,[illegible]	223	95	118	105	1	2	47	43	
2	Killarney, No. 1, W.,	7,[illegible]	4,130	160	171	84	[illegible]	1	1	75	89	.
3	" No. 2,	48,6[illegible]	5,334	1[illegible]	71	[illegible]	79	4	1	31	40	
4	Kilcummin,	83,[illegible]	9,[illegible]	290	122	134	156	1	.	[illegible]	42	
5	Milltown,	24,071	3,[illegible]	163	[illegible]	65	88	1	1	45	44	
6	Molahiffe,	30,744	5,431	145	79	83	62	2	.	41	31	
	99. Listowel.											
1	Ballyduff,	39,[illegible]	7,219	164	101	81	83	.	5	60	41	
2	Ballybunion,	45,547	6,[illegible]	148	74	73	75	1	.	35	39	
3	Ballylongford,	38,[illegible]	3,741	125	68	64	61	.	5	30	38	
4	Listowel, W.,	45,[illegible]	10,727	278	160	137	141	4	5	79	81	
	100. Tralee.											
1	Ardfert,	38,713	7,[illegible]	160	85	75	90	.	.	39	46	
2	[illegible], No. 1,	36,[illegible]	4,300	130	58	64	63	.	.	30	28	
3	" 2,	34,734	4,007	90	59	48	53	.	.	27	31	
4	Castleisland,	80,[illegible]	3,[illegible]	125	70	59	74	1	1	39	38	
5	Castlemaine,	30,110	3,600	60	55	27	33	1	.	30	14	
6	Kilgobbin,	30,400	633	20	8	8	13	.	.	4	4	
7	Tralee, No. 1, W.,	44,[illegible]	9,743	184	207	108	80	6	6	108	104	
8	" 2,	32,149	2,737	233	122	111	123	.	.	47	65	
	Limerick Co.											
	101. Croom.											
1	Adare,	33,241	3,407	64	45	30	35	.	1	20	25	
2	[illegible],	30,142	4,354	85	61	43	43	1	1	33	30	
3	Croom, W.,	30,911	3,[illegible]	73	86	30	43	2	2	67	43	.
	102. Glin, part of.											
1	Shanagolden,	37,345	4,173	85	85	41	44	1	.	25	30	
2	Tarbert No. 1, part of,	3,097	380	8	6	2	6	.	.	1	5	.
3	" No. 2, W.,	23,[illegible]	4,543	187	90	84	43	7	5	49	55	
	103. Kilmallock, part of.											
1	Bruff,	29,[illegible]	4,[illegible]	80	77	43	47	1	1	33	45	
2	Bruree,	30,[illegible]	2,[illegible]	65	43	34	31	1	.	16	25	
3	Charleville, part of,	4,[illegible]	480	17	6	6	11	1	.	9	7	
4	Hospital,	36,[illegible]	4,540	100	85	35	45	3	.	41	46	
5	Kilfinane,	37,460	3,[illegible]	130	80	40	71	2	5	37	41	
6	Kilmallock, W.,	18,876	4,[illegible]	[illegible]	[illegible]	[illegible]	[illegible]	[illegible]	[illegible]	[illegible]	[illegible]	.

BIRTHS AND DEATHS Registered in the Year 1891—REGISTRARS' DISTRICTS, arranged by COUNTIES and SUPERINTENDENT REGISTRARS' DISTRICTS—*continued.*

No.	REGISTRARS' DISTRICTS.	Area in Statute Acres.	Population in 1881.	TOTAL. Births.	TOTAL. Deaths.	BIRTHS. Legitimate (Registered Births). Males.	Females.	Illegitimate Births. Males.	Females.	DEATHS. Males.	Females.	Excess of Births over Deaths.
	III. PROVINCE OF MUNSTER—con.											
	104. [illegible], part of.											
1	Galbally,	[illegible]	4,571	[illegible]	[illegible]	[illegible]	[illegible]	.	.	[illegible]	[illegible]	[illegible]
2	Mitchelstown, part of,	[illegible]	[illegible]	15	[illegible]	[illegible]	[illegible]	.	.	[illegible]	[illegible]	[illegible]
	106. NEWCASTLE.											
1	Abbeyfeale,	[illegible]	[illegible]	[illegible]	[illegible]	[illegible]	111	1	[illegible]	[illegible]	[illegible]	[illegible]
2	Ardagh,	[illegible]	[illegible]	[illegible]	[illegible]	[illegible]	[illegible]	.	1	[illegible]	[illegible]	[illegible]
3	[illegible],	[illegible]	[illegible]	115	[illegible]	[illegible]	[illegible]	1	1	[illegible]	[illegible]	[illegible]
4	[illegible],	[illegible]	[illegible]	[illegible]	[illegible]	[illegible]	[illegible]	1	[illegible]	[illegible]	[illegible]	[illegible]
5	Newcastle, W.	[illegible]	[illegible]	[illegible]	[illegible]	[illegible]	[illegible]	[illegible]	[illegible]	[illegible]	[illegible]	[illegible]
	107. RATHKEALE.											
1	Askeaton,	[illegible]	[illegible]	[illegible]	[illegible]	[illegible]	[illegible]	.	.	[illegible]	[illegible]	[illegible]
2	Pallaskenry,	[illegible]	[illegible]	[illegible]	[illegible]	[illegible]	[illegible]	1	.	[illegible]	[illegible]	[illegible]
3	Rathkeale, No. 1, W.,	[illegible]	[illegible]	[illegible]	[illegible]	[illegible]	[illegible]	[illegible]	[illegible]	[illegible]	[illegible]	[illegible]
4	" No. 2,	[illegible]	[illegible]	[illegible]	[illegible]	[illegible]	[illegible]	.	1	[illegible]	[illegible]	[illegible]
	108. TIPPERARY, part of.											
1	Cappagh, part of,	[illegible]	[illegible]	[illegible]	[illegible]	[illegible]	[illegible]	[illegible]	1	[illegible]	[illegible]	[illegible]
2	Grean, do.,	[illegible]	[illegible]	[illegible]	[illegible]	[illegible]	[illegible]	.	.	[illegible]	[illegible]	[illegible]
	Tipperary Co.											
	109. BORRISOKANE.											
1	Borrisokane, W.	[illegible]	[illegible]	[illegible]	[illegible]	[illegible]	[illegible]	[illegible]	[illegible]	[illegible]	[illegible]	[illegible]
2	Cloughjordan,	[illegible]	[illegible]	[illegible]	[illegible]	[illegible]	[illegible]	.	.	[illegible]	[illegible]	[illegible]
3	Terryglass,	[illegible]	[illegible]	[illegible]	[illegible]	[illegible]	[illegible]	.	.	[illegible]	[illegible]	[illegible]
	110. CALLAN, part of.											
1	Ballingarry,	[illegible]	[illegible]	[illegible]	[illegible]	[illegible]	[illegible]	1	1	[illegible]	[illegible]	[illegible]
2	Mullinahone,	[illegible]	[illegible]	[illegible]	[illegible]	[illegible]	[illegible]	.	1	[illegible]	[illegible]	[illegible]
	111. CARRICK-ON-SUIR, part of.											
1	Carrick-on-Suir, part of, W.	[illegible]	[illegible]	[illegible]	[illegible]	[illegible]	[illegible]	[illegible]	[illegible]	[illegible]	[illegible]	[illegible]
2	Garrangibbon,	[illegible]	[illegible]	[illegible]	[illegible]	[illegible]	[illegible]	.	.	[illegible]	[illegible]	[illegible]
	112. CASHEL.											
1	Cashel, W.	[illegible]	[illegible]	[illegible]	[illegible]	[illegible]	[illegible]	[illegible]	1	[illegible]	[illegible]	[illegible]
2	Fethard,	[illegible]	[illegible]	[illegible]	[illegible]	[illegible]	[illegible]	[illegible]	[illegible]	[illegible]	[illegible]	[illegible]
3	Killenaule,	[illegible]	[illegible]	[illegible]	[illegible]	[illegible]	[illegible]	.	.	[illegible]	[illegible]	[illegible]
4	[illegible],	[illegible]	[illegible]	[illegible]	[illegible]	[illegible]	[illegible]	.	[illegible]	[illegible]	[illegible]	[illegible]
5	Tullamain,	[illegible]	[illegible]	[illegible]	[illegible]	[illegible]	[illegible]	.	.	[illegible]	[illegible]	[illegible]
	113. CLOGHEEN.											
1	Ardfinnan,	[illegible]	[illegible]	[illegible]	[illegible]	[illegible]	[illegible]	.	.	[illegible]	[illegible]	[illegible]
2	Cahir,	[illegible]	[illegible]	[illegible]	[illegible]	[illegible]	[illegible]	1	[illegible]	[illegible]	[illegible]	[illegible]
3	Clogheen, W.	[illegible]	[illegible]	[illegible]	[illegible]	[illegible]	[illegible]	[illegible]	[illegible]	[illegible]	[illegible]	[illegible]
	114. CLONMEL, part of.											
1	Clonmel, W.	[illegible]	[illegible]	[illegible]	[illegible]	[illegible]	[illegible]	[illegible]	[illegible]	[illegible]	[illegible]	[illegible]
2	Kilsheelan, part of,	[illegible]	[illegible]	[illegible]	[illegible]	[illegible]	[illegible]	.	.	[illegible]	[illegible]	[illegible]
3	[illegible],	[illegible]	[illegible]	[illegible]	[illegible]	[illegible]	[illegible]	.	.	[illegible]	[illegible]	[illegible]
4	Marlfield,	[illegible]	[illegible]	[illegible]	[illegible]	[illegible]	[illegible]	.	.	[illegible]	[illegible]	[illegible]
	115. NENAGH.											
1	Nenagh, W.	[illegible]	[illegible]	[illegible]	[illegible]	[illegible]	[illegible]	[illegible]	[illegible]	[illegible]	[illegible]	[illegible]
2	Newport,	[illegible]	[illegible]	[illegible]	[illegible]	[illegible]	[illegible]	.	.	[illegible]	[illegible]	[illegible]
3	Portroe,	[illegible]	[illegible]	[illegible]	[illegible]	[illegible]	[illegible]	.	.	[illegible]	[illegible]	[illegible]
4	Silvermines,	[illegible]	[illegible]	[illegible]	[illegible]	[illegible]	[illegible]	.	.	[illegible]	[illegible]	[illegible]
5	Toomyvara,	[illegible]	[illegible]	[illegible]	[illegible]	[illegible]	[illegible]	1	.	[illegible]	[illegible]	[illegible]
	116. PARSONSTOWN, part of.											
1	[illegible],	[illegible]	[illegible]	[illegible]	[illegible]	[illegible]	[illegible]	.	.	[illegible]	[illegible]	[illegible]

	IX.—[illegible]—*etc.*	
	117. [illegible], part of.	
1	[illegible],	25,[illegible]
2	[illegible], No. 1, part of, W.	28,[illegible]
	118. Thurles.	
1	Borrisoleigh,	[illegible]
2	Holycross,	14,[illegible]
3	Littleton,	[illegible]
4	Moyne,	[illegible]
5	Templemore,	[illegible]
6	Thurles, W.	[illegible]
	119. Tipperary, part of.	
1	Bansha,	41,[illegible]
2	Cappagh, part of,	[illegible]
3	Emly,	24,[illegible]
4	Cullen,	[illegible]
5	[illegible], part of,	4,[illegible]
6	Tipperary, W.	[illegible]
	120. Urlingford, part of.	
1	[illegible],	[illegible]
2	Urlingford, part of,	[illegible]
	Waterford Co.	
	121. Carrick-on-Suir, part of.	
1	Carrick-on-Suir, part of,	7,1[illegible]
2	Portlaw,	[illegible]
3	[illegible],	[illegible]
	122. Clonmel, part of.	
1	Ballymacarbry,	19,[illegible]
2	[illegible], part of,	[illegible]
3	St. Mary's,	[illegible]
	123. Dungarvan.	
1	Dungarvan, W.	[illegible]
2	[illegible],	[illegible]
3	Stradbally,	[illegible]
4	Whitechurch,	[illegible]
	124. Kilmacthomas.	
1	[illegible],	[illegible]
2	Kilmacthomas, W.	[illegible]
	125. Lismore.	
1	Ballyduff,	[illegible]
2	Cappoquin,	[illegible]
3	Lismore, W.	[illegible]
4	Tallow,	[illegible]
	126. Waterford, part of.	
1	Kilmeaden,	[illegible]
2	Tramore,	[illegible]
3	Waterford, No. 1, W.,	[illegible]
4	" No. 2,	4,[illegible]
5	Woodstown,	[illegible]
	127. Youghal, part of.	
1	Ardmore,	[illegible]
2	Clashmore,	[illegible]

BIRTHS AND DEATHS Registered in the Year 1891—REGISTRARS' DISTRICTS, arranged by COUNTIES and SUPERINTENDENT REGISTRARS' DIVISIONS—*continued.*

	Registrars' Districts.	Area in Statute Acres.	Population in 1891.	Total: Births.	Total: Deaths.	Births: [illegible]: Males.	Births: [illegible]: Females.	Births: [illegible]: Males.	Births: [illegible]: Females.	Deaths: Males.	Deaths: Females.	[illegible]
	III.—PROVINCE OF ULSTER.											
	ANTRIM CO.											
	128. ANTRIM.											
	Antrim, W.,	14,278	[illegible]	[illegible]	111	[illegible]	70	4	5	61	[illegible]	14
1	[illegible],	[illegible]	4,176	[illegible]	[illegible]	[illegible]	[illegible]	4	1	[illegible]	[illegible]	47
1	[illegible],	23,[illegible]	[illegible]	[illegible]	71	[illegible]	44	7		[illegible]	[illegible]	[illegible]
	Doagh,	[illegible]	[illegible]	[illegible]	[illegible]	84	105	[illegible]	[illegible]	[illegible]	[illegible]	71
1	Randalstown,	28,[illegible]	[illegible]	[illegible]	[illegible]	[illegible]	48	[illegible]	[illegible]	[illegible]	[illegible]	[illegible]
	Templepatrick,	21,172	[illegible]	[illegible]	71	63	60	[illegible]	[illegible]	[illegible]	[illegible]	[illegible]
	129. BALLYCASTLE.											
	Ballycastle, W.,	[illegible]	[illegible]	[illegible]	[illegible]	61	77	4	[illegible]	[illegible]	[illegible]	[illegible]
1	Clough,	[illegible]	[illegible]	[illegible]	78	[illegible]	61	[illegible]	6	[illegible]	47	[illegible]
1	[illegible],	[illegible]	[illegible]	87	[illegible]	[illegible]	[illegible]		3	[illegible]	[illegible]	61
	130. BALLYMENA.											
	Ahoghill,	14,[illegible]	[illegible]	[illegible]	111	[illegible]	[illegible]	11	4	[illegible]	[illegible]	[illegible]
1	Ballymena, W.,	[illegible]	11,[illegible]	[illegible]	[illegible]	[illegible]	[illegible]	[illegible]	11	[illegible]	[illegible]	[illegible]
1	Broughshane,	[illegible]	[illegible]	[illegible]	64	77	[illegible]	[illegible]	[illegible]	[illegible]	[illegible]	[illegible]
1	Clough,	[illegible]	[illegible]	[illegible]	[illegible]	71	[illegible]	[illegible]	[illegible]	[illegible]	[illegible]	[illegible]
1	Galgorm,	15,[illegible]	[illegible]	[illegible]	[illegible]	[illegible]	[illegible]	10	4	[illegible]	[illegible]	[illegible]
1	[illegible],	[illegible]	[illegible]	[illegible]	[illegible]	85	70	[illegible]	[illegible]	[illegible]	47	[illegible]
1	Portglenone,	17,[illegible]	[illegible]	177	[illegible]	94	[illegible]	[illegible]	4	[illegible]	[illegible]	[illegible]
1	Toome,	15,[illegible]	[illegible]	[illegible]	[illegible]	[illegible]	[illegible]	[illegible]	[illegible]	[illegible]	[illegible]	[illegible]
	131. BALLYMONEY, part of.											
1	Ballymoney, W.	[illegible]	[illegible]	[illegible]	[illegible]	[illegible]	144	17	11	91	[illegible]	[illegible]
2	Castlequarter,	[illegible]	[illegible]	[illegible]	[illegible]	47	[illegible]		[illegible]	[illegible]	[illegible]	[illegible]
3	Dervock,	[illegible]	[illegible]	[illegible]	[illegible]	[illegible]	44	[illegible]	1	[illegible]	[illegible]	[illegible]
4	[illegible],	[illegible]	[illegible]	[illegible]	[illegible]	75	[illegible]	[illegible]	[illegible]	[illegible]	[illegible]	[illegible]
	132. BELFAST, part of.											
1	Belfast, No. 1,	[illegible]	[illegible]	[illegible]	[illegible]	[illegible]	[illegible]	[illegible]	11	191	[illegible]	[illegible]
2	" No. 2,	[illegible]	[illegible]	[illegible]	[illegible]	[illegible]	[illegible]	[illegible]	7	[illegible]	[illegible]	[illegible]
3	" No. 3,	[illegible]	[illegible]	[illegible]	[illegible]	[illegible]	[illegible]	[illegible]	[illegible]	[illegible]	[illegible]	415
4	" No. 4, W.	[illegible]	[illegible]	[illegible]	[illegible]	[illegible]	[illegible]	[illegible]	[illegible]	[illegible]	[illegible]	[illegible]
5	" No. 5,	[illegible]	[illegible]	[illegible]	[illegible]	[illegible]	[illegible]	[illegible]	[illegible]	[illegible]	[illegible]	311
6	" No. 6,	[illegible]	[illegible]	[illegible]	[illegible]	[illegible]	[illegible]	[illegible]	[illegible]	[illegible]	[illegible]	[illegible]
7	" No. 7,	[illegible]	[illegible]	[illegible]	[illegible]	71	71	[illegible]	[illegible]	[illegible]	[illegible]	[illegible]
8	" No. 8,	[illegible]	[illegible]	[illegible]	[illegible]	[illegible]	[illegible]	[illegible]	[illegible]	[illegible]	[illegible]	[illegible]
9	" No. 9,	[illegible]	[illegible]	[illegible]	[illegible]	[illegible]	[illegible]	[illegible]	7	[illegible]	[illegible]	[illegible]
10	" No. 10,	[illegible]	[illegible]	[illegible]	[illegible]	[illegible]	[illegible]	[illegible]	[illegible]	[illegible]	[illegible]	[illegible]
	133. COLERAINE, part of.											
1	Bushmills,	[illegible]	[illegible]	[illegible]	[illegible]	[illegible]	[illegible]	1	[illegible]	[illegible]	[illegible]	[illegible]
2	Portrush, part of,	[illegible]	[illegible]	[illegible]	[illegible]	[illegible]	47	1	4	[illegible]	[illegible]	[illegible]
	134. LARNE.											
1	[illegible],	14,[illegible]	[illegible]	[illegible]	[illegible]	[illegible]	[illegible]	1		[illegible]	47	[illegible]
2	[illegible],	[illegible]	[illegible]	[illegible]	[illegible]	[illegible]	[illegible]	4	[illegible]	[illegible]	[illegible]	[illegible]
3	Carrickfergus,	[illegible]	[illegible]	[illegible]	[illegible]	[illegible]	[illegible]	[illegible]	[illegible]	[illegible]	[illegible]	[illegible]
4	Glenarm,	[illegible]	[illegible]	[illegible]	[illegible]	[illegible]	[illegible]	[illegible]	[illegible]	[illegible]	[illegible]	[illegible]
5	Larne, W.,	[illegible]	[illegible]	[illegible]	[illegible]	[illegible]	[illegible]	[illegible]	[illegible]	[illegible]	[illegible]	[illegible]
6	[illegible],	[illegible]	[illegible]	[illegible]	[illegible]	[illegible]	[illegible]	.	.	4	[illegible]	1
	135. LISBURN, part of.											
1	Dunmurry, part of,	[illegible]	[illegible]	[illegible]	[illegible]	[illegible]	11	1	.	[illegible]	[illegible]	[illegible]
2	Glenavy,	[illegible]	[illegible]	[illegible]	[illegible]	[illegible]	[illegible]	1	7	[illegible]	[illegible]	[illegible]
3	[illegible],	[illegible]	[illegible]	[illegible]	[illegible]	[illegible]	[illegible]	[illegible]	1	[illegible]	[illegible]	[illegible]
4	Lisburn, part of, W.	[illegible]	[illegible]	[illegible]	[illegible]	[illegible]	[illegible]	[illegible]	[illegible]	[illegible]	[illegible]	15

BIRTHS AND DEATHS Registered in the Year 1891—REGISTRARS' DISTRICTS arranged by COUNTIES and SUPERINTENDENT REGISTRARS' DISTRICTS—*continued.*

No.	REGISTRARS' DISTRICTS.	Area in Statute Acres.	Population in 1891.	TOTAL: Births.	TOTAL: Deaths.	BIRTHS: Including Illegitimate Births: Males.	BIRTHS: Including Illegitimate Births: Females.	BIRTHS: Illegitimate Births: Males.	BIRTHS: Illegitimate Births: Females.	DEATHS: Males.	DEATHS: Females.
	III.—PROVINCE OF ULSTER—con.										
	Armagh Co.										
	137. ARMAGH, part of.										
1	Armagh, W.,	[illegible]	[illegible]	[illegible]	[illegible]	[illegible]	[illegible]	[illegible]	[illegible]	[illegible]	171
2	Blackwatertown,	[illegible]	4,7[illegible]	91	[illegible]	[illegible]	[illegible]	[illegible]	1	[illegible]	[illegible]
3	Keady,	[illegible]	11,[illegible]	[illegible]	[illegible]	[illegible]	[illegible]	[illegible]	[illegible]	[illegible]	[illegible]
4	Loughgall,	[illegible]	[illegible]	144	[illegible]	73	73	4	[illegible]	[illegible]	[illegible]
5	Markethill,	[illegible]	7,[illegible]	[illegible]	[illegible]	[illegible]	71	[illegible]	4	[illegible]	[illegible]
6	Rich Hill,	[illegible]	[illegible]	[illegible]	[illegible]	[illegible]	[illegible]	[illegible]	4	[illegible]	[illegible]
7	Tynan,	[illegible]	[illegible]	97	[illegible]	[illegible]	[illegible]	.	.	44	[illegible]
	138. BANBRIDGE, part of.										
1	Tandragee,	[illegible]	[illegible]	[illegible]	[illegible]	[illegible]	[illegible]	[illegible]	[illegible]	[illegible]	[illegible]
	139. CASTLEBLAYNEY, part of.										
1	[illegible], part of,	[illegible]	[illegible]	113	[illegible]	[illegible]	[illegible]	.	.	[illegible]	[illegible]
2	Newtownhamilton, do.,	14,777	[illegible]	[illegible]	[illegible]	[illegible]	[illegible]	1	[illegible]	[illegible]	[illegible]
	140. DUNDALK, part of.										
1	[illegible], part of,	[illegible]	1,7[illegible]	[illegible]	[illegible]	[illegible]	17	[illegible]	.	[illegible]	[illegible]
	141. LURGAN, part of.										
1	Lurgan, No. 1, part of, W.,	[illegible]	[illegible]	[illegible]	[illegible]	[illegible]	[illegible]	17	[illegible]	[illegible]	[illegible]
2	" No. 2,	7,777	[illegible]	[illegible]	77	[illegible]	[illegible]	[illegible]	[illegible]	[illegible]	[illegible]
3	Portadown,	[illegible]	[illegible]	[illegible]	[illegible]	[illegible]	[illegible]	[illegible]	[illegible]	[illegible]	[illegible]
4	Tartaraghan,	[illegible]	[illegible]	[illegible]	[illegible]	[illegible]	[illegible]	[illegible]	[illegible]	[illegible]	[illegible]
	142. NEWRY, part of.										
1	Forkhill,	[illegible]	[illegible]	[illegible]	[illegible]	[illegible]	[illegible]	.	.	[illegible]	[illegible]
2	Meigh,	[illegible]	[illegible]	[illegible]	[illegible]	[illegible]	[illegible]	.	1	[illegible]	[illegible]
3	Mountnorris,	[illegible]	[illegible]	[illegible]	[illegible]	[illegible]	[illegible]	[illegible]	2	[illegible]	[illegible]
4	Mullaghglass,	[illegible]	[illegible]	[illegible]	[illegible]	[illegible]	[illegible]	1	[illegible]	[illegible]	[illegible]
5	Newry, No. 1, part of, W.,	[illegible]	[illegible]	[illegible]	[illegible]	[illegible]	[illegible]	[illegible]	[illegible]	[illegible]	[illegible]
6	Poyntzpass,	[illegible]	[illegible]	[illegible]	[illegible]	[illegible]	[illegible]	1	.	[illegible]	[illegible]
	Cavan Co.										
	143. BAILIEBOROUGH.										
1	Bailieborough, W.,	[illegible]	[illegible]	[illegible]	[illegible]	[illegible]	[illegible]	[illegible]	[illegible]	[illegible]	[illegible]
2	[illegible],	[illegible]	[illegible]	[illegible]	[illegible]	[illegible]	[illegible]	.	.	[illegible]	[illegible]
3	Kingscourt,	[illegible]	[illegible]	47	[illegible]	[illegible]	[illegible]	1	.	[illegible]	[illegible]
4	Shercock,	[illegible]	[illegible]	[illegible]	[illegible]	[illegible]	[illegible]	[illegible]	1	[illegible]	[illegible]
5	[illegible],	4,[illegible]	[illegible]	[illegible]	[illegible]	[illegible]	[illegible]	.	.	[illegible]	[illegible]
	144. BAWNBOY, part of.										
1	Ballyconnell, W.,	[illegible]	[illegible]	[illegible]	[illegible]	[illegible]	[illegible]	[illegible]	[illegible]	[illegible]	[illegible]
2	Newtowngore, part of,	[illegible]	[illegible]	7	4	[illegible]	[illegible]	1	.	[illegible]	[illegible]
3	Swanlinbar,	[illegible]	[illegible]	[illegible]	[illegible]	[illegible]	[illegible]	.	1	[illegible]	[illegible]

	III.—PROVINCE OF ULSTER—con.						
	146. Cootehill, part of.						
1	Cootehill, part of, W., . .	[illegible]	[illegible]	119	[illegible]	[illegible]	[illegible]
2	Drum, part of, .	[illegible]	[illegible]	[illegible]	[illegible]	[illegible]	[illegible]
3	Tullyvin, . . .	[illegible]	[illegible]	[illegible]	[illegible]	[illegible]	[illegible]
	147. Enniskillen, part of.						
1	[illegible], part of, . .	[illegible]	[illegible]	[illegible]	[illegible]	[illegible]	[illegible]
	148. [illegible], part of.						
1	[illegible], part of, . .	[illegible]	[illegible]	77	[illegible]	[illegible]	[illegible]
2	[illegible], do., . .	7,[illegible]	[illegible]	[illegible]	17	[illegible]	14
	149. Kells, part of.						
1	Moynalty, part of, . .	[illegible]	[illegible]	[illegible]	[illegible]	[illegible]	[illegible]
	150. Oldcastle, part of.						
1	Ballyjamesduff, . .	[illegible]	[illegible]	[illegible]	[illegible]	[illegible]	[illegible]
2	Virginia, . . .	[illegible]	[illegible]	[illegible]	[illegible]	[illegible]	[illegible]
	Donegal Co.						
	151. Ballyshannon, part of.						
1	Bundoran, . . .	[illegible]	[illegible]	[illegible]	[illegible]	[illegible]	[illegible]
2	Ballyshannon, W., . .	[illegible]	7,[illegible]	[illegible]	[illegible]	[illegible]	[illegible]
	152. Donegal.						
1	Donegal, W., . . .	[illegible]	[illegible]	[illegible]	[illegible]	[illegible]	[illegible]
2	Dunkineely, . . .	[illegible]	[illegible]	[illegible]	[illegible]	[illegible]	[illegible]
3	Laghy, ...	[illegible]	[illegible]	71	[illegible]	[illegible]	[illegible]
4	Mountcharles, . . .	[illegible]	[illegible]	77	[illegible]	[illegible]	[illegible]
5	Pettigo, . . .	[illegible]	[illegible]	[illegible]	[illegible]	[illegible]	[illegible]
	153. Dunfanaghy.						
1	Creeslough, . . .	[illegible]	[illegible]	[illegible]	[illegible]	[illegible]	[illegible]
2	Dunfanaghy, W. . .	[illegible]	[illegible]	[illegible]	[illegible]	[illegible]	[illegible]
3	Gweedore, . . .	[illegible]	[illegible]	[illegible]	[illegible]	[illegible]	[illegible]
4	Tory Island, . . .	[illegible]	[illegible]	11	7	[illegible]	[illegible]
	154. Glenties.						
1	Ardara, . . .	[illegible]	[illegible]	[illegible]	[illegible]	[illegible]	[illegible]
2	Carrick, . . .	[illegible]	[illegible]	[illegible]	[illegible]	[illegible]	[illegible]
3	Dunglow, . . .	[illegible]	[illegible]	[illegible]	[illegible]	[illegible]	[illegible]
4	Dungloe, . . .	[illegible]	[illegible]	[illegible]	[illegible]	[illegible]	[illegible]
5	Glenties, W., . .	[illegible]	[illegible]	[illegible]	[illegible]	[illegible]	[illegible]
6	Killybegs, . . .	[illegible]	[illegible]	[illegible]	[illegible]	[illegible]	[illegible]
	155. Inishowen.						
1	Buncrana, . . .	[illegible]	[illegible]	[illegible]	[illegible]	[illegible]	[illegible]
2	Carndonagh, W., . .	[illegible]	[illegible]	[illegible]	[illegible]	[illegible]	[illegible]
3	Clonmany, . . .	[illegible]	[illegible]	[illegible]	[illegible]	[illegible]	[illegible]
4	Malin, . . .	[illegible]	[illegible]	[illegible]	[illegible]	[illegible]	[illegible]
5	Moville, . . .	[illegible]	[illegible]	[illegible]	[illegible]	[illegible]	[illegible]
	156. Letterkenny.						
1	Church Hill, . . .	[illegible]	[illegible]	[illegible]	[illegible]	[illegible]	[illegible]
2	Letterkenny, W., . .	[illegible]	[illegible]	[illegible]	[illegible]	[illegible]	[illegible]
3	Manorcunningham, . .	[illegible]	[illegible]	[illegible]	[illegible]	[illegible]	[illegible]

BIRTHS AND DEATHS Registered in the Year 1861—REGISTRARS' DISTRICTS, arranged by COUNTIES and SUPERINTENDENT REGISTRARS' DISTRICTS—continued.

No.	[illegible]	[illegible]	[illegible]	[illegible]	[illegible]	[illegible]	[illegible]	[illegible]	[illegible]	[illegible]	[illegible]
	[illegible]										
	[illegible]										
1	[illegible]	[illegible]	[illegible]	[illegible]	[illegible]	[illegible]	[illegible]	[illegible]	[illegible]	[illegible]	[illegible]
2	[illegible]	[illegible]	[illegible]	[illegible]	[illegible]	[illegible]	[illegible]	[illegible]	[illegible]	[illegible]	[illegible]
3	[illegible]	[illegible]	[illegible]	[illegible]	[illegible]	[illegible]	[illegible]	[illegible]	[illegible]	[illegible]	[illegible]
	[illegible]										
1	[illegible]	[illegible]	[illegible]	[illegible]	[illegible]	[illegible]	[illegible]	[illegible]	[illegible]	[illegible]	[illegible]
2	[illegible]	[illegible]	[illegible]	[illegible]	[illegible]	[illegible]	[illegible]	[illegible]	[illegible]	[illegible]	[illegible]
3	[illegible]	[illegible]	[illegible]	[illegible]	[illegible]	[illegible]	[illegible]	[illegible]	[illegible]	[illegible]	[illegible]
4	[illegible]	[illegible]	[illegible]	[illegible]	[illegible]	[illegible]	[illegible]	[illegible]	[illegible]	[illegible]	[illegible]
5	[illegible]	[illegible]	[illegible]	[illegible]	[illegible]	[illegible]	[illegible]	[illegible]	[illegible]	[illegible]	[illegible]
	[illegible]										
1	[illegible]	[illegible]	[illegible]	[illegible]	[illegible]	[illegible]	[illegible]	[illegible]	[illegible]	[illegible]	[illegible]
2	[illegible]	[illegible]	[illegible]	[illegible]	[illegible]	[illegible]	[illegible]	[illegible]	[illegible]	[illegible]	[illegible]
	[illegible]										
1	[illegible]	[illegible]	[illegible]	[illegible]	[illegible]	[illegible]	[illegible]	[illegible]	[illegible]	[illegible]	[illegible]
2	[illegible]	[illegible]	[illegible]	[illegible]	[illegible]	[illegible]	[illegible]	[illegible]	[illegible]	[illegible]	[illegible]
3	[illegible]	[illegible]	[illegible]	[illegible]	[illegible]	[illegible]	[illegible]	[illegible]	[illegible]	[illegible]	[illegible]
	[illegible]										
	[illegible]										
1	[illegible]	[illegible]	[illegible]	[illegible]	[illegible]	[illegible]	[illegible]	[illegible]	[illegible]	[illegible]	[illegible]
2	[illegible]	[illegible]	[illegible]	[illegible]	[illegible]	[illegible]	[illegible]	[illegible]	[illegible]	[illegible]	[illegible]
3	[illegible]	[illegible]	[illegible]	[illegible]	[illegible]	[illegible]	[illegible]	[illegible]	[illegible]	[illegible]	[illegible]
4	[illegible]	[illegible]	[illegible]	[illegible]	[illegible]	[illegible]	[illegible]	[illegible]	[illegible]	[illegible]	[illegible]
5	[illegible]	[illegible]	[illegible]	[illegible]	[illegible]	[illegible]	[illegible]	[illegible]	[illegible]	[illegible]	[illegible]
	[illegible]										
1	[illegible]	[illegible]	[illegible]	[illegible]	[illegible]	[illegible]	[illegible]	[illegible]	[illegible]	[illegible]	[illegible]
2	[illegible]	[illegible]	[illegible]	[illegible]	[illegible]	[illegible]	[illegible]	[illegible]	[illegible]	[illegible]	[illegible]
3	[illegible]	[illegible]	[illegible]	[illegible]	[illegible]	[illegible]	[illegible]	[illegible]	[illegible]	[illegible]	[illegible]
	[illegible]										
1	[illegible]	[illegible]	[illegible]	[illegible]	[illegible]	[illegible]	[illegible]	[illegible]	[illegible]	[illegible]	[illegible]
2	[illegible]	[illegible]	[illegible]	[illegible]	[illegible]	[illegible]	[illegible]	[illegible]	[illegible]	[illegible]	[illegible]
3	[illegible]	[illegible]	[illegible]	[illegible]	[illegible]	[illegible]	[illegible]	[illegible]	[illegible]	[illegible]	[illegible]
4	[illegible]	[illegible]	[illegible]	[illegible]	[illegible]	[illegible]	[illegible]	[illegible]	[illegible]	[illegible]	[illegible]
5	[illegible]	[illegible]	[illegible]	[illegible]	[illegible]	[illegible]	[illegible]	[illegible]	[illegible]	[illegible]	[illegible]
6	[illegible]	[illegible]	[illegible]	[illegible]	[illegible]	[illegible]	[illegible]	[illegible]	[illegible]	[illegible]	[illegible]
7	[illegible]	[illegible]	[illegible]	[illegible]	[illegible]	[illegible]	[illegible]	[illegible]	[illegible]	[illegible]	[illegible]
	[illegible]										
1	[illegible]	[illegible]	[illegible]	[illegible]	[illegible]	[illegible]	[illegible]	[illegible]	[illegible]	[illegible]	[illegible]
2	[illegible]	[illegible]	[illegible]	[illegible]	[illegible]	[illegible]	[illegible]	[illegible]	[illegible]	[illegible]	[illegible]
3	[illegible]	[illegible]	[illegible]	[illegible]	[illegible]	[illegible]	[illegible]	[illegible]	[illegible]	[illegible]	[illegible]
4	[illegible]	[illegible]	[illegible]	[illegible]	[illegible]	[illegible]	[illegible]	[illegible]	[illegible]	[illegible]	[illegible]
	[illegible]										
1	[illegible]	[illegible]	[illegible]	[illegible]	[illegible]	[illegible]	[illegible]	[illegible]	[illegible]	[illegible]	[illegible]
2	[illegible]	[illegible]	[illegible]	[illegible]	[illegible]	[illegible]	[illegible]	[illegible]	[illegible]	[illegible]	[illegible]
3	[illegible]	[illegible]	[illegible]	[illegible]	[illegible]	[illegible]	[illegible]	[illegible]	[illegible]	[illegible]	[illegible]
4	[illegible]	[illegible]	[illegible]	[illegible]	[illegible]	[illegible]	[illegible]	[illegible]	[illegible]	[illegible]	[illegible]
5	[illegible]	[illegible]	[illegible]	[illegible]	[illegible]	[illegible]	[illegible]	[illegible]	[illegible]	[illegible]	[illegible]
6	[illegible]	[illegible]	[illegible]	[illegible]	[illegible]	[illegible]	[illegible]	[illegible]	[illegible]	[illegible]	[illegible]

BIRTHS AND DEATHS Registered in the Year 1891—Registrars' Districts, arranged by Counties and Superintendent Registrars' Districts—continued.

	Registrars' Districts.	Area in Statute Acres.	Population in 1891.	Total: Births.	Total: Deaths.	Births, including Illegitimate Births: Males.	Births, including Illegitimate Births: Females.	Illegitimate Births: Males.	Illegitimate Births: Females.	Deaths: Males.	Deaths: Females.	Excess of Births over Deaths.
	III.—Province of Ulster—con.											
	166. Lurgan, part of.											
1	Lurgan, No. 2, part of,	1,441	674	11	8	5	6	1	.	4	4	3
2	Moira,	[illegible]	[illegible]	151	[illegible]	75	[illegible]	5	6	[illegible]	[illegible]	[illegible]
3	Waringstown,	11,620	7,[illegible]	[illegible]	141	139	161	9	.	[illegible]	[illegible]	[illegible]
	167. Newry, part of.											
1	Donaghmore,	[illegible]	[illegible]	[illegible]	77	[illegible]	[illegible]	.	2	[illegible]	[illegible]	—[illegible]
2	Newry, No. 1, part of,	2,[illegible]	4,[illegible]	[illegible]	18	[illegible]	[illegible]	.	.	4	[illegible]	4
3	" " 2,	[illegible]	[illegible]	[illegible]	[illegible]	114	[illegible]	6	2	[illegible]	[illegible]	[illegible]
4	Rathfriland,	[illegible]	7,[illegible]	1[illegible]0	[illegible]	[illegible]	[illegible]	2	4	[illegible]	[illegible]	[illegible]
5	Warrenpoint,	15,[illegible]	[illegible]	[illegible]	1[illegible]	[illegible]	[illegible]	2	[illegible]	[illegible]	[illegible]	[illegible]
	168. Newtownards.											
1	Bangor,	17,977	7,[illegible]	[illegible]	[illegible]	[illegible]	1[illegible]	2	4	[illegible]	[illegible]	[illegible]
2	Comber,	16,[illegible]	[illegible]	[illegible]	119	[illegible]	71	3	[illegible]	[illegible]	[illegible]	[illegible]
3	Donaghadee,	9,[illegible]	[illegible]	1[illegible]	[illegible]	[illegible]	47	2	2	[illegible]	[illegible]	[illegible]
4	Greyabbey,	18,[illegible]	[illegible]	[illegible]	[illegible]	[illegible]	[illegible]	[illegible]	4	[illegible]	[illegible]	[illegible]
5	Kircubbin,	14,[illegible]	[illegible]	[illegible]	71	[illegible]	[illegible]	4	2	[illegible]	[illegible]	[illegible]
6	Newtownards, W.,	17,[illegible]	[illegible]	[illegible]	[illegible]	[illegible]	174	[illegible]	[illegible]	[illegible]	[illegible]	[illegible]
	Fermanagh Co.											
	169. Ballyshannon, part of.											
1	Belleek,	11,[illegible]	[illegible]	[illegible]	[illegible]	[illegible]	[illegible]	1	1	[illegible]	[illegible]	[illegible]
2	Church Hill,	[illegible]	[illegible]	[illegible]	[illegible]	[illegible]	[illegible]	.	.	[illegible]	[illegible]	[illegible]
	170. Clones, part of.											
1	Newtown Butler, part of,	[illegible]	[illegible]	[illegible]	[illegible]	[illegible]	[illegible]	.	[illegible]	[illegible]	[illegible]	[illegible]
2	Roslea, do.,	[illegible]	[illegible]	[illegible]	[illegible]	[illegible]	[illegible]	1	1	[illegible]	[illegible]	[illegible]
	171. Enniskillen, part of.											
1	Ely,	[illegible]	[illegible]	[illegible]	[illegible]	[illegible]	[illegible]	[illegible]	1	[illegible]	[illegible]	.
2	Enniskillen, W.,	[illegible]	[illegible]	[illegible]	[illegible]	110	[illegible]	4	[illegible]	110	[illegible]	—[illegible]
3	Florencecourt,	41,[illegible]	4,[illegible]	[illegible]	[illegible]	[illegible]	[illegible]	.	[illegible]	64	[illegible]	[illegible]
4	Holywell, part of,	[illegible]	[illegible]	11	11	7	4	.	.	5	[illegible]	.
5	Lisbellaw,	[illegible]	[illegible]	[illegible]	[illegible]	[illegible]	[illegible]	.	.	17	11	[illegible]
6	Tempo, part of,	[illegible]	[illegible]	[illegible]	[illegible]	[illegible]	[illegible]	[illegible]	1	[illegible]	[illegible]	[illegible]
	172. Irvinestown, part of.											
1	[illegible],	7,[illegible]	[illegible]	14	11	6	9	.	1	[illegible]	6	[illegible]
2	[illegible],	[illegible]	[illegible]	[illegible]	75	[illegible]	[illegible]	[illegible]	[illegible]	[illegible]	[illegible]	[illegible]
3	Irvinestown, No. 1, part of, W.,	[illegible]	[illegible]	[illegible]	[illegible]	[illegible]	[illegible]	[illegible]	[illegible]	[illegible]	[illegible]	[illegible]
4	do. No. 2, part of,	[illegible]	[illegible]	[illegible]	[illegible]	3	5	.	.	[illegible]	4	—[illegible]
	173. Lisnaskea.											
1	Brookeborough,	[illegible]	[illegible]	[illegible]	[illegible]	[illegible]	[illegible]	1	[illegible]	[illegible]	[illegible]	[illegible]
2	Derrylin,	[illegible]	[illegible]	[illegible]	[illegible]	[illegible]	[illegible]	1	3	[illegible]	[illegible]	37
3	Lisnaskea, W.,	[illegible]	[illegible]	[illegible]	[illegible]	[illegible]	[illegible]	1	[illegible]	[illegible]	[illegible]	—[illegible]
4	Maguiresbridge,	11,[illegible]	[illegible]	[illegible]	[illegible]	[illegible]	[illegible]	1	4	[illegible]	[illegible]	[illegible]
	Londonderry Co.											
	174. Ballymoney, part of.											
1	Kilrea,	[illegible]	[illegible]	1[illegible]	[illegible]	[illegible]	[illegible]	[illegible]	[illegible]	[illegible]	[illegible]	[illegible]
	175. Coleraine, part of.											
1	Aghadowey,	[illegible]	[illegible]	1[illegible]	[illegible]	[illegible]	[illegible]	[illegible]	[illegible]	[illegible]	[illegible]	[illegible]
2	Articlave,	[illegible]	[illegible]	[illegible]	[illegible]	[illegible]	[illegible]	[illegible]	1	[illegible]	[illegible]	[illegible]
3	Coleraine, W.,	[illegible]	[illegible]	[illegible]	[illegible]	[illegible]	[illegible]	[illegible]	[illegible]	[illegible]	[illegible]	[illegible]
4	Garvagh,	[illegible]	[illegible]	[illegible]	[illegible]	[illegible]	[illegible]	[illegible]	1	[illegible]	[illegible]	—[illegible]
5	Portrush, part of,	4,7[illegible]	[illegible]	[illegible]	[illegible]	[illegible]	[illegible]	.	[illegible]	14	[illegible]	[illegible]

	177. Londonderry, part of.	
1	County,	[illegible]
2	City of Derry, No. 1,	[illegible]
3	— No. 2,	[illegible]
4	Eglinton,	[illegible]
5	Glendermot, W.,	[illegible]
6	Killea[illegible], part of,	1,71[illegible]
	178. Magherafelt.	
1	Bellaghy,	[illegible]
2	Draperstown,	[illegible]
3	Maghera,	[illegible]
4	Magherafelt, W.,	[illegible]
5	Moneymore,	[illegible]
	Monaghan Co.	
	179. Carrickmacross.	
1	Carrickmacross, W.,	[illegible]
2	Donaghmoyne,	[illegible]
3	[illegible],	[illegible]
	180. Castleblayney, part of.	
1	Ballybay,	[illegible]
2	Castleblayney, W.,	[illegible]
3	[illegible], part of,	[illegible]
4	[illegible], do.	[illegible]
	181. [illegible], part of.	
1	[illegible], part of,	[illegible]
	182. Clones, part of.	
1	Clones, W.,	[illegible]
2	[illegible], part of,	[illegible]
3	[illegible], do.	[illegible]
	183. Cootehill, part of.	
1	[illegible], part of,	[illegible]
2	[illegible],	[illegible]
3	[illegible], part of,	[illegible]
	184. Dundalk, part of.	
1	[illegible], part of,	[illegible]
	185. Monaghan.	
1	[illegible],	[illegible]
2	[illegible],	[illegible]
3	[illegible],	[illegible]

BIRTHS AND DEATHS Registered in the Year 1891—REGISTRARS' DISTRICTS, arranged by COUNTIES and SUPERINTENDENT REGISTRARS' DISTRICTS—*continued.*

No.	REGISTRARS' DISTRICTS.	Area in Statute Acres.	Population in 1891.	TOTAL. BIRTHS.	TOTAL. DEATHS.	BIRTHS. Including Illegitimate Births. Males.	BIRTHS. Including Illegitimate Births. Females.	BIRTHS. Illegitimate Births. Males.	BIRTHS. Illegitimate Births. Females.	DEATHS. Males.	DEATHS. Females.	Excess of Births over Deaths.
	III.—PROVINCE OF ULSTER—con.											
	TYRONE CO.											
	146. ARMAGH, part of.											
1	Caledon,	7,0[illegible]	1,9[illegible]	43	18	27	[illegible]	3	.	13	[illegible]	8
	147. CASTLEDERG.											
1	Castlederg, W.,	23,143	4,4[illegible]	[illegible]	102	60	[illegible]	5	.	46	46	[illegible]
2	Drumquin,	27,784	2,6[illegible]	50	37	27	23	1	1	23	14	13
3	Killeter,	40,[illegible]	4,[illegible]	48	85	34	14	.	3	24	61	8
	148. CLOGHER, part of.											
1	Aughnacloy, part of,	16,170	3,934	63	51	33	30	1	3	23	28	12
2	Ballygawley,	22,494	4,420	86	64	40	46	.	.	30	34	22
3	Clogher, W.,	30,[illegible]	3,[illegible]	121	106	60	61	2	5	42	64	15
4	Fivemiletown,	33,857	3,[illegible]	76	61	37	37	2	1	28	33	15
	149. COOKSTOWN.											
1	Coagh,	11,180	2,[illegible]	90	70	40	36	4	1	29	41	20
2	Cookstown, W.,	35,973	10,377	255	214	117	148	6	8	116	108	41
3	Pomeroy,	36,324	4,424	[illegible]	51	43	20	.	3	29	32	9
4	Stewartstown,	26,257	4,737	[illegible]	61	[illegible]	[illegible]	4	2	43	18	9
	150. DUNGANNON.											
1	Ballymagran,	11,128	1,944	29	37	18	14	2	.	16	21	8
2	Benburb,	17,349	3,732	[illegible]	87	43	47	1		43	[illegible]	13
3	Castlecaulfield,	22,373	4,[illegible]	130	116	43	67	.	3	59	57	14
4	Coal Island,	30,322	4,778	203	154	102	101	.	1	78	77	49
5	Dungannon, W.,	32,150	11,450	244	157	127	117	.	4	51	[illegible]	47
	151. ENNISKILLEN, part of.											
1	Tempo, part of,	[illegible]	[illegible]	23	16	6	[illegible]	1	1	6	10	17
	152. LOWTHERSTOWN, part of.											
1	Irvinestown No. 1, part of,	1,119	247	2	4	1	1	1	.	3	1	—2
2	" No. 2, do.,	17,000	3,710	73	54	39	34	.	2	26	[illegible]	19
	153. OMAGH.											
1	Dromore,	32,145	[illegible]	85	85	45	40	1	1	30	35	[illegible]
2	Drumquin,	18,[illegible]	3,[illegible]	44	31	17	27	1	.	18	13	13
3	Fintona,	27,[illegible]	6,371	120	135	65	55	5	1	64	71	—15
4	Gortin,	33,887	6,446	85	74	38	47	.	.	47	27	11
5	Omagh, No. 1, W.,	38,[illegible]	11,[illegible]	271	325	111	160	11	8	167	158	—54
6	" No. 2,	33,[illegible]	4,344	60	72	33	27	.	.	32	40	—12
7	Mountfield,	23,[illegible]	4,159	[illegible]	47	30	22	2	4	26	21	11
	154. STRABANE, part of.											
1	Dunnamanagh,	42,431	4,[illegible]	84	80	51	33	2	3	40	30	6
2	Newtownstewart,	37,[illegible]	6,[illegible]	149	114	64	65	.	3	54	60	35
3	Plumb Bridge,	34,[illegible]	4,[illegible]	113	88	44	69	.	.	42	46	25
4	Strabane, W.,	19,871	6,[illegible]	244	245	133	110	7	11	129	116	—1

BIRTHS AND DEATHS Registered in the Year 1891—REGISTRARS' DISTRICTS, arranged by COUNTIES and SUPERINTENDENT REGISTRARS' DISTRICTS—*continued.*

No.	REGISTRARS' DISTRICTS.	Area in Statute Acres.	Population in 1881.	TOTAL. Births.	TOTAL. Deaths.	[illegible] Males.	[illegible] Females.	[illegible] Males.	[illegible] Females.	[illegible] Males.	[illegible] Females.
	IV.—PROVINCE OF CONNAUGHT.										
	Galway Co.										
	18. BALLINASLOE, part of.										
1	Ahascragh,	[illegible]	[illegible]	[illegible]	31	[illegible]	[illegible]	-	-	[illegible]	[illegible]
2	Ballinasloe, N.,	[illegible]	[illegible]	[illegible]	[illegible]	70	[illegible]	[illegible]	[illegible]	70	[illegible]
3	Kilconnell,	[illegible]	[illegible]	15	47	[illegible]	[illegible]	-	-	[illegible]	[illegible]
4	Kilreekill,	[illegible]	[illegible]	[illegible]	[illegible]	[illegible]	[illegible]	-	-	[illegible]	[illegible]
5	Lawrencetown,	[illegible]	[illegible]	[illegible]	13	14	11	-	-	[illegible]	[illegible]

BIRTHS AND DEATHS Registered in the Year 1891—REGISTRARS' DISTRICTS, arranged by COUNTIES and SUPERINTENDENT REGISTRARS' DISTRICTS—*continued.*

	REGISTRARS' DISTRICTS.	Area in Statute Acres.	Population in 1891.	TOTAL. Births.	TOTAL. Deaths.	BIRTHS. Including Registered Late. Males.	BIRTHS. Including Registered Late. Females.	BIRTHS. Illegitimate Births. Males.	BIRTHS. Illegitimate Births. Females.	DEATHS. Males.	DEATHS. Females.	[illegible]
	IV.—PROVINCE OF CONNAUGHT—*continued.*											
	[illegible], part of.											
1	[illegible], part of,	[illegible]	[illegible]	[illegible]	[illegible]	[illegible]	[illegible]	-	-	[illegible]	[illegible]	[illegible]
	[illegible], part of.											
1	[illegible], part of,	[illegible]	[illegible]	[illegible]	[illegible]	[illegible]	[illegible]	-	-	[illegible]	[illegible]	[illegible]
	[illegible] TUAM.											
1	Abbey,	[illegible]	[illegible]	[illegible]	[illegible]	[illegible]	[illegible]	-	-	[illegible]	[illegible]	[illegible]
2	Dunmore,	[illegible]	[illegible]	[illegible]	[illegible]	[illegible]	[illegible]	-	-	[illegible]	[illegible]	[illegible]
3	Headford,	[illegible]	[illegible]	[illegible]	[illegible]	[illegible]	[illegible]	-	-	[illegible]	[illegible]	[illegible]
4	Tuam, No. 1, W.	[illegible]	[illegible]	[illegible]	[illegible]	[illegible]	[illegible]	1	[illegible]	[illegible]	[illegible]	[illegible]
5	" No. 2,	[illegible]	[illegible]	[illegible]	[illegible]	[illegible]	[illegible]		[illegible]	[illegible]	[illegible]	[illegible]
	[illegible] Co.											
	[illegible], part of.											
1	[illegible],	[illegible]	[illegible]	[illegible]	[illegible]	[illegible]	[illegible]	-	1	[illegible]	[illegible]	[illegible]
	[illegible], part of.											
1	[illegible],	[illegible]	[illegible]	[illegible]	[illegible]	[illegible]	[illegible]	-	-	[illegible]	[illegible]	[illegible]
2	[illegible], part of,	[illegible]	[illegible]	[illegible]	[illegible]	[illegible]	[illegible]	-	-	[illegible]	[illegible]	[illegible]
	[illegible], part of.											
1	[illegible],	[illegible]	[illegible]	[illegible]	[illegible]	[illegible]	[illegible]	-	-	[illegible]	[illegible]	[illegible]
2	[illegible], part of, W.	[illegible]	[illegible]	[illegible]	[illegible]	[illegible]	[illegible]	[illegible]	[illegible]	[illegible]	[illegible]	[illegible]
3	[illegible], part of,	[illegible]	[illegible]	[illegible]	[illegible]	[illegible]	[illegible]	-	-	[illegible]	[illegible]	[illegible]
	[illegible].											
1	[illegible],	[illegible]	[illegible]	[illegible]	[illegible]	[illegible]	[illegible]	1	-	[illegible]	[illegible]	[illegible]
2	[illegible],	[illegible]	[illegible]	[illegible]	[illegible]	[illegible]	[illegible]	-	1	[illegible]	[illegible]	[illegible]
3	[illegible],	[illegible]	[illegible]	[illegible]	[illegible]	[illegible]	[illegible]	-	-	[illegible]	[illegible]	[illegible]
4	[illegible], W.	[illegible]	[illegible]	[illegible]	[illegible]	[illegible]	[illegible]	[illegible]	[illegible]	[illegible]	[illegible]	[illegible]
	[illegible].											
1	[illegible],	[illegible]	[illegible]	[illegible]	[illegible]	[illegible]	[illegible]	[illegible]	-	[illegible]	[illegible]	[illegible]
2	[illegible], W.	[illegible]	[illegible]	[illegible]	[illegible]	[illegible]	[illegible]	1	[illegible]	[illegible]	[illegible]	[illegible]
3	[illegible],	[illegible]	[illegible]	[illegible]	[illegible]	[illegible]	[illegible]	-	-	[illegible]	[illegible]	[illegible]
4	[illegible],	[illegible]	[illegible]	[illegible]	[illegible]	[illegible]	[illegible]	-	-	[illegible]	[illegible]	[illegible]
	MAYO CO.											
	[illegible] BALLINA, part of.											
1	Ballina, part of, W.	[illegible]	[illegible]	[illegible]	[illegible]	[illegible]	[illegible]	[illegible]	[illegible]	[illegible]	[illegible]	[illegible]
2	[illegible],	[illegible]	7,116	[illegible]	[illegible]	[illegible]	[illegible]	-	-	[illegible]	[illegible]	[illegible]
	[illegible] BALLINROBE, part of.											
1	Ballinrobe, W.	[illegible]	[illegible]	[illegible]	[illegible]	[illegible]	[illegible]	-	1	[illegible]	[illegible]	[illegible]
2	[illegible], part of,	[illegible]	[illegible]	[illegible]	[illegible]	[illegible]	[illegible]	-	-	[illegible]	[illegible]	[illegible]
3	Cong,	[illegible]	[illegible]	[illegible]	[illegible]	[illegible]	[illegible]	-	1	[illegible]	[illegible]	[illegible]
4	Hollymount,	[illegible]	[illegible]	[illegible]	[illegible]	[illegible]	[illegible]	-	1	[illegible]	[illegible]	[illegible]
	[illegible] BELMULLET.											

BIRTHS AND DEATHS Registered in the Year 1881.—REGISTRARS' DISTRICTS, arranged by COUNTIES and SUPERINTENDENT REGISTRARS' DISTRICTS—*continued.*

No.	Registrars' Districts.	Area in Statute Acres.	Population in 1881.	Total: Births.	Total: Deaths.	Births: Including Illegitimate Births: Males.	Births: Including Illegitimate Births: Females.	Illegitimate Births: Males.	Illegitimate Births: Females.	Deaths: Males.	Deaths: Females.
	IV.—PROVINCE OF CONNAUGHT—*continued.*										
	[illegible]. CASTLEBAR.										
1	Balla,	[illegible]	[illegible]	154	[illegible]	[illegible]	[illegible]	.	.	[illegible]	43
2	Castlebar, No. 1, W.	40,254	[illegible]	243	[illegible]	118	127	.	.	125	[illegible]
3	" No. 2,	[illegible]	[illegible]	[illegible]	[illegible]	[illegible]	[illegible]	.	1	[illegible]	[illegible]
	[illegible]. CASTLEREAGH, part of.										
1	Ballaghaderreen, part of,	[illegible]	[illegible]	[illegible]	[illegible]	[illegible]	[illegible]	.	.	[illegible]	44
	[illegible]. CLAREMORRIS.										
1	Ballindine,	[illegible]	[illegible]	[illegible]	173	[illegible]	[illegible]	.	.	104	[illegible]
2	Ballyhaunis,	41,274	11,784	[illegible]	[illegible]	147	[illegible]	2	.	[illegible]	[illegible]
3	Claremorris, W.	[illegible]	[illegible]	[illegible]	[illegible]	[illegible]	[illegible]	.	1	[illegible]	[illegible]
	[illegible]. KILLALA.										
1	[illegible],	[illegible]	[illegible]	[illegible]	47	[illegible]	[illegible]	.	.	[illegible]	[illegible]
2	Killala, W.	[illegible]	[illegible]	77	[illegible]	[illegible]	[illegible]	2	7	[illegible]	[illegible]
	[illegible]. SWINFORD.										
1	Foxford,	[illegible]	[illegible]	[illegible]	[illegible]	[illegible]	[illegible]	.	1	[illegible]	[illegible]
2	Kilkelly,	[illegible]	11,354	[illegible]	[illegible]	[illegible]	[illegible]	1	.	[illegible]	75
3	Kiltimagh,	[illegible]	[illegible]	[illegible]	[illegible]	[illegible]	[illegible]	.	.	77	[illegible]
4	[illegible],	[illegible]	[illegible]	[illegible]	[illegible]	[illegible]	[illegible]	.	.	[illegible]	[illegible]
5	Swinford, W.	[illegible]	[illegible]	[illegible]	170	[illegible]	[illegible]	4	2	[illegible]	[illegible]
	[illegible]. WESTPORT.										
1	Achill,	[illegible]	[illegible]	[illegible]	[illegible]	75	[illegible]	.	.	47	[illegible]
2	[illegible],	[illegible]	[illegible]	[illegible]	[illegible]	[illegible]	[illegible]	.	.	[illegible]	[illegible]
3	[illegible],	[illegible]	[illegible]	[illegible]	78	[illegible]	[illegible]	.	.	[illegible]	41
4	Louisburgh, No. 1,	[illegible]	[illegible]	[illegible]	[illegible]	[illegible]	78	.	.	45	44
5	" No. 2,	[illegible]	[illegible]	[illegible]	2	4	4	.	.	1	1
6	Newport,	[illegible]	[illegible]	[illegible]	77	[illegible]	[illegible]	.	.	[illegible]	[illegible]
7	Westport, No. 1, W.	[illegible]	[illegible]	[illegible]	[illegible]	[illegible]	167	1	.	[illegible]	167
8	No. 2,	[illegible]	[illegible]	1	1	[illegible]	1	.	.	1	1
	ROSCOMMON CO.										
	[illegible]. ATHLONE, part of.										
1	Athlone, No. 2,	[illegible]	[illegible]	[illegible]	[illegible]	[illegible]	[illegible]	.	1	[illegible]	[illegible]
2	[illegible],	[illegible]	[illegible]	[illegible]	[illegible]	[illegible]	[illegible]	.	.	17	[illegible]
3	[illegible],	[illegible]	[illegible]	74	[illegible]	[illegible]	[illegible]	.	.	[illegible]	[illegible]
	[illegible]. BALLINASLOE, part of.										
1	Creagh,	[illegible]	[illegible]	179	[illegible]	[illegible]	[illegible]	.	.	[illegible]	[illegible]
	[illegible]. BOYLE, part of.										
1	[illegible],	[illegible]	[illegible]	[illegible]	[illegible]	72	[illegible]	.	.	[illegible]	[illegible]
2	[illegible], part of,	[illegible]	[illegible]	27	[illegible]	[illegible]	[illegible]	.	.	[illegible]	[illegible]
3	Boyle, do. W.	[illegible]	[illegible]	[illegible]	[illegible]	[illegible]	[illegible]	1	5	[illegible]	[illegible]
4	[illegible],	[illegible]	[illegible]	[illegible]	77	[illegible]	[illegible]	.	.	[illegible]	[illegible]
	[illegible]. CARRICK-ON-SHANNON, part of.										
1	[illegible],	[illegible]	[illegible]	[illegible]	[illegible]	[illegible]	[illegible]	.	.	[illegible]	[illegible]
2	[illegible], part of,	[illegible]	[illegible]	[illegible]	[illegible]	17	16	.	.	14	[illegible]
3	[illegible], do.	[illegible]	[illegible]	[illegible]	[illegible]	[illegible]	[illegible]	.	.	[illegible]	[illegible]

BIRTHS AND DEATHS Registered in the Year 1891—REGISTRARS' DISTRICTS, arranged by COUNTIES and SUPERINTENDENT REGISTRARS' DISTRICTS—continued.

No.	REGISTRARS' DISTRICTS	Area in Statute Acres.	Population in 1891.	TOTAL. Births.	TOTAL. Deaths.	BIRTHS. Legitimate. Males.	BIRTHS. Legitimate. Females.	BIRTHS. Illegitimate. Males.	BIRTHS. Illegitimate. Females.	DEATHS. Males.	DEATHS. Females.	[illegible]
	IV.—PROVINCE OF CONNAUGHT—continued.											
	226. CASTLEREA, part of.											
1	[illegible], part of,	[illegible]	7,[illegible]	[illegible]	[illegible]	74	[illegible]	.	.	[illegible]	[illegible]	[illegible]
2	[illegible],	[illegible]	[illegible]	[illegible]	[illegible]	[illegible]	[illegible]	1	.	[illegible]	[illegible]	[illegible]
3	[illegible], W.	[illegible]	[illegible]	[illegible]	[illegible]	[illegible]	[illegible]	[illegible]	3	[illegible]	[illegible]	[illegible]
4	[illegible],	[illegible]	[illegible]	[illegible]	[illegible]	[illegible]	[illegible]	.	1	[illegible]	[illegible]	[illegible]
	227. [illegible], part of.											
1	[illegible], part of,	[illegible]	[illegible]	[illegible]	[illegible]	[illegible]	[illegible]	.	.	[illegible]	[illegible]	[illegible]
2	[illegible],	[illegible]	[illegible]	[illegible]	[illegible]	[illegible]	[illegible]	.	.	[illegible]	[illegible]	[illegible]
3	[illegible], W.	[illegible]	[illegible]	[illegible]	[illegible]	[illegible]	[illegible]	.	1	[illegible]	[illegible]	[illegible]
	228. [illegible].											
1	[illegible].	[illegible]	[illegible]	[illegible]	[illegible]	[illegible]	[illegible]	.	.	[illegible]	41	[illegible]
2	[illegible],	[illegible]	[illegible]	[illegible]	[illegible]	[illegible]	[illegible]	.	.	[illegible]	[illegible]	[illegible]
3	[illegible], W.	[illegible]	7,[illegible]	[illegible]	[illegible]	[illegible]	[illegible]	1	.	[illegible]	[illegible]	[illegible]
	Sligo Co.											
	229. [illegible], part of.											
1	[illegible], part of,	[illegible]	[illegible]	[illegible]	[illegible]	[illegible]	[illegible]	.	.	[illegible]	[illegible]	[illegible]
	230. [illegible], part of											
1	[illegible], part of,	[illegible]	[illegible]	[illegible]	[illegible]	[illegible]	[illegible]	1	.	[illegible]	[illegible]	[illegible]
2	[illegible], do.,	[illegible]	[illegible]	[illegible]	[illegible]	[illegible]	[illegible]	.	.	[illegible]	[illegible]	[illegible]
3	[illegible],	[illegible]	[illegible]	[illegible]	[illegible]	[illegible]	[illegible]	.	1	[illegible]	[illegible]	[illegible]
	231. [illegible].											
1	[illegible],	[illegible]	[illegible]	[illegible]	[illegible]	[illegible]	[illegible]	.		[illegible]	[illegible]	[illegible]
2	[illegible], W.,	[illegible]	[illegible]	[illegible]	[illegible]	[illegible]	[illegible]	.	.	[illegible]	[illegible]	[illegible]
3	[illegible],	[illegible]	[illegible]	[illegible]	[illegible]	[illegible]	[illegible]	.	.	[illegible]	[illegible]	[illegible]
	232. SLIGO.											
1	[illegible],	[illegible]	[illegible]	[illegible]	[illegible]	[illegible]	[illegible]	.	.	[illegible]	[illegible]	[illegible]
2	[illegible], No. 1,	[illegible]	[illegible]	[illegible]	77	[illegible]	[illegible]	.	.	[illegible]	[illegible]	[illegible]
3	" No. 2,	[illegible]	[illegible]	[illegible]	77	[illegible]	[illegible]	.	1	[illegible]	[illegible]	[illegible]
4	[illegible],	[illegible]	[illegible]	[illegible]	[illegible]	[illegible]	[illegible]	.	.	[illegible]	[illegible]	[illegible]
5	[illegible],	[illegible]	[illegible]	[illegible]	[illegible]	[illegible]	[illegible]	1	.	[illegible]	[illegible]	[illegible]
6	Sligo, No. 1, W.,	[illegible]	[illegible]	[illegible]	[illegible]	[illegible]	[illegible]	[illegible]	3	[illegible]	[illegible]	[illegible]
7	" No. 2,	[illegible]	[illegible]	[illegible]	[illegible]	[illegible]	[illegible]	.	1	[illegible]	[illegible]	[illegible]
	233. [illegible].											
1	[illegible],	[illegible]	[illegible]	[illegible]	[illegible]	[illegible]	[illegible]	.	.	[illegible]	[illegible]	[illegible]
2	[illegible],	[illegible]	[illegible]	[illegible]	[illegible]	[illegible]	[illegible]	.	.	[illegible]	[illegible]	1
3	[illegible], W.,	[illegible]	[illegible]	[illegible]	[illegible]	[illegible]	[illegible]	1	.	[illegible]	[illegible]	[illegible]

[illegible]
[illegible]
[illegible]
[illegible], F.

[illegible]
[illegible]
[illegible]
[illegible] and [illegible], F.
[illegible] and [illegible].

[illegible], F.
[illegible]
[illegible]
[illegible]
[illegible]

[illegible]
[illegible]
[illegible]
[illegible], No. 1, F.
No. 2.

[illegible], F.
[illegible] ([illegible]).
[illegible]
[illegible]
[illegible]
[illegible]

[illegible]
[illegible], F.
[illegible]
[illegible]
[illegible], No. 1, F.

[illegible]
[illegible], F.
[illegible]
[illegible], F.
[illegible]

[illegible], No. 1, F.
[illegible]
[illegible]
[illegible]
[illegible]

[illegible]
[illegible]
[illegible]
[illegible], No. 1, F.
[illegible]
St. Mary's (Drogheda), F.

[illegible]
[illegible]
[illegible], No. 1.

TABLES SHOWING THE NUMBER

OF

BIRTHS

AND

DEATHS

REGISTERED IN EACH OF THE FOUR QUARTERS OF THE YEAR

ALSO

DEATHS AT DIFFERENT AGES,

AND

CAUSES OF DEATH;

IN 1891.

Note.—The Number of Marriages Registered in each Quarter of the Year 1891 will be found stated in the Abstract of Marriages commencing at Page 11.

[illegible] registered in Ireland in the Four Quarters ending
(Exclusive of

No.	Provinces and Counties	Area in Statute Acres	Population in [illegible]	Males and Females: Total	Registered in the Quarter ending the last day of: March	June	Sept.	Dec.
	IRELAND,	[illegible]	[illegible]	[illegible]	[illegible]	[illegible]	[illegible]	[illegible]
	Provinces.							
I.	LEINSTER,	[illegible]	[illegible]	[illegible]	[illegible]	[illegible]	[illegible]	[illegible]
II.	MUNSTER,	[illegible]	[illegible]	[illegible]	[illegible]	[illegible]	[illegible]	[illegible]
III.	ULSTER,	[illegible]	[illegible]	[illegible]	[illegible]	[illegible]	[illegible]	[illegible]
IV.	CONNAUGHT,	[illegible]	[illegible]	[illegible]	[illegible]	[illegible]	[illegible]	[illegible]
	I.—PROVINCE OF							
1	Carlow,	[illegible]	[illegible]	[illegible]	[illegible]	[illegible]	[illegible]	[illegible]
2	Dublin,	[illegible]	[illegible]	[illegible]	[illegible]	[illegible]	[illegible]	[illegible]
3	Kildare,	[illegible]	[illegible]	[illegible]	[illegible]	[illegible]	[illegible]	[illegible]
4	Kilkenny,	[illegible]	[illegible]	[illegible]	[illegible]	[illegible]	[illegible]	[illegible]
5	King's,	[illegible]	[illegible]	[illegible]	[illegible]	[illegible]	[illegible]	[illegible]
6	Longford,	[illegible]	[illegible]	[illegible]	[illegible]	[illegible]	[illegible]	[illegible]
7	Louth, and county of the town of Drogheda,	[illegible]	[illegible]	[illegible]	[illegible]	[illegible]	[illegible]	[illegible]
8	Meath,	[illegible]	[illegible]	[illegible]	[illegible]	[illegible]	[illegible]	[illegible]
9	Queen's,	[illegible]	[illegible]	[illegible]	[illegible]	[illegible]	[illegible]	[illegible]
10	Westmeath,	[illegible]	[illegible]	[illegible]	[illegible]	[illegible]	[illegible]	[illegible]
11	Wexford,	[illegible]	[illegible]	[illegible]	[illegible]	[illegible]	[illegible]	[illegible]
12	Wicklow,	[illegible]	[illegible]	[illegible]	[illegible]	[illegible]	[illegible]	[illegible]
	II.—PROVINCE OF							
13	Clare,	[illegible]	[illegible]	[illegible]	[illegible]	[illegible]	[illegible]	[illegible]
14	Cork,	[illegible]	[illegible]	[illegible]	[illegible]	[illegible]	[illegible]	[illegible]
15	Kerry,	[illegible]	[illegible]	[illegible]	[illegible]	[illegible]	[illegible]	[illegible]
16	Limerick,	[illegible]	[illegible]	[illegible]	[illegible]	[illegible]	[illegible]	[illegible]
17	Tipperary,	[illegible]	[illegible]	[illegible]	[illegible]	[illegible]	[illegible]	[illegible]
18	Waterford,	[illegible]	[illegible]	[illegible]	[illegible]	[illegible]	[illegible]	[illegible]
	III.—PROVINCE OF							
19	Antrim,	[illegible]	[illegible]	[illegible]	[illegible]	[illegible]	[illegible]	[illegible]
20	Armagh,	[illegible]	[illegible]	[illegible]	[illegible]	[illegible]	[illegible]	[illegible]
21	Cavan,	[illegible]	[illegible]	[illegible]	[illegible]	[illegible]	[illegible]	[illegible]
22	Donegal,	[illegible]	[illegible]	[illegible]	[illegible]	[illegible]	[illegible]	[illegible]
23	Down,	[illegible]	[illegible]	[illegible]	[illegible]	[illegible]	[illegible]	[illegible]
24	Fermanagh,	[illegible]	[illegible]	[illegible]	[illegible]	[illegible]	[illegible]	[illegible]
25	Londonderry,	[illegible]	[illegible]	[illegible]	[illegible]	[illegible]	[illegible]	[illegible]
26	Monaghan,	[illegible]	[illegible]	[illegible]	[illegible]	[illegible]	[illegible]	[illegible]
27	Tyrone,	[illegible]	[illegible]	[illegible]	[illegible]	[illegible]	[illegible]	[illegible]
	IV.—PROVINCE OF							
28	Galway,	[illegible]	[illegible]	[illegible]	[illegible]	[illegible]	[illegible]	[illegible]
29	Leitrim,	[illegible]	[illegible]	[illegible]	[illegible]	[illegible]	[illegible]	[illegible]
30	Mayo,	[illegible]	[illegible]	[illegible]	[illegible]	[illegible]	[illegible]	[illegible]
31	Roscommon,	[illegible]	[illegible]	[illegible]	[illegible]	[illegible]	[illegible]	[illegible]
32	Sligo,	[illegible]	[illegible]	[illegible]	[illegible]	[illegible]	[illegible]	[illegible]

March 31st, June 30th, September 30th, and December 31st, 1891.
Still-born).

Males. Registered in the quarters ending the last day of — March.	June.	Sept.	Dec.	Males. Total.	Females. Total.	Females. Registered in the quarters ending the last day of — March.	June.	Sept.	Dec.	Provinces and Counties.
[illegible]	[illegible]	[illegible]	[illegible]	[illegible]	[illegible]	[illegible]	[illegible]	[illegible]	[illegible]	IRELAND.
										Provinces.
[illegible]	[illegible]	[illegible]	[illegible]	[illegible]	[illegible]	[illegible]	[illegible]	[illegible]	[illegible]	LEINSTER.
[illegible]	[illegible]	[illegible]	[illegible]	[illegible]	[illegible]	[illegible]	[illegible]	[illegible]	[illegible]	MUNSTER.
[illegible]	[illegible]	[illegible]	[illegible]	[illegible]	[illegible]	[illegible]	[illegible]	[illegible]	[illegible]	ULSTER.
[illegible]	[illegible]	[illegible]	[illegible]	[illegible]	[illegible]	[illegible]	[illegible]	[illegible]	[illegible]	CONNAUGHT.
LEINSTER.										
[illegible]	[illegible]	[illegible]	[illegible]	[illegible]	[illegible]	[illegible]	[illegible]	[illegible]	[illegible]	Carlow.
[illegible]	[illegible]	[illegible]	[illegible]	[illegible]	[illegible]	[illegible]	[illegible]	[illegible]	[illegible]	Dublin.
[illegible]	[illegible]	[illegible]	[illegible]	[illegible]	[illegible]	[illegible]	[illegible]	[illegible]	[illegible]	Kildare.
[illegible]	[illegible]	[illegible]	[illegible]	[illegible]	[illegible]	[illegible]	[illegible]	[illegible]	[illegible]	Kilkenny.
[illegible]	[illegible]	[illegible]	[illegible]	[illegible]	[illegible]	[illegible]	[illegible]	[illegible]	[illegible]	King's.
[illegible]	[illegible]	[illegible]	[illegible]	[illegible]	[illegible]	[illegible]	[illegible]	[illegible]	[illegible]	Longford.
[illegible]	[illegible]	[illegible]	[illegible]	[illegible]	[illegible]	[illegible]	[illegible]	[illegible]	[illegible]	Louth, and county of the town of Drogheda.
[illegible]	[illegible]	[illegible]	[illegible]	[illegible]	[illegible]	[illegible]	[illegible]	[illegible]	[illegible]	Meath.
[illegible]	[illegible]	[illegible]	[illegible]	[illegible]	[illegible]	[illegible]	[illegible]	[illegible]	[illegible]	Queen's.
[illegible]	[illegible]	[illegible]	[illegible]	[illegible]	[illegible]	[illegible]	[illegible]	[illegible]	[illegible]	Westmeath.
[illegible]	[illegible]	[illegible]	[illegible]	[illegible]	[illegible]	[illegible]	[illegible]	[illegible]	[illegible]	Wexford.
[illegible]	[illegible]	[illegible]	[illegible]	[illegible]	[illegible]	[illegible]	[illegible]	[illegible]	[illegible]	Wicklow.
MUNSTER.										
[illegible]	[illegible]	[illegible]	[illegible]	[illegible]	[illegible]	[illegible]	[illegible]	[illegible]	[illegible]	Clare.
[illegible]	[illegible]	[illegible]	[illegible]	[illegible]	[illegible]	[illegible]	[illegible]	[illegible]	[illegible]	Cork.
[illegible]	[illegible]	[illegible]	[illegible]	[illegible]	[illegible]	[illegible]	[illegible]	[illegible]	[illegible]	Kerry.
[illegible]	[illegible]	[illegible]	[illegible]	[illegible]	[illegible]	[illegible]	[illegible]	[illegible]	[illegible]	Limerick.
[illegible]	[illegible]	[illegible]	[illegible]	[illegible]	[illegible]	[illegible]	[illegible]	[illegible]	[illegible]	Tipperary.
[illegible]	[illegible]	[illegible]	[illegible]	[illegible]	[illegible]	[illegible]	[illegible]	[illegible]	[illegible]	Waterford.
ULSTER.										
[illegible]	[illegible]	[illegible]	[illegible]	[illegible]	[illegible]	[illegible]	[illegible]	[illegible]	[illegible]	Antrim.
[illegible]	[illegible]	[illegible]	[illegible]	[illegible]	[illegible]	[illegible]	[illegible]	[illegible]	[illegible]	Armagh.
[illegible]	[illegible]	[illegible]	[illegible]	[illegible]	[illegible]	[illegible]	[illegible]	[illegible]	[illegible]	Cavan.
[illegible]	[illegible]	[illegible]	[illegible]	[illegible]	[illegible]	[illegible]	[illegible]	[illegible]	[illegible]	Donegal.
[illegible]	[illegible]	[illegible]	[illegible]	[illegible]	[illegible]	[illegible]	[illegible]	[illegible]	[illegible]	Down.
[illegible]	[illegible]	[illegible]	[illegible]	[illegible]	[illegible]	[illegible]	[illegible]	[illegible]	[illegible]	Fermanagh.
[illegible]	[illegible]	[illegible]	[illegible]	[illegible]	[illegible]	[illegible]	[illegible]	[illegible]	[illegible]	Londonderry.
[illegible]	[illegible]	[illegible]	[illegible]	[illegible]	[illegible]	[illegible]	[illegible]	[illegible]	[illegible]	Monaghan.
[illegible]	[illegible]	[illegible]	[illegible]	[illegible]	[illegible]	[illegible]	[illegible]	[illegible]	[illegible]	Tyrone.
CONNAUGHT.										
[illegible]	[illegible]	[illegible]	[illegible]	[illegible]	[illegible]	[illegible]	[illegible]	[illegible]	[illegible]	Galway.
[illegible]	[illegible]	[illegible]	[illegible]	[illegible]	[illegible]	[illegible]	[illegible]	[illegible]	[illegible]	Leitrim.
[illegible]	[illegible]	[illegible]	[illegible]	[illegible]	[illegible]	[illegible]	[illegible]	[illegible]	[illegible]	Mayo.
[illegible]	[illegible]	[illegible]	[illegible]	[illegible]	[illegible]	[illegible]	[illegible]	[illegible]	[illegible]	Roscommon.
[illegible]	[illegible]	[illegible]	[illegible]	[illegible]	[illegible]	[illegible]	[illegible]	[illegible]	[illegible]	Sligo.

BIRTHS registered in Ireland in the Four Quarters ending

I.—PROVINCE OF

No.	SUPERINTENDENT REGISTRAR'S DISTRICT	Area in Statute Acres.	Population in 1871.	MALES AND FEMALES. Total.	Registered in the Quarter ending the last day of March	June	Sept.	Dec.
	Carlow Co.							
1	Baltinglass, part of,	23,139	2,3[illegible]	43	10	12	13	8
2	Carlow, do.,	148,071	30,718	587	144	160	136	148
3	Enniscorthy, do.,	9,838	[illegible]	[illegible]	3	6	7	1
4	New Ross, do.,	[illegible]	[illegible]	[illegible]	[illegible]	[illegible]	[illegible]	[illegible]
5	Shillelagh, do.,	[illegible]	[illegible]	73	11	[illegible]	11	[illegible]
	Dublin Co.							
6	Balrothery,	[illegible]	17,[illegible]	[illegible]	[illegible]	[illegible]	[illegible]	71
7	Celbridge, part of,	[illegible]	[illegible]	[illegible]	[illegible]	[illegible]	[illegible]	[illegible]
8	Dublin, North,	[illegible]	[illegible]	[illegible]	1,127	[illegible]	1,14[illegible]	[illegible]
9	Dublin, South,	[illegible]	[illegible]	[illegible]	[illegible]	[illegible]	[illegible]	1,1[illegible]
10	Dunshaughlin, part of,	8,783	[illegible]	15	[illegible]	[illegible]	[illegible]	1
11	Rathdown, do.,	27,151	[illegible]	[illegible]	[illegible]	277	241	[illegible]
	Kildare Co.							
12	Athy, part of,	118,811	[illegible]	[illegible]	110	[illegible]	[illegible]	[illegible]
13	Baltinglass, do.,	17,133	[illegible]	44	[illegible]	6	[illegible]	9
14	Celbridge, do.,	[illegible]	[illegible]	201	[illegible]	[illegible]	47	44
15	Edenderry, do.,	[illegible]	[illegible]	16[illegible]	37	[illegible]	[illegible]	31
16	Naas, do.,	143,1[illegible]	[illegible]	[illegible]	[illegible]	[illegible]	[illegible]	173
	Kilkenny Co.							
17	Callan, part of,	[illegible]	[illegible]	1[illegible]	[illegible]	[illegible]	[illegible]	[illegible]
18	Carrick-on-Suir, do.,	[illegible]	[illegible]	[illegible]	[illegible]	[illegible]	[illegible]	[illegible]
19	Castlecomer,	[illegible]	11,[illegible]	[illegible]	[illegible]	[illegible]	[illegible]	[illegible]
20	Kilkenny,	[illegible]	[illegible]	[illegible]	[illegible]	145	1[illegible]	[illegible]
21	New Ross, part of,	[illegible]	4,3[illegible]	[illegible]	[illegible]	[illegible]	[illegible]	[illegible]
22	Thomastown,	[illegible]	14,[illegible]	[illegible]	73	[illegible]	[illegible]	75
23	Urlingford, part of,	[illegible]	[illegible]	[illegible]	[illegible]	[illegible]	[illegible]	14
24	Waterford, do.,	[illegible]	[illegible]	174	47	[illegible]	[illegible]	[illegible]
	King's Co.							
25	Edenderry, part of,	[illegible]	[illegible]	171	41	47	[illegible]	[illegible]
26	Mountmellick, do.,	[illegible]	[illegible]	[illegible]	18	[illegible]	19	41
27	Parsonstown, do.,	[illegible]	[illegible]	[illegible]	[illegible]	[illegible]	[illegible]	[illegible]
28	Roscrea, do.,	[illegible]	[illegible]	[illegible]	[illegible]	[illegible]	31	[illegible]
29	Tullamore, do.,	[illegible]	[illegible]	[illegible]	11[illegible]	[illegible]	[illegible]	[illegible]
	Longford Co.							
30	Ballymahon, part of,	[illegible]	10,[illegible]	[illegible]	[illegible]	[illegible]	[illegible]	[illegible]
31	Granard, do.,	77,[illegible]	17,[illegible]	[illegible]	[illegible]	[illegible]	75	[illegible]
32	Longford,	[illegible]	[illegible]	[illegible]	110	[illegible]	[illegible]	[illegible]
	Louth Co. and Co. of Town of Drogheda.							
33	Ardee, part of,	[illegible]	[illegible]	[illegible]	47	[illegible]	[illegible]	[illegible]
34	Dundalk, do.,	41,[illegible]	[illegible]	[illegible]	[illegible]	[illegible]	11[illegible]	[illegible]
35	Drogheda, do.,	[illegible]	[illegible]	[illegible]	[illegible]	[illegible]	[illegible]	[illegible]
	Meath Co.							
36	Ardee, part of,	[illegible]	[illegible]	[illegible]	[illegible]	[illegible]	[illegible]	11
37	Celbridge, do.,	7,[illegible]	[illegible]	9	3	–	1	5
38	Drogheda, do.,	[illegible]	[illegible]	[illegible]	[illegible]	[illegible]	[illegible]	[illegible]
39	Dunshaughlin, do.,	[illegible]	[illegible]	[illegible]	[illegible]	[illegible]	[illegible]	[illegible]
40	Edenderry, do.,	[illegible]	[illegible]	[illegible]	13	[illegible]	6	6
41	Kells, do.,	[illegible]	[illegible]	[illegible]	[illegible]	[illegible]	[illegible]	[illegible]
42	Navan,	[illegible]	[illegible]	[illegible]	[illegible]	[illegible]	[illegible]	[illegible]
43	Oldcastle, part of,	[illegible]	[illegible]	[illegible]	[illegible]	[illegible]	[illegible]	[illegible]
44	Trim,	[illegible]	14,811	[illegible]	[illegible]	[illegible]	[illegible]	[illegible]

Carlow Co.

[illegible] [illegible], part of.
[illegible] Carlow, do.
[illegible] [illegible] do.
[illegible] New Ross, do.
[illegible] [illegible], do.

Dublin Co.

[illegible] Balrothery.
[illegible] [illegible], part of.
[illegible] Dublin, North.
[illegible] Dublin, South
[illegible] [illegible], part of.
[illegible] Rathdown, do.

Kildare Co.

[illegible] Athy, part of.
[illegible] [illegible], do.
[illegible] [illegible], do.
[illegible] [illegible], do.
[illegible] [illegible], do.

Kilkenny Co.

[illegible] Callan, part of.
[illegible] [illegible], do.
[illegible] [illegible].
[illegible] [illegible].
[illegible] New Ross, part of.
[illegible] [illegible].
[illegible] [illegible], part of.
[illegible] Waterford, do.

King's Co.

[illegible] [illegible], part of.
[illegible] [illegible], do.
[illegible] Philipstown, do.
[illegible] [illegible], do.
[illegible] Tullamore, do.

Longford Co.

[illegible] Ballymahon, part of.
[illegible] Granard, do.
[illegible] Longford.

No.	Queen's Co.							
45	[illegible],	127,543	18,[illegible]	262	97	140	[illegible]	67
46	[illegible], part of,	[illegible]	4,[illegible]	1[illegible]	41	[illegible]	27	25
47	[illegible], do.,	82,1[illegible]	6,[illegible]	1[illegible]	[illegible]	43	43	34
48	[illegible], part of,	1[illegible]	[illegible]	[illegible]	271	1[illegible]	141	1[illegible]
49	[illegible], do.,	[illegible]	[illegible]	[illegible]	17	1[illegible]	16	1[illegible]
50	[illegible], do.,	4,1[illegible]	[illegible]	6	5	4	.	1
	Westmeath Co.							
51	[illegible], part of,	47,[illegible]	14,217	[illegible]	41	[illegible]	[illegible]	67
52	[illegible], do.,	[illegible]	4,[illegible]	75	16	[illegible]	25	[illegible]
53	[illegible],	74,[illegible]	[illegible]	[illegible]	[illegible]	47	27	[illegible]
54	[illegible], part of,	[illegible]	4,[illegible]	75	[illegible]	[illegible]	[illegible]	34
55	[illegible],	[illegible]	[illegible]	479	[illegible]	[illegible]	141	141
56	[illegible], part of,	[illegible]	[illegible]	46	13	[illegible]	12	[illegible]
	Wexford Co.							
57	[illegible], part of,	1[illegible]	[illegible]	[illegible]	[illegible]	475	[illegible]	116
58	[illegible],	[illegible]	1[illegible]	444	[illegible]	143	[illegible]	61
59	[illegible], part of,	1[illegible],017	[illegible]	[illegible]	[illegible]	1[illegible]	[illegible]	1[illegible]
60	[illegible], do.,	[illegible]	1[illegible]	5	1	4	1	2
61	[illegible],	[illegible]	15,1[illegible]	1[illegible]	[illegible]	[illegible]	1[illegible]	1[illegible]
	Wicklow Co.							
62	[illegible], part of,	[illegible]	11,[illegible]	[illegible]	4[illegible]	4[illegible]	[illegible]	[illegible]
63	[illegible], do.,	[illegible]	[illegible]	36	[illegible]	11	11	[illegible]
64	[illegible], do.,	[illegible]	[illegible]	1[illegible]	[illegible]	[illegible]	[illegible]	[illegible]
65	[illegible],	[illegible]	77,[illegible]	[illegible]	[illegible]	1[illegible]	1[illegible]	[illegible]
66	[illegible], part of,	[illegible]	[illegible]	1[illegible]	[illegible]	73	47	34

	Clare Co.							
67	[illegible],	71,[illegible]	4,[illegible]	[illegible]	[illegible]	[illegible]	6	[illegible]
68	[illegible],	[illegible]	4,[illegible]	[illegible]	[illegible]	[illegible]	17	[illegible]
69	[illegible],	1[illegible]	71,[illegible]	[illegible]	[illegible]	[illegible]	1[illegible]	[illegible]
70	[illegible],	[illegible]	[illegible]	[illegible]	[illegible]	[illegible]	1[illegible]	67
71	[illegible],	[illegible]	1[illegible]	[illegible]	70	[illegible]	81	47
72	[illegible],	1[illegible]	[illegible]	[illegible]	177	[illegible]	1[illegible]	1[illegible]
73	[illegible], part of,	[illegible]	[illegible]	1[illegible]	40	[illegible]	[illegible]	[illegible]
74	[illegible], do.,	[illegible]	[illegible]	[illegible]	[illegible]	[illegible]	4[illegible]	[illegible]
75	[illegible],	[illegible]	11,[illegible]	[illegible]	[illegible]	[illegible]	[illegible]	[illegible]
	Cork Co.							
76	[illegible],	1[illegible]	[illegible]	[illegible]	176	1[illegible]	1[illegible]	[illegible]
77	[illegible],	1[illegible]	1[illegible]	[illegible]	117	[illegible]	67	[illegible]
78	[illegible],	7[illegible]	1[illegible]	[illegible]	[illegible]	[illegible]	[illegible]	[illegible]
79	[illegible],	[illegible]	[illegible]	[illegible]	1[illegible]	[illegible]	[illegible]	[illegible]
80	[illegible],	[illegible]	[illegible]	1,[illegible]	[illegible]	[illegible]	1[illegible]	172
81	[illegible],	[illegible]	14,[illegible]	[illegible]	[illegible]	[illegible]	11	[illegible]

March 31st, June 30th, September 30th, and December 31st, 1891—*continued.*

[illegible]—*continued.*

MALES.					FEMALES.					SUPERINTENDENT REGISTRARS' DISTRICTS.
Registered in the Quarter ending the last day of				Total.	Total.	Registered in the Quarter ending the last day of				
March.	June.	Sept.	Dec.			March.	June.	Sept.	Dec.	
										[illegible] Co.
[illegible]	[illegible]	[illegible]	[illegible]	[illegible]	[illegible]	[illegible]	[illegible]	[illegible]	41	[illegible]
[illegible]	11	[illegible]	11	[illegible]	[illegible]	[illegible]	17	8	11	[illegible], part of.
[illegible]	[illegible]	[illegible]	[illegible]	[illegible]	[illegible]	10	[illegible]	[illegible]	[illegible]	[illegible], do.
[illegible]	[illegible]	[illegible]	[illegible]	[illegible]	[illegible]	77	[illegible]	[illegible]	71	[illegible], part of.
[illegible]	[illegible]	11	[illegible]	[illegible]	[illegible]	[illegible]	[illegible]	[illegible]	7	[illegible], do.
1	1		1	[illegible]	[illegible]	[illegible]	[illegible]	.	.	[illegible], do.
										[illegible] Co.
[illegible]	[illegible]	[illegible]	[illegible]	[illegible]	[illegible]	[illegible]	[illegible]	[illegible]	[illegible]	[illegible], part of.
19	[illegible]	[illegible]	[illegible]	[illegible]	[illegible]	[illegible]	[illegible]	[illegible]	[illegible]	[illegible], do.
[illegible]	[illegible]	[illegible]	[illegible]	[illegible]	[illegible]	[illegible]	[illegible]	17	[illegible]	[illegible]
[illegible]	[illegible]	7	[illegible]	[illegible]	[illegible]	[illegible]	[illegible]	[illegible]	[illegible]	[illegible], part of.
[illegible]	[illegible]	[illegible]	[illegible]	[illegible]	[illegible]	[illegible]	77	[illegible]	[illegible]	[illegible]
[illegible]	[illegible]	[illegible]	[illegible]	[illegible]	[illegible]	[illegible]	11	[illegible]	[illegible]	[illegible], part of.
										Wexford Co.
[illegible]	[illegible]	[illegible]	[illegible]	[illegible]	[illegible]	[illegible]	[illegible]	[illegible]	[illegible]	[illegible], part of.
[illegible]	[illegible]	[illegible]	[illegible]	101	[illegible]	[illegible]	[illegible]	[illegible]	[illegible]	Gorey.
[illegible]	[illegible]	[illegible]	[illegible]	[illegible]	[illegible]	[illegible]	[illegible]	[illegible]	[illegible]	New Ross, part of.
.	[illegible]	.	[illegible]	[illegible]	[illegible]	1	[illegible]	[illegible]	1	[illegible], do.
[illegible]	[illegible]	[illegible]	[illegible]	[illegible]	[illegible]	[illegible]	[illegible]	[illegible]	[illegible]	Wexford.
										Wicklow Co.
[illegible]	[illegible]	[illegible]	[illegible]	[illegible]	[illegible]	[illegible]	[illegible]	[illegible]	[illegible]	[illegible], part of.
[illegible]	[illegible]	[illegible]	[illegible]	[illegible]	[illegible]	[illegible]	1	[illegible]	[illegible]	[illegible], do.
[illegible]	[illegible]	[illegible]	[illegible]	[illegible]	[illegible]	[illegible]	[illegible]	[illegible]	[illegible]	[illegible], do.
[illegible]	[illegible]	[illegible]	[illegible]	[illegible]	[illegible]	[illegible]	[illegible]	[illegible]	[illegible]	[illegible]
[illegible]	[illegible]	[illegible]	[illegible]	[illegible]	[illegible]	[illegible]	[illegible]	[illegible]	[illegible]	[illegible], part of.

[illegible].

MALES.					FEMALES.					SUPERINTENDENT REGISTRARS' DISTRICTS.
March.	June.	Sept.	Dec.	Total.	Total.	March.	June.	Sept.	Dec.	
										[illegible] Co.
[illegible]	[illegible]	4	7	27	[illegible]	[illegible]	[illegible]	[illegible]	9	[illegible]
[illegible]	[illegible]	[illegible]	[illegible]	[illegible]	[illegible]	[illegible]	[illegible]	[illegible]	[illegible]	[illegible]
[illegible]	[illegible]	67	[illegible]	[illegible]	[illegible]	[illegible]	[illegible]	[illegible]	[illegible]	[illegible]
[illegible]	[illegible]	[illegible]	[illegible]	[illegible]	[illegible]	[illegible]	[illegible]	[illegible]	[illegible]	[illegible]
[illegible]	27	[illegible]	[illegible]	[illegible]	[illegible]	[illegible]	[illegible]	[illegible]	[illegible]	[illegible]
[illegible]	[illegible]	[illegible]	[illegible]	[illegible]	[illegible]	[illegible]	[illegible]	[illegible]	[illegible]	[illegible]
[illegible]	[illegible]	[illegible]	[illegible]	[illegible]	[illegible]	[illegible]	[illegible]	[illegible]	[illegible]	[illegible], part of.
[illegible]	[illegible]	[illegible]	[illegible]	[illegible]	[illegible]	[illegible]	[illegible]	[illegible]	[illegible]	[illegible], do.
[illegible]	[illegible]	[illegible]	[illegible]	[illegible]	[illegible]	[illegible]	[illegible]	[illegible]	[illegible]	Tulla.
										Cork Co.
[illegible]	[illegible]	[illegible]	[illegible]	[illegible]	[illegible]	[illegible]	[illegible]	[illegible]	[illegible]	[illegible]
[illegible]	[illegible]	[illegible]	[illegible]	[illegible]	[illegible]	[illegible]	[illegible]	[illegible]	[illegible]	Bantry.
[illegible]	[illegible]	[illegible]	[illegible]	[illegible]	[illegible]	[illegible]	[illegible]	[illegible]	[illegible]	[illegible]
[illegible]	[illegible]	[illegible]	[illegible]	[illegible]	[illegible]	[illegible]	[illegible]	[illegible]	[illegible]	[illegible]
[illegible]	[illegible]	[illegible]	[illegible]	[illegible]	[illegible]	[illegible]	[illegible]	[illegible]	[illegible]	Cork.
[illegible]	[illegible]	[illegible]	[illegible]	177	[illegible]	[illegible]	[illegible]	[illegible]	[illegible]	[illegible]

No.	Cork Co.—continued.				
82	Fermoy, ...	118,8??	20,3??	620	147
83	Kanturk, ...	168,???	20,171	635	157
84	Kilmallock, part of, . .	10,??4	4,235	135	84
85	Kinsale, ...	70,?11	14,???	4?0	720
86	Macroom, ...	179,???	20,???	[illegible]	[illegible]
87	Mallow, ...	149,??6	21,??6	474	144
88	Midleton, ...	150,???	10,???	167	111
89	Millstreet, ...	74,???	12,153	185	88
90	Mitchelstown, part of, .	40,???	9,???	156	82
91	Skibbereen, ...	21?,???	28,4??	947	173
92	Skull, ...	87,???	11,283	[illegible]	68
93	Youghal, part of, . .	30,???	11,04?	120	44
	Kerry Co.				
94	Cahirciveen, ...	167,?45	25,??4	177	141
95	Dingle, ...	135,270	19,???	629	123
96	Glin, part of, ...	14,???	8,?24	87	30
97	Kenmare, ...	180,1??	10,319	864	60
98	Killarney, ...	2??,???	40,???	[illegible]	184
99	Listowel, ...	1??,???	??,???	714	157
100	Tralee, ...	27?,?47	??,???	148	177
	Limerick Co.				
101	Croom, ...	??,???	12,???	[illegible]	[illegible]
102	Glin, part of, . .	??,???	9,??7	[illegible]	40
103	Kilmallock, do., . .	2??,7??	??,???	[illegible]	167
104	[illegible], do., . .	???,???	??,???	1,???	1??
105	[illegible], &c. . .	??,???	3,???	112	[illegible]
106	Newcastle, ...	14?,??7	??,1??	[illegible]	165
107	Rathkeale, ...	7?,???	11,4??	1??	71
108	Tipperary, part of, . .	??,???	7,???	1??	47
	Tipperary Co.				
109	Borrisokane, ...	??,???	?,1??	373	81
110	Callan, part of, .	41,???	?,2??	1??	40
111	Carrick-on-Suir, do., .	??,??1	?,???	[illegible]	41
112	Cashel, ...	14?,1?7	??,1??	[illegible]	1??
113	Clogheen, ...	127,4??	17,???	?7?	[illegible]
114	Clonmel, part of, . .	??,???	??,???	[illegible]	[illegible]
115	Nenagh, ...	1??,???	17,???	[illegible]	1??
116	Parsonstown, part of, .	17,???	?,???	[illegible]	??
117	Roscrea, do., . .	??,???	?,???	?74	[illegible]
118	Thurles, ...	1??,???	??,???	[illegible]	1??
119	Tipperary, part of, . .	1??,???	??,???	[illegible]	1??
120	Urlingford, do., . .	??,???	?,1??	[illegible]	[illegible]
	Waterford Co.				
121	Carrick-on-Suir, part of,	??,???	7,?1?	1??	[illegible]
122	Clonmel, do.,	??,?7?	?,???	111	[illegible]
123	Dungarvan, ...	??,???	??,???	[illegible]	[illegible]
124	Kilmacthomas, . . .	?1,???	?,???	1??	[illegible]
125	Lismore, ...	??,???	??,???	[illegible]	[illegible]
126	Waterford, part of, . .	7?,??1	??,???	?7	[illegible]
127	Youghal, do., . .	??,???	?,???	1??	[illegible]

March 31st, June 30th, September 30th, and December 31st, 1891—continued.

MUNSTER—continued.

MALES. Registered in the Quarter ending the last day of March.	June.	Sept.	Dec.	Total.	FEMALES. Total.	Registered in the Quarter ending the last day of March.	June.	Sept.	Dec.	Superintendent Registrars' Districts.
										Cork Co.—continued.
[illegible]	[illegible]	[illegible]	[illegible]	[illegible]	[illegible]	[illegible]	[illegible]	[illegible]	[illegible]	Fermoy.
[illegible]	[illegible]	[illegible]	[illegible]	[illegible]	[illegible]	[illegible]	[illegible]	[illegible]	[illegible]	Kanturk.
[illegible]	[illegible]	[illegible]	[illegible]	[illegible]	[illegible]	[illegible]	[illegible]	14	11	Kilmallock, part of.
[illegible]	[illegible]	[illegible]	[illegible]	[illegible]	[illegible]	[illegible]	[illegible]	41	[illegible]	Kinsale.
[illegible]	[illegible]	[illegible]	[illegible]	[illegible]	[illegible]	[illegible]	[illegible]	[illegible]	[illegible]	Macroom.
[illegible]	[illegible]	[illegible]	[illegible]	[illegible]	[illegible]	71	[illegible]	[illegible]	[illegible]	Mallow.
[illegible]	[illegible]	[illegible]	[illegible]	[illegible]	[illegible]	[illegible]	[illegible]	[illegible]	[illegible]	Midleton.
[illegible]	[illegible]	[illegible]	[illegible]	[illegible]	[illegible]	[illegible]	[illegible]	[illegible]	[illegible]	Millstreet.
[illegible]	[illegible]	[illegible]	[illegible]	[illegible]	[illegible]	[illegible]	[illegible]	[illegible]	[illegible]	Mitchelstown, part of.
[illegible]	[illegible]	[illegible]	[illegible]	[illegible]	[illegible]	[illegible]	[illegible]	[illegible]	[illegible]	Skibbereen.
[illegible]	[illegible]	[illegible]	[illegible]	[illegible]	[illegible]	[illegible]	[illegible]	[illegible]	[illegible]	Skull.
[illegible]	[illegible]	[illegible]	[illegible]	[illegible]	[illegible]	[illegible]	[illegible]	[illegible]	[illegible]	Youghal, part of.
										Kerry Co.
[illegible]	[illegible]	[illegible]	[illegible]	[illegible]	[illegible]	[illegible]	[illegible]	[illegible]	[illegible]	Cahersiveen.
[illegible]	[illegible]	[illegible]	[illegible]	[illegible]	[illegible]	[illegible]	[illegible]	[illegible]	[illegible]	Dingle.
[illegible]	[illegible]	11	[illegible]	[illegible]	[illegible]	5	[illegible]	[illegible]	[illegible]	Glin, part of.
[illegible]	[illegible]	[illegible]	[illegible]	[illegible]	[illegible]	[illegible]	[illegible]	[illegible]	41	Kenmare.
[illegible]	[illegible]	[illegible]	[illegible]	[illegible]	[illegible]	[illegible]	[illegible]	[illegible]	[illegible]	Killarney.
[illegible]	[illegible]	[illegible]	[illegible]	[illegible]	[illegible]	[illegible]	[illegible]	[illegible]	[illegible]	Listowel.
[illegible]	[illegible]	[illegible]	[illegible]	[illegible]	[illegible]	[illegible]	[illegible]	[illegible]	[illegible]	Tralee.
										Limerick Co.
[illegible]	[illegible]	[illegible]	[illegible]	[illegible]	[illegible]	[illegible]	[illegible]	[illegible]	17	Croom.
[illegible]	[illegible]	[illegible]	[illegible]	[illegible]	[illegible]	[illegible]	[illegible]	[illegible]	[illegible]	Glin, part of.
[illegible]	[illegible]	[illegible]	[illegible]	[illegible]	[illegible]	[illegible]	[illegible]	[illegible]	[illegible]	Kilmallock, do.
[illegible]	[illegible]	[illegible]	[illegible]	[illegible]	[illegible]	[illegible]	[illegible]	[illegible]	[illegible]	Limerick, do.
[illegible]	[illegible]	11	11	[illegible]	[illegible]	[illegible]	[illegible]	[illegible]	[illegible]	Mitchelstown, do.
[illegible]	[illegible]	[illegible]	[illegible]	[illegible]	[illegible]	[illegible]	[illegible]	[illegible]	[illegible]	Newcastle.
[illegible]	[illegible]	[illegible]	[illegible]	[illegible]	[illegible]	[illegible]	[illegible]	[illegible]	[illegible]	Rathkeale.
[illegible]	[illegible]	[illegible]	[illegible]	[illegible]	[illegible]	[illegible]	[illegible]	[illegible]	[illegible]	Tipperary, part of.
										Tipperary Co.
[illegible]	[illegible]	[illegible]	[illegible]	[illegible]	[illegible]	[illegible]	[illegible]	[illegible]	[illegible]	Borrisokane.
[illegible]	[illegible]	[illegible]	[illegible]	[illegible]	[illegible]	[illegible]	[illegible]	[illegible]	[illegible]	Callan, part of.
17	[illegible]	[illegible]	[illegible]	[illegible]	[illegible]	[illegible]	[illegible]	[illegible]	[illegible]	Carrick-on-Suir, do.
[illegible]	[illegible]	[illegible]	[illegible]	[illegible]	[illegible]	[illegible]	[illegible]	[illegible]	[illegible]	Cashel.
[illegible]	[illegible]	[illegible]	[illegible]	[illegible]	[illegible]	[illegible]	[illegible]	[illegible]	47	Clogheen.
[illegible]	[illegible]	[illegible]	[illegible]	[illegible]	[illegible]	[illegible]	[illegible]	[illegible]	[illegible]	Clonmel, part of.
[illegible]	[illegible]	[illegible]	[illegible]	[illegible]	[illegible]	[illegible]	[illegible]	[illegible]	[illegible]	Nenagh.
6	[illegible]	4	1	[illegible]	[illegible]	4	7	3	4	Parsonstown, part of.
[illegible]	[illegible]	17	[illegible]	[illegible]	[illegible]	[illegible]	[illegible]	[illegible]	[illegible]	Roscrea, do.
[illegible]	[illegible]	[illegible]	[illegible]	[illegible]	[illegible]	[illegible]	[illegible]	[illegible]	[illegible]	Thurles.
[illegible]	[illegible]	[illegible]	[illegible]	[illegible]	[illegible]	[illegible]	[illegible]	[illegible]	[illegible]	Tipperary, part of.
[illegible]	[illegible]	11	4	[illegible]	[illegible]	[illegible]	6	[illegible]	7	Urlingford, do.
										Waterford Co.
[illegible]	[illegible]	[illegible]	[illegible]	[illegible]	[illegible]	[illegible]	71	[illegible]	18	Carrick-on-Suir, pt. of.
17	13	[illegible]	11	[illegible]	[illegible]	[illegible]	[illegible]	16	7	Clonmel, do.
[illegible]	[illegible]	[illegible]	[illegible]	[illegible]	[illegible]	[illegible]	[illegible]	[illegible]	[illegible]	Dungarvan.
[illegible]	[illegible]	[illegible]	[illegible]	[illegible]	[illegible]	[illegible]	11	18	[illegible]	Kilmacthomas.
[illegible]	[illegible]	[illegible]	[illegible]	[illegible]	[illegible]	[illegible]	[illegible]	[illegible]	[illegible]	Lismore.
[illegible]	[illegible]	[illegible]	[illegible]	[illegible]	[illegible]	[illegible]	[illegible]	[illegible]	[illegible]	Waterford, part of.
[illegible]	[illegible]	11	[illegible]	[illegible]	[illegible]	[illegible]	[illegible]	[illegible]	[illegible]	Youghal, do.

[illegible] registered in Ireland in the Four Quarters ending

III.—PROVINCE OF [illegible]

No.	Superintendent Registrars' Districts.	Area in Statute Acres.	Population in 1861.	Males and Females. Total.	Registered in the Quarter ending the last day of March.	June.	Sept.	Dec.
	Antrim Co.							
129	Antrim,	111,927	29,445	[illegible]	[illegible]	[illegible]	179	140
130	Ballycastle,	[illegible]	14,679	333	[illegible]	81	106	75
131	Ballymena,	143,903	[illegible]	[illegible]	[illegible]	[illegible]	[illegible]	[illegible]
132	Ballymoney, part of,	104,553	34,927	549	116	140	122	124
133	Belfast, do.,	21,529	[illegible]	[illegible]	[illegible]	[illegible]	[illegible]	[illegible]
[illegible]	Coleraine, do.,	16,379	8,733	162	46	[illegible]	43	[illegible]
[illegible]	Larne,	117,064	[illegible]	844	243	[illegible]	218	[illegible]
[illegible]	Lisburn, part of,	48,338	[illegible]	614	[illegible]	161	167	[illegible]
[illegible]	Lurgan, do.,	12,824	[illegible]	[illegible]	[illegible]	[illegible]	[illegible]	[illegible]
	Armagh Co.							
[illegible]	Armagh, part of,	[illegible]	[illegible]	1,316	[illegible]	[illegible]	274	[illegible]
[illegible]	Banbridge, do.,	16,175	[illegible]	[illegible]	41	[illegible]	44	37
[illegible]	Castleblayney, do.,	[illegible]	[illegible]	[illegible]	[illegible]	41	[illegible]	41
140	Dundalk, do.,	4,570	1,738	[illegible]	4	4	11	6
141	Lurgan, do.,	[illegible]	48,297	[illegible]	[illegible]	[illegible]	[illegible]	[illegible]
142	Newry, do.,	[illegible]	[illegible]	[illegible]	[illegible]	184	167	171
	Cavan Co.							
143	Bailieborough,	[illegible]	16,731	[illegible]	[illegible]	76	[illegible]	[illegible]
144	Bawnboy, part of,	[illegible]	[illegible]	[illegible]	[illegible]	84	[illegible]	[illegible]
145	Cavan,	[illegible]	[illegible]	676	[illegible]	[illegible]	171	[illegible]
146	Cootehill, part of,	[illegible]	[illegible]	[illegible]	[illegible]	[illegible]	79	[illegible]
147	Enniskillen, do.,	[illegible]	[illegible]	[illegible]	41	47	[illegible]	[illegible]
148	Granard, do.,	[illegible]	[illegible]	[illegible]	43	[illegible]	34	[illegible]
149	Kells, do.,	[illegible]	[illegible]	[illegible]	4	7	6	[illegible]
150	Oldcastle, do.,	[illegible]	[illegible]	[illegible]	[illegible]	[illegible]	41	[illegible]
	Donegal Co.							
[illegible]	Ballyshannon, part of,	[illegible]	[illegible]	[illegible]	66	[illegible]	[illegible]	[illegible]
[illegible]	Donegal,	[illegible]	[illegible]	[illegible]	[illegible]	[illegible]	[illegible]	71
[illegible]	Dunfanaghy,	[illegible]	[illegible]	[illegible]	116	130	76	78
[illegible]	Glenties,	[illegible]	[illegible]	[illegible]	207	[illegible]	147	[illegible]
[illegible]	Inishowen,	[illegible]	[illegible]	[illegible]	176	[illegible]	[illegible]	[illegible]
[illegible]	Letterkenny,	[illegible]	[illegible]	[illegible]	47	[illegible]	[illegible]	47
[illegible]	Londonderry, part of,	[illegible]	[illegible]	[illegible]	47	[illegible]	[illegible]	[illegible]
[illegible]	Milford,	111,334	[illegible]	[illegible]	[illegible]	[illegible]	[illegible]	111
[illegible]	Strabane, part of,	[illegible]	[illegible]	[illegible]	[illegible]	[illegible]	[illegible]	[illegible]
[illegible]	Stranorlar,	[illegible]	[illegible]	[illegible]	[illegible]	[illegible]	[illegible]	[illegible]
	Down Co.							
[illegible]	Banbridge, part of,	[illegible]	[illegible]	[illegible]	[illegible]	[illegible]	[illegible]	[illegible]
[illegible]	Belfast, do.,	[illegible]	[illegible]	[illegible]	[illegible]	[illegible]	[illegible]	[illegible]
[illegible]	Downpatrick,	[illegible]	[illegible]	[illegible]	[illegible]	[illegible]	[illegible]	[illegible]
[illegible]	Kilkeel,	[illegible]	[illegible]	[illegible]	[illegible]	[illegible]	[illegible]	[illegible]
[illegible]	Lisburn, part of,	[illegible]	[illegible]	[illegible]	[illegible]	[illegible]	[illegible]	[illegible]
[illegible]	Lurgan, do.,	27,230	[illegible]	[illegible]	[illegible]	[illegible]	[illegible]	[illegible]
[illegible]	Newry, do.,	[illegible]	[illegible]	[illegible]	[illegible]	[illegible]	[illegible]	[illegible]
[illegible]	Newtownards,	[illegible]	[illegible]	[illegible]	[illegible]	[illegible]	[illegible]	[illegible]
	Fermanagh Co.							
[illegible]	Ballyshannon, part of,	[illegible]	[illegible]	[illegible]	[illegible]	[illegible]	[illegible]	[illegible]
[illegible]	Clones, do.,	[illegible]	[illegible]	[illegible]	[illegible]	[illegible]	[illegible]	[illegible]
171	Enniskillen, do.,	[illegible]	[illegible]	[illegible]	117	[illegible]	[illegible]	[illegible]
[illegible]	Irvinestown, do.,	[illegible]	11,395	[illegible]	[illegible]	61	[illegible]	[illegible]
[illegible]	Lisnaskea,	[illegible]	[illegible]	[illegible]	[illegible]	[illegible]	[illegible]	75

						Antrim Co.
[illegible]	[illegible]	[illegible]	[illegible]	[illegible]	61	Antrim.
177	179	[illegible]	43	35	[illegible]	Ballycastle.
[illegible]	[illegible]	[illegible]	[illegible]	[illegible]	[illegible]	Ballymena.
[illegible]	[illegible]	[illegible]	[illegible]	[illegible]	[illegible]	Ballymoney, part of.
[illegible]	2,716	[illegible]	[illegible]	[illegible]	[illegible]	Belfast, do.
[illegible]	[illegible]	[illegible]	[illegible]	[illegible]	[illegible]	Carrickfergus, do.
[illegible]	[illegible]	[illegible]	[illegible]	[illegible]	[illegible]	Larne.
[illegible]	[illegible]	[illegible]	[illegible]	[illegible]	[illegible]	Lisburn, part of.
46	44	9	5	10	17	Lurgan, do.
						Armagh Co.
[illegible]	[illegible]	[illegible]	[illegible]	[illegible]	[illegible]	Armagh, part of.
[illegible]	[illegible]	17	[illegible]	11	14	Banbridge, do.
[illegible]	[illegible]	[illegible]	[illegible]	[illegible]	17	Castleblayney, do.
17	11	3	2	4	2	Dundalk, do.
[illegible]	[illegible]	[illegible]	[illegible]	[illegible]	[illegible]	Lurgan, do.
[illegible]	[illegible]	[illegible]	[illegible]	[illegible]	[illegible]	Newry, do.
						Cavan Co.
[illegible]	[illegible]	45	[illegible]	[illegible]	47	Bailieborough.
[illegible]	[illegible]	[illegible]	71	[illegible]	14	Bawnboy, part of.
[illegible]	[illegible]	[illegible]	[illegible]	[illegible]	[illegible]	Cavan.
[illegible]	[illegible]	[illegible]	[illegible]	[illegible]	[illegible]	Cootehill, part of.
[illegible]	[illegible]	[illegible]	[illegible]	[illegible]	[illegible]	Enniskillen, do.
[illegible]	[illegible]	[illegible]	9	9	13	Granard, do.
[illegible]	[illegible]	8	4	2	3	Kells, do.
[illegible]	[illegible]	[illegible]	[illegible]	[illegible]	[illegible]	Oldcastle, do.
						Donegal Co.
[illegible]	[illegible]	[illegible]	[illegible]	[illegible]	[illegible]	Ballyshannon, part of
[illegible]	[illegible]	[illegible]	[illegible]	[illegible]	[illegible]	Donegal.
[illegible]	[illegible]	[illegible]	[illegible]	47	[illegible]	Dunfanaghy.
[illegible]	[illegible]	[illegible]	[illegible]	[illegible]	[illegible]	Glenties.
[illegible]	[illegible]	[illegible]	[illegible]	[illegible]	[illegible]	Inishowen.
[illegible]	[illegible]	[illegible]	[illegible]	[illegible]	[illegible]	Letterkenny.
[illegible]	[illegible]	[illegible]	[illegible]	21	[illegible]	Londonderry, part of
[illegible]	[illegible]	71	[illegible]	[illegible]	[illegible]	Milford.
[illegible]	[illegible]	[illegible]	[illegible]	[illegible]	[illegible]	Strabane, part of.
[illegible]	[illegible]	[illegible]	[illegible]	[illegible]	[illegible]	Stranorlar.
						Down Co.
[illegible]	[illegible]	[illegible]	[illegible]	[illegible]	[illegible]	Banbridge, part of.
[illegible]	[illegible]	[illegible]	[illegible]	[illegible]	[illegible]	Belfast, do.
[illegible]	[illegible]	[illegible]	[illegible]	[illegible]	[illegible]	Downpatrick.
[illegible]	[illegible]	64	43	45	[illegible]	Kilkeel.
[illegible]	[illegible]	77	[illegible]	[illegible]	[illegible]	Lisburn, part of.
[illegible]	[illegible]	[illegible]	[illegible]	[illegible]	[illegible]	Lurgan, do.
[illegible]	[illegible]	[illegible]	[illegible]	[illegible]	[illegible]	Newry, do.
[illegible]	[illegible]	[illegible]	[illegible]	[illegible]	[illegible]	Newtownards.
						Fermanagh Co.
73	[illegible]	10	[illegible]	16	13	Ballyshannon, part of
67	61	[illegible]	[illegible]	[illegible]	[illegible]	Clones, do.
[illegible]	[illegible]	[illegible]	[illegible]	[illegible]	[illegible]	Enniskillen, do.
[illegible]	[illegible]	[illegible]	[illegible]	[illegible]	[illegible]	Irvinestown, do.
173	175	[illegible]	[illegible]	[illegible]	[illegible]	Lisnaskea.

[illegible] registered in Ireland in the Four Quarters ending

III.—PROVINCE OF

No.	SUPERINTENDENT REGISTRAR'S DISTRICT.	Area in Statute Acres.	Population in 1861.	MALES AND FEMALES. Total.	Registered in the Quarter ending the last day of March.	June.	Sept.	Dec.
	Londonderry Co.							
174	Ballymoney, part of,	22,581	4,765	135	30	38	39	28
175	Coleraine, do.,	90,434	20,632	636	148	174	157	164
176	Limavady,	123,711	22,386	526	135	153	126	124
177	Londonderry, part of,	66,172	40,347	1,327	348	336	326	310
178	Magherafelt,	166,719	44,679	820	220	226	224	240
	Monaghan Co.							
179	Carrickmacross,	60,482	16,416	300	71	77	81	77
180	Castleblayney, part of,	62,702	19,465	394	67	120	104	103
181	Clones, do.,	21,880	6,860	20	3	6	8	4
182	Cavan, do.,	27,729	6,810	144	45	31	46	32
183	Cootehill, do.,	30,462	7,670	110	29	24	23	33
184	Dundalk, do.,	4,840	1,450	22	6	5	6	4
185	Monaghan,	112,744	39,433	561	139	141	120	125
	Tyrone Co.							
186	Armagh, part of,	7,380	1,625	43	10	18	6	9
187	Castlederg,	94,387	13,130	246	60	45	48	49
188	Clogher, part of,	88,283	16,287	241	61	84	90	63
189	Cookstown,	86,729	27,361	515	131	130	134	115
190	Dungannon,	102,348	34,330	725	166	167	177	175
191	Enniskillen, part of,	4,826	1,137	20	8	4	8	8
192	Lowtherstown, part of,	18,178	3,046	71	25	22	10	12
193	Omagh,	228,246	44,307	860	225	230	775	180
194	Strabane, part of,	130,880	77,163	439	137	134	163	141

IV.—PROVINCE OF

No.	SUPERINTENDENT REGISTRAR'S DISTRICT.	Area in Statute Acres.	Population in 1861.	Total.	March.	June.	Sept.	Dec.
	Galway Co.							
195	Ballinasloe, part of,	183,882	18,235	214	40	61	65	43
196	Ballinrobe, do.,	29,288	7,295	69	25	18	20	6
197	Clifden,	192,851	28,149	420	120	102	99	99
198	Galway,	167,067	38,713	883	261	260	230	222
199	Glennamaddy,	189,214	18,400	413	148	108	73	94
200	Gort,	145,860	14,201	220	40	16	36	43
201	Loughrea,	180,837	32,346	437	118	128	107	99
202	Mountbellew,	88,380	14,477	344	87	79	84	83
203	Oughterard,	173,885	18,875	463	145	131	103	94
204	Portumna,	77,448	16,265	173	41	40	45	40
205	Roscommon, part of,	4,820	840	13	5	1	3	4
206	Scariff, do.,	16,801	1,764	47	7	17	10	19
207	Tuam,	188,440	34,430	762	205	200	173	180
	Leitrim Co.							
208	Ballyshannon, part of,	33,435	6,370	180	30	60	34	20
209	Bawnboy, do.,	42,700	10,827	200	43	60	48	44
210	Carrick-on-Shannon, do.,	62,464	14,867	300	80	71	73	76
211	Manorhamilton,	144,837	29,865	526	144	144	133	109
212	Mohill,	93,864	29,421	483	123	127	120	113

March 31st, June 30th, September 30th, and December 31st, 1891—continued.

ULSTER—continued.

MALES. Registered in the Quarter ending the last day of March.	June.	Sept.	Dec.	Total.	FEMALES. Total.	Registered in the Quarter ending the last day of March.	June.	Sept.	Dec.	Superintendent Registrars' Districts.
										Londonderry Co.
[illegible]	[illegible]	[illegible]	[illegible]	[illegible]	[illegible]	[illegible]	[illegible]	[illegible]	[illegible]	Ballymoney, part of.
[illegible]	[illegible]	[illegible]	[illegible]	[illegible]	[illegible]	[illegible]	[illegible]	[illegible]	[illegible]	Coleraine, do.
[illegible]	[illegible]	[illegible]	[illegible]	[illegible]	[illegible]	[illegible]	[illegible]	[illegible]	[illegible]	Limavady.
[illegible]	[illegible]	[illegible]	[illegible]	[illegible]	[illegible]	[illegible]	[illegible]	[illegible]	[illegible]	Londonderry, part of.
[illegible]	[illegible]	[illegible]	[illegible]	[illegible]	[illegible]	[illegible]	[illegible]	[illegible]	[illegible]	Magherafelt.
										Monaghan Co.
[illegible]	[illegible]	[illegible]	[illegible]	[illegible]	[illegible]	[illegible]	[illegible]	[illegible]	[illegible]	Carrickmacross.
[illegible]	[illegible]	[illegible]	[illegible]	[illegible]	[illegible]	[illegible]	[illegible]	[illegible]	[illegible]	Castleblayney, part of.
[illegible]	[illegible]	[illegible]	[illegible]	[illegible]	[illegible]	[illegible]	[illegible]	[illegible]	[illegible]	Clogher, do.
[illegible]	[illegible]	[illegible]	[illegible]	[illegible]	[illegible]	[illegible]	[illegible]	[illegible]	[illegible]	Clones, do.
[illegible]	[illegible]	[illegible]	[illegible]	[illegible]	[illegible]	[illegible]	[illegible]	[illegible]	[illegible]	Cootehill, do.
[illegible]	[illegible]	[illegible]	[illegible]	[illegible]	[illegible]	[illegible]	[illegible]	[illegible]	[illegible]	Dundalk, do.
[illegible]	[illegible]	[illegible]	[illegible]	[illegible]	[illegible]	[illegible]	[illegible]	[illegible]	[illegible]	Monaghan.
										Tyrone Co.
[illegible]	[illegible]	[illegible]	[illegible]	[illegible]	[illegible]	[illegible]	[illegible]	[illegible]	[illegible]	Armagh, part of.
[illegible]	[illegible]	[illegible]	[illegible]	[illegible]	[illegible]	[illegible]	[illegible]	[illegible]	[illegible]	Castlederg.
[illegible]	[illegible]	[illegible]	[illegible]	[illegible]	[illegible]	[illegible]	[illegible]	[illegible]	[illegible]	Clogher, part of.
[illegible]	[illegible]	[illegible]	[illegible]	[illegible]	[illegible]	[illegible]	[illegible]	[illegible]	[illegible]	Cookstown.
[illegible]	[illegible]	[illegible]	[illegible]	[illegible]	[illegible]	[illegible]	[illegible]	[illegible]	[illegible]	Dungannon.
[illegible]	[illegible]	[illegible]	[illegible]	[illegible]	[illegible]	[illegible]	[illegible]	[illegible]	[illegible]	[illegible], part of.
[illegible]	[illegible]	[illegible]	[illegible]	[illegible]	[illegible]	[illegible]	[illegible]	[illegible]	[illegible]	Irvinestown, part of.
[illegible]	[illegible]	[illegible]	[illegible]	[illegible]	[illegible]	[illegible]	[illegible]	[illegible]	[illegible]	Omagh.
[illegible]	[illegible]	[illegible]	[illegible]	[illegible]	[illegible]	[illegible]	[illegible]	[illegible]	[illegible]	Strabane, part of.

CONNAUGHT.

MALES. Registered in the Quarter ending the last day of March.	June.	Sept.	Dec.	Total.	FEMALES. Total.	Registered in the Quarter ending the last day of March.	June.	Sept.	Dec.	Superintendent Registrars' Districts.
										Galway Co.
[illegible]	[illegible]	[illegible]	[illegible]	[illegible]	[illegible]	[illegible]	[illegible]	[illegible]	[illegible]	Ballinasloe, part of.
[illegible]	[illegible]	[illegible]	[illegible]	[illegible]	[illegible]	[illegible]	[illegible]	[illegible]	[illegible]	Ballinrobe, do.
[illegible]	[illegible]	[illegible]	[illegible]	[illegible]	[illegible]	[illegible]	[illegible]	[illegible]	[illegible]	Clifden.
[illegible]	[illegible]	[illegible]	[illegible]	[illegible]	[illegible]	[illegible]	[illegible]	[illegible]	[illegible]	Galway.
[illegible]	[illegible]	[illegible]	[illegible]	[illegible]	[illegible]	[illegible]	[illegible]	[illegible]	[illegible]	Glenamaddy.
[illegible]	[illegible]	[illegible]	[illegible]	[illegible]	[illegible]	[illegible]	[illegible]	[illegible]	[illegible]	Gort.
[illegible]	[illegible]	[illegible]	[illegible]	[illegible]	[illegible]	[illegible]	[illegible]	[illegible]	[illegible]	Loughrea.
[illegible]	[illegible]	[illegible]	[illegible]	[illegible]	[illegible]	[illegible]	[illegible]	[illegible]	[illegible]	Mount Bellew.
[illegible]	[illegible]	[illegible]	[illegible]	[illegible]	[illegible]	[illegible]	[illegible]	[illegible]	[illegible]	Oughterard.
[illegible]	[illegible]	[illegible]	[illegible]	[illegible]	[illegible]	[illegible]	[illegible]	[illegible]	[illegible]	Portumna.
[illegible]	[illegible]	[illegible]	[illegible]	[illegible]	[illegible]	[illegible]	[illegible]	[illegible]	[illegible]	Roscommon, part of.
[illegible]	[illegible]	[illegible]	[illegible]	[illegible]	[illegible]	[illegible]	[illegible]	[illegible]	[illegible]	Scarriff, do.
[illegible]	[illegible]	[illegible]	[illegible]	[illegible]	[illegible]	[illegible]	[illegible]	[illegible]	[illegible]	Tuam.
										Leitrim Co.
[illegible]	[illegible]	[illegible]	[illegible]	[illegible]	[illegible]	[illegible]	[illegible]	[illegible]	[illegible]	Ballyshannon, part of.
[illegible]	[illegible]	[illegible]	[illegible]	[illegible]	[illegible]	[illegible]	[illegible]	[illegible]	[illegible]	Bawnboy, do.
[illegible]	[illegible]	[illegible]	[illegible]	[illegible]	[illegible]	[illegible]	[illegible]	[illegible]	[illegible]	Carrick-on-Shannon, do.
[illegible]	[illegible]	[illegible]	[illegible]	[illegible]	[illegible]	[illegible]	[illegible]	[illegible]	[illegible]	Manorhamilton.
[illegible]	[illegible]	[illegible]	[illegible]	[illegible]	[illegible]	[illegible]	[illegible]	[illegible]	[illegible]	Mohill.

BIRTHS registered in Ireland in the Four Quarters ending

IV.—PROVINCE OF

SUPERINTENDENT REGISTRARS' DISTRICTS.	Area in Statute Acres.	Population in 1861.	MALES AND FEMALES.				
			Total.	Registered in the Quarter ending the last day of			
				March.	June.	Sept.	Dec.
Mayo Co.							
Ballina, part of,	1[illegible]	[illegible]	[illegible]	[illegible]	[illegible]	1[illegible]	7[illegible]
Ballinrobe, do.,	[illegible]	[illegible]	4[illegible]	1[illegible]	1[illegible]	135	[illegible]
Belmullet,	[illegible]	[illegible]	3[illegible]	[illegible]	1[illegible]	[illegible]	7[illegible]
Castlebar,	[illegible]	[illegible]	[illegible]	[illegible]	1[illegible]	1[illegible]	1[illegible]
[illegible], part of,	[illegible]	[illegible]	1[illegible]	4[illegible]	[illegible]	[illegible]	4[illegible]
Claremorris,	[illegible]	[illegible]	7[illegible]	[illegible]	1[illegible]	[illegible]	[illegible]
Killala,	[illegible]	[illegible]	[illegible]	4[illegible]	3[illegible]	[illegible]	[illegible]
Swinford,	[illegible]	[illegible]	1,2[illegible]	[illegible]	[illegible]	27[illegible]	4[illegible]
Westport,	[illegible]	[illegible]	[illegible]	[illegible]	[illegible]	[illegible]	[illegible]
Roscommon Co.							
Athlone, part of,	[illegible]	[illegible]	[illegible]	17[illegible]	9[illegible]	[illegible]	7[illegible]
Ballinasloe, do.,	[illegible]	[illegible]	17[illegible]	[illegible]	[illegible]	[illegible]	[illegible]
Boyle, do.,	[illegible]	[illegible]	[illegible]	[illegible]	[illegible]	[illegible]	[illegible]
Carrick-on-Shannon, do.,	[illegible]	7,[illegible]	1[illegible]	[illegible]	[illegible]	[illegible]	[illegible]
Castlerea, do.,	14[illegible]	[illegible]	[illegible]	1[illegible]	1[illegible]	1[illegible]	[illegible]
Roscommon, do.,	1[illegible]	[illegible]	[illegible]	[illegible]	[illegible]	[illegible]	[illegible]
Strokestown,	[illegible]	[illegible]	[illegible]	7[illegible]	[illegible]	[illegible]	[illegible]
Sligo Co.							
Ballina, part of,	[illegible]	[illegible]	[illegible]	[illegible]	[illegible]	[illegible]	[illegible]
Boyle, do.,	7[illegible]	[illegible]	[illegible]	7[illegible]	[illegible]	[illegible]	[illegible]
Dromore West,	[illegible]	[illegible]	[illegible]	7[illegible]	[illegible]	[illegible]	[illegible]
Sligo,	[illegible]	[illegible]	[illegible]	[illegible]	[illegible]	[illegible]	[illegible]
Tobercurry,	[illegible]	[illegible]	[illegible]	[illegible]	[illegible]	[illegible]	[illegible]

March 31st, June 30th, September 30th, and December 31st, 1891—*continued.*

CONNAUGHT—*continued.*

MALES.					FEMALES.					SUPERINTENDENT REGISTRARS' DISTRICTS.
Registered in the Quarter ending the last day of				Total.	Total.	Registered in the Quarter ending the last day of				
March.	June.	Sept.	Dec.			March.	June.	Sept.	Dec.	
										Mayo Co.
[illegible]	[illegible]	71	[illegible]	[illegible]	[illegible]	[illegible]	[illegible]	[illegible]	[illegible]	Ballina, part of
[illegible]	[illegible]	[illegible]	[illegible]	[illegible]	[illegible]	[illegible]	[illegible]	[illegible]	[illegible]	Ballinrobe, do.
[illegible]	[illegible]	[illegible]	[illegible]	[illegible]	[illegible]	[illegible]	[illegible]	[illegible]	[illegible]	Belmullet.
[illegible]	[illegible]	[illegible]	[illegible]	[illegible]	311	81	[illegible]	[illegible]	91	Castlebar.
[illegible]	[illegible]	[illegible]	[illegible]	[illegible]	[illegible]	11	[illegible]	[illegible]	24	Castlerea, part of
[illegible]	[illegible]	[illegible]	[illegible]	[illegible]	[illegible]	[illegible]	[illegible]	[illegible]	[illegible]	Claremorris.
[illegible]	[illegible]	[illegible]	[illegible]	[illegible]	[illegible]	14	18	[illegible]	[illegible]	Killala.
170	[illegible]	153	[illegible]	[illegible]	[illegible]	175	[illegible]	[illegible]	191	Swinford.
167	[illegible]	[illegible]	[illegible]	474	[illegible]	[illegible]	[illegible]	[illegible]	[illegible]	Westport.
										Roscommon Co.
[illegible]	41	[illegible]	[illegible]	179	[illegible]	[illegible]	[illegible]	[illegible]	[illegible]	Athlone, part of
[illegible]	[illegible]	24	[illegible]	[illegible]	[illegible]	[illegible]	[illegible]	[illegible]	[illegible]	Ballinasloe, do.
[illegible]	[illegible]	[illegible]	[illegible]	[illegible]	[illegible]	[illegible]	[illegible]	[illegible]	[illegible]	Boyle, do.
[illegible]	16	19	[illegible]	[illegible]	[illegible]	[illegible]	[illegible]	[illegible]	15	Carrick-on-Shannon, do.
[illegible]	[illegible]	[illegible]	[illegible]	[illegible]	[illegible]	[illegible]	[illegible]	[illegible]	[illegible]	Castlerea, do.
[illegible]	[illegible]	[illegible]	[illegible]	[illegible]	[illegible]	[illegible]	[illegible]	[illegible]	[illegible]	Roscommon, do.
[illegible]	[illegible]	[illegible]	[illegible]	[illegible]	[illegible]	[illegible]	[illegible]	[illegible]	[illegible]	Strokestown.
										Sligo Co.
9	[illegible]	[illegible]	[illegible]	[illegible]	[illegible]	14	6	6	[illegible]	Ballina, part of
[illegible]	[illegible]	[illegible]	[illegible]	[illegible]	[illegible]	[illegible]	41	[illegible]	[illegible]	Boyle, do.
[illegible]	[illegible]	[illegible]	[illegible]	[illegible]	[illegible]	[illegible]	[illegible]	[illegible]	[illegible]	Dromore West.
[illegible]	114	113	[illegible]	[illegible]	[illegible]	111	[illegible]	[illegible]	[illegible]	Sligo.
[illegible]	[illegible]	[illegible]	[illegible]	[illegible]	[illegible]	[illegible]	[illegible]	[illegible]	[illegible]	Tobercurry.

BIRTHS Registered in Ireland in the Four Quarters ending March 31st, June 30th, September 30th, and December 31st, 1891, in each SUPERINTENDENT REGISTRAR'S DISTRICT or POOR LAW UNION.

Number or Numbers of Unions in Provincial Abstract	Superintendent Registrar's Districts or Poor Law Unions	Area in Statute Acres	Population in 1891	Males and Females: Total	Males and Females: Registered in the Quarter ending the last day of Mar.	June	Sept.	Dec.	Males: Registered in the Quarter ending the last day of Mar.	June	Sept.	Dec.	Males: Total	Females: Total	Females: Registered in the Quarter ending the last day of Mar.	June	Sept.	Dec.
[illegible]	Abbeyleix,	[illegible]	[illegible]	[illegible]	[illegible]	[illegible]	[illegible]	[illegible]	[illegible]	[illegible]	[illegible]	[illegible]	[illegible]	[illegible]	[illegible]	[illegible]	[illegible]	[illegible]
[illegible]	Antrim,	[illegible]	[illegible]	[illegible]	[illegible]	[illegible]	[illegible]	[illegible]	[illegible]	[illegible]	[illegible]	[illegible]	[illegible]	[illegible]	[illegible]	[illegible]	[illegible]	[illegible]
[illegible]	Ardee,	[illegible]	[illegible]	[illegible]	[illegible]	[illegible]	[illegible]	[illegible]	[illegible]	[illegible]	[illegible]	[illegible]	[illegible]	[illegible]	[illegible]	[illegible]	[illegible]	[illegible]
[illegible]	Armagh,	[illegible]	[illegible]	[illegible]	[illegible]	[illegible]	[illegible]	[illegible]	[illegible]	[illegible]	[illegible]	[illegible]	[illegible]	[illegible]	[illegible]	[illegible]	[illegible]	[illegible]
[illegible]	Athlone,	[illegible]	[illegible]	[illegible]	[illegible]	[illegible]	[illegible]	[illegible]	[illegible]	[illegible]	[illegible]	[illegible]	[illegible]	[illegible]	[illegible]	[illegible]	[illegible]	[illegible]
[illegible]	Athy,	[illegible]	[illegible]	[illegible]	[illegible]	[illegible]	[illegible]	[illegible]	[illegible]	[illegible]	[illegible]	[illegible]	[illegible]	[illegible]	[illegible]	[illegible]	[illegible]	[illegible]
[illegible]	Bailieborough,	[illegible]	[illegible]	[illegible]	[illegible]	[illegible]	[illegible]	[illegible]	[illegible]	[illegible]	[illegible]	[illegible]	[illegible]	[illegible]	[illegible]	[illegible]	[illegible]	[illegible]
[illegible]	Ballina,	[illegible]	[illegible]	[illegible]	[illegible]	[illegible]	[illegible]	[illegible]	[illegible]	[illegible]	[illegible]	[illegible]	[illegible]	[illegible]	[illegible]	[illegible]	[illegible]	[illegible]
[illegible]	Ballinasloe,	[illegible]	[illegible]	[illegible]	[illegible]	[illegible]	[illegible]	[illegible]	[illegible]	[illegible]	[illegible]	[illegible]	[illegible]	[illegible]	[illegible]	[illegible]	[illegible]	[illegible]
[illegible]	Ballinrobe,	[illegible]	[illegible]	[illegible]	[illegible]	[illegible]	[illegible]	[illegible]	[illegible]	[illegible]	[illegible]	[illegible]	[illegible]	[illegible]	[illegible]	[illegible]	[illegible]	[illegible]
[illegible]	Ballycastle,	[illegible]	[illegible]	[illegible]	[illegible]	[illegible]	[illegible]	[illegible]	[illegible]	[illegible]	[illegible]	[illegible]	[illegible]	[illegible]	[illegible]	[illegible]	[illegible]	[illegible]
[illegible]	Ballymahon,	[illegible]	[illegible]	[illegible]	[illegible]	[illegible]	[illegible]	[illegible]	[illegible]	[illegible]	[illegible]	[illegible]	[illegible]	[illegible]	[illegible]	[illegible]	[illegible]	[illegible]
[illegible]	Ballymena,	[illegible]	[illegible]	[illegible]	[illegible]	[illegible]	[illegible]	[illegible]	[illegible]	[illegible]	[illegible]	[illegible]	[illegible]	[illegible]	[illegible]	[illegible]	[illegible]	[illegible]
[illegible]	Ballymoney,	[illegible]	[illegible]	[illegible]	[illegible]	[illegible]	[illegible]	[illegible]	[illegible]	[illegible]	[illegible]	[illegible]	[illegible]	[illegible]	[illegible]	[illegible]	[illegible]	[illegible]
[illegible]	Ballyshannon,	[illegible]	[illegible]	[illegible]	[illegible]	[illegible]	[illegible]	[illegible]	[illegible]	[illegible]	[illegible]	[illegible]	[illegible]	[illegible]	[illegible]	[illegible]	[illegible]	[illegible]
[illegible]	Ballyvaghan,	[illegible]	[illegible]	[illegible]	[illegible]	[illegible]	[illegible]	[illegible]	[illegible]	[illegible]	[illegible]	[illegible]	[illegible]	[illegible]	[illegible]	[illegible]	[illegible]	[illegible]
[illegible]	Balrothery,	[illegible]	[illegible]	[illegible]	[illegible]	[illegible]	[illegible]	[illegible]	[illegible]	[illegible]	[illegible]	[illegible]	[illegible]	[illegible]	[illegible]	[illegible]	[illegible]	[illegible]
[illegible]	Baltinglass,	[illegible]	[illegible]	[illegible]	[illegible]	[illegible]	[illegible]	[illegible]	[illegible]	[illegible]	[illegible]	[illegible]	[illegible]	[illegible]	[illegible]	[illegible]	[illegible]	[illegible]
[illegible]	Banbridge,	[illegible]	[illegible]	[illegible]	[illegible]	[illegible]	[illegible]	[illegible]	[illegible]	[illegible]	[illegible]	[illegible]	[illegible]	[illegible]	[illegible]	[illegible]	[illegible]	[illegible]
[illegible]	Bandon,	[illegible]	[illegible]	[illegible]	[illegible]	[illegible]	[illegible]	[illegible]	[illegible]	[illegible]	[illegible]	[illegible]	[illegible]	[illegible]	[illegible]	[illegible]	[illegible]	[illegible]
[illegible]	Bantry,	[illegible]	[illegible]	[illegible]	[illegible]	[illegible]	[illegible]	[illegible]	[illegible]	[illegible]	[illegible]	[illegible]	[illegible]	[illegible]	[illegible]	[illegible]	[illegible]	[illegible]
[illegible]	Bawnboy,	[illegible]	[illegible]	[illegible]	[illegible]	[illegible]	[illegible]	[illegible]	[illegible]	[illegible]	[illegible]	[illegible]	[illegible]	[illegible]	[illegible]	[illegible]	[illegible]	[illegible]
[illegible]	Belfast,	[illegible]	[illegible]	[illegible]	[illegible]	[illegible]	[illegible]	[illegible]	[illegible]	[illegible]	[illegible]	[illegible]	[illegible]	[illegible]	[illegible]	[illegible]	[illegible]	[illegible]
[illegible]	Belmullet,	[illegible]	[illegible]	[illegible]	[illegible]	[illegible]	[illegible]	[illegible]	[illegible]	[illegible]	[illegible]	[illegible]	[illegible]	[illegible]	[illegible]	[illegible]	[illegible]	[illegible]
[illegible]	Borrisokane,	[illegible]	[illegible]	[illegible]	[illegible]	[illegible]	[illegible]	[illegible]	[illegible]	[illegible]	[illegible]	[illegible]	[illegible]	[illegible]	[illegible]	[illegible]	[illegible]	[illegible]
[illegible]	Boyle,	[illegible]	[illegible]	[illegible]	[illegible]	[illegible]	[illegible]	[illegible]	[illegible]	[illegible]	[illegible]	[illegible]	[illegible]	[illegible]	[illegible]	[illegible]	[illegible]	[illegible]
[illegible]	Cahersiveen,	[illegible]	[illegible]	[illegible]	[illegible]	[illegible]	[illegible]	[illegible]	[illegible]	[illegible]	[illegible]	[illegible]	[illegible]	[illegible]	[illegible]	[illegible]	[illegible]	[illegible]
[illegible]	Callan,	[illegible]	[illegible]	[illegible]	[illegible]	[illegible]	[illegible]	[illegible]	[illegible]	[illegible]	[illegible]	[illegible]	[illegible]	[illegible]	[illegible]	[illegible]	[illegible]	[illegible]
[illegible]	Carlow,	[illegible]	[illegible]	[illegible]	[illegible]	[illegible]	[illegible]	[illegible]	[illegible]	[illegible]	[illegible]	[illegible]	[illegible]	[illegible]	[illegible]	[illegible]	[illegible]	[illegible]
[illegible]	Carrickmacross,	[illegible]	[illegible]	[illegible]	[illegible]	[illegible]	[illegible]	[illegible]	[illegible]	[illegible]	[illegible]	[illegible]	[illegible]	[illegible]	[illegible]	[illegible]	[illegible]	[illegible]
[illegible]	Carrick-on-Shannon,	[illegible]	[illegible]	[illegible]	[illegible]	[illegible]	[illegible]	[illegible]	[illegible]	[illegible]	[illegible]	[illegible]	[illegible]	[illegible]	[illegible]	[illegible]	[illegible]	[illegible]
[illegible]	Carrick-on-Suir,	[illegible]	[illegible]	[illegible]	[illegible]	[illegible]	[illegible]	[illegible]	[illegible]	[illegible]	[illegible]	[illegible]	[illegible]	[illegible]	[illegible]	[illegible]	[illegible]	[illegible]
[illegible]	Cashel,	[illegible]	[illegible]	[illegible]	[illegible]	[illegible]	[illegible]	[illegible]	[illegible]	[illegible]	[illegible]	[illegible]	[illegible]	[illegible]	[illegible]	[illegible]	[illegible]	[illegible]
[illegible]	Castlebar,	[illegible]	[illegible]	[illegible]	[illegible]	[illegible]	[illegible]	[illegible]	[illegible]	[illegible]	[illegible]	[illegible]	[illegible]	[illegible]	[illegible]	[illegible]	[illegible]	[illegible]
[illegible]	Castleblayney,	[illegible]	[illegible]	[illegible]	[illegible]	[illegible]	[illegible]	[illegible]	[illegible]	[illegible]	[illegible]	[illegible]	[illegible]	[illegible]	[illegible]	[illegible]	[illegible]	[illegible]
[illegible]	Castlecomer,	[illegible]	[illegible]	[illegible]	[illegible]	[illegible]	[illegible]	[illegible]	[illegible]	[illegible]	[illegible]	[illegible]	[illegible]	[illegible]	[illegible]	[illegible]	[illegible]	[illegible]
[illegible]	Castlederg,	[illegible]	[illegible]	[illegible]	[illegible]	[illegible]	[illegible]	[illegible]	[illegible]	[illegible]	[illegible]	[illegible]	[illegible]	[illegible]	[illegible]	[illegible]	[illegible]	[illegible]
[illegible]	Castlerea,	[illegible]	[illegible]	[illegible]	[illegible]	[illegible]	[illegible]	[illegible]	[illegible]	[illegible]	[illegible]	[illegible]	[illegible]	[illegible]	[illegible]	[illegible]	[illegible]	[illegible]
[illegible]	Castletown,	[illegible]	[illegible]	[illegible]	[illegible]	[illegible]	[illegible]	[illegible]	[illegible]	[illegible]	[illegible]	[illegible]	[illegible]	[illegible]	[illegible]	[illegible]	[illegible]	[illegible]
[illegible]	Cavan,	[illegible]	[illegible]	[illegible]	[illegible]	[illegible]	[illegible]	[illegible]	[illegible]	[illegible]	[illegible]	[illegible]	[illegible]	[illegible]	[illegible]	[illegible]	[illegible]	[illegible]
[illegible]	Celbridge,	[illegible]	[illegible]	[illegible]	[illegible]	[illegible]	[illegible]	[illegible]	[illegible]	[illegible]	[illegible]	[illegible]	[illegible]	[illegible]	[illegible]	[illegible]	[illegible]	[illegible]
[illegible]	Claremorris,	[illegible]	[illegible]	[illegible]	[illegible]	[illegible]	[illegible]	[illegible]	[illegible]	[illegible]	[illegible]	[illegible]	[illegible]	[illegible]	[illegible]	[illegible]	[illegible]	[illegible]
[illegible]	Clifden,	[illegible]	[illegible]	[illegible]	[illegible]	[illegible]	[illegible]	[illegible]	[illegible]	[illegible]	[illegible]	[illegible]	[illegible]	[illegible]	[illegible]	[illegible]	[illegible]	[illegible]
[illegible]	Clogheen,	[illegible]	[illegible]	[illegible]	[illegible]	[illegible]	[illegible]	[illegible]	[illegible]	[illegible]	[illegible]	[illegible]	[illegible]	[illegible]	[illegible]	[illegible]	[illegible]	[illegible]
[illegible]	Clogher,	[illegible]	[illegible]	[illegible]	[illegible]	[illegible]	[illegible]	[illegible]	[illegible]	[illegible]	[illegible]	[illegible]	[illegible]	[illegible]	[illegible]	[illegible]	[illegible]	[illegible]
[illegible]	Clonakilty,	[illegible]	[illegible]	[illegible]	[illegible]	[illegible]	[illegible]	[illegible]	[illegible]	[illegible]	[illegible]	[illegible]	[illegible]	[illegible]	[illegible]	[illegible]	[illegible]	[illegible]
[illegible]	Clones,	[illegible]	[illegible]	[illegible]	[illegible]	[illegible]	[illegible]	[illegible]	[illegible]	[illegible]	[illegible]	[illegible]	[illegible]	[illegible]	[illegible]	[illegible]	[illegible]	[illegible]
[illegible]	Clonmel,	[illegible]	[illegible]	[illegible]	[illegible]	[illegible]	[illegible]	[illegible]	[illegible]	[illegible]	[illegible]	[illegible]	[illegible]	[illegible]	[illegible]	[illegible]	[illegible]	[illegible]
[illegible]	Coleraine,	[illegible]	[illegible]	[illegible]	[illegible]	[illegible]	[illegible]	[illegible]	[illegible]	[illegible]	[illegible]	[illegible]	[illegible]	[illegible]	[illegible]	[illegible]	[illegible]	[illegible]
[illegible]	Cookstown,	[illegible]	[illegible]	[illegible]	[illegible]	[illegible]	[illegible]	[illegible]	[illegible]	[illegible]	[illegible]	[illegible]	[illegible]	[illegible]	[illegible]	[illegible]	[illegible]	[illegible]
[illegible]	Cootehill,	[illegible]	[illegible]	[illegible]	[illegible]	[illegible]	[illegible]	[illegible]	[illegible]	[illegible]	[illegible]	[illegible]	[illegible]	[illegible]	[illegible]	[illegible]	[illegible]	[illegible]
[illegible]	Cork,	[illegible]	[illegible]	[illegible]	[illegible]	[illegible]	[illegible]	[illegible]	[illegible]	[illegible]	[illegible]	[illegible]	[illegible]	[illegible]	[illegible]	[illegible]	[illegible]	[illegible]
[illegible]	Corrofin,	[illegible]	[illegible]	[illegible]	[illegible]	[illegible]	[illegible]	[illegible]	[illegible]	[illegible]	[illegible]	[illegible]	[illegible]	[illegible]	[illegible]	[illegible]	[illegible]	[illegible]
[illegible]	Croom,	[illegible]	[illegible]	[illegible]	[illegible]	[illegible]	[illegible]	[illegible]	[illegible]	[illegible]	[illegible]	[illegible]	[illegible]	[illegible]	[illegible]	[illegible]	[illegible]	[illegible]
[illegible]	Dingle,	[illegible]	[illegible]	[illegible]	[illegible]	[illegible]	[illegible]	[illegible]	[illegible]	[illegible]	[illegible]	[illegible]	[illegible]	[illegible]	[illegible]	[illegible]	[illegible]	[illegible]

BIRTHS Registered in Ireland in the Four Quarters ending March 31st, June 30th, September 30th, and December 31st, 1891, in each SUPERINTENDENT REGISTRAR'S DISTRICT or POOR LAW UNION—*continued.*

Number or Numbers of Union in [illegible]	Superintendent Registrars' Districts or Poor Law Unions.	Area in Statute Acres.	Population in 1891.	Males and Females: Total	Males and Females: Registered in the Quarter ending the last day of: Mar.	June.	Sept.	Dec.	Males: Registered in the Quarter ending the last day of: Mar.	June.	Sept.	Dec.	Males: Total	Females: Total	Females: Registered in the Quarter ending the last day of: Mar.	June.	Sept.	Dec.
[illegible]	Dingle,	[illegible]	[illegible]	[illegible]	[illegible]	[illegible]	[illegible]	[illegible]	[illegible]	[illegible]	[illegible]	[illegible]	[illegible]	[illegible]	[illegible]	[illegible]	[illegible]	[illegible]
[illegible]	Donegal,	[illegible]	[illegible]	[illegible]	[illegible]	[illegible]	[illegible]	[illegible]	[illegible]	[illegible]	[illegible]	[illegible]	[illegible]	[illegible]	[illegible]	[illegible]	[illegible]	[illegible]
[illegible]	Downpatrick,	[illegible]	[illegible]	[illegible]	[illegible]	[illegible]	[illegible]	[illegible]	[illegible]	[illegible]	[illegible]	[illegible]	[illegible]	[illegible]	[illegible]	[illegible]	[illegible]	[illegible]
[illegible]	Drogheda,	[illegible]	[illegible]	[illegible]	[illegible]	[illegible]	[illegible]	[illegible]	[illegible]	[illegible]	[illegible]	[illegible]	[illegible]	[illegible]	[illegible]	[illegible]	[illegible]	[illegible]
[illegible]	Dromore West,	[illegible]	[illegible]	[illegible]	[illegible]	[illegible]	[illegible]	[illegible]	[illegible]	[illegible]	[illegible]	[illegible]	[illegible]	[illegible]	[illegible]	[illegible]	[illegible]	[illegible]
[illegible]	Dublin, North,	[illegible]	[illegible]	[illegible]	[illegible]	[illegible]	[illegible]	[illegible]	[illegible]	[illegible]	[illegible]	[illegible]	[illegible]	[illegible]	[illegible]	[illegible]	[illegible]	[illegible]
[illegible]	Dublin, South,	[illegible]	[illegible]	[illegible]	[illegible]	[illegible]	[illegible]	[illegible]	[illegible]	[illegible]	[illegible]	[illegible]	[illegible]	[illegible]	[illegible]	[illegible]	[illegible]	[illegible]
[illegible]	Dundalk,	[illegible]	[illegible]	[illegible]	[illegible]	[illegible]	[illegible]	[illegible]	[illegible]	[illegible]	[illegible]	[illegible]	[illegible]	[illegible]	[illegible]	[illegible]	[illegible]	[illegible]
[illegible]	Dunfanaghy,	[illegible]	[illegible]	[illegible]	[illegible]	[illegible]	[illegible]	[illegible]	[illegible]	[illegible]	[illegible]	[illegible]	[illegible]	[illegible]	[illegible]	[illegible]	[illegible]	[illegible]
[illegible]	Dungannon,	[illegible]	[illegible]	[illegible]	[illegible]	[illegible]	[illegible]	[illegible]	[illegible]	[illegible]	[illegible]	[illegible]	[illegible]	[illegible]	[illegible]	[illegible]	[illegible]	[illegible]
[illegible]	Dungarvan,	[illegible]	[illegible]	[illegible]	[illegible]	[illegible]	[illegible]	[illegible]	[illegible]	[illegible]	[illegible]	[illegible]	[illegible]	[illegible]	[illegible]	[illegible]	[illegible]	[illegible]
[illegible]	Dunmanway,	[illegible]	[illegible]	[illegible]	[illegible]	[illegible]	[illegible]	[illegible]	[illegible]	[illegible]	[illegible]	[illegible]	[illegible]	[illegible]	[illegible]	[illegible]	[illegible]	[illegible]
[illegible]	Dunshaughlin,	[illegible]	[illegible]	[illegible]	[illegible]	[illegible]	[illegible]	[illegible]	[illegible]	[illegible]	[illegible]	[illegible]	[illegible]	[illegible]	[illegible]	[illegible]	[illegible]	[illegible]
[illegible]	Edenderry,	[illegible]	[illegible]	[illegible]	[illegible]	[illegible]	[illegible]	[illegible]	[illegible]	[illegible]	[illegible]	[illegible]	[illegible]	[illegible]	[illegible]	[illegible]	[illegible]	[illegible]
[illegible]	Ennis,	[illegible]	[illegible]	[illegible]	[illegible]	[illegible]	[illegible]	[illegible]	[illegible]	[illegible]	[illegible]	[illegible]	[illegible]	[illegible]	[illegible]	[illegible]	[illegible]	[illegible]
[illegible]	Enniscorthy,	[illegible]	[illegible]	[illegible]	[illegible]	[illegible]	[illegible]	[illegible]	[illegible]	[illegible]	[illegible]	[illegible]	[illegible]	[illegible]	[illegible]	[illegible]	[illegible]	[illegible]
[illegible]	Enniskillen,	[illegible]	[illegible]	[illegible]	[illegible]	[illegible]	[illegible]	[illegible]	[illegible]	[illegible]	[illegible]	[illegible]	[illegible]	[illegible]	[illegible]	[illegible]	[illegible]	[illegible]
[illegible]	Ennistimon,	[illegible]	[illegible]	[illegible]	[illegible]	[illegible]	[illegible]	[illegible]	[illegible]	[illegible]	[illegible]	[illegible]	[illegible]	[illegible]	[illegible]	[illegible]	[illegible]	[illegible]
[illegible]	Fermoy,	[illegible]	[illegible]	[illegible]	[illegible]	[illegible]	[illegible]	[illegible]	[illegible]	[illegible]	[illegible]	[illegible]	[illegible]	[illegible]	[illegible]	[illegible]	[illegible]	[illegible]
[illegible]	Galway,	[illegible]	[illegible]	[illegible]	[illegible]	[illegible]	[illegible]	[illegible]	[illegible]	[illegible]	[illegible]	[illegible]	[illegible]	[illegible]	[illegible]	[illegible]	[illegible]	[illegible]
[illegible]	Glenamaddy,	[illegible]	[illegible]	[illegible]	[illegible]	[illegible]	[illegible]	[illegible]	[illegible]	[illegible]	[illegible]	[illegible]	[illegible]	[illegible]	[illegible]	[illegible]	[illegible]	[illegible]
[illegible]	Glenties,	[illegible]	[illegible]	[illegible]	[illegible]	[illegible]	[illegible]	[illegible]	[illegible]	[illegible]	[illegible]	[illegible]	[illegible]	[illegible]	[illegible]	[illegible]	[illegible]	[illegible]
[illegible]	Glin,	[illegible]	[illegible]	[illegible]	[illegible]	[illegible]	[illegible]	[illegible]	[illegible]	[illegible]	[illegible]	[illegible]	[illegible]	[illegible]	[illegible]	[illegible]	[illegible]	[illegible]
[illegible]	Gorey,	[illegible]	[illegible]	[illegible]	[illegible]	[illegible]	[illegible]	[illegible]	[illegible]	[illegible]	[illegible]	[illegible]	[illegible]	[illegible]	[illegible]	[illegible]	[illegible]	[illegible]
[illegible]	Gort,	[illegible]	[illegible]	[illegible]	[illegible]	[illegible]	[illegible]	[illegible]	[illegible]	[illegible]	[illegible]	[illegible]	[illegible]	[illegible]	[illegible]	[illegible]	[illegible]	[illegible]
[illegible]	Granard,	[illegible]	[illegible]	[illegible]	[illegible]	[illegible]	[illegible]	[illegible]	[illegible]	[illegible]	[illegible]	[illegible]	[illegible]	[illegible]	[illegible]	[illegible]	[illegible]	[illegible]
[illegible]	Inishowen,	[illegible]	[illegible]	[illegible]	[illegible]	[illegible]	[illegible]	[illegible]	[illegible]	[illegible]	[illegible]	[illegible]	[illegible]	[illegible]	[illegible]	[illegible]	[illegible]	[illegible]
[illegible]	Irvinestown,	[illegible]	[illegible]	[illegible]	[illegible]	[illegible]	[illegible]	[illegible]	[illegible]	[illegible]	[illegible]	[illegible]	[illegible]	[illegible]	[illegible]	[illegible]	[illegible]	[illegible]
[illegible]	Kanturk,	[illegible]	[illegible]	[illegible]	[illegible]	[illegible]	[illegible]	[illegible]	[illegible]	[illegible]	[illegible]	[illegible]	[illegible]	[illegible]	[illegible]	[illegible]	[illegible]	[illegible]
[illegible]	Kells,	[illegible]	[illegible]	[illegible]	[illegible]	[illegible]	[illegible]	[illegible]	[illegible]	[illegible]	[illegible]	[illegible]	[illegible]	[illegible]	[illegible]	[illegible]	[illegible]	[illegible]
[illegible]	Kenmare,	[illegible]	[illegible]	[illegible]	[illegible]	[illegible]	[illegible]	[illegible]	[illegible]	[illegible]	[illegible]	[illegible]	[illegible]	[illegible]	[illegible]	[illegible]	[illegible]	[illegible]
[illegible]	Kilkeel,	[illegible]	[illegible]	[illegible]	[illegible]	[illegible]	[illegible]	[illegible]	[illegible]	[illegible]	[illegible]	[illegible]	[illegible]	[illegible]	[illegible]	[illegible]	[illegible]	[illegible]
[illegible]	Kilkenny,	[illegible]	[illegible]	[illegible]	[illegible]	[illegible]	[illegible]	[illegible]	[illegible]	[illegible]	[illegible]	[illegible]	[illegible]	[illegible]	[illegible]	[illegible]	[illegible]	[illegible]
[illegible]	Killadysert,	[illegible]	[illegible]	[illegible]	[illegible]	[illegible]	[illegible]	[illegible]	[illegible]	[illegible]	[illegible]	[illegible]	[illegible]	[illegible]	[illegible]	[illegible]	[illegible]	[illegible]
[illegible]	Killala,	[illegible]	[illegible]	[illegible]	[illegible]	[illegible]	[illegible]	[illegible]	[illegible]	[illegible]	[illegible]	[illegible]	[illegible]	[illegible]	[illegible]	[illegible]	[illegible]	[illegible]
[illegible]	Killarney,	[illegible]	[illegible]	[illegible]	[illegible]	[illegible]	[illegible]	[illegible]	[illegible]	[illegible]	[illegible]	[illegible]	[illegible]	[illegible]	[illegible]	[illegible]	[illegible]	[illegible]
[illegible]	Kilmacthomas,	[illegible]	[illegible]	[illegible]	[illegible]	[illegible]	[illegible]	[illegible]	[illegible]	[illegible]	[illegible]	[illegible]	[illegible]	[illegible]	[illegible]	[illegible]	[illegible]	[illegible]
[illegible]	Kilmallock,	[illegible]	[illegible]	[illegible]	[illegible]	[illegible]	[illegible]	[illegible]	[illegible]	[illegible]	[illegible]	[illegible]	[illegible]	[illegible]	[illegible]	[illegible]	[illegible]	[illegible]
[illegible]	Kilrush,	[illegible]	[illegible]	[illegible]	[illegible]	[illegible]	[illegible]	[illegible]	[illegible]	[illegible]	[illegible]	[illegible]	[illegible]	[illegible]	[illegible]	[illegible]	[illegible]	[illegible]
[illegible]	Kinsale,	[illegible]	[illegible]	[illegible]	[illegible]	[illegible]	[illegible]	[illegible]	[illegible]	[illegible]	[illegible]	[illegible]	[illegible]	[illegible]	[illegible]	[illegible]	[illegible]	[illegible]
[illegible]	Larne,	[illegible]	[illegible]	[illegible]	[illegible]	[illegible]	[illegible]	[illegible]	[illegible]	[illegible]	[illegible]	[illegible]	[illegible]	[illegible]	[illegible]	[illegible]	[illegible]	[illegible]
[illegible]	Letterkenny,	[illegible]	[illegible]	[illegible]	[illegible]	[illegible]	[illegible]	[illegible]	[illegible]	[illegible]	[illegible]	[illegible]	[illegible]	[illegible]	[illegible]	[illegible]	[illegible]	[illegible]
[illegible]	Limavady,	[illegible]	[illegible]	[illegible]	[illegible]	[illegible]	[illegible]	[illegible]	[illegible]	[illegible]	[illegible]	[illegible]	[illegible]	[illegible]	[illegible]	[illegible]	[illegible]	[illegible]
[illegible]	Limerick,	[illegible]	[illegible]	[illegible]	[illegible]	[illegible]	[illegible]	[illegible]	[illegible]	[illegible]	[illegible]	[illegible]	[illegible]	[illegible]	[illegible]	[illegible]	[illegible]	[illegible]
[illegible]	Lisburn,	[illegible]	[illegible]	[illegible]	[illegible]	[illegible]	[illegible]	[illegible]	[illegible]	[illegible]	[illegible]	[illegible]	[illegible]	[illegible]	[illegible]	[illegible]	[illegible]	[illegible]
[illegible]	Lismore,	[illegible]	[illegible]	[illegible]	[illegible]	[illegible]	[illegible]	[illegible]	[illegible]	[illegible]	[illegible]	[illegible]	[illegible]	[illegible]	[illegible]	[illegible]	[illegible]	[illegible]
[illegible]	Lisnaskea,	[illegible]	[illegible]	[illegible]	[illegible]	[illegible]	[illegible]	[illegible]	[illegible]	[illegible]	[illegible]	[illegible]	[illegible]	[illegible]	[illegible]	[illegible]	[illegible]	[illegible]
[illegible]	Listowel,	[illegible]	[illegible]	[illegible]	[illegible]	[illegible]	[illegible]	[illegible]	[illegible]	[illegible]	[illegible]	[illegible]	[illegible]	[illegible]	[illegible]	[illegible]	[illegible]	[illegible]
[illegible]	Londonderry,	[illegible]	[illegible]	[illegible]	[illegible]	[illegible]	[illegible]	[illegible]	[illegible]	[illegible]	[illegible]	[illegible]	[illegible]	[illegible]	[illegible]	[illegible]	[illegible]	[illegible]
[illegible]	Longford,	[illegible]	[illegible]	[illegible]	[illegible]	[illegible]	[illegible]	[illegible]	[illegible]	[illegible]	[illegible]	[illegible]	[illegible]	[illegible]	[illegible]	[illegible]	[illegible]	[illegible]
[illegible]	Loughrea,	[illegible]	[illegible]	[illegible]	[illegible]	[illegible]	[illegible]	[illegible]	[illegible]	[illegible]	[illegible]	[illegible]	[illegible]	[illegible]	[illegible]	[illegible]	[illegible]	[illegible]
[illegible]	Lurgan,	[illegible]	[illegible]	[illegible]	[illegible]	[illegible]	[illegible]	[illegible]	[illegible]	[illegible]	[illegible]	[illegible]	[illegible]	[illegible]	[illegible]	[illegible]	[illegible]	[illegible]
[illegible]	Macroom,	[illegible]	[illegible]	[illegible]	[illegible]	[illegible]	[illegible]	[illegible]	[illegible]	[illegible]	[illegible]	[illegible]	[illegible]	[illegible]	[illegible]	[illegible]	[illegible]	[illegible]

BIRTHS Registered in Ireland in the Four Quarters ending March 31st, June 30th, September 30th, and December 31st, 1871, in each Superintendent Registrar's District or Poor Law Union—*continued.*

Number or Numbers of Towns in (Front the) Abstract.	Superintendent Registrars' Districts or Poor Law Unions.	Area in Statute Acres.	Population in 1871.	Males and Females: Total.	Registered in the Quarter ending the last day of: Mar.	June.	Sept.	Dec.	Males: Registered in the Quarter ending the last day of: Mar.	June.	Sept.	Dec.	Total.	Females: Total.	Registered in the Quarter ending the last day of: Mar.	June.	Sept.	Dec.
[illegible]	Magherafelt,	[illegible]	[illegible]	[illegible]	[illegible]	[illegible]	[illegible]	[illegible]	[illegible]	[illegible]	[illegible]	[illegible]	[illegible]	[illegible]	[illegible]	[illegible]	[illegible]	[illegible]
[illegible]	Mallow,	[illegible]	[illegible]	[illegible]	[illegible]	[illegible]	[illegible]	[illegible]	[illegible]	[illegible]	[illegible]	[illegible]	[illegible]	[illegible]	[illegible]	[illegible]	[illegible]	[illegible]
[illegible]	Manorhamilton,	[illegible]	[illegible]	[illegible]	[illegible]	[illegible]	[illegible]	[illegible]	[illegible]	[illegible]	[illegible]	[illegible]	[illegible]	[illegible]	[illegible]	[illegible]	[illegible]	[illegible]
[illegible]	Midleton,	[illegible]	[illegible]	[illegible]	[illegible]	[illegible]	[illegible]	[illegible]	[illegible]	[illegible]	[illegible]	[illegible]	[illegible]	[illegible]	[illegible]	[illegible]	[illegible]	[illegible]
[illegible]	Milford,	[illegible]	[illegible]	[illegible]	[illegible]	[illegible]	[illegible]	[illegible]	[illegible]	[illegible]	[illegible]	[illegible]	[illegible]	[illegible]	[illegible]	[illegible]	[illegible]	[illegible]
[illegible]	Millstreet,	[illegible]	[illegible]	[illegible]	[illegible]	[illegible]	[illegible]	[illegible]	[illegible]	[illegible]	[illegible]	[illegible]	[illegible]	[illegible]	[illegible]	[illegible]	[illegible]	[illegible]
[illegible]	Mitchelstown,	[illegible]	[illegible]	[illegible]	[illegible]	[illegible]	[illegible]	[illegible]	[illegible]	[illegible]	[illegible]	[illegible]	[illegible]	[illegible]	[illegible]	[illegible]	[illegible]	[illegible]
[illegible]	Mohill,	[illegible]	[illegible]	[illegible]	[illegible]	[illegible]	[illegible]	[illegible]	[illegible]	[illegible]	[illegible]	[illegible]	[illegible]	[illegible]	[illegible]	[illegible]	[illegible]	[illegible]
[illegible]	Monaghan,	[illegible]	[illegible]	[illegible]	[illegible]	[illegible]	[illegible]	[illegible]	[illegible]	[illegible]	[illegible]	[illegible]	[illegible]	[illegible]	[illegible]	[illegible]	[illegible]	[illegible]
[illegible]	Mountbellew,	[illegible]	[illegible]	[illegible]	[illegible]	[illegible]	[illegible]	[illegible]	[illegible]	[illegible]	[illegible]	[illegible]	[illegible]	[illegible]	[illegible]	[illegible]	[illegible]	[illegible]
[illegible]	Mountmellick,	[illegible]	[illegible]	[illegible]	[illegible]	[illegible]	[illegible]	[illegible]	[illegible]	[illegible]	[illegible]	[illegible]	[illegible]	[illegible]	[illegible]	[illegible]	[illegible]	[illegible]
[illegible]	Mullingar,	[illegible]	[illegible]	[illegible]	[illegible]	[illegible]	[illegible]	[illegible]	[illegible]	[illegible]	[illegible]	[illegible]	[illegible]	[illegible]	[illegible]	[illegible]	[illegible]	[illegible]
[illegible]	Naas,	[illegible]	[illegible]	[illegible]	[illegible]	[illegible]	[illegible]	[illegible]	[illegible]	[illegible]	[illegible]	[illegible]	[illegible]	[illegible]	[illegible]	[illegible]	[illegible]	[illegible]
[illegible]	Navan,	[illegible]	[illegible]	[illegible]	[illegible]	[illegible]	[illegible]	[illegible]	[illegible]	[illegible]	[illegible]	[illegible]	[illegible]	[illegible]	[illegible]	[illegible]	[illegible]	[illegible]
[illegible]	Nenagh,	[illegible]	[illegible]	[illegible]	[illegible]	[illegible]	[illegible]	[illegible]	[illegible]	[illegible]	[illegible]	[illegible]	[illegible]	[illegible]	[illegible]	[illegible]	[illegible]	[illegible]
[illegible]	Newcastle,	[illegible]	[illegible]	[illegible]	[illegible]	[illegible]	[illegible]	[illegible]	[illegible]	[illegible]	[illegible]	[illegible]	[illegible]	[illegible]	[illegible]	[illegible]	[illegible]	[illegible]
[illegible]	New Ross,	[illegible]	[illegible]	[illegible]	[illegible]	[illegible]	[illegible]	[illegible]	[illegible]	[illegible]	[illegible]	[illegible]	[illegible]	[illegible]	[illegible]	[illegible]	[illegible]	[illegible]
[illegible]	Newry,	[illegible]	[illegible]	[illegible]	[illegible]	[illegible]	[illegible]	[illegible]	[illegible]	[illegible]	[illegible]	[illegible]	[illegible]	[illegible]	[illegible]	[illegible]	[illegible]	[illegible]
[illegible]	Newtownards,	[illegible]	[illegible]	[illegible]	[illegible]	[illegible]	[illegible]	[illegible]	[illegible]	[illegible]	[illegible]	[illegible]	[illegible]	[illegible]	[illegible]	[illegible]	[illegible]	[illegible]
[illegible]	Oldcastle,	[illegible]	[illegible]	[illegible]	[illegible]	[illegible]	[illegible]	[illegible]	[illegible]	[illegible]	[illegible]	[illegible]	[illegible]	[illegible]	[illegible]	[illegible]	[illegible]	[illegible]
[illegible]	Omagh,	[illegible]	[illegible]	[illegible]	[illegible]	[illegible]	[illegible]	[illegible]	[illegible]	[illegible]	[illegible]	[illegible]	[illegible]	[illegible]	[illegible]	[illegible]	[illegible]	[illegible]
[illegible]	Oughterard,	[illegible]	[illegible]	[illegible]	[illegible]	[illegible]	[illegible]	[illegible]	[illegible]	[illegible]	[illegible]	[illegible]	[illegible]	[illegible]	[illegible]	[illegible]	[illegible]	[illegible]
[illegible]	Parsonstown,	[illegible]	[illegible]	[illegible]	[illegible]	[illegible]	[illegible]	[illegible]	[illegible]	[illegible]	[illegible]	[illegible]	[illegible]	[illegible]	[illegible]	[illegible]	[illegible]	[illegible]
[illegible]	Portumna,	[illegible]	[illegible]	[illegible]	[illegible]	[illegible]	[illegible]	[illegible]	[illegible]	[illegible]	[illegible]	[illegible]	[illegible]	[illegible]	[illegible]	[illegible]	[illegible]	[illegible]
[illegible]	Rathdown,	[illegible]	[illegible]	[illegible]	[illegible]	[illegible]	[illegible]	[illegible]	[illegible]	[illegible]	[illegible]	[illegible]	[illegible]	[illegible]	[illegible]	[illegible]	[illegible]	[illegible]
[illegible]	Rathdrum,	[illegible]	[illegible]	[illegible]	[illegible]	[illegible]	[illegible]	[illegible]	[illegible]	[illegible]	[illegible]	[illegible]	[illegible]	[illegible]	[illegible]	[illegible]	[illegible]	[illegible]
[illegible]	Rathkeale,	[illegible]	[illegible]	[illegible]	[illegible]	[illegible]	[illegible]	[illegible]	[illegible]	[illegible]	[illegible]	[illegible]	[illegible]	[illegible]	[illegible]	[illegible]	[illegible]	[illegible]
[illegible]	Roscommon,	[illegible]	[illegible]	[illegible]	[illegible]	[illegible]	[illegible]	[illegible]	[illegible]	[illegible]	[illegible]	[illegible]	[illegible]	[illegible]	[illegible]	[illegible]	[illegible]	[illegible]
[illegible]	Roscrea,	[illegible]	[illegible]	[illegible]	[illegible]	[illegible]	[illegible]	[illegible]	[illegible]	[illegible]	[illegible]	[illegible]	[illegible]	[illegible]	[illegible]	[illegible]	[illegible]	[illegible]
[illegible]	Scariff,	[illegible]	[illegible]	[illegible]	[illegible]	[illegible]	[illegible]	[illegible]	[illegible]	[illegible]	[illegible]	[illegible]	[illegible]	[illegible]	[illegible]	[illegible]	[illegible]	[illegible]
[illegible]	Shillelagh,	[illegible]	[illegible]	[illegible]	[illegible]	[illegible]	[illegible]	[illegible]	[illegible]	[illegible]	[illegible]	[illegible]	[illegible]	[illegible]	[illegible]	[illegible]	[illegible]	[illegible]
[illegible]	Skibbereen,	[illegible]	[illegible]	[illegible]	[illegible]	[illegible]	[illegible]	[illegible]	[illegible]	[illegible]	[illegible]	[illegible]	[illegible]	[illegible]	[illegible]	[illegible]	[illegible]	[illegible]
[illegible]	Skull,	[illegible]	[illegible]	[illegible]	[illegible]	[illegible]	[illegible]	[illegible]	[illegible]	[illegible]	[illegible]	[illegible]	[illegible]	[illegible]	[illegible]	[illegible]	[illegible]	[illegible]
[illegible]	Sligo,	[illegible]	[illegible]	[illegible]	[illegible]	[illegible]	[illegible]	[illegible]	[illegible]	[illegible]	[illegible]	[illegible]	[illegible]	[illegible]	[illegible]	[illegible]	[illegible]	[illegible]
[illegible]	Strabane,	[illegible]	[illegible]	[illegible]	[illegible]	[illegible]	[illegible]	[illegible]	[illegible]	[illegible]	[illegible]	[illegible]	[illegible]	[illegible]	[illegible]	[illegible]	[illegible]	[illegible]
[illegible]	Stranorlar,	[illegible]	[illegible]	[illegible]	[illegible]	[illegible]	[illegible]	[illegible]	[illegible]	[illegible]	[illegible]	[illegible]	[illegible]	[illegible]	[illegible]	[illegible]	[illegible]	[illegible]
[illegible]	Strokestown,	[illegible]	[illegible]	[illegible]	[illegible]	[illegible]	[illegible]	[illegible]	[illegible]	[illegible]	[illegible]	[illegible]	[illegible]	[illegible]	[illegible]	[illegible]	[illegible]	[illegible]
[illegible]	Swineford,	[illegible]	[illegible]	[illegible]	[illegible]	[illegible]	[illegible]	[illegible]	[illegible]	[illegible]	[illegible]	[illegible]	[illegible]	[illegible]	[illegible]	[illegible]	[illegible]	[illegible]
[illegible]	Thomastown,	[illegible]	[illegible]	[illegible]	[illegible]	[illegible]	[illegible]	[illegible]	[illegible]	[illegible]	[illegible]	[illegible]	[illegible]	[illegible]	[illegible]	[illegible]	[illegible]	[illegible]
[illegible]	Thurles,	[illegible]	[illegible]	[illegible]	[illegible]	[illegible]	[illegible]	[illegible]	[illegible]	[illegible]	[illegible]	[illegible]	[illegible]	[illegible]	[illegible]	[illegible]	[illegible]	[illegible]
[illegible]	Tipperary,	[illegible]	[illegible]	[illegible]	[illegible]	[illegible]	[illegible]	[illegible]	[illegible]	[illegible]	[illegible]	[illegible]	[illegible]	[illegible]	[illegible]	[illegible]	[illegible]	[illegible]
[illegible]	Tobercurry,	[illegible]	[illegible]	[illegible]	[illegible]	[illegible]	[illegible]	[illegible]	[illegible]	[illegible]	[illegible]	[illegible]	[illegible]	[illegible]	[illegible]	[illegible]	[illegible]	[illegible]
[illegible]	Tralee,	[illegible]	[illegible]	[illegible]	[illegible]	[illegible]	[illegible]	[illegible]	[illegible]	[illegible]	[illegible]	[illegible]	[illegible]	[illegible]	[illegible]	[illegible]	[illegible]	[illegible]
[illegible]	Trim,	[illegible]	[illegible]	[illegible]	[illegible]	[illegible]	[illegible]	[illegible]	[illegible]	[illegible]	[illegible]	[illegible]	[illegible]	[illegible]	[illegible]	[illegible]	[illegible]	[illegible]
[illegible]	Tuam,	[illegible]	[illegible]	[illegible]	[illegible]	[illegible]	[illegible]	[illegible]	[illegible]	[illegible]	[illegible]	[illegible]	[illegible]	[illegible]	[illegible]	[illegible]	[illegible]	[illegible]
[illegible]	Tulla,	[illegible]	[illegible]	[illegible]	[illegible]	[illegible]	[illegible]	[illegible]	[illegible]	[illegible]	[illegible]	[illegible]	[illegible]	[illegible]	[illegible]	[illegible]	[illegible]	[illegible]
[illegible]	Tullamore,	[illegible]	[illegible]	[illegible]	[illegible]	[illegible]	[illegible]	[illegible]	[illegible]	[illegible]	[illegible]	[illegible]	[illegible]	[illegible]	[illegible]	[illegible]	[illegible]	[illegible]
[illegible]	Urlingford,	[illegible]	[illegible]	[illegible]	[illegible]	[illegible]	[illegible]	[illegible]	[illegible]	[illegible]	[illegible]	[illegible]	[illegible]	[illegible]	[illegible]	[illegible]	[illegible]	[illegible]
[illegible]	Waterford,	[illegible]	[illegible]	[illegible]	[illegible]	[illegible]	[illegible]	[illegible]	[illegible]	[illegible]	[illegible]	[illegible]	[illegible]	[illegible]	[illegible]	[illegible]	[illegible]	[illegible]
[illegible]	Westport,	[illegible]	[illegible]	[illegible]	[illegible]	[illegible]	[illegible]	[illegible]	[illegible]	[illegible]	[illegible]	[illegible]	[illegible]	[illegible]	[illegible]	[illegible]	[illegible]	[illegible]
[illegible]	Wexford,	[illegible]	[illegible]	[illegible]	[illegible]	[illegible]	[illegible]	[illegible]	[illegible]	[illegible]	[illegible]	[illegible]	[illegible]	[illegible]	[illegible]	[illegible]	[illegible]	[illegible]
[illegible]	Youghal,	[illegible]	[illegible]	[illegible]	[illegible]	[illegible]	[illegible]	[illegible]	[illegible]	[illegible]	[illegible]	[illegible]	[illegible]	[illegible]	[illegible]	[illegible]	[illegible]	[illegible]

Deaths in the Four Quarters of 1891.

DEATHS registered in each Province and County in Ireland in the Four Quarters ending March 31st, June 30th, September 30th, and December 31st, 1891.

No.	Provinces and Counties.	Area in Statute Acres.	Population in 1891.	Males and Females: Total.	Registered in the Quarter ending the last day of: March.	June.	Sept.	Dec.	Males: Registered in the Quarter ending the last day of: March.	June.	Sept.	Dec.	Males: Total.	Females: Total.	Registered in the Quarter ending the last day of: March.	June.	Sept.
	IRELAND,	[illegible]	[illegible]	[illegible]	[illegible]	[illegible]	[illegible]	[illegible]	[illegible]	[illegible]	[illegible]	[illegible]	[illegible]	[illegible]	[illegible]	[illegible]	[illegible]
	PROVINCES.																
I.	LEINSTER,	[illegible]	[illegible]	[illegible]	[illegible]	[illegible]	[illegible]	[illegible]	[illegible]	[illegible]	[illegible]	[illegible]	[illegible]	[illegible]	[illegible]	[illegible]	[illegible]
II.	MUNSTER,	[illegible]	[illegible]	[illegible]	[illegible]	[illegible]	[illegible]	[illegible]	[illegible]	[illegible]	[illegible]	[illegible]	[illegible]	[illegible]	[illegible]	[illegible]	[illegible]
III.	ULSTER,	[illegible]	[illegible]	[illegible]	[illegible]	[illegible]	[illegible]	[illegible]	[illegible]	[illegible]	[illegible]	[illegible]	[illegible]	[illegible]	[illegible]	[illegible]	[illegible]
IV.	CONNAUGHT,	[illegible]	[illegible]	[illegible]	[illegible]	[illegible]	[illegible]	[illegible]	[illegible]	[illegible]	[illegible]	[illegible]	[illegible]	[illegible]	[illegible]	[illegible]	[illegible]
	I.—PROVINCE OF LEINSTER.—COUNTIES.																
1	CARLOW,	[illegible]	[illegible]	[illegible]	[illegible]	[illegible]	[illegible]	[illegible]	[illegible]	[illegible]	[illegible]	[illegible]	[illegible]	[illegible]	[illegible]	[illegible]	[illegible]
2	DUBLIN,	[illegible]	[illegible]	[illegible]	[illegible]	[illegible]	[illegible]	[illegible]	[illegible]	[illegible]	[illegible]	[illegible]	[illegible]	[illegible]	[illegible]	[illegible]	[illegible]
3	KILDARE,	[illegible]	[illegible]	[illegible]	[illegible]	[illegible]	[illegible]	[illegible]	[illegible]	[illegible]	[illegible]	[illegible]	[illegible]	[illegible]	[illegible]	[illegible]	[illegible]
4	KILKENNY,	[illegible]	[illegible]	[illegible]	[illegible]	[illegible]	[illegible]	[illegible]	[illegible]	[illegible]	[illegible]	[illegible]	[illegible]	[illegible]	[illegible]	[illegible]	[illegible]
5	KING'S,	[illegible]	[illegible]	[illegible]	[illegible]	[illegible]	[illegible]	[illegible]	[illegible]	[illegible]	[illegible]	[illegible]	[illegible]	[illegible]	[illegible]	[illegible]	[illegible]
6	LONGFORD,	[illegible]	[illegible]	[illegible]	[illegible]	[illegible]	[illegible]	[illegible]	[illegible]	[illegible]	[illegible]	[illegible]	[illegible]	[illegible]	[illegible]	[illegible]	[illegible]
7	LOUTH, excl. of the Town of Drogheda,	[illegible]	[illegible]	[illegible]	[illegible]	[illegible]	[illegible]	[illegible]	[illegible]	[illegible]	[illegible]	[illegible]	[illegible]	[illegible]	[illegible]	[illegible]	[illegible]
8	MEATH,	[illegible]	[illegible]	[illegible]	[illegible]	[illegible]	[illegible]	[illegible]	[illegible]	[illegible]	[illegible]	[illegible]	[illegible]	[illegible]	[illegible]	[illegible]	[illegible]
9	QUEEN'S,	[illegible]	[illegible]	[illegible]	[illegible]	[illegible]	[illegible]	[illegible]	[illegible]	[illegible]	[illegible]	[illegible]	[illegible]	[illegible]	[illegible]	[illegible]	[illegible]
10	WESTMEATH,	[illegible]	[illegible]	[illegible]	[illegible]	[illegible]	[illegible]	[illegible]	[illegible]	[illegible]	[illegible]	[illegible]	[illegible]	[illegible]	[illegible]	[illegible]	[illegible]
11	WEXFORD,	[illegible]	[illegible]	[illegible]	[illegible]	[illegible]	[illegible]	[illegible]	[illegible]	[illegible]	[illegible]	[illegible]	[illegible]	[illegible]	[illegible]	[illegible]	[illegible]
12	WICKLOW,	[illegible]	[illegible]	[illegible]	[illegible]	[illegible]	[illegible]	[illegible]	[illegible]	[illegible]	[illegible]	[illegible]	[illegible]	[illegible]	[illegible]	[illegible]	[illegible]
	II.—PROVINCE OF MUNSTER.—COUNTIES.																
13	CLARE,	[illegible]	[illegible]	[illegible]	[illegible]	[illegible]	[illegible]	[illegible]	[illegible]	[illegible]	[illegible]	[illegible]	[illegible]	[illegible]	[illegible]	[illegible]	[illegible]
14	CORK,	[illegible]	[illegible]	[illegible]	[illegible]	[illegible]	[illegible]	[illegible]	[illegible]	[illegible]	[illegible]	[illegible]	[illegible]	[illegible]	[illegible]	[illegible]	[illegible]
15	KERRY,	[illegible]	[illegible]	[illegible]	[illegible]	[illegible]	[illegible]	[illegible]	[illegible]	[illegible]	[illegible]	[illegible]	[illegible]	[illegible]	[illegible]	[illegible]	[illegible]
16	LIMERICK,	[illegible]	[illegible]	[illegible]	[illegible]	[illegible]	[illegible]	[illegible]	[illegible]	[illegible]	[illegible]	[illegible]	[illegible]	[illegible]	[illegible]	[illegible]	[illegible]
17	TIPPERARY,	[illegible]	[illegible]	[illegible]	[illegible]	[illegible]	[illegible]	[illegible]	[illegible]	[illegible]	[illegible]	[illegible]	[illegible]	[illegible]	[illegible]	[illegible]	[illegible]
18	WATERFORD,	[illegible]	[illegible]	[illegible]	[illegible]	[illegible]	[illegible]	[illegible]	[illegible]	[illegible]	[illegible]	[illegible]	[illegible]	[illegible]	[illegible]	[illegible]	[illegible]
	III.—PROVINCE OF ULSTER.—COUNTIES.																
19	ANTRIM,	[illegible]	[illegible]	[illegible]	[illegible]	[illegible]	[illegible]	[illegible]	[illegible]	[illegible]	[illegible]	[illegible]	[illegible]	[illegible]	[illegible]	[illegible]	[illegible]
20	ARMAGH,	[illegible]	[illegible]	[illegible]	[illegible]	[illegible]	[illegible]	[illegible]	[illegible]	[illegible]	[illegible]	[illegible]	[illegible]	[illegible]	[illegible]	[illegible]	[illegible]
21	CAVAN,	[illegible]	[illegible]	[illegible]	[illegible]	[illegible]	[illegible]	[illegible]	[illegible]	[illegible]	[illegible]	[illegible]	[illegible]	[illegible]	[illegible]	[illegible]	[illegible]
22	DONEGAL,	[illegible]	[illegible]	[illegible]	[illegible]	[illegible]	[illegible]	[illegible]	[illegible]	[illegible]	[illegible]	[illegible]	[illegible]	[illegible]	[illegible]	[illegible]	[illegible]
23	DOWN,	[illegible]	[illegible]	[illegible]	[illegible]	[illegible]	[illegible]	[illegible]	[illegible]	[illegible]	[illegible]	[illegible]	[illegible]	[illegible]	[illegible]	[illegible]	[illegible]
24	FERMANAGH,	[illegible]	[illegible]	[illegible]	[illegible]	[illegible]	[illegible]	[illegible]	[illegible]	[illegible]	[illegible]	[illegible]	[illegible]	[illegible]	[illegible]	[illegible]	[illegible]
25	LONDONDERRY,	[illegible]	[illegible]	[illegible]	[illegible]	[illegible]	[illegible]	[illegible]	[illegible]	[illegible]	[illegible]	[illegible]	[illegible]	[illegible]	[illegible]	[illegible]	[illegible]
26	MONAGHAN,	[illegible]	[illegible]	[illegible]	[illegible]	[illegible]	[illegible]	[illegible]	[illegible]	[illegible]	[illegible]	[illegible]	[illegible]	[illegible]	[illegible]	[illegible]	[illegible]
27	TYRONE,	[illegible]	[illegible]	[illegible]	[illegible]	[illegible]	[illegible]	[illegible]	[illegible]	[illegible]	[illegible]	[illegible]	[illegible]	[illegible]	[illegible]	[illegible]	[illegible]
	IV.—PROVINCE OF CONNAUGHT.—COUNTIES.																
28	GALWAY,	[illegible]	[illegible]	[illegible]	[illegible]	[illegible]	[illegible]	[illegible]	[illegible]	[illegible]	[illegible]	[illegible]	[illegible]	[illegible]	[illegible]	[illegible]	[illegible]
29	LEITRIM,	[illegible]	[illegible]	[illegible]	[illegible]	[illegible]	[illegible]	[illegible]	[illegible]	[illegible]	[illegible]	[illegible]	[illegible]	[illegible]	[illegible]	[illegible]	[illegible]
30	MAYO,	[illegible]	[illegible]	[illegible]	[illegible]	[illegible]	[illegible]	[illegible]	[illegible]	[illegible]	[illegible]	[illegible]	[illegible]	[illegible]	[illegible]	[illegible]	[illegible]
31	ROSCOMMON,	[illegible]	[illegible]	[illegible]	[illegible]	[illegible]	[illegible]	[illegible]	[illegible]	[illegible]	[illegible]	[illegible]	[illegible]	[illegible]	[illegible]	[illegible]	[illegible]
32	SLIGO,	[illegible]	[illegible]	[illegible]	[illegible]	[illegible]	[illegible]	[illegible]	[illegible]	[illegible]	[illegible]	[illegible]	[illegible]	[illegible]	[illegible]	[illegible]	[illegible]

BIRTHS registered in Ireland in the Four Quarters ending

2.—PROVINCE OF

No.	Counties and Superintendent Registrars' Districts.	Area in Statute Acres.	Population in [illegible]	Males and Females. Total.	Registered in the Quarter ending the last day of March.	June.	Sept.	Dec.
	Carlow Co.							
1	Baltinglass, part of,	36,210	7,465	40	9	10	5	15
2	Carlow, do.,	140,423	30,711	495	140	140	128	109
3	[illegible], do.,	9,628	1,640	14	4	1	2	4
4	New Ross, do.,	22,094	5,900	78	25	20	15	15
5	Shillelagh, do.,	22,654	4,645	80	25	29	14	18
	Dublin Co.							
6	Balrothery,	76,330	12,149	256	60	67	67	72
7	Celbridge, part of,	16,827	3,542	47	11	12	17	10
8	Dublin, North,	41,107	140,798	4,419	1,080	925	990	1,182
9	Dublin, South,	46,139	220,760	4,396	1,141	1,389	1,079	1,411
10	Dunshaughlin, part of,	4,501	688	22	5	7	6	4
11	Rathdown, do.,	27,163	44,142	899	227	209	164	210
	Kildare Co.							
12	Athy, part of,	112,111	19,946	327	101	80	82	64
13	Baltinglass, do.,	17,135	3,382	31	8	5	6	12
14	Celbridge, do.,	63,897	9,174	151	40	46	32	33
15	Edenderry, do.,	43,651	6,082	85	30	19	18	20
16	Naas, do.,	165,169	23,073	428	126	144	112	116
	Kilkenny Co.							
17	Callan, part of,	63,148	9,458	180	37	64	38	41
18	Carrick-on-Suir, do.,	22,739	3,578	98	25	28	19	12
19	Castlecomer,	57,620	11,480	173	38	47	40	47
20	Kilkenny,	100,343	25,037	480	130	125	110	115
21	New Ross, part of,	20,670	4,347	65	16	16	10	10
22	Thomastown,	107,577	14,079	190	70	76	33	30
23	Urlingford, part of,	28,860	4,021	140	32	61	34	33
24	Waterford, do.,	55,169	10,453	189	56	49	32	43
	King's Co.							
25	Edenderry, part of,	68,994	6,087	156	41	30	35	46
26	Mountmellick, do.,	44,147	3,080	40	11	11	8	13
27	Parsonstown, do.,	128,344	19,734	420	120	98	87	115
28	Roscrea, do.,	15,853	6,485	86	23	28	27	18
29	Tullamore, do.,	162,844	25,387	380	104	98	80	70
	Longford Co.							
30	Ballymahon, part of,	89,732	16,679	182	40	41	38	30
31	Granard, do.,	77,884	17,040	171	45	77	35	36
32	Longford,	170,876	30,984	371	101	111	86	91
	Louth Co., and Co. of Town of Drogheda.							
33	Ardee, part of,	63,909	14,143	225	64	79	46	35
34	Drogheda, do.,	41,313	19,957	288	80	85	77	85
35	Dundalk, do.,	94,416	40,888	494	127	134	130	101
	Meath Co.							
36	Ardee, part of,	30,483	4,620	50	14	15	15	16
37	Celbridge, do.,	7,238	675	5	3	1	-	1
38	Drogheda, do.,	67,711	8,814	180	44	46	38	43
39	Dunshaughlin, do.,	93,656	8,549	158	35	40	51	30
40	Edenderry, do.,	33,884	2,047	34	10	15	5	6
41	Kells, do.,	143,658	14,890	243	142	80	63	85
42	Navan,	94,676	16,880	318	80	88	82	73
43	Oldcastle, part of,	44,183	6,887	140	35	36	30	18
44	Trim,	118,380	16,811	287	64	88	80	84

March 31st, June 30th, September 30th, and December 31st, 1891.

LEINSTER.

MALES. Registered in the Quarter ending the last day of March.	June.	Sept.	Dec.	Total.	FEMALES. Total.	Registered in the Quarter ending the last day of March.	June.	Sept.	Dec.	SUPERINTENDENT REGISTRARS' DISTRICTS.
										Carlow Co.
5	6	9	[illegible]	17	[illegible]	4	5	8	9	Baltinglass, part of.
[illegible]	79	67	[illegible]	[illegible]	[illegible]	[illegible]	[illegible]	71	72	Carlow, do.
4	[illegible]	1	[illegible]	7	4	3	1	1	5	Enniscorthy, do.
6	[illegible]	5	[illegible]	[illegible]	[illegible]	13	8	6	9	New Ross, do.
7	14	7	[illegible]	[illegible]	[illegible]	14	8	10	3	Shillelagh, do.
										Dublin Co.
[illegible]	[illegible]	[illegible]	[illegible]	[illegible]	[illegible]	[illegible]	[illegible]	[illegible]	[illegible]	Balrothery.
4	12	6	[illegible]	[illegible]	[illegible]	7	15	8	6	Celbridge, part of.
[illegible]	[illegible]	[illegible]	[illegible]	[illegible]	[illegible]	[illegible]	[illegible]	[illegible]	[illegible]	Dublin, North.
[illegible]	[illegible]	[illegible]	[illegible]	[illegible]	[illegible]	[illegible]	[illegible]	[illegible]	[illegible]	Dublin, South.
1	6	3	3	13	8	4	1	0	1	Dunshaughlin, part of.
117	[illegible]	76	[illegible]	[illegible]	[illegible]	[illegible]	[illegible]	[illegible]	111	Rathdown, do.
										Kildare Co.
[illegible]	[illegible]	[illegible]	[illegible]	[illegible]	[illegible]	[illegible]	[illegible]	[illegible]	[illegible]	Athy, part of.
5	4	2	4	[illegible]	15	4	1	4	6	Baltinglass, do.
[illegible]	[illegible]	[illegible]	[illegible]	[illegible]	[illegible]	[illegible]	[illegible]	[illegible]	[illegible]	Celbridge, do.
[illegible]	[illegible]	11	[illegible]	[illegible]	[illegible]	15	8	6	8	Edenderry, do.
[illegible]	[illegible]	[illegible]	[illegible]	[illegible]	[illegible]	[illegible]	[illegible]	35	[illegible]	Naas, do.
										Kilkenny Co.
[illegible]	[illegible]	[illegible]	[illegible]	[illegible]	[illegible]	[illegible]	[illegible]	11	[illegible]	Callan, part of
[illegible]	11	7	5	[illegible]	[illegible]	[illegible]	[illegible]	[illegible]	[illegible]	Carrick-on-Suir, do.
[illegible]	[illegible]	[illegible]	[illegible]	[illegible]	[illegible]	14	[illegible]	[illegible]	[illegible]	Castlecomer.
[illegible]	[illegible]	[illegible]	[illegible]	[illegible]	[illegible]	[illegible]	[illegible]	[illegible]	[illegible]	Kilkenny.
12	[illegible]	3	4	[illegible]	[illegible]	11	[illegible]	7	16	New Ross, part of.
[illegible]	[illegible]	[illegible]	[illegible]	[illegible]	[illegible]	[illegible]	[illegible]	[illegible]	[illegible]	Thomastown.
18	15	9	[illegible]	[illegible]	[illegible]	18	[illegible]	9	[illegible]	Urlingford, part of.
[illegible]	[illegible]	[illegible]	[illegible]	[illegible]	[illegible]	[illegible]	[illegible]	[illegible]	[illegible]	Waterford, do.
										King's Co.
[illegible]	10	13	[illegible]	[illegible]	[illegible]	[illegible]	[illegible]	[illegible]	[illegible]	Edenderry, part of.
6	9	4	[illegible]	[illegible]	[illegible]	6	[illegible]	1	[illegible]	Mountmellick, do.
[illegible]	[illegible]	[illegible]	[illegible]	[illegible]	[illegible]	[illegible]	[illegible]	[illegible]	[illegible]	Parsonstown, do.
14	[illegible]	[illegible]	[illegible]	[illegible]	[illegible]	4	[illegible]	[illegible]	[illegible]	Roscrea, do.
[illegible]	[illegible]	[illegible]	[illegible]	[illegible]	[illegible]	[illegible]	[illegible]	[illegible]	[illegible]	Tullamore, do.
										Longford Co.
[illegible]	[illegible]	13	[illegible]	[illegible]	[illegible]	[illegible]	[illegible]	[illegible]	[illegible]	Ballymahon, part of.
[illegible]	[illegible]	[illegible]	[illegible]	[illegible]	[illegible]	[illegible]	[illegible]	[illegible]	[illegible]	Granard, do.
[illegible]	[illegible]	[illegible]	[illegible]	[illegible]	[illegible]	[illegible]	[illegible]	[illegible]	[illegible]	Longford.
										Louth Co. and Co. of Town of Drogheda.
[illegible]	[illegible]	[illegible]	[illegible]	[illegible]	[illegible]	[illegible]	[illegible]	[illegible]	[illegible]	Ardee, part of.
[illegible]	[illegible]	[illegible]	[illegible]	[illegible]	[illegible]	[illegible]	[illegible]	41	[illegible]	Drogheda, do.
[illegible]	[illegible]	[illegible]	[illegible]	[illegible]	[illegible]	[illegible]	[illegible]	[illegible]	[illegible]	Dundalk, do.
										Meath Co.
[illegible]	[illegible]	[illegible]	[illegible]	[illegible]	[illegible]	[illegible]	[illegible]	[illegible]	[illegible]	Ardee, part of.
5	[illegible]	[illegible]	[illegible]	5	3	[illegible]	1	[illegible]	1	Celbridge, do.
[illegible]	[illegible]	[illegible]	[illegible]	[illegible]	[illegible]	[illegible]	[illegible]	14	[illegible]	Drogheda, do.
[illegible]	[illegible]	[illegible]	[illegible]	[illegible]	[illegible]	15	[illegible]	[illegible]	11	Dunshaughlin, do.
7	7	3	1	[illegible]	12	3	4	9	3	Edenderry, do.
[illegible]	[illegible]	10	[illegible]	[illegible]	[illegible]	[illegible]	[illegible]	[illegible]	13	Kells, do.
[illegible]	[illegible]	[illegible]	[illegible]	[illegible]	[illegible]	[illegible]	[illegible]	[illegible]	[illegible]	Navan.
14	11	11	[illegible]	[illegible]	[illegible]	[illegible]	[illegible]	8	4	Oldcastle, part of.
[illegible]	[illegible]	[illegible]	[illegible]	[illegible]	[illegible]	[illegible]	[illegible]	[illegible]	[illegible]	Trim.

[illegible] registered in Ireland in the Four Quarters ending

I.—PROVINCE OF

No.	SUPERINTENDENT REGISTRARS' DISTRICTS.	Area in Statute Acres.	Population in 1861.	MALES and FEMALES				
				Total.	Registered in the Quarter ending the last day of			
					March.	June.	Sept.	Dec.
	Queen's Co.							
45	Abbeyleix,	177,447	19,600	216	42	67	49	76
46	Athy, part of,	14,830	4,720	85	33	71	23	18
47	Carlow, do.	27,135	3,340	85	25	23	14	29
48	Mountmellick, part of,	179,682	32,871	430	133	119	83	79
49	Roscrea, do.	30,415	6,316	44	25	30	6	15
50	Urlingford, do.	8,111	480	8	.	3	1	5
	Westmeath Co.							
51	Athlone, part of,	57,483	14,257	130	30	19	42	47
52	Ballymahon, do.	30,410	3,827	38	20	10	17	9
53	Delvin,	74,330	6,384	140	40	35	30	33
54	Granard, part of,	38,470	4,303	35	13	20	6	16
55	Mullingar,	200,691	32,634	563	148	160	130	135
56	Tullamore, part of,	33,440	3,030	41	10	7	4	10
	Wexford Co.							
57	Enniscorthy, part of,	157,684	33,743	545	150	143	154	138
58	Gorey,	135,683	30,135	351	103	90	44	90
59	New Ross, part of,	170,317	38,385	430	130	101	100	85
60	Shillelagh, do.	5,187	410	6	2	1	1	2
61	Wexford,	128,099	46,147	640	200	200	100	140
	Wicklow Co.							
62	Baltinglass, part of,	103,035	11,273	200	73	45	30	55
63	Naas, do.	33,687	4,350	50	13	14	7	13
64	Rathdown, do.	54,302	9,067	187	48	27	27	65
65	Rathdrum,	227,467	37,238	486	133	135	100	121
66	Shillelagh, part of,	65,873	14,040	180	62	46	30	35

II.—PROVINCE OF

No.	SUPERINTENDENT REGISTRARS' DISTRICTS.	Area in Statute Acres.	Population in 1861.	Total.	March.	June.	Sept.	Dec.
	Clare Co.							
67	Ballyvaughan,	73,433	4,897	80	30	27	26	7
68	Corrofin,	67,380	3,600	40	17	23	11	10
69	Ennis,	112,400	22,771	270	127	83	50	60
70	Ennistymon,	90,281	20,140	280	60	73	47	73
71	Killadysert,	62,414	10,330	163	42	40	30	34
72	Kilrush,	105,300	32,483	400	116	120	100	60
73	Limerick, part of,	44,700	6,163	130	43	35	30	27
74	Scarriff, do.	47,420	4,934	140	48	44	41	30
75	Tulla,	80,235	11,035	148	44	40	20	46
	Cork Co.							
76	Bandon,	101,146	30,300	260	90	64	60	60
77	Bantry,	146,000	31,440	186	73	48	46	40
78	Castletown,	80,445	23,000	150	35	44	37	30
79	Clonakilty,	82,461	32,005	340	100	118	78	37
80	Cork,	240,710	133,797	4,173	900	760	540	1,050
81	Dunmanway,	140,037	14,197	200	74	63	41	44
82	Fermoy,	149,380	93,463	467	150	130	60	140
83	Kanturk,	154,464	33,171	480	167	184	79	80
84	Kilmallock, part of,	73,284	4,500	35	13	14	13	43
85	Kinsale,	79,083	24,433	434	116	107	87	123
86	Macroom,	173,140	30,000	304	114	300	73	140
87	Mallow,	140,035	32,404	473	130	160	60	100

March 31st, June 30th, September 30th, and December 31st, 1891—continued.

LEINSTER—continued.

MALES. Registered in the Quarter ending the last day of March.	June.	Sept.	Dec.	Total.	FEMALES. Total.	Registered in the Quarter ending the last day of March.	June.	Sept.	Dec.	SUPERINTENDENT REGISTRAR'S DISTRICTS.
										Queen's Co.
[illegible]	[illegible]	[illegible]	[illegible]	[illegible]	[illegible]	[illegible]	[illegible]	[illegible]	[illegible]	Abbeyleix.
[illegible]	[illegible]	[illegible]	[illegible]	[illegible]	[illegible]	15	[illegible]	[illegible]	6	Athy, part of.
[illegible]	11	11	[illegible]	43	[illegible]	11	11	7	10	Carlow, do.
[illegible]	[illegible]	[illegible]	[illegible]	[illegible]	[illegible]	[illegible]	[illegible]	[illegible]	[illegible]	Mountmellick, part of.
[illegible]	[illegible]	3	[illegible]	[illegible]	[illegible]	6	7	6	7	Roscrea, do.
...	1	...	...	1	[illegible]	...	1	...	1	[illegible], do.
										Westmeath Co.
[illegible]	[illegible]	[illegible]	[illegible]	[illegible]	[illegible]	[illegible]	[illegible]	[illegible]	[illegible]	Athlone, part of.
[illegible]	[illegible]	[illegible]	[illegible]	[illegible]	[illegible]	[illegible]	[illegible]	[illegible]	[illegible]	Ballymahon, do.
[illegible]	[illegible]	[illegible]	[illegible]	[illegible]	[illegible]	[illegible]	[illegible]	[illegible]	[illegible]	Delvin.
4	11	4	16	[illegible]	[illegible]	[illegible]	8	[illegible]	8	Granard, part of.
[illegible]	[illegible]	[illegible]	[illegible]	[illegible]	[illegible]	[illegible]	[illegible]	[illegible]	[illegible]	Mullingar.
[illegible]	[illegible]	9	[illegible]	[illegible]	[illegible]	[illegible]	1	[illegible]	[illegible]	Tullamore, part of.
										Wexford Co.
[illegible]	[illegible]	[illegible]	[illegible]	[illegible]	[illegible]	[illegible]	[illegible]	[illegible]	[illegible]	Enniscorthy, part of.
[illegible]	[illegible]	[illegible]	[illegible]	[illegible]	[illegible]	[illegible]	[illegible]	[illegible]	[illegible]	Gorey.
[illegible]	[illegible]	[illegible]	[illegible]	[illegible]	[illegible]	[illegible]	[illegible]	[illegible]	[illegible]	New Ross, part of.
3	...	1	1	4	[illegible]	...	1	...	1	Shillelagh, do.
[illegible]	[illegible]	[illegible]	[illegible]	[illegible]	[illegible]	[illegible]	[illegible]	[illegible]	[illegible]	Wexford.
										Wicklow Co.
[illegible]	[illegible]	[illegible]	[illegible]	[illegible]	[illegible]	[illegible]	[illegible]	[illegible]	[illegible]	Baltinglass, part of.
[illegible]	[illegible]	[illegible]	[illegible]	[illegible]	[illegible]	[illegible]	4	4	4	Naas, do.
[illegible]	[illegible]	[illegible]	[illegible]	[illegible]	[illegible]	[illegible]	[illegible]	[illegible]	[illegible]	Rathdown, do.
[illegible]	[illegible]	[illegible]	[illegible]	[illegible]	[illegible]	[illegible]	[illegible]	[illegible]	[illegible]	Rathdrum.
[illegible]	[illegible]	[illegible]	[illegible]	[illegible]	[illegible]	[illegible]	[illegible]	[illegible]	[illegible]	Shillelagh, part of.

MUNSTER.

March.	June.	Sept.	Dec.	Total.	Total.	March.	June.	Sept.	Dec.	SUPERINTENDENT REGISTRAR'S DISTRICTS.
										Clare Co.
[illegible]	[illegible]	[illegible]	[illegible]	[illegible]	[illegible]	[illegible]	[illegible]	11	[illegible]	Ballyvaghan.
7	[illegible]	[illegible]	[illegible]	[illegible]	[illegible]	[illegible]	[illegible]	[illegible]	[illegible]	Corofin.
[illegible]	[illegible]	[illegible]	[illegible]	[illegible]	[illegible]	[illegible]	[illegible]	[illegible]	[illegible]	Ennis.
[illegible]	[illegible]	[illegible]	[illegible]	[illegible]	[illegible]	[illegible]	[illegible]	[illegible]	[illegible]	Ennistimon.
[illegible]	[illegible]	[illegible]	[illegible]	[illegible]	[illegible]	[illegible]	[illegible]	14	[illegible]	Killadysert.
[illegible]	[illegible]	[illegible]	[illegible]	[illegible]	[illegible]	[illegible]	[illegible]	[illegible]	[illegible]	Kilrush.
[illegible]	[illegible]	[illegible]	11	[illegible]	[illegible]	[illegible]	[illegible]	[illegible]	[illegible]	Limerick, part of.
[illegible]	[illegible]	[illegible]	[illegible]	[illegible]	[illegible]	[illegible]	[illegible]	[illegible]	[illegible]	Scariff, do.
[illegible]	[illegible]	[illegible]	[illegible]	[illegible]	[illegible]	[illegible]	[illegible]	16	[illegible]	Tulla.
										Cork Co.
[illegible]	[illegible]	[illegible]	[illegible]	[illegible]	[illegible]	[illegible]	[illegible]	[illegible]	[illegible]	Bandon.
[illegible]	[illegible]	[illegible]	[illegible]	[illegible]	[illegible]	[illegible]	[illegible]	[illegible]	[illegible]	Bantry.
11	[illegible]	[illegible]	[illegible]	[illegible]	[illegible]	[illegible]	[illegible]	[illegible]	[illegible]	Castletown.
[illegible]	[illegible]	[illegible]	[illegible]	[illegible]	[illegible]	[illegible]	[illegible]	[illegible]	[illegible]	Clonakilty.
[illegible]	[illegible]	[illegible]	[illegible]	[illegible]	[illegible]	[illegible]	[illegible]	[illegible]	[illegible]	Cork.
[illegible]	[illegible]	[illegible]	[illegible]	[illegible]	[illegible]	[illegible]	[illegible]	[illegible]	[illegible]	Dunmanway.
77	[illegible]	[illegible]	[illegible]	[illegible]	[illegible]	[illegible]	[illegible]	[illegible]	[illegible]	Fermoy.
[illegible]	[illegible]	[illegible]	[illegible]	[illegible]	[illegible]	[illegible]	[illegible]	[illegible]	[illegible]	Kanturk.
[illegible]	[illegible]	7	[illegible]	[illegible]	[illegible]	[illegible]	[illegible]	[illegible]	[illegible]	Kilmallock, part of.
[illegible]	[illegible]	[illegible]	[illegible]	[illegible]	[illegible]	[illegible]	[illegible]	[illegible]	[illegible]	Kinsale.
[illegible]	[illegible]	[illegible]	[illegible]	[illegible]	[illegible]	[illegible]	[illegible]	[illegible]	[illegible]	Macroom.
[illegible]	[illegible]	[illegible]	[illegible]	[illegible]	[illegible]	[illegible]	[illegible]	[illegible]	[illegible]	Mallow.

DEATHS registered in Ireland in the Four Quarters ending

III.—PROVINCE OF

No.	Superintendent Registrars' Districts.	Area in Statute Acres.	Population in 1861.	Males and Females. Total.	Registered in the Quarter ending the last day of March.	June.	Sept.	Dec.
	Cork Co.—continued.							
88	Midleton,	[illegible]	[illegible]	[illegible]	[illegible]	[illegible]	[illegible]	[illegible]
89	Millstreet,	[illegible]	[illegible]	[illegible]	[illegible]	[illegible]	[illegible]	[illegible]
90	Mitchelstown, part of,	[illegible]	[illegible]	[illegible]	[illegible]	[illegible]	[illegible]	[illegible]
91	Skibbereen,	[illegible]	[illegible]	[illegible]	[illegible]	[illegible]	[illegible]	[illegible]
92	Skull,	[illegible]	[illegible]	[illegible]	[illegible]	[illegible]	[illegible]	[illegible]
93	Youghal, part of,	[illegible]	[illegible]	[illegible]	[illegible]	[illegible]	[illegible]	[illegible]
	Kerry Co.							
94	Cahersiveen,	[illegible]	[illegible]	[illegible]	[illegible]	[illegible]	[illegible]	[illegible]
95	Dingle,	[illegible]	[illegible]	[illegible]	[illegible]	[illegible]	[illegible]	[illegible]
96	Glin, part of,	[illegible]	[illegible]	[illegible]	[illegible]	[illegible]	7	[illegible]
97	Kenmare,	[illegible]	[illegible]	[illegible]	[illegible]	[illegible]	[illegible]	[illegible]
98	Killarney,	[illegible]	[illegible]	[illegible]	[illegible]	[illegible]	[illegible]	[illegible]
99	Listowel,	[illegible]	[illegible]	[illegible]	[illegible]	[illegible]	[illegible]	114
100	Tralee,	[illegible]	[illegible]	[illegible]	[illegible]	[illegible]	[illegible]	[illegible]
	Limerick Co.							
101	Croom,	[illegible]	[illegible]	[illegible]	[illegible]	[illegible]	[illegible]	[illegible]
102	Glin, part of	[illegible]	[illegible]	[illegible]	[illegible]	[illegible]	[illegible]	[illegible]
103	Kilmallock, do.,	[illegible]	[illegible]	[illegible]	[illegible]	[illegible]	[illegible]	[illegible]
104	Limerick, do.,	[illegible]	[illegible]	[illegible]	[illegible]	[illegible]	[illegible]	[illegible]
105	Mitchelstown, do.,	[illegible]	[illegible]	[illegible]	[illegible]	[illegible]	[illegible]	[illegible]
106	Newcastle,	[illegible]	[illegible]	[illegible]	[illegible]	[illegible]	[illegible]	[illegible]
107	Rathkeale,	[illegible]	[illegible]	[illegible]	[illegible]	[illegible]	[illegible]	[illegible]
108	Tipperary, part of,	[illegible]	[illegible]	[illegible]	[illegible]	[illegible]	[illegible]	[illegible]
	Tipperary Co.							
109	Borrisokane, part of,	[illegible]	[illegible]	[illegible]	[illegible]	[illegible]	[illegible]	[illegible]
110	Callan, part of,	[illegible]	[illegible]	[illegible]	[illegible]	[illegible]	[illegible]	[illegible]
111	Carrick-on-Suir, do.,	[illegible]	[illegible]	[illegible]	[illegible]	[illegible]	[illegible]	[illegible]
112	Cashel,	[illegible]	[illegible]	[illegible]	[illegible]	[illegible]	[illegible]	[illegible]
113	Clogheen,	[illegible]	[illegible]	[illegible]	[illegible]	[illegible]	[illegible]	[illegible]
114	Clonmel, part of,	[illegible]	[illegible]	[illegible]	[illegible]	[illegible]	[illegible]	[illegible]
115	Nenagh,	[illegible]	[illegible]	[illegible]	[illegible]	[illegible]	116	[illegible]
116	Parsonstown, part of,	[illegible]	[illegible]	[illegible]	[illegible]	[illegible]	4	[illegible]
117	Roscrea, do.,	[illegible]	[illegible]	[illegible]	[illegible]	[illegible]	[illegible]	[illegible]
118	Thurles,	[illegible]	[illegible]	[illegible]	[illegible]	[illegible]	[illegible]	[illegible]
119	Tipperary, part of,	[illegible]	[illegible]	[illegible]	[illegible]	[illegible]	[illegible]	[illegible]
120	Urlingford, do.,	[illegible]	[illegible]	[illegible]	[illegible]	[illegible]	[illegible]	[illegible]
	Waterford Co.							
121	Carrick-on-Suir, part of,	[illegible]	[illegible]	[illegible]	[illegible]	[illegible]	[illegible]	[illegible]
122	Clonmel, do.,	[illegible]	[illegible]	[illegible]	[illegible]	[illegible]	[illegible]	[illegible]
123	Dungarvan,	[illegible]	[illegible]	[illegible]	[illegible]	[illegible]	[illegible]	[illegible]
124	Kilmacthomas,	[illegible]	[illegible]	[illegible]	[illegible]	[illegible]	[illegible]	[illegible]
125	Lismore,	[illegible]	[illegible]	[illegible]	[illegible]	[illegible]	[illegible]	[illegible]
126	Waterford, part of,	[illegible]	[illegible]	[illegible]	[illegible]	[illegible]	[illegible]	[illegible]
127	Youghal, do.,	[illegible]	[illegible]	[illegible]	[illegible]	[illegible]	18	[illegible]

March 31st, June 30th, September 30th, and December 31st, 1891—*continued.*

MUNSTER—*continued.*

MALES.					FEMALES.					SUPERINTENDENT REGISTRAR'S DISTRICT.
Registered in the Quarter ending the last day of				Total.	Total.	Registered in the Quarter ending the last day of				
March.	June.	Sept.	Dec.			March.	June.	Sept.	Dec.	
										Cork Co.—*continued.*
[illegible]	[illegible]	[illegible]	[illegible]	[illegible]	[illegible]	[illegible]	[illegible]	[illegible]	[illegible]	[illegible]
[illegible]	[illegible]	[illegible]	[illegible]	[illegible]	[illegible]	[illegible]	[illegible]	[illegible]	[illegible]	[illegible]
[illegible]	[illegible]	[illegible]	[illegible]	[illegible]	[illegible]	[illegible]	[illegible]	[illegible]	[illegible]	Kilmallock, part of.
[illegible]	[illegible]	[illegible]	[illegible]	[illegible]	[illegible]	[illegible]	[illegible]	[illegible]	[illegible]	Skibbereen.
[illegible]	[illegible]	[illegible]	[illegible]	[illegible]	[illegible]	[illegible]	[illegible]	[illegible]	[illegible]	Skull.
[illegible]	[illegible]	[illegible]	[illegible]	[illegible]	[illegible]	[illegible]	[illegible]	[illegible]	[illegible]	Youghal, part of.
										Kerry Co.
[illegible]	[illegible]	[illegible]	[illegible]	[illegible]	[illegible]	[illegible]	[illegible]	[illegible]	[illegible]	Cahersiveen.
[illegible]	[illegible]	[illegible]	[illegible]	[illegible]	[illegible]	[illegible]	[illegible]	[illegible]	[illegible]	Dingle.
[illegible]	[illegible]	[illegible]	[illegible]	[illegible]	[illegible]	[illegible]	[illegible]	[illegible]	[illegible]	Glin, part of.
[illegible]	[illegible]	[illegible]	[illegible]	[illegible]	[illegible]	[illegible]	[illegible]	[illegible]	[illegible]	Kenmare.
[illegible]	[illegible]	[illegible]	[illegible]	[illegible]	[illegible]	[illegible]	[illegible]	[illegible]	[illegible]	Killarney.
[illegible]	[illegible]	[illegible]	[illegible]	[illegible]	[illegible]	[illegible]	[illegible]	[illegible]	[illegible]	Listowel.
[illegible]	[illegible]	[illegible]	[illegible]	[illegible]	[illegible]	[illegible]	[illegible]	[illegible]	[illegible]	Tralee.
										Limerick Co.
[illegible]	[illegible]	[illegible]	[illegible]	[illegible]	[illegible]	[illegible]	[illegible]	[illegible]	[illegible]	Croom.
[illegible]	[illegible]	[illegible]	[illegible]	[illegible]	[illegible]	[illegible]	[illegible]	[illegible]	[illegible]	Glin, part of.
[illegible]	[illegible]	[illegible]	[illegible]	[illegible]	[illegible]	[illegible]	[illegible]	[illegible]	[illegible]	Kilmallock, do.
[illegible]	[illegible]	[illegible]	[illegible]	[illegible]	[illegible]	[illegible]	[illegible]	[illegible]	[illegible]	Limerick, do.
[illegible]	[illegible]	[illegible]	[illegible]	[illegible]	[illegible]	[illegible]	[illegible]	[illegible]	[illegible]	Mitchelstown, do.
[illegible]	[illegible]	[illegible]	[illegible]	[illegible]	[illegible]	[illegible]	[illegible]	[illegible]	[illegible]	Newcastle.
[illegible]	[illegible]	[illegible]	[illegible]	[illegible]	[illegible]	[illegible]	[illegible]	[illegible]	[illegible]	Rathkeale.
[illegible]	[illegible]	[illegible]	[illegible]	[illegible]	[illegible]	[illegible]	[illegible]	[illegible]	[illegible]	Tipperary, part of.
										Tipperary Co.
[illegible]	[illegible]	[illegible]	[illegible]	[illegible]	[illegible]	[illegible]	[illegible]	[illegible]	[illegible]	Borrisokane.
[illegible]	[illegible]	[illegible]	[illegible]	[illegible]	[illegible]	[illegible]	[illegible]	[illegible]	[illegible]	Callan, part of.
[illegible]	[illegible]	[illegible]	[illegible]	[illegible]	[illegible]	[illegible]	[illegible]	[illegible]	[illegible]	Carrick-on-Suir, do.
[illegible]	[illegible]	[illegible]	[illegible]	[illegible]	[illegible]	[illegible]	[illegible]	[illegible]	[illegible]	Cashel.
[illegible]	[illegible]	[illegible]	[illegible]	[illegible]	[illegible]	[illegible]	[illegible]	[illegible]	[illegible]	Clogheen.
[illegible]	[illegible]	[illegible]	[illegible]	[illegible]	[illegible]	[illegible]	[illegible]	[illegible]	[illegible]	Clonmel, part of.
[illegible]	[illegible]	[illegible]	[illegible]	[illegible]	[illegible]	[illegible]	[illegible]	[illegible]	[illegible]	Nenagh.
[illegible]	[illegible]	[illegible]	[illegible]	[illegible]	[illegible]	[illegible]	[illegible]	[illegible]	[illegible]	Parsonstown, part of.
[illegible]	[illegible]	[illegible]	[illegible]	[illegible]	[illegible]	[illegible]	[illegible]	[illegible]	[illegible]	Roscrea, do.
[illegible]	[illegible]	[illegible]	[illegible]	[illegible]	[illegible]	[illegible]	[illegible]	[illegible]	[illegible]	Thurles.
[illegible]	[illegible]	[illegible]	[illegible]	[illegible]	[illegible]	[illegible]	[illegible]	[illegible]	[illegible]	Tipperary, part of.
[illegible]	[illegible]	[illegible]	[illegible]	[illegible]	[illegible]	[illegible]	[illegible]	[illegible]	[illegible]	Thomastown, do.
										Waterford Co.
[illegible]	[illegible]	[illegible]	[illegible]	[illegible]	[illegible]	[illegible]	[illegible]	[illegible]	[illegible]	Carrick-on-Suir, pt of.
[illegible]	[illegible]	[illegible]	[illegible]	[illegible]	[illegible]	[illegible]	[illegible]	[illegible]	[illegible]	Clonmel, do.
[illegible]	[illegible]	[illegible]	[illegible]	[illegible]	[illegible]	[illegible]	[illegible]	[illegible]	[illegible]	Dungarvan.
[illegible]	[illegible]	[illegible]	[illegible]	[illegible]	[illegible]	[illegible]	[illegible]	[illegible]	[illegible]	Kilmacthomas.
[illegible]	[illegible]	[illegible]	[illegible]	[illegible]	[illegible]	[illegible]	[illegible]	[illegible]	[illegible]	Lismore.
[illegible]	[illegible]	[illegible]	[illegible]	[illegible]	[illegible]	[illegible]	[illegible]	[illegible]	[illegible]	Waterford, part of.
[illegible]	[illegible]	[illegible]	[illegible]	[illegible]	[illegible]	[illegible]	[illegible]	[illegible]	[illegible]	Youghal, do.

[illegible] registered in Ireland in the Four Quarters ending

[illegible]—PROVINCE OF [illegible]

No.	Superintendent Registrars' Districts.	Area in Statute Acres.	Population in [illegible].	Males and Females. Total.	Registered in the Quarters ending the last day of March.	June.	Sept.	Dec.
	Antrim Co.							
128	Antrim,	[illegible]	[illegible]	[illegible]	[illegible]	[illegible]	[illegible]	[illegible]
129	Ballycastle,	[illegible]	[illegible]	[illegible]	[illegible]	[illegible]	[illegible]	[illegible]
130	Ballymena,	[illegible]	[illegible]	[illegible]	[illegible]	[illegible]	[illegible]	[illegible]
131	Ballymoney, part of,	[illegible]	[illegible]	[illegible]	[illegible]	[illegible]	[illegible]	[illegible]
132	Belfast, do.	[illegible]	[illegible]	[illegible]	[illegible]	[illegible]	[illegible]	[illegible]
133	Coleraine, do.	[illegible]	[illegible]	[illegible]	[illegible]	[illegible]	[illegible]	[illegible]
134	Larne,	[illegible]	[illegible]	[illegible]	[illegible]	[illegible]	[illegible]	[illegible]
135	Lisburn, part of,	[illegible]	[illegible]	[illegible]	[illegible]	[illegible]	[illegible]	[illegible]
136	Lurgan, do.	[illegible]	[illegible]	[illegible]	[illegible]	[illegible]	[illegible]	[illegible]
	Armagh Co.							
137	Armagh, part of,	[illegible]	[illegible]	[illegible]	[illegible]	[illegible]	[illegible]	[illegible]
138	Banbridge, do.	[illegible]	[illegible]	[illegible]	[illegible]	[illegible]	[illegible]	[illegible]
139	Castleblayney, do.	[illegible]	[illegible]	[illegible]	[illegible]	[illegible]	[illegible]	[illegible]
140	Dundalk, do.	[illegible]	[illegible]	[illegible]	[illegible]	4	3	[illegible]
141	Lurgan, do.	[illegible]	[illegible]	[illegible]	[illegible]	[illegible]	[illegible]	[illegible]
142	Newry do.	[illegible]	[illegible]	[illegible]	[illegible]	[illegible]	[illegible]	[illegible]
	Cavan Co.							
143	Bailieborough,	[illegible]	[illegible]	[illegible]	[illegible]	77	[illegible]	[illegible]
144	Bawnboy, part of,	[illegible]	[illegible]	[illegible]	[illegible]	[illegible]	[illegible]	[illegible]
145	Cavan,	[illegible]	[illegible]	[illegible]	[illegible]	[illegible]	[illegible]	[illegible]
146	Cootehill, part of,	[illegible]	[illegible]	[illegible]	[illegible]	[illegible]	[illegible]	[illegible]
147	Enniskillen, do.	[illegible]	[illegible]	[illegible]	[illegible]	14	[illegible]	[illegible]
148	Granard, do.	[illegible]	[illegible]	[illegible]	[illegible]	[illegible]	[illegible]	[illegible]
149	Kells, do.	[illegible]	[illegible]	[illegible]	[illegible]	1	[illegible]	[illegible]
150	Oldcastle, do.	[illegible]	[illegible]	[illegible]	[illegible]	[illegible]	[illegible]	[illegible]
	Donegal Co.							
151	Ballyshannon, part of,	[illegible]	[illegible]	[illegible]	[illegible]	[illegible]	[illegible]	[illegible]
152	Donegal,	[illegible]	[illegible]	[illegible]	111	[illegible]	[illegible]	[illegible]
153	Dunfanaghy,	[illegible]	[illegible]	[illegible]	[illegible]	[illegible]	[illegible]	[illegible]
154	Glenties,	[illegible]	[illegible]	[illegible]	[illegible]	[illegible]	[illegible]	[illegible]
155	Inishowen,	[illegible]	[illegible]	[illegible]	[illegible]	[illegible]	[illegible]	[illegible]
156	Letterkenny,	[illegible]	[illegible]	[illegible]	[illegible]	[illegible]	[illegible]	[illegible]
157	Londonderry, part of,	[illegible]	[illegible]	[illegible]	[illegible]	[illegible]	[illegible]	[illegible]
158	Milford,	[illegible]	[illegible]	[illegible]	[illegible]	[illegible]	[illegible]	[illegible]
159	Strabane, part of,	[illegible]	[illegible]	[illegible]	[illegible]	[illegible]	[illegible]	[illegible]
160	Stranorlar,	[illegible]	[illegible]	[illegible]	[illegible]	[illegible]	[illegible]	[illegible]
	Down Co.							
161	Banbridge, part of,	[illegible]	[illegible]	[illegible]	[illegible]	[illegible]	[illegible]	[illegible]
162	Belfast, do.	[illegible]	[illegible]	[illegible]	[illegible]	[illegible]	[illegible]	[illegible]
163	Downpatrick,	[illegible]	[illegible]	[illegible]	[illegible]	[illegible]	[illegible]	[illegible]
164	Kilkeel,	[illegible]	[illegible]	[illegible]	[illegible]	[illegible]	[illegible]	74
165	Lisburn, part of,	[illegible]	[illegible]	[illegible]	[illegible]	[illegible]	[illegible]	[illegible]
166	Lurgan, do.	[illegible]	[illegible]	[illegible]	[illegible]	[illegible]	[illegible]	[illegible]
167	Newry, do.	[illegible]	[illegible]	[illegible]	[illegible]	[illegible]	[illegible]	[illegible]
168	Newtownards,	[illegible]	[illegible]	[illegible]	[illegible]	[illegible]	[illegible]	[illegible]
	Fermanagh Co.							
169	Ballyshannon, part of,	[illegible]	[illegible]	79	[illegible]	[illegible]	[illegible]	[illegible]
170	Clones, do.	[illegible]	[illegible]	[illegible]	[illegible]	[illegible]	[illegible]	[illegible]
171	Enniskillen, do.	[illegible]	[illegible]	[illegible]	[illegible]	[illegible]	[illegible]	[illegible]
172	Irvinestown, do.	[illegible]	[illegible]	[illegible]	[illegible]	[illegible]	[illegible]	[illegible]
173	Lisnaskea,	[illegible]	[illegible]	[illegible]	[illegible]	[illegible]	[illegible]	[illegible]

March 31st, June 30th, September 30th, and December 31st, 1891—*continued.*

OF ULSTER.

MALES. Registered in the Quarter ending the last day of March.	June.	Sept.	Dec.	Total.	FEMALES. Total.	Registered in the Quarter ending the last day of March.	June.	Sept.	Dec.	SUPERINTENDENT REGISTRARS' DISTRICTS.
										Antrim Co.
[illegible]	[illegible]	47	[illegible]	[illegible]	[illegible]	[illegible]	[illegible]	[illegible]	[illegible]	Antrim.
[illegible]	[illegible]	[illegible]	[illegible]	[illegible]	115	[illegible]	[illegible]	[illegible]	[illegible]	Ballycastle.
[illegible]	[illegible]	[illegible]	[illegible]	[illegible]	[illegible]	[illegible]	[illegible]	[illegible]	[illegible]	Ballymena.
[illegible]	[illegible]	41	[illegible]	[illegible]	[illegible]	[illegible]	[illegible]	[illegible]	[illegible]	Ballymoney, part of
[illegible]	[illegible]	[illegible]	[illegible]	[illegible]	[illegible]	[illegible]	[illegible]	[illegible]	[illegible]	Belfast, do.
[illegible]	[illegible]	[illegible]	[illegible]	[illegible]	[illegible]	[illegible]	[illegible]	[illegible]	[illegible]	Coleraine, do.
71	71	47	[illegible]	[illegible]	[illegible]	[illegible]	[illegible]	[illegible]	[illegible]	Larne.
[illegible]	[illegible]	[illegible]	[illegible]	[illegible]	[illegible]	[illegible]	[illegible]	[illegible]	[illegible]	Lisburn, part of
4	4	7	[illegible]	[illegible]	[illegible]	[illegible]	[illegible]	9	[illegible]	Lurgan, do.
										Armagh Co.
[illegible]	[illegible]	[illegible]	104	[illegible]	[illegible]	[illegible]	[illegible]	[illegible]	[illegible]	Armagh, part of
[illegible]	21	15	16	[illegible]	71	[illegible]	[illegible]	[illegible]	[illegible]	Banbridge, do.
[illegible]	[illegible]	[illegible]	[illegible]	[illegible]	[illegible]	[illegible]	17	71	[illegible]	Castleblayney, do.
[illegible]	[illegible]	.	[illegible]	[illegible]	[illegible]	[illegible]	[illegible]	9	[illegible]	Dundalk, do.
[illegible]	[illegible]	[illegible]	[illegible]	[illegible]	[illegible]	[illegible]	[illegible]	[illegible]	[illegible]	Lurgan, do.
[illegible]	[illegible]	[illegible]	[illegible]	[illegible]	[illegible]	[illegible]	[illegible]	[illegible]	[illegible]	Newry, do.
										Cavan Co.
[illegible]	[illegible]	[illegible]	16	[illegible]	[illegible]	[illegible]	[illegible]	[illegible]	[illegible]	Bailieborough.
[illegible]	[illegible]	[illegible]	[illegible]	[illegible]	[illegible]	[illegible]	[illegible]	17	[illegible]	Bawnboy, part of
[illegible]	[illegible]	[illegible]	[illegible]	[illegible]	[illegible]	[illegible]	[illegible]	[illegible]	[illegible]	Cavan.
[illegible]	[illegible]	47	[illegible]	[illegible]	[illegible]	[illegible]	[illegible]	[illegible]	[illegible]	Cootehill, part of
[illegible]	[illegible]	[illegible]	[illegible]	[illegible]	[illegible]	17	[illegible]	[illegible]	[illegible]	Enniskillen, do.
[illegible]	[illegible]	[illegible]	[illegible]	[illegible]	[illegible]	11	[illegible]	4	[illegible]	Granard, do.
1	1	1	1	4	13	[illegible]	.	[illegible]	[illegible]	Kells, do.
[illegible]	[illegible]	[illegible]	[illegible]	[illegible]	[illegible]	[illegible]	[illegible]	[illegible]	[illegible]	Oldcastle, do.
										Donegal Co.
[illegible]	[illegible]	11	[illegible]	[illegible]	[illegible]	[illegible]	[illegible]	[illegible]	[illegible]	Ballyshannon, part of
[illegible]	[illegible]	[illegible]	[illegible]	[illegible]	[illegible]	47	[illegible]	[illegible]	[illegible]	Donegal.
[illegible]	[illegible]	[illegible]	[illegible]	[illegible]	[illegible]	[illegible]	[illegible]	[illegible]	[illegible]	Dunfanaghy.
[illegible]	[illegible]	44	[illegible]	[illegible]	[illegible]	[illegible]	[illegible]	[illegible]	45	Glenties.
71	[illegible]	[illegible]	[illegible]	[illegible]	[illegible]	[illegible]	[illegible]	[illegible]	71	Inishowen.
[illegible]	[illegible]	[illegible]	[illegible]	[illegible]	[illegible]	[illegible]	[illegible]	[illegible]	[illegible]	Letterkenny.
[illegible]	[illegible]	[illegible]	[illegible]	[illegible]	[illegible]	[illegible]	[illegible]	11	[illegible]	Londonderry, part of
[illegible]	[illegible]	[illegible]	[illegible]	[illegible]	[illegible]	[illegible]	[illegible]	[illegible]	[illegible]	Milford.
[illegible]	[illegible]	[illegible]	[illegible]	[illegible]	[illegible]	[illegible]	[illegible]	19	[illegible]	Strabane, part of
[illegible]	[illegible]	[illegible]	[illegible]	[illegible]	[illegible]	[illegible]	[illegible]	[illegible]	[illegible]	Stranorlar.
										Down Co.
[illegible]	[illegible]	[illegible]	[illegible]	[illegible]	[illegible]	[illegible]	[illegible]	[illegible]	[illegible]	Banbridge, part of
[illegible]	[illegible]	[illegible]	[illegible]	[illegible]	[illegible]	[illegible]	[illegible]	[illegible]	[illegible]	Belfast, do.
[illegible]	[illegible]	[illegible]	[illegible]	[illegible]	[illegible]	[illegible]	[illegible]	[illegible]	[illegible]	Downpatrick.
[illegible]	[illegible]	[illegible]	[illegible]	[illegible]	[illegible]	[illegible]	[illegible]	[illegible]	[illegible]	Kilkeel.
[illegible]	[illegible]	[illegible]	[illegible]	[illegible]	[illegible]	[illegible]	[illegible]	[illegible]	[illegible]	Lisburn, part of
[illegible]	[illegible]	[illegible]	[illegible]	[illegible]	[illegible]	[illegible]	[illegible]	[illegible]	[illegible]	Lurgan, do.
[illegible]	[illegible]	[illegible]	[illegible]	[illegible]	[illegible]	[illegible]	[illegible]	[illegible]	[illegible]	Newry, do.
[illegible]	[illegible]	[illegible]	[illegible]	[illegible]	[illegible]	[illegible]	[illegible]	[illegible]	[illegible]	Newtownards.
										Fermanagh Co.
[illegible]	[illegible]	[illegible]	[illegible]	[illegible]	[illegible]	17	[illegible]	[illegible]	7	Ballyshannon, part of
[illegible]	[illegible]	[illegible]	[illegible]	[illegible]	[illegible]	[illegible]	[illegible]	15	15	Clones, do.
[illegible]	[illegible]	[illegible]	[illegible]	[illegible]	[illegible]	[illegible]	[illegible]	[illegible]	[illegible]	Enniskillen, do.
[illegible]	[illegible]	[illegible]	[illegible]	[illegible]	[illegible]	[illegible]	[illegible]	[illegible]	[illegible]	Irvinestown, do.
[illegible]	[illegible]	47	[illegible]	[illegible]	[illegible]	[illegible]	[illegible]	[illegible]	[illegible]	Lisnaskea.

DEATHS registered in Ireland in the Four Quarters ending

III.—PROVINCE OF

No.	SUPERINTENDENT REGISTRARS' DISTRICTS	Area in Statute Acres.	Population in 1861.	MALES AND FEMALES. Total.	Registered in the Quarter ending the last day of March.	June.	Sept.	Dec.
	Londonderry Co.							
175	Ballymoney, part of,	[illegible]	[illegible]	[illegible]	[illegible]	[illegible]	[illegible]	[illegible]
176	Coleraine, do.	[illegible]	[illegible]	[illegible]	111	146	111	[illegible]
176	Limavady,	[illegible]	[illegible]	[illegible]	[illegible]	[illegible]	78	[illegible]
177	Londonderry, part of,	[illegible]	[illegible]	1,011	[illegible]	270	[illegible]	[illegible]
178	Magherafelt,	[illegible]	[illegible]	[illegible]	[illegible]	[illegible]	143	[illegible]
	Monaghan Co.							
179	Carrickmacross,	[illegible]	[illegible]	[illegible]	71	[illegible]	[illegible]	[illegible]
180	Castleblayney, part of,	[illegible]	[illegible]	[illegible]	[illegible]	[illegible]	77	[illegible]
181	Clones, do.	[illegible]	[illegible]	[illegible]	16	[illegible]	11	[illegible]
182	Cootehill, do.	[illegible]	[illegible]	[illegible]	46	[illegible]	[illegible]	[illegible]
183	Dundalk, do.	[illegible]	[illegible]	[illegible]	[illegible]	[illegible]	[illegible]	[illegible]
184	Dunleer, do.	4,500	1,400	24	4	6	5	[illegible]
185	Monaghan,	[illegible]	[illegible]	[illegible]	[illegible]	[illegible]	114	[illegible]
	Tyrone Co.							
186	Armagh, part of,	[illegible]	[illegible]	[illegible]	16	11	6	6
187	Castlederg,	41,7[illegible]	[illegible]	[illegible]	[illegible]	[illegible]	[illegible]	[illegible]
188	Clogher, part of,	[illegible]	[illegible]	[illegible]	[illegible]	[illegible]	[illegible]	[illegible]
189	Cookstown,	[illegible]	37,143	[illegible]	[illegible]	112	[illegible]	[illegible]
190	Dungannon,	[illegible]	[illegible]	[illegible]	[illegible]	[illegible]	119	[illegible]
191	Enniskillen, part of,	[illegible]	1,137	[illegible]	7	[illegible]	1	[illegible]
192	Londonderry, part of,	[illegible]	[illegible]	[illegible]	[illegible]	13	16	[illegible]
193	Omagh,	[illegible]	[illegible]	[illegible]	[illegible]	[illegible]	148	[illegible]
194	Strabane, part of,	[illegible]	27,[illegible]	[illegible]	147	[illegible]	[illegible]	[illegible]

IV.—PROVINCE

No.	SUPERINTENDENT REGISTRARS' DISTRICTS	Area in Statute Acres.	Population in 1861.	Total.	March.	June.	Sept.	Dec.
	Galway Co.							
195	Ballinasloe, part of,	[illegible]	[illegible]	[illegible]	[illegible]	[illegible]	[illegible]	[illegible]
196	Ballinrobe, do.	[illegible]	[illegible]	[illegible]	[illegible]	[illegible]	[illegible]	[illegible]
197	Clifden,	[illegible]	[illegible]	[illegible]	76	100	47	[illegible]
198	Galway,	187,[illegible]	[illegible]	716	[illegible]	[illegible]	[illegible]	[illegible]
199	Glennamaddy,	[illegible]	[illegible]	[illegible]	[illegible]	[illegible]	[illegible]	[illegible]
200	Gort,	[illegible]	11,[illegible]	[illegible]	[illegible]	[illegible]	[illegible]	[illegible]
201	Loughrea,	[illegible]	[illegible]	[illegible]	[illegible]	[illegible]	[illegible]	[illegible]
202	Mountbellew,	[illegible]	16,471	[illegible]	77	44	44	[illegible]
203	Oughterard,	[illegible]	[illegible]	[illegible]	[illegible]	[illegible]	[illegible]	[illegible]
204	Portumna,	77,[illegible]	[illegible]	[illegible]	47	41	[illegible]	[illegible]
205	Roscommon, part of,	[illegible]	[illegible]	4	?	1	-	[illegible]
206	Scariff, do.	14,[illegible]	1,7[illegible]	[illegible]	[illegible]	[illegible]	[illegible]	11
207	Tuam,	[illegible]	[illegible]	[illegible]	[illegible]	174	[illegible]	[illegible]
	Leitrim Co.							
208	Ballyshannon, part of,	[illegible]	[illegible]	113	[illegible]	[illegible]	17	[illegible]
209	Bawnboy, do.	[illegible]	[illegible]	[illegible]	[illegible]	41	45	[illegible]
210	Carrick-on-Shannon, do.	[illegible]	[illegible]	[illegible]	[illegible]	[illegible]	[illegible]	[illegible]
211	Manorhamilton,	[illegible]	[illegible]	[illegible]	111	[illegible]	[illegible]	[illegible]
212	Mohill,	[illegible]	[illegible]	[illegible]	[illegible]	[illegible]	61	71

DEATHS registered in Ireland in the Four Quarters ending

IV.—PROVINCE OF

No.	Superintendent Registrars' Districts.	Area in Statute Acres.	Population in 1891.	Males and Females. Total.	Registered in the Quarter ending the last day of Mar.	June.	Sept.	Dec.
	Mayo Co.							
[illegible]	Ballina, part of, . .	[illegible]	[illegible]	[illegible]	[illegible]	[illegible]	[illegible]	[illegible]
[illegible]	Ballinrobe, do., . .	[illegible]	[illegible]	[illegible]	[illegible]	[illegible]	[illegible]	[illegible]
[illegible]	Belmullet, . . .	[illegible]	[illegible]	[illegible]	[illegible]	[illegible]	[illegible]	[illegible]
[illegible]	Castlebar, . . .	[illegible]	[illegible]	[illegible]	[illegible]	[illegible]	[illegible]	[illegible]
[illegible]	Castlerea, part of, . .	[illegible]	[illegible]	[illegible]	[illegible]	[illegible]	[illegible]	[illegible]
[illegible]	Claremorris, . . .	[illegible]	[illegible]	[illegible]	[illegible]	[illegible]	[illegible]	[illegible]
[illegible]	Killala, . . .	[illegible]	[illegible]	[illegible]	[illegible]	[illegible]	[illegible]	[illegible]
[illegible]	Newport, . . .	[illegible]	[illegible]	[illegible]	[illegible]	[illegible]	[illegible]	[illegible]
[illegible]	Westport, . . .	[illegible]	[illegible]	[illegible]	[illegible]	[illegible]	[illegible]	[illegible]
	Roscommon Co.							
[illegible]	Athlone, part of,	[illegible]	[illegible]	[illegible]	[illegible]	[illegible]	[illegible]	[illegible]
[illegible]	Ballinasloe, do.	[illegible]	[illegible]	[illegible]	[illegible]	[illegible]	[illegible]	[illegible]
[illegible]	Boyle, do.	[illegible]	[illegible]	[illegible]	[illegible]	[illegible]	[illegible]	[illegible]
[illegible]	Carrick-on-Shannon, do.	[illegible]	[illegible]	[illegible]	[illegible]	[illegible]	[illegible]	[illegible]
[illegible]	Castlerea, do.	[illegible]	[illegible]	[illegible]	[illegible]	[illegible]	[illegible]	[illegible]
[illegible]	Roscommon, do.	[illegible]	[illegible]	[illegible]	[illegible]	[illegible]	[illegible]	[illegible]
[illegible]	Strokestown, . . .	[illegible]	[illegible]	[illegible]	[illegible]	[illegible]	[illegible]	[illegible]
	Sligo Co.							
[illegible]	Ballina, part of, . .	[illegible]	[illegible]	[illegible]	[illegible]	[illegible]	[illegible]	[illegible]
[illegible]	Boyle, do. . .	[illegible]	[illegible]	[illegible]	[illegible]	[illegible]	[illegible]	[illegible]
[illegible]	Dromore West, . .	[illegible]	[illegible]	[illegible]	[illegible]	[illegible]	[illegible]	[illegible]
[illegible]	Sligo, . . .	[illegible]	[illegible]	[illegible]	[illegible]	[illegible]	[illegible]	[illegible]
[illegible]	Tobercurry, . . .	[illegible]	[illegible]	[illegible]	[illegible]	[illegible]	[illegible]	[illegible]

DEATHS Registered in Ireland in the Four Quarters ending March 31st, June 30th, September 30th, and December 31st, 1891, in each Superintendent Registrar's District or Poor Law Union.

Registry or Number of Cases [illegible]	Superintendent Registrars' Districts or Poor Law Unions.	Area in Statute Acres.	Population in 1891.	Males and Females. Total.	Registered in the Quarter ending the last day of Mar.	June.	Sept.	Dec.	Males. Registered in the Quarter ending the last day of Mar.	June.	Sept.	Dec.	Total.	Females. Total.	Registered in the Quarter ending the last day of Mar.	June.	Sept.	Dec.
[illegible]	Abbeyleix, . .	[illegible]	[illegible]	[illegible]	[illegible]	[illegible]	[illegible]	[illegible]	[illegible]	[illegible]	[illegible]	[illegible]	[illegible]	[illegible]	[illegible]	[illegible]	[illegible]	[illegible]
[illegible]	Antrim, . .	[illegible]	[illegible]	[illegible]	[illegible]	[illegible]	[illegible]	[illegible]	[illegible]	[illegible]	[illegible]	[illegible]	[illegible]	[illegible]	[illegible]	[illegible]	[illegible]	[illegible]
[illegible]	Ardee, . .	[illegible]	[illegible]	[illegible]	[illegible]	[illegible]	[illegible]	[illegible]	[illegible]	[illegible]	[illegible]	[illegible]	[illegible]	[illegible]	[illegible]	[illegible]	[illegible]	[illegible]
[illegible]	Armagh, . .	[illegible]	[illegible]	[illegible]	[illegible]	[illegible]	[illegible]	[illegible]	[illegible]	[illegible]	[illegible]	[illegible]	[illegible]	[illegible]	[illegible]	[illegible]	[illegible]	[illegible]
[illegible]	Athlone, . .	[illegible]	[illegible]	[illegible]	[illegible]	[illegible]	[illegible]	[illegible]	[illegible]	[illegible]	[illegible]	[illegible]	[illegible]	[illegible]	[illegible]	[illegible]	[illegible]	[illegible]
[illegible]	Athy, . .	[illegible]	[illegible]	[illegible]	[illegible]	[illegible]	[illegible]	[illegible]	[illegible]	[illegible]	[illegible]	[illegible]	[illegible]	[illegible]	[illegible]	[illegible]	[illegible]	[illegible]
[illegible]	Bailieborough, .	[illegible]	[illegible]	[illegible]	[illegible]	[illegible]	[illegible]	[illegible]	[illegible]	[illegible]	[illegible]	[illegible]	[illegible]	[illegible]	[illegible]	[illegible]	[illegible]	[illegible]
[illegible]	Ballina, . .	[illegible]	[illegible]	[illegible]	[illegible]	[illegible]	[illegible]	[illegible]	[illegible]	[illegible]	[illegible]	[illegible]	[illegible]	[illegible]	[illegible]	[illegible]	[illegible]	[illegible]
[illegible]	Ballinasloe, . .	[illegible]	[illegible]	[illegible]	[illegible]	[illegible]	[illegible]	[illegible]	[illegible]	[illegible]	[illegible]	[illegible]	[illegible]	[illegible]	[illegible]	[illegible]	[illegible]	[illegible]
[illegible]	Ballinrobe, . .	[illegible]	[illegible]	[illegible]	[illegible]	[illegible]	[illegible]	[illegible]	[illegible]	[illegible]	[illegible]	[illegible]	[illegible]	[illegible]	[illegible]	[illegible]	[illegible]	[illegible]
[illegible]	Ballycastle, . .	[illegible]	[illegible]	[illegible]	[illegible]	[illegible]	[illegible]	[illegible]	[illegible]	[illegible]	[illegible]	[illegible]	[illegible]	[illegible]	[illegible]	[illegible]	[illegible]	[illegible]
[illegible]	Ballymahon, . .	[illegible]	[illegible]	[illegible]	[illegible]	[illegible]	[illegible]	[illegible]	[illegible]	[illegible]	[illegible]	[illegible]	[illegible]	[illegible]	[illegible]	[illegible]	[illegible]	[illegible]
[illegible]	Ballymena, . .	[illegible]	[illegible]	[illegible]	[illegible]	[illegible]	[illegible]	[illegible]	[illegible]	[illegible]	[illegible]	[illegible]	[illegible]	[illegible]	[illegible]	[illegible]	[illegible]	[illegible]
[illegible]	Ballymoney, . .	[illegible]	[illegible]	[illegible]	[illegible]	[illegible]	[illegible]	[illegible]	[illegible]	[illegible]	[illegible]	[illegible]	[illegible]	[illegible]	[illegible]	[illegible]	[illegible]	[illegible]
[illegible]	Ballyshannon, .	[illegible]	[illegible]	[illegible]	[illegible]	[illegible]	[illegible]	[illegible]	[illegible]	[illegible]	[illegible]	[illegible]	[illegible]	[illegible]	[illegible]	[illegible]	[illegible]	[illegible]
[illegible]	Ballyvaghan, .	[illegible]	[illegible]	[illegible]	[illegible]	[illegible]	[illegible]	[illegible]	[illegible]	[illegible]	[illegible]	[illegible]	[illegible]	[illegible]	[illegible]	[illegible]	[illegible]	[illegible]
[illegible]	Balrothery, . .	[illegible]	[illegible]	[illegible]	[illegible]	[illegible]	[illegible]	[illegible]	[illegible]	[illegible]	[illegible]	[illegible]	[illegible]	[illegible]	[illegible]	[illegible]	[illegible]	[illegible]
[illegible]	Baltinglass, . .	[illegible]	[illegible]	[illegible]	[illegible]	[illegible]	[illegible]	[illegible]	[illegible]	[illegible]	[illegible]	[illegible]	[illegible]	[illegible]	[illegible]	[illegible]	[illegible]	[illegible]
[illegible]	Banbridge, . .	[illegible]	[illegible]	[illegible]	[illegible]	[illegible]	[illegible]	[illegible]	[illegible]	[illegible]	[illegible]	[illegible]	[illegible]	[illegible]	[illegible]	[illegible]	[illegible]	[illegible]
[illegible]	Bantry, . .	[illegible]	[illegible]	[illegible]	[illegible]	[illegible]	[illegible]	[illegible]	[illegible]	[illegible]	[illegible]	[illegible]	[illegible]	[illegible]	[illegible]	[illegible]	[illegible]	[illegible]

March 31st, June 30th, September 30th, and December 31st, 1891—*continued.*

CONNAUGHT—*continued.*

Males: Registered in the Quarter ending the last day of — March	June	Sept.	Dec.	Males: Total	Females: Total	Females: Registered in the Quarter ending the last day of — March	June	Sept.	Dec.	Superintendent Registrars' Districts
										Mayo Co.
43	[illegible]	[illegible]	[illegible]	[illegible]	[illegible]	[illegible]	[illegible]	[illegible]	[illegible]	Ballina, part of.
[illegible]	[illegible]	[illegible]	[illegible]	[illegible]	[illegible]	[illegible]	[illegible]	[illegible]	[illegible]	Ballinrobe, do.
[illegible]	[illegible]	[illegible]	[illegible]	[illegible]	[illegible]	[illegible]	[illegible]	[illegible]	[illegible]	Belmullet.
[illegible]	[illegible]	[illegible]	[illegible]	[illegible]	[illegible]	[illegible]	[illegible]	[illegible]	[illegible]	Castlebar.
[illegible]	[illegible]	[illegible]	[illegible]	[illegible]	[illegible]	11	[illegible]	[illegible]	[illegible]	Castlereagh, part of.
[illegible]	[illegible]	[illegible]	[illegible]	[illegible]	[illegible]	[illegible]	[illegible]	[illegible]	[illegible]	Claremorris.
[illegible]	[illegible]	[illegible]	[illegible]	[illegible]	[illegible]	[illegible]	[illegible]	[illegible]	[illegible]	Killala.
[illegible]	[illegible]	[illegible]	[illegible]	[illegible]	[illegible]	[illegible]	[illegible]	[illegible]	[illegible]	Newport.
[illegible]	[illegible]	[illegible]	[illegible]	[illegible]	[illegible]	[illegible]	[illegible]	[illegible]	[illegible]	Westport.
										Roscommon Co.
[illegible]	[illegible]	[illegible]	[illegible]	[illegible]	[illegible]	[illegible]	[illegible]	[illegible]	[illegible]	Athlone, part of.
[illegible]	[illegible]	[illegible]	[illegible]	[illegible]	[illegible]	[illegible]	[illegible]	[illegible]	[illegible]	Ballinasloe, do.
[illegible]	[illegible]	[illegible]	[illegible]	[illegible]	[illegible]	[illegible]	[illegible]	[illegible]	[illegible]	Boyle, do.
[illegible]	[illegible]	[illegible]	[illegible]	[illegible]	[illegible]	[illegible]	[illegible]	[illegible]	[illegible]	Carrick-on-Shan. do.
[illegible]	[illegible]	[illegible]	[illegible]	[illegible]	[illegible]	[illegible]	[illegible]	[illegible]	[illegible]	Castlerea, do.
[illegible]	[illegible]	[illegible]	[illegible]	[illegible]	[illegible]	[illegible]	[illegible]	[illegible]	[illegible]	Roscommon, do.
[illegible]	[illegible]	[illegible]	[illegible]	[illegible]	[illegible]	[illegible]	[illegible]	[illegible]	[illegible]	Strokestown.
										Sligo Co.
[illegible]	4	[illegible]	[illegible]	[illegible]	[illegible]	[illegible]	7	[illegible]	[illegible]	Ballina, part of.
[illegible]	[illegible]	[illegible]	[illegible]	[illegible]	[illegible]	[illegible]	[illegible]	11	[illegible]	Boyle, do.
[illegible]	[illegible]	77	[illegible]	[illegible]	[illegible]	[illegible]	[illegible]	[illegible]	[illegible]	Dromore West.
[illegible]	[illegible]	[illegible]	[illegible]	[illegible]	[illegible]	[illegible]	[illegible]	[illegible]	[illegible]	Sligo.
[illegible]	[illegible]	[illegible]	[illegible]	[illegible]	144	[illegible]	[illegible]	[illegible]	[illegible]	Tobercurry.

DEATHS Registered in Ireland in the Four Quarters ending March 31st, June 30th, September 30th, and December 31st, 1891, in each Superintendent Registrar's District or Poor Law Union—*continued.*

[illegible]	Superintendent Registrars' Districts or Poor Law Unions	Area in Statute Acres	Population in 1891	Males and Females: Total	Registered in the Quarter ending the last day of — Mar.	June	Sept.	Dec.	Males: Registered in the Quarter ending the last day of — Mar.	June	Sept.	Dec.	Males: Total	Females: Total	Registered in the Quarter ending the last day of — Mar.	June	Sept.	Dec.
[illegible]	Bantry,	[illegible]	[illegible]	[illegible]	[illegible]	[illegible]	[illegible]	[illegible]	[illegible]	[illegible]	[illegible]	[illegible]	[illegible]	[illegible]	[illegible]	[illegible]	[illegible]	[illegible]
[illegible]	Bawnboy,	[illegible]	[illegible]	[illegible]	[illegible]	[illegible]	[illegible]	[illegible]	[illegible]	[illegible]	[illegible]	[illegible]	[illegible]	[illegible]	[illegible]	[illegible]	[illegible]	[illegible]
[illegible]	Belfast,	[illegible]	[illegible]	[illegible]	[illegible]	[illegible]	[illegible]	[illegible]	[illegible]	[illegible]	[illegible]	[illegible]	[illegible]	[illegible]	[illegible]	[illegible]	[illegible]	[illegible]
[illegible]	Belmullet,	[illegible]	[illegible]	[illegible]	[illegible]	[illegible]	[illegible]	[illegible]	[illegible]	[illegible]	[illegible]	[illegible]	[illegible]	[illegible]	[illegible]	[illegible]	[illegible]	[illegible]
[illegible]	Borrisokane,	[illegible]	[illegible]	[illegible]	[illegible]	[illegible]	[illegible]	[illegible]	[illegible]	[illegible]	[illegible]	[illegible]	[illegible]	[illegible]	[illegible]	[illegible]	[illegible]	[illegible]
[illegible]	Boyle,	[illegible]	[illegible]	[illegible]	[illegible]	[illegible]	[illegible]	[illegible]	[illegible]	[illegible]	[illegible]	[illegible]	[illegible]	[illegible]	[illegible]	[illegible]	[illegible]	[illegible]
[illegible]	Cahirciveen,	[illegible]	[illegible]	[illegible]	[illegible]	[illegible]	[illegible]	[illegible]	[illegible]	[illegible]	[illegible]	[illegible]	[illegible]	[illegible]	[illegible]	[illegible]	[illegible]	[illegible]
[illegible]	Callan,	[illegible]	[illegible]	[illegible]	[illegible]	[illegible]	[illegible]	[illegible]	[illegible]	[illegible]	[illegible]	[illegible]	[illegible]	[illegible]	[illegible]	[illegible]	[illegible]	[illegible]
[illegible]	Carlow,	[illegible]	[illegible]	[illegible]	[illegible]	[illegible]	[illegible]	[illegible]	[illegible]	[illegible]	[illegible]	[illegible]	[illegible]	[illegible]	[illegible]	[illegible]	[illegible]	[illegible]
[illegible]	Carrickmacross,	[illegible]	[illegible]	[illegible]	[illegible]	[illegible]	[illegible]	[illegible]	[illegible]	[illegible]	[illegible]	[illegible]	[illegible]	[illegible]	[illegible]	[illegible]	[illegible]	[illegible]
[illegible]	Carrick-on-Shan.,	[illegible]	[illegible]	[illegible]	[illegible]	[illegible]	[illegible]	[illegible]	[illegible]	[illegible]	[illegible]	[illegible]	[illegible]	[illegible]	[illegible]	[illegible]	[illegible]	[illegible]
[illegible]	Carrick-on-Suir,	[illegible]	[illegible]	[illegible]	[illegible]	[illegible]	[illegible]	[illegible]	[illegible]	[illegible]	[illegible]	[illegible]	[illegible]	[illegible]	[illegible]	[illegible]	[illegible]	[illegible]
[illegible]	Cashel,	[illegible]	[illegible]	[illegible]	[illegible]	[illegible]	[illegible]	[illegible]	[illegible]	[illegible]	[illegible]	[illegible]	[illegible]	[illegible]	[illegible]	[illegible]	[illegible]	[illegible]
[illegible]	Castlebar,	[illegible]	[illegible]	[illegible]	[illegible]	[illegible]	[illegible]	[illegible]	[illegible]	[illegible]	[illegible]	[illegible]	[illegible]	[illegible]	[illegible]	[illegible]	[illegible]	[illegible]
[illegible]	Castleblayney,	[illegible]	[illegible]	[illegible]	[illegible]	[illegible]	[illegible]	[illegible]	[illegible]	[illegible]	[illegible]	[illegible]	[illegible]	[illegible]	[illegible]	[illegible]	[illegible]	[illegible]
[illegible]	Castlecomer,	[illegible]	[illegible]	[illegible]	[illegible]	[illegible]	[illegible]	[illegible]	[illegible]	[illegible]	[illegible]	[illegible]	[illegible]	[illegible]	[illegible]	[illegible]	[illegible]	[illegible]
[illegible]	Castlederg,	[illegible]	[illegible]	[illegible]	[illegible]	[illegible]	[illegible]	[illegible]	[illegible]	[illegible]	[illegible]	[illegible]	[illegible]	[illegible]	[illegible]	[illegible]	[illegible]	[illegible]
[illegible]	Castlerea,	[illegible]	[illegible]	[illegible]	[illegible]	[illegible]	[illegible]	[illegible]	[illegible]	[illegible]	[illegible]	[illegible]	[illegible]	[illegible]	[illegible]	[illegible]	[illegible]	[illegible]
[illegible]	Castletown,	[illegible]	[illegible]	[illegible]	[illegible]	[illegible]	[illegible]	[illegible]	[illegible]	[illegible]	[illegible]	[illegible]	[illegible]	[illegible]	[illegible]	[illegible]	[illegible]	[illegible]
[illegible]	Cavan,	[illegible]	[illegible]	[illegible]	[illegible]	[illegible]	[illegible]	[illegible]	[illegible]	[illegible]	[illegible]	[illegible]	[illegible]	[illegible]	[illegible]	[illegible]	[illegible]	[illegible]

DEATHS Registered in Ireland in the Four Quarters ending March 31st, June 30th, September 30th, and December 31st, 1881, in each SUPERINTENDENT REGISTRAR'S DISTRICT OF POOR LAW UNION—*continued.*

[illegible]	Superintendent Registrars' Districts or Poor Law Unions.	Area in Statute Acres.	Population in 1881.	Males and Females					Males					Females				
				Total.	Registered in the Quarter ending the last day of				Registered in the Quarter ending the last day of				Total.	Total.	Registered in the Quarter ending the last day of			
					Mar.	June.	Sept.	Dec.	Mar.	June.	Sept.	Dec.			Mar.	June.	Sept.	Dec.
[illegible]	Celbridge,	[illegible]	[illegible]	[illegible]	[illegible]	[illegible]	[illegible]	[illegible]	[illegible]	[illegible]	[illegible]	[illegible]	[illegible]	[illegible]	[illegible]	[illegible]	[illegible]	[illegible]
[illegible]	[illegible]	[illegible]	[illegible]	[illegible]	[illegible]	[illegible]	[illegible]	[illegible]	[illegible]	[illegible]	[illegible]	[illegible]	[illegible]	[illegible]	[illegible]	[illegible]	[illegible]	[illegible]
[illegible]	Clifden,	[illegible]	[illegible]	[illegible]	[illegible]	[illegible]	[illegible]	[illegible]	[illegible]	[illegible]	[illegible]	[illegible]	[illegible]	[illegible]	[illegible]	[illegible]	[illegible]	[illegible]
[illegible]	Clogheen,	[illegible]	[illegible]	[illegible]	[illegible]	[illegible]	[illegible]	[illegible]	[illegible]	[illegible]	[illegible]	[illegible]	[illegible]	[illegible]	[illegible]	[illegible]	[illegible]	[illegible]
[illegible]	Clogher,	[illegible]	[illegible]	[illegible]	[illegible]	[illegible]	[illegible]	[illegible]	[illegible]	[illegible]	[illegible]	[illegible]	[illegible]	[illegible]	[illegible]	[illegible]	[illegible]	[illegible]
[illegible]	Clonakilty,	[illegible]	[illegible]	[illegible]	[illegible]	[illegible]	[illegible]	[illegible]	[illegible]	[illegible]	[illegible]	[illegible]	[illegible]	[illegible]	[illegible]	[illegible]	[illegible]	[illegible]
[illegible]	Clones,	[illegible]	[illegible]	[illegible]	[illegible]	[illegible]	[illegible]	[illegible]	[illegible]	[illegible]	[illegible]	[illegible]	[illegible]	[illegible]	[illegible]	[illegible]	[illegible]	[illegible]
[illegible]	Clonmel,	[illegible]	[illegible]	[illegible]	[illegible]	[illegible]	[illegible]	[illegible]	[illegible]	[illegible]	[illegible]	[illegible]	[illegible]	[illegible]	[illegible]	[illegible]	[illegible]	[illegible]
[illegible]	Coleraine,	[illegible]	[illegible]	[illegible]	[illegible]	[illegible]	[illegible]	[illegible]	[illegible]	[illegible]	[illegible]	[illegible]	[illegible]	[illegible]	[illegible]	[illegible]	[illegible]	[illegible]
[illegible]	Cookstown,	[illegible]	[illegible]	[illegible]	[illegible]	[illegible]	[illegible]	[illegible]	[illegible]	[illegible]	[illegible]	[illegible]	[illegible]	[illegible]	[illegible]	[illegible]	[illegible]	[illegible]
[illegible]	Cootehill,	[illegible]	[illegible]	[illegible]	[illegible]	[illegible]	[illegible]	[illegible]	[illegible]	[illegible]	[illegible]	[illegible]	[illegible]	[illegible]	[illegible]	[illegible]	[illegible]	[illegible]
[illegible]	Cork,	[illegible]	[illegible]	[illegible]	[illegible]	[illegible]	[illegible]	[illegible]	[illegible]	[illegible]	[illegible]	[illegible]	[illegible]	[illegible]	[illegible]	[illegible]	[illegible]	[illegible]
[illegible]	Corrofin,	[illegible]	[illegible]	[illegible]	[illegible]	[illegible]	[illegible]	[illegible]	[illegible]	[illegible]	[illegible]	[illegible]	[illegible]	[illegible]	[illegible]	[illegible]	[illegible]	[illegible]
[illegible]	Croom,	[illegible]	[illegible]	[illegible]	[illegible]	[illegible]	[illegible]	[illegible]	[illegible]	[illegible]	[illegible]	[illegible]	[illegible]	[illegible]	[illegible]	[illegible]	[illegible]	[illegible]
[illegible]	[illegible]	[illegible]	[illegible]	[illegible]	[illegible]	[illegible]	[illegible]	[illegible]	[illegible]	[illegible]	[illegible]	[illegible]	[illegible]	[illegible]	[illegible]	[illegible]	[illegible]	[illegible]
[illegible]	Dingle,	[illegible]	[illegible]	[illegible]	[illegible]	[illegible]	[illegible]	[illegible]	[illegible]	[illegible]	[illegible]	[illegible]	[illegible]	[illegible]	[illegible]	[illegible]	[illegible]	[illegible]
[illegible]	Donegal,	[illegible]	[illegible]	[illegible]	[illegible]	[illegible]	[illegible]	[illegible]	[illegible]	[illegible]	[illegible]	[illegible]	[illegible]	[illegible]	[illegible]	[illegible]	[illegible]	[illegible]
[illegible]	Downpatrick,	[illegible]	[illegible]	[illegible]	[illegible]	[illegible]	[illegible]	[illegible]	[illegible]	[illegible]	[illegible]	[illegible]	[illegible]	[illegible]	[illegible]	[illegible]	[illegible]	[illegible]
[illegible]	Drogheda,	[illegible]	[illegible]	[illegible]	[illegible]	[illegible]	[illegible]	[illegible]	[illegible]	[illegible]	[illegible]	[illegible]	[illegible]	[illegible]	[illegible]	[illegible]	[illegible]	[illegible]
[illegible]	Dromore West,	[illegible]	[illegible]	[illegible]	[illegible]	[illegible]	[illegible]	[illegible]	[illegible]	[illegible]	[illegible]	[illegible]	[illegible]	[illegible]	[illegible]	[illegible]	[illegible]	[illegible]
[illegible]	Dublin, North,	[illegible]	[illegible]	[illegible]	[illegible]	[illegible]	[illegible]	[illegible]	[illegible]	[illegible]	[illegible]	[illegible]	[illegible]	[illegible]	[illegible]	[illegible]	[illegible]	[illegible]
[illegible]	Dublin, South,	[illegible]	[illegible]	[illegible]	[illegible]	[illegible]	[illegible]	[illegible]	[illegible]	[illegible]	[illegible]	[illegible]	[illegible]	[illegible]	[illegible]	[illegible]	[illegible]	[illegible]
[illegible]	Dundalk,	[illegible]	[illegible]	[illegible]	[illegible]	[illegible]	[illegible]	[illegible]	[illegible]	[illegible]	[illegible]	[illegible]	[illegible]	[illegible]	[illegible]	[illegible]	[illegible]	[illegible]
[illegible]	Dunfanaghy,	[illegible]	[illegible]	[illegible]	[illegible]	[illegible]	[illegible]	[illegible]	[illegible]	[illegible]	[illegible]	[illegible]	[illegible]	[illegible]	[illegible]	[illegible]	[illegible]	[illegible]
[illegible]	Dungannon,	[illegible]	[illegible]	[illegible]	[illegible]	[illegible]	[illegible]	[illegible]	[illegible]	[illegible]	[illegible]	[illegible]	[illegible]	[illegible]	[illegible]	[illegible]	[illegible]	[illegible]
[illegible]	[illegible]	[illegible]	[illegible]	[illegible]	[illegible]	[illegible]	[illegible]	[illegible]	[illegible]	[illegible]	[illegible]	[illegible]	[illegible]	[illegible]	[illegible]	[illegible]	[illegible]	[illegible]
[illegible]	[illegible]	[illegible]	[illegible]	[illegible]	[illegible]	[illegible]	[illegible]	[illegible]	[illegible]	[illegible]	[illegible]	[illegible]	[illegible]	[illegible]	[illegible]	[illegible]	[illegible]	[illegible]
[illegible]	Dunshaughlin,	[illegible]	[illegible]	[illegible]	[illegible]	[illegible]	[illegible]	[illegible]	[illegible]	[illegible]	[illegible]	[illegible]	[illegible]	[illegible]	[illegible]	[illegible]	[illegible]	[illegible]
[illegible]	Edenderry,	[illegible]	[illegible]	[illegible]	[illegible]	[illegible]	[illegible]	[illegible]	[illegible]	[illegible]	[illegible]	[illegible]	[illegible]	[illegible]	[illegible]	[illegible]	[illegible]	[illegible]
[illegible]	Ennis,	[illegible]	[illegible]	[illegible]	[illegible]	[illegible]	[illegible]	[illegible]	[illegible]	[illegible]	[illegible]	[illegible]	[illegible]	[illegible]	[illegible]	[illegible]	[illegible]	[illegible]
[illegible]	Enniscorthy,	[illegible]	[illegible]	[illegible]	[illegible]	[illegible]	[illegible]	[illegible]	[illegible]	[illegible]	[illegible]	[illegible]	[illegible]	[illegible]	[illegible]	[illegible]	[illegible]	[illegible]
[illegible]	Enniskillen,	[illegible]	[illegible]	[illegible]	[illegible]	[illegible]	[illegible]	[illegible]	[illegible]	[illegible]	[illegible]	[illegible]	[illegible]	[illegible]	[illegible]	[illegible]	[illegible]	[illegible]
[illegible]	Ennistymon,	[illegible]	[illegible]	[illegible]	[illegible]	[illegible]	[illegible]	[illegible]	[illegible]	[illegible]	[illegible]	[illegible]	[illegible]	[illegible]	[illegible]	[illegible]	[illegible]	[illegible]
[illegible]	Fermoy,	[illegible]	[illegible]	[illegible]	[illegible]	[illegible]	[illegible]	[illegible]	[illegible]	[illegible]	[illegible]	[illegible]	[illegible]	[illegible]	[illegible]	[illegible]	[illegible]	[illegible]
[illegible]	Galway,	[illegible]	[illegible]	[illegible]	[illegible]	[illegible]	[illegible]	[illegible]	[illegible]	[illegible]	[illegible]	[illegible]	[illegible]	[illegible]	[illegible]	[illegible]	[illegible]	[illegible]
[illegible]	Glenamaddy,	[illegible]	[illegible]	[illegible]	[illegible]	[illegible]	[illegible]	[illegible]	[illegible]	[illegible]	[illegible]	[illegible]	[illegible]	[illegible]	[illegible]	[illegible]	[illegible]	[illegible]
[illegible]	Glenties,	[illegible]	[illegible]	[illegible]	[illegible]	[illegible]	[illegible]	[illegible]	[illegible]	[illegible]	[illegible]	[illegible]	[illegible]	[illegible]	[illegible]	[illegible]	[illegible]	[illegible]
[illegible]	Glin,	[illegible]	[illegible]	[illegible]	[illegible]	[illegible]	[illegible]	[illegible]	[illegible]	[illegible]	[illegible]	[illegible]	[illegible]	[illegible]	[illegible]	[illegible]	[illegible]	[illegible]
[illegible]	Gorey,	[illegible]	[illegible]	[illegible]	[illegible]	[illegible]	[illegible]	[illegible]	[illegible]	[illegible]	[illegible]	[illegible]	[illegible]	[illegible]	[illegible]	[illegible]	[illegible]	[illegible]
[illegible]	Gort,	[illegible]	[illegible]	[illegible]	[illegible]	[illegible]	[illegible]	[illegible]	[illegible]	[illegible]	[illegible]	[illegible]	[illegible]	[illegible]	[illegible]	[illegible]	[illegible]	[illegible]
[illegible]	Granard,	[illegible]	[illegible]	[illegible]	[illegible]	[illegible]	[illegible]	[illegible]	[illegible]	[illegible]	[illegible]	[illegible]	[illegible]	[illegible]	[illegible]	[illegible]	[illegible]	[illegible]
[illegible]	Inishowen,	[illegible]	[illegible]	[illegible]	[illegible]	[illegible]	[illegible]	[illegible]	[illegible]	[illegible]	[illegible]	[illegible]	[illegible]	[illegible]	[illegible]	[illegible]	[illegible]	[illegible]
[illegible]	Irvinestown,	[illegible]	[illegible]	[illegible]	[illegible]	[illegible]	[illegible]	[illegible]	[illegible]	[illegible]	[illegible]	[illegible]	[illegible]	[illegible]	[illegible]	[illegible]	[illegible]	[illegible]
[illegible]	Kanturk,	[illegible]	[illegible]	[illegible]	[illegible]	[illegible]	[illegible]	[illegible]	[illegible]	[illegible]	[illegible]	[illegible]	[illegible]	[illegible]	[illegible]	[illegible]	[illegible]	[illegible]
[illegible]	Kells,	[illegible]	[illegible]	[illegible]	[illegible]	[illegible]	[illegible]	[illegible]	[illegible]	[illegible]	[illegible]	[illegible]	[illegible]	[illegible]	[illegible]	[illegible]	[illegible]	[illegible]
[illegible]	Kenmare,	[illegible]	[illegible]	[illegible]	[illegible]	[illegible]	[illegible]	[illegible]	[illegible]	[illegible]	[illegible]	[illegible]	[illegible]	[illegible]	[illegible]	[illegible]	[illegible]	[illegible]
[illegible]	Kilkeel,	[illegible]	[illegible]	[illegible]	[illegible]	[illegible]	[illegible]	[illegible]	[illegible]	[illegible]	[illegible]	[illegible]	[illegible]	[illegible]	[illegible]	[illegible]	[illegible]	[illegible]
[illegible]	Kilkenny,	[illegible]	[illegible]	[illegible]	[illegible]	[illegible]	[illegible]	[illegible]	[illegible]	[illegible]	[illegible]	[illegible]	[illegible]	[illegible]	[illegible]	[illegible]	[illegible]	[illegible]
[illegible]	Killadysert,	[illegible]	[illegible]	[illegible]	[illegible]	[illegible]	[illegible]	[illegible]	[illegible]	[illegible]	[illegible]	[illegible]	[illegible]	[illegible]	[illegible]	[illegible]	[illegible]	[illegible]
[illegible]	Killala,	[illegible]	[illegible]	[illegible]	[illegible]	[illegible]	[illegible]	[illegible]	[illegible]	[illegible]	[illegible]	[illegible]	[illegible]	[illegible]	[illegible]	[illegible]	[illegible]	[illegible]
[illegible]	Killarney,	[illegible]	[illegible]	[illegible]	[illegible]	[illegible]	[illegible]	[illegible]	[illegible]	[illegible]	[illegible]	[illegible]	[illegible]	[illegible]	[illegible]	[illegible]	[illegible]	[illegible]
[illegible]	Kilmacthomas,	[illegible]	[illegible]	[illegible]	[illegible]	[illegible]	[illegible]	[illegible]	[illegible]	[illegible]	[illegible]	[illegible]	[illegible]	[illegible]	[illegible]	[illegible]	[illegible]	[illegible]
[illegible]	Kilmallock,	[illegible]	[illegible]	[illegible]	[illegible]	[illegible]	[illegible]	[illegible]	[illegible]	[illegible]	[illegible]	[illegible]	[illegible]	[illegible]	[illegible]	[illegible]	[illegible]	[illegible]
[illegible]	Kilrush,	[illegible]	[illegible]	[illegible]	[illegible]	[illegible]	[illegible]	[illegible]	[illegible]	[illegible]	[illegible]	[illegible]	[illegible]	[illegible]	[illegible]	[illegible]	[illegible]	[illegible]
[illegible]	Kinsale,	[illegible]	[illegible]	[illegible]	[illegible]	[illegible]	[illegible]	[illegible]	[illegible]	[illegible]	[illegible]	[illegible]	[illegible]	[illegible]	[illegible]	[illegible]	[illegible]	[illegible]
[illegible]	Larne,	[illegible]	[illegible]	[illegible]	[illegible]	[illegible]	[illegible]	[illegible]	[illegible]	[illegible]	[illegible]	[illegible]	[illegible]	[illegible]	[illegible]	[illegible]	[illegible]	[illegible]
[illegible]	Letterkenny,	[illegible]	[illegible]	[illegible]	[illegible]	[illegible]	[illegible]	[illegible]	[illegible]	[illegible]	[illegible]	[illegible]	[illegible]	[illegible]	[illegible]	[illegible]	[illegible]	[illegible]
[illegible]	Limerick,	[illegible]	[illegible]	[illegible]	[illegible]	[illegible]	[illegible]	[illegible]	[illegible]	[illegible]	[illegible]	[illegible]	[illegible]	[illegible]	[illegible]	[illegible]	[illegible]	[illegible]

DEATHS Registered in Ireland in the Four Quarters ending March 31st, June 30th, September 30th, and December 31st, 1891, in each Superintendent Registrar's District or Poor Law Union—*continued.*

Number of Inquests of Cases in preceding columns.	Superintendent Registrar's Districts or Poor Law Unions.	Area in Statute Acres.	Population in 1891.	Males and Females: Total.	Registered in the Quarter ending the last day of: Mar.	June.	Sept.	Dec.	Males: Registered in the Quarter ending the last day of: Mar.	June.	Sept.	Dec.	Total.	Females: Total.	Registered in the Quarter ending the last day of: Mar.	June.	Sept.	Dec.
[illegible]	Limerick	[illegible]	[illegible]	[illegible]	[illegible]	[illegible]	[illegible]	[illegible]	[illegible]	[illegible]	[illegible]	[illegible]	[illegible]	[illegible]	[illegible]	[illegible]	[illegible]	[illegible]
[illegible]	Lisburn	[illegible]	[illegible]	[illegible]	[illegible]	[illegible]	[illegible]	[illegible]	[illegible]	[illegible]	[illegible]	[illegible]	[illegible]	[illegible]	[illegible]	[illegible]	[illegible]	[illegible]
[illegible]	Lismore	[illegible]	[illegible]	[illegible]	[illegible]	[illegible]	[illegible]	[illegible]	[illegible]	[illegible]	[illegible]	[illegible]	[illegible]	[illegible]	[illegible]	[illegible]	[illegible]	[illegible]
[illegible]	Lisnaskea	[illegible]	[illegible]	[illegible]	[illegible]	[illegible]	[illegible]	[illegible]	[illegible]	[illegible]	[illegible]	[illegible]	[illegible]	[illegible]	[illegible]	[illegible]	[illegible]	[illegible]
[illegible]	Listowel	[illegible]	[illegible]	[illegible]	[illegible]	[illegible]	[illegible]	[illegible]	[illegible]	[illegible]	[illegible]	[illegible]	[illegible]	[illegible]	[illegible]	[illegible]	[illegible]	[illegible]
[illegible]	Londonderry	[illegible]	[illegible]	[illegible]	[illegible]	[illegible]	[illegible]	[illegible]	[illegible]	[illegible]	[illegible]	[illegible]	[illegible]	[illegible]	[illegible]	[illegible]	[illegible]	[illegible]
[illegible]	Longford	[illegible]	[illegible]	[illegible]	[illegible]	[illegible]	[illegible]	[illegible]	[illegible]	[illegible]	[illegible]	[illegible]	[illegible]	[illegible]	[illegible]	[illegible]	[illegible]	[illegible]
[illegible]	Loughrea	[illegible]	[illegible]	[illegible]	[illegible]	[illegible]	[illegible]	[illegible]	[illegible]	[illegible]	[illegible]	[illegible]	[illegible]	[illegible]	[illegible]	[illegible]	[illegible]	[illegible]
[illegible]	Lurgan	[illegible]	[illegible]	[illegible]	[illegible]	[illegible]	[illegible]	[illegible]	[illegible]	[illegible]	[illegible]	[illegible]	[illegible]	[illegible]	[illegible]	[illegible]	[illegible]	[illegible]
[illegible]	Macroom	[illegible]	[illegible]	[illegible]	[illegible]	[illegible]	[illegible]	[illegible]	[illegible]	[illegible]	[illegible]	[illegible]	[illegible]	[illegible]	[illegible]	[illegible]	[illegible]	[illegible]
[illegible]	Magherafelt	[illegible]	[illegible]	[illegible]	[illegible]	[illegible]	[illegible]	[illegible]	[illegible]	[illegible]	[illegible]	[illegible]	[illegible]	[illegible]	[illegible]	[illegible]	[illegible]	[illegible]
[illegible]	Mallow	[illegible]	[illegible]	[illegible]	[illegible]	[illegible]	[illegible]	[illegible]	[illegible]	[illegible]	[illegible]	[illegible]	[illegible]	[illegible]	[illegible]	[illegible]	[illegible]	[illegible]
[illegible]	Manorhamilton	[illegible]	[illegible]	[illegible]	[illegible]	[illegible]	[illegible]	[illegible]	[illegible]	[illegible]	[illegible]	[illegible]	[illegible]	[illegible]	[illegible]	[illegible]	[illegible]	[illegible]
[illegible]	Midleton	[illegible]	[illegible]	[illegible]	[illegible]	[illegible]	[illegible]	[illegible]	[illegible]	[illegible]	[illegible]	[illegible]	[illegible]	[illegible]	[illegible]	[illegible]	[illegible]	[illegible]
[illegible]	Milford	[illegible]	[illegible]	[illegible]	[illegible]	[illegible]	[illegible]	[illegible]	[illegible]	[illegible]	[illegible]	[illegible]	[illegible]	[illegible]	[illegible]	[illegible]	[illegible]	[illegible]
[illegible]	Millstreet	[illegible]	[illegible]	[illegible]	[illegible]	[illegible]	[illegible]	[illegible]	[illegible]	[illegible]	[illegible]	[illegible]	[illegible]	[illegible]	[illegible]	[illegible]	[illegible]	[illegible]
[illegible]	Mitchelstown	[illegible]	[illegible]	[illegible]	[illegible]	[illegible]	[illegible]	[illegible]	[illegible]	[illegible]	[illegible]	[illegible]	[illegible]	[illegible]	[illegible]	[illegible]	[illegible]	[illegible]
[illegible]	Mohill	[illegible]	[illegible]	[illegible]	[illegible]	[illegible]	[illegible]	[illegible]	[illegible]	[illegible]	[illegible]	[illegible]	[illegible]	[illegible]	[illegible]	[illegible]	[illegible]	[illegible]
[illegible]	Monaghan	[illegible]	[illegible]	[illegible]	[illegible]	[illegible]	[illegible]	[illegible]	[illegible]	[illegible]	[illegible]	[illegible]	[illegible]	[illegible]	[illegible]	[illegible]	[illegible]	[illegible]
[illegible]	Mountbellew	[illegible]	[illegible]	[illegible]	[illegible]	[illegible]	[illegible]	[illegible]	[illegible]	[illegible]	[illegible]	[illegible]	[illegible]	[illegible]	[illegible]	[illegible]	[illegible]	[illegible]
[illegible]	Mountmellick	[illegible]	[illegible]	[illegible]	[illegible]	[illegible]	[illegible]	[illegible]	[illegible]	[illegible]	[illegible]	[illegible]	[illegible]	[illegible]	[illegible]	[illegible]	[illegible]	[illegible]
[illegible]	Mullingar	[illegible]	[illegible]	[illegible]	[illegible]	[illegible]	[illegible]	[illegible]	[illegible]	[illegible]	[illegible]	[illegible]	[illegible]	[illegible]	[illegible]	[illegible]	[illegible]	[illegible]
[illegible]	Naas	[illegible]	[illegible]	[illegible]	[illegible]	[illegible]	[illegible]	[illegible]	[illegible]	[illegible]	[illegible]	[illegible]	[illegible]	[illegible]	[illegible]	[illegible]	[illegible]	[illegible]
[illegible]	Navan	[illegible]	[illegible]	[illegible]	[illegible]	[illegible]	[illegible]	[illegible]	[illegible]	[illegible]	[illegible]	[illegible]	[illegible]	[illegible]	[illegible]	[illegible]	[illegible]	[illegible]
[illegible]	Nenagh	[illegible]	[illegible]	[illegible]	[illegible]	[illegible]	[illegible]	[illegible]	[illegible]	[illegible]	[illegible]	[illegible]	[illegible]	[illegible]	[illegible]	[illegible]	[illegible]	[illegible]
[illegible]	Newcastle	[illegible]	[illegible]	[illegible]	[illegible]	[illegible]	[illegible]	[illegible]	[illegible]	[illegible]	[illegible]	[illegible]	[illegible]	[illegible]	[illegible]	[illegible]	[illegible]	[illegible]
[illegible]	New Ross	[illegible]	[illegible]	[illegible]	[illegible]	[illegible]	[illegible]	[illegible]	[illegible]	[illegible]	[illegible]	[illegible]	[illegible]	[illegible]	[illegible]	[illegible]	[illegible]	[illegible]
[illegible]	Newry	[illegible]	[illegible]	[illegible]	[illegible]	[illegible]	[illegible]	[illegible]	[illegible]	[illegible]	[illegible]	[illegible]	[illegible]	[illegible]	[illegible]	[illegible]	[illegible]	[illegible]
[illegible]	Newtownards	[illegible]	[illegible]	[illegible]	[illegible]	[illegible]	[illegible]	[illegible]	[illegible]	[illegible]	[illegible]	[illegible]	[illegible]	[illegible]	[illegible]	[illegible]	[illegible]	[illegible]
[illegible]	Oldcastle	[illegible]	[illegible]	[illegible]	[illegible]	[illegible]	[illegible]	[illegible]	[illegible]	[illegible]	[illegible]	[illegible]	[illegible]	[illegible]	[illegible]	[illegible]	[illegible]	[illegible]
[illegible]	Omagh	[illegible]	[illegible]	[illegible]	[illegible]	[illegible]	[illegible]	[illegible]	[illegible]	[illegible]	[illegible]	[illegible]	[illegible]	[illegible]	[illegible]	[illegible]	[illegible]	[illegible]
[illegible]	Oughterard	[illegible]	[illegible]	[illegible]	[illegible]	[illegible]	[illegible]	[illegible]	[illegible]	[illegible]	[illegible]	[illegible]	[illegible]	[illegible]	[illegible]	[illegible]	[illegible]	[illegible]
[illegible]	Parsonstown	[illegible]	[illegible]	[illegible]	[illegible]	[illegible]	[illegible]	[illegible]	[illegible]	[illegible]	[illegible]	[illegible]	[illegible]	[illegible]	[illegible]	[illegible]	[illegible]	[illegible]
[illegible]	Portumna	[illegible]	[illegible]	[illegible]	[illegible]	[illegible]	[illegible]	[illegible]	[illegible]	[illegible]	[illegible]	[illegible]	[illegible]	[illegible]	[illegible]	[illegible]	[illegible]	[illegible]
[illegible]	Rathdown	[illegible]	[illegible]	[illegible]	[illegible]	[illegible]	[illegible]	[illegible]	[illegible]	[illegible]	[illegible]	[illegible]	[illegible]	[illegible]	[illegible]	[illegible]	[illegible]	[illegible]
[illegible]	Rathdrum	[illegible]	[illegible]	[illegible]	[illegible]	[illegible]	[illegible]	[illegible]	[illegible]	[illegible]	[illegible]	[illegible]	[illegible]	[illegible]	[illegible]	[illegible]	[illegible]	[illegible]
[illegible]	Rathkeale	[illegible]	[illegible]	[illegible]	[illegible]	[illegible]	[illegible]	[illegible]	[illegible]	[illegible]	[illegible]	[illegible]	[illegible]	[illegible]	[illegible]	[illegible]	[illegible]	[illegible]
[illegible]	Roscommon	[illegible]	[illegible]	[illegible]	[illegible]	[illegible]	[illegible]	[illegible]	[illegible]	[illegible]	[illegible]	[illegible]	[illegible]	[illegible]	[illegible]	[illegible]	[illegible]	[illegible]
[illegible]	Roscrea	[illegible]	[illegible]	[illegible]	[illegible]	[illegible]	[illegible]	[illegible]	[illegible]	[illegible]	[illegible]	[illegible]	[illegible]	[illegible]	[illegible]	[illegible]	[illegible]	[illegible]
[illegible]	Scarriff	[illegible]	[illegible]	[illegible]	[illegible]	[illegible]	[illegible]	[illegible]	[illegible]	[illegible]	[illegible]	[illegible]	[illegible]	[illegible]	[illegible]	[illegible]	[illegible]	[illegible]
[illegible]	Shillelagh	[illegible]	[illegible]	[illegible]	[illegible]	[illegible]	[illegible]	[illegible]	[illegible]	[illegible]	[illegible]	[illegible]	[illegible]	[illegible]	[illegible]	[illegible]	[illegible]	[illegible]
[illegible]	Skibbereen	[illegible]	[illegible]	[illegible]	[illegible]	[illegible]	[illegible]	[illegible]	[illegible]	[illegible]	[illegible]	[illegible]	[illegible]	[illegible]	[illegible]	[illegible]	[illegible]	[illegible]
[illegible]	Skull	[illegible]	[illegible]	[illegible]	[illegible]	[illegible]	[illegible]	[illegible]	[illegible]	[illegible]	[illegible]	[illegible]	[illegible]	[illegible]	[illegible]	[illegible]	[illegible]	[illegible]
[illegible]	Sligo	[illegible]	[illegible]	[illegible]	[illegible]	[illegible]	[illegible]	[illegible]	[illegible]	[illegible]	[illegible]	[illegible]	[illegible]	[illegible]	[illegible]	[illegible]	[illegible]	[illegible]
[illegible]	Strabane	[illegible]	[illegible]	[illegible]	[illegible]	[illegible]	[illegible]	[illegible]	[illegible]	[illegible]	[illegible]	[illegible]	[illegible]	[illegible]	[illegible]	[illegible]	[illegible]	[illegible]
[illegible]	Stranorlar	[illegible]	[illegible]	[illegible]	[illegible]	[illegible]	[illegible]	[illegible]	[illegible]	[illegible]	[illegible]	[illegible]	[illegible]	[illegible]	[illegible]	[illegible]	[illegible]	[illegible]
[illegible]	Strokestown	[illegible]	[illegible]	[illegible]	[illegible]	[illegible]	[illegible]	[illegible]	[illegible]	[illegible]	[illegible]	[illegible]	[illegible]	[illegible]	[illegible]	[illegible]	[illegible]	[illegible]
[illegible]	Swineford	[illegible]	[illegible]	[illegible]	[illegible]	[illegible]	[illegible]	[illegible]	[illegible]	[illegible]	[illegible]	[illegible]	[illegible]	[illegible]	[illegible]	[illegible]	[illegible]	[illegible]
[illegible]	Thomastown	[illegible]	[illegible]	[illegible]	[illegible]	[illegible]	[illegible]	[illegible]	[illegible]	[illegible]	[illegible]	[illegible]	[illegible]	[illegible]	[illegible]	[illegible]	[illegible]	[illegible]
[illegible]	Thurles	[illegible]	[illegible]	[illegible]	[illegible]	[illegible]	[illegible]	[illegible]	[illegible]	[illegible]	[illegible]	[illegible]	[illegible]	[illegible]	[illegible]	[illegible]	[illegible]	[illegible]
[illegible]	Tipperary	[illegible]	[illegible]	[illegible]	[illegible]	[illegible]	[illegible]	[illegible]	[illegible]	[illegible]	[illegible]	[illegible]	[illegible]	[illegible]	[illegible]	[illegible]	[illegible]	[illegible]
[illegible]	Tobercurry	[illegible]	[illegible]	[illegible]	[illegible]	[illegible]	[illegible]	[illegible]	[illegible]	[illegible]	[illegible]	[illegible]	[illegible]	[illegible]	[illegible]	[illegible]	[illegible]	[illegible]
[illegible]	Tralee	[illegible]	[illegible]	[illegible]	[illegible]	[illegible]	[illegible]	[illegible]	[illegible]	[illegible]	[illegible]	[illegible]	[illegible]	[illegible]	[illegible]	[illegible]	[illegible]	[illegible]
[illegible]	Trim	[illegible]	[illegible]	[illegible]	[illegible]	[illegible]	[illegible]	[illegible]	[illegible]	[illegible]	[illegible]	[illegible]	[illegible]	[illegible]	[illegible]	[illegible]	[illegible]	[illegible]
[illegible]	Tuam	[illegible]	[illegible]	[illegible]	[illegible]	[illegible]	[illegible]	[illegible]	[illegible]	[illegible]	[illegible]	[illegible]	[illegible]	[illegible]	[illegible]	[illegible]	[illegible]	[illegible]
[illegible]	Tulla	[illegible]	[illegible]	[illegible]	[illegible]	[illegible]	[illegible]	[illegible]	[illegible]	[illegible]	[illegible]	[illegible]	[illegible]	[illegible]	[illegible]	[illegible]	[illegible]	[illegible]
[illegible]	Tullamore	[illegible]	[illegible]	[illegible]	[illegible]	[illegible]	[illegible]	[illegible]	[illegible]	[illegible]	[illegible]	[illegible]	[illegible]	[illegible]	[illegible]	[illegible]	[illegible]	[illegible]
[illegible]	Urlingford	[illegible]	[illegible]	[illegible]	[illegible]	[illegible]	[illegible]	[illegible]	[illegible]	[illegible]	[illegible]	[illegible]	[illegible]	[illegible]	[illegible]	[illegible]	[illegible]	[illegible]
[illegible]	Waterford	[illegible]	[illegible]	[illegible]	[illegible]	[illegible]	[illegible]	[illegible]	[illegible]	[illegible]	[illegible]	[illegible]	[illegible]	[illegible]	[illegible]	[illegible]	[illegible]	[illegible]
[illegible]	Westport	[illegible]	[illegible]	[illegible]	[illegible]	[illegible]	[illegible]	[illegible]	[illegible]	[illegible]	[illegible]	[illegible]	[illegible]	[illegible]	[illegible]	[illegible]	[illegible]	[illegible]
[illegible]	Wexford	[illegible]	[illegible]	[illegible]	[illegible]	[illegible]	[illegible]	[illegible]	[illegible]	[illegible]	[illegible]	[illegible]	[illegible]	[illegible]	[illegible]	[illegible]	[illegible]	[illegible]
[illegible]	Youghal	[illegible]	[illegible]	[illegible]	[illegible]	[illegible]	[illegible]	[illegible]	[illegible]	[illegible]	[illegible]	[illegible]	[illegible]	[illegible]	[illegible]	[illegible]	[illegible]	[illegible]

IRELAND.—Deaths at different Ages registered in the Year 1891—in the Provinces and Counties—Males.

No.	Provinces and Counties	Males.																			
				Ages at Death.																	
		[illegible]	[illegible]	[illegible]	1	2	3	4	[illegible]	[illegible]	[illegible]	[illegible]	[illegible]	[illegible]	[illegible]	[illegible]	[illegible]	[illegible]	[illegible]	[illegible]	[illegible]
	IRELAND,	[illegible]	[illegible]	[illegible]	[illegible]	[illegible]	[illegible]	[illegible]	[illegible]	[illegible]	[illegible]	[illegible]	[illegible]	[illegible]	[illegible]	[illegible]	[illegible]	[illegible]	[illegible]	[illegible]	[illegible]
No.	PROVINCES.																				
I.	LEINSTER,	[illegible]	[illegible]	[illegible]	[illegible]	[illegible]	[illegible]	[illegible]	[illegible]	[illegible]	[illegible]	[illegible]	[illegible]	[illegible]	[illegible]	[illegible]	[illegible]	[illegible]	[illegible]	[illegible]	[illegible]
II.	MUNSTER,	[illegible]	[illegible]	[illegible]	[illegible]	[illegible]	[illegible]	[illegible]	[illegible]	[illegible]	[illegible]	[illegible]	[illegible]	[illegible]	[illegible]	[illegible]	[illegible]	[illegible]	[illegible]	[illegible]	[illegible]
III.	ULSTER,	[illegible]	[illegible]	[illegible]	[illegible]	[illegible]	[illegible]	[illegible]	[illegible]	[illegible]	[illegible]	[illegible]	[illegible]	[illegible]	[illegible]	[illegible]	[illegible]	[illegible]	[illegible]	[illegible]	[illegible]
IV.	CONNAUGHT,	[illegible]	[illegible]	[illegible]	[illegible]	[illegible]	[illegible]	[illegible]	[illegible]	[illegible]	[illegible]	[illegible]	[illegible]	[illegible]	[illegible]	[illegible]	[illegible]	[illegible]	[illegible]	[illegible]	[illegible]
	I.—LEINSTER.																				
1	Carlow,	[illegible]	[illegible]	[illegible]	[illegible]	[illegible]	[illegible]	[illegible]	[illegible]	[illegible]	[illegible]	[illegible]	[illegible]	[illegible]	[illegible]	[illegible]	[illegible]	[illegible]	[illegible]	[illegible]	[illegible]
2	Dublin,	[illegible]	[illegible]	[illegible]	[illegible]	[illegible]	[illegible]	[illegible]	[illegible]	[illegible]	[illegible]	[illegible]	[illegible]	[illegible]	[illegible]	[illegible]	[illegible]	[illegible]	[illegible]	[illegible]	[illegible]
3	Kildare,	[illegible]	[illegible]	[illegible]	[illegible]	[illegible]	[illegible]	[illegible]	[illegible]	[illegible]	[illegible]	[illegible]	[illegible]	[illegible]	[illegible]	[illegible]	[illegible]	[illegible]	[illegible]	[illegible]	[illegible]
4	Kilkenny,	[illegible]	[illegible]	[illegible]	[illegible]	[illegible]	[illegible]	[illegible]	[illegible]	[illegible]	[illegible]	[illegible]	[illegible]	[illegible]	[illegible]	[illegible]	[illegible]	[illegible]	[illegible]	[illegible]	[illegible]
5	King's,	[illegible]	[illegible]	[illegible]	[illegible]	[illegible]	[illegible]	[illegible]	[illegible]	[illegible]	[illegible]	[illegible]	[illegible]	[illegible]	[illegible]	[illegible]	[illegible]	[illegible]	[illegible]	[illegible]	[illegible]
6	Longford,	[illegible]	[illegible]	[illegible]	[illegible]	[illegible]	[illegible]	[illegible]	[illegible]	[illegible]	[illegible]	[illegible]	[illegible]	[illegible]	[illegible]	[illegible]	[illegible]	[illegible]	[illegible]	[illegible]	[illegible]
7	Louth, and Co. of the Town of Drogheda,	[illegible]	[illegible]	[illegible]	[illegible]	[illegible]	[illegible]	[illegible]	[illegible]	[illegible]	[illegible]	[illegible]	[illegible]	[illegible]	[illegible]	[illegible]	[illegible]	[illegible]	[illegible]	[illegible]	[illegible]
8	Meath,	[illegible]	[illegible]	[illegible]	[illegible]	[illegible]	[illegible]	[illegible]	[illegible]	[illegible]	[illegible]	[illegible]	[illegible]	[illegible]	[illegible]	[illegible]	[illegible]	[illegible]	[illegible]	[illegible]	[illegible]
9	Queen's,	[illegible]	[illegible]	[illegible]	[illegible]	[illegible]	[illegible]	[illegible]	[illegible]	[illegible]	[illegible]	[illegible]	[illegible]	[illegible]	[illegible]	[illegible]	[illegible]	[illegible]	[illegible]	[illegible]	[illegible]
10	Westmeath,	[illegible]	[illegible]	[illegible]	[illegible]	[illegible]	[illegible]	[illegible]	[illegible]	[illegible]	[illegible]	[illegible]	[illegible]	[illegible]	[illegible]	[illegible]	[illegible]	[illegible]	[illegible]	[illegible]	[illegible]
11	Wexford,	[illegible]	[illegible]	[illegible]	[illegible]	[illegible]	[illegible]	[illegible]	[illegible]	[illegible]	[illegible]	[illegible]	[illegible]	[illegible]	[illegible]	[illegible]	[illegible]	[illegible]	[illegible]	[illegible]	[illegible]
12	Wicklow,	[illegible]	[illegible]	[illegible]	[illegible]	[illegible]	[illegible]	[illegible]	[illegible]	[illegible]	[illegible]	[illegible]	[illegible]	[illegible]	[illegible]	[illegible]	[illegible]	[illegible]	[illegible]	[illegible]	[illegible]
	II.—MUNSTER.																				
13	Clare,	[illegible]	[illegible]	[illegible]	[illegible]	[illegible]	[illegible]	[illegible]	[illegible]	[illegible]	[illegible]	[illegible]	[illegible]	[illegible]	[illegible]	[illegible]	[illegible]	[illegible]	[illegible]	[illegible]	[illegible]
14	Cork,	[illegible]	[illegible]	[illegible]	[illegible]	[illegible]	[illegible]	[illegible]	[illegible]	[illegible]	[illegible]	[illegible]	[illegible]	[illegible]	[illegible]	[illegible]	[illegible]	[illegible]	[illegible]	[illegible]	[illegible]
15	Kerry,	[illegible]	[illegible]	[illegible]	[illegible]	[illegible]	[illegible]	[illegible]	[illegible]	[illegible]	[illegible]	[illegible]	[illegible]	[illegible]	[illegible]	[illegible]	[illegible]	[illegible]	[illegible]	[illegible]	[illegible]
16	Limerick,	[illegible]	[illegible]	[illegible]	[illegible]	[illegible]	[illegible]	[illegible]	[illegible]	[illegible]	[illegible]	[illegible]	[illegible]	[illegible]	[illegible]	[illegible]	[illegible]	[illegible]	[illegible]	[illegible]	[illegible]
17	Tipperary,	[illegible]	[illegible]	[illegible]	[illegible]	[illegible]	[illegible]	[illegible]	[illegible]	[illegible]	[illegible]	[illegible]	[illegible]	[illegible]	[illegible]	[illegible]	[illegible]	[illegible]	[illegible]	[illegible]	[illegible]
18	Waterford,	[illegible]	[illegible]	[illegible]	[illegible]	[illegible]	[illegible]	[illegible]	[illegible]	[illegible]	[illegible]	[illegible]	[illegible]	[illegible]	[illegible]	[illegible]	[illegible]	[illegible]	[illegible]	[illegible]	[illegible]
	III.—ULSTER.																				
19	Antrim,	[illegible]	[illegible]	[illegible]	[illegible]	[illegible]	[illegible]	[illegible]	[illegible]	[illegible]	[illegible]	[illegible]	[illegible]	[illegible]	[illegible]	[illegible]	[illegible]	[illegible]	[illegible]	[illegible]	[illegible]
20	Armagh,	[illegible]	[illegible]	[illegible]	[illegible]	[illegible]	[illegible]	[illegible]	[illegible]	[illegible]	[illegible]	[illegible]	[illegible]	[illegible]	[illegible]	[illegible]	[illegible]	[illegible]	[illegible]	[illegible]	[illegible]
21	Cavan,	[illegible]	[illegible]	[illegible]	[illegible]	[illegible]	[illegible]	[illegible]	[illegible]	[illegible]	[illegible]	[illegible]	[illegible]	[illegible]	[illegible]	[illegible]	[illegible]	[illegible]	[illegible]	[illegible]	[illegible]
22	Donegal,	[illegible]	[illegible]	[illegible]	[illegible]	[illegible]	[illegible]	[illegible]	[illegible]	[illegible]	[illegible]	[illegible]	[illegible]	[illegible]	[illegible]	[illegible]	[illegible]	[illegible]	[illegible]	[illegible]	[illegible]
23	Down,	[illegible]	[illegible]	[illegible]	[illegible]	[illegible]	[illegible]	[illegible]	[illegible]	[illegible]	[illegible]	[illegible]	[illegible]	[illegible]	[illegible]	[illegible]	[illegible]	[illegible]	[illegible]	[illegible]	[illegible]
24	Fermanagh,	[illegible]	[illegible]	[illegible]	[illegible]	[illegible]	[illegible]	[illegible]	[illegible]	[illegible]	[illegible]	[illegible]	[illegible]	[illegible]	[illegible]	[illegible]	[illegible]	[illegible]	[illegible]	[illegible]	[illegible]
25	Londonderry,	[illegible]	[illegible]	[illegible]	[illegible]	[illegible]	[illegible]	[illegible]	[illegible]	[illegible]	[illegible]	[illegible]	[illegible]	[illegible]	[illegible]	[illegible]	[illegible]	[illegible]	[illegible]	[illegible]	[illegible]
26	Monaghan,	[illegible]	[illegible]	[illegible]	[illegible]	[illegible]	[illegible]	[illegible]	[illegible]	[illegible]	[illegible]	[illegible]	[illegible]	[illegible]	[illegible]	[illegible]	[illegible]	[illegible]	[illegible]	[illegible]	[illegible]
27	Tyrone,	[illegible]	[illegible]	[illegible]	[illegible]	[illegible]	[illegible]	[illegible]	[illegible]	[illegible]	[illegible]	[illegible]	[illegible]	[illegible]	[illegible]	[illegible]	[illegible]	[illegible]	[illegible]	[illegible]	[illegible]
	IV.—CONNAUGHT.																				
28	Galway,	[illegible]	[illegible]	[illegible]	[illegible]	[illegible]	[illegible]	[illegible]	[illegible]	[illegible]	[illegible]	[illegible]	[illegible]	[illegible]	[illegible]	[illegible]	[illegible]	[illegible]	[illegible]	[illegible]	[illegible]
29	Leitrim,	[illegible]	[illegible]	[illegible]	[illegible]	[illegible]	[illegible]	[illegible]	[illegible]	[illegible]	[illegible]	[illegible]	[illegible]	[illegible]	[illegible]	[illegible]	[illegible]	[illegible]	[illegible]	[illegible]	[illegible]
30	Mayo,	[illegible]	[illegible]	[illegible]	[illegible]	[illegible]	[illegible]	[illegible]	[illegible]	[illegible]	[illegible]	[illegible]	[illegible]	[illegible]	[illegible]	[illegible]	[illegible]	[illegible]	[illegible]	[illegible]	[illegible]
31	Roscommon,	[illegible]	[illegible]	[illegible]	[illegible]	[illegible]	[illegible]	[illegible]	[illegible]	[illegible]	[illegible]	[illegible]	[illegible]	[illegible]	[illegible]	[illegible]	[illegible]	[illegible]	[illegible]	[illegible]	[illegible]
32	Sligo,	[illegible]	[illegible]	[illegible]	[illegible]	[illegible]	[illegible]	[illegible]	[illegible]	[illegible]	[illegible]	[illegible]	[illegible]	[illegible]	[illegible]	[illegible]	[illegible]	[illegible]	[illegible]	[illegible]	[illegible]

IRELAND.—DEATHS at different AGES registered in the Year 1891—in the PROVINCES and COUNTIES.—FEMALES.

No.	PROVINCES AND COUNTIES.	Births	Total Deaths	Under 1 year	1	2	3	4	Under 5 years	5-	10-	15-	20-	25-	35-	45-	55-	65-	75-	85-	95 and upwards
	IRELAND,	[illegible]	[illegible]	[illegible]	[illegible]	[illegible]	[illegible]	[illegible]	[illegible]	[illegible]	[illegible]	[illegible]	[illegible]	[illegible]	[illegible]	[illegible]	[illegible]	[illegible]	[illegible]	[illegible]	[illegible]
No.	PROVINCES.																				
I.	LEINSTER,	[illegible]	[illegible]	[illegible]	[illegible]	[illegible]	[illegible]	[illegible]	[illegible]	[illegible]	[illegible]	[illegible]	[illegible]	[illegible]	[illegible]	[illegible]	[illegible]	[illegible]	[illegible]	[illegible]	[illegible]
II.	MUNSTER,	[illegible]	[illegible]	[illegible]	[illegible]	[illegible]	[illegible]	[illegible]	[illegible]	[illegible]	[illegible]	[illegible]	[illegible]	[illegible]	[illegible]	[illegible]	[illegible]	[illegible]	[illegible]	[illegible]	[illegible]
III.	ULSTER,	[illegible]	[illegible]	[illegible]	[illegible]	[illegible]	[illegible]	[illegible]	[illegible]	[illegible]	[illegible]	[illegible]	[illegible]	[illegible]	[illegible]	[illegible]	[illegible]	[illegible]	[illegible]	[illegible]	[illegible]
IV.	CONNAUGHT,	[illegible]	[illegible]	[illegible]	[illegible]	[illegible]	[illegible]	[illegible]	[illegible]	[illegible]	[illegible]	[illegible]	[illegible]	[illegible]	[illegible]	[illegible]	[illegible]	[illegible]	[illegible]	[illegible]	[illegible]
	I.—LEINSTER.																				
1	Carlow,	[illegible]	[illegible]	[illegible]	[illegible]	[illegible]	[illegible]	[illegible]	[illegible]	[illegible]	[illegible]	[illegible]	[illegible]	[illegible]	[illegible]	[illegible]	[illegible]	[illegible]	[illegible]	[illegible]	[illegible]
2	Dublin,	[illegible]	[illegible]	[illegible]	[illegible]	[illegible]	[illegible]	[illegible]	[illegible]	[illegible]	[illegible]	[illegible]	[illegible]	[illegible]	[illegible]	[illegible]	[illegible]	[illegible]	[illegible]	[illegible]	[illegible]
3	Kildare,	[illegible]	[illegible]	[illegible]	[illegible]	[illegible]	[illegible]	[illegible]	[illegible]	[illegible]	[illegible]	[illegible]	[illegible]	[illegible]	[illegible]	[illegible]	[illegible]	[illegible]	[illegible]	[illegible]	[illegible]
4	Kilkenny,	[illegible]	[illegible]	[illegible]	[illegible]	[illegible]	[illegible]	[illegible]	[illegible]	[illegible]	[illegible]	[illegible]	[illegible]	[illegible]	[illegible]	[illegible]	[illegible]	[illegible]	[illegible]	[illegible]	[illegible]
5	King's,	[illegible]	[illegible]	[illegible]	[illegible]	[illegible]	[illegible]	[illegible]	[illegible]	[illegible]	[illegible]	[illegible]	[illegible]	[illegible]	[illegible]	[illegible]	[illegible]	[illegible]	[illegible]	[illegible]	[illegible]
6	Longford,	[illegible]	[illegible]	[illegible]	[illegible]	[illegible]	[illegible]	[illegible]	[illegible]	[illegible]	[illegible]	[illegible]	[illegible]	[illegible]	[illegible]	[illegible]	[illegible]	[illegible]	[illegible]	[illegible]	[illegible]
7	Louth, and Co. of the Town of Drogheda,	[illegible]	[illegible]	[illegible]	[illegible]	[illegible]	[illegible]	[illegible]	[illegible]	[illegible]	[illegible]	[illegible]	[illegible]	[illegible]	[illegible]	[illegible]	[illegible]	[illegible]	[illegible]	[illegible]	[illegible]
8	Meath,	[illegible]	[illegible]	[illegible]	[illegible]	[illegible]	[illegible]	[illegible]	[illegible]	[illegible]	[illegible]	[illegible]	[illegible]	[illegible]	[illegible]	[illegible]	[illegible]	[illegible]	[illegible]	[illegible]	[illegible]
9	Queen's,	[illegible]	[illegible]	[illegible]	[illegible]	[illegible]	[illegible]	[illegible]	[illegible]	[illegible]	[illegible]	[illegible]	[illegible]	[illegible]	[illegible]	[illegible]	[illegible]	[illegible]	[illegible]	[illegible]	[illegible]
10	Westmeath,	[illegible]	[illegible]	[illegible]	[illegible]	[illegible]	[illegible]	[illegible]	[illegible]	[illegible]	[illegible]	[illegible]	[illegible]	[illegible]	[illegible]	[illegible]	[illegible]	[illegible]	[illegible]	[illegible]	[illegible]
11	Wexford,	[illegible]	[illegible]	[illegible]	[illegible]	[illegible]	[illegible]	[illegible]	[illegible]	[illegible]	[illegible]	[illegible]	[illegible]	[illegible]	[illegible]	[illegible]	[illegible]	[illegible]	[illegible]	[illegible]	[illegible]
12	Wicklow,	[illegible]	[illegible]	[illegible]	[illegible]	[illegible]	[illegible]	[illegible]	[illegible]	[illegible]	[illegible]	[illegible]	[illegible]	[illegible]	[illegible]	[illegible]	[illegible]	[illegible]	[illegible]	[illegible]	[illegible]
	II.—MUNSTER.																				
13	Clare,	[illegible]	[illegible]	[illegible]	[illegible]	[illegible]	[illegible]	[illegible]	[illegible]	[illegible]	[illegible]	[illegible]	[illegible]	[illegible]	[illegible]	[illegible]	[illegible]	[illegible]	[illegible]	[illegible]	[illegible]
14	Cork,	[illegible]	[illegible]	[illegible]	[illegible]	[illegible]	[illegible]	[illegible]	[illegible]	[illegible]	[illegible]	[illegible]	[illegible]	[illegible]	[illegible]	[illegible]	[illegible]	[illegible]	[illegible]	[illegible]	[illegible]
15	Kerry,	[illegible]	[illegible]	[illegible]	[illegible]	[illegible]	[illegible]	[illegible]	[illegible]	[illegible]	[illegible]	[illegible]	[illegible]	[illegible]	[illegible]	[illegible]	[illegible]	[illegible]	[illegible]	[illegible]	[illegible]
16	Limerick,	[illegible]	[illegible]	[illegible]	[illegible]	[illegible]	[illegible]	[illegible]	[illegible]	[illegible]	[illegible]	[illegible]	[illegible]	[illegible]	[illegible]	[illegible]	[illegible]	[illegible]	[illegible]	[illegible]	[illegible]
17	Tipperary,	[illegible]	[illegible]	[illegible]	[illegible]	[illegible]	[illegible]	[illegible]	[illegible]	[illegible]	[illegible]	[illegible]	[illegible]	[illegible]	[illegible]	[illegible]	[illegible]	[illegible]	[illegible]	[illegible]	[illegible]
18	Waterford,	[illegible]	[illegible]	[illegible]	[illegible]	[illegible]	[illegible]	[illegible]	[illegible]	[illegible]	[illegible]	[illegible]	[illegible]	[illegible]	[illegible]	[illegible]	[illegible]	[illegible]	[illegible]	[illegible]	[illegible]
	III.—ULSTER.																				
19	Antrim,	[illegible]	[illegible]	[illegible]	[illegible]	[illegible]	[illegible]	[illegible]	[illegible]	[illegible]	[illegible]	[illegible]	[illegible]	[illegible]	[illegible]	[illegible]	[illegible]	[illegible]	[illegible]	[illegible]	[illegible]
20	Armagh,	[illegible]	[illegible]	[illegible]	[illegible]	[illegible]	[illegible]	[illegible]	[illegible]	[illegible]	[illegible]	[illegible]	[illegible]	[illegible]	[illegible]	[illegible]	[illegible]	[illegible]	[illegible]	[illegible]	[illegible]
21	Cavan,	[illegible]	[illegible]	[illegible]	[illegible]	[illegible]	[illegible]	[illegible]	[illegible]	[illegible]	[illegible]	[illegible]	[illegible]	[illegible]	[illegible]	[illegible]	[illegible]	[illegible]	[illegible]	[illegible]	[illegible]
22	Donegal,	[illegible]	[illegible]	[illegible]	[illegible]	[illegible]	[illegible]	[illegible]	[illegible]	[illegible]	[illegible]	[illegible]	[illegible]	[illegible]	[illegible]	[illegible]	[illegible]	[illegible]	[illegible]	[illegible]	[illegible]
23	Down,	[illegible]	[illegible]	[illegible]	[illegible]	[illegible]	[illegible]	[illegible]	[illegible]	[illegible]	[illegible]	[illegible]	[illegible]	[illegible]	[illegible]	[illegible]	[illegible]	[illegible]	[illegible]	[illegible]	[illegible]
24	Fermanagh,	[illegible]	[illegible]	[illegible]	[illegible]	[illegible]	[illegible]	[illegible]	[illegible]	[illegible]	[illegible]	[illegible]	[illegible]	[illegible]	[illegible]	[illegible]	[illegible]	[illegible]	[illegible]	[illegible]	[illegible]
25	Londonderry,	[illegible]	[illegible]	[illegible]	[illegible]	[illegible]	[illegible]	[illegible]	[illegible]	[illegible]	[illegible]	[illegible]	[illegible]	[illegible]	[illegible]	[illegible]	[illegible]	[illegible]	[illegible]	[illegible]	[illegible]
26	Monaghan,	[illegible]	[illegible]	[illegible]	[illegible]	[illegible]	[illegible]	[illegible]	[illegible]	[illegible]	[illegible]	[illegible]	[illegible]	[illegible]	[illegible]	[illegible]	[illegible]	[illegible]	[illegible]	[illegible]	[illegible]
27	Tyrone,	[illegible]	[illegible]	[illegible]	[illegible]	[illegible]	[illegible]	[illegible]	[illegible]	[illegible]	[illegible]	[illegible]	[illegible]	[illegible]	[illegible]	[illegible]	[illegible]	[illegible]	[illegible]	[illegible]	[illegible]
	IV.—CONNAUGHT.																				
28	Galway,	[illegible]	[illegible]	[illegible]	[illegible]	[illegible]	[illegible]	[illegible]	[illegible]	[illegible]	[illegible]	[illegible]	[illegible]	[illegible]	[illegible]	[illegible]	[illegible]	[illegible]	[illegible]	[illegible]	[illegible]
29	Leitrim,	[illegible]	[illegible]	[illegible]	[illegible]	[illegible]	[illegible]	[illegible]	[illegible]	[illegible]	[illegible]	[illegible]	[illegible]	[illegible]	[illegible]	[illegible]	[illegible]	[illegible]	[illegible]	[illegible]	[illegible]
30	Mayo,	[illegible]	[illegible]	[illegible]	[illegible]	[illegible]	[illegible]	[illegible]	[illegible]	[illegible]	[illegible]	[illegible]	[illegible]	[illegible]	[illegible]	[illegible]	[illegible]	[illegible]	[illegible]	[illegible]	[illegible]
31	Roscommon,	[illegible]	[illegible]	[illegible]	[illegible]	[illegible]	[illegible]	[illegible]	[illegible]	[illegible]	[illegible]	[illegible]	[illegible]	[illegible]	[illegible]	[illegible]	[illegible]	[illegible]	[illegible]	[illegible]	[illegible]
32	Sligo,	[illegible]	[illegible]	[illegible]	[illegible]	[illegible]	[illegible]	[illegible]	[illegible]	[illegible]	[illegible]	[illegible]	[illegible]	[illegible]	[illegible]	[illegible]	[illegible]	[illegible]	[illegible]	[illegible]	[illegible]

IRELAND.—[illegible] at different Ages registered in the year 1891—in the Superintendent Registrars' Districts in each County.—Males.

I.—Province of Leinster.

No.	Superintendent Registrars' Districts and Parts of Districts	Total Births	Total Deaths	Under 1 year	1	2	3	4	Under 5	5-	10-	15-	20-	25-	35-	45-	55-	65-	75-	85-	[illegible]
	1. Carlow Co.																				
1	[illegible], part of	[illegible]	[illegible]	[illegible]	[illegible]	[illegible]	[illegible]	[illegible]	[illegible]	[illegible]	[illegible]	[illegible]	[illegible]	[illegible]	[illegible]	[illegible]	[illegible]	[illegible]	[illegible]	[illegible]	[illegible]
2	[illegible], do.	[illegible]	[illegible]	[illegible]	[illegible]	[illegible]	[illegible]	[illegible]	[illegible]	[illegible]	[illegible]	[illegible]	[illegible]	[illegible]	[illegible]	[illegible]	[illegible]	[illegible]	[illegible]	[illegible]	[illegible]
3	[illegible], do.	[illegible]	[illegible]	[illegible]	[illegible]	[illegible]	[illegible]	[illegible]	[illegible]	[illegible]	[illegible]	[illegible]	[illegible]	[illegible]	[illegible]	[illegible]	[illegible]	[illegible]	[illegible]	[illegible]	[illegible]
4	New Ross, do.	[illegible]	[illegible]	[illegible]	[illegible]	[illegible]	[illegible]	[illegible]	[illegible]	[illegible]	[illegible]	[illegible]	[illegible]	[illegible]	[illegible]	[illegible]	[illegible]	[illegible]	[illegible]	[illegible]	[illegible]
5	[illegible], do.	[illegible]	[illegible]	[illegible]	[illegible]	[illegible]	[illegible]	[illegible]	[illegible]	[illegible]	[illegible]	[illegible]	[illegible]	[illegible]	[illegible]	[illegible]	[illegible]	[illegible]	[illegible]	[illegible]	[illegible]
	2. Dublin Co.																				
6	[illegible]	[illegible]	[illegible]	[illegible]	[illegible]	[illegible]	[illegible]	[illegible]	[illegible]	[illegible]	[illegible]	[illegible]	[illegible]	[illegible]	[illegible]	[illegible]	[illegible]	[illegible]	[illegible]	[illegible]	[illegible]
7	[illegible], part of	[illegible]	[illegible]	[illegible]	[illegible]	[illegible]	[illegible]	[illegible]	[illegible]	[illegible]	[illegible]	[illegible]	[illegible]	[illegible]	[illegible]	[illegible]	[illegible]	[illegible]	[illegible]	[illegible]	[illegible]
8	Dublin, North	[illegible]	[illegible]	[illegible]	[illegible]	[illegible]	[illegible]	[illegible]	[illegible]	[illegible]	[illegible]	[illegible]	[illegible]	[illegible]	[illegible]	[illegible]	[illegible]	[illegible]	[illegible]	[illegible]	[illegible]
9	Dublin, South	[illegible]	[illegible]	[illegible]	[illegible]	[illegible]	[illegible]	[illegible]	[illegible]	[illegible]	[illegible]	[illegible]	[illegible]	[illegible]	[illegible]	[illegible]	[illegible]	[illegible]	[illegible]	[illegible]	[illegible]
10	[illegible], part of	[illegible]	[illegible]	[illegible]	[illegible]	[illegible]	[illegible]	[illegible]	[illegible]	[illegible]	[illegible]	[illegible]	[illegible]	[illegible]	[illegible]	[illegible]	[illegible]	[illegible]	[illegible]	[illegible]	[illegible]
11	[illegible], do.	[illegible]	[illegible]	[illegible]	[illegible]	[illegible]	[illegible]	[illegible]	[illegible]	[illegible]	[illegible]	[illegible]	[illegible]	[illegible]	[illegible]	[illegible]	[illegible]	[illegible]	[illegible]	[illegible]	[illegible]
	3. Kildare Co.																				
12	Athy, part of	[illegible]	[illegible]	[illegible]	[illegible]	[illegible]	[illegible]	[illegible]	[illegible]	[illegible]	[illegible]	[illegible]	[illegible]	[illegible]	[illegible]	[illegible]	[illegible]	[illegible]	[illegible]	[illegible]	[illegible]
13	[illegible], do.	[illegible]	[illegible]	[illegible]	[illegible]	[illegible]	[illegible]	[illegible]	[illegible]	[illegible]	[illegible]	[illegible]	[illegible]	[illegible]	[illegible]	[illegible]	[illegible]	[illegible]	[illegible]	[illegible]	[illegible]
14	[illegible], do.	[illegible]	[illegible]	[illegible]	[illegible]	[illegible]	[illegible]	[illegible]	[illegible]	[illegible]	[illegible]	[illegible]	[illegible]	[illegible]	[illegible]	[illegible]	[illegible]	[illegible]	[illegible]	[illegible]	[illegible]
15	[illegible], do.	[illegible]	[illegible]	[illegible]	[illegible]	[illegible]	[illegible]	[illegible]	[illegible]	[illegible]	[illegible]	[illegible]	[illegible]	[illegible]	[illegible]	[illegible]	[illegible]	[illegible]	[illegible]	[illegible]	[illegible]
16	Naas, do.	[illegible]	[illegible]	[illegible]	[illegible]	[illegible]	[illegible]	[illegible]	[illegible]	[illegible]	[illegible]	[illegible]	[illegible]	[illegible]	[illegible]	[illegible]	[illegible]	[illegible]	[illegible]	[illegible]	[illegible]
	4. Kilkenny Co.																				
17	Callan, part of	[illegible]	[illegible]	[illegible]	[illegible]	[illegible]	[illegible]	[illegible]	[illegible]	[illegible]	[illegible]	[illegible]	[illegible]	[illegible]	[illegible]	[illegible]	[illegible]	[illegible]	[illegible]	[illegible]	[illegible]
18	Carrick on Suir, do.	[illegible]	[illegible]	[illegible]	[illegible]	[illegible]	[illegible]	[illegible]	[illegible]	[illegible]	[illegible]	[illegible]	[illegible]	[illegible]	[illegible]	[illegible]	[illegible]	[illegible]	[illegible]	[illegible]	[illegible]
19	Castlecomer	[illegible]	[illegible]	[illegible]	[illegible]	[illegible]	[illegible]	[illegible]	[illegible]	[illegible]	[illegible]	[illegible]	[illegible]	[illegible]	[illegible]	[illegible]	[illegible]	[illegible]	[illegible]	[illegible]	[illegible]
20	Kilkenny	[illegible]	[illegible]	[illegible]	[illegible]	[illegible]	[illegible]	[illegible]	[illegible]	[illegible]	[illegible]	[illegible]	[illegible]	[illegible]	[illegible]	[illegible]	[illegible]	[illegible]	[illegible]	[illegible]	[illegible]
21	New Ross, part of	[illegible]	[illegible]	[illegible]	[illegible]	[illegible]	[illegible]	[illegible]	[illegible]	[illegible]	[illegible]	[illegible]	[illegible]	[illegible]	[illegible]	[illegible]	[illegible]	[illegible]	[illegible]	[illegible]	[illegible]
22	[illegible]	[illegible]	[illegible]	[illegible]	[illegible]	[illegible]	[illegible]	[illegible]	[illegible]	[illegible]	[illegible]	[illegible]	[illegible]	[illegible]	[illegible]	[illegible]	[illegible]	[illegible]	[illegible]	[illegible]	[illegible]
23	[illegible], part of	[illegible]	[illegible]	[illegible]	[illegible]	[illegible]	[illegible]	[illegible]	[illegible]	[illegible]	[illegible]	[illegible]	[illegible]	[illegible]	[illegible]	[illegible]	[illegible]	[illegible]	[illegible]	[illegible]	[illegible]
24	Waterford, do.	[illegible]	[illegible]	[illegible]	[illegible]	[illegible]	[illegible]	[illegible]	[illegible]	[illegible]	[illegible]	[illegible]	[illegible]	[illegible]	[illegible]	[illegible]	[illegible]	[illegible]	[illegible]	[illegible]	[illegible]
	5. King's Co.																				
25	[illegible], part of	[illegible]	[illegible]	[illegible]	[illegible]	[illegible]	[illegible]	[illegible]	[illegible]	[illegible]	[illegible]	[illegible]	[illegible]	[illegible]	[illegible]	[illegible]	[illegible]	[illegible]	[illegible]	[illegible]	[illegible]
26	[illegible], do.	[illegible]	[illegible]	[illegible]	[illegible]	[illegible]	[illegible]	[illegible]	[illegible]	[illegible]	[illegible]	[illegible]	[illegible]	[illegible]	[illegible]	[illegible]	[illegible]	[illegible]	[illegible]	[illegible]	[illegible]
27	[illegible], do.	[illegible]	[illegible]	[illegible]	[illegible]	[illegible]	[illegible]	[illegible]	[illegible]	[illegible]	[illegible]	[illegible]	[illegible]	[illegible]	[illegible]	[illegible]	[illegible]	[illegible]	[illegible]	[illegible]	[illegible]
28	[illegible], do.	[illegible]	[illegible]	[illegible]	[illegible]	[illegible]	[illegible]	[illegible]	[illegible]	[illegible]	[illegible]	[illegible]	[illegible]	[illegible]	[illegible]	[illegible]	[illegible]	[illegible]	[illegible]	[illegible]	[illegible]
29	Tullamore, do.	[illegible]	[illegible]	[illegible]	[illegible]	[illegible]	[illegible]	[illegible]	[illegible]	[illegible]	[illegible]	[illegible]	[illegible]	[illegible]	[illegible]	[illegible]	[illegible]	[illegible]	[illegible]	[illegible]	[illegible]
	6. Longford Co.																				
30	Ballymahon, part of	[illegible]	[illegible]	[illegible]	[illegible]	[illegible]	[illegible]	[illegible]	[illegible]	[illegible]	[illegible]	[illegible]	[illegible]	[illegible]	[illegible]	[illegible]	[illegible]	[illegible]	[illegible]	[illegible]	[illegible]
31	Granard, do.	[illegible]	[illegible]	[illegible]	[illegible]	[illegible]	[illegible]	[illegible]	[illegible]	[illegible]	[illegible]	[illegible]	[illegible]	[illegible]	[illegible]	[illegible]	[illegible]	[illegible]	[illegible]	[illegible]	[illegible]
32	Longford	[illegible]	[illegible]	[illegible]	[illegible]	[illegible]	[illegible]	[illegible]	[illegible]	[illegible]	[illegible]	[illegible]	[illegible]	[illegible]	[illegible]	[illegible]	[illegible]	[illegible]	[illegible]	[illegible]	[illegible]
	7. Louth Co. and Co. of Town of Drogheda.																				
33	Ardee, part of	[illegible]	[illegible]	[illegible]	[illegible]	[illegible]	[illegible]	[illegible]	[illegible]	[illegible]	[illegible]	[illegible]	[illegible]	[illegible]	[illegible]	[illegible]	[illegible]	[illegible]	[illegible]	[illegible]	[illegible]
34	Drogheda, do.	[illegible]	[illegible]	[illegible]	[illegible]	[illegible]	[illegible]	[illegible]	[illegible]	[illegible]	[illegible]	[illegible]	[illegible]	[illegible]	[illegible]	[illegible]	[illegible]	[illegible]	[illegible]	[illegible]	[illegible]
35	Dundalk, do.	[illegible]	[illegible]	[illegible]	[illegible]	[illegible]	[illegible]	[illegible]	[illegible]	[illegible]	[illegible]	[illegible]	[illegible]	[illegible]	[illegible]	[illegible]	[illegible]	[illegible]	[illegible]	[illegible]	[illegible]
	8. Meath Co.																				
36	Ardee, part of	[illegible]	[illegible]	[illegible]	[illegible]	[illegible]	[illegible]	[illegible]	[illegible]	[illegible]	[illegible]	[illegible]	[illegible]	[illegible]	[illegible]	[illegible]	[illegible]	[illegible]	[illegible]	[illegible]	[illegible]
37	[illegible], do.	[illegible]	[illegible]	[illegible]	[illegible]	[illegible]	[illegible]	[illegible]	[illegible]	[illegible]	[illegible]	[illegible]	[illegible]	[illegible]	[illegible]	[illegible]	[illegible]	[illegible]	[illegible]	[illegible]	[illegible]
38	Drogheda, do.	[illegible]	[illegible]	[illegible]	[illegible]	[illegible]	[illegible]	[illegible]	[illegible]	[illegible]	[illegible]	[illegible]	[illegible]	[illegible]	[illegible]	[illegible]	[illegible]	[illegible]	[illegible]	[illegible]	[illegible]
39	Dunshaughlin, do.	[illegible]	[illegible]	[illegible]	[illegible]	[illegible]	[illegible]	[illegible]	[illegible]	[illegible]	[illegible]	[illegible]	[illegible]	[illegible]	[illegible]	[illegible]	[illegible]	[illegible]	[illegible]	[illegible]	[illegible]
40	[illegible], do.	[illegible]	[illegible]	[illegible]	[illegible]	[illegible]	[illegible]	[illegible]	[illegible]	[illegible]	[illegible]	[illegible]	[illegible]	[illegible]	[illegible]	[illegible]	[illegible]	[illegible]	[illegible]	[illegible]	[illegible]
41	Kells, do.	[illegible]	[illegible]	[illegible]	[illegible]	[illegible]	[illegible]	[illegible]	[illegible]	[illegible]	[illegible]	[illegible]	[illegible]	[illegible]	[illegible]	[illegible]	[illegible]	[illegible]	[illegible]	[illegible]	[illegible]
42	Navan	[illegible]	[illegible]	[illegible]	[illegible]	[illegible]	[illegible]	[illegible]	[illegible]	[illegible]	[illegible]	[illegible]	[illegible]	[illegible]	[illegible]	[illegible]	[illegible]	[illegible]	[illegible]	[illegible]	[illegible]
43	Oldcastle, part of	[illegible]	[illegible]	[illegible]	[illegible]	[illegible]	[illegible]	[illegible]	[illegible]	[illegible]	[illegible]	[illegible]	[illegible]	[illegible]	[illegible]	[illegible]	[illegible]	[illegible]	[illegible]	[illegible]	[illegible]
44	Trim	[illegible]	[illegible]	[illegible]	[illegible]	[illegible]	[illegible]	[illegible]	[illegible]	[illegible]	[illegible]	[illegible]	[illegible]	[illegible]	[illegible]	[illegible]	[illegible]	[illegible]	[illegible]	[illegible]	[illegible]

IRELAND.—Females at different Ages registered in Ireland in the year 1891—in the Superintendent Registrars' Districts and Parts of Districts.—Females.

I.—Province of Leinster.

No.	Superintendent Registrars' Districts and Parts of Districts	[illegible]	[illegible]	Under 1 Year	1	2	3	4	Total under 5 Years	5-	10-	15-	20-	25-	35-	45-	55-	65-	75-	85-	[illegible]
	1. Carlow Co.																				
1	Baltinglass, part of,	[illegible]	[illegible]	[illegible]	[illegible]	[illegible]	[illegible]	[illegible]	[illegible]	[illegible]	[illegible]	[illegible]	[illegible]	[illegible]	[illegible]	[illegible]	[illegible]	[illegible]	[illegible]	[illegible]	[illegible]
2	Carlow, do.	[illegible]	[illegible]	[illegible]	[illegible]	[illegible]	[illegible]	[illegible]	[illegible]	[illegible]	[illegible]	[illegible]	[illegible]	[illegible]	[illegible]	[illegible]	[illegible]	[illegible]	[illegible]	[illegible]	[illegible]
3	[illegible], do.	[illegible]	[illegible]	[illegible]	[illegible]	[illegible]	[illegible]	[illegible]	[illegible]	[illegible]	[illegible]	[illegible]	[illegible]	[illegible]	[illegible]	[illegible]	[illegible]	[illegible]	[illegible]	[illegible]	[illegible]
4	New Ross, do.	[illegible]	[illegible]	[illegible]	[illegible]	[illegible]	[illegible]	[illegible]	[illegible]	[illegible]	[illegible]	[illegible]	[illegible]	[illegible]	[illegible]	[illegible]	[illegible]	[illegible]	[illegible]	[illegible]	[illegible]
5	Shillelagh, do.	[illegible]	[illegible]	[illegible]	[illegible]	[illegible]	[illegible]	[illegible]	[illegible]	[illegible]	[illegible]	[illegible]	[illegible]	[illegible]	[illegible]	[illegible]	[illegible]	[illegible]	[illegible]	[illegible]	[illegible]
	2. Dublin Co.																				
6	Balrothery,	[illegible]	[illegible]	[illegible]	[illegible]	[illegible]	[illegible]	[illegible]	[illegible]	[illegible]	[illegible]	[illegible]	[illegible]	[illegible]	[illegible]	[illegible]	[illegible]	[illegible]	[illegible]	[illegible]	[illegible]
7	Celbridge, part of,	[illegible]	[illegible]	[illegible]	[illegible]	[illegible]	[illegible]	[illegible]	[illegible]	[illegible]	[illegible]	[illegible]	[illegible]	[illegible]	[illegible]	[illegible]	[illegible]	[illegible]	[illegible]	[illegible]	[illegible]
8	Dublin, North,	[illegible]	[illegible]	[illegible]	[illegible]	[illegible]	[illegible]	[illegible]	[illegible]	[illegible]	[illegible]	[illegible]	[illegible]	[illegible]	[illegible]	[illegible]	[illegible]	[illegible]	[illegible]	[illegible]	[illegible]
9	Dublin, South,	[illegible]	[illegible]	[illegible]	[illegible]	[illegible]	[illegible]	[illegible]	[illegible]	[illegible]	[illegible]	[illegible]	[illegible]	[illegible]	[illegible]	[illegible]	[illegible]	[illegible]	[illegible]	[illegible]	[illegible]
10	[illegible], part of,	[illegible]	[illegible]	[illegible]	[illegible]	[illegible]	[illegible]	[illegible]	[illegible]	[illegible]	[illegible]	[illegible]	[illegible]	[illegible]	[illegible]	[illegible]	[illegible]	[illegible]	[illegible]	[illegible]	[illegible]
11	Rathdown, do.	[illegible]	[illegible]	[illegible]	[illegible]	[illegible]	[illegible]	[illegible]	[illegible]	[illegible]	[illegible]	[illegible]	[illegible]	[illegible]	[illegible]	[illegible]	[illegible]	[illegible]	[illegible]	[illegible]	[illegible]
	3. Kildare Co.																				
12	Athy, part of,	[illegible]	[illegible]	[illegible]	[illegible]	[illegible]	[illegible]	[illegible]	[illegible]	[illegible]	[illegible]	[illegible]	[illegible]	[illegible]	[illegible]	[illegible]	[illegible]	[illegible]	[illegible]	[illegible]	[illegible]
13	Baltinglass, do.	[illegible]	[illegible]	[illegible]	[illegible]	[illegible]	[illegible]	[illegible]	[illegible]	[illegible]	[illegible]	[illegible]	[illegible]	[illegible]	[illegible]	[illegible]	[illegible]	[illegible]	[illegible]	[illegible]	[illegible]
14	Celbridge, do.	[illegible]	[illegible]	[illegible]	[illegible]	[illegible]	[illegible]	[illegible]	[illegible]	[illegible]	[illegible]	[illegible]	[illegible]	[illegible]	[illegible]	[illegible]	[illegible]	[illegible]	[illegible]	[illegible]	[illegible]
15	Edenderry, do.	[illegible]	[illegible]	[illegible]	[illegible]	[illegible]	[illegible]	[illegible]	[illegible]	[illegible]	[illegible]	[illegible]	[illegible]	[illegible]	[illegible]	[illegible]	[illegible]	[illegible]	[illegible]	[illegible]	[illegible]
16	Naas, do.	[illegible]	[illegible]	[illegible]	[illegible]	[illegible]	[illegible]	[illegible]	[illegible]	[illegible]	[illegible]	[illegible]	[illegible]	[illegible]	[illegible]	[illegible]	[illegible]	[illegible]	[illegible]	[illegible]	[illegible]
	4. Kilkenny Co.																				
17	Callan, part of,	[illegible]	[illegible]	[illegible]	[illegible]	[illegible]	[illegible]	[illegible]	[illegible]	[illegible]	[illegible]	[illegible]	[illegible]	[illegible]	[illegible]	[illegible]	[illegible]	[illegible]	[illegible]	[illegible]	[illegible]
18	Carrick-on-Suir, part of,	[illegible]	[illegible]	[illegible]	[illegible]	[illegible]	[illegible]	[illegible]	[illegible]	[illegible]	[illegible]	[illegible]	[illegible]	[illegible]	[illegible]	[illegible]	[illegible]	[illegible]	[illegible]	[illegible]	[illegible]
19	Castlecomer,	[illegible]	[illegible]	[illegible]	[illegible]	[illegible]	[illegible]	[illegible]	[illegible]	[illegible]	[illegible]	[illegible]	[illegible]	[illegible]	[illegible]	[illegible]	[illegible]	[illegible]	[illegible]	[illegible]	[illegible]
20	Kilkenny,	[illegible]	[illegible]	[illegible]	[illegible]	[illegible]	[illegible]	[illegible]	[illegible]	[illegible]	[illegible]	[illegible]	[illegible]	[illegible]	[illegible]	[illegible]	[illegible]	[illegible]	[illegible]	[illegible]	[illegible]
21	New Ross, part of,	[illegible]	[illegible]	[illegible]	[illegible]	[illegible]	[illegible]	[illegible]	[illegible]	[illegible]	[illegible]	[illegible]	[illegible]	[illegible]	[illegible]	[illegible]	[illegible]	[illegible]	[illegible]	[illegible]	[illegible]
22	Thomastown,	[illegible]	[illegible]	[illegible]	[illegible]	[illegible]	[illegible]	[illegible]	[illegible]	[illegible]	[illegible]	[illegible]	[illegible]	[illegible]	[illegible]	[illegible]	[illegible]	[illegible]	[illegible]	[illegible]	[illegible]
23	Urlingford, part of,	[illegible]	[illegible]	[illegible]	[illegible]	[illegible]	[illegible]	[illegible]	[illegible]	[illegible]	[illegible]	[illegible]	[illegible]	[illegible]	[illegible]	[illegible]	[illegible]	[illegible]	[illegible]	[illegible]	[illegible]
24	Waterford, do.	[illegible]	[illegible]	[illegible]	[illegible]	[illegible]	[illegible]	[illegible]	[illegible]	[illegible]	[illegible]	[illegible]	[illegible]	[illegible]	[illegible]	[illegible]	[illegible]	[illegible]	[illegible]	[illegible]	[illegible]
	5. King's Co.																				
25	Edenderry, part of,	[illegible]	[illegible]	[illegible]	[illegible]	[illegible]	[illegible]	[illegible]	[illegible]	[illegible]	[illegible]	[illegible]	[illegible]	[illegible]	[illegible]	[illegible]	[illegible]	[illegible]	[illegible]	[illegible]	[illegible]
26	Mountmellick, do.	[illegible]	[illegible]	[illegible]	[illegible]	[illegible]	[illegible]	[illegible]	[illegible]	[illegible]	[illegible]	[illegible]	[illegible]	[illegible]	[illegible]	[illegible]	[illegible]	[illegible]	[illegible]	[illegible]	[illegible]
27	Parsonstown, do.	[illegible]	[illegible]	[illegible]	[illegible]	[illegible]	[illegible]	[illegible]	[illegible]	[illegible]	[illegible]	[illegible]	[illegible]	[illegible]	[illegible]	[illegible]	[illegible]	[illegible]	[illegible]	[illegible]	[illegible]
28	Roscrea, do.	[illegible]	[illegible]	[illegible]	[illegible]	[illegible]	[illegible]	[illegible]	[illegible]	[illegible]	[illegible]	[illegible]	[illegible]	[illegible]	[illegible]	[illegible]	[illegible]	[illegible]	[illegible]	[illegible]	[illegible]
29	Tullamore, do.	[illegible]	[illegible]	[illegible]	[illegible]	[illegible]	[illegible]	[illegible]	[illegible]	[illegible]	[illegible]	[illegible]	[illegible]	[illegible]	[illegible]	[illegible]	[illegible]	[illegible]	[illegible]	[illegible]	[illegible]
	6. Longford Co.																				
30	Ballymahon, part of,	[illegible]	[illegible]	[illegible]	[illegible]	[illegible]	[illegible]	[illegible]	[illegible]	[illegible]	[illegible]	[illegible]	[illegible]	[illegible]	[illegible]	[illegible]	[illegible]	[illegible]	[illegible]	[illegible]	[illegible]
31	Granard, do.	[illegible]	[illegible]	[illegible]	[illegible]	[illegible]	[illegible]	[illegible]	[illegible]	[illegible]	[illegible]	[illegible]	[illegible]	[illegible]	[illegible]	[illegible]	[illegible]	[illegible]	[illegible]	[illegible]	[illegible]
32	Longford,	[illegible]	[illegible]	[illegible]	[illegible]	[illegible]	[illegible]	[illegible]	[illegible]	[illegible]	[illegible]	[illegible]	[illegible]	[illegible]	[illegible]	[illegible]	[illegible]	[illegible]	[illegible]	[illegible]	[illegible]
	7. Louth Co. & Co. of Town of Drogheda.																				
33	Ardee, part of,	[illegible]	[illegible]	[illegible]	[illegible]	[illegible]	[illegible]	[illegible]	[illegible]	[illegible]	[illegible]	[illegible]	[illegible]	[illegible]	[illegible]	[illegible]	[illegible]	[illegible]	[illegible]	[illegible]	[illegible]
34	Dundalk, do.	[illegible]	[illegible]	[illegible]	[illegible]	[illegible]	[illegible]	[illegible]	[illegible]	[illegible]	[illegible]	[illegible]	[illegible]	[illegible]	[illegible]	[illegible]	[illegible]	[illegible]	[illegible]	[illegible]	[illegible]
35	Drogheda, do.	[illegible]	[illegible]	[illegible]	[illegible]	[illegible]	[illegible]	[illegible]	[illegible]	[illegible]	[illegible]	[illegible]	[illegible]	[illegible]	[illegible]	[illegible]	[illegible]	[illegible]	[illegible]	[illegible]	[illegible]
	8. Meath Co.																				
36	Ardee, part of,	[illegible]	[illegible]	[illegible]	[illegible]	[illegible]	[illegible]	[illegible]	[illegible]	[illegible]	[illegible]	[illegible]	[illegible]	[illegible]	[illegible]	[illegible]	[illegible]	[illegible]	[illegible]	[illegible]	[illegible]
37	[illegible], do.	[illegible]	[illegible]	[illegible]	[illegible]	[illegible]	[illegible]	[illegible]	[illegible]	[illegible]	[illegible]	[illegible]	[illegible]	[illegible]	[illegible]	[illegible]	[illegible]	[illegible]	[illegible]	[illegible]	[illegible]
38	[illegible], do.	[illegible]	[illegible]	[illegible]	[illegible]	[illegible]	[illegible]	[illegible]	[illegible]	[illegible]	[illegible]	[illegible]	[illegible]	[illegible]	[illegible]	[illegible]	[illegible]	[illegible]	[illegible]	[illegible]	[illegible]
39	Dunshaughlin, do.	[illegible]	[illegible]	[illegible]	[illegible]	[illegible]	[illegible]	[illegible]	[illegible]	[illegible]	[illegible]	[illegible]	[illegible]	[illegible]	[illegible]	[illegible]	[illegible]	[illegible]	[illegible]	[illegible]	[illegible]
40	[illegible], do.	[illegible]	[illegible]	[illegible]	[illegible]	[illegible]	[illegible]	[illegible]	[illegible]	[illegible]	[illegible]	[illegible]	[illegible]	[illegible]	[illegible]	[illegible]	[illegible]	[illegible]	[illegible]	[illegible]	[illegible]
41	Kells, do.	[illegible]	[illegible]	[illegible]	[illegible]	[illegible]	[illegible]	[illegible]	[illegible]	[illegible]	[illegible]	[illegible]	[illegible]	[illegible]	[illegible]	[illegible]	[illegible]	[illegible]	[illegible]	[illegible]	[illegible]
42	Navan,	[illegible]	[illegible]	[illegible]	[illegible]	[illegible]	[illegible]	[illegible]	[illegible]	[illegible]	[illegible]	[illegible]	[illegible]	[illegible]	[illegible]	[illegible]	[illegible]	[illegible]	[illegible]	[illegible]	[illegible]
43	Oldcastle, part of,	[illegible]	[illegible]	[illegible]	[illegible]	[illegible]	[illegible]	[illegible]	[illegible]	[illegible]	[illegible]	[illegible]	[illegible]	[illegible]	[illegible]	[illegible]	[illegible]	[illegible]	[illegible]	[illegible]	[illegible]
44	Trim,	[illegible]	[illegible]	[illegible]	[illegible]	[illegible]	[illegible]	[illegible]	[illegible]	[illegible]	[illegible]	[illegible]	[illegible]	[illegible]	[illegible]	[illegible]	[illegible]	[illegible]	[illegible]	[illegible]	[illegible]

IRELAND.—DEATHS at different AGES registered in the year 1891—in the SUPERINTENDENT REGISTRARS' DISTRICTS in each COUNTY.—MALES—continued.

I.—PROVINCE OF LEINSTER—continued.

No.	Superintendent Registrars' Districts and Parts of Districts	Total Births	Total Deaths	Under 1 year	1	2	3	4	Under 5 years	5-	10-	15-	20-	25-	35-	45-	55-	65-	75-	85-	[illegible]
	8. Queen's Co.																				
45	Abbeyleix,	[illegible]	[illegible]	[illegible]	[illegible]	[illegible]	[illegible]	[illegible]	[illegible]	[illegible]	[illegible]	[illegible]	[illegible]	[illegible]	[illegible]	[illegible]	[illegible]	[illegible]	[illegible]	[illegible]	[illegible]
46	Athy, part of,	[illegible]	[illegible]	[illegible]	[illegible]	[illegible]	[illegible]	[illegible]	[illegible]	[illegible]	[illegible]	[illegible]	[illegible]	[illegible]	[illegible]	[illegible]	[illegible]	[illegible]	[illegible]	[illegible]	[illegible]
47	Carlow, do.	[illegible]	[illegible]	[illegible]	[illegible]	[illegible]	[illegible]	[illegible]	[illegible]	[illegible]	[illegible]	[illegible]	[illegible]	[illegible]	[illegible]	[illegible]	[illegible]	[illegible]	[illegible]	[illegible]	[illegible]
48	Mountmellick, part of,	[illegible]	[illegible]	[illegible]	[illegible]	[illegible]	[illegible]	[illegible]	[illegible]	[illegible]	[illegible]	[illegible]	[illegible]	[illegible]	[illegible]	[illegible]	[illegible]	[illegible]	[illegible]	[illegible]	[illegible]
49	Roscrea, do.	[illegible]	[illegible]	[illegible]	[illegible]	[illegible]	[illegible]	[illegible]	[illegible]	[illegible]	[illegible]	[illegible]	[illegible]	[illegible]	[illegible]	[illegible]	[illegible]	[illegible]	[illegible]	[illegible]	[illegible]
50	[illegible], do.	[illegible]	[illegible]	[illegible]	[illegible]	[illegible]	[illegible]	[illegible]	[illegible]	[illegible]	[illegible]	[illegible]	[illegible]	[illegible]	[illegible]	[illegible]	[illegible]	[illegible]	[illegible]	[illegible]	[illegible]
	10. Westmeath Co.																				
51	Athlone, part of,	[illegible]	[illegible]	[illegible]	[illegible]	[illegible]	[illegible]	[illegible]	[illegible]	[illegible]	[illegible]	[illegible]	[illegible]	[illegible]	[illegible]	[illegible]	[illegible]	[illegible]	[illegible]	[illegible]	[illegible]
52	Ballymahon, do.	[illegible]	[illegible]	[illegible]	[illegible]	[illegible]	[illegible]	[illegible]	[illegible]	[illegible]	[illegible]	[illegible]	[illegible]	[illegible]	[illegible]	[illegible]	[illegible]	[illegible]	[illegible]	[illegible]	[illegible]
53	Delvin,	[illegible]	[illegible]	[illegible]	[illegible]	[illegible]	[illegible]	[illegible]	[illegible]	[illegible]	[illegible]	[illegible]	[illegible]	[illegible]	[illegible]	[illegible]	[illegible]	[illegible]	[illegible]	[illegible]	[illegible]
54	Granard, part of,	[illegible]	[illegible]	[illegible]	[illegible]	[illegible]	[illegible]	[illegible]	[illegible]	[illegible]	[illegible]	[illegible]	[illegible]	[illegible]	[illegible]	[illegible]	[illegible]	[illegible]	[illegible]	[illegible]	[illegible]
55	Mullingar,	[illegible]	[illegible]	[illegible]	[illegible]	[illegible]	[illegible]	[illegible]	[illegible]	[illegible]	[illegible]	[illegible]	[illegible]	[illegible]	[illegible]	[illegible]	[illegible]	[illegible]	[illegible]	[illegible]	[illegible]
56	Tullamore, part of,	[illegible]	[illegible]	[illegible]	[illegible]	[illegible]	[illegible]	[illegible]	[illegible]	[illegible]	[illegible]	[illegible]	[illegible]	[illegible]	[illegible]	[illegible]	[illegible]	[illegible]	[illegible]	[illegible]	[illegible]
	11. Wexford Co.																				
57	Enniscorthy, part of,	[illegible]	[illegible]	[illegible]	[illegible]	[illegible]	[illegible]	[illegible]	[illegible]	[illegible]	[illegible]	[illegible]	[illegible]	[illegible]	[illegible]	[illegible]	[illegible]	[illegible]	[illegible]	[illegible]	[illegible]
58	Gorey,	[illegible]	[illegible]	[illegible]	[illegible]	[illegible]	[illegible]	[illegible]	[illegible]	[illegible]	[illegible]	[illegible]	[illegible]	[illegible]	[illegible]	[illegible]	[illegible]	[illegible]	[illegible]	[illegible]	[illegible]
59	New Ross, part of,	[illegible]	[illegible]	[illegible]	[illegible]	[illegible]	[illegible]	[illegible]	[illegible]	[illegible]	[illegible]	[illegible]	[illegible]	[illegible]	[illegible]	[illegible]	[illegible]	[illegible]	[illegible]	[illegible]	[illegible]
60	Shillelagh, do.	[illegible]	[illegible]	[illegible]	[illegible]	[illegible]	[illegible]	[illegible]	[illegible]	[illegible]	[illegible]	[illegible]	[illegible]	[illegible]	[illegible]	[illegible]	[illegible]	[illegible]	[illegible]	[illegible]	[illegible]
61	Wexford,	[illegible]	[illegible]	[illegible]	[illegible]	[illegible]	[illegible]	[illegible]	[illegible]	[illegible]	[illegible]	[illegible]	[illegible]	[illegible]	[illegible]	[illegible]	[illegible]	[illegible]	[illegible]	[illegible]	[illegible]
	12. Wicklow Co.																				
62	Baltinglass, part of,	[illegible]	[illegible]	[illegible]	[illegible]	[illegible]	[illegible]	[illegible]	[illegible]	[illegible]	[illegible]	[illegible]	[illegible]	[illegible]	[illegible]	[illegible]	[illegible]	[illegible]	[illegible]	[illegible]	[illegible]
63	Naas, do.	[illegible]	[illegible]	[illegible]	[illegible]	[illegible]	[illegible]	[illegible]	[illegible]	[illegible]	[illegible]	[illegible]	[illegible]	[illegible]	[illegible]	[illegible]	[illegible]	[illegible]	[illegible]	[illegible]	[illegible]
64	[illegible], do.	[illegible]	[illegible]	[illegible]	[illegible]	[illegible]	[illegible]	[illegible]	[illegible]	[illegible]	[illegible]	[illegible]	[illegible]	[illegible]	[illegible]	[illegible]	[illegible]	[illegible]	[illegible]	[illegible]	[illegible]
65	Rathdrum,	[illegible]	[illegible]	[illegible]	[illegible]	[illegible]	[illegible]	[illegible]	[illegible]	[illegible]	[illegible]	[illegible]	[illegible]	[illegible]	[illegible]	[illegible]	[illegible]	[illegible]	[illegible]	[illegible]	[illegible]
66	Shillelagh, part of,	[illegible]	[illegible]	[illegible]	[illegible]	[illegible]	[illegible]	[illegible]	[illegible]	[illegible]	[illegible]	[illegible]	[illegible]	[illegible]	[illegible]	[illegible]	[illegible]	[illegible]	[illegible]	[illegible]	[illegible]

II. PROVINCE OF MUNSTER.

No.	Superintendent Registrars' Districts and Parts of Districts	Total Births	Total Deaths	Under 1 year	1	2	3	4	Under 5 years	5-	10-	15-	20-	25-	35-	45-	55-	65-	75-	85-	[illegible]
	13. Clare Co.																				
67	Ballyvaghan,	[illegible]	[illegible]	[illegible]	[illegible]	[illegible]	[illegible]	[illegible]	[illegible]	[illegible]	[illegible]	[illegible]	[illegible]	[illegible]	[illegible]	[illegible]	[illegible]	[illegible]	[illegible]	[illegible]	[illegible]
68	Corofin,	[illegible]	[illegible]	[illegible]	[illegible]	[illegible]	[illegible]	[illegible]	[illegible]	[illegible]	[illegible]	[illegible]	[illegible]	[illegible]	[illegible]	[illegible]	[illegible]	[illegible]	[illegible]	[illegible]	[illegible]
69	Ennis,	[illegible]	[illegible]	[illegible]	[illegible]	[illegible]	[illegible]	[illegible]	[illegible]	[illegible]	[illegible]	[illegible]	[illegible]	[illegible]	[illegible]	[illegible]	[illegible]	[illegible]	[illegible]	[illegible]	[illegible]
70	Ennistymon,	[illegible]	[illegible]	[illegible]	[illegible]	[illegible]	[illegible]	[illegible]	[illegible]	[illegible]	[illegible]	[illegible]	[illegible]	[illegible]	[illegible]	[illegible]	[illegible]	[illegible]	[illegible]	[illegible]	[illegible]
71	Killadysert,	[illegible]	[illegible]	[illegible]	[illegible]	[illegible]	[illegible]	[illegible]	[illegible]	[illegible]	[illegible]	[illegible]	[illegible]	[illegible]	[illegible]	[illegible]	[illegible]	[illegible]	[illegible]	[illegible]	[illegible]
72	Kilrush,	[illegible]	[illegible]	[illegible]	[illegible]	[illegible]	[illegible]	[illegible]	[illegible]	[illegible]	[illegible]	[illegible]	[illegible]	[illegible]	[illegible]	[illegible]	[illegible]	[illegible]	[illegible]	[illegible]	[illegible]
73	Limerick, part of,	[illegible]	[illegible]	[illegible]	[illegible]	[illegible]	[illegible]	[illegible]	[illegible]	[illegible]	[illegible]	[illegible]	[illegible]	[illegible]	[illegible]	[illegible]	[illegible]	[illegible]	[illegible]	[illegible]	[illegible]
74	Scariff, do.	[illegible]	[illegible]	[illegible]	[illegible]	[illegible]	[illegible]	[illegible]	[illegible]	[illegible]	[illegible]	[illegible]	[illegible]	[illegible]	[illegible]	[illegible]	[illegible]	[illegible]	[illegible]	[illegible]	[illegible]
75	Tulla,	[illegible]	[illegible]	[illegible]	[illegible]	[illegible]	[illegible]	[illegible]	[illegible]	[illegible]	[illegible]	[illegible]	[illegible]	[illegible]	[illegible]	[illegible]	[illegible]	[illegible]	[illegible]	[illegible]	[illegible]
	14. Cork Co.																				
76	Bandon,	[illegible]	[illegible]	[illegible]	[illegible]	[illegible]	[illegible]	[illegible]	[illegible]	[illegible]	[illegible]	[illegible]	[illegible]	[illegible]	[illegible]	[illegible]	[illegible]	[illegible]	[illegible]	[illegible]	[illegible]
77	Bantry,	[illegible]	[illegible]	[illegible]	[illegible]	[illegible]	[illegible]	[illegible]	[illegible]	[illegible]	[illegible]	[illegible]	[illegible]	[illegible]	[illegible]	[illegible]	[illegible]	[illegible]	[illegible]	[illegible]	[illegible]
78	Castletown,	[illegible]	[illegible]	[illegible]	[illegible]	[illegible]	[illegible]	[illegible]	[illegible]	[illegible]	[illegible]	[illegible]	[illegible]	[illegible]	[illegible]	[illegible]	[illegible]	[illegible]	[illegible]	[illegible]	[illegible]
79	Clonakilty,	[illegible]	[illegible]	[illegible]	[illegible]	[illegible]	[illegible]	[illegible]	[illegible]	[illegible]	[illegible]	[illegible]	[illegible]	[illegible]	[illegible]	[illegible]	[illegible]	[illegible]	[illegible]	[illegible]	[illegible]
80	Cork,	[illegible]	[illegible]	[illegible]	[illegible]	[illegible]	[illegible]	[illegible]	[illegible]	[illegible]	[illegible]	[illegible]	[illegible]	[illegible]	[illegible]	[illegible]	[illegible]	[illegible]	[illegible]	[illegible]	[illegible]
81	Dunmanway,	[illegible]	[illegible]	[illegible]	[illegible]	[illegible]	[illegible]	[illegible]	[illegible]	[illegible]	[illegible]	[illegible]	[illegible]	[illegible]	[illegible]	[illegible]	[illegible]	[illegible]	[illegible]	[illegible]	[illegible]

IRELAND.—DEATHS at different AGES registered in the year 1891—in the SUPERINTENDENT REGISTRARS' DISTRICTS in each COUNTY—FEMALES—*continued*.

II.—PROVINCE OF LEINSTER—*continued*.

No.	Superintendent Registrars' District and Parts of Districts	Total Deaths	Total Births	Under 1 year	1	2	3	4	Total under 5 years	5-	10-	15-	20-	25-	35-	45-	55-	65-	75-	85-	95 and upwards
	9. Queen's Co.																				
45	Abbeyleix,	[illegible]	[illegible]	[illegible]	[illegible]	[illegible]	[illegible]	[illegible]	[illegible]	[illegible]	[illegible]	[illegible]	[illegible]	[illegible]	[illegible]	[illegible]	[illegible]	[illegible]	[illegible]	[illegible]	[illegible]
46	Athy, part of,	[illegible]	[illegible]	[illegible]	[illegible]	[illegible]	[illegible]	[illegible]	[illegible]	[illegible]	[illegible]	[illegible]	[illegible]	[illegible]	[illegible]	[illegible]	[illegible]	[illegible]	[illegible]	[illegible]	[illegible]
47	Carlow, do.	[illegible]	[illegible]	[illegible]	[illegible]	[illegible]	[illegible]	[illegible]	[illegible]	[illegible]	[illegible]	[illegible]	[illegible]	[illegible]	[illegible]	[illegible]	[illegible]	[illegible]	[illegible]	[illegible]	[illegible]
48	Mountmellick, do.	[illegible]	[illegible]	[illegible]	[illegible]	[illegible]	[illegible]	[illegible]	[illegible]	[illegible]	[illegible]	[illegible]	[illegible]	[illegible]	[illegible]	[illegible]	[illegible]	[illegible]	[illegible]	[illegible]	[illegible]
49	Roscrea, do.	[illegible]	[illegible]	[illegible]	[illegible]	[illegible]	[illegible]	[illegible]	[illegible]	[illegible]	[illegible]	[illegible]	[illegible]	[illegible]	[illegible]	[illegible]	[illegible]	[illegible]	[illegible]	[illegible]	[illegible]
50	Tullamore, do.	[illegible]	[illegible]	[illegible]	[illegible]	[illegible]	[illegible]	[illegible]	[illegible]	[illegible]	[illegible]	[illegible]	[illegible]	[illegible]	[illegible]	[illegible]	[illegible]	[illegible]	[illegible]	[illegible]	[illegible]
	10. Westmeath Co.																				
51	Athlone, part of,	[illegible]	[illegible]	[illegible]	[illegible]	[illegible]	[illegible]	[illegible]	[illegible]	[illegible]	[illegible]	[illegible]	[illegible]	[illegible]	[illegible]	[illegible]	[illegible]	[illegible]	[illegible]	[illegible]	[illegible]
52	Ballymahon, do.	[illegible]	[illegible]	[illegible]	[illegible]	[illegible]	[illegible]	[illegible]	[illegible]	[illegible]	[illegible]	[illegible]	[illegible]	[illegible]	[illegible]	[illegible]	[illegible]	[illegible]	[illegible]	[illegible]	[illegible]
53	Delvin,	[illegible]	[illegible]	[illegible]	[illegible]	[illegible]	[illegible]	[illegible]	[illegible]	[illegible]	[illegible]	[illegible]	[illegible]	[illegible]	[illegible]	[illegible]	[illegible]	[illegible]	[illegible]	[illegible]	[illegible]
54	Granard, part of,	[illegible]	[illegible]	[illegible]	[illegible]	[illegible]	[illegible]	[illegible]	[illegible]	[illegible]	[illegible]	[illegible]	[illegible]	[illegible]	[illegible]	[illegible]	[illegible]	[illegible]	[illegible]	[illegible]	[illegible]
55	Mullingar,	[illegible]	[illegible]	[illegible]	[illegible]	[illegible]	[illegible]	[illegible]	[illegible]	[illegible]	[illegible]	[illegible]	[illegible]	[illegible]	[illegible]	[illegible]	[illegible]	[illegible]	[illegible]	[illegible]	[illegible]
56	Tullamore, part of,	[illegible]	[illegible]	[illegible]	[illegible]	[illegible]	[illegible]	[illegible]	[illegible]	[illegible]	[illegible]	[illegible]	[illegible]	[illegible]	[illegible]	[illegible]	[illegible]	[illegible]	[illegible]	[illegible]	[illegible]
	11. Wexford Co.																				
57	Enniscorthy, part of,	[illegible]	[illegible]	[illegible]	[illegible]	[illegible]	[illegible]	[illegible]	[illegible]	[illegible]	[illegible]	[illegible]	[illegible]	[illegible]	[illegible]	[illegible]	[illegible]	[illegible]	[illegible]	[illegible]	[illegible]
58	Gorey,	[illegible]	[illegible]	[illegible]	[illegible]	[illegible]	[illegible]	[illegible]	[illegible]	[illegible]	[illegible]	[illegible]	[illegible]	[illegible]	[illegible]	[illegible]	[illegible]	[illegible]	[illegible]	[illegible]	[illegible]
59	New Ross, part of,	[illegible]	[illegible]	[illegible]	[illegible]	[illegible]	[illegible]	[illegible]	[illegible]	[illegible]	[illegible]	[illegible]	[illegible]	[illegible]	[illegible]	[illegible]	[illegible]	[illegible]	[illegible]	[illegible]	[illegible]
60	Shillelagh, do.	[illegible]	[illegible]	[illegible]	[illegible]	[illegible]	[illegible]	[illegible]	[illegible]	[illegible]	[illegible]	[illegible]	[illegible]	[illegible]	[illegible]	[illegible]	[illegible]	[illegible]	[illegible]	[illegible]	[illegible]
61	Wexford,	[illegible]	[illegible]	[illegible]	[illegible]	[illegible]	[illegible]	[illegible]	[illegible]	[illegible]	[illegible]	[illegible]	[illegible]	[illegible]	[illegible]	[illegible]	[illegible]	[illegible]	[illegible]	[illegible]	[illegible]
	12. Wicklow Co.																				
62	Baltinglass, part of,	[illegible]	[illegible]	[illegible]	[illegible]	[illegible]	[illegible]	[illegible]	[illegible]	[illegible]	[illegible]	[illegible]	[illegible]	[illegible]	[illegible]	[illegible]	[illegible]	[illegible]	[illegible]	[illegible]	[illegible]
63	Naas, do.	[illegible]	[illegible]	[illegible]	[illegible]	[illegible]	[illegible]	[illegible]	[illegible]	[illegible]	[illegible]	[illegible]	[illegible]	[illegible]	[illegible]	[illegible]	[illegible]	[illegible]	[illegible]	[illegible]	[illegible]
64	Rathdown, do.	[illegible]	[illegible]	[illegible]	[illegible]	[illegible]	[illegible]	[illegible]	[illegible]	[illegible]	[illegible]	[illegible]	[illegible]	[illegible]	[illegible]	[illegible]	[illegible]	[illegible]	[illegible]	[illegible]	[illegible]
65	Rathdrum,	[illegible]	[illegible]	[illegible]	[illegible]	[illegible]	[illegible]	[illegible]	[illegible]	[illegible]	[illegible]	[illegible]	[illegible]	[illegible]	[illegible]	[illegible]	[illegible]	[illegible]	[illegible]	[illegible]	[illegible]
66	Shillelagh, part of,	[illegible]	[illegible]	[illegible]	[illegible]	[illegible]	[illegible]	[illegible]	[illegible]	[illegible]	[illegible]	[illegible]	[illegible]	[illegible]	[illegible]	[illegible]	[illegible]	[illegible]	[illegible]	[illegible]	[illegible]
	III.—PROVINCE OF MUNSTER.																				
	13. Clare Co.																				
67	Ballyvaughan,	[illegible]	[illegible]	[illegible]	[illegible]	[illegible]	[illegible]	[illegible]	[illegible]	[illegible]	[illegible]	[illegible]	[illegible]	[illegible]	[illegible]	[illegible]	[illegible]	[illegible]	[illegible]	[illegible]	[illegible]
68	Corrofin,	[illegible]	[illegible]	[illegible]	[illegible]	[illegible]	[illegible]	[illegible]	[illegible]	[illegible]	[illegible]	[illegible]	[illegible]	[illegible]	[illegible]	[illegible]	[illegible]	[illegible]	[illegible]	[illegible]	[illegible]
69	Ennis,	[illegible]	[illegible]	[illegible]	[illegible]	[illegible]	[illegible]	[illegible]	[illegible]	[illegible]	[illegible]	[illegible]	[illegible]	[illegible]	[illegible]	[illegible]	[illegible]	[illegible]	[illegible]	[illegible]	[illegible]
70	Ennistymon,	[illegible]	[illegible]	[illegible]	[illegible]	[illegible]	[illegible]	[illegible]	[illegible]	[illegible]	[illegible]	[illegible]	[illegible]	[illegible]	[illegible]	[illegible]	[illegible]	[illegible]	[illegible]	[illegible]	[illegible]
71	Kiladysert,	[illegible]	[illegible]	[illegible]	[illegible]	[illegible]	[illegible]	[illegible]	[illegible]	[illegible]	[illegible]	[illegible]	[illegible]	[illegible]	[illegible]	[illegible]	[illegible]	[illegible]	[illegible]	[illegible]	[illegible]
72	Kilrush,	[illegible]	[illegible]	[illegible]	[illegible]	[illegible]	[illegible]	[illegible]	[illegible]	[illegible]	[illegible]	[illegible]	[illegible]	[illegible]	[illegible]	[illegible]	[illegible]	[illegible]	[illegible]	[illegible]	[illegible]
73	Limerick, part of,	[illegible]	[illegible]	[illegible]	[illegible]	[illegible]	[illegible]	[illegible]	[illegible]	[illegible]	[illegible]	[illegible]	[illegible]	[illegible]	[illegible]	[illegible]	[illegible]	[illegible]	[illegible]	[illegible]	[illegible]
74	Scarriff, do.	[illegible]	[illegible]	[illegible]	[illegible]	[illegible]	[illegible]	[illegible]	[illegible]	[illegible]	[illegible]	[illegible]	[illegible]	[illegible]	[illegible]	[illegible]	[illegible]	[illegible]	[illegible]	[illegible]	[illegible]
75	Tulla,	[illegible]	[illegible]	[illegible]	[illegible]	[illegible]	[illegible]	[illegible]	[illegible]	[illegible]	[illegible]	[illegible]	[illegible]	[illegible]	[illegible]	[illegible]	[illegible]	[illegible]	[illegible]	[illegible]	[illegible]
	14. Cork Co.																				
76	Bandon,	[illegible]	[illegible]	[illegible]	[illegible]	[illegible]	[illegible]	[illegible]	[illegible]	[illegible]	[illegible]	[illegible]	[illegible]	[illegible]	[illegible]	[illegible]	[illegible]	[illegible]	[illegible]	[illegible]	[illegible]
77	Bantry,	[illegible]	[illegible]	[illegible]	[illegible]	[illegible]	[illegible]	[illegible]	[illegible]	[illegible]	[illegible]	[illegible]	[illegible]	[illegible]	[illegible]	[illegible]	[illegible]	[illegible]	[illegible]	[illegible]	[illegible]
78	Castletown,	[illegible]	[illegible]	[illegible]	[illegible]	[illegible]	[illegible]	[illegible]	[illegible]	[illegible]	[illegible]	[illegible]	[illegible]	[illegible]	[illegible]	[illegible]	[illegible]	[illegible]	[illegible]	[illegible]	[illegible]
79	Clonakilty,	[illegible]	[illegible]	[illegible]	[illegible]	[illegible]	[illegible]	[illegible]	[illegible]	[illegible]	[illegible]	[illegible]	[illegible]	[illegible]	[illegible]	[illegible]	[illegible]	[illegible]	[illegible]	[illegible]	[illegible]
80	Cork,	[illegible]	[illegible]	[illegible]	[illegible]	[illegible]	[illegible]	[illegible]	[illegible]	[illegible]	[illegible]	[illegible]	[illegible]	[illegible]	[illegible]	[illegible]	[illegible]	[illegible]	[illegible]	[illegible]	[illegible]
81	Dunmanway,	[illegible]	[illegible]	[illegible]	[illegible]	[illegible]	[illegible]	[illegible]	[illegible]	[illegible]	[illegible]	[illegible]	[illegible]	[illegible]	[illegible]	[illegible]	[illegible]	[illegible]	[illegible]	[illegible]	[illegible]

IRELAND.—DEATHS at different AGES registered in the year 1891—in the SUPERINTENDENT REGISTRARS' DISTRICTS in each COUNTY.—MALES—continued.

II.—PROVINCE OF MUNSTER—continued.

No.	Superintendent Registrars' Districts and Parts of Districts	Total Births	Total Deaths	Under 1 year	1	2	3	4	Under 5 years	5-	10-	15-	20-	25-	35-	45-	55-	65-	75-	85-	[illegible]
	14. Clare Co.—continued.																				
[illegible]	[illegible]	[illegible]	[illegible]	[illegible]	[illegible]	[illegible]	[illegible]	[illegible]	[illegible]	[illegible]	[illegible]	[illegible]	[illegible]	[illegible]	[illegible]	[illegible]	[illegible]	[illegible]	[illegible]	[illegible]	[illegible]
[illegible]	[illegible]	[illegible]	[illegible]	[illegible]	[illegible]	[illegible]	[illegible]	[illegible]	[illegible]	[illegible]	[illegible]	[illegible]	[illegible]	[illegible]	[illegible]	[illegible]	[illegible]	[illegible]	[illegible]	[illegible]	[illegible]
[illegible]	[illegible]	[illegible]	[illegible]	[illegible]	[illegible]	[illegible]	[illegible]	[illegible]	[illegible]	[illegible]	[illegible]	[illegible]	[illegible]	[illegible]	[illegible]	[illegible]	[illegible]	[illegible]	[illegible]	[illegible]	[illegible]
[illegible]	[illegible]	[illegible]	[illegible]	[illegible]	[illegible]	[illegible]	[illegible]	[illegible]	[illegible]	[illegible]	[illegible]	[illegible]	[illegible]	[illegible]	[illegible]	[illegible]	[illegible]	[illegible]	[illegible]	[illegible]	[illegible]
[illegible]	[illegible]	[illegible]	[illegible]	[illegible]	[illegible]	[illegible]	[illegible]	[illegible]	[illegible]	[illegible]	[illegible]	[illegible]	[illegible]	[illegible]	[illegible]	[illegible]	[illegible]	[illegible]	[illegible]	[illegible]	[illegible]
[illegible]	[illegible]	[illegible]	[illegible]	[illegible]	[illegible]	[illegible]	[illegible]	[illegible]	[illegible]	[illegible]	[illegible]	[illegible]	[illegible]	[illegible]	[illegible]	[illegible]	[illegible]	[illegible]	[illegible]	[illegible]	[illegible]
[illegible]	[illegible]	[illegible]	[illegible]	[illegible]	[illegible]	[illegible]	[illegible]	[illegible]	[illegible]	[illegible]	[illegible]	[illegible]	[illegible]	[illegible]	[illegible]	[illegible]	[illegible]	[illegible]	[illegible]	[illegible]	[illegible]
[illegible]	[illegible]	[illegible]	[illegible]	[illegible]	[illegible]	[illegible]	[illegible]	[illegible]	[illegible]	[illegible]	[illegible]	[illegible]	[illegible]	[illegible]	[illegible]	[illegible]	[illegible]	[illegible]	[illegible]	[illegible]	[illegible]
[illegible]	[illegible]	[illegible]	[illegible]	[illegible]	[illegible]	[illegible]	[illegible]	[illegible]	[illegible]	[illegible]	[illegible]	[illegible]	[illegible]	[illegible]	[illegible]	[illegible]	[illegible]	[illegible]	[illegible]	[illegible]	[illegible]
[illegible]	[illegible]	[illegible]	[illegible]	[illegible]	[illegible]	[illegible]	[illegible]	[illegible]	[illegible]	[illegible]	[illegible]	[illegible]	[illegible]	[illegible]	[illegible]	[illegible]	[illegible]	[illegible]	[illegible]	[illegible]	[illegible]
[illegible]	[illegible]	[illegible]	[illegible]	[illegible]	[illegible]	[illegible]	[illegible]	[illegible]	[illegible]	[illegible]	[illegible]	[illegible]	[illegible]	[illegible]	[illegible]	[illegible]	[illegible]	[illegible]	[illegible]	[illegible]	[illegible]
[illegible]	[illegible]	[illegible]	[illegible]	[illegible]	[illegible]	[illegible]	[illegible]	[illegible]	[illegible]	[illegible]	[illegible]	[illegible]	[illegible]	[illegible]	[illegible]	[illegible]	[illegible]	[illegible]	[illegible]	[illegible]	[illegible]
	15. Kerry Co.																				
[illegible]	[illegible]	[illegible]	[illegible]	[illegible]	[illegible]	[illegible]	[illegible]	[illegible]	[illegible]	[illegible]	[illegible]	[illegible]	[illegible]	[illegible]	[illegible]	[illegible]	[illegible]	[illegible]	[illegible]	[illegible]	[illegible]
[illegible]	[illegible]	[illegible]	[illegible]	[illegible]	[illegible]	[illegible]	[illegible]	[illegible]	[illegible]	[illegible]	[illegible]	[illegible]	[illegible]	[illegible]	[illegible]	[illegible]	[illegible]	[illegible]	[illegible]	[illegible]	[illegible]
[illegible]	[illegible]	[illegible]	[illegible]	[illegible]	[illegible]	[illegible]	[illegible]	[illegible]	[illegible]	[illegible]	[illegible]	[illegible]	[illegible]	[illegible]	[illegible]	[illegible]	[illegible]	[illegible]	[illegible]	[illegible]	[illegible]
[illegible]	[illegible]	[illegible]	[illegible]	[illegible]	[illegible]	[illegible]	[illegible]	[illegible]	[illegible]	[illegible]	[illegible]	[illegible]	[illegible]	[illegible]	[illegible]	[illegible]	[illegible]	[illegible]	[illegible]	[illegible]	[illegible]
[illegible]	[illegible]	[illegible]	[illegible]	[illegible]	[illegible]	[illegible]	[illegible]	[illegible]	[illegible]	[illegible]	[illegible]	[illegible]	[illegible]	[illegible]	[illegible]	[illegible]	[illegible]	[illegible]	[illegible]	[illegible]	[illegible]
[illegible]	[illegible]	[illegible]	[illegible]	[illegible]	[illegible]	[illegible]	[illegible]	[illegible]	[illegible]	[illegible]	[illegible]	[illegible]	[illegible]	[illegible]	[illegible]	[illegible]	[illegible]	[illegible]	[illegible]	[illegible]	[illegible]
[illegible]	[illegible]	[illegible]	[illegible]	[illegible]	[illegible]	[illegible]	[illegible]	[illegible]	[illegible]	[illegible]	[illegible]	[illegible]	[illegible]	[illegible]	[illegible]	[illegible]	[illegible]	[illegible]	[illegible]	[illegible]	[illegible]
	16. Limerick Co.																				
[illegible]	[illegible]	[illegible]	[illegible]	[illegible]	[illegible]	[illegible]	[illegible]	[illegible]	[illegible]	[illegible]	[illegible]	[illegible]	[illegible]	[illegible]	[illegible]	[illegible]	[illegible]	[illegible]	[illegible]	[illegible]	[illegible]
[illegible]	[illegible]	[illegible]	[illegible]	[illegible]	[illegible]	[illegible]	[illegible]	[illegible]	[illegible]	[illegible]	[illegible]	[illegible]	[illegible]	[illegible]	[illegible]	[illegible]	[illegible]	[illegible]	[illegible]	[illegible]	[illegible]
[illegible]	[illegible]	[illegible]	[illegible]	[illegible]	[illegible]	[illegible]	[illegible]	[illegible]	[illegible]	[illegible]	[illegible]	[illegible]	[illegible]	[illegible]	[illegible]	[illegible]	[illegible]	[illegible]	[illegible]	[illegible]	[illegible]
[illegible]	[illegible]	[illegible]	[illegible]	[illegible]	[illegible]	[illegible]	[illegible]	[illegible]	[illegible]	[illegible]	[illegible]	[illegible]	[illegible]	[illegible]	[illegible]	[illegible]	[illegible]	[illegible]	[illegible]	[illegible]	[illegible]
[illegible]	[illegible]	[illegible]	[illegible]	[illegible]	[illegible]	[illegible]	[illegible]	[illegible]	[illegible]	[illegible]	[illegible]	[illegible]	[illegible]	[illegible]	[illegible]	[illegible]	[illegible]	[illegible]	[illegible]	[illegible]	[illegible]
[illegible]	[illegible]	[illegible]	[illegible]	[illegible]	[illegible]	[illegible]	[illegible]	[illegible]	[illegible]	[illegible]	[illegible]	[illegible]	[illegible]	[illegible]	[illegible]	[illegible]	[illegible]	[illegible]	[illegible]	[illegible]	[illegible]
[illegible]	[illegible]	[illegible]	[illegible]	[illegible]	[illegible]	[illegible]	[illegible]	[illegible]	[illegible]	[illegible]	[illegible]	[illegible]	[illegible]	[illegible]	[illegible]	[illegible]	[illegible]	[illegible]	[illegible]	[illegible]	[illegible]
[illegible]	[illegible]	[illegible]	[illegible]	[illegible]	[illegible]	[illegible]	[illegible]	[illegible]	[illegible]	[illegible]	[illegible]	[illegible]	[illegible]	[illegible]	[illegible]	[illegible]	[illegible]	[illegible]	[illegible]	[illegible]	[illegible]
	17. Tipperary Co.																				
[illegible]	[illegible]	[illegible]	[illegible]	[illegible]	[illegible]	[illegible]	[illegible]	[illegible]	[illegible]	[illegible]	[illegible]	[illegible]	[illegible]	[illegible]	[illegible]	[illegible]	[illegible]	[illegible]	[illegible]	[illegible]	[illegible]
[illegible]	[illegible]	[illegible]	[illegible]	[illegible]	[illegible]	[illegible]	[illegible]	[illegible]	[illegible]	[illegible]	[illegible]	[illegible]	[illegible]	[illegible]	[illegible]	[illegible]	[illegible]	[illegible]	[illegible]	[illegible]	[illegible]
[illegible]	[illegible]	[illegible]	[illegible]	[illegible]	[illegible]	[illegible]	[illegible]	[illegible]	[illegible]	[illegible]	[illegible]	[illegible]	[illegible]	[illegible]	[illegible]	[illegible]	[illegible]	[illegible]	[illegible]	[illegible]	[illegible]
[illegible]	[illegible]	[illegible]	[illegible]	[illegible]	[illegible]	[illegible]	[illegible]	[illegible]	[illegible]	[illegible]	[illegible]	[illegible]	[illegible]	[illegible]	[illegible]	[illegible]	[illegible]	[illegible]	[illegible]	[illegible]	[illegible]
[illegible]	[illegible]	[illegible]	[illegible]	[illegible]	[illegible]	[illegible]	[illegible]	[illegible]	[illegible]	[illegible]	[illegible]	[illegible]	[illegible]	[illegible]	[illegible]	[illegible]	[illegible]	[illegible]	[illegible]	[illegible]	[illegible]
[illegible]	[illegible]	[illegible]	[illegible]	[illegible]	[illegible]	[illegible]	[illegible]	[illegible]	[illegible]	[illegible]	[illegible]	[illegible]	[illegible]	[illegible]	[illegible]	[illegible]	[illegible]	[illegible]	[illegible]	[illegible]	[illegible]
[illegible]	[illegible]	[illegible]	[illegible]	[illegible]	[illegible]	[illegible]	[illegible]	[illegible]	[illegible]	[illegible]	[illegible]	[illegible]	[illegible]	[illegible]	[illegible]	[illegible]	[illegible]	[illegible]	[illegible]	[illegible]	[illegible]
[illegible]	[illegible]	[illegible]	[illegible]	[illegible]	[illegible]	[illegible]	[illegible]	[illegible]	[illegible]	[illegible]	[illegible]	[illegible]	[illegible]	[illegible]	[illegible]	[illegible]	[illegible]	[illegible]	[illegible]	[illegible]	[illegible]
[illegible]	[illegible]	[illegible]	[illegible]	[illegible]	[illegible]	[illegible]	[illegible]	[illegible]	[illegible]	[illegible]	[illegible]	[illegible]	[illegible]	[illegible]	[illegible]	[illegible]	[illegible]	[illegible]	[illegible]	[illegible]	[illegible]
[illegible]	[illegible]	[illegible]	[illegible]	[illegible]	[illegible]	[illegible]	[illegible]	[illegible]	[illegible]	[illegible]	[illegible]	[illegible]	[illegible]	[illegible]	[illegible]	[illegible]	[illegible]	[illegible]	[illegible]	[illegible]	[illegible]
[illegible]	[illegible]	[illegible]	[illegible]	[illegible]	[illegible]	[illegible]	[illegible]	[illegible]	[illegible]	[illegible]	[illegible]	[illegible]	[illegible]	[illegible]	[illegible]	[illegible]	[illegible]	[illegible]	[illegible]	[illegible]	[illegible]
[illegible]	[illegible]	[illegible]	[illegible]	[illegible]	[illegible]	[illegible]	[illegible]	[illegible]	[illegible]	[illegible]	[illegible]	[illegible]	[illegible]	[illegible]	[illegible]	[illegible]	[illegible]	[illegible]	[illegible]	[illegible]	[illegible]
	18. Waterford Co.																				
[illegible]	[illegible]	[illegible]	[illegible]	[illegible]	[illegible]	[illegible]	[illegible]	[illegible]	[illegible]	[illegible]	[illegible]	[illegible]	[illegible]	[illegible]	[illegible]	[illegible]	[illegible]	[illegible]	[illegible]	[illegible]	[illegible]
[illegible]	[illegible]	[illegible]	[illegible]	[illegible]	[illegible]	[illegible]	[illegible]	[illegible]	[illegible]	[illegible]	[illegible]	[illegible]	[illegible]	[illegible]	[illegible]	[illegible]	[illegible]	[illegible]	[illegible]	[illegible]	[illegible]
[illegible]	[illegible]	[illegible]	[illegible]	[illegible]	[illegible]	[illegible]	[illegible]	[illegible]	[illegible]	[illegible]	[illegible]	[illegible]	[illegible]	[illegible]	[illegible]	[illegible]	[illegible]	[illegible]	[illegible]	[illegible]	[illegible]
[illegible]	[illegible]	[illegible]	[illegible]	[illegible]	[illegible]	[illegible]	[illegible]	[illegible]	[illegible]	[illegible]	[illegible]	[illegible]	[illegible]	[illegible]	[illegible]	[illegible]	[illegible]	[illegible]	[illegible]	[illegible]	[illegible]
[illegible]	[illegible]	[illegible]	[illegible]	[illegible]	[illegible]	[illegible]	[illegible]	[illegible]	[illegible]	[illegible]	[illegible]	[illegible]	[illegible]	[illegible]	[illegible]	[illegible]	[illegible]	[illegible]	[illegible]	[illegible]	[illegible]
[illegible]	[illegible]	[illegible]	[illegible]	[illegible]	[illegible]	[illegible]	[illegible]	[illegible]	[illegible]	[illegible]	[illegible]	[illegible]	[illegible]	[illegible]	[illegible]	[illegible]	[illegible]	[illegible]	[illegible]	[illegible]	[illegible]
[illegible]	[illegible]	[illegible]	[illegible]	[illegible]	[illegible]	[illegible]	[illegible]	[illegible]	[illegible]	[illegible]	[illegible]	[illegible]	[illegible]	[illegible]	[illegible]	[illegible]	[illegible]	[illegible]	[illegible]	[illegible]	[illegible]

IRELAND.—DEATHS at different AGES registered in the year 1891—in the SUPERINTENDENT REGISTRARS' DISTRICTS in each COUNTY.—FEMALES—continued.

II.—PROVINCE OF MUNSTER—continued.

No.	Superintendent Registrars' Districts and Parts of Districts	[illegible]	[illegible]	Under 1	1	2	3	4	Under 5	[illegible]	[illegible]	[illegible]	[illegible]	[illegible]	[illegible]	[illegible]	[illegible]	[illegible]	[illegible]	[illegible]	[illegible]	[illegible]
	Cork Co.—continued.																					
[illegible]	[illegible]	[illegible]	[illegible]	[illegible]	[illegible]	[illegible]	[illegible]	[illegible]	[illegible]	[illegible]	[illegible]	[illegible]	[illegible]	[illegible]	[illegible]	[illegible]	[illegible]	[illegible]	[illegible]	[illegible]	[illegible]	[illegible]
[illegible]	[illegible]	[illegible]	[illegible]	[illegible]	[illegible]	[illegible]	[illegible]	[illegible]	[illegible]	[illegible]	[illegible]	[illegible]	[illegible]	[illegible]	[illegible]	[illegible]	[illegible]	[illegible]	[illegible]	[illegible]	[illegible]	[illegible]
[illegible]	[illegible]	[illegible]	[illegible]	[illegible]	[illegible]	[illegible]	[illegible]	[illegible]	[illegible]	[illegible]	[illegible]	[illegible]	[illegible]	[illegible]	[illegible]	[illegible]	[illegible]	[illegible]	[illegible]	[illegible]	[illegible]	[illegible]
[illegible]	[illegible]	[illegible]	[illegible]	[illegible]	[illegible]	[illegible]	[illegible]	[illegible]	[illegible]	[illegible]	[illegible]	[illegible]	[illegible]	[illegible]	[illegible]	[illegible]	[illegible]	[illegible]	[illegible]	[illegible]	[illegible]	[illegible]
[illegible]	[illegible]	[illegible]	[illegible]	[illegible]	[illegible]	[illegible]	[illegible]	[illegible]	[illegible]	[illegible]	[illegible]	[illegible]	[illegible]	[illegible]	[illegible]	[illegible]	[illegible]	[illegible]	[illegible]	[illegible]	[illegible]	[illegible]
[illegible]	[illegible]	[illegible]	[illegible]	[illegible]	[illegible]	[illegible]	[illegible]	[illegible]	[illegible]	[illegible]	[illegible]	[illegible]	[illegible]	[illegible]	[illegible]	[illegible]	[illegible]	[illegible]	[illegible]	[illegible]	[illegible]	[illegible]
[illegible]	[illegible]	[illegible]	[illegible]	[illegible]	[illegible]	[illegible]	[illegible]	[illegible]	[illegible]	[illegible]	[illegible]	[illegible]	[illegible]	[illegible]	[illegible]	[illegible]	[illegible]	[illegible]	[illegible]	[illegible]	[illegible]	[illegible]
[illegible]	[illegible]	[illegible]	[illegible]	[illegible]	[illegible]	[illegible]	[illegible]	[illegible]	[illegible]	[illegible]	[illegible]	[illegible]	[illegible]	[illegible]	[illegible]	[illegible]	[illegible]	[illegible]	[illegible]	[illegible]	[illegible]	[illegible]
[illegible]	[illegible]	[illegible]	[illegible]	[illegible]	[illegible]	[illegible]	[illegible]	[illegible]	[illegible]	[illegible]	[illegible]	[illegible]	[illegible]	[illegible]	[illegible]	[illegible]	[illegible]	[illegible]	[illegible]	[illegible]	[illegible]	[illegible]
[illegible]	[illegible]	[illegible]	[illegible]	[illegible]	[illegible]	[illegible]	[illegible]	[illegible]	[illegible]	[illegible]	[illegible]	[illegible]	[illegible]	[illegible]	[illegible]	[illegible]	[illegible]	[illegible]	[illegible]	[illegible]	[illegible]	[illegible]
[illegible]	[illegible]	[illegible]	[illegible]	[illegible]	[illegible]	[illegible]	[illegible]	[illegible]	[illegible]	[illegible]	[illegible]	[illegible]	[illegible]	[illegible]	[illegible]	[illegible]	[illegible]	[illegible]	[illegible]	[illegible]	[illegible]	[illegible]
[illegible]	[illegible]	[illegible]	[illegible]	[illegible]	[illegible]	[illegible]	[illegible]	[illegible]	[illegible]	[illegible]	[illegible]	[illegible]	[illegible]	[illegible]	[illegible]	[illegible]	[illegible]	[illegible]	[illegible]	[illegible]	[illegible]	[illegible]
	Kerry Co.																					
[illegible]	[illegible]	[illegible]	[illegible]	[illegible]	[illegible]	[illegible]	[illegible]	[illegible]	[illegible]	[illegible]	[illegible]	[illegible]	[illegible]	[illegible]	[illegible]	[illegible]	[illegible]	[illegible]	[illegible]	[illegible]	[illegible]	[illegible]
[illegible]	[illegible]	[illegible]	[illegible]	[illegible]	[illegible]	[illegible]	[illegible]	[illegible]	[illegible]	[illegible]	[illegible]	[illegible]	[illegible]	[illegible]	[illegible]	[illegible]	[illegible]	[illegible]	[illegible]	[illegible]	[illegible]	[illegible]
[illegible]	[illegible]	[illegible]	[illegible]	[illegible]	[illegible]	[illegible]	[illegible]	[illegible]	[illegible]	[illegible]	[illegible]	[illegible]	[illegible]	[illegible]	[illegible]	[illegible]	[illegible]	[illegible]	[illegible]	[illegible]	[illegible]	[illegible]
[illegible]	[illegible]	[illegible]	[illegible]	[illegible]	[illegible]	[illegible]	[illegible]	[illegible]	[illegible]	[illegible]	[illegible]	[illegible]	[illegible]	[illegible]	[illegible]	[illegible]	[illegible]	[illegible]	[illegible]	[illegible]	[illegible]	[illegible]
[illegible]	[illegible]	[illegible]	[illegible]	[illegible]	[illegible]	[illegible]	[illegible]	[illegible]	[illegible]	[illegible]	[illegible]	[illegible]	[illegible]	[illegible]	[illegible]	[illegible]	[illegible]	[illegible]	[illegible]	[illegible]	[illegible]	[illegible]
[illegible]	[illegible]	[illegible]	[illegible]	[illegible]	[illegible]	[illegible]	[illegible]	[illegible]	[illegible]	[illegible]	[illegible]	[illegible]	[illegible]	[illegible]	[illegible]	[illegible]	[illegible]	[illegible]	[illegible]	[illegible]	[illegible]	[illegible]
[illegible]	[illegible]	[illegible]	[illegible]	[illegible]	[illegible]	[illegible]	[illegible]	[illegible]	[illegible]	[illegible]	[illegible]	[illegible]	[illegible]	[illegible]	[illegible]	[illegible]	[illegible]	[illegible]	[illegible]	[illegible]	[illegible]	[illegible]
	Limerick Co.																					
[illegible]	[illegible]	[illegible]	[illegible]	[illegible]	[illegible]	[illegible]	[illegible]	[illegible]	[illegible]	[illegible]	[illegible]	[illegible]	[illegible]	[illegible]	[illegible]	[illegible]	[illegible]	[illegible]	[illegible]	[illegible]	[illegible]	[illegible]
[illegible]	[illegible]	[illegible]	[illegible]	[illegible]	[illegible]	[illegible]	[illegible]	[illegible]	[illegible]	[illegible]	[illegible]	[illegible]	[illegible]	[illegible]	[illegible]	[illegible]	[illegible]	[illegible]	[illegible]	[illegible]	[illegible]	[illegible]
[illegible]	[illegible]	[illegible]	[illegible]	[illegible]	[illegible]	[illegible]	[illegible]	[illegible]	[illegible]	[illegible]	[illegible]	[illegible]	[illegible]	[illegible]	[illegible]	[illegible]	[illegible]	[illegible]	[illegible]	[illegible]	[illegible]	[illegible]
[illegible]	[illegible]	[illegible]	[illegible]	[illegible]	[illegible]	[illegible]	[illegible]	[illegible]	[illegible]	[illegible]	[illegible]	[illegible]	[illegible]	[illegible]	[illegible]	[illegible]	[illegible]	[illegible]	[illegible]	[illegible]	[illegible]	[illegible]
[illegible]	[illegible]	[illegible]	[illegible]	[illegible]	[illegible]	[illegible]	[illegible]	[illegible]	[illegible]	[illegible]	[illegible]	[illegible]	[illegible]	[illegible]	[illegible]	[illegible]	[illegible]	[illegible]	[illegible]	[illegible]	[illegible]	[illegible]
[illegible]	[illegible]	[illegible]	[illegible]	[illegible]	[illegible]	[illegible]	[illegible]	[illegible]	[illegible]	[illegible]	[illegible]	[illegible]	[illegible]	[illegible]	[illegible]	[illegible]	[illegible]	[illegible]	[illegible]	[illegible]	[illegible]	[illegible]
[illegible]	[illegible]	[illegible]	[illegible]	[illegible]	[illegible]	[illegible]	[illegible]	[illegible]	[illegible]	[illegible]	[illegible]	[illegible]	[illegible]	[illegible]	[illegible]	[illegible]	[illegible]	[illegible]	[illegible]	[illegible]	[illegible]	[illegible]
[illegible]	[illegible]	[illegible]	[illegible]	[illegible]	[illegible]	[illegible]	[illegible]	[illegible]	[illegible]	[illegible]	[illegible]	[illegible]	[illegible]	[illegible]	[illegible]	[illegible]	[illegible]	[illegible]	[illegible]	[illegible]	[illegible]	[illegible]
	17. Tipperary Co.																					
[illegible]	[illegible]	[illegible]	[illegible]	[illegible]	[illegible]	[illegible]	[illegible]	[illegible]	[illegible]	[illegible]	[illegible]	[illegible]	[illegible]	[illegible]	[illegible]	[illegible]	[illegible]	[illegible]	[illegible]	[illegible]	[illegible]	[illegible]
[illegible]	[illegible]	[illegible]	[illegible]	[illegible]	[illegible]	[illegible]	[illegible]	[illegible]	[illegible]	[illegible]	[illegible]	[illegible]	[illegible]	[illegible]	[illegible]	[illegible]	[illegible]	[illegible]	[illegible]	[illegible]	[illegible]	[illegible]
[illegible]	[illegible]	[illegible]	[illegible]	[illegible]	[illegible]	[illegible]	[illegible]	[illegible]	[illegible]	[illegible]	[illegible]	[illegible]	[illegible]	[illegible]	[illegible]	[illegible]	[illegible]	[illegible]	[illegible]	[illegible]	[illegible]	[illegible]
[illegible]	[illegible]	[illegible]	[illegible]	[illegible]	[illegible]	[illegible]	[illegible]	[illegible]	[illegible]	[illegible]	[illegible]	[illegible]	[illegible]	[illegible]	[illegible]	[illegible]	[illegible]	[illegible]	[illegible]	[illegible]	[illegible]	[illegible]
[illegible]	[illegible]	[illegible]	[illegible]	[illegible]	[illegible]	[illegible]	[illegible]	[illegible]	[illegible]	[illegible]	[illegible]	[illegible]	[illegible]	[illegible]	[illegible]	[illegible]	[illegible]	[illegible]	[illegible]	[illegible]	[illegible]	[illegible]
[illegible]	[illegible]	[illegible]	[illegible]	[illegible]	[illegible]	[illegible]	[illegible]	[illegible]	[illegible]	[illegible]	[illegible]	[illegible]	[illegible]	[illegible]	[illegible]	[illegible]	[illegible]	[illegible]	[illegible]	[illegible]	[illegible]	[illegible]
[illegible]	[illegible]	[illegible]	[illegible]	[illegible]	[illegible]	[illegible]	[illegible]	[illegible]	[illegible]	[illegible]	[illegible]	[illegible]	[illegible]	[illegible]	[illegible]	[illegible]	[illegible]	[illegible]	[illegible]	[illegible]	[illegible]	[illegible]
[illegible]	[illegible]	[illegible]	[illegible]	[illegible]	[illegible]	[illegible]	[illegible]	[illegible]	[illegible]	[illegible]	[illegible]	[illegible]	[illegible]	[illegible]	[illegible]	[illegible]	[illegible]	[illegible]	[illegible]	[illegible]	[illegible]	[illegible]
[illegible]	[illegible]	[illegible]	[illegible]	[illegible]	[illegible]	[illegible]	[illegible]	[illegible]	[illegible]	[illegible]	[illegible]	[illegible]	[illegible]	[illegible]	[illegible]	[illegible]	[illegible]	[illegible]	[illegible]	[illegible]	[illegible]	[illegible]
[illegible]	[illegible]	[illegible]	[illegible]	[illegible]	[illegible]	[illegible]	[illegible]	[illegible]	[illegible]	[illegible]	[illegible]	[illegible]	[illegible]	[illegible]	[illegible]	[illegible]	[illegible]	[illegible]	[illegible]	[illegible]	[illegible]	[illegible]
[illegible]	[illegible]	[illegible]	[illegible]	[illegible]	[illegible]	[illegible]	[illegible]	[illegible]	[illegible]	[illegible]	[illegible]	[illegible]	[illegible]	[illegible]	[illegible]	[illegible]	[illegible]	[illegible]	[illegible]	[illegible]	[illegible]	[illegible]
[illegible]	[illegible]	[illegible]	[illegible]	[illegible]	[illegible]	[illegible]	[illegible]	[illegible]	[illegible]	[illegible]	[illegible]	[illegible]	[illegible]	[illegible]	[illegible]	[illegible]	[illegible]	[illegible]	[illegible]	[illegible]	[illegible]	[illegible]
	18. Waterford Co.																					
[illegible]	[illegible]	[illegible]	[illegible]	[illegible]	[illegible]	[illegible]	[illegible]	[illegible]	[illegible]	[illegible]	[illegible]	[illegible]	[illegible]	[illegible]	[illegible]	[illegible]	[illegible]	[illegible]	[illegible]	[illegible]	[illegible]	[illegible]
[illegible]	[illegible]	[illegible]	[illegible]	[illegible]	[illegible]	[illegible]	[illegible]	[illegible]	[illegible]	[illegible]	[illegible]	[illegible]	[illegible]	[illegible]	[illegible]	[illegible]	[illegible]	[illegible]	[illegible]	[illegible]	[illegible]	[illegible]
[illegible]	[illegible]	[illegible]	[illegible]	[illegible]	[illegible]	[illegible]	[illegible]	[illegible]	[illegible]	[illegible]	[illegible]	[illegible]	[illegible]	[illegible]	[illegible]	[illegible]	[illegible]	[illegible]	[illegible]	[illegible]	[illegible]	[illegible]
[illegible]	[illegible]	[illegible]	[illegible]	[illegible]	[illegible]	[illegible]	[illegible]	[illegible]	[illegible]	[illegible]	[illegible]	[illegible]	[illegible]	[illegible]	[illegible]	[illegible]	[illegible]	[illegible]	[illegible]	[illegible]	[illegible]	[illegible]
[illegible]	[illegible]	[illegible]	[illegible]	[illegible]	[illegible]	[illegible]	[illegible]	[illegible]	[illegible]	[illegible]	[illegible]	[illegible]	[illegible]	[illegible]	[illegible]	[illegible]	[illegible]	[illegible]	[illegible]	[illegible]	[illegible]	[illegible]
[illegible]	[illegible]	[illegible]	[illegible]	[illegible]	[illegible]	[illegible]	[illegible]	[illegible]	[illegible]	[illegible]	[illegible]	[illegible]	[illegible]	[illegible]	[illegible]	[illegible]	[illegible]	[illegible]	[illegible]	[illegible]	[illegible]	[illegible]
[illegible]	[illegible]	[illegible]	[illegible]	[illegible]	[illegible]	[illegible]	[illegible]	[illegible]	[illegible]	[illegible]	[illegible]	[illegible]	[illegible]	[illegible]	[illegible]	[illegible]	[illegible]	[illegible]	[illegible]	[illegible]	[illegible]	[illegible]

IRELAND.—[illegible] at different Ages registered in the year 1891—in the Superintendent Registrars' Districts and Parts of Districts.—Males—continued.

III.—Province of Ulster.

Superintendent Registrars' Districts and Parts of Districts.		Males.																			
		[illegible]	[illegible]	Ages at Death.																	
				[illegible]	1	2	3	4	[illegible]	[illegible]	[illegible]	[illegible]	[illegible]	[illegible]	[illegible]	[illegible]	[illegible]	[illegible]	[illegible]	[illegible]	[illegible]
No.	[illegible] Antrim Co.																				
[illegible]	Antrim	[illegible]	[illegible]	[illegible]	[illegible]	[illegible]	[illegible]	[illegible]	[illegible]	[illegible]	[illegible]	[illegible]	[illegible]	[illegible]	[illegible]	[illegible]	[illegible]	[illegible]	[illegible]	[illegible]	[illegible]
[illegible]	[illegible]	[illegible]	[illegible]	[illegible]	[illegible]	[illegible]	[illegible]	[illegible]	[illegible]	[illegible]	[illegible]	[illegible]	[illegible]	[illegible]	[illegible]	[illegible]	[illegible]	[illegible]	[illegible]	[illegible]	[illegible]
[illegible]	[illegible]	[illegible]	[illegible]	[illegible]	[illegible]	[illegible]	[illegible]	[illegible]	[illegible]	[illegible]	[illegible]	[illegible]	[illegible]	[illegible]	[illegible]	[illegible]	[illegible]	[illegible]	[illegible]	[illegible]	[illegible]
[illegible]	[illegible], part of	[illegible]	[illegible]	[illegible]	[illegible]	[illegible]	[illegible]	[illegible]	[illegible]	[illegible]	[illegible]	[illegible]	[illegible]	[illegible]	[illegible]	[illegible]	[illegible]	[illegible]	[illegible]	[illegible]	[illegible]
[illegible]	Belfast, do.	[illegible]	[illegible]	[illegible]	[illegible]	[illegible]	[illegible]	[illegible]	[illegible]	[illegible]	[illegible]	[illegible]	[illegible]	[illegible]	[illegible]	[illegible]	[illegible]	[illegible]	[illegible]	[illegible]	[illegible]
[illegible]	[illegible], do.	[illegible]	[illegible]	[illegible]	[illegible]	[illegible]	[illegible]	[illegible]	[illegible]	[illegible]	[illegible]	[illegible]	[illegible]	[illegible]	[illegible]	[illegible]	[illegible]	[illegible]	[illegible]	[illegible]	[illegible]
[illegible]	Larne	[illegible]	[illegible]	[illegible]	[illegible]	[illegible]	[illegible]	[illegible]	[illegible]	[illegible]	[illegible]	[illegible]	[illegible]	[illegible]	[illegible]	[illegible]	[illegible]	[illegible]	[illegible]	[illegible]	[illegible]
[illegible]	[illegible], part of	[illegible]	[illegible]	[illegible]	[illegible]	[illegible]	[illegible]	[illegible]	[illegible]	[illegible]	[illegible]	[illegible]	[illegible]	[illegible]	[illegible]	[illegible]	[illegible]	[illegible]	[illegible]	[illegible]	[illegible]
[illegible]	[illegible], do.	[illegible]	[illegible]	[illegible]	[illegible]	[illegible]	[illegible]	[illegible]	[illegible]	[illegible]	[illegible]	[illegible]	[illegible]	[illegible]	[illegible]	[illegible]	[illegible]	[illegible]	[illegible]	[illegible]	[illegible]
	[illegible] Armagh Co.																				
[illegible]	Armagh, part of	[illegible]	[illegible]	[illegible]	[illegible]	[illegible]	[illegible]	[illegible]	[illegible]	[illegible]	[illegible]	[illegible]	[illegible]	[illegible]	[illegible]	[illegible]	[illegible]	[illegible]	[illegible]	[illegible]	[illegible]
[illegible]	[illegible], do.	[illegible]	[illegible]	[illegible]	[illegible]	[illegible]	[illegible]	[illegible]	[illegible]	[illegible]	[illegible]	[illegible]	[illegible]	[illegible]	[illegible]	[illegible]	[illegible]	[illegible]	[illegible]	[illegible]	[illegible]
[illegible]	[illegible], do.	[illegible]	[illegible]	[illegible]	[illegible]	[illegible]	[illegible]	[illegible]	[illegible]	[illegible]	[illegible]	[illegible]	[illegible]	[illegible]	[illegible]	[illegible]	[illegible]	[illegible]	[illegible]	[illegible]	[illegible]
[illegible]	Dundalk, do.	[illegible]	[illegible]	[illegible]	[illegible]	[illegible]	[illegible]	[illegible]	[illegible]	[illegible]	[illegible]	[illegible]	[illegible]	[illegible]	[illegible]	[illegible]	[illegible]	[illegible]	[illegible]	[illegible]	[illegible]
[illegible]	[illegible], do.	[illegible]	[illegible]	[illegible]	[illegible]	[illegible]	[illegible]	[illegible]	[illegible]	[illegible]	[illegible]	[illegible]	[illegible]	[illegible]	[illegible]	[illegible]	[illegible]	[illegible]	[illegible]	[illegible]	[illegible]
[illegible]	Newry, do.	[illegible]	[illegible]	[illegible]	[illegible]	[illegible]	[illegible]	[illegible]	[illegible]	[illegible]	[illegible]	[illegible]	[illegible]	[illegible]	[illegible]	[illegible]	[illegible]	[illegible]	[illegible]	[illegible]	[illegible]
	[illegible] Cavan Co.																				
[illegible]	[illegible]	[illegible]	[illegible]	[illegible]	[illegible]	[illegible]	[illegible]	[illegible]	[illegible]	[illegible]	[illegible]	[illegible]	[illegible]	[illegible]	[illegible]	[illegible]	[illegible]	[illegible]	[illegible]	[illegible]	[illegible]
[illegible]	[illegible], part of	[illegible]	[illegible]	[illegible]	[illegible]	[illegible]	[illegible]	[illegible]	[illegible]	[illegible]	[illegible]	[illegible]	[illegible]	[illegible]	[illegible]	[illegible]	[illegible]	[illegible]	[illegible]	[illegible]	[illegible]
[illegible]	Cavan	[illegible]	[illegible]	[illegible]	[illegible]	[illegible]	[illegible]	[illegible]	[illegible]	[illegible]	[illegible]	[illegible]	[illegible]	[illegible]	[illegible]	[illegible]	[illegible]	[illegible]	[illegible]	[illegible]	[illegible]
[illegible]	[illegible], part of	[illegible]	[illegible]	[illegible]	[illegible]	[illegible]	[illegible]	[illegible]	[illegible]	[illegible]	[illegible]	[illegible]	[illegible]	[illegible]	[illegible]	[illegible]	[illegible]	[illegible]	[illegible]	[illegible]	[illegible]
[illegible]	[illegible], do.	[illegible]	[illegible]	[illegible]	[illegible]	[illegible]	[illegible]	[illegible]	[illegible]	[illegible]	[illegible]	[illegible]	[illegible]	[illegible]	[illegible]	[illegible]	[illegible]	[illegible]	[illegible]	[illegible]	[illegible]
[illegible]	[illegible], do.	[illegible]	[illegible]	[illegible]	[illegible]	[illegible]	[illegible]	[illegible]	[illegible]	[illegible]	[illegible]	[illegible]	[illegible]	[illegible]	[illegible]	[illegible]	[illegible]	[illegible]	[illegible]	[illegible]	[illegible]
[illegible]	[illegible], do.	[illegible]	[illegible]	[illegible]	[illegible]	[illegible]	[illegible]	[illegible]	[illegible]	[illegible]	[illegible]	[illegible]	[illegible]	[illegible]	[illegible]	[illegible]	[illegible]	[illegible]	[illegible]	[illegible]	[illegible]
[illegible]	[illegible], do.	[illegible]	[illegible]	[illegible]	[illegible]	[illegible]	[illegible]	[illegible]	[illegible]	[illegible]	[illegible]	[illegible]	[illegible]	[illegible]	[illegible]	[illegible]	[illegible]	[illegible]	[illegible]	[illegible]	[illegible]
	[illegible] Donegal Co.																				
[illegible]	[illegible], part of	[illegible]	[illegible]	[illegible]	[illegible]	[illegible]	[illegible]	[illegible]	[illegible]	[illegible]	[illegible]	[illegible]	[illegible]	[illegible]	[illegible]	[illegible]	[illegible]	[illegible]	[illegible]	[illegible]	[illegible]
[illegible]	[illegible]	[illegible]	[illegible]	[illegible]	[illegible]	[illegible]	[illegible]	[illegible]	[illegible]	[illegible]	[illegible]	[illegible]	[illegible]	[illegible]	[illegible]	[illegible]	[illegible]	[illegible]	[illegible]	[illegible]	[illegible]
[illegible]	[illegible]	[illegible]	[illegible]	[illegible]	[illegible]	[illegible]	[illegible]	[illegible]	[illegible]	[illegible]	[illegible]	[illegible]	[illegible]	[illegible]	[illegible]	[illegible]	[illegible]	[illegible]	[illegible]	[illegible]	[illegible]
[illegible]	[illegible]	[illegible]	[illegible]	[illegible]	[illegible]	[illegible]	[illegible]	[illegible]	[illegible]	[illegible]	[illegible]	[illegible]	[illegible]	[illegible]	[illegible]	[illegible]	[illegible]	[illegible]	[illegible]	[illegible]	[illegible]
[illegible]	[illegible]	[illegible]	[illegible]	[illegible]	[illegible]	[illegible]	[illegible]	[illegible]	[illegible]	[illegible]	[illegible]	[illegible]	[illegible]	[illegible]	[illegible]	[illegible]	[illegible]	[illegible]	[illegible]	[illegible]	[illegible]
[illegible]	[illegible]	[illegible]	[illegible]	[illegible]	[illegible]	[illegible]	[illegible]	[illegible]	[illegible]	[illegible]	[illegible]	[illegible]	[illegible]	[illegible]	[illegible]	[illegible]	[illegible]	[illegible]	[illegible]	[illegible]	[illegible]
[illegible]	[illegible], part of	[illegible]	[illegible]	[illegible]	[illegible]	[illegible]	[illegible]	[illegible]	[illegible]	[illegible]	[illegible]	[illegible]	[illegible]	[illegible]	[illegible]	[illegible]	[illegible]	[illegible]	[illegible]	[illegible]	[illegible]
[illegible]	[illegible]	[illegible]	[illegible]	[illegible]	[illegible]	[illegible]	[illegible]	[illegible]	[illegible]	[illegible]	[illegible]	[illegible]	[illegible]	[illegible]	[illegible]	[illegible]	[illegible]	[illegible]	[illegible]	[illegible]	[illegible]
[illegible]	[illegible], part of	[illegible]	[illegible]	[illegible]	[illegible]	[illegible]	[illegible]	[illegible]	[illegible]	[illegible]	[illegible]	[illegible]	[illegible]	[illegible]	[illegible]	[illegible]	[illegible]	[illegible]	[illegible]	[illegible]	[illegible]
[illegible]	[illegible]	[illegible]	[illegible]	[illegible]	[illegible]	[illegible]	[illegible]	[illegible]	[illegible]	[illegible]	[illegible]	[illegible]	[illegible]	[illegible]	[illegible]	[illegible]	[illegible]	[illegible]	[illegible]	[illegible]	[illegible]
	[illegible] Down Co.																				
[illegible]	[illegible], part of	[illegible]	[illegible]	[illegible]	[illegible]	[illegible]	[illegible]	[illegible]	[illegible]	[illegible]	[illegible]	[illegible]	[illegible]	[illegible]	[illegible]	[illegible]	[illegible]	[illegible]	[illegible]	[illegible]	[illegible]
[illegible]	[illegible], do.	[illegible]	[illegible]	[illegible]	[illegible]	[illegible]	[illegible]	[illegible]	[illegible]	[illegible]	[illegible]	[illegible]	[illegible]	[illegible]	[illegible]	[illegible]	[illegible]	[illegible]	[illegible]	[illegible]	[illegible]
[illegible]	[illegible]	[illegible]	[illegible]	[illegible]	[illegible]	[illegible]	[illegible]	[illegible]	[illegible]	[illegible]	[illegible]	[illegible]	[illegible]	[illegible]	[illegible]	[illegible]	[illegible]	[illegible]	[illegible]	[illegible]	[illegible]
[illegible]	[illegible]	[illegible]	[illegible]	[illegible]	[illegible]	[illegible]	[illegible]	[illegible]	[illegible]	[illegible]	[illegible]	[illegible]	[illegible]	[illegible]	[illegible]	[illegible]	[illegible]	[illegible]	[illegible]	[illegible]	[illegible]
[illegible]	[illegible], part of	[illegible]	[illegible]	[illegible]	[illegible]	[illegible]	[illegible]	[illegible]	[illegible]	[illegible]	[illegible]	[illegible]	[illegible]	[illegible]	[illegible]	[illegible]	[illegible]	[illegible]	[illegible]	[illegible]	[illegible]
[illegible]	[illegible], do.	[illegible]	[illegible]	[illegible]	[illegible]	[illegible]	[illegible]	[illegible]	[illegible]	[illegible]	[illegible]	[illegible]	[illegible]	[illegible]	[illegible]	[illegible]	[illegible]	[illegible]	[illegible]	[illegible]	[illegible]
[illegible]	[illegible], do.	[illegible]	[illegible]	[illegible]	[illegible]	[illegible]	[illegible]	[illegible]	[illegible]	[illegible]	[illegible]	[illegible]	[illegible]	[illegible]	[illegible]	[illegible]	[illegible]	[illegible]	[illegible]	[illegible]	[illegible]
[illegible]	[illegible]	[illegible]	[illegible]	[illegible]	[illegible]	[illegible]	[illegible]	[illegible]	[illegible]	[illegible]	[illegible]	[illegible]	[illegible]	[illegible]	[illegible]	[illegible]	[illegible]	[illegible]	[illegible]	[illegible]	[illegible]

IRELAND.—[illegible] at different Ages registered in the year 1891—in the Superintendent Registrars' Districts and Parts of Districts in each County.—Males—*continued.*

III.—Province of Ulster—*continued.*

Superintendent Registrars' Districts and Parts of Districts.		Males.																			
		[illegible]	[illegible]	Ages at Death.																	
No.				[illegible]	1	2	3	4	[illegible]	5-	10-	15-	20-	25-	[illegible]	[illegible]	[illegible]	[illegible]	[illegible]	[illegible]	[illegible]
	[illegible] Fermanagh Co.																				
[illegible]	[illegible]	[illegible]	[illegible]	[illegible]	[illegible]	[illegible]	[illegible]	[illegible]	[illegible]	[illegible]	[illegible]	[illegible]	[illegible]	[illegible]	[illegible]	[illegible]	[illegible]	[illegible]	[illegible]	[illegible]	[illegible]
[illegible]	[illegible]	[illegible]	[illegible]	[illegible]	[illegible]	[illegible]	[illegible]	[illegible]	[illegible]	[illegible]	[illegible]	[illegible]	[illegible]	[illegible]	[illegible]	[illegible]	[illegible]	[illegible]	[illegible]	[illegible]	[illegible]
[illegible]	[illegible]	[illegible]	[illegible]	[illegible]	[illegible]	[illegible]	[illegible]	[illegible]	[illegible]	[illegible]	[illegible]	[illegible]	[illegible]	[illegible]	[illegible]	[illegible]	[illegible]	[illegible]	[illegible]	[illegible]	[illegible]
[illegible]	[illegible]	[illegible]	[illegible]	[illegible]	[illegible]	[illegible]	[illegible]	[illegible]	[illegible]	[illegible]	[illegible]	[illegible]	[illegible]	[illegible]	[illegible]	[illegible]	[illegible]	[illegible]	[illegible]	[illegible]	[illegible]
[illegible]	[illegible]	[illegible]	[illegible]	[illegible]	[illegible]	[illegible]	[illegible]	[illegible]	[illegible]	[illegible]	[illegible]	[illegible]	[illegible]	[illegible]	[illegible]	[illegible]	[illegible]	[illegible]	[illegible]	[illegible]	[illegible]
	[illegible] Londonderry Co.																				
[illegible]	[illegible]	[illegible]	[illegible]	[illegible]	[illegible]	[illegible]	[illegible]	[illegible]	[illegible]	[illegible]	[illegible]	[illegible]	[illegible]	[illegible]	[illegible]	[illegible]	[illegible]	[illegible]	[illegible]	[illegible]	[illegible]
[illegible]	[illegible]	[illegible]	[illegible]	[illegible]	[illegible]	[illegible]	[illegible]	[illegible]	[illegible]	[illegible]	[illegible]	[illegible]	[illegible]	[illegible]	[illegible]	[illegible]	[illegible]	[illegible]	[illegible]	[illegible]	[illegible]
[illegible]	[illegible]	[illegible]	[illegible]	[illegible]	[illegible]	[illegible]	[illegible]	[illegible]	[illegible]	[illegible]	[illegible]	[illegible]	[illegible]	[illegible]	[illegible]	[illegible]	[illegible]	[illegible]	[illegible]	[illegible]	[illegible]
[illegible]	[illegible]	[illegible]	[illegible]	[illegible]	[illegible]	[illegible]	[illegible]	[illegible]	[illegible]	[illegible]	[illegible]	[illegible]	[illegible]	[illegible]	[illegible]	[illegible]	[illegible]	[illegible]	[illegible]	[illegible]	[illegible]
[illegible]	[illegible]	[illegible]	[illegible]	[illegible]	[illegible]	[illegible]	[illegible]	[illegible]	[illegible]	[illegible]	[illegible]	[illegible]	[illegible]	[illegible]	[illegible]	[illegible]	[illegible]	[illegible]	[illegible]	[illegible]	[illegible]
	[illegible] Monaghan Co.																				
[illegible]	[illegible]	[illegible]	[illegible]	[illegible]	[illegible]	[illegible]	[illegible]	[illegible]	[illegible]	[illegible]	[illegible]	[illegible]	[illegible]	[illegible]	[illegible]	[illegible]	[illegible]	[illegible]	[illegible]	[illegible]	[illegible]
[illegible]	[illegible]	[illegible]	[illegible]	[illegible]	[illegible]	[illegible]	[illegible]	[illegible]	[illegible]	[illegible]	[illegible]	[illegible]	[illegible]	[illegible]	[illegible]	[illegible]	[illegible]	[illegible]	[illegible]	[illegible]	[illegible]
[illegible]	[illegible]	[illegible]	[illegible]	[illegible]	[illegible]	[illegible]	[illegible]	[illegible]	[illegible]	[illegible]	[illegible]	[illegible]	[illegible]	[illegible]	[illegible]	[illegible]	[illegible]	[illegible]	[illegible]	[illegible]	[illegible]
[illegible]	[illegible]	[illegible]	[illegible]	[illegible]	[illegible]	[illegible]	[illegible]	[illegible]	[illegible]	[illegible]	[illegible]	[illegible]	[illegible]	[illegible]	[illegible]	[illegible]	[illegible]	[illegible]	[illegible]	[illegible]	[illegible]
[illegible]	[illegible]	[illegible]	[illegible]	[illegible]	[illegible]	[illegible]	[illegible]	[illegible]	[illegible]	[illegible]	[illegible]	[illegible]	[illegible]	[illegible]	[illegible]	[illegible]	[illegible]	[illegible]	[illegible]	[illegible]	[illegible]
[illegible]	[illegible]	[illegible]	[illegible]	[illegible]	[illegible]	[illegible]	[illegible]	[illegible]	[illegible]	[illegible]	[illegible]	[illegible]	[illegible]	[illegible]	[illegible]	[illegible]	[illegible]	[illegible]	[illegible]	[illegible]	[illegible]
[illegible]	[illegible]	[illegible]	[illegible]	[illegible]	[illegible]	[illegible]	[illegible]	[illegible]	[illegible]	[illegible]	[illegible]	[illegible]	[illegible]	[illegible]	[illegible]	[illegible]	[illegible]	[illegible]	[illegible]	[illegible]	[illegible]
	[illegible] Tyrone Co.																				
[illegible]	[illegible]	[illegible]	[illegible]	[illegible]	[illegible]	[illegible]	[illegible]	[illegible]	[illegible]	[illegible]	[illegible]	[illegible]	[illegible]	[illegible]	[illegible]	[illegible]	[illegible]	[illegible]	[illegible]	[illegible]	[illegible]
[illegible]	[illegible]	[illegible]	[illegible]	[illegible]	[illegible]	[illegible]	[illegible]	[illegible]	[illegible]	[illegible]	[illegible]	[illegible]	[illegible]	[illegible]	[illegible]	[illegible]	[illegible]	[illegible]	[illegible]	[illegible]	[illegible]
[illegible]	[illegible]	[illegible]	[illegible]	[illegible]	[illegible]	[illegible]	[illegible]	[illegible]	[illegible]	[illegible]	[illegible]	[illegible]	[illegible]	[illegible]	[illegible]	[illegible]	[illegible]	[illegible]	[illegible]	[illegible]	[illegible]
[illegible]	[illegible]	[illegible]	[illegible]	[illegible]	[illegible]	[illegible]	[illegible]	[illegible]	[illegible]	[illegible]	[illegible]	[illegible]	[illegible]	[illegible]	[illegible]	[illegible]	[illegible]	[illegible]	[illegible]	[illegible]	[illegible]
[illegible]	[illegible]	[illegible]	[illegible]	[illegible]	[illegible]	[illegible]	[illegible]	[illegible]	[illegible]	[illegible]	[illegible]	[illegible]	[illegible]	[illegible]	[illegible]	[illegible]	[illegible]	[illegible]	[illegible]	[illegible]	[illegible]
[illegible]	[illegible]	[illegible]	[illegible]	[illegible]	[illegible]	[illegible]	[illegible]	[illegible]	[illegible]	[illegible]	[illegible]	[illegible]	[illegible]	[illegible]	[illegible]	[illegible]	[illegible]	[illegible]	[illegible]	[illegible]	[illegible]
[illegible]	[illegible]	[illegible]	[illegible]	[illegible]	[illegible]	[illegible]	[illegible]	[illegible]	[illegible]	[illegible]	[illegible]	[illegible]	[illegible]	[illegible]	[illegible]	[illegible]	[illegible]	[illegible]	[illegible]	[illegible]	[illegible]
[illegible]	[illegible]	[illegible]	[illegible]	[illegible]	[illegible]	[illegible]	[illegible]	[illegible]	[illegible]	[illegible]	[illegible]	[illegible]	[illegible]	[illegible]	[illegible]	[illegible]	[illegible]	[illegible]	[illegible]	[illegible]	[illegible]
[illegible]	[illegible]	[illegible]	[illegible]	[illegible]	[illegible]	[illegible]	[illegible]	[illegible]	[illegible]	[illegible]	[illegible]	[illegible]	[illegible]	[illegible]	[illegible]	[illegible]	[illegible]	[illegible]	[illegible]	[illegible]	[illegible]

IV.—Province of Connaught.

No.	District																				
	[illegible] Galway Co.																				
[illegible]	[illegible]	[illegible]	[illegible]	[illegible]	[illegible]	[illegible]	[illegible]	[illegible]	[illegible]	[illegible]	[illegible]	[illegible]	[illegible]	[illegible]	[illegible]	[illegible]	[illegible]	[illegible]	[illegible]	[illegible]	[illegible]
[illegible]	[illegible]	[illegible]	[illegible]	[illegible]	[illegible]	[illegible]	[illegible]	[illegible]	[illegible]	[illegible]	[illegible]	[illegible]	[illegible]	[illegible]	[illegible]	[illegible]	[illegible]	[illegible]	[illegible]	[illegible]	[illegible]
[illegible]	[illegible]	[illegible]	[illegible]	[illegible]	[illegible]	[illegible]	[illegible]	[illegible]	[illegible]	[illegible]	[illegible]	[illegible]	[illegible]	[illegible]	[illegible]	[illegible]	[illegible]	[illegible]	[illegible]	[illegible]	[illegible]
[illegible]	[illegible]	[illegible]	[illegible]	[illegible]	[illegible]	[illegible]	[illegible]	[illegible]	[illegible]	[illegible]	[illegible]	[illegible]	[illegible]	[illegible]	[illegible]	[illegible]	[illegible]	[illegible]	[illegible]	[illegible]	[illegible]
[illegible]	[illegible]	[illegible]	[illegible]	[illegible]	[illegible]	[illegible]	[illegible]	[illegible]	[illegible]	[illegible]	[illegible]	[illegible]	[illegible]	[illegible]	[illegible]	[illegible]	[illegible]	[illegible]	[illegible]	[illegible]	[illegible]
[illegible]	[illegible]	[illegible]	[illegible]	[illegible]	[illegible]	[illegible]	[illegible]	[illegible]	[illegible]	[illegible]	[illegible]	[illegible]	[illegible]	[illegible]	[illegible]	[illegible]	[illegible]	[illegible]	[illegible]	[illegible]	[illegible]
[illegible]	[illegible]	[illegible]	[illegible]	[illegible]	[illegible]	[illegible]	[illegible]	[illegible]	[illegible]	[illegible]	[illegible]	[illegible]	[illegible]	[illegible]	[illegible]	[illegible]	[illegible]	[illegible]	[illegible]	[illegible]	[illegible]
[illegible]	[illegible]	[illegible]	[illegible]	[illegible]	[illegible]	[illegible]	[illegible]	[illegible]	[illegible]	[illegible]	[illegible]	[illegible]	[illegible]	[illegible]	[illegible]	[illegible]	[illegible]	[illegible]	[illegible]	[illegible]	[illegible]
[illegible]	[illegible]	[illegible]	[illegible]	[illegible]	[illegible]	[illegible]	[illegible]	[illegible]	[illegible]	[illegible]	[illegible]	[illegible]	[illegible]	[illegible]	[illegible]	[illegible]	[illegible]	[illegible]	[illegible]	[illegible]	[illegible]
[illegible]	[illegible]	[illegible]	[illegible]	[illegible]	[illegible]	[illegible]	[illegible]	[illegible]	[illegible]	[illegible]	[illegible]	[illegible]	[illegible]	[illegible]	[illegible]	[illegible]	[illegible]	[illegible]	[illegible]	[illegible]	[illegible]
[illegible]	[illegible]	[illegible]	[illegible]	[illegible]	[illegible]	[illegible]	[illegible]	[illegible]	[illegible]	[illegible]	[illegible]	[illegible]	[illegible]	[illegible]	[illegible]	[illegible]	[illegible]	[illegible]	[illegible]	[illegible]	[illegible]
[illegible]	[illegible]	[illegible]	[illegible]	[illegible]	[illegible]	[illegible]	[illegible]	[illegible]	[illegible]	[illegible]	[illegible]	[illegible]	[illegible]	[illegible]	[illegible]	[illegible]	[illegible]	[illegible]	[illegible]	[illegible]	[illegible]
[illegible]	[illegible]	[illegible]	[illegible]	[illegible]	[illegible]	[illegible]	[illegible]	[illegible]	[illegible]	[illegible]	[illegible]	[illegible]	[illegible]	[illegible]	[illegible]	[illegible]	[illegible]	[illegible]	[illegible]	[illegible]	[illegible]
[illegible]	[illegible]	[illegible]	[illegible]	[illegible]	[illegible]	[illegible]	[illegible]	[illegible]	[illegible]	[illegible]	[illegible]	[illegible]	[illegible]	[illegible]	[illegible]	[illegible]	[illegible]	[illegible]	[illegible]	[illegible]	[illegible]

	Fermanagh Co.															
[illegible]	[illegible]	[illegible]	[illegible]	[illegible]	[illegible]	[illegible]	[illegible]	[illegible]	[illegible]	[illegible]	[illegible]	[illegible]	[illegible]	[illegible]	[illegible]	[illegible]
[illegible]	[illegible]	[illegible]	[illegible]	[illegible]	[illegible]	[illegible]	[illegible]	[illegible]	[illegible]	[illegible]	[illegible]	[illegible]	[illegible]	[illegible]	[illegible]	[illegible]
[illegible]	[illegible]	[illegible]	[illegible]	[illegible]	[illegible]	[illegible]	[illegible]	[illegible]	[illegible]	[illegible]	[illegible]	[illegible]	[illegible]	[illegible]	[illegible]	[illegible]
[illegible]	[illegible]	[illegible]	[illegible]	[illegible]	[illegible]	[illegible]	[illegible]	[illegible]	[illegible]	[illegible]	[illegible]	[illegible]	[illegible]	[illegible]	[illegible]	[illegible]
[illegible]	[illegible]	[illegible]	[illegible]	[illegible]	[illegible]	[illegible]	[illegible]	[illegible]	[illegible]	[illegible]	[illegible]	[illegible]	[illegible]	[illegible]	[illegible]	[illegible]
	Londonderry Co.															
[illegible]	[illegible]	[illegible]	[illegible]	[illegible]	[illegible]	[illegible]	[illegible]	[illegible]	[illegible]	[illegible]	[illegible]	[illegible]	[illegible]	[illegible]	[illegible]	[illegible]
[illegible]	[illegible]	[illegible]	[illegible]	[illegible]	[illegible]	[illegible]	[illegible]	[illegible]	[illegible]	[illegible]	[illegible]	[illegible]	[illegible]	[illegible]	[illegible]	[illegible]
[illegible]	[illegible]	[illegible]	[illegible]	[illegible]	[illegible]	[illegible]	[illegible]	[illegible]	[illegible]	[illegible]	[illegible]	[illegible]	[illegible]	[illegible]	[illegible]	[illegible]
[illegible]	[illegible]	[illegible]	[illegible]	[illegible]	[illegible]	[illegible]	[illegible]	[illegible]	[illegible]	[illegible]	[illegible]	[illegible]	[illegible]	[illegible]	[illegible]	[illegible]
[illegible]	[illegible]	[illegible]	[illegible]	[illegible]	[illegible]	[illegible]	[illegible]	[illegible]	[illegible]	[illegible]	[illegible]	[illegible]	[illegible]	[illegible]	[illegible]	[illegible]
	Monaghan Co.															
[illegible]	[illegible]	[illegible]	[illegible]	[illegible]	[illegible]	[illegible]	[illegible]	[illegible]	[illegible]	[illegible]	[illegible]	[illegible]	[illegible]	[illegible]	[illegible]	[illegible]
[illegible]	[illegible]	[illegible]	[illegible]	[illegible]	[illegible]	[illegible]	[illegible]	[illegible]	[illegible]	[illegible]	[illegible]	[illegible]	[illegible]	[illegible]	[illegible]	[illegible]
[illegible]	[illegible]	[illegible]	[illegible]	[illegible]	[illegible]	[illegible]	[illegible]	[illegible]	[illegible]	[illegible]	[illegible]	[illegible]	[illegible]	[illegible]	[illegible]	[illegible]
[illegible]	[illegible]	[illegible]	[illegible]	[illegible]	[illegible]	[illegible]	[illegible]	[illegible]	[illegible]	[illegible]	[illegible]	[illegible]	[illegible]	[illegible]	[illegible]	[illegible]
[illegible]	[illegible]	[illegible]	[illegible]	[illegible]	[illegible]	[illegible]	[illegible]	[illegible]	[illegible]	[illegible]	[illegible]	[illegible]	[illegible]	[illegible]	[illegible]	[illegible]
[illegible]	[illegible]	[illegible]	[illegible]	[illegible]	[illegible]	[illegible]	[illegible]	[illegible]	[illegible]	[illegible]	[illegible]	[illegible]	[illegible]	[illegible]	[illegible]	[illegible]
[illegible]	[illegible]	[illegible]	[illegible]	[illegible]	[illegible]	[illegible]	[illegible]	[illegible]	[illegible]	[illegible]	[illegible]	[illegible]	[illegible]	[illegible]	[illegible]	[illegible]
	Tyrone Co.															
[illegible]	[illegible]	[illegible]	[illegible]	[illegible]	[illegible]	[illegible]	[illegible]	[illegible]	[illegible]	[illegible]	[illegible]	[illegible]	[illegible]	[illegible]	[illegible]	[illegible]
[illegible]	[illegible]	[illegible]	[illegible]	[illegible]	[illegible]	[illegible]	[illegible]	[illegible]	[illegible]	[illegible]	[illegible]	[illegible]	[illegible]	[illegible]	[illegible]	[illegible]
[illegible]	[illegible]	[illegible]	[illegible]	[illegible]	[illegible]	[illegible]	[illegible]	[illegible]	[illegible]	[illegible]	[illegible]	[illegible]	[illegible]	[illegible]	[illegible]	[illegible]
[illegible]	[illegible]	[illegible]	[illegible]	[illegible]	[illegible]	[illegible]	[illegible]	[illegible]	[illegible]	[illegible]	[illegible]	[illegible]	[illegible]	[illegible]	[illegible]	[illegible]
[illegible]	[illegible]	[illegible]	[illegible]	[illegible]	[illegible]	[illegible]	[illegible]	[illegible]	[illegible]	[illegible]	[illegible]	[illegible]	[illegible]	[illegible]	[illegible]	[illegible]
[illegible]	[illegible]	[illegible]	[illegible]	[illegible]	[illegible]	[illegible]	[illegible]	[illegible]	[illegible]	[illegible]	[illegible]	[illegible]	[illegible]	[illegible]	[illegible]	[illegible]
[illegible]	[illegible]	[illegible]	[illegible]	[illegible]	[illegible]	[illegible]	[illegible]	[illegible]	[illegible]	[illegible]	[illegible]	[illegible]	[illegible]	[illegible]	[illegible]	[illegible]
[illegible]	[illegible]	[illegible]	[illegible]	[illegible]	[illegible]	[illegible]	[illegible]	[illegible]	[illegible]	[illegible]	[illegible]	[illegible]	[illegible]	[illegible]	[illegible]	[illegible]
[illegible]	[illegible]	[illegible]	[illegible]	[illegible]	[illegible]	[illegible]	[illegible]	[illegible]	[illegible]	[illegible]	[illegible]	[illegible]	[illegible]	[illegible]	[illegible]	[illegible]

IV.—PROVINCE OF CONNAUGHT.

	Galway Co.															
[illegible]	[illegible]	[illegible]	[illegible]	[illegible]	[illegible]	[illegible]	[illegible]	[illegible]	[illegible]	[illegible]	[illegible]	[illegible]	[illegible]	[illegible]	[illegible]	[illegible]
[illegible]	[illegible]	[illegible]	[illegible]	[illegible]	[illegible]	[illegible]	[illegible]	[illegible]	[illegible]	[illegible]	[illegible]	[illegible]	[illegible]	[illegible]	[illegible]	[illegible]
[illegible]	[illegible]	[illegible]	[illegible]	[illegible]	[illegible]	[illegible]	[illegible]	[illegible]	[illegible]	[illegible]	[illegible]	[illegible]	[illegible]	[illegible]	[illegible]	[illegible]
[illegible]	[illegible]	[illegible]	[illegible]	[illegible]	[illegible]	[illegible]	[illegible]	[illegible]	[illegible]	[illegible]	[illegible]	[illegible]	[illegible]	[illegible]	[illegible]	[illegible]
[illegible]	[illegible]	[illegible]	[illegible]	[illegible]	[illegible]	[illegible]	[illegible]	[illegible]	[illegible]	[illegible]	[illegible]	[illegible]	[illegible]	[illegible]	[illegible]	[illegible]
[illegible]	[illegible]	[illegible]	[illegible]	[illegible]	[illegible]	[illegible]	[illegible]	[illegible]	[illegible]	[illegible]	[illegible]	[illegible]	[illegible]	[illegible]	[illegible]	[illegible]
[illegible]	[illegible]	[illegible]	[illegible]	[illegible]	[illegible]	[illegible]	[illegible]	[illegible]	[illegible]	[illegible]	[illegible]	[illegible]	[illegible]	[illegible]	[illegible]	[illegible]
[illegible]	[illegible]	[illegible]	[illegible]	[illegible]	[illegible]	[illegible]	[illegible]	[illegible]	[illegible]	[illegible]	[illegible]	[illegible]	[illegible]	[illegible]	[illegible]	[illegible]
[illegible]	[illegible]	[illegible]	[illegible]	[illegible]	[illegible]	[illegible]	[illegible]	[illegible]	[illegible]	[illegible]	[illegible]	[illegible]	[illegible]	[illegible]	[illegible]	[illegible]
[illegible]	[illegible]	[illegible]	[illegible]	[illegible]	[illegible]	[illegible]	[illegible]	[illegible]	[illegible]	[illegible]	[illegible]	[illegible]	[illegible]	[illegible]	[illegible]	[illegible]
[illegible]	[illegible]	[illegible]	[illegible]	[illegible]	[illegible]	[illegible]	[illegible]	[illegible]	[illegible]	[illegible]	[illegible]	[illegible]	[illegible]	[illegible]	[illegible]	[illegible]
[illegible]	[illegible]	[illegible]	[illegible]	[illegible]	[illegible]	[illegible]	[illegible]	[illegible]	[illegible]	[illegible]	[illegible]	[illegible]	[illegible]	[illegible]	[illegible]	[illegible]
[illegible]	[illegible]	[illegible]	[illegible]	[illegible]	[illegible]	[illegible]	[illegible]	[illegible]	[illegible]	[illegible]	[illegible]	[illegible]	[illegible]	[illegible]	[illegible]	[illegible]

IRELAND.—DEATHS at different AGES registered in the year 1891—in the SUPERINTENDENT REGISTRARS' DISTRICTS and PARTS of DISTRICTS in each COUNTY.—MALES—continued.

IV.—PROVINCE OF CONNAUGHT—continued.

No.	Superintendent Registrars' Districts and Parts of Districts	[illegible]	[illegible]	[illegible]	1	2	3	4	[illegible]	5-	10-	15-	20-	25-	35-	45-	55-	65-	75-	85-	[illegible]
	[illegible] Co.																				
[illegible]	[illegible]	[illegible]	[illegible]	[illegible]	[illegible]	[illegible]	[illegible]	[illegible]	[illegible]	[illegible]	[illegible]	[illegible]	[illegible]	[illegible]	[illegible]	[illegible]	[illegible]	[illegible]	[illegible]	[illegible]	[illegible]
[illegible]	[illegible]	[illegible]	[illegible]	[illegible]	[illegible]	[illegible]	[illegible]	[illegible]	[illegible]	[illegible]	[illegible]	[illegible]	[illegible]	[illegible]	[illegible]	[illegible]	[illegible]	[illegible]	[illegible]	[illegible]	[illegible]
[illegible]	[illegible]	[illegible]	[illegible]	[illegible]	[illegible]	[illegible]	[illegible]	[illegible]	[illegible]	[illegible]	[illegible]	[illegible]	[illegible]	[illegible]	[illegible]	[illegible]	[illegible]	[illegible]	[illegible]	[illegible]	[illegible]
[illegible]	[illegible]	[illegible]	[illegible]	[illegible]	[illegible]	[illegible]	[illegible]	[illegible]	[illegible]	[illegible]	[illegible]	[illegible]	[illegible]	[illegible]	[illegible]	[illegible]	[illegible]	[illegible]	[illegible]	[illegible]	[illegible]
[illegible]	[illegible]	[illegible]	[illegible]	[illegible]	[illegible]	[illegible]	[illegible]	[illegible]	[illegible]	[illegible]	[illegible]	[illegible]	[illegible]	[illegible]	[illegible]	[illegible]	[illegible]	[illegible]	[illegible]	[illegible]	[illegible]
	[illegible] Mayo Co.																				
[illegible]	[illegible]	[illegible]	[illegible]	[illegible]	[illegible]	[illegible]	[illegible]	[illegible]	[illegible]	[illegible]	[illegible]	[illegible]	[illegible]	[illegible]	[illegible]	[illegible]	[illegible]	[illegible]	[illegible]	[illegible]	[illegible]
[illegible]	[illegible]	[illegible]	[illegible]	[illegible]	[illegible]	[illegible]	[illegible]	[illegible]	[illegible]	[illegible]	[illegible]	[illegible]	[illegible]	[illegible]	[illegible]	[illegible]	[illegible]	[illegible]	[illegible]	[illegible]	[illegible]
[illegible]	[illegible]	[illegible]	[illegible]	[illegible]	[illegible]	[illegible]	[illegible]	[illegible]	[illegible]	[illegible]	[illegible]	[illegible]	[illegible]	[illegible]	[illegible]	[illegible]	[illegible]	[illegible]	[illegible]	[illegible]	[illegible]
[illegible]	[illegible]	[illegible]	[illegible]	[illegible]	[illegible]	[illegible]	[illegible]	[illegible]	[illegible]	[illegible]	[illegible]	[illegible]	[illegible]	[illegible]	[illegible]	[illegible]	[illegible]	[illegible]	[illegible]	[illegible]	[illegible]
[illegible]	[illegible]	[illegible]	[illegible]	[illegible]	[illegible]	[illegible]	[illegible]	[illegible]	[illegible]	[illegible]	[illegible]	[illegible]	[illegible]	[illegible]	[illegible]	[illegible]	[illegible]	[illegible]	[illegible]	[illegible]	[illegible]
[illegible]	[illegible]	[illegible]	[illegible]	[illegible]	[illegible]	[illegible]	[illegible]	[illegible]	[illegible]	[illegible]	[illegible]	[illegible]	[illegible]	[illegible]	[illegible]	[illegible]	[illegible]	[illegible]	[illegible]	[illegible]	[illegible]
[illegible]	[illegible]	[illegible]	[illegible]	[illegible]	[illegible]	[illegible]	[illegible]	[illegible]	[illegible]	[illegible]	[illegible]	[illegible]	[illegible]	[illegible]	[illegible]	[illegible]	[illegible]	[illegible]	[illegible]	[illegible]	[illegible]
[illegible]	[illegible]	[illegible]	[illegible]	[illegible]	[illegible]	[illegible]	[illegible]	[illegible]	[illegible]	[illegible]	[illegible]	[illegible]	[illegible]	[illegible]	[illegible]	[illegible]	[illegible]	[illegible]	[illegible]	[illegible]	[illegible]
[illegible]	[illegible]	[illegible]	[illegible]	[illegible]	[illegible]	[illegible]	[illegible]	[illegible]	[illegible]	[illegible]	[illegible]	[illegible]	[illegible]	[illegible]	[illegible]	[illegible]	[illegible]	[illegible]	[illegible]	[illegible]	[illegible]
[illegible]	[illegible]	[illegible]	[illegible]	[illegible]	[illegible]	[illegible]	[illegible]	[illegible]	[illegible]	[illegible]	[illegible]	[illegible]	[illegible]	[illegible]	[illegible]	[illegible]	[illegible]	[illegible]	[illegible]	[illegible]	[illegible]
	[illegible] Co.																				
[illegible]	[illegible]	[illegible]	[illegible]	[illegible]	[illegible]	[illegible]	[illegible]	[illegible]	[illegible]	[illegible]	[illegible]	[illegible]	[illegible]	[illegible]	[illegible]	[illegible]	[illegible]	[illegible]	[illegible]	[illegible]	[illegible]
[illegible]	[illegible]	[illegible]	[illegible]	[illegible]	[illegible]	[illegible]	[illegible]	[illegible]	[illegible]	[illegible]	[illegible]	[illegible]	[illegible]	[illegible]	[illegible]	[illegible]	[illegible]	[illegible]	[illegible]	[illegible]	[illegible]
[illegible]	[illegible]	[illegible]	[illegible]	[illegible]	[illegible]	[illegible]	[illegible]	[illegible]	[illegible]	[illegible]	[illegible]	[illegible]	[illegible]	[illegible]	[illegible]	[illegible]	[illegible]	[illegible]	[illegible]	[illegible]	[illegible]
[illegible]	[illegible]	[illegible]	[illegible]	[illegible]	[illegible]	[illegible]	[illegible]	[illegible]	[illegible]	[illegible]	[illegible]	[illegible]	[illegible]	[illegible]	[illegible]	[illegible]	[illegible]	[illegible]	[illegible]	[illegible]	[illegible]
[illegible]	[illegible]	[illegible]	[illegible]	[illegible]	[illegible]	[illegible]	[illegible]	[illegible]	[illegible]	[illegible]	[illegible]	[illegible]	[illegible]	[illegible]	[illegible]	[illegible]	[illegible]	[illegible]	[illegible]	[illegible]	[illegible]
[illegible]	[illegible]	[illegible]	[illegible]	[illegible]	[illegible]	[illegible]	[illegible]	[illegible]	[illegible]	[illegible]	[illegible]	[illegible]	[illegible]	[illegible]	[illegible]	[illegible]	[illegible]	[illegible]	[illegible]	[illegible]	[illegible]
[illegible]	[illegible]	[illegible]	[illegible]	[illegible]	[illegible]	[illegible]	[illegible]	[illegible]	[illegible]	[illegible]	[illegible]	[illegible]	[illegible]	[illegible]	[illegible]	[illegible]	[illegible]	[illegible]	[illegible]	[illegible]	[illegible]
	[illegible] Co.																				
[illegible]	[illegible]	[illegible]	[illegible]	[illegible]	[illegible]	[illegible]	[illegible]	[illegible]	[illegible]	[illegible]	[illegible]	[illegible]	[illegible]	[illegible]	[illegible]	[illegible]	[illegible]	[illegible]	[illegible]	[illegible]	[illegible]
[illegible]	[illegible]	[illegible]	[illegible]	[illegible]	[illegible]	[illegible]	[illegible]	[illegible]	[illegible]	[illegible]	[illegible]	[illegible]	[illegible]	[illegible]	[illegible]	[illegible]	[illegible]	[illegible]	[illegible]	[illegible]	[illegible]
[illegible]	[illegible]	[illegible]	[illegible]	[illegible]	[illegible]	[illegible]	[illegible]	[illegible]	[illegible]	[illegible]	[illegible]	[illegible]	[illegible]	[illegible]	[illegible]	[illegible]	[illegible]	[illegible]	[illegible]	[illegible]	[illegible]
[illegible]	[illegible]	[illegible]	[illegible]	[illegible]	[illegible]	[illegible]	[illegible]	[illegible]	[illegible]	[illegible]	[illegible]	[illegible]	[illegible]	[illegible]	[illegible]	[illegible]	[illegible]	[illegible]	[illegible]	[illegible]	[illegible]
[illegible]	[illegible]	[illegible]	[illegible]	[illegible]	[illegible]	[illegible]	[illegible]	[illegible]	[illegible]	[illegible]	[illegible]	[illegible]	[illegible]	[illegible]	[illegible]	[illegible]	[illegible]	[illegible]	[illegible]	[illegible]	[illegible]

IRELAND.—Deaths at different Ages registered in the year 1891—in the Superintendent Registrars' Districts and Parts of Districts in each County.—Females—continued.

IV.—Province of Connaught—continued.

Superintendent Registrars' Districts and Parts of Districts.		Total Births.	Total Deaths.	Females. Ages at Death. Under 1 year	1	2	3	4	Under 5	5-	10-	15-	20-	25-	35-	45-	55-	65-	75-	85-	[illegible]
No.	[illegible] Co.																				
[illegible]	[illegible]	[illegible]	[illegible]	[illegible]	[illegible]	[illegible]	[illegible]	[illegible]	[illegible]	[illegible]	[illegible]	[illegible]	[illegible]	[illegible]	[illegible]	[illegible]	[illegible]	[illegible]	[illegible]	[illegible]	[illegible]
[illegible]	[illegible]	[illegible]	[illegible]	[illegible]	[illegible]	[illegible]	[illegible]	[illegible]	[illegible]	[illegible]	[illegible]	[illegible]	[illegible]	[illegible]	[illegible]	[illegible]	[illegible]	[illegible]	[illegible]	[illegible]	[illegible]
[illegible]	[illegible]	[illegible]	[illegible]	[illegible]	[illegible]	[illegible]	[illegible]	[illegible]	[illegible]	[illegible]	[illegible]	[illegible]	[illegible]	[illegible]	[illegible]	[illegible]	[illegible]	[illegible]	[illegible]	[illegible]	[illegible]
[illegible]	[illegible]	[illegible]	[illegible]	[illegible]	[illegible]	[illegible]	[illegible]	[illegible]	[illegible]	[illegible]	[illegible]	[illegible]	[illegible]	[illegible]	[illegible]	[illegible]	[illegible]	[illegible]	[illegible]	[illegible]	[illegible]
[illegible]	[illegible]	[illegible]	[illegible]	[illegible]	[illegible]	[illegible]	[illegible]	[illegible]	[illegible]	[illegible]	[illegible]	[illegible]	[illegible]	[illegible]	[illegible]	[illegible]	[illegible]	[illegible]	[illegible]	[illegible]	[illegible]
	[illegible] Co.																				
[illegible]	[illegible]	[illegible]	[illegible]	[illegible]	[illegible]	[illegible]	[illegible]	[illegible]	[illegible]	[illegible]	[illegible]	[illegible]	[illegible]	[illegible]	[illegible]	[illegible]	[illegible]	[illegible]	[illegible]	[illegible]	[illegible]
[illegible]	[illegible]	[illegible]	[illegible]	[illegible]	[illegible]	[illegible]	[illegible]	[illegible]	[illegible]	[illegible]	[illegible]	[illegible]	[illegible]	[illegible]	[illegible]	[illegible]	[illegible]	[illegible]	[illegible]	[illegible]	[illegible]
[illegible]	[illegible]	[illegible]	[illegible]	[illegible]	[illegible]	[illegible]	[illegible]	[illegible]	[illegible]	[illegible]	[illegible]	[illegible]	[illegible]	[illegible]	[illegible]	[illegible]	[illegible]	[illegible]	[illegible]	[illegible]	[illegible]
[illegible]	[illegible]	[illegible]	[illegible]	[illegible]	[illegible]	[illegible]	[illegible]	[illegible]	[illegible]	[illegible]	[illegible]	[illegible]	[illegible]	[illegible]	[illegible]	[illegible]	[illegible]	[illegible]	[illegible]	[illegible]	[illegible]
[illegible]	[illegible]	[illegible]	[illegible]	[illegible]	[illegible]	[illegible]	[illegible]	[illegible]	[illegible]	[illegible]	[illegible]	[illegible]	[illegible]	[illegible]	[illegible]	[illegible]	[illegible]	[illegible]	[illegible]	[illegible]	[illegible]
[illegible]	[illegible]	[illegible]	[illegible]	[illegible]	[illegible]	[illegible]	[illegible]	[illegible]	[illegible]	[illegible]	[illegible]	[illegible]	[illegible]	[illegible]	[illegible]	[illegible]	[illegible]	[illegible]	[illegible]	[illegible]	[illegible]
[illegible]	[illegible]	[illegible]	[illegible]	[illegible]	[illegible]	[illegible]	[illegible]	[illegible]	[illegible]	[illegible]	[illegible]	[illegible]	[illegible]	[illegible]	[illegible]	[illegible]	[illegible]	[illegible]	[illegible]	[illegible]	[illegible]
[illegible]	[illegible]	[illegible]	[illegible]	[illegible]	[illegible]	[illegible]	[illegible]	[illegible]	[illegible]	[illegible]	[illegible]	[illegible]	[illegible]	[illegible]	[illegible]	[illegible]	[illegible]	[illegible]	[illegible]	[illegible]	[illegible]
[illegible]	[illegible]	[illegible]	[illegible]	[illegible]	[illegible]	[illegible]	[illegible]	[illegible]	[illegible]	[illegible]	[illegible]	[illegible]	[illegible]	[illegible]	[illegible]	[illegible]	[illegible]	[illegible]	[illegible]	[illegible]	[illegible]
[illegible]	[illegible]	[illegible]	[illegible]	[illegible]	[illegible]	[illegible]	[illegible]	[illegible]	[illegible]	[illegible]	[illegible]	[illegible]	[illegible]	[illegible]	[illegible]	[illegible]	[illegible]	[illegible]	[illegible]	[illegible]	[illegible]
	[illegible] Co.																				
[illegible]	[illegible]	[illegible]	[illegible]	[illegible]	[illegible]	[illegible]	[illegible]	[illegible]	[illegible]	[illegible]	[illegible]	[illegible]	[illegible]	[illegible]	[illegible]	[illegible]	[illegible]	[illegible]	[illegible]	[illegible]	[illegible]
[illegible]	[illegible]	[illegible]	[illegible]	[illegible]	[illegible]	[illegible]	[illegible]	[illegible]	[illegible]	[illegible]	[illegible]	[illegible]	[illegible]	[illegible]	[illegible]	[illegible]	[illegible]	[illegible]	[illegible]	[illegible]	[illegible]
[illegible]	[illegible]	[illegible]	[illegible]	[illegible]	[illegible]	[illegible]	[illegible]	[illegible]	[illegible]	[illegible]	[illegible]	[illegible]	[illegible]	[illegible]	[illegible]	[illegible]	[illegible]	[illegible]	[illegible]	[illegible]	[illegible]
[illegible]	[illegible]	[illegible]	[illegible]	[illegible]	[illegible]	[illegible]	[illegible]	[illegible]	[illegible]	[illegible]	[illegible]	[illegible]	[illegible]	[illegible]	[illegible]	[illegible]	[illegible]	[illegible]	[illegible]	[illegible]	[illegible]
[illegible]	[illegible]	[illegible]	[illegible]	[illegible]	[illegible]	[illegible]	[illegible]	[illegible]	[illegible]	[illegible]	[illegible]	[illegible]	[illegible]	[illegible]	[illegible]	[illegible]	[illegible]	[illegible]	[illegible]	[illegible]	[illegible]
[illegible]	[illegible]	[illegible]	[illegible]	[illegible]	[illegible]	[illegible]	[illegible]	[illegible]	[illegible]	[illegible]	[illegible]	[illegible]	[illegible]	[illegible]	[illegible]	[illegible]	[illegible]	[illegible]	[illegible]	[illegible]	[illegible]
[illegible]	[illegible]	[illegible]	[illegible]	[illegible]	[illegible]	[illegible]	[illegible]	[illegible]	[illegible]	[illegible]	[illegible]	[illegible]	[illegible]	[illegible]	[illegible]	[illegible]	[illegible]	[illegible]	[illegible]	[illegible]	[illegible]
	[illegible] Co.																				
[illegible]	[illegible]	[illegible]	[illegible]	[illegible]	[illegible]	[illegible]	[illegible]	[illegible]	[illegible]	[illegible]	[illegible]	[illegible]	[illegible]	[illegible]	[illegible]	[illegible]	[illegible]	[illegible]	[illegible]	[illegible]	[illegible]
[illegible]	[illegible]	[illegible]	[illegible]	[illegible]	[illegible]	[illegible]	[illegible]	[illegible]	[illegible]	[illegible]	[illegible]	[illegible]	[illegible]	[illegible]	[illegible]	[illegible]	[illegible]	[illegible]	[illegible]	[illegible]	[illegible]
[illegible]	[illegible]	[illegible]	[illegible]	[illegible]	[illegible]	[illegible]	[illegible]	[illegible]	[illegible]	[illegible]	[illegible]	[illegible]	[illegible]	[illegible]	[illegible]	[illegible]	[illegible]	[illegible]	[illegible]	[illegible]	[illegible]
[illegible]	[illegible]	[illegible]	[illegible]	[illegible]	[illegible]	[illegible]	[illegible]	[illegible]	[illegible]	[illegible]	[illegible]	[illegible]	[illegible]	[illegible]	[illegible]	[illegible]	[illegible]	[illegible]	[illegible]	[illegible]	[illegible]
[illegible]	[illegible]	[illegible]	[illegible]	[illegible]	[illegible]	[illegible]	[illegible]	[illegible]	[illegible]	[illegible]	[illegible]	[illegible]	[illegible]	[illegible]	[illegible]	[illegible]	[illegible]	[illegible]	[illegible]	[illegible]	[illegible]

IRELAND.—[illegible] at different Ages registered in the year 1851—in the Superintendent Registrars' Districts—Males.

[illegible]	[illegible]	[illegible]	[illegible]	[illegible]	[illegible]	[illegible]	[illegible]	[illegible]	[illegible]	[illegible]	[illegible]	[illegible]	[illegible]	[illegible]	[illegible]	[illegible]	[illegible]	[illegible]	[illegible]	[illegible]	[illegible]
[illegible]	[illegible]	[illegible]	[illegible]	[illegible]	[illegible]	[illegible]	[illegible]	[illegible]	[illegible]	[illegible]	[illegible]	[illegible]	[illegible]	[illegible]	[illegible]	[illegible]	[illegible]	[illegible]	[illegible]	[illegible]	[illegible]

IRELAND.—Deaths at different Ages registered in the year 1891—in the Superintendent Registrars' Districts—Females.

IRELAND.—Deaths at different Ages registered in the year 1891—in the Superintendent Registrars' Districts.—Males—*continued.*

[illegible]	Superintendent Registrars' Districts	Total Births	Total Deaths	Ages at Death																	
				Under 1	1	2	3	4	Total under 5	5-	10-	15-	20-	25-	35-	45-	55-	65-	75-	85-	[illegible]
[illegible]	Dingle	[illegible]	[illegible]	[illegible]	[illegible]	[illegible]	[illegible]	[illegible]	[illegible]	[illegible]	[illegible]	[illegible]	[illegible]	[illegible]	[illegible]	[illegible]	[illegible]	[illegible]	[illegible]	[illegible]	[illegible]
[illegible]	Donegal	[illegible]	[illegible]	[illegible]	[illegible]	[illegible]	[illegible]	[illegible]	[illegible]	[illegible]	[illegible]	[illegible]	[illegible]	[illegible]	[illegible]	[illegible]	[illegible]	[illegible]	[illegible]	[illegible]	[illegible]
[illegible]	Downpatrick	[illegible]	[illegible]	[illegible]	[illegible]	[illegible]	[illegible]	[illegible]	[illegible]	[illegible]	[illegible]	[illegible]	[illegible]	[illegible]	[illegible]	[illegible]	[illegible]	[illegible]	[illegible]	[illegible]	[illegible]
[illegible]	Drogheda	[illegible]	[illegible]	[illegible]	[illegible]	[illegible]	[illegible]	[illegible]	[illegible]	[illegible]	[illegible]	[illegible]	[illegible]	[illegible]	[illegible]	[illegible]	[illegible]	[illegible]	[illegible]	[illegible]	[illegible]
[illegible]	Dromore West	[illegible]	[illegible]	[illegible]	[illegible]	[illegible]	[illegible]	[illegible]	[illegible]	[illegible]	[illegible]	[illegible]	[illegible]	[illegible]	[illegible]	[illegible]	[illegible]	[illegible]	[illegible]	[illegible]	[illegible]
[illegible]	Dublin, North	[illegible]	[illegible]	[illegible]	[illegible]	[illegible]	[illegible]	[illegible]	[illegible]	[illegible]	[illegible]	[illegible]	[illegible]	[illegible]	[illegible]	[illegible]	[illegible]	[illegible]	[illegible]	[illegible]	[illegible]
[illegible]	Dublin, South	[illegible]	[illegible]	[illegible]	[illegible]	[illegible]	[illegible]	[illegible]	[illegible]	[illegible]	[illegible]	[illegible]	[illegible]	[illegible]	[illegible]	[illegible]	[illegible]	[illegible]	[illegible]	[illegible]	[illegible]
[illegible]	Dundalk	[illegible]	[illegible]	[illegible]	[illegible]	[illegible]	[illegible]	[illegible]	[illegible]	[illegible]	[illegible]	[illegible]	[illegible]	[illegible]	[illegible]	[illegible]	[illegible]	[illegible]	[illegible]	[illegible]	[illegible]
[illegible]	Dunfanaghy	[illegible]	[illegible]	[illegible]	[illegible]	[illegible]	[illegible]	[illegible]	[illegible]	[illegible]	[illegible]	[illegible]	[illegible]	[illegible]	[illegible]	[illegible]	[illegible]	[illegible]	[illegible]	[illegible]	[illegible]
[illegible]	Dungannon	[illegible]	[illegible]	[illegible]	[illegible]	[illegible]	[illegible]	[illegible]	[illegible]	[illegible]	[illegible]	[illegible]	[illegible]	[illegible]	[illegible]	[illegible]	[illegible]	[illegible]	[illegible]	[illegible]	[illegible]
[illegible]	Dungarvan	[illegible]	[illegible]	[illegible]	[illegible]	[illegible]	[illegible]	[illegible]	[illegible]	[illegible]	[illegible]	[illegible]	[illegible]	[illegible]	[illegible]	[illegible]	[illegible]	[illegible]	[illegible]	[illegible]	[illegible]
[illegible]	Dunmanway	[illegible]	[illegible]	[illegible]	[illegible]	[illegible]	[illegible]	[illegible]	[illegible]	[illegible]	[illegible]	[illegible]	[illegible]	[illegible]	[illegible]	[illegible]	[illegible]	[illegible]	[illegible]	[illegible]	[illegible]
[illegible]	Dunshaughlin	[illegible]	[illegible]	[illegible]	[illegible]	[illegible]	[illegible]	[illegible]	[illegible]	[illegible]	[illegible]	[illegible]	[illegible]	[illegible]	[illegible]	[illegible]	[illegible]	[illegible]	[illegible]	[illegible]	[illegible]
[illegible]	Edenderry	[illegible]	[illegible]	[illegible]	[illegible]	[illegible]	[illegible]	[illegible]	[illegible]	[illegible]	[illegible]	[illegible]	[illegible]	[illegible]	[illegible]	[illegible]	[illegible]	[illegible]	[illegible]	[illegible]	[illegible]
[illegible]	Ennis	[illegible]	[illegible]	[illegible]	[illegible]	[illegible]	[illegible]	[illegible]	[illegible]	[illegible]	[illegible]	[illegible]	[illegible]	[illegible]	[illegible]	[illegible]	[illegible]	[illegible]	[illegible]	[illegible]	[illegible]
[illegible]	Enniscorthy	[illegible]	[illegible]	[illegible]	[illegible]	[illegible]	[illegible]	[illegible]	[illegible]	[illegible]	[illegible]	[illegible]	[illegible]	[illegible]	[illegible]	[illegible]	[illegible]	[illegible]	[illegible]	[illegible]	[illegible]
[illegible]	Enniskillen	[illegible]	[illegible]	[illegible]	[illegible]	[illegible]	[illegible]	[illegible]	[illegible]	[illegible]	[illegible]	[illegible]	[illegible]	[illegible]	[illegible]	[illegible]	[illegible]	[illegible]	[illegible]	[illegible]	[illegible]
[illegible]	Ennistimon	[illegible]	[illegible]	[illegible]	[illegible]	[illegible]	[illegible]	[illegible]	[illegible]	[illegible]	[illegible]	[illegible]	[illegible]	[illegible]	[illegible]	[illegible]	[illegible]	[illegible]	[illegible]	[illegible]	[illegible]
[illegible]	Fermoy	[illegible]	[illegible]	[illegible]	[illegible]	[illegible]	[illegible]	[illegible]	[illegible]	[illegible]	[illegible]	[illegible]	[illegible]	[illegible]	[illegible]	[illegible]	[illegible]	[illegible]	[illegible]	[illegible]	[illegible]
[illegible]	Galway	[illegible]	[illegible]	[illegible]	[illegible]	[illegible]	[illegible]	[illegible]	[illegible]	[illegible]	[illegible]	[illegible]	[illegible]	[illegible]	[illegible]	[illegible]	[illegible]	[illegible]	[illegible]	[illegible]	[illegible]
[illegible]	Glenamaddy	[illegible]	[illegible]	[illegible]	[illegible]	[illegible]	[illegible]	[illegible]	[illegible]	[illegible]	[illegible]	[illegible]	[illegible]	[illegible]	[illegible]	[illegible]	[illegible]	[illegible]	[illegible]	[illegible]	[illegible]
[illegible]	Glenties	[illegible]	[illegible]	[illegible]	[illegible]	[illegible]	[illegible]	[illegible]	[illegible]	[illegible]	[illegible]	[illegible]	[illegible]	[illegible]	[illegible]	[illegible]	[illegible]	[illegible]	[illegible]	[illegible]	[illegible]
[illegible]	Glin	[illegible]	[illegible]	[illegible]	[illegible]	[illegible]	[illegible]	[illegible]	[illegible]	[illegible]	[illegible]	[illegible]	[illegible]	[illegible]	[illegible]	[illegible]	[illegible]	[illegible]	[illegible]	[illegible]	[illegible]
[illegible]	Gorey	[illegible]	[illegible]	[illegible]	[illegible]	[illegible]	[illegible]	[illegible]	[illegible]	[illegible]	[illegible]	[illegible]	[illegible]	[illegible]	[illegible]	[illegible]	[illegible]	[illegible]	[illegible]	[illegible]	[illegible]
[illegible]	Gort	[illegible]	[illegible]	[illegible]	[illegible]	[illegible]	[illegible]	[illegible]	[illegible]	[illegible]	[illegible]	[illegible]	[illegible]	[illegible]	[illegible]	[illegible]	[illegible]	[illegible]	[illegible]	[illegible]	[illegible]
[illegible]	Granard	[illegible]	[illegible]	[illegible]	[illegible]	[illegible]	[illegible]	[illegible]	[illegible]	[illegible]	[illegible]	[illegible]	[illegible]	[illegible]	[illegible]	[illegible]	[illegible]	[illegible]	[illegible]	[illegible]	[illegible]
[illegible]	Inishowen	[illegible]	[illegible]	[illegible]	[illegible]	[illegible]	[illegible]	[illegible]	[illegible]	[illegible]	[illegible]	[illegible]	[illegible]	[illegible]	[illegible]	[illegible]	[illegible]	[illegible]	[illegible]	[illegible]	[illegible]
[illegible]	Irvinestown	[illegible]	[illegible]	[illegible]	[illegible]	[illegible]	[illegible]	[illegible]	[illegible]	[illegible]	[illegible]	[illegible]	[illegible]	[illegible]	[illegible]	[illegible]	[illegible]	[illegible]	[illegible]	[illegible]	[illegible]
[illegible]	Kanturk	[illegible]	[illegible]	[illegible]	[illegible]	[illegible]	[illegible]	[illegible]	[illegible]	[illegible]	[illegible]	[illegible]	[illegible]	[illegible]	[illegible]	[illegible]	[illegible]	[illegible]	[illegible]	[illegible]	[illegible]
[illegible]	Kells	[illegible]	[illegible]	[illegible]	[illegible]	[illegible]	[illegible]	[illegible]	[illegible]	[illegible]	[illegible]	[illegible]	[illegible]	[illegible]	[illegible]	[illegible]	[illegible]	[illegible]	[illegible]	[illegible]	[illegible]
[illegible]	Kenmare	[illegible]	[illegible]	[illegible]	[illegible]	[illegible]	[illegible]	[illegible]	[illegible]	[illegible]	[illegible]	[illegible]	[illegible]	[illegible]	[illegible]	[illegible]	[illegible]	[illegible]	[illegible]	[illegible]	[illegible]
[illegible]	Kilkeel	[illegible]	[illegible]	[illegible]	[illegible]	[illegible]	[illegible]	[illegible]	[illegible]	[illegible]	[illegible]	[illegible]	[illegible]	[illegible]	[illegible]	[illegible]	[illegible]	[illegible]	[illegible]	[illegible]	[illegible]
[illegible]	Kilkenny	[illegible]	[illegible]	[illegible]	[illegible]	[illegible]	[illegible]	[illegible]	[illegible]	[illegible]	[illegible]	[illegible]	[illegible]	[illegible]	[illegible]	[illegible]	[illegible]	[illegible]	[illegible]	[illegible]	[illegible]
[illegible]	Killadysert	[illegible]	[illegible]	[illegible]	[illegible]	[illegible]	[illegible]	[illegible]	[illegible]	[illegible]	[illegible]	[illegible]	[illegible]	[illegible]	[illegible]	[illegible]	[illegible]	[illegible]	[illegible]	[illegible]	[illegible]
[illegible]	Killala	[illegible]	[illegible]	[illegible]	[illegible]	[illegible]	[illegible]	[illegible]	[illegible]	[illegible]	[illegible]	[illegible]	[illegible]	[illegible]	[illegible]	[illegible]	[illegible]	[illegible]	[illegible]	[illegible]	[illegible]
[illegible]	Killarney	[illegible]	[illegible]	[illegible]	[illegible]	[illegible]	[illegible]	[illegible]	[illegible]	[illegible]	[illegible]	[illegible]	[illegible]	[illegible]	[illegible]	[illegible]	[illegible]	[illegible]	[illegible]	[illegible]	[illegible]
[illegible]	Kilmacthomas	[illegible]	[illegible]	[illegible]	[illegible]	[illegible]	[illegible]	[illegible]	[illegible]	[illegible]	[illegible]	[illegible]	[illegible]	[illegible]	[illegible]	[illegible]	[illegible]	[illegible]	[illegible]	[illegible]	[illegible]
[illegible]	Kilmallock	[illegible]	[illegible]	[illegible]	[illegible]	[illegible]	[illegible]	[illegible]	[illegible]	[illegible]	[illegible]	[illegible]	[illegible]	[illegible]	[illegible]	[illegible]	[illegible]	[illegible]	[illegible]	[illegible]	[illegible]
[illegible]	Kilrush	[illegible]	[illegible]	[illegible]	[illegible]	[illegible]	[illegible]	[illegible]	[illegible]	[illegible]	[illegible]	[illegible]	[illegible]	[illegible]	[illegible]	[illegible]	[illegible]	[illegible]	[illegible]	[illegible]	[illegible]
[illegible]	Kinsale	[illegible]	[illegible]	[illegible]	[illegible]	[illegible]	[illegible]	[illegible]	[illegible]	[illegible]	[illegible]	[illegible]	[illegible]	[illegible]	[illegible]	[illegible]	[illegible]	[illegible]	[illegible]	[illegible]	[illegible]
[illegible]	Larne	[illegible]	[illegible]	[illegible]	[illegible]	[illegible]	[illegible]	[illegible]	[illegible]	[illegible]	[illegible]	[illegible]	[illegible]	[illegible]	[illegible]	[illegible]	[illegible]	[illegible]	[illegible]	[illegible]	[illegible]
[illegible]	Letterkenny	[illegible]	[illegible]	[illegible]	[illegible]	[illegible]	[illegible]	[illegible]	[illegible]	[illegible]	[illegible]	[illegible]	[illegible]	[illegible]	[illegible]	[illegible]	[illegible]	[illegible]	[illegible]	[illegible]	[illegible]
[illegible]	Limavady	[illegible]	[illegible]	[illegible]	[illegible]	[illegible]	[illegible]	[illegible]	[illegible]	[illegible]	[illegible]	[illegible]	[illegible]	[illegible]	[illegible]	[illegible]	[illegible]	[illegible]	[illegible]	[illegible]	[illegible]
[illegible]	Limerick	[illegible]	[illegible]	[illegible]	[illegible]	[illegible]	[illegible]	[illegible]	[illegible]	[illegible]	[illegible]	[illegible]	[illegible]	[illegible]	[illegible]	[illegible]	[illegible]	[illegible]	[illegible]	[illegible]	[illegible]
[illegible]	Lisburn	[illegible]	[illegible]	[illegible]	[illegible]	[illegible]	[illegible]	[illegible]	[illegible]	[illegible]	[illegible]	[illegible]	[illegible]	[illegible]	[illegible]	[illegible]	[illegible]	[illegible]	[illegible]	[illegible]	[illegible]
[illegible]	Lismore	[illegible]	[illegible]	[illegible]	[illegible]	[illegible]	[illegible]	[illegible]	[illegible]	[illegible]	[illegible]	[illegible]	[illegible]	[illegible]	[illegible]	[illegible]	[illegible]	[illegible]	[illegible]	[illegible]	[illegible]
[illegible]	Lisnaskea	[illegible]	[illegible]	[illegible]	[illegible]	[illegible]	[illegible]	[illegible]	[illegible]	[illegible]	[illegible]	[illegible]	[illegible]	[illegible]	[illegible]	[illegible]	[illegible]	[illegible]	[illegible]	[illegible]	[illegible]
[illegible]	Listowel	[illegible]	[illegible]	[illegible]	[illegible]	[illegible]	[illegible]	[illegible]	[illegible]	[illegible]	[illegible]	[illegible]	[illegible]	[illegible]	[illegible]	[illegible]	[illegible]	[illegible]	[illegible]	[illegible]	[illegible]
[illegible]	Londonderry	[illegible]	[illegible]	[illegible]	[illegible]	[illegible]	[illegible]	[illegible]	[illegible]	[illegible]	[illegible]	[illegible]	[illegible]	[illegible]	[illegible]	[illegible]	[illegible]	[illegible]	[illegible]	[illegible]	[illegible]
[illegible]	Longford	[illegible]	[illegible]	[illegible]	[illegible]	[illegible]	[illegible]	[illegible]	[illegible]	[illegible]	[illegible]	[illegible]	[illegible]	[illegible]	[illegible]	[illegible]	[illegible]	[illegible]	[illegible]	[illegible]	[illegible]
[illegible]	Loughrea	[illegible]	[illegible]	[illegible]	[illegible]	[illegible]	[illegible]	[illegible]	[illegible]	[illegible]	[illegible]	[illegible]	[illegible]	[illegible]	[illegible]	[illegible]	[illegible]	[illegible]	[illegible]	[illegible]	[illegible]
[illegible]	Lurgan	[illegible]	[illegible]	[illegible]	[illegible]	[illegible]	[illegible]	[illegible]	[illegible]	[illegible]	[illegible]	[illegible]	[illegible]	[illegible]	[illegible]	[illegible]	[illegible]	[illegible]	[illegible]	[illegible]	[illegible]
[illegible]	Macroom	[illegible]	[illegible]	[illegible]	[illegible]	[illegible]	[illegible]	[illegible]	[illegible]	[illegible]	[illegible]	[illegible]	[illegible]	[illegible]	[illegible]	[illegible]	[illegible]	[illegible]	[illegible]	[illegible]	[illegible]

IRELAND.—DEATHS at different AGES registered in the year 1891—in the SUPERINTENDENT REGISTRARS' DISTRICTS.—FEMALES—*continued.*

Number or Numbers of Union in preceding Abstract.	Superintendent Registrars' Districts.	Total Births.	Total Deaths.	Under 1 year.	1	2	3	4	Under 5 years.	5-	10-	15-	20-	25-	35-	45-	55-	65-	75-	85-	95 and upwards.
[illegible]	Dingle,	[illegible]	[illegible]	[illegible]	[illegible]	[illegible]	[illegible]	[illegible]	[illegible]	[illegible]	[illegible]	[illegible]	[illegible]	[illegible]	[illegible]	[illegible]	[illegible]	[illegible]	[illegible]	[illegible]	[illegible]
[illegible]	Donegal,	[illegible]	[illegible]	[illegible]	[illegible]	[illegible]	[illegible]	[illegible]	[illegible]	[illegible]	[illegible]	[illegible]	[illegible]	[illegible]	[illegible]	[illegible]	[illegible]	[illegible]	[illegible]	[illegible]	[illegible]
[illegible]	Downpatrick,	[illegible]	[illegible]	[illegible]	[illegible]	[illegible]	[illegible]	[illegible]	[illegible]	[illegible]	[illegible]	[illegible]	[illegible]	[illegible]	[illegible]	[illegible]	[illegible]	[illegible]	[illegible]	[illegible]	[illegible]
[illegible]	Drogheda,	[illegible]	[illegible]	[illegible]	[illegible]	[illegible]	[illegible]	[illegible]	[illegible]	[illegible]	[illegible]	[illegible]	[illegible]	[illegible]	[illegible]	[illegible]	[illegible]	[illegible]	[illegible]	[illegible]	[illegible]
[illegible]	Dromore West,	[illegible]	[illegible]	[illegible]	[illegible]	[illegible]	[illegible]	[illegible]	[illegible]	[illegible]	[illegible]	[illegible]	[illegible]	[illegible]	[illegible]	[illegible]	[illegible]	[illegible]	[illegible]	[illegible]	[illegible]
[illegible]	Dublin, North,	[illegible]	[illegible]	[illegible]	[illegible]	[illegible]	[illegible]	[illegible]	[illegible]	[illegible]	[illegible]	[illegible]	[illegible]	[illegible]	[illegible]	[illegible]	[illegible]	[illegible]	[illegible]	[illegible]	[illegible]
[illegible]	Dublin, South,	[illegible]	[illegible]	[illegible]	[illegible]	[illegible]	[illegible]	[illegible]	[illegible]	[illegible]	[illegible]	[illegible]	[illegible]	[illegible]	[illegible]	[illegible]	[illegible]	[illegible]	[illegible]	[illegible]	[illegible]
[illegible]	Dundalk,	[illegible]	[illegible]	[illegible]	[illegible]	[illegible]	[illegible]	[illegible]	[illegible]	[illegible]	[illegible]	[illegible]	[illegible]	[illegible]	[illegible]	[illegible]	[illegible]	[illegible]	[illegible]	[illegible]	[illegible]
[illegible]	Dunfanaghy,	[illegible]	[illegible]	[illegible]	[illegible]	[illegible]	[illegible]	[illegible]	[illegible]	[illegible]	[illegible]	[illegible]	[illegible]	[illegible]	[illegible]	[illegible]	[illegible]	[illegible]	[illegible]	[illegible]	[illegible]
[illegible]	Dungannon,	[illegible]	[illegible]	[illegible]	[illegible]	[illegible]	[illegible]	[illegible]	[illegible]	[illegible]	[illegible]	[illegible]	[illegible]	[illegible]	[illegible]	[illegible]	[illegible]	[illegible]	[illegible]	[illegible]	[illegible]
[illegible]	Dungarvan,	[illegible]	[illegible]	[illegible]	[illegible]	[illegible]	[illegible]	[illegible]	[illegible]	[illegible]	[illegible]	[illegible]	[illegible]	[illegible]	[illegible]	[illegible]	[illegible]	[illegible]	[illegible]	[illegible]	[illegible]
[illegible]	Dunmanway,	[illegible]	[illegible]	[illegible]	[illegible]	[illegible]	[illegible]	[illegible]	[illegible]	[illegible]	[illegible]	[illegible]	[illegible]	[illegible]	[illegible]	[illegible]	[illegible]	[illegible]	[illegible]	[illegible]	[illegible]
[illegible]	Dunshaughlin,	[illegible]	[illegible]	[illegible]	[illegible]	[illegible]	[illegible]	[illegible]	[illegible]	[illegible]	[illegible]	[illegible]	[illegible]	[illegible]	[illegible]	[illegible]	[illegible]	[illegible]	[illegible]	[illegible]	[illegible]
[illegible]	Edenderry,	[illegible]	[illegible]	[illegible]	[illegible]	[illegible]	[illegible]	[illegible]	[illegible]	[illegible]	[illegible]	[illegible]	[illegible]	[illegible]	[illegible]	[illegible]	[illegible]	[illegible]	[illegible]	[illegible]	[illegible]
[illegible]	Ennis,	[illegible]	[illegible]	[illegible]	[illegible]	[illegible]	[illegible]	[illegible]	[illegible]	[illegible]	[illegible]	[illegible]	[illegible]	[illegible]	[illegible]	[illegible]	[illegible]	[illegible]	[illegible]	[illegible]	[illegible]
[illegible]	Enniscorthy,	[illegible]	[illegible]	[illegible]	[illegible]	[illegible]	[illegible]	[illegible]	[illegible]	[illegible]	[illegible]	[illegible]	[illegible]	[illegible]	[illegible]	[illegible]	[illegible]	[illegible]	[illegible]	[illegible]	[illegible]
[illegible]	Enniskillen,	[illegible]	[illegible]	[illegible]	[illegible]	[illegible]	[illegible]	[illegible]	[illegible]	[illegible]	[illegible]	[illegible]	[illegible]	[illegible]	[illegible]	[illegible]	[illegible]	[illegible]	[illegible]	[illegible]	[illegible]
[illegible]	Ennistimon,	[illegible]	[illegible]	[illegible]	[illegible]	[illegible]	[illegible]	[illegible]	[illegible]	[illegible]	[illegible]	[illegible]	[illegible]	[illegible]	[illegible]	[illegible]	[illegible]	[illegible]	[illegible]	[illegible]	[illegible]
[illegible]	Fermoy,	[illegible]	[illegible]	[illegible]	[illegible]	[illegible]	[illegible]	[illegible]	[illegible]	[illegible]	[illegible]	[illegible]	[illegible]	[illegible]	[illegible]	[illegible]	[illegible]	[illegible]	[illegible]	[illegible]	[illegible]
[illegible]	Galway,	[illegible]	[illegible]	[illegible]	[illegible]	[illegible]	[illegible]	[illegible]	[illegible]	[illegible]	[illegible]	[illegible]	[illegible]	[illegible]	[illegible]	[illegible]	[illegible]	[illegible]	[illegible]	[illegible]	[illegible]
[illegible]	Glenamaddy,	[illegible]	[illegible]	[illegible]	[illegible]	[illegible]	[illegible]	[illegible]	[illegible]	[illegible]	[illegible]	[illegible]	[illegible]	[illegible]	[illegible]	[illegible]	[illegible]	[illegible]	[illegible]	[illegible]	[illegible]
[illegible]	Glenties,	[illegible]	[illegible]	[illegible]	[illegible]	[illegible]	[illegible]	[illegible]	[illegible]	[illegible]	[illegible]	[illegible]	[illegible]	[illegible]	[illegible]	[illegible]	[illegible]	[illegible]	[illegible]	[illegible]	[illegible]
[illegible]	Glin,	[illegible]	[illegible]	[illegible]	[illegible]	[illegible]	[illegible]	[illegible]	[illegible]	[illegible]	[illegible]	[illegible]	[illegible]	[illegible]	[illegible]	[illegible]	[illegible]	[illegible]	[illegible]	[illegible]	[illegible]
[illegible]	Gorey,	[illegible]	[illegible]	[illegible]	[illegible]	[illegible]	[illegible]	[illegible]	[illegible]	[illegible]	[illegible]	[illegible]	[illegible]	[illegible]	[illegible]	[illegible]	[illegible]	[illegible]	[illegible]	[illegible]	[illegible]
[illegible]	Gort,	[illegible]	[illegible]	[illegible]	[illegible]	[illegible]	[illegible]	[illegible]	[illegible]	[illegible]	[illegible]	[illegible]	[illegible]	[illegible]	[illegible]	[illegible]	[illegible]	[illegible]	[illegible]	[illegible]	[illegible]
[illegible]	Granard,	[illegible]	[illegible]	[illegible]	[illegible]	[illegible]	[illegible]	[illegible]	[illegible]	[illegible]	[illegible]	[illegible]	[illegible]	[illegible]	[illegible]	[illegible]	[illegible]	[illegible]	[illegible]	[illegible]	[illegible]
[illegible]	Inishowen,	[illegible]	[illegible]	[illegible]	[illegible]	[illegible]	[illegible]	[illegible]	[illegible]	[illegible]	[illegible]	[illegible]	[illegible]	[illegible]	[illegible]	[illegible]	[illegible]	[illegible]	[illegible]	[illegible]	[illegible]
[illegible]	Irvinestown,	[illegible]	[illegible]	[illegible]	[illegible]	[illegible]	[illegible]	[illegible]	[illegible]	[illegible]	[illegible]	[illegible]	[illegible]	[illegible]	[illegible]	[illegible]	[illegible]	[illegible]	[illegible]	[illegible]	[illegible]
[illegible]	Kanturk,	[illegible]	[illegible]	[illegible]	[illegible]	[illegible]	[illegible]	[illegible]	[illegible]	[illegible]	[illegible]	[illegible]	[illegible]	[illegible]	[illegible]	[illegible]	[illegible]	[illegible]	[illegible]	[illegible]	[illegible]
[illegible]	Kells,	[illegible]	[illegible]	[illegible]	[illegible]	[illegible]	[illegible]	[illegible]	[illegible]	[illegible]	[illegible]	[illegible]	[illegible]	[illegible]	[illegible]	[illegible]	[illegible]	[illegible]	[illegible]	[illegible]	[illegible]
[illegible]	Kenmare,	[illegible]	[illegible]	[illegible]	[illegible]	[illegible]	[illegible]	[illegible]	[illegible]	[illegible]	[illegible]	[illegible]	[illegible]	[illegible]	[illegible]	[illegible]	[illegible]	[illegible]	[illegible]	[illegible]	[illegible]
[illegible]	Kilkeel,	[illegible]	[illegible]	[illegible]	[illegible]	[illegible]	[illegible]	[illegible]	[illegible]	[illegible]	[illegible]	[illegible]	[illegible]	[illegible]	[illegible]	[illegible]	[illegible]	[illegible]	[illegible]	[illegible]	[illegible]
[illegible]	Kilkenny,	[illegible]	[illegible]	[illegible]	[illegible]	[illegible]	[illegible]	[illegible]	[illegible]	[illegible]	[illegible]	[illegible]	[illegible]	[illegible]	[illegible]	[illegible]	[illegible]	[illegible]	[illegible]	[illegible]	[illegible]
[illegible]	Killadysert,	[illegible]	[illegible]	[illegible]	[illegible]	[illegible]	[illegible]	[illegible]	[illegible]	[illegible]	[illegible]	[illegible]	[illegible]	[illegible]	[illegible]	[illegible]	[illegible]	[illegible]	[illegible]	[illegible]	[illegible]
[illegible]	Killala,	[illegible]	[illegible]	[illegible]	[illegible]	[illegible]	[illegible]	[illegible]	[illegible]	[illegible]	[illegible]	[illegible]	[illegible]	[illegible]	[illegible]	[illegible]	[illegible]	[illegible]	[illegible]	[illegible]	[illegible]
[illegible]	Killarney,	[illegible]	[illegible]	[illegible]	[illegible]	[illegible]	[illegible]	[illegible]	[illegible]	[illegible]	[illegible]	[illegible]	[illegible]	[illegible]	[illegible]	[illegible]	[illegible]	[illegible]	[illegible]	[illegible]	[illegible]
[illegible]	Kilmacthomas,	[illegible]	[illegible]	[illegible]	[illegible]	[illegible]	[illegible]	[illegible]	[illegible]	[illegible]	[illegible]	[illegible]	[illegible]	[illegible]	[illegible]	[illegible]	[illegible]	[illegible]	[illegible]	[illegible]	[illegible]
[illegible]	Kilmallock,	[illegible]	[illegible]	[illegible]	[illegible]	[illegible]	[illegible]	[illegible]	[illegible]	[illegible]	[illegible]	[illegible]	[illegible]	[illegible]	[illegible]	[illegible]	[illegible]	[illegible]	[illegible]	[illegible]	[illegible]
[illegible]	Kilrush,	[illegible]	[illegible]	[illegible]	[illegible]	[illegible]	[illegible]	[illegible]	[illegible]	[illegible]	[illegible]	[illegible]	[illegible]	[illegible]	[illegible]	[illegible]	[illegible]	[illegible]	[illegible]	[illegible]	[illegible]
[illegible]	Kinsale,	[illegible]	[illegible]	[illegible]	[illegible]	[illegible]	[illegible]	[illegible]	[illegible]	[illegible]	[illegible]	[illegible]	[illegible]	[illegible]	[illegible]	[illegible]	[illegible]	[illegible]	[illegible]	[illegible]	[illegible]
[illegible]	Larne,	[illegible]	[illegible]	[illegible]	[illegible]	[illegible]	[illegible]	[illegible]	[illegible]	[illegible]	[illegible]	[illegible]	[illegible]	[illegible]	[illegible]	[illegible]	[illegible]	[illegible]	[illegible]	[illegible]	[illegible]
[illegible]	Letterkenny,	[illegible]	[illegible]	[illegible]	[illegible]	[illegible]	[illegible]	[illegible]	[illegible]	[illegible]	[illegible]	[illegible]	[illegible]	[illegible]	[illegible]	[illegible]	[illegible]	[illegible]	[illegible]	[illegible]	[illegible]
[illegible]	Limavady,	[illegible]	[illegible]	[illegible]	[illegible]	[illegible]	[illegible]	[illegible]	[illegible]	[illegible]	[illegible]	[illegible]	[illegible]	[illegible]	[illegible]	[illegible]	[illegible]	[illegible]	[illegible]	[illegible]	[illegible]
[illegible]	Limerick,	[illegible]	[illegible]	[illegible]	[illegible]	[illegible]	[illegible]	[illegible]	[illegible]	[illegible]	[illegible]	[illegible]	[illegible]	[illegible]	[illegible]	[illegible]	[illegible]	[illegible]	[illegible]	[illegible]	[illegible]
[illegible]	Lisburn,	[illegible]	[illegible]	[illegible]	[illegible]	[illegible]	[illegible]	[illegible]	[illegible]	[illegible]	[illegible]	[illegible]	[illegible]	[illegible]	[illegible]	[illegible]	[illegible]	[illegible]	[illegible]	[illegible]	[illegible]
[illegible]	Lismore,	[illegible]	[illegible]	[illegible]	[illegible]	[illegible]	[illegible]	[illegible]	[illegible]	[illegible]	[illegible]	[illegible]	[illegible]	[illegible]	[illegible]	[illegible]	[illegible]	[illegible]	[illegible]	[illegible]	[illegible]
[illegible]	Lisnaskea,	[illegible]	[illegible]	[illegible]	[illegible]	[illegible]	[illegible]	[illegible]	[illegible]	[illegible]	[illegible]	[illegible]	[illegible]	[illegible]	[illegible]	[illegible]	[illegible]	[illegible]	[illegible]	[illegible]	[illegible]
[illegible]	Listowel,	[illegible]	[illegible]	[illegible]	[illegible]	[illegible]	[illegible]	[illegible]	[illegible]	[illegible]	[illegible]	[illegible]	[illegible]	[illegible]	[illegible]	[illegible]	[illegible]	[illegible]	[illegible]	[illegible]	[illegible]
[illegible]	Londonderry,	[illegible]	[illegible]	[illegible]	[illegible]	[illegible]	[illegible]	[illegible]	[illegible]	[illegible]	[illegible]	[illegible]	[illegible]	[illegible]	[illegible]	[illegible]	[illegible]	[illegible]	[illegible]	[illegible]	[illegible]
[illegible]	Longford,	[illegible]	[illegible]	[illegible]	[illegible]	[illegible]	[illegible]	[illegible]	[illegible]	[illegible]	[illegible]	[illegible]	[illegible]	[illegible]	[illegible]	[illegible]	[illegible]	[illegible]	[illegible]	[illegible]	[illegible]
[illegible]	Loughrea,	[illegible]	[illegible]	[illegible]	[illegible]	[illegible]	[illegible]	[illegible]	[illegible]	[illegible]	[illegible]	[illegible]	[illegible]	[illegible]	[illegible]	[illegible]	[illegible]	[illegible]	[illegible]	[illegible]	[illegible]
[illegible]	Lurgan,	[illegible]	[illegible]	[illegible]	[illegible]	[illegible]	[illegible]	[illegible]	[illegible]	[illegible]	[illegible]	[illegible]	[illegible]	[illegible]	[illegible]	[illegible]	[illegible]	[illegible]	[illegible]	[illegible]	[illegible]
[illegible]	Macroom,	[illegible]	[illegible]	[illegible]	[illegible]	[illegible]	[illegible]	[illegible]	[illegible]	[illegible]	[illegible]	[illegible]	[illegible]	[illegible]	[illegible]	[illegible]	[illegible]	[illegible]	[illegible]	[illegible]	[illegible]

IRELAND.—DEATHS at different AGES registered in the year 1891—in the SUPERINTENDENT REGISTRARS' DISTRICTS.—MALES—continued.

Number of District of Union in preceding Abstract	Superintendent Registrars' Districts	Total Births	Total Deaths	Under 1	1	2	3	4	Total under 5	5–	10–	15–	20–	25–	35–	45–	55–	65–	75–	85–	Age not stated
[illegible]	[illegible]	[illegible]	[illegible]	[illegible]	[illegible]	[illegible]	[illegible]	[illegible]	[illegible]	[illegible]	[illegible]	[illegible]	[illegible]	[illegible]	[illegible]	[illegible]	[illegible]	[illegible]	[illegible]	[illegible]	[illegible]
[illegible]	Tipperary,	[illegible]	[illegible]	[illegible]	[illegible]	[illegible]	[illegible]	[illegible]	[illegible]	[illegible]	[illegible]	[illegible]	[illegible]	[illegible]	[illegible]	[illegible]	[illegible]	[illegible]	[illegible]	[illegible]	[illegible]
[illegible]	Tobercurry,	[illegible]	[illegible]	[illegible]	[illegible]	[illegible]	[illegible]	[illegible]	[illegible]	[illegible]	[illegible]	[illegible]	[illegible]	[illegible]	[illegible]	[illegible]	[illegible]	[illegible]	[illegible]	[illegible]	[illegible]
[illegible]	Tralee,	[illegible]	[illegible]	[illegible]	[illegible]	[illegible]	[illegible]	[illegible]	[illegible]	[illegible]	[illegible]	[illegible]	[illegible]	[illegible]	[illegible]	[illegible]	[illegible]	[illegible]	[illegible]	[illegible]	[illegible]
[illegible]	Trim,	[illegible]	[illegible]	[illegible]	[illegible]	[illegible]	[illegible]	[illegible]	[illegible]	[illegible]	[illegible]	[illegible]	[illegible]	[illegible]	[illegible]	[illegible]	[illegible]	[illegible]	[illegible]	[illegible]	[illegible]
[illegible]	Tuam,	[illegible]	[illegible]	[illegible]	[illegible]	[illegible]	[illegible]	[illegible]	[illegible]	[illegible]	[illegible]	[illegible]	[illegible]	[illegible]	[illegible]	[illegible]	[illegible]	[illegible]	[illegible]	[illegible]	[illegible]
[illegible]	Tulla,	[illegible]	[illegible]	[illegible]	[illegible]	[illegible]	[illegible]	[illegible]	[illegible]	[illegible]	[illegible]	[illegible]	[illegible]	[illegible]	[illegible]	[illegible]	[illegible]	[illegible]	[illegible]	[illegible]	[illegible]
[illegible]	Tullamore,	[illegible]	[illegible]	[illegible]	[illegible]	[illegible]	[illegible]	[illegible]	[illegible]	[illegible]	[illegible]	[illegible]	[illegible]	[illegible]	[illegible]	[illegible]	[illegible]	[illegible]	[illegible]	[illegible]	[illegible]
[illegible]	[illegible]	[illegible]	[illegible]	[illegible]	[illegible]	[illegible]	[illegible]	[illegible]	[illegible]	[illegible]	[illegible]	[illegible]	[illegible]	[illegible]	[illegible]	[illegible]	[illegible]	[illegible]	[illegible]	[illegible]	[illegible]
[illegible]	Waterford,	[illegible]	[illegible]	[illegible]	[illegible]	[illegible]	[illegible]	[illegible]	[illegible]	[illegible]	[illegible]	[illegible]	[illegible]	[illegible]	[illegible]	[illegible]	[illegible]	[illegible]	[illegible]	[illegible]	[illegible]
[illegible]	Westport,	[illegible]	[illegible]	[illegible]	[illegible]	[illegible]	[illegible]	[illegible]	[illegible]	[illegible]	[illegible]	[illegible]	[illegible]	[illegible]	[illegible]	[illegible]	[illegible]	[illegible]	[illegible]	[illegible]	[illegible]
[illegible]	Wexford,	[illegible]	[illegible]	[illegible]	[illegible]	[illegible]	[illegible]	[illegible]	[illegible]	[illegible]	[illegible]	[illegible]	[illegible]	[illegible]	[illegible]	[illegible]	[illegible]	[illegible]	[illegible]	[illegible]	[illegible]
[illegible]	Youghal,	[illegible]	[illegible]	[illegible]	[illegible]	[illegible]	[illegible]	[illegible]	[illegible]	[illegible]	[illegible]	[illegible]	[illegible]	[illegible]	[illegible]	[illegible]	[illegible]	[illegible]	[illegible]	[illegible]	[illegible]

[illegible]	[illegible]	[illegible]	[illegible]	[illegible]	[illegible]	[illegible]	[illegible]	[illegible]	[illegible]	[illegible]
[illegible]	[illegible]	[illegible]	[illegible]	[illegible]	[illegible]	[illegible]	[illegible]	[illegible]	[illegible]	[illegible]
[illegible]	[illegible]	[illegible]	[illegible]	[illegible]	[illegible]	[illegible]	[illegible]	[illegible]	[illegible]	[illegible]
[illegible]	[illegible]	[illegible]	[illegible]	[illegible]	[illegible]	[illegible]	[illegible]	[illegible]	[illegible]	[illegible]
[illegible]	[illegible]	[illegible]	[illegible]	[illegible]	[illegible]	[illegible]	[illegible]	[illegible]	[illegible]	[illegible]
[illegible]	[illegible]	[illegible]	[illegible]	[illegible]	[illegible]	[illegible]	[illegible]	[illegible]	[illegible]	[illegible]
[illegible]	[illegible]	[illegible]	[illegible]	[illegible]	[illegible]	[illegible]	[illegible]	[illegible]	[illegible]	[illegible]
[illegible]	[illegible]	[illegible]	[illegible]	[illegible]	[illegible]	[illegible]	[illegible]	[illegible]	[illegible]	[illegible]
[illegible]	[illegible]	[illegible]	[illegible]	[illegible]	[illegible]	[illegible]	[illegible]	[illegible]	[illegible]	[illegible]
[illegible]	[illegible]	[illegible]	[illegible]	[illegible]	[illegible]	[illegible]	[illegible]	[illegible]	[illegible]	[illegible]
[illegible]	[illegible]	[illegible]	[illegible]	[illegible]	[illegible]	[illegible]	[illegible]	[illegible]	[illegible]	[illegible]
[illegible]	[illegible]	[illegible]	[illegible]	[illegible]	[illegible]	[illegible]	[illegible]	[illegible]	[illegible]	[illegible]
								[illegible]	[illegible]	[illegible]

IRELAND.—CAUSES of DEATH at different Periods of Life in the Year 1891.—MALES.

Class.	CAUSES OF DEATH.	All Ages.	Under 1 year	1	2	3	4	Total under 5 years.	5-	10-	15-	20-	25-	35-	45-	55-	65-	75-	85-	95 and upwards
	ALL CAUSES,	[illegible]	[illegible]	[illegible]	[illegible]	[illegible]	[illegible]	[illegible]	[illegible]	[illegible]	[illegible]	[illegible]	[illegible]	[illegible]	[illegible]	[illegible]	[illegible]	[illegible]	[illegible]	[illegible]
	(CLASSES.)																			
I.	SPECIFIC FEBRILE or ZYMOTIC DISEASES,	[illegible]	[illegible]	[illegible]	[illegible]	[illegible]	[illegible]	[illegible]	[illegible]	[illegible]	[illegible]	[illegible]	[illegible]	[illegible]	[illegible]	[illegible]	[illegible]	[illegible]	[illegible]	[illegible]
II.	PARASITIC DISEASES,	[illegible]	[illegible]	[illegible]	[illegible]	[illegible]	[illegible]	[illegible]	[illegible]	[illegible]	[illegible]	[illegible]	[illegible]	[illegible]	[illegible]	[illegible]	[illegible]	[illegible]	[illegible]	[illegible]
III.	DIETETIC	[illegible]	[illegible]	[illegible]	[illegible]	[illegible]	[illegible]	[illegible]	[illegible]	[illegible]	[illegible]	[illegible]	[illegible]	[illegible]	[illegible]	[illegible]	[illegible]	[illegible]	[illegible]	[illegible]
IV.	CONSTITUTIONAL	[illegible]	[illegible]	[illegible]	[illegible]	[illegible]	[illegible]	[illegible]	[illegible]	[illegible]	[illegible]	[illegible]	[illegible]	[illegible]	[illegible]	[illegible]	[illegible]	[illegible]	[illegible]	[illegible]
V.	DEVELOPMENTAL	[illegible]	[illegible]	[illegible]	[illegible]	[illegible]	[illegible]	[illegible]	[illegible]	[illegible]	[illegible]	[illegible]	[illegible]	[illegible]	[illegible]	[illegible]	[illegible]	[illegible]	[illegible]	[illegible]
VI.	LOCAL	[illegible]	[illegible]	[illegible]	[illegible]	[illegible]	[illegible]	[illegible]	[illegible]	[illegible]	[illegible]	[illegible]	[illegible]	[illegible]	[illegible]	[illegible]	[illegible]	[illegible]	[illegible]	[illegible]
VII.	VIOLENCE,	[illegible]	[illegible]	[illegible]	[illegible]	[illegible]	[illegible]	[illegible]	[illegible]	[illegible]	[illegible]	[illegible]	[illegible]	[illegible]	[illegible]	[illegible]	[illegible]	[illegible]	[illegible]	[illegible]
VIII.	ILL-DEFINED AND NOT SPECIFIED CAUSES,	[illegible]	[illegible]	[illegible]	[illegible]	[illegible]	[illegible]	[illegible]	[illegible]	[illegible]	[illegible]	[illegible]	[illegible]	[illegible]	[illegible]	[illegible]	[illegible]	[illegible]	[illegible]	[illegible]
	(ORDERS.)																			
I.	1. Miasmatic Diseases,	[illegible]	[illegible]	[illegible]	[illegible]	[illegible]	[illegible]	[illegible]	[illegible]	[illegible]	[illegible]	[illegible]	[illegible]	[illegible]	[illegible]	[illegible]	[illegible]	[illegible]	[illegible]	[illegible]
	2. Diarrhoeal,	[illegible]	[illegible]	[illegible]	[illegible]	[illegible]	[illegible]	[illegible]	[illegible]	[illegible]	[illegible]	[illegible]	[illegible]	[illegible]	[illegible]	[illegible]	[illegible]	[illegible]	[illegible]	[illegible]
	3. Malarial,	[illegible]	[illegible]	[illegible]	[illegible]	[illegible]	[illegible]	[illegible]	[illegible]	[illegible]	[illegible]	[illegible]	[illegible]	[illegible]	[illegible]	[illegible]	[illegible]	[illegible]	[illegible]	[illegible]
	4. Zoogenous,	[illegible]	[illegible]	[illegible]	[illegible]	[illegible]	[illegible]	[illegible]	[illegible]	[illegible]	[illegible]	[illegible]	[illegible]	[illegible]	[illegible]	[illegible]	[illegible]	[illegible]	[illegible]	[illegible]
	5. Venereal,	[illegible]	[illegible]	[illegible]	[illegible]	[illegible]	[illegible]	[illegible]	[illegible]	[illegible]	[illegible]	[illegible]	[illegible]	[illegible]	[illegible]	[illegible]	[illegible]	[illegible]	[illegible]	[illegible]
	6. Septic,	[illegible]	[illegible]	[illegible]	[illegible]	[illegible]	[illegible]	[illegible]	[illegible]	[illegible]	[illegible]	[illegible]	[illegible]	[illegible]	[illegible]	[illegible]	[illegible]	[illegible]	[illegible]	[illegible]
II.	Parasitic	[illegible]	[illegible]	[illegible]	[illegible]	[illegible]	[illegible]	[illegible]	[illegible]	[illegible]	[illegible]	[illegible]	[illegible]	[illegible]	[illegible]	[illegible]	[illegible]	[illegible]	[illegible]	[illegible]
III.	Dietetic	[illegible]	[illegible]	[illegible]	[illegible]	[illegible]	[illegible]	[illegible]	[illegible]	[illegible]	[illegible]	[illegible]	[illegible]	[illegible]	[illegible]	[illegible]	[illegible]	[illegible]	[illegible]	[illegible]
IV.	Constitutional	[illegible]	[illegible]	[illegible]	[illegible]	[illegible]	[illegible]	[illegible]	[illegible]	[illegible]	[illegible]	[illegible]	[illegible]	[illegible]	[illegible]	[illegible]	[illegible]	[illegible]	[illegible]	[illegible]
V.	Developmental	[illegible]	[illegible]	[illegible]	[illegible]	[illegible]	[illegible]	[illegible]	[illegible]	[illegible]	[illegible]	[illegible]	[illegible]	[illegible]	[illegible]	[illegible]	[illegible]	[illegible]	[illegible]	[illegible]
VI.	1. Diseases of Nervous System,	[illegible]	[illegible]	[illegible]	[illegible]	[illegible]	[illegible]	[illegible]	[illegible]	[illegible]	[illegible]	[illegible]	[illegible]	[illegible]	[illegible]	[illegible]	[illegible]	[illegible]	[illegible]	[illegible]
	2. " Organs of Special Sense,	[illegible]	[illegible]	[illegible]	[illegible]	[illegible]	[illegible]	[illegible]	[illegible]	[illegible]	[illegible]	[illegible]	[illegible]	[illegible]	[illegible]	[illegible]	[illegible]	[illegible]	[illegible]	[illegible]
	3. " Circulatory System,	[illegible]	[illegible]	[illegible]	[illegible]	[illegible]	[illegible]	[illegible]	[illegible]	[illegible]	[illegible]	[illegible]	[illegible]	[illegible]	[illegible]	[illegible]	[illegible]	[illegible]	[illegible]	[illegible]
	4. " Respiratory System,	[illegible]	[illegible]	[illegible]	[illegible]	[illegible]	[illegible]	[illegible]	[illegible]	[illegible]	[illegible]	[illegible]	[illegible]	[illegible]	[illegible]	[illegible]	[illegible]	[illegible]	[illegible]	[illegible]
	5. " Digestive System,	[illegible]	[illegible]	[illegible]	[illegible]	[illegible]	[illegible]	[illegible]	[illegible]	[illegible]	[illegible]	[illegible]	[illegible]	[illegible]	[illegible]	[illegible]	[illegible]	[illegible]	[illegible]	[illegible]
	6. " Lymphatic System, and Ductless Glands,	[illegible]	[illegible]	[illegible]	[illegible]	[illegible]	[illegible]	[illegible]	[illegible]	[illegible]	[illegible]	[illegible]	[illegible]	[illegible]	[illegible]	[illegible]	[illegible]	[illegible]	[illegible]	[illegible]
	7. " Urinary System,	[illegible]	[illegible]	[illegible]	[illegible]	[illegible]	[illegible]	[illegible]	[illegible]	[illegible]	[illegible]	[illegible]	[illegible]	[illegible]	[illegible]	[illegible]	[illegible]	[illegible]	[illegible]	[illegible]
	8. " Reproductive System:—																			
	(a) " Organs of Generation,	[illegible]	[illegible]	[illegible]	[illegible]	[illegible]	[illegible]	[illegible]	[illegible]	[illegible]	[illegible]	[illegible]	[illegible]	[illegible]	[illegible]	[illegible]	[illegible]	[illegible]	[illegible]	[illegible]
	(b) " Parturition,	[illegible]	[illegible]	[illegible]	[illegible]	[illegible]	[illegible]	[illegible]	[illegible]	[illegible]	[illegible]	[illegible]	[illegible]	[illegible]	[illegible]	[illegible]	[illegible]	[illegible]	[illegible]	[illegible]
	9. " Locomotive System,	[illegible]	[illegible]	[illegible]	[illegible]	[illegible]	[illegible]	[illegible]	[illegible]	[illegible]	[illegible]	[illegible]	[illegible]	[illegible]	[illegible]	[illegible]	[illegible]	[illegible]	[illegible]	[illegible]
	10. " Integumentary System,	[illegible]	[illegible]	[illegible]	[illegible]	[illegible]	[illegible]	[illegible]	[illegible]	[illegible]	[illegible]	[illegible]	[illegible]	[illegible]	[illegible]	[illegible]	[illegible]	[illegible]	[illegible]	[illegible]
VII.	1. Accident or Negligence,	[illegible]	[illegible]	[illegible]	[illegible]	[illegible]	[illegible]	[illegible]	[illegible]	[illegible]	[illegible]	[illegible]	[illegible]	[illegible]	[illegible]	[illegible]	[illegible]	[illegible]	[illegible]	[illegible]
	2. Homicide,	[illegible]	[illegible]	[illegible]	[illegible]	[illegible]	[illegible]	[illegible]	[illegible]	[illegible]	[illegible]	[illegible]	[illegible]	[illegible]	[illegible]	[illegible]	[illegible]	[illegible]	[illegible]	[illegible]
	3. Suicide,	[illegible]	[illegible]	[illegible]	[illegible]	[illegible]	[illegible]	[illegible]	[illegible]	[illegible]	[illegible]	[illegible]	[illegible]	[illegible]	[illegible]	[illegible]	[illegible]	[illegible]	[illegible]	[illegible]
	4. Execution,	[illegible]	[illegible]	[illegible]	[illegible]	[illegible]	[illegible]	[illegible]	[illegible]	[illegible]	[illegible]	[illegible]	[illegible]	[illegible]	[illegible]	[illegible]	[illegible]	[illegible]	[illegible]	[illegible]
VIII.	Ill-Defined and not Specified Causes,	[illegible]	[illegible]	[illegible]	[illegible]	[illegible]	[illegible]	[illegible]	[illegible]	[illegible]	[illegible]	[illegible]	[illegible]	[illegible]	[illegible]	[illegible]	[illegible]	[illegible]	[illegible]	[illegible]

(continued at page 150.)

IRELAND.—CAUSES of DEATH at different Periods of Life in the Year 1891.—FEMALES.

Class.	CAUSES OF DEATH.	All Ages.	Under 1 year.	1	2	3	4	Total under 5 Years.	[illegible]	[illegible]	[illegible]	[illegible]	[illegible]	[illegible]	[illegible]	[illegible]	[illegible]	[illegible]	[illegible]	[illegible]
	ALL CAUSES,	[illegible]	[illegible]	[illegible]	[illegible]	[illegible]	[illegible]	[illegible]	[illegible]	[illegible]	[illegible]	[illegible]	[illegible]	[illegible]	[illegible]	[illegible]	[illegible]	[illegible]	[illegible]	[illegible]
	(CLASSES.)																			
I.	SPECIFIC FEBRILE or ZYMOTIC DISEASES,	[illegible]	[illegible]	[illegible]	[illegible]	[illegible]	[illegible]	[illegible]	[illegible]	[illegible]	[illegible]	[illegible]	[illegible]	[illegible]	[illegible]	[illegible]	[illegible]	[illegible]	[illegible]	[illegible]
II.	PARASITIC DISEASES,	[illegible]	[illegible]	[illegible]	[illegible]	[illegible]	[illegible]	[illegible]	[illegible]	[illegible]	[illegible]	[illegible]	[illegible]	[illegible]	[illegible]	[illegible]	[illegible]	[illegible]	[illegible]	[illegible]
III.	DIETETIC	[illegible]	[illegible]	[illegible]	[illegible]	[illegible]	[illegible]	[illegible]	[illegible]	[illegible]	[illegible]	[illegible]	[illegible]	[illegible]	[illegible]	[illegible]	[illegible]	[illegible]	[illegible]	[illegible]
IV.	CONSTITUTIONAL	[illegible]	[illegible]	[illegible]	[illegible]	[illegible]	[illegible]	[illegible]	[illegible]	[illegible]	[illegible]	[illegible]	[illegible]	[illegible]	[illegible]	[illegible]	[illegible]	[illegible]	[illegible]	[illegible]
V.	DEVELOPMENTAL	[illegible]	[illegible]	[illegible]	[illegible]	[illegible]	[illegible]	[illegible]	[illegible]	[illegible]	[illegible]	[illegible]	[illegible]	[illegible]	[illegible]	[illegible]	[illegible]	[illegible]	[illegible]	[illegible]
VI.	LOCAL	[illegible]	[illegible]	[illegible]	[illegible]	[illegible]	[illegible]	[illegible]	[illegible]	[illegible]	[illegible]	[illegible]	[illegible]	[illegible]	[illegible]	[illegible]	[illegible]	[illegible]	[illegible]	[illegible]
VII.	VIOLENCE,	[illegible]	[illegible]	[illegible]	[illegible]	[illegible]	[illegible]	[illegible]	[illegible]	[illegible]	[illegible]	[illegible]	[illegible]	[illegible]	[illegible]	[illegible]	[illegible]	[illegible]	[illegible]	[illegible]
VIII.	ILL-DEFINED AND NOT SPECIFIED CAUSES,	[illegible]	[illegible]	[illegible]	[illegible]	[illegible]	[illegible]	[illegible]	[illegible]	[illegible]	[illegible]	[illegible]	[illegible]	[illegible]	[illegible]	[illegible]	[illegible]	[illegible]	[illegible]	[illegible]
	(ORDERS.)																			
I.	1. [illegible]	[illegible]	[illegible]	[illegible]	[illegible]	[illegible]	[illegible]	[illegible]	[illegible]	[illegible]	[illegible]	[illegible]	[illegible]	[illegible]	[illegible]	[illegible]	[illegible]	[illegible]	[illegible]	[illegible]
	2. [illegible]	[illegible]	[illegible]	[illegible]	[illegible]	[illegible]	[illegible]	[illegible]	[illegible]	[illegible]	[illegible]	[illegible]	[illegible]	[illegible]	[illegible]	[illegible]	[illegible]	[illegible]	[illegible]	[illegible]
	3. [illegible]	[illegible]	[illegible]	[illegible]	[illegible]	[illegible]	[illegible]	[illegible]	[illegible]	[illegible]	[illegible]	[illegible]	[illegible]	[illegible]	[illegible]	[illegible]	[illegible]	[illegible]	[illegible]	[illegible]
	4. [illegible]	[illegible]	[illegible]	[illegible]	[illegible]	[illegible]	[illegible]	[illegible]	[illegible]	[illegible]	[illegible]	[illegible]	[illegible]	[illegible]	[illegible]	[illegible]	[illegible]	[illegible]	[illegible]	[illegible]
	5. [illegible]	[illegible]	[illegible]	[illegible]	[illegible]	[illegible]	[illegible]	[illegible]	[illegible]	[illegible]	[illegible]	[illegible]	[illegible]	[illegible]	[illegible]	[illegible]	[illegible]	[illegible]	[illegible]	[illegible]
	6. [illegible]	[illegible]	[illegible]	[illegible]	[illegible]	[illegible]	[illegible]	[illegible]	[illegible]	[illegible]	[illegible]	[illegible]	[illegible]	[illegible]	[illegible]	[illegible]	[illegible]	[illegible]	[illegible]	[illegible]
II.	[illegible]	[illegible]	[illegible]	[illegible]	[illegible]	[illegible]	[illegible]	[illegible]	[illegible]	[illegible]	[illegible]	[illegible]	[illegible]	[illegible]	[illegible]	[illegible]	[illegible]	[illegible]	[illegible]	[illegible]
III.	[illegible]	[illegible]	[illegible]	[illegible]	[illegible]	[illegible]	[illegible]	[illegible]	[illegible]	[illegible]	[illegible]	[illegible]	[illegible]	[illegible]	[illegible]	[illegible]	[illegible]	[illegible]	[illegible]	[illegible]
IV.	[illegible]	[illegible]	[illegible]	[illegible]	[illegible]	[illegible]	[illegible]	[illegible]	[illegible]	[illegible]	[illegible]	[illegible]	[illegible]	[illegible]	[illegible]	[illegible]	[illegible]	[illegible]	[illegible]	[illegible]
V.	[illegible]	[illegible]	[illegible]	[illegible]	[illegible]	[illegible]	[illegible]	[illegible]	[illegible]	[illegible]	[illegible]	[illegible]	[illegible]	[illegible]	[illegible]	[illegible]	[illegible]	[illegible]	[illegible]	[illegible]
VI.	1. [illegible]	[illegible]	[illegible]	[illegible]	[illegible]	[illegible]	[illegible]	[illegible]	[illegible]	[illegible]	[illegible]	[illegible]	[illegible]	[illegible]	[illegible]	[illegible]	[illegible]	[illegible]	[illegible]	[illegible]
	2. [illegible]	[illegible]	[illegible]	[illegible]	[illegible]	[illegible]	[illegible]	[illegible]	[illegible]	[illegible]	[illegible]	[illegible]	[illegible]	[illegible]	[illegible]	[illegible]	[illegible]	[illegible]	[illegible]	[illegible]
	3. [illegible]	[illegible]	[illegible]	[illegible]	[illegible]	[illegible]	[illegible]	[illegible]	[illegible]	[illegible]	[illegible]	[illegible]	[illegible]	[illegible]	[illegible]	[illegible]	[illegible]	[illegible]	[illegible]	[illegible]
	4. [illegible]	[illegible]	[illegible]	[illegible]	[illegible]	[illegible]	[illegible]	[illegible]	[illegible]	[illegible]	[illegible]	[illegible]	[illegible]	[illegible]	[illegible]	[illegible]	[illegible]	[illegible]	[illegible]	[illegible]
	5. [illegible]	[illegible]	[illegible]	[illegible]	[illegible]	[illegible]	[illegible]	[illegible]	[illegible]	[illegible]	[illegible]	[illegible]	[illegible]	[illegible]	[illegible]	[illegible]	[illegible]	[illegible]	[illegible]	[illegible]
	6. [illegible]	[illegible]	[illegible]	[illegible]	[illegible]	[illegible]	[illegible]	[illegible]	[illegible]	[illegible]	[illegible]	[illegible]	[illegible]	[illegible]	[illegible]	[illegible]	[illegible]	[illegible]	[illegible]	[illegible]
	7. [illegible]	[illegible]	[illegible]	[illegible]	[illegible]	[illegible]	[illegible]	[illegible]	[illegible]	[illegible]	[illegible]	[illegible]	[illegible]	[illegible]	[illegible]	[illegible]	[illegible]	[illegible]	[illegible]	[illegible]
	8. [illegible] (a) [illegible]	[illegible]	[illegible]	[illegible]	[illegible]	[illegible]	[illegible]	[illegible]	[illegible]	[illegible]	[illegible]	[illegible]	[illegible]	[illegible]	[illegible]	[illegible]	[illegible]	[illegible]	[illegible]	[illegible]
	(b) [illegible]	[illegible]	[illegible]	[illegible]	[illegible]	[illegible]	[illegible]	[illegible]	[illegible]	[illegible]	[illegible]	[illegible]	[illegible]	[illegible]	[illegible]	[illegible]	[illegible]	[illegible]	[illegible]	[illegible]
	9. [illegible]	[illegible]	[illegible]	[illegible]	[illegible]	[illegible]	[illegible]	[illegible]	[illegible]	[illegible]	[illegible]	[illegible]	[illegible]	[illegible]	[illegible]	[illegible]	[illegible]	[illegible]	[illegible]	[illegible]
	10. [illegible]	[illegible]	[illegible]	[illegible]	[illegible]	[illegible]	[illegible]	[illegible]	[illegible]	[illegible]	[illegible]	[illegible]	[illegible]	[illegible]	[illegible]	[illegible]	[illegible]	[illegible]	[illegible]	[illegible]
VII.	1. [illegible]	[illegible]	[illegible]	[illegible]	[illegible]	[illegible]	[illegible]	[illegible]	[illegible]	[illegible]	[illegible]	[illegible]	[illegible]	[illegible]	[illegible]	[illegible]	[illegible]	[illegible]	[illegible]	[illegible]
	2. [illegible]	[illegible]	[illegible]	[illegible]	[illegible]	[illegible]	[illegible]	[illegible]	[illegible]	[illegible]	[illegible]	[illegible]	[illegible]	[illegible]	[illegible]	[illegible]	[illegible]	[illegible]	[illegible]	[illegible]
	3. [illegible]	[illegible]	[illegible]	[illegible]	[illegible]	[illegible]	[illegible]	[illegible]	[illegible]	[illegible]	[illegible]	[illegible]	[illegible]	[illegible]	[illegible]	[illegible]	[illegible]	[illegible]	[illegible]	[illegible]
	4. [illegible]	[illegible]	[illegible]	[illegible]	[illegible]	[illegible]	[illegible]	[illegible]	[illegible]	[illegible]	[illegible]	[illegible]	[illegible]	[illegible]	[illegible]	[illegible]	[illegible]	[illegible]	[illegible]	[illegible]
VIII.	[illegible]	[illegible]	[illegible]	[illegible]	[illegible]	[illegible]	[illegible]	[illegible]	[illegible]	[illegible]	[illegible]	[illegible]	[illegible]	[illegible]	[illegible]	[illegible]	[illegible]	[illegible]	[illegible]	[illegible]

[continued at page 150.]

IRELAND.—CAUSES of [illegible] at different Periods of Life in the Year 1891—MALES.

Class	Causes of Death	All Ages	Under 1 year	1	2	3	4	Total under 5 years	5-	10-	15-	20-	25-	35-	45-	55-	65-	75-	85-	[illegible]
I.	Class 1.																			
	[illegible]	[illegible]	[illegible]	[illegible]	[illegible]	[illegible]	[illegible]	[illegible]	[illegible]	[illegible]	[illegible]	[illegible]	[illegible]	[illegible]	[illegible]	[illegible]	[illegible]	[illegible]	[illegible]	[illegible]
	[illegible]	[illegible]	[illegible]	[illegible]	[illegible]	[illegible]	[illegible]	[illegible]	[illegible]	[illegible]	[illegible]	[illegible]	[illegible]	[illegible]	[illegible]	[illegible]	[illegible]	[illegible]	[illegible]	[illegible]
	[illegible]	[illegible]	[illegible]	[illegible]	[illegible]	[illegible]	[illegible]	[illegible]	[illegible]	[illegible]	[illegible]	[illegible]	[illegible]	[illegible]	[illegible]	[illegible]	[illegible]	[illegible]	[illegible]	[illegible]
	[illegible]	[illegible]	[illegible]	[illegible]	[illegible]	[illegible]	[illegible]	[illegible]	[illegible]	[illegible]	[illegible]	[illegible]	[illegible]	[illegible]	[illegible]	[illegible]	[illegible]	[illegible]	[illegible]	[illegible]
	[illegible]	[illegible]	[illegible]	[illegible]	[illegible]	[illegible]	[illegible]	[illegible]	[illegible]	[illegible]	[illegible]	[illegible]	[illegible]	[illegible]	[illegible]	[illegible]	[illegible]	[illegible]	[illegible]	[illegible]
	[illegible]	[illegible]	[illegible]	[illegible]	[illegible]	[illegible]	[illegible]	[illegible]	[illegible]	[illegible]	[illegible]	[illegible]	[illegible]	[illegible]	[illegible]	[illegible]	[illegible]	[illegible]	[illegible]	[illegible]
	Scarlet Fever,	[illegible]	16	[illegible]	[illegible]	[illegible]	[illegible]	[illegible]	[illegible]	[illegible]	[illegible]	[illegible]	[illegible]	[illegible]	[illegible]	[illegible]	[illegible]	[illegible]	[illegible]	[illegible]
	Typhus,	[illegible]	[illegible]	[illegible]	[illegible]	[illegible]	[illegible]	[illegible]	[illegible]	[illegible]	[illegible]	[illegible]	[illegible]	[illegible]	[illegible]	[illegible]	[illegible]	[illegible]	[illegible]	[illegible]
	[illegible] Fever,	[illegible]	[illegible]	[illegible]	[illegible]	[illegible]	[illegible]	[illegible]	[illegible]	[illegible]	[illegible]	[illegible]	[illegible]	[illegible]	[illegible]	[illegible]	[illegible]	[illegible]	[illegible]	[illegible]
	[illegible]	[illegible]	[illegible]	[illegible]	[illegible]	[illegible]	[illegible]	[illegible]	[illegible]	[illegible]	[illegible]	[illegible]	[illegible]	[illegible]	[illegible]	[illegible]	[illegible]	[illegible]	[illegible]	[illegible]
	Whooping-cough,	[illegible]	[illegible]	[illegible]	[illegible]	[illegible]	[illegible]	[illegible]	[illegible]	[illegible]	[illegible]	[illegible]	[illegible]	[illegible]	[illegible]	[illegible]	[illegible]	[illegible]	[illegible]	[illegible]
	[illegible]	[illegible]	[illegible]	[illegible]	[illegible]	[illegible]	[illegible]	[illegible]	[illegible]	[illegible]	[illegible]	[illegible]	[illegible]	[illegible]	[illegible]	[illegible]	[illegible]	[illegible]	[illegible]	[illegible]
	[illegible]	[illegible]	[illegible]	[illegible]	[illegible]	[illegible]	[illegible]	[illegible]	[illegible]	[illegible]	[illegible]	[illegible]	[illegible]	[illegible]	[illegible]	[illegible]	[illegible]	[illegible]	[illegible]	[illegible]
	[illegible] Fever,	[illegible]	[illegible]	[illegible]	[illegible]	[illegible]	[illegible]	[illegible]	[illegible]	[illegible]	[illegible]	[illegible]	[illegible]	[illegible]	[illegible]	[illegible]	[illegible]	[illegible]	[illegible]	[illegible]
	[illegible] Fever,	[illegible]	[illegible]	[illegible]	[illegible]	[illegible]	[illegible]	[illegible]	[illegible]	[illegible]	[illegible]	[illegible]	[illegible]	[illegible]	[illegible]	[illegible]	[illegible]	[illegible]	[illegible]	[illegible]
	[illegible] Fever,	[illegible]	[illegible]	[illegible]	[illegible]	[illegible]	[illegible]	[illegible]	[illegible]	[illegible]	[illegible]	[illegible]	[illegible]	[illegible]	[illegible]	[illegible]	[illegible]	[illegible]	[illegible]	[illegible]
	Other [illegible] Diseases	[illegible]	[illegible]	[illegible]	[illegible]	[illegible]	[illegible]	[illegible]	[illegible]	[illegible]	[illegible]	[illegible]	[illegible]	[illegible]	[illegible]	[illegible]	[illegible]	[illegible]	[illegible]	[illegible]
	Class 2.																			
	[illegible]	[illegible]	14	[illegible]	[illegible]	[illegible]	[illegible]	[illegible]	[illegible]	[illegible]	[illegible]	[illegible]	[illegible]	[illegible]	[illegible]	[illegible]	[illegible]	[illegible]	[illegible]	[illegible]
	[illegible]	[illegible]	[illegible]	[illegible]	[illegible]	[illegible]	[illegible]	[illegible]	[illegible]	[illegible]	[illegible]	[illegible]	[illegible]	[illegible]	[illegible]	[illegible]	[illegible]	[illegible]	[illegible]	[illegible]
	Class 3.																			
	[illegible]	[illegible]	[illegible]	[illegible]	[illegible]	[illegible]	[illegible]	[illegible]	[illegible]	[illegible]	[illegible]	[illegible]	[illegible]	[illegible]	[illegible]	[illegible]	[illegible]	[illegible]	[illegible]	[illegible]
	[illegible]	[illegible]	[illegible]	[illegible]	[illegible]	[illegible]	[illegible]	[illegible]	[illegible]	[illegible]	[illegible]	[illegible]	[illegible]	[illegible]	[illegible]	[illegible]	[illegible]	[illegible]	[illegible]	[illegible]
	Class 4.																			
	[illegible]	[illegible]	[illegible]	[illegible]	[illegible]	[illegible]	[illegible]	[illegible]	[illegible]	[illegible]	[illegible]	[illegible]	[illegible]	[illegible]	[illegible]	[illegible]	[illegible]	[illegible]	[illegible]	[illegible]
	[illegible]	[illegible]	[illegible]	[illegible]	[illegible]	[illegible]	[illegible]	[illegible]	[illegible]	[illegible]	[illegible]	[illegible]	[illegible]	[illegible]	[illegible]	[illegible]	[illegible]	[illegible]	[illegible]	[illegible]
	[illegible]	[illegible]	[illegible]	[illegible]	[illegible]	[illegible]	[illegible]	[illegible]	[illegible]	[illegible]	[illegible]	[illegible]	[illegible]	[illegible]	[illegible]	[illegible]	[illegible]	[illegible]	[illegible]	[illegible]
	[illegible]	[illegible]	[illegible]	[illegible]	[illegible]	[illegible]	[illegible]	[illegible]	[illegible]	[illegible]	[illegible]	[illegible]	[illegible]	[illegible]	[illegible]	[illegible]	[illegible]	[illegible]	[illegible]	[illegible]
	Class 5.																			
	[illegible]	[illegible]	[illegible]	[illegible]	[illegible]	[illegible]	[illegible]	[illegible]	[illegible]	[illegible]	[illegible]	[illegible]	[illegible]	[illegible]	[illegible]	[illegible]	[illegible]	[illegible]	[illegible]	[illegible]
	[illegible]	[illegible]	[illegible]	[illegible]	[illegible]	[illegible]	[illegible]	[illegible]	[illegible]	[illegible]	[illegible]	[illegible]	[illegible]	[illegible]	[illegible]	[illegible]	[illegible]	[illegible]	[illegible]	[illegible]
	Class 6.																			
	[illegible]	[illegible]	[illegible]	[illegible]	[illegible]	[illegible]	[illegible]	[illegible]	[illegible]	[illegible]	[illegible]	[illegible]	[illegible]	[illegible]	[illegible]	[illegible]	[illegible]	[illegible]	[illegible]	[illegible]
	[illegible]	[illegible]	[illegible]	[illegible]	[illegible]	[illegible]	[illegible]	[illegible]	[illegible]	[illegible]	[illegible]	[illegible]	[illegible]	[illegible]	[illegible]	[illegible]	[illegible]	[illegible]	[illegible]	[illegible]
	[illegible]	[illegible]	[illegible]	[illegible]	[illegible]	[illegible]	[illegible]	[illegible]	[illegible]	[illegible]	[illegible]	[illegible]	[illegible]	[illegible]	[illegible]	[illegible]	[illegible]	[illegible]	[illegible]	[illegible]
	[illegible]	[illegible]	[illegible]	[illegible]	[illegible]	[illegible]	[illegible]	[illegible]	[illegible]	[illegible]	[illegible]	[illegible]	[illegible]	[illegible]	[illegible]	[illegible]	[illegible]	[illegible]	[illegible]	[illegible]
II.	[illegible]	[illegible]	[illegible]	[illegible]	[illegible]	[illegible]	[illegible]	[illegible]	[illegible]	[illegible]	[illegible]	[illegible]	[illegible]	[illegible]	[illegible]	[illegible]	[illegible]	[illegible]	[illegible]	[illegible]
	[illegible]	[illegible]	[illegible]	[illegible]	[illegible]	[illegible]	[illegible]	[illegible]	[illegible]	[illegible]	[illegible]	[illegible]	[illegible]	[illegible]	[illegible]	[illegible]	[illegible]	[illegible]	[illegible]	[illegible]
	[illegible]	[illegible]	[illegible]	[illegible]	[illegible]	[illegible]	[illegible]	[illegible]	[illegible]	[illegible]	[illegible]	[illegible]	[illegible]	[illegible]	[illegible]	[illegible]	[illegible]	[illegible]	[illegible]	[illegible]
	[illegible]	[illegible]	[illegible]	[illegible]	[illegible]	[illegible]	[illegible]	[illegible]	[illegible]	[illegible]	[illegible]	[illegible]	[illegible]	[illegible]	[illegible]	[illegible]	[illegible]	[illegible]	[illegible]	[illegible]
III.	[illegible]	[illegible]	[illegible]	[illegible]	[illegible]	[illegible]	[illegible]	[illegible]	[illegible]	[illegible]	[illegible]	[illegible]	[illegible]	[illegible]	[illegible]	[illegible]	[illegible]	[illegible]	[illegible]	[illegible]
	[illegible]	[illegible]	[illegible]	[illegible]	[illegible]	[illegible]	[illegible]	[illegible]	[illegible]	[illegible]	[illegible]	[illegible]	[illegible]	[illegible]	[illegible]	[illegible]	[illegible]	[illegible]	[illegible]	[illegible]
	[illegible]	[illegible]	[illegible]	[illegible]	[illegible]	[illegible]	[illegible]	[illegible]	[illegible]	[illegible]	[illegible]	[illegible]	[illegible]	[illegible]	[illegible]	[illegible]	[illegible]	[illegible]	[illegible]	[illegible]
	[illegible]	[illegible]	[illegible]	[illegible]	[illegible]	[illegible]	[illegible]	[illegible]	[illegible]	[illegible]	[illegible]	[illegible]	[illegible]	[illegible]	[illegible]	[illegible]	[illegible]	[illegible]	[illegible]	[illegible]
IV.	[illegible]	[illegible]	[illegible]	[illegible]	[illegible]	[illegible]	[illegible]	[illegible]	[illegible]	[illegible]	[illegible]	[illegible]	[illegible]	[illegible]	[illegible]	[illegible]	[illegible]	[illegible]	[illegible]	[illegible]
	[illegible]	[illegible]	[illegible]	[illegible]	[illegible]	[illegible]	[illegible]	[illegible]	[illegible]	[illegible]	[illegible]	[illegible]	[illegible]	[illegible]	[illegible]	[illegible]	[illegible]	[illegible]	[illegible]	[illegible]
	[illegible]	[illegible]	[illegible]	[illegible]	[illegible]	[illegible]	[illegible]	[illegible]	[illegible]	[illegible]	[illegible]	[illegible]	[illegible]	[illegible]	[illegible]	[illegible]	[illegible]	[illegible]	[illegible]	[illegible]
	[illegible]	[illegible]	[illegible]	[illegible]	[illegible]	[illegible]	[illegible]	[illegible]	[illegible]	[illegible]	[illegible]	[illegible]	[illegible]	[illegible]	[illegible]	[illegible]	[illegible]	[illegible]	[illegible]	[illegible]
	[illegible]	[illegible]	[illegible]	[illegible]	[illegible]	[illegible]	[illegible]	[illegible]	[illegible]	[illegible]	[illegible]	[illegible]	[illegible]	[illegible]	[illegible]	[illegible]	[illegible]	[illegible]	[illegible]	[illegible]

[Continued at page 152.]

IRELAND.—CAUSES of DEATH at different Periods of Life in the Year 1891—FEMALES.

Class.	CAUSES OF DEATH.	FEMALES. All Ages.	Ages at Death. Under 1 year.	1	2	3	4	Total under 5 years.	5-	10-	15-	20-	25-	35-	45-	55-	65-	75-	85-	95 and upwards.
I.	ORDER 1.																			
	Smallpox: Vaccinated,	-	-	-	-	-	-	-	-	-	-	-	-	-	-	-	-	-	-	-
	Smallpox: Unvaccinated,	[illegible]	1	-	-	-	-	[illegible]	-	-	-	1	-	-	-	-	-	-	-	-
	Smallpox: No Statement,	-	-	-	-	-	-	-	-	-	-	-	-	-	-	-	-	-	-	-
	Chicken-pox,	[illegible]	[illegible]	[illegible]	-	-	-	[illegible]	[illegible]	-	-	-	-	-	-	-	-	-	-	-
	Measles,	[illegible]	[illegible]	[illegible]	[illegible]	[illegible]	[illegible]	[illegible]	[illegible]	[illegible]	[illegible]	[illegible]	[illegible]	[illegible]	-	-	-	-	-	-
	Epidemic Rose Rash,	[illegible]	[illegible]	[illegible]	-	-	-	[illegible]	-	-	-	-	[illegible]	-	-	-	-	-	-	-
	Scarlet Fever,	[illegible]	[illegible]	[illegible]	[illegible]	[illegible]	[illegible]	[illegible]	[illegible]	[illegible]	7	-	[illegible]	[illegible]	[illegible]	-	-	-	-	-
	Typhus,	[illegible]	-	-	[illegible]	-	-	[illegible]	1	1	[illegible]	[illegible]	[illegible]	[illegible]	[illegible]	[illegible]	1	-	1	-
	Relapsing Fever,	1	-	-	-	-	-	-	-	-	-	-	[illegible]	-	-	-	-	-	-	-
	Influenza,	[illegible]	[illegible]	[illegible]	[illegible]	[illegible]	[illegible]	[illegible]	[illegible]	[illegible]	[illegible]	[illegible]	[illegible]	[illegible]	[illegible]	[illegible]	[illegible]	[illegible]	[illegible]	-
	Whooping Cough,	[illegible]	[illegible]	[illegible]	[illegible]	[illegible]	[illegible]	[illegible]	[illegible]	[illegible]	[illegible]	-	-	-	-	-	-	-	-	-
	Mumps,	[illegible]	-	1	-	[illegible]	-	[illegible]	1	-	-	-	-	-	-	-	-	-	-	-
	Diphtheria,	[illegible]	7	[illegible]	[illegible]	[illegible]	[illegible]	[illegible]	[illegible]	[illegible]	[illegible]	[illegible]	[illegible]	[illegible]	[illegible]	-	[illegible]	-	-	-
	Continued Fever,	[illegible]	4	[illegible]	[illegible]	[illegible]	-	[illegible]	[illegible]	[illegible]	[illegible]	[illegible]	[illegible]	-	[illegible]	[illegible]	[illegible]	-	-	-
	Simple and ill-defined Fever,	[illegible]	1	[illegible]	[illegible]	[illegible]	[illegible]	11	[illegible]	[illegible]	[illegible]	[illegible]	[illegible]	[illegible]	[illegible]	[illegible]	[illegible]	[illegible]	-	-
	Enteric Fever,	[illegible]	[illegible]	[illegible]	[illegible]	11	[illegible]	[illegible]	[illegible]	[illegible]	[illegible]	[illegible]	[illegible]	[illegible]	[illegible]	[illegible]	[illegible]	[illegible]	-	-
	Other Miasmatic Diseases,	[illegible]	-	1	-	-	-	1	-	-	-	-	-	-	-	-	1	-	-	-
	ORDER 2.																			
	Simple Cholera,	[illegible]	[illegible]	[illegible]	[illegible]	-	1	[illegible]	[illegible]	-	-	-	[illegible]	[illegible]	-	[illegible]	[illegible]	[illegible]	-	-
	Diarrhoea, Dysentery,	[illegible]	[illegible]	[illegible]	[illegible]	[illegible]	11	[illegible]	[illegible]	[illegible]	[illegible]	[illegible]	[illegible]	[illegible]	[illegible]	[illegible]	[illegible]	[illegible]	1	[illegible]
	ORDER 3.																			
	Remittent Fever,	-	-	-	-	-	-	-	-	-	-	-	-	-	-	-	-	-	-	-
	Ague,	-	-	-	-	-	-	-	-	-	-	-	-	-	-	-	-	-	-	-
	ORDER 4.																			
	Hydrophobia,	1	-	-	-	-	-	-	-	-	-	-	-	-	-	-	[illegible]	-	-	-
	Glanders,	-	-	-	-	-	-	-	-	-	-	-	-	-	-	-	-	-	-	-
	Splenic Fever,	-	-	-	-	-	-	-	-	-	-	-	-	-	-	-	-	-	-	-
	Cowpox and other effects of Vaccination,	-	-	-	-	-	-	-	-	-	-	-	-	-	-	-	-	-	-	-
	ORDER 5.																			
	Syphilis,	[illegible]	[illegible]	[illegible]	-	-	-	[illegible]	-	-	[illegible]	-	[illegible]	[illegible]	[illegible]	-	[illegible]	-	-	-
	Gonorrhoea, Stricture of Urethra,	-	-	-	-	-	-	-	-	-	-	-	-	-	-	-	-	-	-	-
	ORDER 6.																			
	Phagedaena,	1	-	-	-	1	-	1	-	-	-	-	-	-	-	-	-	-	-	-
	Erysipelas,	[illegible]	[illegible]	[illegible]	[illegible]	[illegible]	-	[illegible]	[illegible]	[illegible]	[illegible]	[illegible]	[illegible]	[illegible]	[illegible]	[illegible]	[illegible]	[illegible]	[illegible]	-
	Pyaemia, Septicaemia,	[illegible]	1	[illegible]	-	-	-	[illegible]	[illegible]	[illegible]	[illegible]	[illegible]	[illegible]	[illegible]	[illegible]	[illegible]	[illegible]	[illegible]	-	-
	Puerperal Fever,	[illegible]	-	-	-	-	-	-	-	-	[illegible]	[illegible]	[illegible]	[illegible]	[illegible]	-	-	-	-	-
II.	Thrush,	[illegible]	[illegible]	-	-	-	-	[illegible]	-	-	-	-	-	-	-	-	-	-	-	-
	Other Diseases from Vegetable Parasites,	-	-	-	-	-	-	-	-	-	-	-	-	-	-	-	-	-	-	-
	Hydatid Disease,	-	-	-	-	-	-	-	-	-	-	-	-	-	-	-	-	-	-	-
	Other Diseases from Animal Parasites,	[illegible]	-	1	[illegible]	-	1	1	1	[illegible]	-	-	-	-	-	-	-	-	-	-
III.	Starvation, Want of Breast Milk,	[illegible]	[illegible]	-	-	-	-	[illegible]	-	-	-	-	-	-	-	1	-	-	-	-
	Scurvy,	1	-	-	-	-	-	-	-	-	-	-	-	-	-	1	-	-	-	-
	Intemperance: Chronic Alcoholism,	[illegible]	-	-	-	-	-	-	-	-	-	-	[illegible]	[illegible]	[illegible]	[illegible]	[illegible]	-	-	-
	Intemperance: Delirium Tremens,	1	-	-	-	-	-	-	-	-	-	-	-	-	-	1	-	-	-	-
IV.	Rheumatic Fever, Rheumatism of Heart,	[illegible]	-	-	-	-	-	-	[illegible]	[illegible]	[illegible]	[illegible]	[illegible]	[illegible]	[illegible]	[illegible]	[illegible]	[illegible]	-	-
	Rheumatism,	[illegible]	1	-	-	-	-	1	[illegible]	[illegible]	1	1	[illegible]	[illegible]	[illegible]	[illegible]	[illegible]	[illegible]	1	-
	Gout,	10	-	-	-	-	-	-	-	-	-	-	-	-	1	1	[illegible]	1	-	-
	Rickets,	[illegible]	[illegible]	[illegible]	[illegible]	1	[illegible]	[illegible]	[illegible]	1	-	-	-	-	-	-	-	-	-	-
	Cancer,	[illegible]	-	-	1	[illegible]	-	[illegible]	1	1	1	[illegible]	[illegible]	[illegible]	[illegible]	[illegible]	[illegible]	[illegible]	[illegible]	1

[continued at page 152.]

IRELAND.—CAUSES of DEATHS at different Periods of Life in the Year 1891—MALES—con.

Class.	CAUSES OF DEATH.	MALES.																			
		All Ages.	Under 1 year.	1	2	3	4	Total under 5 years.	5-	10-	15-	20-	25-	35-	45-	55-	65-	75-	85-	95 and upwards.	
IV.—con.	Tabes Mesenterica,	[illegible]	[illegible]	[illegible]	[illegible]	[illegible]	[illegible]	[illegible]	[illegible]	[illegible]	[illegible]	[illegible]	[illegible]	[illegible]	[illegible]	[illegible]	[illegible]	[illegible]	[illegible]	[illegible]	
	Tubercular Meningitis (Acute Hydrocephalus),	[illegible]	[illegible]	[illegible]	[illegible]	[illegible]	[illegible]	[illegible]	[illegible]	[illegible]	[illegible]	[illegible]	[illegible]	[illegible]	[illegible]	[illegible]	[illegible]	[illegible]	[illegible]	[illegible]	
	Phthisis,	[illegible]	[illegible]	[illegible]	[illegible]	[illegible]	[illegible]	[illegible]	[illegible]	[illegible]	[illegible]	[illegible]	[illegible]	[illegible]	[illegible]	[illegible]	[illegible]	[illegible]	[illegible]	[illegible]	
	Tuberculosis, other forms of Scrofula,	[illegible]	[illegible]	[illegible]	[illegible]	[illegible]	[illegible]	[illegible]	[illegible]	[illegible]	[illegible]	[illegible]	[illegible]	[illegible]	[illegible]	[illegible]	[illegible]	[illegible]	[illegible]	[illegible]	
	Purpura, Hæmorrhagic Diathesis,	[illegible]	[illegible]	[illegible]	[illegible]	[illegible]	[illegible]	[illegible]	[illegible]	[illegible]	[illegible]	[illegible]	[illegible]	[illegible]	[illegible]	[illegible]	[illegible]	[illegible]	[illegible]	[illegible]	
	Anæmia, Chlorosis, Leucocythæmia,	[illegible]	[illegible]	[illegible]	[illegible]	[illegible]	[illegible]	[illegible]	[illegible]	[illegible]	[illegible]	[illegible]	[illegible]	[illegible]	[illegible]	[illegible]	[illegible]	[illegible]	[illegible]	[illegible]	
	Diabetes Mellitus,	[illegible]	[illegible]	[illegible]	[illegible]	[illegible]	[illegible]	[illegible]	[illegible]	[illegible]	[illegible]	[illegible]	[illegible]	[illegible]	[illegible]	[illegible]	[illegible]	[illegible]	[illegible]	[illegible]	
	Other Constitutional Diseases,	[illegible]	[illegible]	[illegible]	[illegible]	[illegible]	[illegible]	[illegible]	[illegible]	[illegible]	[illegible]	[illegible]	[illegible]	[illegible]	[illegible]	[illegible]	[illegible]	[illegible]	[illegible]	[illegible]	
V.	Premature Birth,	[illegible]	[illegible]	[illegible]	[illegible]	[illegible]	[illegible]	[illegible]	[illegible]	[illegible]	[illegible]	[illegible]	[illegible]	[illegible]	[illegible]	[illegible]	[illegible]	[illegible]	[illegible]	[illegible]	
	Atelectasis,	[illegible]	[illegible]	[illegible]	[illegible]	[illegible]	[illegible]	[illegible]	[illegible]	[illegible]	[illegible]	[illegible]	[illegible]	[illegible]	[illegible]	[illegible]	[illegible]	[illegible]	[illegible]	[illegible]	
	Cyanosis,	[illegible]	[illegible]	[illegible]	[illegible]	[illegible]	[illegible]	[illegible]	[illegible]	[illegible]	[illegible]	[illegible]	[illegible]	[illegible]	[illegible]	[illegible]	[illegible]	[illegible]	[illegible]	[illegible]	
	Spina Bifida,	[illegible]	[illegible]	[illegible]	[illegible]	[illegible]	[illegible]	[illegible]	[illegible]	[illegible]	[illegible]	[illegible]	[illegible]	[illegible]	[illegible]	[illegible]	[illegible]	[illegible]	[illegible]	[illegible]	
	Imperforate Anus,	[illegible]	[illegible]	[illegible]	[illegible]	[illegible]	[illegible]	[illegible]	[illegible]	[illegible]	[illegible]	[illegible]	[illegible]	[illegible]	[illegible]	[illegible]	[illegible]	[illegible]	[illegible]	[illegible]	
	Cleft Palate, Harelip,	[illegible]	[illegible]	[illegible]	[illegible]	[illegible]	[illegible]	[illegible]	[illegible]	[illegible]	[illegible]	[illegible]	[illegible]	[illegible]	[illegible]	[illegible]	[illegible]	[illegible]	[illegible]	[illegible]	
	Other Congenital Defects,	[illegible]	[illegible]	[illegible]	[illegible]	[illegible]	[illegible]	[illegible]	[illegible]	[illegible]	[illegible]	[illegible]	[illegible]	[illegible]	[illegible]	[illegible]	[illegible]	[illegible]	[illegible]	[illegible]	
	Old Age,	[illegible]	[illegible]	[illegible]	[illegible]	[illegible]	[illegible]	[illegible]	[illegible]	[illegible]	[illegible]	[illegible]	[illegible]	[illegible]	[illegible]	[illegible]	[illegible]	[illegible]	[illegible]	[illegible]	
	GROUP 1.																				
VI.	Inflammation of Brain or its Membranes,	[illegible]	[illegible]	[illegible]	[illegible]	[illegible]	[illegible]	[illegible]	[illegible]	[illegible]	[illegible]	[illegible]	[illegible]	[illegible]	[illegible]	[illegible]	[illegible]	[illegible]	[illegible]	[illegible]	
	Apoplexy,	[illegible]	[illegible]	[illegible]	[illegible]	[illegible]	[illegible]	[illegible]	[illegible]	[illegible]	[illegible]	[illegible]	[illegible]	[illegible]	[illegible]	[illegible]	[illegible]	[illegible]	[illegible]	[illegible]	
	Softening of Brain,	[illegible]	[illegible]	[illegible]	[illegible]	[illegible]	[illegible]	[illegible]	[illegible]	[illegible]	[illegible]	[illegible]	[illegible]	[illegible]	[illegible]	[illegible]	[illegible]	[illegible]	[illegible]	[illegible]	
	Hemiplegia, Brain Paralysis,	[illegible]	[illegible]	[illegible]	[illegible]	[illegible]	[illegible]	[illegible]	[illegible]	[illegible]	[illegible]	[illegible]	[illegible]	[illegible]	[illegible]	[illegible]	[illegible]	[illegible]	[illegible]	[illegible]	
	Paralysis agitans,	[illegible]	[illegible]	[illegible]	[illegible]	[illegible]	[illegible]	[illegible]	[illegible]	[illegible]	[illegible]	[illegible]	[illegible]	[illegible]	[illegible]	[illegible]	[illegible]	[illegible]	[illegible]	[illegible]	
	Insanity, General Paralysis of Insane,	[illegible]	[illegible]	[illegible]	[illegible]	[illegible]	[illegible]	[illegible]	[illegible]	[illegible]	[illegible]	[illegible]	[illegible]	[illegible]	[illegible]	[illegible]	[illegible]	[illegible]	[illegible]	[illegible]	
	Chorea,	[illegible]	[illegible]	[illegible]	[illegible]	[illegible]	[illegible]	[illegible]	[illegible]	[illegible]	[illegible]	[illegible]	[illegible]	[illegible]	[illegible]	[illegible]	[illegible]	[illegible]	[illegible]	[illegible]	
	Epilepsy,	[illegible]	[illegible]	[illegible]	[illegible]	[illegible]	[illegible]	[illegible]	[illegible]	[illegible]	[illegible]	[illegible]	[illegible]	[illegible]	[illegible]	[illegible]	[illegible]	[illegible]	[illegible]	[illegible]	
	Convulsions,	[illegible]	[illegible]	[illegible]	[illegible]	[illegible]	[illegible]	[illegible]	[illegible]	[illegible]	[illegible]	[illegible]	[illegible]	[illegible]	[illegible]	[illegible]	[illegible]	[illegible]	[illegible]	[illegible]	
	Laryngismus Stridulus,	[illegible]	[illegible]	[illegible]	[illegible]	[illegible]	[illegible]	[illegible]	[illegible]	[illegible]	[illegible]	[illegible]	[illegible]	[illegible]	[illegible]	[illegible]	[illegible]	[illegible]	[illegible]	[illegible]	
	Idiopathic Tetanus,	[illegible]	[illegible]	[illegible]	[illegible]	[illegible]	[illegible]	[illegible]	[illegible]	[illegible]	[illegible]	[illegible]	[illegible]	[illegible]	[illegible]	[illegible]	[illegible]	[illegible]	[illegible]	[illegible]	
	Paraplegia, Diseases of Spinal Cord,	[illegible]	[illegible]	[illegible]	[illegible]	[illegible]	[illegible]	[illegible]	[illegible]	[illegible]	[illegible]	[illegible]	[illegible]	[illegible]	[illegible]	[illegible]	[illegible]	[illegible]	[illegible]	[illegible]	
	Other Diseases of Nervous System,	[illegible]	[illegible]	[illegible]	[illegible]	[illegible]	[illegible]	[illegible]	[illegible]	[illegible]	[illegible]	[illegible]	[illegible]	[illegible]	[illegible]	[illegible]	[illegible]	[illegible]	[illegible]	[illegible]	
	GROUP 2.																				
	Otitis, Otorrhœa,	[illegible]	[illegible]	[illegible]	[illegible]	[illegible]	[illegible]	[illegible]	[illegible]	[illegible]	[illegible]	[illegible]	[illegible]	[illegible]	[illegible]	[illegible]	[illegible]	[illegible]	[illegible]	[illegible]	
	Epistaxis and Diseases of Nose,	[illegible]	[illegible]	[illegible]	[illegible]	[illegible]	[illegible]	[illegible]	[illegible]	[illegible]	[illegible]	[illegible]	[illegible]	[illegible]	[illegible]	[illegible]	[illegible]	[illegible]	[illegible]	[illegible]	
	Ophthalmia and Diseases of Eye,	[illegible]	[illegible]	[illegible]	[illegible]	[illegible]	[illegible]	[illegible]	[illegible]	[illegible]	[illegible]	[illegible]	[illegible]	[illegible]	[illegible]	[illegible]	[illegible]	[illegible]	[illegible]	[illegible]	
	GROUP 3.																				
	Endocarditis, Valvular Disease,	[illegible]	[illegible]	[illegible]	[illegible]	[illegible]	[illegible]	[illegible]	[illegible]	[illegible]	[illegible]	[illegible]	[illegible]	[illegible]	[illegible]	[illegible]	[illegible]	[illegible]	[illegible]	[illegible]	
	Pericarditis,	[illegible]	[illegible]	[illegible]	[illegible]	[illegible]	[illegible]	[illegible]	[illegible]	[illegible]	[illegible]	[illegible]	[illegible]	[illegible]	[illegible]	[illegible]	[illegible]	[illegible]	[illegible]	[illegible]	
	Hypertrophy of Heart,	[illegible]	[illegible]	[illegible]	[illegible]	[illegible]	[illegible]	[illegible]	[illegible]	[illegible]	[illegible]	[illegible]	[illegible]	[illegible]	[illegible]	[illegible]	[illegible]	[illegible]	[illegible]	[illegible]	
	Angina Pectoris,	[illegible]	[illegible]	[illegible]	[illegible]	[illegible]	[illegible]	[illegible]	[illegible]	[illegible]	[illegible]	[illegible]	[illegible]	[illegible]	[illegible]	[illegible]	[illegible]	[illegible]	[illegible]	[illegible]	
	Syncope,	[illegible]	[illegible]	[illegible]	[illegible]	[illegible]	[illegible]	[illegible]	[illegible]	[illegible]	[illegible]	[illegible]	[illegible]	[illegible]	[illegible]	[illegible]	[illegible]	[illegible]	[illegible]	[illegible]	
	Aneurism,	[illegible]	[illegible]	[illegible]	[illegible]	[illegible]	[illegible]	[illegible]	[illegible]	[illegible]	[illegible]	[illegible]	[illegible]	[illegible]	[illegible]	[illegible]	[illegible]	[illegible]	[illegible]	[illegible]	
	Senile Gangrene,	[illegible]	[illegible]	[illegible]	[illegible]	[illegible]	[illegible]	[illegible]	[illegible]	[illegible]	[illegible]	[illegible]	[illegible]	[illegible]	[illegible]	[illegible]	[illegible]	[illegible]	[illegible]	[illegible]	
	Embolism, Thrombosis,	[illegible]	[illegible]	[illegible]	[illegible]	[illegible]	[illegible]	[illegible]	[illegible]	[illegible]	[illegible]	[illegible]	[illegible]	[illegible]	[illegible]	[illegible]	[illegible]	[illegible]	[illegible]	[illegible]	
	Phlebitis,	[illegible]	[illegible]	[illegible]	[illegible]	[illegible]	[illegible]	[illegible]	[illegible]	[illegible]	[illegible]	[illegible]	[illegible]	[illegible]	[illegible]	[illegible]	[illegible]	[illegible]	[illegible]	[illegible]	
	Varicose Veins,	[illegible]	[illegible]	[illegible]	[illegible]	[illegible]	[illegible]	[illegible]	[illegible]	[illegible]	[illegible]	[illegible]	[illegible]	[illegible]	[illegible]	[illegible]	[illegible]	[illegible]	[illegible]	[illegible]	
	Other Diseases of Circulatory System,	[illegible]	[illegible]	[illegible]	[illegible]	[illegible]	[illegible]	[illegible]	[illegible]	[illegible]	[illegible]	[illegible]	[illegible]	[illegible]	[illegible]	[illegible]	[illegible]	[illegible]	[illegible]	[illegible]	
	GROUP 4.																				
	Laryngitis,	[illegible]	[illegible]	[illegible]	[illegible]	[illegible]	[illegible]	[illegible]	[illegible]	[illegible]	[illegible]	[illegible]	[illegible]	[illegible]	[illegible]	[illegible]	[illegible]	[illegible]	[illegible]	[illegible]	
	Croup,	[illegible]	[illegible]	[illegible]	[illegible]	[illegible]	[illegible]	[illegible]	[illegible]	[illegible]	[illegible]	[illegible]	[illegible]	[illegible]	[illegible]	[illegible]	[illegible]	[illegible]	[illegible]	[illegible]	
	Other Diseases of Larynx and Trachea,	[illegible]	[illegible]	[illegible]	[illegible]	[illegible]	[illegible]	[illegible]	[illegible]	[illegible]	[illegible]	[illegible]	[illegible]	[illegible]	[illegible]	[illegible]	[illegible]	[illegible]	[illegible]	[illegible]	
	Emphysema, Asthma,	[illegible]	[illegible]	[illegible]	[illegible]	[illegible]	[illegible]	[illegible]	[illegible]	[illegible]	[illegible]	[illegible]	[illegible]	[illegible]	[illegible]	[illegible]	[illegible]	[illegible]	[illegible]	[illegible]	

(continued at page [illegible].)

IRELAND.—CAUSES of DEATHS at different Periods of Life in the Year 1891—FEMALES—con.

Class	CAUSES OF DEATH.	FEMALES. All Ages.	Ages at Death. Under 1 year	1	2	3	4	Total under 5 years	5-	10-	15-	20-	25-	35-	45-	55-	65-	75-	85-	95 and upwards
IV.—con.	Tabes Mesenterica,	[illegible]	[illegible]	[illegible]	[illegible]	[illegible]	[illegible]	[illegible]	[illegible]	[illegible]	[illegible]	[illegible]	[illegible]	[illegible]	[illegible]	[illegible]	[illegible]	[illegible]	[illegible]	[illegible]
	Tubercular Meningitis (Acute Hydrocephalus),	[illegible]	[illegible]	[illegible]	[illegible]	[illegible]	[illegible]	[illegible]	[illegible]	[illegible]	[illegible]	[illegible]	[illegible]	[illegible]	[illegible]	[illegible]	[illegible]	[illegible]	[illegible]	[illegible]
	Phthisis,	[illegible]	[illegible]	[illegible]	[illegible]	[illegible]	[illegible]	[illegible]	[illegible]	[illegible]	[illegible]	[illegible]	[illegible]	[illegible]	[illegible]	[illegible]	[illegible]	[illegible]	[illegible]	[illegible]
	Other forms of Tuberculosis, Scrofula,	[illegible]	[illegible]	[illegible]	[illegible]	[illegible]	[illegible]	[illegible]	[illegible]	[illegible]	[illegible]	[illegible]	[illegible]	[illegible]	[illegible]	[illegible]	[illegible]	[illegible]	[illegible]	[illegible]
	Purpura, Haemorrhagic Diathesis,	[illegible]	[illegible]	[illegible]	[illegible]	[illegible]	[illegible]	[illegible]	[illegible]	[illegible]	[illegible]	[illegible]	[illegible]	[illegible]	[illegible]	[illegible]	[illegible]	[illegible]	[illegible]	[illegible]
	Anaemia, Chlorosis, Leucocythaemia,	[illegible]	[illegible]	[illegible]	[illegible]	[illegible]	[illegible]	[illegible]	[illegible]	[illegible]	[illegible]	[illegible]	[illegible]	[illegible]	[illegible]	[illegible]	[illegible]	[illegible]	[illegible]	[illegible]
	Diabetes Mellitus,	[illegible]	[illegible]	[illegible]	[illegible]	[illegible]	[illegible]	[illegible]	[illegible]	[illegible]	[illegible]	[illegible]	[illegible]	[illegible]	[illegible]	[illegible]	[illegible]	[illegible]	[illegible]	[illegible]
	Other Constitutional Diseases,	[illegible]	[illegible]	[illegible]	[illegible]	[illegible]	[illegible]	[illegible]	[illegible]	[illegible]	[illegible]	[illegible]	[illegible]	[illegible]	[illegible]	[illegible]	[illegible]	[illegible]	[illegible]	[illegible]
V.	Premature Birth,	[illegible]	[illegible]	[illegible]	[illegible]	[illegible]	[illegible]	[illegible]	[illegible]	[illegible]	[illegible]	[illegible]	[illegible]	[illegible]	[illegible]	[illegible]	[illegible]	[illegible]	[illegible]	[illegible]
	Atelectasis,	[illegible]	[illegible]	[illegible]	[illegible]	[illegible]	[illegible]	[illegible]	[illegible]	[illegible]	[illegible]	[illegible]	[illegible]	[illegible]	[illegible]	[illegible]	[illegible]	[illegible]	[illegible]	[illegible]
	Cyanosis,	[illegible]	[illegible]	[illegible]	[illegible]	[illegible]	[illegible]	[illegible]	[illegible]	[illegible]	[illegible]	[illegible]	[illegible]	[illegible]	[illegible]	[illegible]	[illegible]	[illegible]	[illegible]	[illegible]
	Spina Bifida,	[illegible]	[illegible]	[illegible]	[illegible]	[illegible]	[illegible]	[illegible]	[illegible]	[illegible]	[illegible]	[illegible]	[illegible]	[illegible]	[illegible]	[illegible]	[illegible]	[illegible]	[illegible]	[illegible]
	Imperforate Anus,	[illegible]	[illegible]	[illegible]	[illegible]	[illegible]	[illegible]	[illegible]	[illegible]	[illegible]	[illegible]	[illegible]	[illegible]	[illegible]	[illegible]	[illegible]	[illegible]	[illegible]	[illegible]	[illegible]
	Cleft Palate, Harelip,	[illegible]	[illegible]	[illegible]	[illegible]	[illegible]	[illegible]	[illegible]	[illegible]	[illegible]	[illegible]	[illegible]	[illegible]	[illegible]	[illegible]	[illegible]	[illegible]	[illegible]	[illegible]	[illegible]
	Other Congenital Defects,	[illegible]	[illegible]	[illegible]	[illegible]	[illegible]	[illegible]	[illegible]	[illegible]	[illegible]	[illegible]	[illegible]	[illegible]	[illegible]	[illegible]	[illegible]	[illegible]	[illegible]	[illegible]	[illegible]
	Old Age,	[illegible]	[illegible]	[illegible]	[illegible]	[illegible]	[illegible]	[illegible]	[illegible]	[illegible]	[illegible]	[illegible]	[illegible]	[illegible]	[illegible]	[illegible]	[illegible]	[illegible]	[illegible]	[illegible]
VI.	Order 1.																			
	Inflammation of Brain or its Membranes,	[illegible]	[illegible]	[illegible]	[illegible]	[illegible]	[illegible]	[illegible]	[illegible]	[illegible]	[illegible]	[illegible]	[illegible]	[illegible]	[illegible]	[illegible]	[illegible]	[illegible]	[illegible]	[illegible]
	Apoplexy,	[illegible]	[illegible]	[illegible]	[illegible]	[illegible]	[illegible]	[illegible]	[illegible]	[illegible]	[illegible]	[illegible]	[illegible]	[illegible]	[illegible]	[illegible]	[illegible]	[illegible]	[illegible]	[illegible]
	Softening of Brain,	[illegible]	[illegible]	[illegible]	[illegible]	[illegible]	[illegible]	[illegible]	[illegible]	[illegible]	[illegible]	[illegible]	[illegible]	[illegible]	[illegible]	[illegible]	[illegible]	[illegible]	[illegible]	[illegible]
	Hemiplegia, Brain Paralysis,	[illegible]	[illegible]	[illegible]	[illegible]	[illegible]	[illegible]	[illegible]	[illegible]	[illegible]	[illegible]	[illegible]	[illegible]	[illegible]	[illegible]	[illegible]	[illegible]	[illegible]	[illegible]	[illegible]
	Paralysis Agitans,	[illegible]	[illegible]	[illegible]	[illegible]	[illegible]	[illegible]	[illegible]	[illegible]	[illegible]	[illegible]	[illegible]	[illegible]	[illegible]	[illegible]	[illegible]	[illegible]	[illegible]	[illegible]	[illegible]
	Insanity, General Paralysis of Insane,	[illegible]	[illegible]	[illegible]	[illegible]	[illegible]	[illegible]	[illegible]	[illegible]	[illegible]	[illegible]	[illegible]	[illegible]	[illegible]	[illegible]	[illegible]	[illegible]	[illegible]	[illegible]	[illegible]
	Chorea,	[illegible]	[illegible]	[illegible]	[illegible]	[illegible]	[illegible]	[illegible]	[illegible]	[illegible]	[illegible]	[illegible]	[illegible]	[illegible]	[illegible]	[illegible]	[illegible]	[illegible]	[illegible]	[illegible]
	Epilepsy,	[illegible]	[illegible]	[illegible]	[illegible]	[illegible]	[illegible]	[illegible]	[illegible]	[illegible]	[illegible]	[illegible]	[illegible]	[illegible]	[illegible]	[illegible]	[illegible]	[illegible]	[illegible]	[illegible]
	Convulsions,	[illegible]	[illegible]	[illegible]	[illegible]	[illegible]	[illegible]	[illegible]	[illegible]	[illegible]	[illegible]	[illegible]	[illegible]	[illegible]	[illegible]	[illegible]	[illegible]	[illegible]	[illegible]	[illegible]
	Laryngismus Stridulus,	[illegible]	[illegible]	[illegible]	[illegible]	[illegible]	[illegible]	[illegible]	[illegible]	[illegible]	[illegible]	[illegible]	[illegible]	[illegible]	[illegible]	[illegible]	[illegible]	[illegible]	[illegible]	[illegible]
	Idiopathic Tetanus,	[illegible]	[illegible]	[illegible]	[illegible]	[illegible]	[illegible]	[illegible]	[illegible]	[illegible]	[illegible]	[illegible]	[illegible]	[illegible]	[illegible]	[illegible]	[illegible]	[illegible]	[illegible]	[illegible]
	Paraplegia, Diseases of Spinal Cord,	[illegible]	[illegible]	[illegible]	[illegible]	[illegible]	[illegible]	[illegible]	[illegible]	[illegible]	[illegible]	[illegible]	[illegible]	[illegible]	[illegible]	[illegible]	[illegible]	[illegible]	[illegible]	[illegible]
	Other Diseases of Nervous System,	[illegible]	[illegible]	[illegible]	[illegible]	[illegible]	[illegible]	[illegible]	[illegible]	[illegible]	[illegible]	[illegible]	[illegible]	[illegible]	[illegible]	[illegible]	[illegible]	[illegible]	[illegible]	[illegible]
	Order 2.																			
	Otitis, Otorrhoea,	[illegible]	[illegible]	[illegible]	[illegible]	[illegible]	[illegible]	[illegible]	[illegible]	[illegible]	[illegible]	[illegible]	[illegible]	[illegible]	[illegible]	[illegible]	[illegible]	[illegible]	[illegible]	[illegible]
	Epistaxis and Diseases of Nose,	[illegible]	[illegible]	[illegible]	[illegible]	[illegible]	[illegible]	[illegible]	[illegible]	[illegible]	[illegible]	[illegible]	[illegible]	[illegible]	[illegible]	[illegible]	[illegible]	[illegible]	[illegible]	[illegible]
	Ophthalmia and Diseases of Eye,	[illegible]	[illegible]	[illegible]	[illegible]	[illegible]	[illegible]	[illegible]	[illegible]	[illegible]	[illegible]	[illegible]	[illegible]	[illegible]	[illegible]	[illegible]	[illegible]	[illegible]	[illegible]	[illegible]
	Order 3.																			
	Endocarditis, Valvular Disease,	[illegible]	[illegible]	[illegible]	[illegible]	[illegible]	[illegible]	[illegible]	[illegible]	[illegible]	[illegible]	[illegible]	[illegible]	[illegible]	[illegible]	[illegible]	[illegible]	[illegible]	[illegible]	[illegible]
	Pericarditis,	[illegible]	[illegible]	[illegible]	[illegible]	[illegible]	[illegible]	[illegible]	[illegible]	[illegible]	[illegible]	[illegible]	[illegible]	[illegible]	[illegible]	[illegible]	[illegible]	[illegible]	[illegible]	[illegible]
	Hypertrophy of Heart,	[illegible]	[illegible]	[illegible]	[illegible]	[illegible]	[illegible]	[illegible]	[illegible]	[illegible]	[illegible]	[illegible]	[illegible]	[illegible]	[illegible]	[illegible]	[illegible]	[illegible]	[illegible]	[illegible]
	Angina Pectoris,	[illegible]	[illegible]	[illegible]	[illegible]	[illegible]	[illegible]	[illegible]	[illegible]	[illegible]	[illegible]	[illegible]	[illegible]	[illegible]	[illegible]	[illegible]	[illegible]	[illegible]	[illegible]	[illegible]
	Syncope,	[illegible]	[illegible]	[illegible]	[illegible]	[illegible]	[illegible]	[illegible]	[illegible]	[illegible]	[illegible]	[illegible]	[illegible]	[illegible]	[illegible]	[illegible]	[illegible]	[illegible]	[illegible]	[illegible]
	Aneurysm,	[illegible]	[illegible]	[illegible]	[illegible]	[illegible]	[illegible]	[illegible]	[illegible]	[illegible]	[illegible]	[illegible]	[illegible]	[illegible]	[illegible]	[illegible]	[illegible]	[illegible]	[illegible]	[illegible]
	Senile Gangrene,	[illegible]	[illegible]	[illegible]	[illegible]	[illegible]	[illegible]	[illegible]	[illegible]	[illegible]	[illegible]	[illegible]	[illegible]	[illegible]	[illegible]	[illegible]	[illegible]	[illegible]	[illegible]	[illegible]
	Embolism, Thrombosis,	[illegible]	[illegible]	[illegible]	[illegible]	[illegible]	[illegible]	[illegible]	[illegible]	[illegible]	[illegible]	[illegible]	[illegible]	[illegible]	[illegible]	[illegible]	[illegible]	[illegible]	[illegible]	[illegible]
	Phlebitis,	[illegible]	[illegible]	[illegible]	[illegible]	[illegible]	[illegible]	[illegible]	[illegible]	[illegible]	[illegible]	[illegible]	[illegible]	[illegible]	[illegible]	[illegible]	[illegible]	[illegible]	[illegible]	[illegible]
	Varicose Veins,	[illegible]	[illegible]	[illegible]	[illegible]	[illegible]	[illegible]	[illegible]	[illegible]	[illegible]	[illegible]	[illegible]	[illegible]	[illegible]	[illegible]	[illegible]	[illegible]	[illegible]	[illegible]	[illegible]
	Other Diseases of Circulatory System,	[illegible]	[illegible]	[illegible]	[illegible]	[illegible]	[illegible]	[illegible]	[illegible]	[illegible]	[illegible]	[illegible]	[illegible]	[illegible]	[illegible]	[illegible]	[illegible]	[illegible]	[illegible]	[illegible]
	Order 4.																			
	Laryngitis,	[illegible]	[illegible]	[illegible]	[illegible]	[illegible]	[illegible]	[illegible]	[illegible]	[illegible]	[illegible]	[illegible]	[illegible]	[illegible]	[illegible]	[illegible]	[illegible]	[illegible]	[illegible]	[illegible]
	Croup,	[illegible]	[illegible]	[illegible]	[illegible]	[illegible]	[illegible]	[illegible]	[illegible]	[illegible]	[illegible]	[illegible]	[illegible]	[illegible]	[illegible]	[illegible]	[illegible]	[illegible]	[illegible]	[illegible]
	Other Diseases of Larynx and Trachea,	[illegible]	[illegible]	[illegible]	[illegible]	[illegible]	[illegible]	[illegible]	[illegible]	[illegible]	[illegible]	[illegible]	[illegible]	[illegible]	[illegible]	[illegible]	[illegible]	[illegible]	[illegible]	[illegible]
	Emphysema, Asthma,	[illegible]	[illegible]	[illegible]	[illegible]	[illegible]	[illegible]	[illegible]	[illegible]	[illegible]	[illegible]	[illegible]	[illegible]	[illegible]	[illegible]	[illegible]	[illegible]	[illegible]	[illegible]	[illegible]

[continued on page 154.]

IRELAND.—CAUSES of DEATH at different Periods of Life in the Year 1891—MALES—con.

Class	CAUSES OF DEATH	MALES: All Ages	Ages at Death: Under 1 year	1	2	3	4	Total under 5 years	5-	10-	15-	20-	25-	35-	45-	55-	65-	75-	85-	Age not stated
	Order 4 (continued).																			
VI.—con.	Bronchitis,	[illegible]	[illegible]	[illegible]	[illegible]	[illegible]	[illegible]	[illegible]	[illegible]	[illegible]	[illegible]	[illegible]	[illegible]	[illegible]	[illegible]	[illegible]	[illegible]	[illegible]	[illegible]	[illegible]
	Pneumonia,	[illegible]	[illegible]	[illegible]	[illegible]	[illegible]	[illegible]	[illegible]	[illegible]	[illegible]	[illegible]	[illegible]	[illegible]	[illegible]	[illegible]	[illegible]	[illegible]	[illegible]	[illegible]	[illegible]
	Pleurisy,	[illegible]	[illegible]	[illegible]	[illegible]	[illegible]	[illegible]	[illegible]	[illegible]	[illegible]	[illegible]	[illegible]	[illegible]	[illegible]	[illegible]	[illegible]	[illegible]	[illegible]	[illegible]	[illegible]
	Other Diseases of Respiratory System,	[illegible]	[illegible]	[illegible]	[illegible]	[illegible]	[illegible]	[illegible]	[illegible]	[illegible]	[illegible]	[illegible]	[illegible]	[illegible]	[illegible]	[illegible]	[illegible]	[illegible]	[illegible]	[illegible]
	Order 5.																			
	[illegible]	[illegible]	[illegible]	[illegible]	[illegible]	[illegible]	[illegible]	[illegible]	[illegible]	[illegible]	[illegible]	[illegible]	[illegible]	[illegible]	[illegible]	[illegible]	[illegible]	[illegible]	[illegible]	[illegible]
	Dentition,	[illegible]	[illegible]	[illegible]	[illegible]	[illegible]	[illegible]	[illegible]	[illegible]	[illegible]	[illegible]	[illegible]	[illegible]	[illegible]	[illegible]	[illegible]	[illegible]	[illegible]	[illegible]	[illegible]
	Sore-throat, Quinsy,	[illegible]	[illegible]	[illegible]	[illegible]	[illegible]	[illegible]	[illegible]	[illegible]	[illegible]	[illegible]	[illegible]	[illegible]	[illegible]	[illegible]	[illegible]	[illegible]	[illegible]	[illegible]	[illegible]
	Dyspepsia,	[illegible]	[illegible]	[illegible]	[illegible]	[illegible]	[illegible]	[illegible]	[illegible]	[illegible]	[illegible]	[illegible]	[illegible]	[illegible]	[illegible]	[illegible]	[illegible]	[illegible]	[illegible]	[illegible]
	Haematemesis,	[illegible]	[illegible]	[illegible]	[illegible]	[illegible]	[illegible]	[illegible]	[illegible]	[illegible]	[illegible]	[illegible]	[illegible]	[illegible]	[illegible]	[illegible]	[illegible]	[illegible]	[illegible]	[illegible]
	Melaena,	[illegible]	[illegible]	[illegible]	[illegible]	[illegible]	[illegible]	[illegible]	[illegible]	[illegible]	[illegible]	[illegible]	[illegible]	[illegible]	[illegible]	[illegible]	[illegible]	[illegible]	[illegible]	[illegible]
	Diseases of Stomach,	[illegible]	[illegible]	[illegible]	[illegible]	[illegible]	[illegible]	[illegible]	[illegible]	[illegible]	[illegible]	[illegible]	[illegible]	[illegible]	[illegible]	[illegible]	[illegible]	[illegible]	[illegible]	[illegible]
	Enteritis,	[illegible]	[illegible]	[illegible]	[illegible]	[illegible]	[illegible]	[illegible]	[illegible]	[illegible]	[illegible]	[illegible]	[illegible]	[illegible]	[illegible]	[illegible]	[illegible]	[illegible]	[illegible]	[illegible]
	Ulceration of Intestine,	[illegible]	[illegible]	[illegible]	[illegible]	[illegible]	[illegible]	[illegible]	[illegible]	[illegible]	[illegible]	[illegible]	[illegible]	[illegible]	[illegible]	[illegible]	[illegible]	[illegible]	[illegible]	[illegible]
	Ileus, Obstruction of Intestine,	[illegible]	[illegible]	[illegible]	[illegible]	[illegible]	[illegible]	[illegible]	[illegible]	[illegible]	[illegible]	[illegible]	[illegible]	[illegible]	[illegible]	[illegible]	[illegible]	[illegible]	[illegible]	[illegible]
	Stricture or Strangulation of Intestine,	[illegible]	[illegible]	[illegible]	[illegible]	[illegible]	[illegible]	[illegible]	[illegible]	[illegible]	[illegible]	[illegible]	[illegible]	[illegible]	[illegible]	[illegible]	[illegible]	[illegible]	[illegible]	[illegible]
	Intussusception of Intestine,	[illegible]	[illegible]	[illegible]	[illegible]	[illegible]	[illegible]	[illegible]	[illegible]	[illegible]	[illegible]	[illegible]	[illegible]	[illegible]	[illegible]	[illegible]	[illegible]	[illegible]	[illegible]	[illegible]
	Hernia,	[illegible]	[illegible]	[illegible]	[illegible]	[illegible]	[illegible]	[illegible]	[illegible]	[illegible]	[illegible]	[illegible]	[illegible]	[illegible]	[illegible]	[illegible]	[illegible]	[illegible]	[illegible]	[illegible]
	Fistula,	[illegible]	[illegible]	[illegible]	[illegible]	[illegible]	[illegible]	[illegible]	[illegible]	[illegible]	[illegible]	[illegible]	[illegible]	[illegible]	[illegible]	[illegible]	[illegible]	[illegible]	[illegible]	[illegible]
	Peritonitis,	[illegible]	[illegible]	[illegible]	[illegible]	[illegible]	[illegible]	[illegible]	[illegible]	[illegible]	[illegible]	[illegible]	[illegible]	[illegible]	[illegible]	[illegible]	[illegible]	[illegible]	[illegible]	[illegible]
	Ascites,	[illegible]	[illegible]	[illegible]	[illegible]	[illegible]	[illegible]	[illegible]	[illegible]	[illegible]	[illegible]	[illegible]	[illegible]	[illegible]	[illegible]	[illegible]	[illegible]	[illegible]	[illegible]	[illegible]
	Gall-stones,	[illegible]	[illegible]	[illegible]	[illegible]	[illegible]	[illegible]	[illegible]	[illegible]	[illegible]	[illegible]	[illegible]	[illegible]	[illegible]	[illegible]	[illegible]	[illegible]	[illegible]	[illegible]	[illegible]
	Cirrhosis of Liver,	[illegible]	[illegible]	[illegible]	[illegible]	[illegible]	[illegible]	[illegible]	[illegible]	[illegible]	[illegible]	[illegible]	[illegible]	[illegible]	[illegible]	[illegible]	[illegible]	[illegible]	[illegible]	[illegible]
	Other Diseases of Liver,	[illegible]	[illegible]	[illegible]	[illegible]	[illegible]	[illegible]	[illegible]	[illegible]	[illegible]	[illegible]	[illegible]	[illegible]	[illegible]	[illegible]	[illegible]	[illegible]	[illegible]	[illegible]	[illegible]
	Other Diseases of Digestive System,	[illegible]	[illegible]	[illegible]	[illegible]	[illegible]	[illegible]	[illegible]	[illegible]	[illegible]	[illegible]	[illegible]	[illegible]	[illegible]	[illegible]	[illegible]	[illegible]	[illegible]	[illegible]	[illegible]
	Order 6.																			
	Diseases of Spleen,	[illegible]	[illegible]	[illegible]	[illegible]	[illegible]	[illegible]	[illegible]	[illegible]	[illegible]	[illegible]	[illegible]	[illegible]	[illegible]	[illegible]	[illegible]	[illegible]	[illegible]	[illegible]	[illegible]
	[illegible]	[illegible]	[illegible]	[illegible]	[illegible]	[illegible]	[illegible]	[illegible]	[illegible]	[illegible]	[illegible]	[illegible]	[illegible]	[illegible]	[illegible]	[illegible]	[illegible]	[illegible]	[illegible]	[illegible]
	Diseases of Thyroid Body,	[illegible]	[illegible]	[illegible]	[illegible]	[illegible]	[illegible]	[illegible]	[illegible]	[illegible]	[illegible]	[illegible]	[illegible]	[illegible]	[illegible]	[illegible]	[illegible]	[illegible]	[illegible]	[illegible]
	Diseases of Suprarenal Capsules,	[illegible]	[illegible]	[illegible]	[illegible]	[illegible]	[illegible]	[illegible]	[illegible]	[illegible]	[illegible]	[illegible]	[illegible]	[illegible]	[illegible]	[illegible]	[illegible]	[illegible]	[illegible]	[illegible]
	Order 7.																			
	Acute Nephritis,	[illegible]	[illegible]	[illegible]	[illegible]	[illegible]	[illegible]	[illegible]	[illegible]	[illegible]	[illegible]	[illegible]	[illegible]	[illegible]	[illegible]	[illegible]	[illegible]	[illegible]	[illegible]	[illegible]
	Bright's Disease,	[illegible]	[illegible]	[illegible]	[illegible]	[illegible]	[illegible]	[illegible]	[illegible]	[illegible]	[illegible]	[illegible]	[illegible]	[illegible]	[illegible]	[illegible]	[illegible]	[illegible]	[illegible]	[illegible]
	Uraemia,	[illegible]	[illegible]	[illegible]	[illegible]	[illegible]	[illegible]	[illegible]	[illegible]	[illegible]	[illegible]	[illegible]	[illegible]	[illegible]	[illegible]	[illegible]	[illegible]	[illegible]	[illegible]	[illegible]
	Suppression of Urine,	[illegible]	[illegible]	[illegible]	[illegible]	[illegible]	[illegible]	[illegible]	[illegible]	[illegible]	[illegible]	[illegible]	[illegible]	[illegible]	[illegible]	[illegible]	[illegible]	[illegible]	[illegible]	[illegible]
	Calculus,	[illegible]	[illegible]	[illegible]	[illegible]	[illegible]	[illegible]	[illegible]	[illegible]	[illegible]	[illegible]	[illegible]	[illegible]	[illegible]	[illegible]	[illegible]	[illegible]	[illegible]	[illegible]	[illegible]
	Haematuria,	[illegible]	[illegible]	[illegible]	[illegible]	[illegible]	[illegible]	[illegible]	[illegible]	[illegible]	[illegible]	[illegible]	[illegible]	[illegible]	[illegible]	[illegible]	[illegible]	[illegible]	[illegible]	[illegible]
	Diseases of Bladder and of Prostate,	[illegible]	[illegible]	[illegible]	[illegible]	[illegible]	[illegible]	[illegible]	[illegible]	[illegible]	[illegible]	[illegible]	[illegible]	[illegible]	[illegible]	[illegible]	[illegible]	[illegible]	[illegible]	[illegible]
	Other Diseases of Urinary System,	[illegible]	[illegible]	[illegible]	[illegible]	[illegible]	[illegible]	[illegible]	[illegible]	[illegible]	[illegible]	[illegible]	[illegible]	[illegible]	[illegible]	[illegible]	[illegible]	[illegible]	[illegible]	[illegible]
	Order 8 (a).																			
	Ovarian Disease,	[illegible]	[illegible]	[illegible]	[illegible]	[illegible]	[illegible]	[illegible]	[illegible]	[illegible]	[illegible]	[illegible]	[illegible]	[illegible]	[illegible]	[illegible]	[illegible]	[illegible]	[illegible]	[illegible]
	Diseases of Uterus and Vagina,	[illegible]	[illegible]	[illegible]	[illegible]	[illegible]	[illegible]	[illegible]	[illegible]	[illegible]	[illegible]	[illegible]	[illegible]	[illegible]	[illegible]	[illegible]	[illegible]	[illegible]	[illegible]	[illegible]
	Disorders of Menstruation,	[illegible]	[illegible]	[illegible]	[illegible]	[illegible]	[illegible]	[illegible]	[illegible]	[illegible]	[illegible]	[illegible]	[illegible]	[illegible]	[illegible]	[illegible]	[illegible]	[illegible]	[illegible]	[illegible]
	Pelvic Abscess,	[illegible]	[illegible]	[illegible]	[illegible]	[illegible]	[illegible]	[illegible]	[illegible]	[illegible]	[illegible]	[illegible]	[illegible]	[illegible]	[illegible]	[illegible]	[illegible]	[illegible]	[illegible]	[illegible]
	Perineal Abscess,	[illegible]	[illegible]	[illegible]	[illegible]	[illegible]	[illegible]	[illegible]	[illegible]	[illegible]	[illegible]	[illegible]	[illegible]	[illegible]	[illegible]	[illegible]	[illegible]	[illegible]	[illegible]	[illegible]
	Diseases of Penis, Testis, Scrotum, &c.	[illegible]	[illegible]	[illegible]	[illegible]	[illegible]	[illegible]	[illegible]	[illegible]	[illegible]	[illegible]	[illegible]	[illegible]	[illegible]	[illegible]	[illegible]	[illegible]	[illegible]	[illegible]	[illegible]

[continued on page 1[illegible].]

IRELAND.—CAUSES of DEATH at different Periods of Life in the Year 1891—FEMALES—con.

Class.	CAUSES OF DEATH.	All Ages.	Under 1 year.	1	2	3	4	Total under 5 years.	5-	10-	15-	20-	25-	35-	45-	55-	65-	75-	85-	Age not stated.
	ORDER 4—con.																			
VI.—con.	Bronchitis,	[illegible]	[illegible]	[illegible]	[illegible]	[illegible]	[illegible]	[illegible]	[illegible]	[illegible]	[illegible]	[illegible]	[illegible]	[illegible]	[illegible]	[illegible]	[illegible]	[illegible]	[illegible]	[illegible]
	Pneumonia,	[illegible]	[illegible]	[illegible]	[illegible]	[illegible]	[illegible]	[illegible]	[illegible]	[illegible]	[illegible]	[illegible]	[illegible]	[illegible]	[illegible]	[illegible]	[illegible]	[illegible]	[illegible]	[illegible]
	Pleurisy,	[illegible]	[illegible]	[illegible]	[illegible]	[illegible]	[illegible]	[illegible]	[illegible]	[illegible]	[illegible]	[illegible]	[illegible]	[illegible]	[illegible]	[illegible]	[illegible]	[illegible]	[illegible]	[illegible]
	Other Diseases of Respiratory System,	[illegible]	[illegible]	[illegible]	[illegible]	[illegible]	[illegible]	[illegible]	[illegible]	[illegible]	[illegible]	[illegible]	[illegible]	[illegible]	[illegible]	[illegible]	[illegible]	[illegible]	[illegible]	[illegible]
	ORDER 5.																			
	[illegible]	[illegible]	[illegible]	[illegible]	[illegible]	[illegible]	[illegible]	[illegible]	[illegible]	[illegible]	[illegible]	[illegible]	[illegible]	[illegible]	[illegible]	[illegible]	[illegible]	[illegible]	[illegible]	[illegible]
	Dentition,	[illegible]	[illegible]	[illegible]	[illegible]	[illegible]	[illegible]	[illegible]	[illegible]	[illegible]	[illegible]	[illegible]	[illegible]	[illegible]	[illegible]	[illegible]	[illegible]	[illegible]	[illegible]	[illegible]
	Sore-throat, Quinsy,	[illegible]	[illegible]	[illegible]	[illegible]	[illegible]	[illegible]	[illegible]	[illegible]	[illegible]	[illegible]	[illegible]	[illegible]	[illegible]	[illegible]	[illegible]	[illegible]	[illegible]	[illegible]	[illegible]
	Dyspepsia,	[illegible]	[illegible]	[illegible]	[illegible]	[illegible]	[illegible]	[illegible]	[illegible]	[illegible]	[illegible]	[illegible]	[illegible]	[illegible]	[illegible]	[illegible]	[illegible]	[illegible]	[illegible]	[illegible]
	Haematemesis,	[illegible]	[illegible]	[illegible]	[illegible]	[illegible]	[illegible]	[illegible]	[illegible]	[illegible]	[illegible]	[illegible]	[illegible]	[illegible]	[illegible]	[illegible]	[illegible]	[illegible]	[illegible]	[illegible]
	Melaena,	[illegible]	[illegible]	[illegible]	[illegible]	[illegible]	[illegible]	[illegible]	[illegible]	[illegible]	[illegible]	[illegible]	[illegible]	[illegible]	[illegible]	[illegible]	[illegible]	[illegible]	[illegible]	[illegible]
	Diseases of Stomach,	[illegible]	[illegible]	[illegible]	[illegible]	[illegible]	[illegible]	[illegible]	[illegible]	[illegible]	[illegible]	[illegible]	[illegible]	[illegible]	[illegible]	[illegible]	[illegible]	[illegible]	[illegible]	[illegible]
	Enteritis,	[illegible]	[illegible]	[illegible]	[illegible]	[illegible]	[illegible]	[illegible]	[illegible]	[illegible]	[illegible]	[illegible]	[illegible]	[illegible]	[illegible]	[illegible]	[illegible]	[illegible]	[illegible]	[illegible]
	Ulceration of Intestine,	[illegible]	[illegible]	[illegible]	[illegible]	[illegible]	[illegible]	[illegible]	[illegible]	[illegible]	[illegible]	[illegible]	[illegible]	[illegible]	[illegible]	[illegible]	[illegible]	[illegible]	[illegible]	[illegible]
	Ileus, Obstruction of Intestine,	[illegible]	[illegible]	[illegible]	[illegible]	[illegible]	[illegible]	[illegible]	[illegible]	[illegible]	[illegible]	[illegible]	[illegible]	[illegible]	[illegible]	[illegible]	[illegible]	[illegible]	[illegible]	[illegible]
	[illegible] of Intestine,	[illegible]	[illegible]	[illegible]	[illegible]	[illegible]	[illegible]	[illegible]	[illegible]	[illegible]	[illegible]	[illegible]	[illegible]	[illegible]	[illegible]	[illegible]	[illegible]	[illegible]	[illegible]	[illegible]
	[illegible] of Intestine,	[illegible]	[illegible]	[illegible]	[illegible]	[illegible]	[illegible]	[illegible]	[illegible]	[illegible]	[illegible]	[illegible]	[illegible]	[illegible]	[illegible]	[illegible]	[illegible]	[illegible]	[illegible]	[illegible]
	Hernia,	[illegible]	[illegible]	[illegible]	[illegible]	[illegible]	[illegible]	[illegible]	[illegible]	[illegible]	[illegible]	[illegible]	[illegible]	[illegible]	[illegible]	[illegible]	[illegible]	[illegible]	[illegible]	[illegible]
	Fistula,	[illegible]	[illegible]	[illegible]	[illegible]	[illegible]	[illegible]	[illegible]	[illegible]	[illegible]	[illegible]	[illegible]	[illegible]	[illegible]	[illegible]	[illegible]	[illegible]	[illegible]	[illegible]	[illegible]
	Peritonitis,	[illegible]	[illegible]	[illegible]	[illegible]	[illegible]	[illegible]	[illegible]	[illegible]	[illegible]	[illegible]	[illegible]	[illegible]	[illegible]	[illegible]	[illegible]	[illegible]	[illegible]	[illegible]	[illegible]
	Ascites,	[illegible]	[illegible]	[illegible]	[illegible]	[illegible]	[illegible]	[illegible]	[illegible]	[illegible]	[illegible]	[illegible]	[illegible]	[illegible]	[illegible]	[illegible]	[illegible]	[illegible]	[illegible]	[illegible]
	Gall-stones,	[illegible]	[illegible]	[illegible]	[illegible]	[illegible]	[illegible]	[illegible]	[illegible]	[illegible]	[illegible]	[illegible]	[illegible]	[illegible]	[illegible]	[illegible]	[illegible]	[illegible]	[illegible]	[illegible]
	Cirrhosis of Liver,	[illegible]	[illegible]	[illegible]	[illegible]	[illegible]	[illegible]	[illegible]	[illegible]	[illegible]	[illegible]	[illegible]	[illegible]	[illegible]	[illegible]	[illegible]	[illegible]	[illegible]	[illegible]	[illegible]
	Other Diseases of Liver,	[illegible]	[illegible]	[illegible]	[illegible]	[illegible]	[illegible]	[illegible]	[illegible]	[illegible]	[illegible]	[illegible]	[illegible]	[illegible]	[illegible]	[illegible]	[illegible]	[illegible]	[illegible]	[illegible]
	Other Diseases of Digestive System,	[illegible]	[illegible]	[illegible]	[illegible]	[illegible]	[illegible]	[illegible]	[illegible]	[illegible]	[illegible]	[illegible]	[illegible]	[illegible]	[illegible]	[illegible]	[illegible]	[illegible]	[illegible]	[illegible]
	ORDER 6.																			
	Diseases of Spleen,	[illegible]	[illegible]	[illegible]	[illegible]	[illegible]	[illegible]	[illegible]	[illegible]	[illegible]	[illegible]	[illegible]	[illegible]	[illegible]	[illegible]	[illegible]	[illegible]	[illegible]	[illegible]	[illegible]
	Diseases of Lymphatic System,	[illegible]	[illegible]	[illegible]	[illegible]	[illegible]	[illegible]	[illegible]	[illegible]	[illegible]	[illegible]	[illegible]	[illegible]	[illegible]	[illegible]	[illegible]	[illegible]	[illegible]	[illegible]	[illegible]
	Diseases of Thyroid Body,	[illegible]	[illegible]	[illegible]	[illegible]	[illegible]	[illegible]	[illegible]	[illegible]	[illegible]	[illegible]	[illegible]	[illegible]	[illegible]	[illegible]	[illegible]	[illegible]	[illegible]	[illegible]	[illegible]
	Diseases of Suprarenal Capsules,	[illegible]	[illegible]	[illegible]	[illegible]	[illegible]	[illegible]	[illegible]	[illegible]	[illegible]	[illegible]	[illegible]	[illegible]	[illegible]	[illegible]	[illegible]	[illegible]	[illegible]	[illegible]	[illegible]
	ORDER 7.																			
	Acute Nephritis,	[illegible]	[illegible]	[illegible]	[illegible]	[illegible]	[illegible]	[illegible]	[illegible]	[illegible]	[illegible]	[illegible]	[illegible]	[illegible]	[illegible]	[illegible]	[illegible]	[illegible]	[illegible]	[illegible]
	Bright's Disease,	[illegible]	[illegible]	[illegible]	[illegible]	[illegible]	[illegible]	[illegible]	[illegible]	[illegible]	[illegible]	[illegible]	[illegible]	[illegible]	[illegible]	[illegible]	[illegible]	[illegible]	[illegible]	[illegible]
	Uraemia,	[illegible]	[illegible]	[illegible]	[illegible]	[illegible]	[illegible]	[illegible]	[illegible]	[illegible]	[illegible]	[illegible]	[illegible]	[illegible]	[illegible]	[illegible]	[illegible]	[illegible]	[illegible]	[illegible]
	Suppression of Urine,	[illegible]	[illegible]	[illegible]	[illegible]	[illegible]	[illegible]	[illegible]	[illegible]	[illegible]	[illegible]	[illegible]	[illegible]	[illegible]	[illegible]	[illegible]	[illegible]	[illegible]	[illegible]	[illegible]
	Calculus,	[illegible]	[illegible]	[illegible]	[illegible]	[illegible]	[illegible]	[illegible]	[illegible]	[illegible]	[illegible]	[illegible]	[illegible]	[illegible]	[illegible]	[illegible]	[illegible]	[illegible]	[illegible]	[illegible]
	Haematuria,	[illegible]	[illegible]	[illegible]	[illegible]	[illegible]	[illegible]	[illegible]	[illegible]	[illegible]	[illegible]	[illegible]	[illegible]	[illegible]	[illegible]	[illegible]	[illegible]	[illegible]	[illegible]	[illegible]
	Diseases of Bladder and of Prostate,	[illegible]	[illegible]	[illegible]	[illegible]	[illegible]	[illegible]	[illegible]	[illegible]	[illegible]	[illegible]	[illegible]	[illegible]	[illegible]	[illegible]	[illegible]	[illegible]	[illegible]	[illegible]	[illegible]
	Other Diseases of Urinary System,	[illegible]	[illegible]	[illegible]	[illegible]	[illegible]	[illegible]	[illegible]	[illegible]	[illegible]	[illegible]	[illegible]	[illegible]	[illegible]	[illegible]	[illegible]	[illegible]	[illegible]	[illegible]	[illegible]
	ORDER 8 (a).																			
	Ovarian Disease,	[illegible]	[illegible]	[illegible]	[illegible]	[illegible]	[illegible]	[illegible]	[illegible]	[illegible]	[illegible]	[illegible]	[illegible]	[illegible]	[illegible]	[illegible]	[illegible]	[illegible]	[illegible]	[illegible]
	Diseases of Uterus and Vagina,	[illegible]	[illegible]	[illegible]	[illegible]	[illegible]	[illegible]	[illegible]	[illegible]	[illegible]	[illegible]	[illegible]	[illegible]	[illegible]	[illegible]	[illegible]	[illegible]	[illegible]	[illegible]	[illegible]
	Disorders of Menstruation,	[illegible]	[illegible]	[illegible]	[illegible]	[illegible]	[illegible]	[illegible]	[illegible]	[illegible]	[illegible]	[illegible]	[illegible]	[illegible]	[illegible]	[illegible]	[illegible]	[illegible]	[illegible]	[illegible]
	[illegible]	[illegible]	[illegible]	[illegible]	[illegible]	[illegible]	[illegible]	[illegible]	[illegible]	[illegible]	[illegible]	[illegible]	[illegible]	[illegible]	[illegible]	[illegible]	[illegible]	[illegible]	[illegible]	[illegible]
	[illegible]	[illegible]	[illegible]	[illegible]	[illegible]	[illegible]	[illegible]	[illegible]	[illegible]	[illegible]	[illegible]	[illegible]	[illegible]	[illegible]	[illegible]	[illegible]	[illegible]	[illegible]	[illegible]	[illegible]
	Diseases of Testes, Penis, Scrotum, &c.	[illegible]	[illegible]	[illegible]	[illegible]	[illegible]	[illegible]	[illegible]	[illegible]	[illegible]	[illegible]	[illegible]	[illegible]	[illegible]	[illegible]	[illegible]	[illegible]	[illegible]	[illegible]	[illegible]

[continued on page 157.]

IRELAND.—CAUSES of DEATH at different Periods of Life in the Year 1891—MALES—con.

Class.	CAUSES OF DEATH.	All Ages.	Under 1 Year.	1	2	3	4	Total under 5 Years.	5-	10-	15-	20-	25-	35-	45-	55-	65-	75-	85-	95 and upwards.
		MALES.																		
			Ages at Death.																	
VI.—con.	ORDER 4 (b).																			
	Abortion, Miscarriage,	[illegible]	[illegible]	[illegible]	[illegible]	[illegible]	[illegible]	[illegible]	[illegible]	[illegible]	[illegible]	[illegible]	[illegible]	[illegible]	[illegible]	[illegible]	[illegible]	[illegible]	[illegible]	[illegible]
	Puerperal Mania,	[illegible]	[illegible]	[illegible]	[illegible]	[illegible]	[illegible]	[illegible]	[illegible]	[illegible]	[illegible]	[illegible]	[illegible]	[illegible]	[illegible]	[illegible]	[illegible]	[illegible]	[illegible]	[illegible]
	Puerperal Convulsions,	[illegible]	[illegible]	[illegible]	[illegible]	[illegible]	[illegible]	[illegible]	[illegible]	[illegible]	[illegible]	[illegible]	[illegible]	[illegible]	[illegible]	[illegible]	[illegible]	[illegible]	[illegible]	[illegible]
	Placenta praevia, Flooding,	[illegible]	[illegible]	[illegible]	[illegible]	[illegible]	[illegible]	[illegible]	[illegible]	[illegible]	[illegible]	[illegible]	[illegible]	[illegible]	[illegible]	[illegible]	[illegible]	[illegible]	[illegible]	[illegible]
	Phlegmasia Dolens,	[illegible]	[illegible]	[illegible]	[illegible]	[illegible]	[illegible]	[illegible]	[illegible]	[illegible]	[illegible]	[illegible]	[illegible]	[illegible]	[illegible]	[illegible]	[illegible]	[illegible]	[illegible]	[illegible]
	Other Accidents of Childbirth,	[illegible]	[illegible]	[illegible]	[illegible]	[illegible]	[illegible]	[illegible]	[illegible]	[illegible]	[illegible]	[illegible]	[illegible]	[illegible]	[illegible]	[illegible]	[illegible]	[illegible]	[illegible]	[illegible]
	ORDER 5.																			
	Caries, Necrosis,	[illegible]	[illegible]	[illegible]	[illegible]	[illegible]	[illegible]	[illegible]	[illegible]	[illegible]	[illegible]	[illegible]	[illegible]	[illegible]	[illegible]	[illegible]	[illegible]	[illegible]	[illegible]	[illegible]
	Arthritis, Ostitis, Periostitis,	[illegible]	[illegible]	[illegible]	[illegible]	[illegible]	[illegible]	[illegible]	[illegible]	[illegible]	[illegible]	[illegible]	[illegible]	[illegible]	[illegible]	[illegible]	[illegible]	[illegible]	[illegible]	[illegible]
	Other Diseases of Organs of Locomotion,	[illegible]	[illegible]	[illegible]	[illegible]	[illegible]	[illegible]	[illegible]	[illegible]	[illegible]	[illegible]	[illegible]	[illegible]	[illegible]	[illegible]	[illegible]	[illegible]	[illegible]	[illegible]	[illegible]
	ORDER 6.																			
	Carbuncle,	[illegible]	[illegible]	[illegible]	[illegible]	[illegible]	[illegible]	[illegible]	[illegible]	[illegible]	[illegible]	[illegible]	[illegible]	[illegible]	[illegible]	[illegible]	[illegible]	[illegible]	[illegible]	[illegible]
	Phlegmon, Cellulitis,	[illegible]	[illegible]	[illegible]	[illegible]	[illegible]	[illegible]	[illegible]	[illegible]	[illegible]	[illegible]	[illegible]	[illegible]	[illegible]	[illegible]	[illegible]	[illegible]	[illegible]	[illegible]	[illegible]
	Lupus,	[illegible]	[illegible]	[illegible]	[illegible]	[illegible]	[illegible]	[illegible]	[illegible]	[illegible]	[illegible]	[illegible]	[illegible]	[illegible]	[illegible]	[illegible]	[illegible]	[illegible]	[illegible]	[illegible]
	Ulcer, Bedsore,	[illegible]	[illegible]	[illegible]	[illegible]	[illegible]	[illegible]	[illegible]	[illegible]	[illegible]	[illegible]	[illegible]	[illegible]	[illegible]	[illegible]	[illegible]	[illegible]	[illegible]	[illegible]	[illegible]
	Eczema,	[illegible]	[illegible]	[illegible]	[illegible]	[illegible]	[illegible]	[illegible]	[illegible]	[illegible]	[illegible]	[illegible]	[illegible]	[illegible]	[illegible]	[illegible]	[illegible]	[illegible]	[illegible]	[illegible]
	Pemphigus,	[illegible]	[illegible]	[illegible]	[illegible]	[illegible]	[illegible]	[illegible]	[illegible]	[illegible]	[illegible]	[illegible]	[illegible]	[illegible]	[illegible]	[illegible]	[illegible]	[illegible]	[illegible]	[illegible]
	Other Diseases of Integumentary System,	[illegible]	[illegible]	[illegible]	[illegible]	[illegible]	[illegible]	[illegible]	[illegible]	[illegible]	[illegible]	[illegible]	[illegible]	[illegible]	[illegible]	[illegible]	[illegible]	[illegible]	[illegible]	[illegible]
VII.	ORDER 1.																			
	In Mines and Quarries,	[illegible]	[illegible]	[illegible]	[illegible]	[illegible]	[illegible]	[illegible]	[illegible]	[illegible]	[illegible]	[illegible]	[illegible]	[illegible]	[illegible]	[illegible]	[illegible]	[illegible]	[illegible]	[illegible]
	Vehicles and Horses,	[illegible]	[illegible]	[illegible]	[illegible]	[illegible]	[illegible]	[illegible]	[illegible]	[illegible]	[illegible]	[illegible]	[illegible]	[illegible]	[illegible]	[illegible]	[illegible]	[illegible]	[illegible]	[illegible]
	Ships, Boats, Docks and Harbours,	[illegible]	[illegible]	[illegible]	[illegible]	[illegible]	[illegible]	[illegible]	[illegible]	[illegible]	[illegible]	[illegible]	[illegible]	[illegible]	[illegible]	[illegible]	[illegible]	[illegible]	[illegible]	[illegible]
	Building Operations,	[illegible]	[illegible]	[illegible]	[illegible]	[illegible]	[illegible]	[illegible]	[illegible]	[illegible]	[illegible]	[illegible]	[illegible]	[illegible]	[illegible]	[illegible]	[illegible]	[illegible]	[illegible]	[illegible]
	Machinery,	[illegible]	[illegible]	[illegible]	[illegible]	[illegible]	[illegible]	[illegible]	[illegible]	[illegible]	[illegible]	[illegible]	[illegible]	[illegible]	[illegible]	[illegible]	[illegible]	[illegible]	[illegible]	[illegible]
	Weapons & Implements,	[illegible]	[illegible]	[illegible]	[illegible]	[illegible]	[illegible]	[illegible]	[illegible]	[illegible]	[illegible]	[illegible]	[illegible]	[illegible]	[illegible]	[illegible]	[illegible]	[illegible]	[illegible]	[illegible]
	Burns and Scalds,	[illegible]	[illegible]	[illegible]	[illegible]	[illegible]	[illegible]	[illegible]	[illegible]	[illegible]	[illegible]	[illegible]	[illegible]	[illegible]	[illegible]	[illegible]	[illegible]	[illegible]	[illegible]	[illegible]
	Poison, Poisonous Vapours,	[illegible]	[illegible]	[illegible]	[illegible]	[illegible]	[illegible]	[illegible]	[illegible]	[illegible]	[illegible]	[illegible]	[illegible]	[illegible]	[illegible]	[illegible]	[illegible]	[illegible]	[illegible]	[illegible]
	Drowning,	[illegible]	[illegible]	[illegible]	[illegible]	[illegible]	[illegible]	[illegible]	[illegible]	[illegible]	[illegible]	[illegible]	[illegible]	[illegible]	[illegible]	[illegible]	[illegible]	[illegible]	[illegible]	[illegible]
	Suffocation,	[illegible]	[illegible]	[illegible]	[illegible]	[illegible]	[illegible]	[illegible]	[illegible]	[illegible]	[illegible]	[illegible]	[illegible]	[illegible]	[illegible]	[illegible]	[illegible]	[illegible]	[illegible]	[illegible]
	Falls,	[illegible]	[illegible]	[illegible]	[illegible]	[illegible]	[illegible]	[illegible]	[illegible]	[illegible]	[illegible]	[illegible]	[illegible]	[illegible]	[illegible]	[illegible]	[illegible]	[illegible]	[illegible]	[illegible]
	Weather Agencies,	[illegible]	[illegible]	[illegible]	[illegible]	[illegible]	[illegible]	[illegible]	[illegible]	[illegible]	[illegible]	[illegible]	[illegible]	[illegible]	[illegible]	[illegible]	[illegible]	[illegible]	[illegible]	[illegible]
	Otherwise or not Stated,	[illegible]	[illegible]	[illegible]	[illegible]	[illegible]	[illegible]	[illegible]	[illegible]	[illegible]	[illegible]	[illegible]	[illegible]	[illegible]	[illegible]	[illegible]	[illegible]	[illegible]	[illegible]	[illegible]
	ORDER 2.																			
	Homicide,	[illegible]	[illegible]	[illegible]	[illegible]	[illegible]	[illegible]	[illegible]	[illegible]	[illegible]	[illegible]	[illegible]	[illegible]	[illegible]	[illegible]	[illegible]	[illegible]	[illegible]	[illegible]	[illegible]
	ORDER 3.																			
	Suicide,	[illegible]	[illegible]	[illegible]	[illegible]	[illegible]	[illegible]	[illegible]	[illegible]	[illegible]	[illegible]	[illegible]	[illegible]	[illegible]	[illegible]	[illegible]	[illegible]	[illegible]	[illegible]	[illegible]
	ORDER 4.																			
	Execution,	[illegible]	[illegible]	[illegible]	[illegible]	[illegible]	[illegible]	[illegible]	[illegible]	[illegible]	[illegible]	[illegible]	[illegible]	[illegible]	[illegible]	[illegible]	[illegible]	[illegible]	[illegible]	[illegible]
VIII.	Dropsy,	[illegible]	[illegible]	[illegible]	[illegible]	[illegible]	[illegible]	[illegible]	[illegible]	[illegible]	[illegible]	[illegible]	[illegible]	[illegible]	[illegible]	[illegible]	[illegible]	[illegible]	[illegible]	[illegible]
	Debility, Atrophy, Inanition,	[illegible]	[illegible]	[illegible]	[illegible]	[illegible]	[illegible]	[illegible]	[illegible]	[illegible]	[illegible]	[illegible]	[illegible]	[illegible]	[illegible]	[illegible]	[illegible]	[illegible]	[illegible]	[illegible]
	Mortification,	[illegible]	[illegible]	[illegible]	[illegible]	[illegible]	[illegible]	[illegible]	[illegible]	[illegible]	[illegible]	[illegible]	[illegible]	[illegible]	[illegible]	[illegible]	[illegible]	[illegible]	[illegible]	[illegible]
	Tumour,	[illegible]	[illegible]	[illegible]	[illegible]	[illegible]	[illegible]	[illegible]	[illegible]	[illegible]	[illegible]	[illegible]	[illegible]	[illegible]	[illegible]	[illegible]	[illegible]	[illegible]	[illegible]	[illegible]
	Abscess,	[illegible]	[illegible]	[illegible]	[illegible]	[illegible]	[illegible]	[illegible]	[illegible]	[illegible]	[illegible]	[illegible]	[illegible]	[illegible]	[illegible]	[illegible]	[illegible]	[illegible]	[illegible]	[illegible]
	Haemorrhage,	[illegible]	[illegible]	[illegible]	[illegible]	[illegible]	[illegible]	[illegible]	[illegible]	[illegible]	[illegible]	[illegible]	[illegible]	[illegible]	[illegible]	[illegible]	[illegible]	[illegible]	[illegible]	[illegible]
	Sudden (cause unascertained),	[illegible]	[illegible]	[illegible]	[illegible]	[illegible]	[illegible]	[illegible]	[illegible]	[illegible]	[illegible]	[illegible]	[illegible]	[illegible]	[illegible]	[illegible]	[illegible]	[illegible]	[illegible]	[illegible]
	Cause ill-defined and not specified,	[illegible]	[illegible]	[illegible]	[illegible]	[illegible]	[illegible]	[illegible]	[illegible]	[illegible]	[illegible]	[illegible]	[illegible]	[illegible]	[illegible]	[illegible]	[illegible]	[illegible]	[illegible]	[illegible]

IRELAND.—CAUSES of Deaths at different Periods of Life in the Year 1891—Females—con.

Class.	Causes of Death.	All Ages.	Under 1 year	1	2	3	4	Total under 5 years.	5-	10-	15-	20-	25-	35-	45-	55-	65-	75-	85-	95 and upwards.
VI.—con.	Order 6 (8).																			
	Abortion, Miscarriage,	[illegible]	[illegible]	[illegible]	[illegible]	[illegible]	[illegible]	[illegible]	[illegible]	[illegible]	[illegible]	[illegible]	[illegible]	[illegible]	[illegible]	[illegible]	[illegible]	[illegible]	[illegible]	[illegible]
	Puerperal Mania,	[illegible]	[illegible]	[illegible]	[illegible]	[illegible]	[illegible]	[illegible]	[illegible]	[illegible]	[illegible]	[illegible]	[illegible]	[illegible]	[illegible]	[illegible]	[illegible]	[illegible]	[illegible]	[illegible]
	Puerperal Convulsions,	[illegible]	[illegible]	[illegible]	[illegible]	[illegible]	[illegible]	[illegible]	[illegible]	[illegible]	[illegible]	[illegible]	[illegible]	[illegible]	[illegible]	[illegible]	[illegible]	[illegible]	[illegible]	[illegible]
	Placenta praevia, Flooding,	[illegible]	[illegible]	[illegible]	[illegible]	[illegible]	[illegible]	[illegible]	[illegible]	[illegible]	[illegible]	[illegible]	[illegible]	[illegible]	[illegible]	[illegible]	[illegible]	[illegible]	[illegible]	[illegible]
	Phlegmasia dolens,	7	[illegible]	[illegible]	[illegible]	[illegible]	[illegible]	[illegible]	[illegible]	[illegible]	[illegible]	[illegible]	[illegible]	[illegible]	[illegible]	[illegible]	[illegible]	[illegible]	[illegible]	[illegible]
	Other Accidents of Childbirth,	[illegible]	[illegible]	[illegible]	[illegible]	[illegible]	[illegible]	[illegible]	[illegible]	[illegible]	[illegible]	[illegible]	[illegible]	[illegible]	[illegible]	[illegible]	[illegible]	[illegible]	[illegible]	[illegible]
	Order 9.																			
	Caries, Necrosis,	[illegible]	[illegible]	[illegible]	[illegible]	[illegible]	[illegible]	[illegible]	[illegible]	[illegible]	[illegible]	[illegible]	[illegible]	[illegible]	[illegible]	[illegible]	[illegible]	[illegible]	[illegible]	[illegible]
	Arthritis, Ostitis, Periostitis,	[illegible]	[illegible]	[illegible]	[illegible]	[illegible]	[illegible]	[illegible]	[illegible]	[illegible]	[illegible]	[illegible]	[illegible]	[illegible]	[illegible]	[illegible]	[illegible]	[illegible]	[illegible]	[illegible]
	Other Diseases of Organs of Locomotion,	[illegible]	[illegible]	[illegible]	[illegible]	[illegible]	[illegible]	[illegible]	[illegible]	[illegible]	[illegible]	[illegible]	[illegible]	[illegible]	[illegible]	[illegible]	[illegible]	[illegible]	[illegible]	[illegible]
	Order 10.																			
	Carbuncle,	[illegible]	[illegible]	[illegible]	[illegible]	[illegible]	[illegible]	[illegible]	[illegible]	[illegible]	[illegible]	[illegible]	[illegible]	[illegible]	[illegible]	[illegible]	[illegible]	[illegible]	[illegible]	[illegible]
	Phlegmon, Cellulitis,	[illegible]	[illegible]	[illegible]	[illegible]	[illegible]	[illegible]	[illegible]	[illegible]	[illegible]	[illegible]	[illegible]	[illegible]	[illegible]	[illegible]	[illegible]	[illegible]	[illegible]	[illegible]	[illegible]
	Lupus,	[illegible]	[illegible]	[illegible]	[illegible]	[illegible]	[illegible]	[illegible]	[illegible]	[illegible]	[illegible]	[illegible]	[illegible]	[illegible]	[illegible]	[illegible]	[illegible]	[illegible]	[illegible]	[illegible]
	Ulcer, Bedsore,	[illegible]	[illegible]	[illegible]	[illegible]	[illegible]	[illegible]	[illegible]	[illegible]	[illegible]	[illegible]	[illegible]	[illegible]	[illegible]	[illegible]	[illegible]	[illegible]	[illegible]	[illegible]	[illegible]
	Eczema,	[illegible]	[illegible]	[illegible]	[illegible]	[illegible]	[illegible]	[illegible]	[illegible]	[illegible]	[illegible]	[illegible]	[illegible]	[illegible]	[illegible]	[illegible]	[illegible]	[illegible]	[illegible]	[illegible]
	Pemphigus,	[illegible]	[illegible]	[illegible]	[illegible]	[illegible]	[illegible]	[illegible]	[illegible]	[illegible]	[illegible]	[illegible]	[illegible]	[illegible]	[illegible]	[illegible]	[illegible]	[illegible]	[illegible]	[illegible]
	Other Diseases of Integumentary System,	[illegible]	[illegible]	[illegible]	[illegible]	[illegible]	[illegible]	[illegible]	[illegible]	[illegible]	[illegible]	[illegible]	[illegible]	[illegible]	[illegible]	[illegible]	[illegible]	[illegible]	[illegible]	[illegible]
VII.	Order 1.																			
	In Mines and Quarries,	[illegible]	[illegible]	[illegible]	[illegible]	[illegible]	[illegible]	[illegible]	[illegible]	[illegible]	[illegible]	[illegible]	[illegible]	[illegible]	[illegible]	[illegible]	[illegible]	[illegible]	[illegible]	[illegible]
	Vehicles and Horses,	[illegible]	[illegible]	[illegible]	[illegible]	[illegible]	[illegible]	[illegible]	[illegible]	[illegible]	[illegible]	[illegible]	[illegible]	[illegible]	[illegible]	[illegible]	[illegible]	[illegible]	[illegible]	[illegible]
	Ships, Boats, Docks (not Drowning),	[illegible]	[illegible]	[illegible]	[illegible]	[illegible]	[illegible]	[illegible]	[illegible]	[illegible]	[illegible]	[illegible]	[illegible]	[illegible]	[illegible]	[illegible]	[illegible]	[illegible]	[illegible]	[illegible]
	Building Operations,	[illegible]	[illegible]	[illegible]	[illegible]	[illegible]	[illegible]	[illegible]	[illegible]	[illegible]	[illegible]	[illegible]	[illegible]	[illegible]	[illegible]	[illegible]	[illegible]	[illegible]	[illegible]	[illegible]
	Machinery,	[illegible]	[illegible]	[illegible]	[illegible]	[illegible]	[illegible]	[illegible]	[illegible]	[illegible]	[illegible]	[illegible]	[illegible]	[illegible]	[illegible]	[illegible]	[illegible]	[illegible]	[illegible]	[illegible]
	Weapons & Implements,	[illegible]	[illegible]	[illegible]	[illegible]	[illegible]	[illegible]	[illegible]	[illegible]	[illegible]	[illegible]	[illegible]	[illegible]	[illegible]	[illegible]	[illegible]	[illegible]	[illegible]	[illegible]	[illegible]
	Burns and Scalds,	[illegible]	[illegible]	[illegible]	[illegible]	[illegible]	[illegible]	[illegible]	[illegible]	[illegible]	[illegible]	[illegible]	[illegible]	[illegible]	[illegible]	[illegible]	[illegible]	[illegible]	[illegible]	[illegible]
	Poison, Poisonous Vapour,	[illegible]	[illegible]	[illegible]	[illegible]	[illegible]	[illegible]	[illegible]	[illegible]	[illegible]	[illegible]	[illegible]	[illegible]	[illegible]	[illegible]	[illegible]	[illegible]	[illegible]	[illegible]	[illegible]
	Drowning,	[illegible]	[illegible]	[illegible]	[illegible]	[illegible]	[illegible]	[illegible]	[illegible]	[illegible]	[illegible]	[illegible]	[illegible]	[illegible]	[illegible]	[illegible]	[illegible]	[illegible]	[illegible]	[illegible]
	Suffocation,	[illegible]	[illegible]	[illegible]	[illegible]	[illegible]	[illegible]	[illegible]	[illegible]	[illegible]	[illegible]	[illegible]	[illegible]	[illegible]	[illegible]	[illegible]	[illegible]	[illegible]	[illegible]	[illegible]
	Falls,	[illegible]	[illegible]	[illegible]	[illegible]	[illegible]	[illegible]	[illegible]	[illegible]	[illegible]	[illegible]	[illegible]	[illegible]	[illegible]	[illegible]	[illegible]	[illegible]	[illegible]	[illegible]	[illegible]
	Weather Agencies,	[illegible]	[illegible]	[illegible]	[illegible]	[illegible]	[illegible]	[illegible]	[illegible]	[illegible]	[illegible]	[illegible]	[illegible]	[illegible]	[illegible]	[illegible]	[illegible]	[illegible]	[illegible]	[illegible]
	Otherwise, or not Stated,	[illegible]	[illegible]	[illegible]	[illegible]	[illegible]	[illegible]	[illegible]	[illegible]	[illegible]	[illegible]	[illegible]	[illegible]	[illegible]	[illegible]	[illegible]	[illegible]	[illegible]	[illegible]	[illegible]
	Order 2.																			
	Homicide,	[illegible]	[illegible]	[illegible]	[illegible]	[illegible]	[illegible]	[illegible]	[illegible]	[illegible]	[illegible]	[illegible]	[illegible]	[illegible]	[illegible]	[illegible]	[illegible]	[illegible]	[illegible]	[illegible]
	Order 3.																			
	Suicide,	[illegible]	[illegible]	[illegible]	[illegible]	[illegible]	[illegible]	[illegible]	[illegible]	[illegible]	[illegible]	[illegible]	[illegible]	[illegible]	[illegible]	[illegible]	[illegible]	[illegible]	[illegible]	[illegible]
	Order 4.																			
	Execution,	[illegible]	[illegible]	[illegible]	[illegible]	[illegible]	[illegible]	[illegible]	[illegible]	[illegible]	[illegible]	[illegible]	[illegible]	[illegible]	[illegible]	[illegible]	[illegible]	[illegible]	[illegible]	[illegible]
VIII.	Dropsy,	[illegible]	[illegible]	[illegible]	[illegible]	[illegible]	[illegible]	[illegible]	[illegible]	[illegible]	[illegible]	[illegible]	[illegible]	[illegible]	[illegible]	[illegible]	[illegible]	[illegible]	[illegible]	[illegible]
	Debility, Atrophy, Inanition,	[illegible]	[illegible]	[illegible]	[illegible]	[illegible]	[illegible]	[illegible]	[illegible]	[illegible]	[illegible]	[illegible]	[illegible]	[illegible]	[illegible]	[illegible]	[illegible]	[illegible]	[illegible]	[illegible]
	Mortification,	[illegible]	[illegible]	[illegible]	[illegible]	[illegible]	[illegible]	[illegible]	[illegible]	[illegible]	[illegible]	[illegible]	[illegible]	[illegible]	[illegible]	[illegible]	[illegible]	[illegible]	[illegible]	[illegible]
	Tumour,	[illegible]	[illegible]	[illegible]	[illegible]	[illegible]	[illegible]	[illegible]	[illegible]	[illegible]	[illegible]	[illegible]	[illegible]	[illegible]	[illegible]	[illegible]	[illegible]	[illegible]	[illegible]	[illegible]
	Abscess,	[illegible]	[illegible]	[illegible]	[illegible]	[illegible]	[illegible]	[illegible]	[illegible]	[illegible]	[illegible]	[illegible]	[illegible]	[illegible]	[illegible]	[illegible]	[illegible]	[illegible]	[illegible]	[illegible]
	Haemorrhage,	[illegible]	[illegible]	[illegible]	[illegible]	[illegible]	[illegible]	[illegible]	[illegible]	[illegible]	[illegible]	[illegible]	[illegible]	[illegible]	[illegible]	[illegible]	[illegible]	[illegible]	[illegible]	[illegible]
	Sudden (cause unascertained),	[illegible]	[illegible]	[illegible]	[illegible]	[illegible]	[illegible]	[illegible]	[illegible]	[illegible]	[illegible]	[illegible]	[illegible]	[illegible]	[illegible]	[illegible]	[illegible]	[illegible]	[illegible]	[illegible]
	Other ill-defined and not specified causes,	[illegible]	[illegible]	[illegible]	[illegible]	[illegible]	[illegible]	[illegible]	[illegible]	[illegible]	[illegible]	[illegible]	[illegible]	[illegible]	[illegible]	[illegible]	[illegible]	[illegible]	[illegible]	[illegible]

IRELAND.—CAUSES of DEATH at different Periods of Life, in the Year 1891.—
MALES and FEMALES.

Class.	Causes of Death.	All Ages.	Under 1 Year.	1	2	3	4	Total under 5 Years.	5-	10-	15-	20-	25-	35-	45-	55-	65-	75-	85-	95 and upwards.
	ALL CAUSES,	[illegible]	[illegible]	[illegible]	[illegible]	[illegible]	[illegible]	[illegible]	[illegible]	[illegible]	[illegible]	[illegible]	[illegible]	[illegible]	[illegible]	[illegible]	[illegible]	[illegible]	[illegible]	[illegible]
	(Classes.)																			
I.	Specific Febrile or Zymotic Diseases,	[illegible]	[illegible]	[illegible]	[illegible]	[illegible]	[illegible]	[illegible]	[illegible]	[illegible]	[illegible]	[illegible]	[illegible]	[illegible]	[illegible]	[illegible]	[illegible]	[illegible]	[illegible]	[illegible]
II.	Parasitic Diseases,	[illegible]	[illegible]	[illegible]	[illegible]	[illegible]	[illegible]	[illegible]	[illegible]	[illegible]	[illegible]	[illegible]	[illegible]	[illegible]	[illegible]	[illegible]	[illegible]	[illegible]	[illegible]	[illegible]
III.	Dietetic,	[illegible]	[illegible]	[illegible]	[illegible]	[illegible]	[illegible]	[illegible]	[illegible]	[illegible]	[illegible]	[illegible]	[illegible]	[illegible]	[illegible]	[illegible]	[illegible]	[illegible]	[illegible]	[illegible]
IV.	Constitutional,	[illegible]	[illegible]	[illegible]	[illegible]	[illegible]	[illegible]	[illegible]	[illegible]	[illegible]	[illegible]	[illegible]	[illegible]	[illegible]	[illegible]	[illegible]	[illegible]	[illegible]	[illegible]	[illegible]
V.	Developmental,	[illegible]	[illegible]	[illegible]	[illegible]	[illegible]	[illegible]	[illegible]	[illegible]	[illegible]	[illegible]	[illegible]	[illegible]	[illegible]	[illegible]	[illegible]	[illegible]	[illegible]	[illegible]	[illegible]
VI.	Local,	[illegible]	[illegible]	[illegible]	[illegible]	[illegible]	[illegible]	[illegible]	[illegible]	[illegible]	[illegible]	[illegible]	[illegible]	[illegible]	[illegible]	[illegible]	[illegible]	[illegible]	[illegible]	[illegible]
VII.	Violence,	[illegible]	[illegible]	[illegible]	[illegible]	[illegible]	[illegible]	[illegible]	[illegible]	[illegible]	[illegible]	[illegible]	[illegible]	[illegible]	[illegible]	[illegible]	[illegible]	[illegible]	[illegible]	[illegible]
VIII.	Ill-defined and not specified causes,	[illegible]	[illegible]	[illegible]	[illegible]	[illegible]	[illegible]	[illegible]	[illegible]	[illegible]	[illegible]	[illegible]	[illegible]	[illegible]	[illegible]	[illegible]	[illegible]	[illegible]	[illegible]	[illegible]
	(Orders.)																			
I.	1. Miasmatic Diseases,	[illegible]	[illegible]	[illegible]	[illegible]	[illegible]	[illegible]	[illegible]	[illegible]	[illegible]	[illegible]	[illegible]	[illegible]	[illegible]	[illegible]	[illegible]	[illegible]	[illegible]	[illegible]	[illegible]
	2. Diarrhoeal,	[illegible]	[illegible]	[illegible]	[illegible]	[illegible]	[illegible]	[illegible]	[illegible]	[illegible]	[illegible]	[illegible]	[illegible]	[illegible]	[illegible]	[illegible]	[illegible]	[illegible]	[illegible]	[illegible]
	3. Malarial,	[illegible]	[illegible]	[illegible]	[illegible]	[illegible]	[illegible]	[illegible]	[illegible]	[illegible]	[illegible]	[illegible]	[illegible]	[illegible]	[illegible]	[illegible]	[illegible]	[illegible]	[illegible]	[illegible]
	4. Zoogenous,	[illegible]	[illegible]	[illegible]	[illegible]	[illegible]	[illegible]	[illegible]	[illegible]	[illegible]	[illegible]	[illegible]	[illegible]	[illegible]	[illegible]	[illegible]	[illegible]	[illegible]	[illegible]	[illegible]
	5. Venereal,	[illegible]	[illegible]	[illegible]	[illegible]	[illegible]	[illegible]	[illegible]	[illegible]	[illegible]	[illegible]	[illegible]	[illegible]	[illegible]	[illegible]	[illegible]	[illegible]	[illegible]	[illegible]	[illegible]
	6. Septic,	[illegible]	[illegible]	[illegible]	[illegible]	[illegible]	[illegible]	[illegible]	[illegible]	[illegible]	[illegible]	[illegible]	[illegible]	[illegible]	[illegible]	[illegible]	[illegible]	[illegible]	[illegible]	[illegible]
II.	Parasitic,	[illegible]	[illegible]	[illegible]	[illegible]	[illegible]	[illegible]	[illegible]	[illegible]	[illegible]	[illegible]	[illegible]	[illegible]	[illegible]	[illegible]	[illegible]	[illegible]	[illegible]	[illegible]	[illegible]
III.	Dietetic,	[illegible]	[illegible]	[illegible]	[illegible]	[illegible]	[illegible]	[illegible]	[illegible]	[illegible]	[illegible]	[illegible]	[illegible]	[illegible]	[illegible]	[illegible]	[illegible]	[illegible]	[illegible]	[illegible]
IV.	Constitutional,	[illegible]	[illegible]	[illegible]	[illegible]	[illegible]	[illegible]	[illegible]	[illegible]	[illegible]	[illegible]	[illegible]	[illegible]	[illegible]	[illegible]	[illegible]	[illegible]	[illegible]	[illegible]	[illegible]
V.	Developmental,	[illegible]	[illegible]	[illegible]	[illegible]	[illegible]	[illegible]	[illegible]	[illegible]	[illegible]	[illegible]	[illegible]	[illegible]	[illegible]	[illegible]	[illegible]	[illegible]	[illegible]	[illegible]	[illegible]
VI.	1. Diseases of Nervous System,	[illegible]	[illegible]	[illegible]	[illegible]	[illegible]	[illegible]	[illegible]	[illegible]	[illegible]	[illegible]	[illegible]	[illegible]	[illegible]	[illegible]	[illegible]	[illegible]	[illegible]	[illegible]	[illegible]
	2. „ Organs of Special Sense,	[illegible]	[illegible]	[illegible]	[illegible]	[illegible]	[illegible]	[illegible]	[illegible]	[illegible]	[illegible]	[illegible]	[illegible]	[illegible]	[illegible]	[illegible]	[illegible]	[illegible]	[illegible]	[illegible]
	3. „ Circulatory System,	[illegible]	[illegible]	[illegible]	[illegible]	[illegible]	[illegible]	[illegible]	[illegible]	[illegible]	[illegible]	[illegible]	[illegible]	[illegible]	[illegible]	[illegible]	[illegible]	[illegible]	[illegible]	[illegible]
	4. „ Respiratory System,	[illegible]	[illegible]	[illegible]	[illegible]	[illegible]	[illegible]	[illegible]	[illegible]	[illegible]	[illegible]	[illegible]	[illegible]	[illegible]	[illegible]	[illegible]	[illegible]	[illegible]	[illegible]	[illegible]
	5. „ Digestive System,	[illegible]	[illegible]	[illegible]	[illegible]	[illegible]	[illegible]	[illegible]	[illegible]	[illegible]	[illegible]	[illegible]	[illegible]	[illegible]	[illegible]	[illegible]	[illegible]	[illegible]	[illegible]	[illegible]
	6. „ Lymphatic System and Ductless Glands,	[illegible]	[illegible]	[illegible]	[illegible]	[illegible]	[illegible]	[illegible]	[illegible]	[illegible]	[illegible]	[illegible]	[illegible]	[illegible]	[illegible]	[illegible]	[illegible]	[illegible]	[illegible]	[illegible]
	7. „ Urinary System,	[illegible]	[illegible]	[illegible]	[illegible]	[illegible]	[illegible]	[illegible]	[illegible]	[illegible]	[illegible]	[illegible]	[illegible]	[illegible]	[illegible]	[illegible]	[illegible]	[illegible]	[illegible]	[illegible]
	8. „ Reproductive System:—																			
	(a) „ Organs of Generation,	[illegible]	[illegible]	[illegible]	[illegible]	[illegible]	[illegible]	[illegible]	[illegible]	[illegible]	[illegible]	[illegible]	[illegible]	[illegible]	[illegible]	[illegible]	[illegible]	[illegible]	[illegible]	[illegible]
	(b) „ Parturition,	[illegible]	[illegible]	[illegible]	[illegible]	[illegible]	[illegible]	[illegible]	[illegible]	[illegible]	[illegible]	[illegible]	[illegible]	[illegible]	[illegible]	[illegible]	[illegible]	[illegible]	[illegible]	[illegible]
	9. „ Locomotive System,	[illegible]	[illegible]	[illegible]	[illegible]	[illegible]	[illegible]	[illegible]	[illegible]	[illegible]	[illegible]	[illegible]	[illegible]	[illegible]	[illegible]	[illegible]	[illegible]	[illegible]	[illegible]	[illegible]
	10. „ Integumentary System,	[illegible]	[illegible]	[illegible]	[illegible]	[illegible]	[illegible]	[illegible]	[illegible]	[illegible]	[illegible]	[illegible]	[illegible]	[illegible]	[illegible]	[illegible]	[illegible]	[illegible]	[illegible]	[illegible]
VII.	1. Accident or Negligence,	[illegible]	[illegible]	[illegible]	[illegible]	[illegible]	[illegible]	[illegible]	[illegible]	[illegible]	[illegible]	[illegible]	[illegible]	[illegible]	[illegible]	[illegible]	[illegible]	[illegible]	[illegible]	[illegible]
	2. Homicide,	[illegible]	[illegible]	[illegible]	[illegible]	[illegible]	[illegible]	[illegible]	[illegible]	[illegible]	[illegible]	[illegible]	[illegible]	[illegible]	[illegible]	[illegible]	[illegible]	[illegible]	[illegible]	[illegible]
	3. Suicide,	[illegible]	[illegible]	[illegible]	[illegible]	[illegible]	[illegible]	[illegible]	[illegible]	[illegible]	[illegible]	[illegible]	[illegible]	[illegible]	[illegible]	[illegible]	[illegible]	[illegible]	[illegible]	[illegible]
	4. Execution,	[illegible]	[illegible]	[illegible]	[illegible]	[illegible]	[illegible]	[illegible]	[illegible]	[illegible]	[illegible]	[illegible]	[illegible]	[illegible]	[illegible]	[illegible]	[illegible]	[illegible]	[illegible]	[illegible]
VIII.	Ill-defined and not specified Causes,	[illegible]	[illegible]	[illegible]	[illegible]	[illegible]	[illegible]	[illegible]	[illegible]	[illegible]	[illegible]	[illegible]	[illegible]	[illegible]	[illegible]	[illegible]	[illegible]	[illegible]	[illegible]	[illegible]

IRELAND.—CAUSES of DEATH at different Periods of Life in the Year 1891.—MALES and FEMALES—*continued*.

Class	SPECIFIED CAUSE	MALES AND FEMALES: All Ages	AGE AT DEATH: Under 1 year	1	2	3	4	Total under 5 years	5–	10–	15–	20–	25–	35–	45–	55–	65–	75–	85–	95–	Age not stated
I.	ORDER 1.																				
	Small-pox: Vaccinated	[illegible]	[illegible]	[illegible]	[illegible]	[illegible]	[illegible]	[illegible]	[illegible]	[illegible]	[illegible]	[illegible]	[illegible]	[illegible]	[illegible]	[illegible]	[illegible]	[illegible]	[illegible]	[illegible]	[illegible]
	Small-pox: Unvaccinated	[illegible]	[illegible]	[illegible]	[illegible]	[illegible]	[illegible]	[illegible]	[illegible]	[illegible]	[illegible]	[illegible]	[illegible]	[illegible]	[illegible]	[illegible]	[illegible]	[illegible]	[illegible]	[illegible]	[illegible]
	Small-pox: No statement	[illegible]	[illegible]	[illegible]	[illegible]	[illegible]	[illegible]	[illegible]	[illegible]	[illegible]	[illegible]	[illegible]	[illegible]	[illegible]	[illegible]	[illegible]	[illegible]	[illegible]	[illegible]	[illegible]	[illegible]
	Chicken-pox	[illegible]	[illegible]	[illegible]	[illegible]	[illegible]	[illegible]	[illegible]	[illegible]	[illegible]	[illegible]	[illegible]	[illegible]	[illegible]	[illegible]	[illegible]	[illegible]	[illegible]	[illegible]	[illegible]	[illegible]
	Measles	[illegible]	[illegible]	[illegible]	[illegible]	[illegible]	[illegible]	[illegible]	[illegible]	[illegible]	[illegible]	[illegible]	[illegible]	[illegible]	[illegible]	[illegible]	[illegible]	[illegible]	[illegible]	[illegible]	[illegible]
	Epidemic Rose-Rash	[illegible]	[illegible]	[illegible]	[illegible]	[illegible]	[illegible]	[illegible]	[illegible]	[illegible]	[illegible]	[illegible]	[illegible]	[illegible]	[illegible]	[illegible]	[illegible]	[illegible]	[illegible]	[illegible]	[illegible]
	Scarlet Fever	[illegible]	[illegible]	[illegible]	[illegible]	[illegible]	[illegible]	[illegible]	[illegible]	[illegible]	[illegible]	[illegible]	[illegible]	[illegible]	[illegible]	[illegible]	[illegible]	[illegible]	[illegible]	[illegible]	[illegible]
	Typhus	[illegible]	[illegible]	[illegible]	[illegible]	[illegible]	[illegible]	[illegible]	[illegible]	[illegible]	[illegible]	[illegible]	[illegible]	[illegible]	[illegible]	[illegible]	[illegible]	[illegible]	[illegible]	[illegible]	[illegible]
	Relapsing Fever	[illegible]	[illegible]	[illegible]	[illegible]	[illegible]	[illegible]	[illegible]	[illegible]	[illegible]	[illegible]	[illegible]	[illegible]	[illegible]	[illegible]	[illegible]	[illegible]	[illegible]	[illegible]	[illegible]	[illegible]
	Influenza	[illegible]	[illegible]	[illegible]	[illegible]	[illegible]	[illegible]	[illegible]	[illegible]	[illegible]	[illegible]	[illegible]	[illegible]	[illegible]	[illegible]	[illegible]	[illegible]	[illegible]	[illegible]	[illegible]	[illegible]
	Whooping-cough	[illegible]	[illegible]	[illegible]	[illegible]	[illegible]	[illegible]	[illegible]	[illegible]	[illegible]	[illegible]	[illegible]	[illegible]	[illegible]	[illegible]	[illegible]	[illegible]	[illegible]	[illegible]	[illegible]	[illegible]
	Mumps	[illegible]	[illegible]	[illegible]	[illegible]	[illegible]	[illegible]	[illegible]	[illegible]	[illegible]	[illegible]	[illegible]	[illegible]	[illegible]	[illegible]	[illegible]	[illegible]	[illegible]	[illegible]	[illegible]	[illegible]
	Diphtheria	[illegible]	[illegible]	[illegible]	[illegible]	[illegible]	[illegible]	[illegible]	[illegible]	[illegible]	[illegible]	[illegible]	[illegible]	[illegible]	[illegible]	[illegible]	[illegible]	[illegible]	[illegible]	[illegible]	[illegible]
	Cerebro-spinal Fever	[illegible]	[illegible]	[illegible]	[illegible]	[illegible]	[illegible]	[illegible]	[illegible]	[illegible]	[illegible]	[illegible]	[illegible]	[illegible]	[illegible]	[illegible]	[illegible]	[illegible]	[illegible]	[illegible]	[illegible]
	Simple and ill-defined Fever	[illegible]	[illegible]	[illegible]	[illegible]	[illegible]	[illegible]	[illegible]	[illegible]	[illegible]	[illegible]	[illegible]	[illegible]	[illegible]	[illegible]	[illegible]	[illegible]	[illegible]	[illegible]	[illegible]	[illegible]
	Enteric Fever	[illegible]	[illegible]	[illegible]	[illegible]	[illegible]	[illegible]	[illegible]	[illegible]	[illegible]	[illegible]	[illegible]	[illegible]	[illegible]	[illegible]	[illegible]	[illegible]	[illegible]	[illegible]	[illegible]	[illegible]
	Other Miasmatic Diseases	[illegible]	[illegible]	[illegible]	[illegible]	[illegible]	[illegible]	[illegible]	[illegible]	[illegible]	[illegible]	[illegible]	[illegible]	[illegible]	[illegible]	[illegible]	[illegible]	[illegible]	[illegible]	[illegible]	[illegible]
	ORDER 2.																				
	Simple Cholera	[illegible]	[illegible]	[illegible]	[illegible]	[illegible]	[illegible]	[illegible]	[illegible]	[illegible]	[illegible]	[illegible]	[illegible]	[illegible]	[illegible]	[illegible]	[illegible]	[illegible]	[illegible]	[illegible]	[illegible]
	Diarrhoea, Dysentery	[illegible]	[illegible]	[illegible]	[illegible]	[illegible]	[illegible]	[illegible]	[illegible]	[illegible]	[illegible]	[illegible]	[illegible]	[illegible]	[illegible]	[illegible]	[illegible]	[illegible]	[illegible]	[illegible]	[illegible]
	ORDER 3.																				
	Remittent Fever	[illegible]	[illegible]	[illegible]	[illegible]	[illegible]	[illegible]	[illegible]	[illegible]	[illegible]	[illegible]	[illegible]	[illegible]	[illegible]	[illegible]	[illegible]	[illegible]	[illegible]	[illegible]	[illegible]	[illegible]
	Ague	[illegible]	[illegible]	[illegible]	[illegible]	[illegible]	[illegible]	[illegible]	[illegible]	[illegible]	[illegible]	[illegible]	[illegible]	[illegible]	[illegible]	[illegible]	[illegible]	[illegible]	[illegible]	[illegible]	[illegible]
	ORDER 4.																				
	Hydrophobia	[illegible]	[illegible]	[illegible]	[illegible]	[illegible]	[illegible]	[illegible]	[illegible]	[illegible]	[illegible]	[illegible]	[illegible]	[illegible]	[illegible]	[illegible]	[illegible]	[illegible]	[illegible]	[illegible]	[illegible]
	Glanders	[illegible]	[illegible]	[illegible]	[illegible]	[illegible]	[illegible]	[illegible]	[illegible]	[illegible]	[illegible]	[illegible]	[illegible]	[illegible]	[illegible]	[illegible]	[illegible]	[illegible]	[illegible]	[illegible]	[illegible]
	Splenic Fever	[illegible]	[illegible]	[illegible]	[illegible]	[illegible]	[illegible]	[illegible]	[illegible]	[illegible]	[illegible]	[illegible]	[illegible]	[illegible]	[illegible]	[illegible]	[illegible]	[illegible]	[illegible]	[illegible]	[illegible]
	Cowpox and other effects of Vaccination	[illegible]	[illegible]	[illegible]	[illegible]	[illegible]	[illegible]	[illegible]	[illegible]	[illegible]	[illegible]	[illegible]	[illegible]	[illegible]	[illegible]	[illegible]	[illegible]	[illegible]	[illegible]	[illegible]	[illegible]
	ORDER 5.																				
	Syphilis	[illegible]	[illegible]	[illegible]	[illegible]	[illegible]	[illegible]	[illegible]	[illegible]	[illegible]	[illegible]	[illegible]	[illegible]	[illegible]	[illegible]	[illegible]	[illegible]	[illegible]	[illegible]	[illegible]	[illegible]
	Gonorrhoea, Stricture of Urethra	[illegible]	[illegible]	[illegible]	[illegible]	[illegible]	[illegible]	[illegible]	[illegible]	[illegible]	[illegible]	[illegible]	[illegible]	[illegible]	[illegible]	[illegible]	[illegible]	[illegible]	[illegible]	[illegible]	[illegible]
	ORDER 6.																				
	Phagedaena	[illegible]	[illegible]	[illegible]	[illegible]	[illegible]	[illegible]	[illegible]	[illegible]	[illegible]	[illegible]	[illegible]	[illegible]	[illegible]	[illegible]	[illegible]	[illegible]	[illegible]	[illegible]	[illegible]	[illegible]
	Erysipelas	[illegible]	[illegible]	[illegible]	[illegible]	[illegible]	[illegible]	[illegible]	[illegible]	[illegible]	[illegible]	[illegible]	[illegible]	[illegible]	[illegible]	[illegible]	[illegible]	[illegible]	[illegible]	[illegible]	[illegible]
	Pyaemia, Septicaemia	[illegible]	[illegible]	[illegible]	[illegible]	[illegible]	[illegible]	[illegible]	[illegible]	[illegible]	[illegible]	[illegible]	[illegible]	[illegible]	[illegible]	[illegible]	[illegible]	[illegible]	[illegible]	[illegible]	[illegible]
	Puerperal Fever	[illegible]	[illegible]	[illegible]	[illegible]	[illegible]	[illegible]	[illegible]	[illegible]	[illegible]	[illegible]	[illegible]	[illegible]	[illegible]	[illegible]	[illegible]	[illegible]	[illegible]	[illegible]	[illegible]	[illegible]
II.	Thrush	[illegible]	[illegible]	[illegible]	[illegible]	[illegible]	[illegible]	[illegible]	[illegible]	[illegible]	[illegible]	[illegible]	[illegible]	[illegible]	[illegible]	[illegible]	[illegible]	[illegible]	[illegible]	[illegible]	[illegible]
	Other Dis. from Vegetable Parasites	[illegible]	[illegible]	[illegible]	[illegible]	[illegible]	[illegible]	[illegible]	[illegible]	[illegible]	[illegible]	[illegible]	[illegible]	[illegible]	[illegible]	[illegible]	[illegible]	[illegible]	[illegible]	[illegible]	[illegible]
	Hydatid Disease	[illegible]	[illegible]	[illegible]	[illegible]	[illegible]	[illegible]	[illegible]	[illegible]	[illegible]	[illegible]	[illegible]	[illegible]	[illegible]	[illegible]	[illegible]	[illegible]	[illegible]	[illegible]	[illegible]	[illegible]
	Other Dis. from Animal Parasites	[illegible]	[illegible]	[illegible]	[illegible]	[illegible]	[illegible]	[illegible]	[illegible]	[illegible]	[illegible]	[illegible]	[illegible]	[illegible]	[illegible]	[illegible]	[illegible]	[illegible]	[illegible]	[illegible]	[illegible]
III.	Starvation, Want of Breast Milk	[illegible]	[illegible]	[illegible]	[illegible]	[illegible]	[illegible]	[illegible]	[illegible]	[illegible]	[illegible]	[illegible]	[illegible]	[illegible]	[illegible]	[illegible]	[illegible]	[illegible]	[illegible]	[illegible]	[illegible]
	Scurvy	[illegible]	[illegible]	[illegible]	[illegible]	[illegible]	[illegible]	[illegible]	[illegible]	[illegible]	[illegible]	[illegible]	[illegible]	[illegible]	[illegible]	[illegible]	[illegible]	[illegible]	[illegible]	[illegible]	[illegible]
	Intemperance—Chronic Alcoholism	[illegible]	[illegible]	[illegible]	[illegible]	[illegible]	[illegible]	[illegible]	[illegible]	[illegible]	[illegible]	[illegible]	[illegible]	[illegible]	[illegible]	[illegible]	[illegible]	[illegible]	[illegible]	[illegible]	[illegible]
	Intemperance—Delirium Tremens	[illegible]	[illegible]	[illegible]	[illegible]	[illegible]	[illegible]	[illegible]	[illegible]	[illegible]	[illegible]	[illegible]	[illegible]	[illegible]	[illegible]	[illegible]	[illegible]	[illegible]	[illegible]	[illegible]	[illegible]
IV.	Rheumatic Fever; Rheumatism of Heart	[illegible]	[illegible]	[illegible]	[illegible]	[illegible]	[illegible]	[illegible]	[illegible]	[illegible]	[illegible]	[illegible]	[illegible]	[illegible]	[illegible]	[illegible]	[illegible]	[illegible]	[illegible]	[illegible]	[illegible]
	Rheumatism	[illegible]	[illegible]	[illegible]	[illegible]	[illegible]	[illegible]	[illegible]	[illegible]	[illegible]	[illegible]	[illegible]	[illegible]	[illegible]	[illegible]	[illegible]	[illegible]	[illegible]	[illegible]	[illegible]	[illegible]
	Gout	[illegible]	[illegible]	[illegible]	[illegible]	[illegible]	[illegible]	[illegible]	[illegible]	[illegible]	[illegible]	[illegible]	[illegible]	[illegible]	[illegible]	[illegible]	[illegible]	[illegible]	[illegible]	[illegible]	[illegible]
	Rickets	[illegible]	[illegible]	[illegible]	[illegible]	[illegible]	[illegible]	[illegible]	[illegible]	[illegible]	[illegible]	[illegible]	[illegible]	[illegible]	[illegible]	[illegible]	[illegible]	[illegible]	[illegible]	[illegible]	[illegible]
	Cancer	[illegible]	[illegible]	[illegible]	[illegible]	[illegible]	[illegible]	[illegible]	[illegible]	[illegible]	[illegible]	[illegible]	[illegible]	[illegible]	[illegible]	[illegible]	[illegible]	[illegible]	[illegible]	[illegible]	[illegible]

IRELAND—CAUSES of DEATHS at different Periods of Life in the Year 1891—MALES and FEMALES—continued.

Class.	CAUSES OF DEATH.	MALES and FEMALES. All Ages.	Age at Death: Under 1 year.	1	2	3	4	Total under 5 years.	5-	10-	15-	20-	25-	35-	45-	55-	65-	75-	85-	95 and upwards.
IV.—con.	Tabes Mesenterica,	[illegible]	[illegible]	[illegible]	[illegible]	[illegible]	[illegible]	[illegible]	[illegible]	[illegible]	[illegible]	[illegible]	[illegible]	[illegible]	[illegible]	[illegible]	[illegible]	[illegible]	[illegible]	[illegible]
	Tubercular Meningitis, Acute Hydrocephalus,	[illegible]	[illegible]	[illegible]	[illegible]	[illegible]	[illegible]	[illegible]	[illegible]	[illegible]	[illegible]	[illegible]	[illegible]	[illegible]	[illegible]	[illegible]	[illegible]	[illegible]	[illegible]	[illegible]
	Phthisis,	[illegible]	[illegible]	[illegible]	[illegible]	[illegible]	[illegible]	[illegible]	[illegible]	[illegible]	[illegible]	[illegible]	[illegible]	[illegible]	[illegible]	[illegible]	[illegible]	[illegible]	[illegible]	[illegible]
	Other forms of Tuberculosis, Scrofula,	[illegible]	[illegible]	[illegible]	[illegible]	[illegible]	[illegible]	[illegible]	[illegible]	[illegible]	[illegible]	[illegible]	[illegible]	[illegible]	[illegible]	[illegible]	[illegible]	[illegible]	[illegible]	[illegible]
	Purpura, Haemorrhagic Diathesis,	[illegible]	[illegible]	[illegible]	[illegible]	[illegible]	[illegible]	[illegible]	[illegible]	[illegible]	[illegible]	[illegible]	[illegible]	[illegible]	[illegible]	[illegible]	[illegible]	[illegible]	[illegible]	[illegible]
	Anaemia, Chlorosis, Leucocythaemia,	[illegible]	[illegible]	[illegible]	[illegible]	[illegible]	[illegible]	[illegible]	[illegible]	[illegible]	[illegible]	[illegible]	[illegible]	[illegible]	[illegible]	[illegible]	[illegible]	[illegible]	[illegible]	[illegible]
	Diabetes Mellitus,	[illegible]	[illegible]	[illegible]	[illegible]	[illegible]	[illegible]	[illegible]	[illegible]	[illegible]	[illegible]	[illegible]	[illegible]	[illegible]	[illegible]	[illegible]	[illegible]	[illegible]	[illegible]	[illegible]
	Other Constitutional Diseases,	[illegible]	[illegible]	[illegible]	[illegible]	[illegible]	[illegible]	[illegible]	[illegible]	[illegible]	[illegible]	[illegible]	[illegible]	[illegible]	[illegible]	[illegible]	[illegible]	[illegible]	[illegible]	[illegible]
V.	Premature Birth,	[illegible]	[illegible]	[illegible]	[illegible]	[illegible]	[illegible]	[illegible]	[illegible]	[illegible]	[illegible]	[illegible]	[illegible]	[illegible]	[illegible]	[illegible]	[illegible]	[illegible]	[illegible]	[illegible]
	Atelectasis,	[illegible]	[illegible]	[illegible]	[illegible]	[illegible]	[illegible]	[illegible]	[illegible]	[illegible]	[illegible]	[illegible]	[illegible]	[illegible]	[illegible]	[illegible]	[illegible]	[illegible]	[illegible]	[illegible]
	Cyanosis,	[illegible]	[illegible]	[illegible]	[illegible]	[illegible]	[illegible]	[illegible]	[illegible]	[illegible]	[illegible]	[illegible]	[illegible]	[illegible]	[illegible]	[illegible]	[illegible]	[illegible]	[illegible]	[illegible]
	Spina Bifida,	[illegible]	[illegible]	[illegible]	[illegible]	[illegible]	[illegible]	[illegible]	[illegible]	[illegible]	[illegible]	[illegible]	[illegible]	[illegible]	[illegible]	[illegible]	[illegible]	[illegible]	[illegible]	[illegible]
	Imperforate Anus,	[illegible]	[illegible]	[illegible]	[illegible]	[illegible]	[illegible]	[illegible]	[illegible]	[illegible]	[illegible]	[illegible]	[illegible]	[illegible]	[illegible]	[illegible]	[illegible]	[illegible]	[illegible]	[illegible]
	Cleft Palate, Harelip,	[illegible]	[illegible]	[illegible]	[illegible]	[illegible]	[illegible]	[illegible]	[illegible]	[illegible]	[illegible]	[illegible]	[illegible]	[illegible]	[illegible]	[illegible]	[illegible]	[illegible]	[illegible]	[illegible]
	Other Congenital Defects,	[illegible]	[illegible]	[illegible]	[illegible]	[illegible]	[illegible]	[illegible]	[illegible]	[illegible]	[illegible]	[illegible]	[illegible]	[illegible]	[illegible]	[illegible]	[illegible]	[illegible]	[illegible]	[illegible]
	Old Age,	[illegible]	[illegible]	[illegible]	[illegible]	[illegible]	[illegible]	[illegible]	[illegible]	[illegible]	[illegible]	[illegible]	[illegible]	[illegible]	[illegible]	[illegible]	[illegible]	[illegible]	[illegible]	[illegible]
VI.	ORDER 1.																			
	Inflammation of Brain, or its Membranes,	[illegible]	[illegible]	[illegible]	[illegible]	[illegible]	[illegible]	[illegible]	[illegible]	[illegible]	[illegible]	[illegible]	[illegible]	[illegible]	[illegible]	[illegible]	[illegible]	[illegible]	[illegible]	[illegible]
	Apoplexy,	[illegible]	[illegible]	[illegible]	[illegible]	[illegible]	[illegible]	[illegible]	[illegible]	[illegible]	[illegible]	[illegible]	[illegible]	[illegible]	[illegible]	[illegible]	[illegible]	[illegible]	[illegible]	[illegible]
	Softening of Brain,	[illegible]	[illegible]	[illegible]	[illegible]	[illegible]	[illegible]	[illegible]	[illegible]	[illegible]	[illegible]	[illegible]	[illegible]	[illegible]	[illegible]	[illegible]	[illegible]	[illegible]	[illegible]	[illegible]
	Hemiplegia, Brain Paralysis,	[illegible]	[illegible]	[illegible]	[illegible]	[illegible]	[illegible]	[illegible]	[illegible]	[illegible]	[illegible]	[illegible]	[illegible]	[illegible]	[illegible]	[illegible]	[illegible]	[illegible]	[illegible]	[illegible]
	Paralysis Agitans,	[illegible]	[illegible]	[illegible]	[illegible]	[illegible]	[illegible]	[illegible]	[illegible]	[illegible]	[illegible]	[illegible]	[illegible]	[illegible]	[illegible]	[illegible]	[illegible]	[illegible]	[illegible]	[illegible]
	Insanity, General Paralysis of Insane,	[illegible]	[illegible]	[illegible]	[illegible]	[illegible]	[illegible]	[illegible]	[illegible]	[illegible]	[illegible]	[illegible]	[illegible]	[illegible]	[illegible]	[illegible]	[illegible]	[illegible]	[illegible]	[illegible]
	Chorea,	[illegible]	[illegible]	[illegible]	[illegible]	[illegible]	[illegible]	[illegible]	[illegible]	[illegible]	[illegible]	[illegible]	[illegible]	[illegible]	[illegible]	[illegible]	[illegible]	[illegible]	[illegible]	[illegible]
	Epilepsy,	[illegible]	[illegible]	[illegible]	[illegible]	[illegible]	[illegible]	[illegible]	[illegible]	[illegible]	[illegible]	[illegible]	[illegible]	[illegible]	[illegible]	[illegible]	[illegible]	[illegible]	[illegible]	[illegible]
	Convulsions,	[illegible]	[illegible]	[illegible]	[illegible]	[illegible]	[illegible]	[illegible]	[illegible]	[illegible]	[illegible]	[illegible]	[illegible]	[illegible]	[illegible]	[illegible]	[illegible]	[illegible]	[illegible]	[illegible]
	Laryngismus Stridulus,	[illegible]	[illegible]	[illegible]	[illegible]	[illegible]	[illegible]	[illegible]	[illegible]	[illegible]	[illegible]	[illegible]	[illegible]	[illegible]	[illegible]	[illegible]	[illegible]	[illegible]	[illegible]	[illegible]
	Idiopathic Tetanus,	[illegible]	[illegible]	[illegible]	[illegible]	[illegible]	[illegible]	[illegible]	[illegible]	[illegible]	[illegible]	[illegible]	[illegible]	[illegible]	[illegible]	[illegible]	[illegible]	[illegible]	[illegible]	[illegible]
	Paraplegia, Diseases of Spinal Cord,	[illegible]	[illegible]	[illegible]	[illegible]	[illegible]	[illegible]	[illegible]	[illegible]	[illegible]	[illegible]	[illegible]	[illegible]	[illegible]	[illegible]	[illegible]	[illegible]	[illegible]	[illegible]	[illegible]
	Other Diseases of Nervous System,	[illegible]	[illegible]	[illegible]	[illegible]	[illegible]	[illegible]	[illegible]	[illegible]	[illegible]	[illegible]	[illegible]	[illegible]	[illegible]	[illegible]	[illegible]	[illegible]	[illegible]	[illegible]	[illegible]
	ORDER 2.																			
	Otitis, Otorrhoea,	[illegible]	[illegible]	[illegible]	[illegible]	[illegible]	[illegible]	[illegible]	[illegible]	[illegible]	[illegible]	[illegible]	[illegible]	[illegible]	[illegible]	[illegible]	[illegible]	[illegible]	[illegible]	[illegible]
	Epistaxis and Dis. of Nose,	[illegible]	[illegible]	[illegible]	[illegible]	[illegible]	[illegible]	[illegible]	[illegible]	[illegible]	[illegible]	[illegible]	[illegible]	[illegible]	[illegible]	[illegible]	[illegible]	[illegible]	[illegible]	[illegible]
	Ophthalmia and Dis. of Eye,	[illegible]	[illegible]	[illegible]	[illegible]	[illegible]	[illegible]	[illegible]	[illegible]	[illegible]	[illegible]	[illegible]	[illegible]	[illegible]	[illegible]	[illegible]	[illegible]	[illegible]	[illegible]	[illegible]
	ORDER 3.																			
	Endocarditis, Valvular Disease,	[illegible]	[illegible]	[illegible]	[illegible]	[illegible]	[illegible]	[illegible]	[illegible]	[illegible]	[illegible]	[illegible]	[illegible]	[illegible]	[illegible]	[illegible]	[illegible]	[illegible]	[illegible]	[illegible]
	Pericarditis,	[illegible]	[illegible]	[illegible]	[illegible]	[illegible]	[illegible]	[illegible]	[illegible]	[illegible]	[illegible]	[illegible]	[illegible]	[illegible]	[illegible]	[illegible]	[illegible]	[illegible]	[illegible]	[illegible]
	Hypertrophy of Heart,	[illegible]	[illegible]	[illegible]	[illegible]	[illegible]	[illegible]	[illegible]	[illegible]	[illegible]	[illegible]	[illegible]	[illegible]	[illegible]	[illegible]	[illegible]	[illegible]	[illegible]	[illegible]	[illegible]
	Angina Pectoris,	[illegible]	[illegible]	[illegible]	[illegible]	[illegible]	[illegible]	[illegible]	[illegible]	[illegible]	[illegible]	[illegible]	[illegible]	[illegible]	[illegible]	[illegible]	[illegible]	[illegible]	[illegible]	[illegible]
	Syncope,	[illegible]	[illegible]	[illegible]	[illegible]	[illegible]	[illegible]	[illegible]	[illegible]	[illegible]	[illegible]	[illegible]	[illegible]	[illegible]	[illegible]	[illegible]	[illegible]	[illegible]	[illegible]	[illegible]
	Aneurism,	[illegible]	[illegible]	[illegible]	[illegible]	[illegible]	[illegible]	[illegible]	[illegible]	[illegible]	[illegible]	[illegible]	[illegible]	[illegible]	[illegible]	[illegible]	[illegible]	[illegible]	[illegible]	[illegible]
	Senile Gangrene,	[illegible]	[illegible]	[illegible]	[illegible]	[illegible]	[illegible]	[illegible]	[illegible]	[illegible]	[illegible]	[illegible]	[illegible]	[illegible]	[illegible]	[illegible]	[illegible]	[illegible]	[illegible]	[illegible]
	Embolism, Thrombosis,	[illegible]	[illegible]	[illegible]	[illegible]	[illegible]	[illegible]	[illegible]	[illegible]	[illegible]	[illegible]	[illegible]	[illegible]	[illegible]	[illegible]	[illegible]	[illegible]	[illegible]	[illegible]	[illegible]
	Phlebitis,	[illegible]	[illegible]	[illegible]	[illegible]	[illegible]	[illegible]	[illegible]	[illegible]	[illegible]	[illegible]	[illegible]	[illegible]	[illegible]	[illegible]	[illegible]	[illegible]	[illegible]	[illegible]	[illegible]
	Varicose Veins,	[illegible]	[illegible]	[illegible]	[illegible]	[illegible]	[illegible]	[illegible]	[illegible]	[illegible]	[illegible]	[illegible]	[illegible]	[illegible]	[illegible]	[illegible]	[illegible]	[illegible]	[illegible]	[illegible]
	Other Diseases of Circulatory System,	[illegible]	[illegible]	[illegible]	[illegible]	[illegible]	[illegible]	[illegible]	[illegible]	[illegible]	[illegible]	[illegible]	[illegible]	[illegible]	[illegible]	[illegible]	[illegible]	[illegible]	[illegible]	[illegible]
	ORDER 4.																			
	Laryngitis,	[illegible]	[illegible]	[illegible]	[illegible]	[illegible]	[illegible]	[illegible]	[illegible]	[illegible]	[illegible]	[illegible]	[illegible]	[illegible]	[illegible]	[illegible]	[illegible]	[illegible]	[illegible]	[illegible]
	Croup,	[illegible]	[illegible]	[illegible]	[illegible]	[illegible]	[illegible]	[illegible]	[illegible]	[illegible]	[illegible]	[illegible]	[illegible]	[illegible]	[illegible]	[illegible]	[illegible]	[illegible]	[illegible]	[illegible]
	Other Diseases of Larynx and Trachea,	[illegible]	[illegible]	[illegible]	[illegible]	[illegible]	[illegible]	[illegible]	[illegible]	[illegible]	[illegible]	[illegible]	[illegible]	[illegible]	[illegible]	[illegible]	[illegible]	[illegible]	[illegible]	[illegible]

IRELAND.—CAUSES of DEATH at different Periods of Life in the Year 1891—MALES and FEMALES—*continued*.

Class.	CAUSES OF DEATH.	All Ages.	Under 1 year.	1	2	3	4	Total under 5 years.	5-	10-	15-	20-	25-	35-	45-	55-	65-	75-	85-	95 and upwards.
	[illegible]—*continued*.																			
[illegible]	[illegible]	[illegible]	[illegible]	[illegible]	[illegible]	[illegible]	[illegible]	[illegible]	[illegible]	[illegible]	[illegible]	[illegible]	[illegible]	[illegible]	[illegible]	[illegible]	[illegible]	[illegible]	[illegible]	[illegible]
	[illegible]	[illegible]	[illegible]	[illegible]	[illegible]	[illegible]	[illegible]	[illegible]	[illegible]	[illegible]	[illegible]	[illegible]	[illegible]	[illegible]	[illegible]	[illegible]	[illegible]	[illegible]	[illegible]	[illegible]
	[illegible]	[illegible]	[illegible]	[illegible]	[illegible]	[illegible]	[illegible]	[illegible]	[illegible]	[illegible]	[illegible]	[illegible]	[illegible]	[illegible]	[illegible]	[illegible]	[illegible]	[illegible]	[illegible]	[illegible]
	[illegible]	[illegible]	[illegible]	[illegible]	[illegible]	[illegible]	[illegible]	[illegible]	[illegible]	[illegible]	[illegible]	[illegible]	[illegible]	[illegible]	[illegible]	[illegible]	[illegible]	[illegible]	[illegible]	[illegible]
	[illegible]	[illegible]	[illegible]	[illegible]	[illegible]	[illegible]	[illegible]	[illegible]	[illegible]	[illegible]	[illegible]	[illegible]	[illegible]	[illegible]	[illegible]	[illegible]	[illegible]	[illegible]	[illegible]	[illegible]

IRELAND.—CAUSES of DEATH at different Periods of Life in the Year 1891—MALES and FEMALES—continued.

Class.	CAUSES OF DEATH.	MALES AND FEMALES. All Ages.	Under 1 year.	1	2	3	4	Total under 5 years.	5-	10-	15-	20-	25-	35-	45-	55-	65-	75-	85-	95-
	[illegible]																			
VI.—[illegible]	[illegible]	[illegible]	[illegible]	[illegible]	[illegible]	[illegible]	[illegible]	[illegible]	[illegible]	[illegible]	[illegible]	[illegible]	[illegible]	[illegible]	[illegible]	[illegible]	[illegible]	[illegible]	[illegible]	[illegible]
	[illegible]	[illegible]	[illegible]	[illegible]	[illegible]	[illegible]	[illegible]	[illegible]	[illegible]	[illegible]	[illegible]	[illegible]	[illegible]	[illegible]	[illegible]	[illegible]	[illegible]	[illegible]	[illegible]	[illegible]
	[illegible]	[illegible]	[illegible]	[illegible]	[illegible]	[illegible]	[illegible]	[illegible]	[illegible]	[illegible]	[illegible]	[illegible]	[illegible]	[illegible]	[illegible]	[illegible]	[illegible]	[illegible]	[illegible]	[illegible]
	[illegible]	[illegible]	[illegible]	[illegible]	[illegible]	[illegible]	[illegible]	[illegible]	[illegible]	[illegible]	[illegible]	[illegible]	[illegible]	[illegible]	[illegible]	[illegible]	[illegible]	[illegible]	[illegible]	[illegible]
	[illegible]	[illegible]	[illegible]	[illegible]	[illegible]	[illegible]	[illegible]	[illegible]	[illegible]	[illegible]	[illegible]	[illegible]	[illegible]	[illegible]	[illegible]	[illegible]	[illegible]	[illegible]	[illegible]	[illegible]
	[illegible]	[illegible]	[illegible]	[illegible]	[illegible]	[illegible]	[illegible]	[illegible]	[illegible]	[illegible]	[illegible]	[illegible]	[illegible]	[illegible]	[illegible]	[illegible]	[illegible]	[illegible]	[illegible]	[illegible]
	[illegible]																			
	[illegible]	[illegible]	[illegible]	[illegible]	[illegible]	[illegible]	[illegible]	[illegible]	[illegible]	[illegible]	[illegible]	[illegible]	[illegible]	[illegible]	[illegible]	[illegible]	[illegible]	[illegible]	[illegible]	[illegible]
	[illegible]	[illegible]	[illegible]	[illegible]	[illegible]	[illegible]	[illegible]	[illegible]	[illegible]	[illegible]	[illegible]	[illegible]	[illegible]	[illegible]	[illegible]	[illegible]	[illegible]	[illegible]	[illegible]	[illegible]
	[illegible]	[illegible]	[illegible]	[illegible]	[illegible]	[illegible]	[illegible]	[illegible]	[illegible]	[illegible]	[illegible]	[illegible]	[illegible]	[illegible]	[illegible]	[illegible]	[illegible]	[illegible]	[illegible]	[illegible]
	[illegible]																			
	[illegible]	[illegible]	[illegible]	[illegible]	[illegible]	[illegible]	[illegible]	[illegible]	[illegible]	[illegible]	[illegible]	[illegible]	[illegible]	[illegible]	[illegible]	[illegible]	[illegible]	[illegible]	[illegible]	[illegible]
	[illegible]	[illegible]	[illegible]	[illegible]	[illegible]	[illegible]	[illegible]	[illegible]	[illegible]	[illegible]	[illegible]	[illegible]	[illegible]	[illegible]	[illegible]	[illegible]	[illegible]	[illegible]	[illegible]	[illegible]
	[illegible]	[illegible]	[illegible]	[illegible]	[illegible]	[illegible]	[illegible]	[illegible]	[illegible]	[illegible]	[illegible]	[illegible]	[illegible]	[illegible]	[illegible]	[illegible]	[illegible]	[illegible]	[illegible]	[illegible]
	[illegible]	[illegible]	[illegible]	[illegible]	[illegible]	[illegible]	[illegible]	[illegible]	[illegible]	[illegible]	[illegible]	[illegible]	[illegible]	[illegible]	[illegible]	[illegible]	[illegible]	[illegible]	[illegible]	[illegible]
	[illegible]	[illegible]	[illegible]	[illegible]	[illegible]	[illegible]	[illegible]	[illegible]	[illegible]	[illegible]	[illegible]	[illegible]	[illegible]	[illegible]	[illegible]	[illegible]	[illegible]	[illegible]	[illegible]	[illegible]
	[illegible]	[illegible]	[illegible]	[illegible]	[illegible]	[illegible]	[illegible]	[illegible]	[illegible]	[illegible]	[illegible]	[illegible]	[illegible]	[illegible]	[illegible]	[illegible]	[illegible]	[illegible]	[illegible]	[illegible]
	[illegible]	[illegible]	[illegible]	[illegible]	[illegible]	[illegible]	[illegible]	[illegible]	[illegible]	[illegible]	[illegible]	[illegible]	[illegible]	[illegible]	[illegible]	[illegible]	[illegible]	[illegible]	[illegible]	[illegible]
	[illegible]																			
VII.	[illegible]	[illegible]	[illegible]	[illegible]	[illegible]	[illegible]	[illegible]	[illegible]	[illegible]	[illegible]	[illegible]	[illegible]	[illegible]	[illegible]	[illegible]	[illegible]	[illegible]	[illegible]	[illegible]	[illegible]
	[illegible]	[illegible]	[illegible]	[illegible]	[illegible]	[illegible]	[illegible]	[illegible]	[illegible]	[illegible]	[illegible]	[illegible]	[illegible]	[illegible]	[illegible]	[illegible]	[illegible]	[illegible]	[illegible]	[illegible]
	[illegible]	[illegible]	[illegible]	[illegible]	[illegible]	[illegible]	[illegible]	[illegible]	[illegible]	[illegible]	[illegible]	[illegible]	[illegible]	[illegible]	[illegible]	[illegible]	[illegible]	[illegible]	[illegible]	[illegible]
	[illegible]	[illegible]	[illegible]	[illegible]	[illegible]	[illegible]	[illegible]	[illegible]	[illegible]	[illegible]	[illegible]	[illegible]	[illegible]	[illegible]	[illegible]	[illegible]	[illegible]	[illegible]	[illegible]	[illegible]
	[illegible]	[illegible]	[illegible]	[illegible]	[illegible]	[illegible]	[illegible]	[illegible]	[illegible]	[illegible]	[illegible]	[illegible]	[illegible]	[illegible]	[illegible]	[illegible]	[illegible]	[illegible]	[illegible]	[illegible]
	[illegible]	[illegible]	[illegible]	[illegible]	[illegible]	[illegible]	[illegible]	[illegible]	[illegible]	[illegible]	[illegible]	[illegible]	[illegible]	[illegible]	[illegible]	[illegible]	[illegible]	[illegible]	[illegible]	[illegible]
	[illegible]	[illegible]	[illegible]	[illegible]	[illegible]	[illegible]	[illegible]	[illegible]	[illegible]	[illegible]	[illegible]	[illegible]	[illegible]	[illegible]	[illegible]	[illegible]	[illegible]	[illegible]	[illegible]	[illegible]
	[illegible]	[illegible]	[illegible]	[illegible]	[illegible]	[illegible]	[illegible]	[illegible]	[illegible]	[illegible]	[illegible]	[illegible]	[illegible]	[illegible]	[illegible]	[illegible]	[illegible]	[illegible]	[illegible]	[illegible]
	[illegible]	[illegible]	[illegible]	[illegible]	[illegible]	[illegible]	[illegible]	[illegible]	[illegible]	[illegible]	[illegible]	[illegible]	[illegible]	[illegible]	[illegible]	[illegible]	[illegible]	[illegible]	[illegible]	[illegible]
	[illegible]	[illegible]	[illegible]	[illegible]	[illegible]	[illegible]	[illegible]	[illegible]	[illegible]	[illegible]	[illegible]	[illegible]	[illegible]	[illegible]	[illegible]	[illegible]	[illegible]	[illegible]	[illegible]	[illegible]
	[illegible]	[illegible]	[illegible]	[illegible]	[illegible]	[illegible]	[illegible]	[illegible]	[illegible]	[illegible]	[illegible]	[illegible]	[illegible]	[illegible]	[illegible]	[illegible]	[illegible]	[illegible]	[illegible]	[illegible]
	[illegible]	[illegible]	[illegible]	[illegible]	[illegible]	[illegible]	[illegible]	[illegible]	[illegible]	[illegible]	[illegible]	[illegible]	[illegible]	[illegible]	[illegible]	[illegible]	[illegible]	[illegible]	[illegible]	[illegible]
	[illegible]	[illegible]	[illegible]	[illegible]	[illegible]	[illegible]	[illegible]	[illegible]	[illegible]	[illegible]	[illegible]	[illegible]	[illegible]	[illegible]	[illegible]	[illegible]	[illegible]	[illegible]	[illegible]	[illegible]
	[illegible]																			
	[illegible]	[illegible]	[illegible]	[illegible]	[illegible]	[illegible]	[illegible]	[illegible]	[illegible]	[illegible]	[illegible]	[illegible]	[illegible]	[illegible]	[illegible]	[illegible]	[illegible]	[illegible]	[illegible]	[illegible]
	[illegible]																			
	[illegible]	[illegible]	[illegible]	[illegible]	[illegible]	[illegible]	[illegible]	[illegible]	[illegible]	[illegible]	[illegible]	[illegible]	[illegible]	[illegible]	[illegible]	[illegible]	[illegible]	[illegible]	[illegible]	[illegible]
	[illegible]																			
	[illegible]	[illegible]	[illegible]	[illegible]	[illegible]	[illegible]	[illegible]	[illegible]	[illegible]	[illegible]	[illegible]	[illegible]	[illegible]	[illegible]	[illegible]	[illegible]	[illegible]	[illegible]	[illegible]	[illegible]
VIII.	[illegible]	[illegible]	[illegible]	[illegible]	[illegible]	[illegible]	[illegible]	[illegible]	[illegible]	[illegible]	[illegible]	[illegible]	[illegible]	[illegible]	[illegible]	[illegible]	[illegible]	[illegible]	[illegible]	[illegible]
	[illegible]	[illegible]	[illegible]	[illegible]	[illegible]	[illegible]	[illegible]	[illegible]	[illegible]	[illegible]	[illegible]	[illegible]	[illegible]	[illegible]	[illegible]	[illegible]	[illegible]	[illegible]	[illegible]	[illegible]
	[illegible]	[illegible]	[illegible]	[illegible]	[illegible]	[illegible]	[illegible]	[illegible]	[illegible]	[illegible]	[illegible]	[illegible]	[illegible]	[illegible]	[illegible]	[illegible]	[illegible]	[illegible]	[illegible]	[illegible]
	[illegible]	[illegible]	[illegible]	[illegible]	[illegible]	[illegible]	[illegible]	[illegible]	[illegible]	[illegible]	[illegible]	[illegible]	[illegible]	[illegible]	[illegible]	[illegible]	[illegible]	[illegible]	[illegible]	[illegible]
	[illegible]	[illegible]	[illegible]	[illegible]	[illegible]	[illegible]	[illegible]	[illegible]	[illegible]	[illegible]	[illegible]	[illegible]	[illegible]	[illegible]	[illegible]	[illegible]	[illegible]	[illegible]	[illegible]	[illegible]
	[illegible]	[illegible]	[illegible]	[illegible]	[illegible]	[illegible]	[illegible]	[illegible]	[illegible]	[illegible]	[illegible]	[illegible]	[illegible]	[illegible]	[illegible]	[illegible]	[illegible]	[illegible]	[illegible]	[illegible]
	[illegible]	[illegible]	[illegible]	[illegible]	[illegible]	[illegible]	[illegible]	[illegible]	[illegible]	[illegible]	[illegible]	[illegible]	[illegible]	[illegible]	[illegible]	[illegible]	[illegible]	[illegible]	[illegible]	[illegible]
	[illegible]	[illegible]	[illegible]	[illegible]	[illegible]	[illegible]	[illegible]	[illegible]	[illegible]	[illegible]	[illegible]	[illegible]	[illegible]	[illegible]	[illegible]	[illegible]	[illegible]	[illegible]	[illegible]	[illegible]

DEATHS of Males and Females from different CAUSES registered in IRELAND, and in each of the FOUR PROVINCES, in the Year 1891.

Class.	CAUSES OF DEATH.	IRELAND.			LEINSTER.			MUNSTER.			ULSTER.			CONNAUGHT.		
		Males.	Fem.	Total.	Males.	Fem.	Total.	Males.	Fem.	Total.	Males.	Fem.	Total.	Males.	Fem.	Total.
	ALL CAUSES,	[illegible]	[illegible]	[illegible]	[illegible]	[illegible]	[illegible]	[illegible]	[illegible]	[illegible]	[illegible]	[illegible]	[illegible]	[illegible]	[illegible]	[illegible]
	(CLASSES.)															
I.	SPECIFIC FEBRILE OR ZYMOTIC DISEASES,	[illegible]	[illegible]	[illegible]	[illegible]	[illegible]	[illegible]	[illegible]	[illegible]	[illegible]	[illegible]	[illegible]	[illegible]	[illegible]	[illegible]	[illegible]
II.	PARASITIC DISEASES,	[illegible]	[illegible]	[illegible]	[illegible]	[illegible]	[illegible]	[illegible]	[illegible]	[illegible]	[illegible]	[illegible]	[illegible]	[illegible]	[illegible]	[illegible]
III.	DIETETIC	[illegible]	[illegible]	[illegible]	[illegible]	[illegible]	[illegible]	[illegible]	[illegible]	[illegible]	[illegible]	[illegible]	[illegible]	[illegible]	[illegible]	[illegible]
IV.	CONSTITUTIONAL,	[illegible]	[illegible]	[illegible]	[illegible]	[illegible]	[illegible]	[illegible]	[illegible]	[illegible]	[illegible]	[illegible]	[illegible]	[illegible]	[illegible]	[illegible]
V.	DEVELOPMENTAL,	[illegible]	[illegible]	[illegible]	[illegible]	[illegible]	[illegible]	[illegible]	[illegible]	[illegible]	[illegible]	[illegible]	[illegible]	[illegible]	[illegible]	[illegible]
VI.	LOCAL	[illegible]	[illegible]	[illegible]	[illegible]	[illegible]	[illegible]	[illegible]	[illegible]	[illegible]	[illegible]	[illegible]	[illegible]	[illegible]	[illegible]	[illegible]
VII.	VIOLENCE,	[illegible]	[illegible]	[illegible]	[illegible]	[illegible]	[illegible]	[illegible]	[illegible]	[illegible]	[illegible]	[illegible]	[illegible]	[illegible]	[illegible]	[illegible]
VIII.	ILL-DEFINED AND NOT SPECIFIED CAUSES,	[illegible]	[illegible]	[illegible]	[illegible]	[illegible]	[illegible]	[illegible]	[illegible]	[illegible]	[illegible]	[illegible]	[illegible]	[illegible]	[illegible]	[illegible]
	(ORDERS.)															
I.	1. Miasmatic Diseases,	[illegible]	[illegible]	[illegible]	[illegible]	[illegible]	[illegible]	[illegible]	[illegible]	[illegible]	[illegible]	[illegible]	[illegible]	[illegible]	[illegible]	[illegible]
	2. Diarrhoeal	[illegible]	[illegible]	[illegible]	[illegible]	[illegible]	[illegible]	[illegible]	[illegible]	[illegible]	[illegible]	[illegible]	[illegible]	[illegible]	[illegible]	[illegible]
	3. Malarial	[illegible]	[illegible]	[illegible]	[illegible]	[illegible]	[illegible]	[illegible]	[illegible]	[illegible]	[illegible]	[illegible]	[illegible]	[illegible]	[illegible]	[illegible]
	4. Zoogenous	[illegible]	[illegible]	[illegible]	[illegible]	[illegible]	[illegible]	[illegible]	[illegible]	[illegible]	[illegible]	[illegible]	[illegible]	[illegible]	[illegible]	[illegible]
	5. Venereal	[illegible]	[illegible]	[illegible]	[illegible]	[illegible]	[illegible]	[illegible]	[illegible]	[illegible]	[illegible]	[illegible]	[illegible]	[illegible]	[illegible]	[illegible]
	6. Septic	[illegible]	[illegible]	[illegible]	[illegible]	[illegible]	[illegible]	[illegible]	[illegible]	[illegible]	[illegible]	[illegible]	[illegible]	[illegible]	[illegible]	[illegible]
II.	Parasitic Diseases,	[illegible]	[illegible]	[illegible]	[illegible]	[illegible]	[illegible]	[illegible]	[illegible]	[illegible]	[illegible]	[illegible]	[illegible]	[illegible]	[illegible]	[illegible]
III.	Dietetic Diseases,	[illegible]	[illegible]	[illegible]	[illegible]	[illegible]	[illegible]	[illegible]	[illegible]	[illegible]	[illegible]	[illegible]	[illegible]	[illegible]	[illegible]	[illegible]
IV.	Constitutional Diseases,	[illegible]	[illegible]	[illegible]	[illegible]	[illegible]	[illegible]	[illegible]	[illegible]	[illegible]	[illegible]	[illegible]	[illegible]	[illegible]	[illegible]	[illegible]
V.	Developmental Diseases,	[illegible]	[illegible]	[illegible]	[illegible]	[illegible]	[illegible]	[illegible]	[illegible]	[illegible]	[illegible]	[illegible]	[illegible]	[illegible]	[illegible]	[illegible]
VI.	1. Diseases of Nervous System,	[illegible]	[illegible]	[illegible]	[illegible]	[illegible]	[illegible]	[illegible]	[illegible]	[illegible]	[illegible]	[illegible]	[illegible]	[illegible]	[illegible]	[illegible]
	2. " Organs of Special Sense,	[illegible]	[illegible]	[illegible]	[illegible]	[illegible]	[illegible]	[illegible]	[illegible]	[illegible]	[illegible]	[illegible]	[illegible]	[illegible]	[illegible]	[illegible]
	3. " Circulatory System,	[illegible]	[illegible]	[illegible]	[illegible]	[illegible]	[illegible]	[illegible]	[illegible]	[illegible]	[illegible]	[illegible]	[illegible]	[illegible]	[illegible]	[illegible]
	4. " Respiratory System,	[illegible]	[illegible]	[illegible]	[illegible]	[illegible]	[illegible]	[illegible]	[illegible]	[illegible]	[illegible]	[illegible]	[illegible]	[illegible]	[illegible]	[illegible]
	5. " Digestive System,	[illegible]	[illegible]	[illegible]	[illegible]	[illegible]	[illegible]	[illegible]	[illegible]	[illegible]	[illegible]	[illegible]	[illegible]	[illegible]	[illegible]	[illegible]
	6. " Lymphatic System and Ductless Glands,	[illegible]	[illegible]	[illegible]	[illegible]	[illegible]	[illegible]	[illegible]	[illegible]	[illegible]	[illegible]	[illegible]	[illegible]	[illegible]	[illegible]	[illegible]
	7. " Urinary System,	[illegible]	[illegible]	[illegible]	[illegible]	[illegible]	[illegible]	[illegible]	[illegible]	[illegible]	[illegible]	[illegible]	[illegible]	[illegible]	[illegible]	[illegible]
	8. " Reproductive System:—															
	(a) " Organs of Generation,	[illegible]	[illegible]	[illegible]	[illegible]	[illegible]	[illegible]	[illegible]	[illegible]	[illegible]	[illegible]	[illegible]	[illegible]	[illegible]	[illegible]	[illegible]
	(b) " Parturition,	[illegible]	[illegible]	[illegible]	[illegible]	[illegible]	[illegible]	[illegible]	[illegible]	[illegible]	[illegible]	[illegible]	[illegible]	[illegible]	[illegible]	[illegible]
	9. " Locomotive System,	[illegible]	[illegible]	[illegible]	[illegible]	[illegible]	[illegible]	[illegible]	[illegible]	[illegible]	[illegible]	[illegible]	[illegible]	[illegible]	[illegible]	[illegible]
	10. " Integumentary System,	[illegible]	[illegible]	[illegible]	[illegible]	[illegible]	[illegible]	[illegible]	[illegible]	[illegible]	[illegible]	[illegible]	[illegible]	[illegible]	[illegible]	[illegible]
VII.	1. Accident or Negligence,	[illegible]	[illegible]	[illegible]	[illegible]	[illegible]	[illegible]	[illegible]	[illegible]	[illegible]	[illegible]	[illegible]	[illegible]	[illegible]	[illegible]	[illegible]
	2. Homicide,	[illegible]	[illegible]	[illegible]	[illegible]	[illegible]	[illegible]	[illegible]	[illegible]	[illegible]	[illegible]	[illegible]	[illegible]	[illegible]	[illegible]	[illegible]
	3. Suicide,	[illegible]	[illegible]	[illegible]	[illegible]	[illegible]	[illegible]	[illegible]	[illegible]	[illegible]	[illegible]	[illegible]	[illegible]	[illegible]	[illegible]	[illegible]
	4. Execution,	[illegible]	[illegible]	[illegible]	[illegible]	[illegible]	[illegible]	[illegible]	[illegible]	[illegible]	[illegible]	[illegible]	[illegible]	[illegible]	[illegible]	[illegible]
VIII.	Ill-Defined and not Specified Causes,	[illegible]	[illegible]	[illegible]	[illegible]	[illegible]	[illegible]	[illegible]	[illegible]	[illegible]	[illegible]	[illegible]	[illegible]	[illegible]	[illegible]	[illegible]

[illegible] from different causes registered in IRELAND, and in each of the FOUR PROVINCES, in the Year 1881—*continued.*

Class.	CAUSES OF DEATH.	IRELAND.			LEINSTER.			MUNSTER.			ULSTER.			CONNAUGHT.		
		Males.	Fem.	Total.	Males.	Fem.	Total.	Males.	Fem.	Total.	Males.	Fem.	Total.	Males.	Fem.	Total.
I.	ORDER 1.															
	Small-pox: Vaccinated,	[illegible]	[illegible]	[illegible]	[illegible]	[illegible]	[illegible]	[illegible]	[illegible]	[illegible]	[illegible]	[illegible]	[illegible]	[illegible]	[illegible]	[illegible]
	Small-pox: Unvaccinated,	[illegible]	[illegible]	[illegible]	[illegible]	[illegible]	[illegible]	[illegible]	[illegible]	[illegible]	[illegible]	[illegible]	[illegible]	[illegible]	[illegible]	[illegible]
	Small-pox: No Statement,	[illegible]	[illegible]	[illegible]	[illegible]	[illegible]	[illegible]	[illegible]	[illegible]	[illegible]	[illegible]	[illegible]	[illegible]	[illegible]	[illegible]	[illegible]
	Chicken-pox,	[illegible]	[illegible]	[illegible]	[illegible]	[illegible]	[illegible]	[illegible]	[illegible]	[illegible]	[illegible]	[illegible]	[illegible]	[illegible]	[illegible]	[illegible]
	Measles,	[illegible]	[illegible]	[illegible]	[illegible]	[illegible]	[illegible]	[illegible]	[illegible]	[illegible]	[illegible]	[illegible]	[illegible]	[illegible]	[illegible]	[illegible]
	Epidemic Rose Rash,	[illegible]	[illegible]	[illegible]	[illegible]	[illegible]	[illegible]	[illegible]	[illegible]	[illegible]	[illegible]	[illegible]	[illegible]	[illegible]	[illegible]	[illegible]
	Scarlet Fever,	[illegible]	[illegible]	[illegible]	[illegible]	[illegible]	[illegible]	[illegible]	[illegible]	[illegible]	[illegible]	[illegible]	[illegible]	[illegible]	[illegible]	[illegible]
	Typhus,	[illegible]	[illegible]	[illegible]	[illegible]	[illegible]	[illegible]	[illegible]	[illegible]	[illegible]	[illegible]	[illegible]	[illegible]	[illegible]	[illegible]	[illegible]
	Relapsing Fever,	[illegible]	[illegible]	[illegible]	[illegible]	[illegible]	[illegible]	[illegible]	[illegible]	[illegible]	[illegible]	[illegible]	[illegible]	[illegible]	[illegible]	[illegible]
	Influenza,	[illegible]	[illegible]	[illegible]	[illegible]	[illegible]	[illegible]	[illegible]	[illegible]	[illegible]	[illegible]	[illegible]	[illegible]	[illegible]	[illegible]	[illegible]
	Whooping Cough,	[illegible]	[illegible]	[illegible]	[illegible]	[illegible]	[illegible]	[illegible]	[illegible]	[illegible]	[illegible]	[illegible]	[illegible]	[illegible]	[illegible]	[illegible]
	Mumps,	[illegible]	[illegible]	[illegible]	[illegible]	[illegible]	[illegible]	[illegible]	[illegible]	[illegible]	[illegible]	[illegible]	[illegible]	[illegible]	[illegible]	[illegible]
	Diphtheria,	[illegible]	[illegible]	[illegible]	[illegible]	[illegible]	[illegible]	[illegible]	[illegible]	[illegible]	[illegible]	[illegible]	[illegible]	[illegible]	[illegible]	[illegible]
	Cerebro-spinal Fever,	[illegible]	[illegible]	[illegible]	[illegible]	[illegible]	[illegible]	[illegible]	[illegible]	[illegible]	[illegible]	[illegible]	[illegible]	[illegible]	[illegible]	[illegible]
	Simple and ill-defined Fever,	[illegible]	[illegible]	[illegible]	[illegible]	[illegible]	[illegible]	[illegible]	[illegible]	[illegible]	[illegible]	[illegible]	[illegible]	[illegible]	[illegible]	[illegible]
	Enteric Fever,	[illegible]	[illegible]	[illegible]	[illegible]	[illegible]	[illegible]	[illegible]	[illegible]	[illegible]	[illegible]	[illegible]	[illegible]	[illegible]	[illegible]	[illegible]
	Other Miasmatic Diseases,	[illegible]	[illegible]	[illegible]	[illegible]	[illegible]	[illegible]	[illegible]	[illegible]	[illegible]	[illegible]	[illegible]	[illegible]	[illegible]	[illegible]	[illegible]
	ORDER 2.															
	Simple Cholera,	[illegible]	[illegible]	[illegible]	[illegible]	[illegible]	[illegible]	[illegible]	[illegible]	[illegible]	[illegible]	[illegible]	[illegible]	[illegible]	[illegible]	[illegible]
	Diarrhoea, Dysentery,	[illegible]	[illegible]	[illegible]	[illegible]	[illegible]	[illegible]	[illegible]	[illegible]	[illegible]	[illegible]	[illegible]	[illegible]	[illegible]	[illegible]	116
	ORDER 3.															
	Remittent Fever,	[illegible]	[illegible]	[illegible]	[illegible]	[illegible]	[illegible]	[illegible]	[illegible]	[illegible]	[illegible]	[illegible]	[illegible]	[illegible]	[illegible]	[illegible]
	Ague,	[illegible]	[illegible]	[illegible]	[illegible]	[illegible]	[illegible]	[illegible]	[illegible]	[illegible]	[illegible]	[illegible]	[illegible]	[illegible]	[illegible]	[illegible]
	ORDER 4.															
	Hydrophobia,	[illegible]	[illegible]	[illegible]	[illegible]	[illegible]	[illegible]	[illegible]	[illegible]	[illegible]	[illegible]	[illegible]	[illegible]	[illegible]	[illegible]	[illegible]
	Glanders,	[illegible]	[illegible]	[illegible]	[illegible]	[illegible]	[illegible]	[illegible]	[illegible]	[illegible]	[illegible]	[illegible]	[illegible]	[illegible]	[illegible]	[illegible]
	Splenic Fever,	[illegible]	[illegible]	[illegible]	[illegible]	[illegible]	[illegible]	[illegible]	[illegible]	[illegible]	[illegible]	[illegible]	[illegible]	[illegible]	[illegible]	[illegible]
	Cowpox and other effects of Vaccination,	[illegible]	[illegible]	[illegible]	[illegible]	[illegible]	[illegible]	[illegible]	[illegible]	[illegible]	[illegible]	[illegible]	[illegible]	[illegible]	[illegible]	[illegible]
	ORDER 5.															
	Syphilis,	[illegible]	[illegible]	[illegible]	[illegible]	[illegible]	[illegible]	[illegible]	[illegible]	[illegible]	[illegible]	[illegible]	[illegible]	[illegible]	[illegible]	[illegible]
	Gonorrhoea, Stricture of Urethra,	[illegible]	[illegible]	[illegible]	[illegible]	[illegible]	[illegible]	[illegible]	[illegible]	[illegible]	[illegible]	[illegible]	[illegible]	[illegible]	[illegible]	[illegible]
	ORDER 6.															
	Phagedaena,	[illegible]	[illegible]	[illegible]	[illegible]	[illegible]	[illegible]	[illegible]	[illegible]	[illegible]	[illegible]	[illegible]	[illegible]	[illegible]	[illegible]	[illegible]
	Erysipelas,	[illegible]	[illegible]	[illegible]	[illegible]	[illegible]	[illegible]	[illegible]	[illegible]	[illegible]	[illegible]	[illegible]	[illegible]	[illegible]	[illegible]	[illegible]
	Pyaemia, Septicaemia,	[illegible]	[illegible]	[illegible]	[illegible]	[illegible]	[illegible]	[illegible]	[illegible]	[illegible]	[illegible]	[illegible]	[illegible]	[illegible]	[illegible]	[illegible]
	Puerperal Fever,	[illegible]	[illegible]	[illegible]	[illegible]	[illegible]	[illegible]	[illegible]	[illegible]	[illegible]	[illegible]	[illegible]	[illegible]	[illegible]	[illegible]	[illegible]
II.	Thrush,	[illegible]	[illegible]	[illegible]	[illegible]	[illegible]	[illegible]	[illegible]	[illegible]	[illegible]	[illegible]	[illegible]	[illegible]	[illegible]	[illegible]	[illegible]
	Other Dis. from Vegetable Parasites,	[illegible]	[illegible]	[illegible]	[illegible]	[illegible]	[illegible]	[illegible]	[illegible]	[illegible]	[illegible]	[illegible]	[illegible]	[illegible]	[illegible]	[illegible]
	Hydatid Disease,	[illegible]	[illegible]	[illegible]	[illegible]	[illegible]	[illegible]	[illegible]	[illegible]	[illegible]	[illegible]	[illegible]	[illegible]	[illegible]	[illegible]	[illegible]
	Other Dis. from Animal Parasites,	[illegible]	[illegible]	[illegible]	[illegible]	[illegible]	[illegible]	[illegible]	[illegible]	[illegible]	[illegible]	[illegible]	[illegible]	[illegible]	[illegible]	[illegible]
III.	Starvation, Want of Breast Milk,	[illegible]	[illegible]	[illegible]	[illegible]	[illegible]	[illegible]	[illegible]	[illegible]	[illegible]	[illegible]	[illegible]	[illegible]	[illegible]	[illegible]	[illegible]
	Scurvy,	[illegible]	[illegible]	[illegible]	[illegible]	[illegible]	[illegible]	[illegible]	[illegible]	[illegible]	[illegible]	[illegible]	[illegible]	[illegible]	[illegible]	[illegible]
	Intemperance—Chronic Alcoholism,	[illegible]	[illegible]	[illegible]	[illegible]	[illegible]	[illegible]	[illegible]	[illegible]	[illegible]	[illegible]	[illegible]	[illegible]	[illegible]	[illegible]	[illegible]
	Intemperance—Delirium Tremens,	[illegible]	[illegible]	[illegible]	[illegible]	[illegible]	[illegible]	[illegible]	[illegible]	[illegible]	[illegible]	[illegible]	[illegible]	[illegible]	[illegible]	[illegible]
IV.	Rheumatic Fever, Rheumatism of Heart,	[illegible]	[illegible]	[illegible]	[illegible]	[illegible]	[illegible]	[illegible]	[illegible]	[illegible]	[illegible]	[illegible]	[illegible]	[illegible]	[illegible]	[illegible]
	Rheumatism,	[illegible]	[illegible]	[illegible]	[illegible]	[illegible]	[illegible]	[illegible]	[illegible]	[illegible]	[illegible]	[illegible]	[illegible]	[illegible]	[illegible]	[illegible]
	Gout,	[illegible]	[illegible]	[illegible]	[illegible]	[illegible]	[illegible]	[illegible]	[illegible]	[illegible]	[illegible]	[illegible]	[illegible]	[illegible]	[illegible]	[illegible]
	Rickets,	[illegible]	[illegible]	[illegible]	[illegible]	[illegible]	[illegible]	[illegible]	[illegible]	[illegible]	[illegible]	[illegible]	[illegible]	[illegible]	[illegible]	[illegible]
	Cancer,	[illegible]	[illegible]	[illegible]	[illegible]	[illegible]	[illegible]	[illegible]	[illegible]	[illegible]	[illegible]	[illegible]	[illegible]	[illegible]	[illegible]	[illegible]
	Tabes Mesenterica,	[illegible]	[illegible]	[illegible]	[illegible]	[illegible]	[illegible]	[illegible]	[illegible]	[illegible]	[illegible]	[illegible]	[illegible]	[illegible]	[illegible]	[illegible]
	Tubercular Meningitis, Acute Hydrocephalus,	[illegible]	[illegible]	[illegible]	[illegible]	[illegible]	[illegible]	[illegible]	[illegible]	[illegible]	[illegible]	[illegible]	[illegible]	[illegible]	[illegible]	[illegible]

DEATHS from different CAUSES registered in IRELAND, and in each of the FOUR PROVINCES, in the year 1891—*continued.*

Class	CAUSES OF DEATH.	IRELAND.			LEINSTER.			MUNSTER.			ULSTER.			CONNAUGHT.		
		Males.	Fem.	Total	Males.	Fem.	Total	Males.	Fem.	Total	Males.	Fem.	Total	Males.	Fem.	Total
IV. (con.)	Phthisis,	[illegible]	[illegible]	[illegible]	[illegible]	[illegible]	[illegible]	[illegible]	[illegible]	[illegible]	[illegible]	[illegible]	[illegible]	[illegible]	[illegible]	[illegible]
	Other forms of Tuberculous Scrofula,	[illegible]	[illegible]	[illegible]	[illegible]	[illegible]	[illegible]	[illegible]	[illegible]	[illegible]	[illegible]	[illegible]	[illegible]	[illegible]	[illegible]	[illegible]
	Purpura, Haemorrhagic Diathesis,	[illegible]	[illegible]	[illegible]	[illegible]	[illegible]	[illegible]	[illegible]	[illegible]	[illegible]	[illegible]	[illegible]	[illegible]	[illegible]	.	[illegible]
	Anaemia, Chlorosis, Leucocythaemia,	[illegible]	[illegible]	[illegible]	[illegible]	[illegible]	[illegible]	[illegible]	[illegible]	[illegible]	[illegible]	[illegible]	[illegible]	[illegible]	[illegible]	[illegible]
	Diabetes Mellitus,	[illegible]	[illegible]	[illegible]	[illegible]	[illegible]	[illegible]	[illegible]	[illegible]	[illegible]	[illegible]	[illegible]	[illegible]	[illegible]	[illegible]	[illegible]
	Other Constitutional Diseases,	-	[illegible]	[illegible]	.	[illegible]	[illegible]	.	[illegible]	[illegible]	-	[illegible]	[illegible]	-	-	.
V.	Premature Birth,	[illegible]	[illegible]	[illegible]	[illegible]	[illegible]	[illegible]	[illegible]	[illegible]	[illegible]	[illegible]	[illegible]	[illegible]	[illegible]	[illegible]	[illegible]
	Atelectasis,	[illegible]	[illegible]	[illegible]	[illegible]	[illegible]	[illegible]	[illegible]	.	[illegible]	[illegible]	[illegible]	[illegible]	[illegible]	[illegible]	[illegible]
	Cyanosis,	[illegible]	[illegible]	[illegible]	[illegible]	[illegible]	[illegible]	-	-	-	[illegible]	[illegible]	[illegible]	-	.	.
	Spina Bifida,	[illegible]	[illegible]	[illegible]	[illegible]	[illegible]	[illegible]	[illegible]	.	[illegible]	[illegible]	[illegible]	[illegible]	-	[illegible]	[illegible]
	Imperforate Anus,	[illegible]	[illegible]	[illegible]	-	[illegible]	[illegible]	.	-	.	[illegible]	-	[illegible]	-	.	.
	Cleft Palate, Harelip,	[illegible]	[illegible]	[illegible]	[illegible]	.	[illegible]	.	.	.	.	[illegible]	[illegible]	[illegible]	.	.
	Other Congenital defects,	[illegible]	[illegible]	[illegible]	[illegible]	[illegible]	[illegible]	[illegible]	[illegible]	[illegible]	[illegible]	[illegible]	[illegible]	[illegible]	-	[illegible]
	Old Age,	[illegible]	[illegible]	[illegible]	[illegible]	[illegible]	[illegible]	[illegible]	[illegible]	[illegible]	[illegible]	[illegible]	[illegible]	[illegible]	[illegible]	[illegible]
	ORDER 1.															
VI.	Inflammation of Brain or its Membranes,	[illegible]	[illegible]	[illegible]	[illegible]	[illegible]	[illegible]	[illegible]	[illegible]	[illegible]	[illegible]	[illegible]	[illegible]	[illegible]	[illegible]	[illegible]
	Apoplexy,	[illegible]	[illegible]	[illegible]	[illegible]	[illegible]	[illegible]	[illegible]	[illegible]	[illegible]	[illegible]	[illegible]	[illegible]	[illegible]	[illegible]	[illegible]
	Softening of Brain,	[illegible]	[illegible]	[illegible]	[illegible]	[illegible]	[illegible]	[illegible]	[illegible]	[illegible]	[illegible]	[illegible]	[illegible]	[illegible]	[illegible]	[illegible]
	Hemiplegia, Brain Paralysis,	[illegible]	[illegible]	[illegible]	[illegible]	[illegible]	[illegible]	[illegible]	[illegible]	[illegible]	[illegible]	[illegible]	[illegible]	[illegible]	[illegible]	[illegible]
	Paralysis agitans,	[illegible]	[illegible]	[illegible]	[illegible]	[illegible]	[illegible]	[illegible]	[illegible]	[illegible]	[illegible]	[illegible]	[illegible]		[illegible]	[illegible]
	Insanity, General Paralysis of Insane,	[illegible]	[illegible]	[illegible]	[illegible]	[illegible]	[illegible]	[illegible]	[illegible]	[illegible]	[illegible]	[illegible]	[illegible]	[illegible]	[illegible]	[illegible]
	Chorea,	.	[illegible]	[illegible]	-	[illegible]	[illegible]	.	[illegible]	[illegible]	-	[illegible]	[illegible]	.	[illegible]	[illegible]
	Epilepsy,	[illegible]	[illegible]	[illegible]	[illegible]	[illegible]	[illegible]	[illegible]	[illegible]	[illegible]	[illegible]	[illegible]	[illegible]	[illegible]	[illegible]	[illegible]
	Convulsions,	[illegible]	[illegible]	[illegible]	[illegible]	[illegible]	[illegible]	[illegible]	[illegible]	[illegible]	[illegible]	[illegible]	[illegible]	[illegible]	[illegible]	[illegible]
	Laryngismus Stridulus,	[illegible]	[illegible]	[illegible]	[illegible]	[illegible]	[illegible]	.	.	-	[illegible]	[illegible]	[illegible]	.	-	.
	Idiopathic Tetanus,	[illegible]	[illegible]	[illegible]	-	[illegible]	[illegible]	.	.	.	[illegible]	.	[illegible]	.	-	-
	Paraplegia and Diseases of Spinal Cord,	[illegible]	[illegible]	[illegible]	[illegible]	[illegible]	[illegible]	[illegible]	[illegible]	[illegible]	[illegible]	[illegible]	[illegible]	[illegible]	[illegible]	[illegible]
	Other Diseases of Nervous System,	[illegible]	[illegible]	[illegible]	[illegible]	[illegible]	[illegible]	[illegible]	[illegible]	[illegible]	[illegible]	[illegible]	[illegible]	[illegible]	[illegible]	[illegible]
	ORDER 2.															
	Otitis, Otorrhoea,	[illegible]	[illegible]	[illegible]	[illegible]	[illegible]	[illegible]	[illegible]	[illegible]	[illegible]	[illegible]	[illegible]	[illegible]	[illegible]	[illegible]	[illegible]
	Epistaxis and Dis. of Nose,	[illegible]	[illegible]	[illegible]	.	-	.	.	[illegible]	[illegible]	[illegible]	[illegible]	[illegible]	.	[illegible]	[illegible]
	Ophthalmia and Dis. of Eye,	[illegible]	[illegible]	[illegible]	[illegible]	[illegible]	[illegible]	.	[illegible]	[illegible]	[illegible]	.	[illegible]	[illegible]	[illegible]	[illegible]
	ORDER 3.															
	Endocarditis, Valvular Disease,	[illegible]	[illegible]	[illegible]	[illegible]	[illegible]	[illegible]	[illegible]	[illegible]	[illegible]	[illegible]	[illegible]	[illegible]	[illegible]	[illegible]	[illegible]
	Pericarditis,	[illegible]	[illegible]	[illegible]	[illegible]	[illegible]	[illegible]	[illegible]	[illegible]	[illegible]	[illegible]	[illegible]	[illegible]	[illegible]	.	[illegible]
	Hypertrophy of Heart,	[illegible]	[illegible]	[illegible]	[illegible]	[illegible]	[illegible]	[illegible]	[illegible]	[illegible]	[illegible]	[illegible]	[illegible]	[illegible]	.	[illegible]
	Angina Pectoris,	[illegible]	[illegible]	[illegible]	[illegible]	[illegible]	[illegible]	[illegible]	[illegible]	[illegible]	[illegible]	[illegible]	[illegible]	[illegible]	[illegible]	[illegible]
	Syncope,	[illegible]	[illegible]	[illegible]	[illegible]	[illegible]	[illegible]	[illegible]	[illegible]	[illegible]	[illegible]	[illegible]	[illegible]	[illegible]	[illegible]	[illegible]
	Aneurism,	[illegible]	[illegible]	[illegible]	[illegible]	[illegible]	[illegible]	[illegible]	[illegible]	[illegible]	[illegible]	[illegible]	[illegible]	[illegible]	[illegible]	[illegible]
	Senile Gangrene,	[illegible]	[illegible]	[illegible]	[illegible]	[illegible]	[illegible]	[illegible]	[illegible]	[illegible]	[illegible]	[illegible]	[illegible]	[illegible]	[illegible]	[illegible]
	Embolism, Thrombosis,	[illegible]	[illegible]	[illegible]	[illegible]	[illegible]	[illegible]	[illegible]	-	[illegible]	[illegible]	[illegible]	[illegible]	[illegible]	[illegible]	[illegible]
	Phlebitis,	[illegible]	[illegible]	[illegible]	[illegible]	[illegible]	[illegible]	-	.	-	[illegible]	[illegible]	[illegible]	-	.	.
	Varicose Veins,	[illegible]	[illegible]	[illegible]	[illegible]	[illegible]	[illegible]	.	.	-	.	[illegible]	[illegible]	[illegible]	-	[illegible]
	Other Diseases of Circulatory System,	[illegible]	[illegible]	[illegible]	[illegible]	[illegible]	[illegible]	[illegible]	[illegible]	[illegible]	[illegible]	[illegible]	[illegible]	[illegible]	[illegible]	[illegible]
	ORDER 4.															
	Laryngitis,	[illegible]	[illegible]	[illegible]	[illegible]	[illegible]	[illegible]	[illegible]	[illegible]	[illegible]	[illegible]	[illegible]	[illegible]	[illegible]	[illegible]	[illegible]
	Croup,	[illegible]	[illegible]	[illegible]	[illegible]	[illegible]	[illegible]	[illegible]	[illegible]	[illegible]	[illegible]	[illegible]	[illegible]	[illegible]	[illegible]	[illegible]
	Other Diseases of Larynx and Trachea,	[illegible]	[illegible]	[illegible]	[illegible]	[illegible]	[illegible]	[illegible]	.	[illegible]	[illegible]	[illegible]	[illegible]	.	[illegible]	[illegible]
	Emphysema, Asthma,	[illegible]	[illegible]	[illegible]	[illegible]	[illegible]	[illegible]	[illegible]	[illegible]	[illegible]	[illegible]	[illegible]	[illegible]	[illegible]	[illegible]	[illegible]
	Bronchitis,	[illegible]	[illegible]	[illegible]	[illegible]	[illegible]	[illegible]	[illegible]	[illegible]	[illegible]	[illegible]	[illegible]	[illegible]	[illegible]	[illegible]	[illegible]
	Pneumonia,	[illegible]	[illegible]	[illegible]	[illegible]	[illegible]	[illegible]	[illegible]	[illegible]	[illegible]	[illegible]	[illegible]	[illegible]	[illegible]	[illegible]	[illegible]
	Pleurisy,	[illegible]	[illegible]	[illegible]	[illegible]	[illegible]	[illegible]	[illegible]	[illegible]	[illegible]	[illegible]	[illegible]	[illegible]	[illegible]	[illegible]	[illegible]
	Other Diseases of Respiratory System,	[illegible]	[illegible]	[illegible]	[illegible]	[illegible]	[illegible]	[illegible]	[illegible]	[illegible]	[illegible]	[illegible]	[illegible]	[illegible]	[illegible]	[illegible]

DEATHS from different Causes registered in IRELAND, and in each of the FOUR PROVINCES, in the Year 1891—*continued.*

Class	Causes of Death.	Ireland.			Leinster.			Munster.			Ulster.			Connaught.		
		Males.	Fem.	Total.	Males.	Fem.	Total.	Males.	Fem.	Total.	Males.	Fem.	Total.	Males.	Fem.	Total.
[illegible]	ORDER 4.															
	Dentition,	[illegible]	[illegible]	[illegible]	[illegible]	[illegible]	[illegible]	[illegible]	[illegible]	[illegible]	[illegible]	[illegible]	[illegible]	[illegible]	[illegible]	[illegible]
	Sore Throat, Quinsy,	[illegible]	[illegible]	[illegible]	[illegible]	[illegible]	[illegible]	[illegible]	[illegible]	[illegible]	[illegible]	[illegible]	[illegible]	[illegible]	[illegible]	[illegible]
	Dyspepsia,	[illegible]	[illegible]	[illegible]	[illegible]	[illegible]	[illegible]	[illegible]	[illegible]	[illegible]	[illegible]	[illegible]	[illegible]	[illegible]	[illegible]	[illegible]
	Haematemesis,	[illegible]	[illegible]	[illegible]	[illegible]	[illegible]	[illegible]	[illegible]	[illegible]	[illegible]	[illegible]	[illegible]	[illegible]	[illegible]	[illegible]	[illegible]
	Melaena,	[illegible]	[illegible]	[illegible]	[illegible]	[illegible]	[illegible]	[illegible]	[illegible]	[illegible]	[illegible]	[illegible]	[illegible]	[illegible]	[illegible]	[illegible]
	Diseases of Stomach,	[illegible]	[illegible]	[illegible]	[illegible]	[illegible]	[illegible]	[illegible]	[illegible]	[illegible]	[illegible]	[illegible]	[illegible]	[illegible]	[illegible]	[illegible]
	Enteritis,	[illegible]	[illegible]	[illegible]	[illegible]	[illegible]	[illegible]	[illegible]	[illegible]	[illegible]	[illegible]	[illegible]	[illegible]	[illegible]	[illegible]	[illegible]
	Ulceration of Intestines,	[illegible]	[illegible]	[illegible]	[illegible]	[illegible]	[illegible]	[illegible]	[illegible]	[illegible]	[illegible]	[illegible]	[illegible]	[illegible]	[illegible]	[illegible]
	Ileus, Obstruction of Intestines,	[illegible]	[illegible]	[illegible]	[illegible]	[illegible]	[illegible]	[illegible]	[illegible]	[illegible]	[illegible]	[illegible]	[illegible]	[illegible]	[illegible]	[illegible]
	Stricture or Strangulation of Intestines,	[illegible]	[illegible]	[illegible]	[illegible]	[illegible]	[illegible]	[illegible]	[illegible]	[illegible]	[illegible]	[illegible]	[illegible]	[illegible]	[illegible]	[illegible]
	Intussusception of Intestines,	[illegible]	[illegible]	[illegible]	[illegible]	[illegible]	[illegible]	[illegible]	[illegible]	[illegible]	[illegible]	[illegible]	[illegible]	[illegible]	[illegible]	[illegible]
	Hernia,	[illegible]	[illegible]	[illegible]	[illegible]	[illegible]	[illegible]	[illegible]	[illegible]	[illegible]	[illegible]	[illegible]	[illegible]	[illegible]	[illegible]	[illegible]
	Fistula,	[illegible]	[illegible]	[illegible]	[illegible]	[illegible]	[illegible]	[illegible]	[illegible]	[illegible]	[illegible]	[illegible]	[illegible]	[illegible]	[illegible]	[illegible]
	Peritonitis,	[illegible]	[illegible]	[illegible]	[illegible]	[illegible]	[illegible]	[illegible]	[illegible]	[illegible]	[illegible]	[illegible]	[illegible]	[illegible]	[illegible]	[illegible]
	Ascites,	[illegible]	[illegible]	[illegible]	[illegible]	[illegible]	[illegible]	[illegible]	[illegible]	[illegible]	[illegible]	[illegible]	[illegible]	[illegible]	[illegible]	[illegible]
	Gallstones,	[illegible]	[illegible]	[illegible]	[illegible]	[illegible]	[illegible]	[illegible]	[illegible]	[illegible]	[illegible]	[illegible]	[illegible]	[illegible]	[illegible]	[illegible]
	Cirrhosis of Liver,	[illegible]	[illegible]	[illegible]	[illegible]	[illegible]	[illegible]	[illegible]	[illegible]	[illegible]	[illegible]	[illegible]	[illegible]	[illegible]	[illegible]	[illegible]
	Other Diseases of Liver,	[illegible]	[illegible]	[illegible]	[illegible]	[illegible]	[illegible]	[illegible]	[illegible]	[illegible]	[illegible]	[illegible]	[illegible]	[illegible]	[illegible]	[illegible]
	Other Diseases of Digestive System,	[illegible]	[illegible]	[illegible]	[illegible]	[illegible]	[illegible]	[illegible]	[illegible]	[illegible]	[illegible]	[illegible]	[illegible]	[illegible]	[illegible]	[illegible]
	ORDER 6.															
	Diseases of Spleen,	[illegible]	[illegible]	[illegible]	[illegible]	[illegible]	[illegible]	[illegible]	[illegible]	[illegible]	[illegible]	[illegible]	[illegible]	[illegible]	[illegible]	[illegible]
	Dis. of Lymphatic System,	[illegible]	[illegible]	[illegible]	[illegible]	[illegible]	[illegible]	[illegible]	[illegible]	[illegible]	[illegible]	[illegible]	[illegible]	[illegible]	[illegible]	[illegible]
	Dis. of Thyroid Body,	[illegible]	[illegible]	[illegible]	[illegible]	[illegible]	[illegible]	[illegible]	[illegible]	[illegible]	[illegible]	[illegible]	[illegible]	[illegible]	[illegible]	[illegible]
	Dis. of Suprarenal Capsules,	[illegible]	[illegible]	[illegible]	[illegible]	[illegible]	[illegible]	[illegible]	[illegible]	[illegible]	[illegible]	[illegible]	[illegible]	[illegible]	[illegible]	[illegible]
	ORDER 7.															
	Acute Nephritis,	[illegible]	[illegible]	[illegible]	[illegible]	[illegible]	[illegible]	[illegible]	[illegible]	[illegible]	[illegible]	[illegible]	[illegible]	[illegible]	[illegible]	[illegible]
	Bright's Disease,	[illegible]	[illegible]	[illegible]	[illegible]	[illegible]	[illegible]	[illegible]	[illegible]	[illegible]	[illegible]	[illegible]	[illegible]	[illegible]	[illegible]	[illegible]
	Calculus,	[illegible]	[illegible]	[illegible]	[illegible]	[illegible]	[illegible]	[illegible]	[illegible]	[illegible]	[illegible]	[illegible]	[illegible]	[illegible]	[illegible]	[illegible]
	Suppression of Urine,	[illegible]	[illegible]	[illegible]	[illegible]	[illegible]	[illegible]	[illegible]	[illegible]	[illegible]	[illegible]	[illegible]	[illegible]	[illegible]	[illegible]	[illegible]
	Cystitis,	[illegible]	[illegible]	[illegible]	[illegible]	[illegible]	[illegible]	[illegible]	[illegible]	[illegible]	[illegible]	[illegible]	[illegible]	[illegible]	[illegible]	[illegible]
	Haematuria,	[illegible]	[illegible]	[illegible]	[illegible]	[illegible]	[illegible]	[illegible]	[illegible]	[illegible]	[illegible]	[illegible]	[illegible]	[illegible]	[illegible]	[illegible]
	Diseases of Bladder and of Prostate,	[illegible]	[illegible]	[illegible]	[illegible]	[illegible]	[illegible]	[illegible]	[illegible]	[illegible]	[illegible]	[illegible]	[illegible]	[illegible]	[illegible]	[illegible]
	Other Diseases of Urinary System,	[illegible]	[illegible]	[illegible]	[illegible]	[illegible]	[illegible]	[illegible]	[illegible]	[illegible]	[illegible]	[illegible]	[illegible]	[illegible]	[illegible]	[illegible]
	ORDER 8 (a).															
	Ovarian Disease,	[illegible]	[illegible]	[illegible]	[illegible]	[illegible]	[illegible]	[illegible]	[illegible]	[illegible]	[illegible]	[illegible]	[illegible]	[illegible]	[illegible]	[illegible]
	Diseases of Uterus and Vagina,	[illegible]	[illegible]	[illegible]	[illegible]	[illegible]	[illegible]	[illegible]	[illegible]	[illegible]	[illegible]	[illegible]	[illegible]	[illegible]	[illegible]	[illegible]
	Disorders of Menstruation,	[illegible]	[illegible]	[illegible]	[illegible]	[illegible]	[illegible]	[illegible]	[illegible]	[illegible]	[illegible]	[illegible]	[illegible]	[illegible]	[illegible]	[illegible]
	Pelvic Abscess,	[illegible]	[illegible]	[illegible]	[illegible]	[illegible]	[illegible]	[illegible]	[illegible]	[illegible]	[illegible]	[illegible]	[illegible]	[illegible]	[illegible]	[illegible]
	Perineal Abscess,	[illegible]	[illegible]	[illegible]	[illegible]	[illegible]	[illegible]	[illegible]	[illegible]	[illegible]	[illegible]	[illegible]	[illegible]	[illegible]	[illegible]	[illegible]
	Diseases of Testes, Penis, Scrotum, &c.	[illegible]	[illegible]	[illegible]	[illegible]	[illegible]	[illegible]	[illegible]	[illegible]	[illegible]	[illegible]	[illegible]	[illegible]	[illegible]	[illegible]	[illegible]
	ORDER 8 (b).															
	Abortion, Miscarriage,	[illegible]	[illegible]	[illegible]	[illegible]	[illegible]	[illegible]	[illegible]	[illegible]	[illegible]	[illegible]	[illegible]	[illegible]	[illegible]	[illegible]	[illegible]
	Puerperal Mania,	[illegible]	[illegible]	[illegible]	[illegible]	[illegible]	[illegible]	[illegible]	[illegible]	[illegible]	[illegible]	[illegible]	[illegible]	[illegible]	[illegible]	[illegible]
	Puerperal Convulsions,	[illegible]	[illegible]	[illegible]	[illegible]	[illegible]	[illegible]	[illegible]	[illegible]	[illegible]	[illegible]	[illegible]	[illegible]	[illegible]	[illegible]	[illegible]
	Placenta praevia, Flooding,	[illegible]	[illegible]	[illegible]	[illegible]	[illegible]	[illegible]	[illegible]	[illegible]	[illegible]	[illegible]	[illegible]	[illegible]	[illegible]	[illegible]	[illegible]
	Phlegmasia Dolens,	[illegible]	[illegible]	[illegible]	[illegible]	[illegible]	[illegible]	[illegible]	[illegible]	[illegible]	[illegible]	[illegible]	[illegible]	[illegible]	[illegible]	[illegible]
	Other Accidents of Childbirth,	[illegible]	[illegible]	[illegible]	[illegible]	[illegible]	[illegible]	[illegible]	[illegible]	[illegible]	[illegible]	[illegible]	[illegible]	[illegible]	[illegible]	[illegible]
	ORDER 9.															
	Caries, Necrosis,	[illegible]	[illegible]	[illegible]	[illegible]	[illegible]	[illegible]	[illegible]	[illegible]	[illegible]	[illegible]	[illegible]	[illegible]	[illegible]	[illegible]	[illegible]
	Arthritis, Ostitis, Periostitis,	[illegible]	[illegible]	[illegible]	[illegible]	[illegible]	[illegible]	[illegible]	[illegible]	[illegible]	[illegible]	[illegible]	[illegible]	[illegible]	[illegible]	[illegible]
	Other Diseases of Organs of Locomotion,	[illegible]	[illegible]	[illegible]	[illegible]	[illegible]	[illegible]	[illegible]	[illegible]	[illegible]	[illegible]	[illegible]	[illegible]	[illegible]	[illegible]	[illegible]

DEATHS from different Causes registered in IRELAND, and in each of the FOUR PROVINCES, in the Year 1891—*continued.*

Class.	CAUSES OF DEATH.	IRELAND.			LEINSTER.			MUNSTER.			ULSTER.			CONNAUGHT.		
		Males.	Fem.	Total.	Males.	Fem.	Total.	Males.	Fem.	Total.	Males.	Fem.	Total.	Males.	Fem.	Total.
VI.—*cont.*	Diseases of Skin.															
	Carbuncle,	[illegible]	[illegible]	[illegible]	[illegible]	[illegible]	[illegible]	[illegible]	[illegible]	[illegible]	[illegible]	[illegible]	[illegible]	[illegible]	[illegible]	[illegible]
	Phlegmon, Cellulitis,	[illegible]	[illegible]	[illegible]	[illegible]	[illegible]	[illegible]	[illegible]	[illegible]	[illegible]	[illegible]	[illegible]	[illegible]	[illegible]	[illegible]	[illegible]
	Lupus,	[illegible]	[illegible]	[illegible]	[illegible]	[illegible]	[illegible]	[illegible]	[illegible]	[illegible]	[illegible]	[illegible]	[illegible]	[illegible]	[illegible]	[illegible]
	Ulcer, Bedsore,	[illegible]	[illegible]	[illegible]	[illegible]	[illegible]	[illegible]	[illegible]	[illegible]	[illegible]	[illegible]	[illegible]	[illegible]	[illegible]	[illegible]	[illegible]
	Eczema,	[illegible]	[illegible]	[illegible]	[illegible]	[illegible]	[illegible]	[illegible]	[illegible]	[illegible]	[illegible]	[illegible]	[illegible]	[illegible]	[illegible]	[illegible]
	Pemphigus,	[illegible]	[illegible]	[illegible]	[illegible]	[illegible]	[illegible]	[illegible]	[illegible]	[illegible]	[illegible]	[illegible]	[illegible]	[illegible]	[illegible]	[illegible]
	Other Diseases of Integumentary System,	[illegible]	[illegible]	[illegible]	[illegible]	[illegible]	[illegible]	[illegible]	[illegible]	[illegible]	[illegible]	[illegible]	[illegible]	[illegible]	[illegible]	[illegible]
	Accident or Negligence.															
VII.	In Mines and Quarries,	[illegible]	[illegible]	[illegible]	[illegible]	[illegible]	[illegible]	[illegible]	[illegible]	[illegible]	[illegible]	[illegible]	[illegible]	[illegible]	[illegible]	[illegible]
	Vehicles and Horses,	[illegible]	[illegible]	[illegible]	[illegible]	[illegible]	[illegible]	[illegible]	[illegible]	[illegible]	[illegible]	[illegible]	[illegible]	[illegible]	[illegible]	[illegible]
	Ships, Boats, Docks and Drowning,	[illegible]	[illegible]	[illegible]	[illegible]	[illegible]	[illegible]	[illegible]	[illegible]	[illegible]	[illegible]	[illegible]	[illegible]	[illegible]	[illegible]	[illegible]
	Building Operations,	[illegible]	[illegible]	[illegible]	[illegible]	[illegible]	[illegible]	[illegible]	[illegible]	[illegible]	[illegible]	[illegible]	[illegible]	[illegible]	[illegible]	[illegible]
	Machinery,	[illegible]	[illegible]	[illegible]	[illegible]	[illegible]	[illegible]	[illegible]	[illegible]	[illegible]	[illegible]	[illegible]	[illegible]	[illegible]	[illegible]	[illegible]
	Weapons & Implements,	[illegible]	[illegible]	[illegible]	[illegible]	[illegible]	[illegible]	[illegible]	[illegible]	[illegible]	[illegible]	[illegible]	[illegible]	[illegible]	[illegible]	[illegible]
	Burns and Scalds,	[illegible]	[illegible]	[illegible]	[illegible]	[illegible]	[illegible]	[illegible]	[illegible]	[illegible]	[illegible]	[illegible]	[illegible]	[illegible]	[illegible]	[illegible]
	Poison, Pois. Vapours,	[illegible]	[illegible]	[illegible]	[illegible]	[illegible]	[illegible]	[illegible]	[illegible]	[illegible]	[illegible]	[illegible]	[illegible]	[illegible]	[illegible]	[illegible]
	Drowning,	[illegible]	[illegible]	[illegible]	[illegible]	[illegible]	[illegible]	[illegible]	[illegible]	[illegible]	[illegible]	[illegible]	[illegible]	[illegible]	[illegible]	[illegible]
	Suffocation,	[illegible]	[illegible]	[illegible]	[illegible]	[illegible]	[illegible]	[illegible]	[illegible]	[illegible]	[illegible]	[illegible]	[illegible]	[illegible]	[illegible]	[illegible]
	Falls,	[illegible]	[illegible]	[illegible]	[illegible]	[illegible]	[illegible]	[illegible]	[illegible]	[illegible]	[illegible]	[illegible]	[illegible]	[illegible]	[illegible]	[illegible]
	Weather Agencies,	[illegible]	[illegible]	[illegible]	[illegible]	[illegible]	[illegible]	[illegible]	[illegible]	[illegible]	[illegible]	[illegible]	[illegible]	[illegible]	[illegible]	[illegible]
	Otherwise, or not stated,	[illegible]	[illegible]	[illegible]	[illegible]	[illegible]	[illegible]	[illegible]	[illegible]	[illegible]	[illegible]	[illegible]	[illegible]	[illegible]	[illegible]	[illegible]
	Homicide.															
	Homicide,	[illegible]	[illegible]	[illegible]	[illegible]	[illegible]	[illegible]	[illegible]	[illegible]	[illegible]	[illegible]	[illegible]	[illegible]	[illegible]	[illegible]	[illegible]
	Suicide.															
	Suicide,	[illegible]	[illegible]	[illegible]	[illegible]	[illegible]	[illegible]	[illegible]	[illegible]	[illegible]	[illegible]	[illegible]	[illegible]	[illegible]	[illegible]	[illegible]
	Execution.															
	Execution,	[illegible]	—	[illegible]	[illegible]	[illegible]	[illegible]	[illegible]	[illegible]	[illegible]	[illegible]	[illegible]	—	—	[illegible]	[illegible]
VIII.	Dropsy,	[illegible]	[illegible]	[illegible]	[illegible]	[illegible]	[illegible]	[illegible]	[illegible]	[illegible]	[illegible]	[illegible]	[illegible]	[illegible]	[illegible]	[illegible]
	Debility, Atrophy, Inanition,	[illegible]	[illegible]	[illegible]	[illegible]	[illegible]	[illegible]	[illegible]	[illegible]	[illegible]	[illegible]	[illegible]	[illegible]	[illegible]	[illegible]	[illegible]
	Mortification,	[illegible]	[illegible]	[illegible]	[illegible]	[illegible]	[illegible]	[illegible]	[illegible]	[illegible]	[illegible]	[illegible]	[illegible]	[illegible]	[illegible]	[illegible]
	Tumour,	[illegible]	[illegible]	[illegible]	[illegible]	[illegible]	[illegible]	[illegible]	[illegible]	[illegible]	[illegible]	[illegible]	[illegible]	[illegible]	[illegible]	[illegible]
	Abscess,	[illegible]	[illegible]	[illegible]	[illegible]	[illegible]	[illegible]	[illegible]	[illegible]	[illegible]	[illegible]	[illegible]	[illegible]	[illegible]	[illegible]	[illegible]
	Haemorrhage,	[illegible]	[illegible]	[illegible]	[illegible]	[illegible]	[illegible]	—	[illegible]	[illegible]	[illegible]	[illegible]	[illegible]	[illegible]	[illegible]	[illegible]
	Sudden (cause unascertained),	[illegible]	[illegible]	[illegible]	[illegible]	[illegible]	[illegible]	[illegible]	[illegible]	[illegible]	[illegible]	[illegible]	[illegible]	[illegible]	[illegible]	[illegible]
	Not specified or ill-defined,	[illegible]	[illegible]	[illegible]	[illegible]	[illegible]	[illegible]	[illegible]	[illegible]	[illegible]	[illegible]	[illegible]	[illegible]	[illegible]	[illegible]	[illegible]

TOTAL NUMBER OF DEATHS.—NUMBER of PERSONS who died (1), in INFIRMARIES and GENERAL [illegible] OWN HOMES, &c.; NUMBER of DEATHS from the PRINCIPAL CAUSES; and [illegible] REGISTRARS' DISTRICTS

No.	PROVINCES and COUNTIES.	Total Number of Deaths.	Number of Persons who Died: [illegible]	[illegible]	[illegible]	[illegible]	CAUSES OF [illegible]: [illegible]	[illegible]	[illegible]	[illegible]	[illegible]	[illegible]	[illegible]	[illegible]	[illegible]	[illegible]	[illegible]	[illegible]	[illegible]	[illegible]	[illegible]	[illegible]
	IRELAND,	[illegible]	[illegible]	[illegible]	[illegible]	[illegible]	[illegible]	[illegible]	[illegible]	[illegible]	[illegible]	[illegible]	[illegible]	[illegible]	[illegible]	[illegible]	[illegible]	[illegible]	[illegible]	[illegible]	[illegible]	[illegible]
No.	PROVINCES.																					
I.	LEINSTER,	[illegible]	[illegible]	[illegible]	[illegible]	[illegible]	[illegible]	[illegible]	[illegible]	[illegible]	[illegible]	[illegible]	[illegible]	[illegible]	[illegible]	[illegible]	[illegible]	[illegible]	[illegible]	[illegible]	[illegible]	[illegible]
II.	MUNSTER,	[illegible]	[illegible]	[illegible]	[illegible]	[illegible]	[illegible]	[illegible]	[illegible]	[illegible]	[illegible]	[illegible]	[illegible]	[illegible]	[illegible]	[illegible]	[illegible]	[illegible]	[illegible]	[illegible]	[illegible]	[illegible]
III.	ULSTER,	[illegible]	[illegible]	[illegible]	[illegible]	[illegible]	[illegible]	[illegible]	[illegible]	[illegible]	[illegible]	[illegible]	[illegible]	[illegible]	[illegible]	[illegible]	[illegible]	[illegible]	[illegible]	[illegible]	[illegible]	[illegible]
IV.	CONNAUGHT,	[illegible]	[illegible]	[illegible]	[illegible]	[illegible]	[illegible]	[illegible]	[illegible]	[illegible]	[illegible]	[illegible]	[illegible]	[illegible]	[illegible]	[illegible]	[illegible]	[illegible]	[illegible]	[illegible]	[illegible]	[illegible]
	I.—PROVINCE [illegible]																					
1	Carlow,	[illegible]	[illegible]	[illegible]	[illegible]	[illegible]	[illegible]	[illegible]	[illegible]	[illegible]	[illegible]	[illegible]	[illegible]	[illegible]	[illegible]	[illegible]	[illegible]	[illegible]	[illegible]	[illegible]	[illegible]	[illegible]
2	Dublin,	[illegible]	[illegible]	[illegible]	[illegible]	[illegible]	[illegible]	[illegible]	[illegible]	[illegible]	[illegible]	[illegible]	[illegible]	[illegible]	[illegible]	[illegible]	[illegible]	[illegible]	[illegible]	[illegible]	[illegible]	[illegible]
3	Kildare,	[illegible]	[illegible]	[illegible]	[illegible]	[illegible]	[illegible]	[illegible]	[illegible]	[illegible]	[illegible]	[illegible]	[illegible]	[illegible]	[illegible]	[illegible]	[illegible]	[illegible]	[illegible]	[illegible]	[illegible]	[illegible]
4	Kilkenny,	[illegible]	[illegible]	[illegible]	[illegible]	[illegible]	[illegible]	[illegible]	[illegible]	[illegible]	[illegible]	[illegible]	[illegible]	[illegible]	[illegible]	[illegible]	[illegible]	[illegible]	[illegible]	[illegible]	[illegible]	[illegible]
5	King's,	[illegible]	[illegible]	[illegible]	[illegible]	[illegible]	[illegible]	[illegible]	[illegible]	[illegible]	[illegible]	[illegible]	[illegible]	[illegible]	[illegible]	[illegible]	[illegible]	[illegible]	[illegible]	[illegible]	[illegible]	[illegible]
6	Longford,	[illegible]	[illegible]	[illegible]	[illegible]	[illegible]	[illegible]	[illegible]	[illegible]	[illegible]	[illegible]	[illegible]	[illegible]	[illegible]	[illegible]	[illegible]	[illegible]	[illegible]	[illegible]	[illegible]	[illegible]	[illegible]
7	Louth, and Co. of the Town of Drogheda,	[illegible]	[illegible]	[illegible]	[illegible]	[illegible]	[illegible]	[illegible]	[illegible]	[illegible]	[illegible]	[illegible]	[illegible]	[illegible]	[illegible]	[illegible]	[illegible]	[illegible]	[illegible]	[illegible]	[illegible]	[illegible]
8	Meath,	[illegible]	[illegible]	[illegible]	[illegible]	[illegible]	[illegible]	[illegible]	[illegible]	[illegible]	[illegible]	[illegible]	[illegible]	[illegible]	[illegible]	[illegible]	[illegible]	[illegible]	[illegible]	[illegible]	[illegible]	[illegible]
9	Queen's,	[illegible]	[illegible]	[illegible]	[illegible]	[illegible]	[illegible]	[illegible]	[illegible]	[illegible]	[illegible]	[illegible]	[illegible]	[illegible]	[illegible]	[illegible]	[illegible]	[illegible]	[illegible]	[illegible]	[illegible]	[illegible]
10	Westmeath,	[illegible]	[illegible]	[illegible]	[illegible]	[illegible]	[illegible]	[illegible]	[illegible]	[illegible]	[illegible]	[illegible]	[illegible]	[illegible]	[illegible]	[illegible]	[illegible]	[illegible]	[illegible]	[illegible]	[illegible]	[illegible]
11	Wexford,	[illegible]	[illegible]	[illegible]	[illegible]	[illegible]	[illegible]	[illegible]	[illegible]	[illegible]	[illegible]	[illegible]	[illegible]	[illegible]	[illegible]	[illegible]	[illegible]	[illegible]	[illegible]	[illegible]	[illegible]	[illegible]
12	Wicklow,	[illegible]	[illegible]	[illegible]	[illegible]	[illegible]	[illegible]	[illegible]	[illegible]	[illegible]	[illegible]	[illegible]	[illegible]	[illegible]	[illegible]	[illegible]	[illegible]	[illegible]	[illegible]	[illegible]	[illegible]	[illegible]
	II.—PROVINCE [illegible]																					
13	Clare,	[illegible]	[illegible]	[illegible]	[illegible]	[illegible]	[illegible]	[illegible]	[illegible]	[illegible]	[illegible]	[illegible]	[illegible]	[illegible]	[illegible]	[illegible]	[illegible]	[illegible]	[illegible]	[illegible]	[illegible]	[illegible]
14	Cork,	[illegible]	[illegible]	[illegible]	[illegible]	[illegible]	[illegible]	[illegible]	[illegible]	[illegible]	[illegible]	[illegible]	[illegible]	[illegible]	[illegible]	[illegible]	[illegible]	[illegible]	[illegible]	[illegible]	[illegible]	[illegible]
15	Kerry,	[illegible]	[illegible]	[illegible]	[illegible]	[illegible]	[illegible]	[illegible]	[illegible]	[illegible]	[illegible]	[illegible]	[illegible]	[illegible]	[illegible]	[illegible]	[illegible]	[illegible]	[illegible]	[illegible]	[illegible]	[illegible]
16	Limerick,	[illegible]	[illegible]	[illegible]	[illegible]	[illegible]	[illegible]	[illegible]	[illegible]	[illegible]	[illegible]	[illegible]	[illegible]	[illegible]	[illegible]	[illegible]	[illegible]	[illegible]	[illegible]	[illegible]	[illegible]	[illegible]
17	Tipperary,	[illegible]	[illegible]	[illegible]	[illegible]	[illegible]	[illegible]	[illegible]	[illegible]	[illegible]	[illegible]	[illegible]	[illegible]	[illegible]	[illegible]	[illegible]	[illegible]	[illegible]	[illegible]	[illegible]	[illegible]	[illegible]
18	Waterford,	[illegible]	[illegible]	[illegible]	[illegible]	[illegible]	[illegible]	[illegible]	[illegible]	[illegible]	[illegible]	[illegible]	[illegible]	[illegible]	[illegible]	[illegible]	[illegible]	[illegible]	[illegible]	[illegible]	[illegible]	[illegible]
	III.—PROVINCE [illegible]																					
19	Antrim,	[illegible]	[illegible]	[illegible]	[illegible]	[illegible]	[illegible]	[illegible]	[illegible]	[illegible]	[illegible]	[illegible]	[illegible]	[illegible]	[illegible]	[illegible]	[illegible]	[illegible]	[illegible]	[illegible]	[illegible]	[illegible]
20	Armagh,	[illegible]	[illegible]	[illegible]	[illegible]	[illegible]	[illegible]	[illegible]	[illegible]	[illegible]	[illegible]	[illegible]	[illegible]	[illegible]	[illegible]	[illegible]	[illegible]	[illegible]	[illegible]	[illegible]	[illegible]	[illegible]
21	Cavan,	[illegible]	[illegible]	[illegible]	[illegible]	[illegible]	[illegible]	[illegible]	[illegible]	[illegible]	[illegible]	[illegible]	[illegible]	[illegible]	[illegible]	[illegible]	[illegible]	[illegible]	[illegible]	[illegible]	[illegible]	[illegible]
22	Donegal,	[illegible]	[illegible]	[illegible]	[illegible]	[illegible]	[illegible]	[illegible]	[illegible]	[illegible]	[illegible]	[illegible]	[illegible]	[illegible]	[illegible]	[illegible]	[illegible]	[illegible]	[illegible]	[illegible]	[illegible]	[illegible]
23	Down,	[illegible]	[illegible]	[illegible]	[illegible]	[illegible]	[illegible]	[illegible]	[illegible]	[illegible]	[illegible]	[illegible]	[illegible]	[illegible]	[illegible]	[illegible]	[illegible]	[illegible]	[illegible]	[illegible]	[illegible]	[illegible]
24	Fermanagh,	[illegible]	[illegible]	[illegible]	[illegible]	[illegible]	[illegible]	[illegible]	[illegible]	[illegible]	[illegible]	[illegible]	[illegible]	[illegible]	[illegible]	[illegible]	[illegible]	[illegible]	[illegible]	[illegible]	[illegible]	[illegible]
25	Londonderry,	[illegible]	[illegible]	[illegible]	[illegible]	[illegible]	[illegible]	[illegible]	[illegible]	[illegible]	[illegible]	[illegible]	[illegible]	[illegible]	[illegible]	[illegible]	[illegible]	[illegible]	[illegible]	[illegible]	[illegible]	[illegible]
26	Monaghan,	[illegible]	[illegible]	[illegible]	[illegible]	[illegible]	[illegible]	[illegible]	[illegible]	[illegible]	[illegible]	[illegible]	[illegible]	[illegible]	[illegible]	[illegible]	[illegible]	[illegible]	[illegible]	[illegible]	[illegible]	[illegible]
27	Tyrone,	[illegible]	[illegible]	[illegible]	[illegible]	[illegible]	[illegible]	[illegible]	[illegible]	[illegible]	[illegible]	[illegible]	[illegible]	[illegible]	[illegible]	[illegible]	[illegible]	[illegible]	[illegible]	[illegible]	[illegible]	[illegible]
	IV.—PROVINCE [illegible]																					
28	Galway,	[illegible]	[illegible]	[illegible]	[illegible]	[illegible]	[illegible]	[illegible]	[illegible]	[illegible]	[illegible]	[illegible]	[illegible]	[illegible]	[illegible]	[illegible]	[illegible]	[illegible]	[illegible]	[illegible]	[illegible]	[illegible]
29	Leitrim,	[illegible]	[illegible]	[illegible]	[illegible]	[illegible]	[illegible]	[illegible]	[illegible]	[illegible]	[illegible]	[illegible]	[illegible]	[illegible]	[illegible]	[illegible]	[illegible]	[illegible]	[illegible]	[illegible]	[illegible]	[illegible]
30	Mayo,	[illegible]	[illegible]	[illegible]	[illegible]	[illegible]	[illegible]	[illegible]	[illegible]	[illegible]	[illegible]	[illegible]	[illegible]	[illegible]	[illegible]	[illegible]	[illegible]	[illegible]	[illegible]	[illegible]	[illegible]	[illegible]
31	Roscommon,	[illegible]	[illegible]	[illegible]	[illegible]	[illegible]	[illegible]	[illegible]	[illegible]	[illegible]	[illegible]	[illegible]	[illegible]	[illegible]	[illegible]	[illegible]	[illegible]	[illegible]	[illegible]	[illegible]	[illegible]	[illegible]
32	Sligo,	[illegible]	[illegible]	[illegible]	[illegible]	[illegible]	[illegible]	[illegible]	[illegible]	[illegible]	[illegible]	[illegible]	[illegible]	[illegible]	[illegible]	[illegible]	[illegible]	[illegible]	[illegible]	[illegible]	[illegible]	[illegible]

and Special Hospitals; (2), in Public Lunatic Asylums; (3), in Workhouses; and (4), at their Number of Inquests in the Provinces, Counties, and Superintendent in Ireland in 1891.

Deaths.

Constitutional Diseases.					Local Diseases.							Violence.				All causes	Number of Inquests	Provinces and Counties.
[illegible]	[illegible]	[illegible]	[illegible]	[illegible]	[illegible]	[illegible]	[illegible]	[illegible]	[illegible]	[illegible]	[illegible]	[illegible]	[illegible]	[illegible]	[illegible]	[illegible]	[illegible]	IRELAND.
																		PROVINCES.
[illegible]	[illegible]	[illegible]	[illegible]	[illegible]	[illegible]	[illegible]	[illegible]	[illegible]	[illegible]	[illegible]	[illegible]	[illegible]	[illegible]	[illegible]	[illegible]	[illegible]	[illegible]	LEINSTER.
[illegible]	[illegible]	[illegible]	[illegible]	[illegible]	[illegible]	[illegible]	[illegible]	[illegible]	[illegible]	[illegible]	[illegible]	[illegible]	[illegible]	[illegible]	[illegible]	[illegible]	[illegible]	MUNSTER.
[illegible]	[illegible]	[illegible]	[illegible]	[illegible]	[illegible]	[illegible]	[illegible]	[illegible]	[illegible]	[illegible]	[illegible]	[illegible]	[illegible]	[illegible]	[illegible]	[illegible]	[illegible]	ULSTER.
[illegible]	[illegible]	[illegible]	[illegible]	[illegible]	[illegible]	[illegible]	[illegible]	[illegible]	[illegible]	[illegible]	[illegible]	[illegible]	[illegible]	[illegible]	[illegible]	[illegible]	[illegible]	CONNAUGHT.

OF LEINSTER.

[illegible]	[illegible]	[illegible]	[illegible]	[illegible]	[illegible]	[illegible]	[illegible]	[illegible]	[illegible]	[illegible]	[illegible]	[illegible]	[illegible]	[illegible]	[illegible]	[illegible]	[illegible]	Carlow.
[illegible]	[illegible]	[illegible]	[illegible]	[illegible]	[illegible]	[illegible]	[illegible]	[illegible]	[illegible]	[illegible]	[illegible]	[illegible]	[illegible]	[illegible]	[illegible]	[illegible]	[illegible]	Dublin.
[illegible]	[illegible]	[illegible]	[illegible]	[illegible]	[illegible]	[illegible]	[illegible]	[illegible]	[illegible]	[illegible]	[illegible]	[illegible]	[illegible]	[illegible]	[illegible]	[illegible]	[illegible]	Kildare.
[illegible]	[illegible]	[illegible]	[illegible]	[illegible]	[illegible]	[illegible]	[illegible]	[illegible]	[illegible]	[illegible]	[illegible]	[illegible]	[illegible]	[illegible]	[illegible]	[illegible]	[illegible]	Kilkenny.
[illegible]	[illegible]	[illegible]	[illegible]	[illegible]	[illegible]	[illegible]	[illegible]	[illegible]	[illegible]	[illegible]	[illegible]	[illegible]	[illegible]	[illegible]	[illegible]	[illegible]	[illegible]	King's.
[illegible]	[illegible]	[illegible]	[illegible]	[illegible]	[illegible]	[illegible]	[illegible]	[illegible]	[illegible]	[illegible]	[illegible]	[illegible]	[illegible]	[illegible]	[illegible]	[illegible]	[illegible]	Longford.
[illegible]	[illegible]	[illegible]	[illegible]	[illegible]	[illegible]	[illegible]	[illegible]	[illegible]	[illegible]	[illegible]	[illegible]	[illegible]	[illegible]	[illegible]	[illegible]	[illegible]	[illegible]	Louth, & Co. of the Town of Drogheda.
[illegible]	[illegible]	[illegible]	[illegible]	[illegible]	[illegible]	[illegible]	[illegible]	[illegible]	[illegible]	[illegible]	[illegible]	[illegible]	[illegible]	[illegible]	[illegible]	[illegible]	[illegible]	Meath.
[illegible]	[illegible]	[illegible]	[illegible]	[illegible]	[illegible]	[illegible]	[illegible]	[illegible]	[illegible]	[illegible]	[illegible]	[illegible]	[illegible]	[illegible]	[illegible]	[illegible]	[illegible]	Queen's.
[illegible]	[illegible]	[illegible]	[illegible]	[illegible]	[illegible]	[illegible]	[illegible]	[illegible]	[illegible]	[illegible]	[illegible]	[illegible]	[illegible]	[illegible]	[illegible]	[illegible]	[illegible]	Westmeath.
[illegible]	[illegible]	[illegible]	[illegible]	[illegible]	[illegible]	[illegible]	[illegible]	[illegible]	[illegible]	[illegible]	[illegible]	[illegible]	[illegible]	[illegible]	[illegible]	[illegible]	[illegible]	Wexford.
[illegible]	[illegible]	[illegible]	[illegible]	[illegible]	[illegible]	[illegible]	[illegible]	[illegible]	[illegible]	[illegible]	[illegible]	[illegible]	[illegible]	[illegible]	[illegible]	[illegible]	[illegible]	Wicklow.

OF MUNSTER.

[illegible]	[illegible]	[illegible]	[illegible]	[illegible]	[illegible]	[illegible]	[illegible]	[illegible]	[illegible]	[illegible]	[illegible]	[illegible]	[illegible]	[illegible]	[illegible]	[illegible]	[illegible]	Clare.
[illegible]	[illegible]	[illegible]	[illegible]	[illegible]	[illegible]	[illegible]	[illegible]	[illegible]	[illegible]	[illegible]	[illegible]	[illegible]	[illegible]	[illegible]	[illegible]	[illegible]	[illegible]	Cork.
[illegible]	[illegible]	[illegible]	[illegible]	[illegible]	[illegible]	[illegible]	[illegible]	[illegible]	[illegible]	[illegible]	[illegible]	[illegible]	[illegible]	[illegible]	[illegible]	[illegible]	[illegible]	Kerry.
[illegible]	[illegible]	[illegible]	[illegible]	[illegible]	[illegible]	[illegible]	[illegible]	[illegible]	[illegible]	[illegible]	[illegible]	[illegible]	[illegible]	[illegible]	[illegible]	[illegible]	[illegible]	Limerick.
[illegible]	[illegible]	[illegible]	[illegible]	[illegible]	[illegible]	[illegible]	[illegible]	[illegible]	[illegible]	[illegible]	[illegible]	[illegible]	[illegible]	[illegible]	[illegible]	[illegible]	[illegible]	Tipperary.
[illegible]	[illegible]	[illegible]	[illegible]	[illegible]	[illegible]	[illegible]	[illegible]	[illegible]	[illegible]	[illegible]	[illegible]	[illegible]	[illegible]	[illegible]	[illegible]	[illegible]	[illegible]	Waterford.

OF ULSTER.

[illegible]	[illegible]	[illegible]	[illegible]	[illegible]	[illegible]	[illegible]	[illegible]	[illegible]	[illegible]	[illegible]	[illegible]	[illegible]	[illegible]	[illegible]	[illegible]	[illegible]	[illegible]	Antrim.
[illegible]	[illegible]	[illegible]	[illegible]	[illegible]	[illegible]	[illegible]	[illegible]	[illegible]	[illegible]	[illegible]	[illegible]	[illegible]	[illegible]	[illegible]	[illegible]	[illegible]	[illegible]	Armagh.
[illegible]	[illegible]	[illegible]	[illegible]	[illegible]	[illegible]	[illegible]	[illegible]	[illegible]	[illegible]	[illegible]	[illegible]	[illegible]	[illegible]	[illegible]	[illegible]	[illegible]	[illegible]	Cavan.
[illegible]	[illegible]	[illegible]	[illegible]	[illegible]	[illegible]	[illegible]	[illegible]	[illegible]	[illegible]	[illegible]	[illegible]	[illegible]	[illegible]	[illegible]	[illegible]	[illegible]	[illegible]	Donegal.
[illegible]	[illegible]	[illegible]	[illegible]	[illegible]	[illegible]	[illegible]	[illegible]	[illegible]	[illegible]	[illegible]	[illegible]	[illegible]	[illegible]	[illegible]	[illegible]	[illegible]	[illegible]	Down.
[illegible]	[illegible]	[illegible]	[illegible]	[illegible]	[illegible]	[illegible]	[illegible]	[illegible]	[illegible]	[illegible]	[illegible]	[illegible]	[illegible]	[illegible]	[illegible]	[illegible]	[illegible]	Fermanagh.
[illegible]	[illegible]	[illegible]	[illegible]	[illegible]	[illegible]	[illegible]	[illegible]	[illegible]	[illegible]	[illegible]	[illegible]	[illegible]	[illegible]	[illegible]	[illegible]	[illegible]	[illegible]	Londonderry.
[illegible]	[illegible]	[illegible]	[illegible]	[illegible]	[illegible]	[illegible]	[illegible]	[illegible]	[illegible]	[illegible]	[illegible]	[illegible]	[illegible]	[illegible]	[illegible]	[illegible]	[illegible]	Monaghan.
[illegible]	[illegible]	[illegible]	[illegible]	[illegible]	[illegible]	[illegible]	[illegible]	[illegible]	[illegible]	[illegible]	[illegible]	[illegible]	[illegible]	[illegible]	[illegible]	[illegible]	[illegible]	Tyrone.

OF CONNAUGHT.

[illegible]	[illegible]	[illegible]	[illegible]	[illegible]	[illegible]	[illegible]	[illegible]	[illegible]	[illegible]	[illegible]	[illegible]	[illegible]	[illegible]	[illegible]	[illegible]	[illegible]	[illegible]	Galway.
[illegible]	[illegible]	[illegible]	[illegible]	[illegible]	[illegible]	[illegible]	[illegible]	[illegible]	[illegible]	[illegible]	[illegible]	[illegible]	[illegible]	[illegible]	[illegible]	[illegible]	[illegible]	Leitrim.
[illegible]	[illegible]	[illegible]	[illegible]	[illegible]	[illegible]	[illegible]	[illegible]	[illegible]	[illegible]	[illegible]	[illegible]	[illegible]	[illegible]	[illegible]	[illegible]	[illegible]	[illegible]	Mayo.
[illegible]	[illegible]	[illegible]	[illegible]	[illegible]	[illegible]	[illegible]	[illegible]	[illegible]	[illegible]	[illegible]	[illegible]	[illegible]	[illegible]	[illegible]	[illegible]	[illegible]	[illegible]	Roscommon.
[illegible]	[illegible]	[illegible]	[illegible]	[illegible]	[illegible]	[illegible]	[illegible]	[illegible]	[illegible]	[illegible]	[illegible]	[illegible]	[illegible]	[illegible]	[illegible]	[illegible]	[illegible]	Sligo.

TOTAL NUMBER OF DEATHS.—NUMBER of PERSONS who died (1), in INFIRMARIES and GENERAL … OWN HOMES, &c.; NUMBER of DEATHS from the PRINCIPAL CAUSES; and … REGISTRARS' DISTRICTS

SUPERINTENDENT REGISTRARS' DISTRICTS OR …

SUPERINTENDENT REGISTRARS' DISTRICTS or POOR LAW UNIONS.	Total Number of Deaths.	Number of Persons who Died [illegible]				CAUSES OF [illegible]
[illegible]	[illegible]	[illegible]	[illegible]	[illegible]	[illegible]	[illegible]

and SPECIAL HOSPITALS; (3), in PUBLIC LUNATIC ASYLUMS; (3), in WORKHOUSES, and (4), at their NUMBER of INQUESTS in the PROVINCES, COUNTIES, and SUPERINTENDENT in IRELAND in 1891—*continued.*

POOR LAW UNIONS ARRANGED ALPHABETICALLY.

[illegible]	[illegible]

TOTAL NUMBER OF DEATHS.—NUMBER of PERSONS who died (1), in INFIRMARIES and GENERAL … OWN HOMES, &c.; NUMBER of DEATHS from the PRINCIPAL CAUSES; and … REGISTRARS' DISTRICTS

SUPERINTENDENT REGISTRARS' DISTRICTS, OR …

SUPERINTENDENT REGISTRARS' DISTRICTS OR POOR LAW UNIONS.	Total Number of Deaths.	Number of Persons who Died				CAUSES OF
[illegible]	[illegible]	[illegible]	[illegible]	[illegible]	[illegible]	[illegible]

and Special Hospitals; (2), in Public Lunatic Asylums; (3), in Workhouses; and (4), at their Number of Inquests in the Provinces, Counties, and Superintendent in Ireland in 1891—continued.

Poor Law Unions arranged Alphabetically.

Males.

Constitutional Diseases					Local Diseases							Violence				Ill-defined Causes	Number of Inquests	Superintendent Registrars' Districts or Poor Law Unions
[illegible]	[illegible]	[illegible]	[illegible]	[illegible]	[illegible]	[illegible]	[illegible]	[illegible]	[illegible]	[illegible]	[illegible]	[illegible]	[illegible]	[illegible]	[illegible]			
[illegible]	[illegible]	[illegible]	[illegible]	[illegible]	[illegible]	[illegible]	[illegible]	[illegible]	[illegible]	[illegible]	[illegible]	[illegible]	[illegible]	[illegible]	[illegible]	[illegible]	[illegible]	[illegible]
[illegible]	[illegible]	[illegible]	[illegible]	[illegible]	[illegible]	[illegible]	[illegible]	[illegible]	[illegible]	[illegible]	[illegible]	[illegible]	[illegible]	[illegible]	[illegible]	[illegible]	[illegible]	[illegible]
[illegible]	[illegible]	[illegible]	[illegible]	[illegible]	[illegible]	[illegible]	[illegible]	[illegible]	[illegible]	[illegible]	[illegible]	[illegible]	[illegible]	[illegible]	[illegible]	[illegible]	[illegible]	[illegible]
[illegible]	[illegible]	[illegible]	[illegible]	[illegible]	[illegible]	[illegible]	[illegible]	[illegible]	[illegible]	[illegible]	[illegible]	[illegible]	[illegible]	[illegible]	[illegible]	[illegible]	[illegible]	[illegible]
[illegible]	[illegible]	[illegible]	[illegible]	[illegible]	[illegible]	[illegible]	[illegible]	[illegible]	[illegible]	[illegible]	[illegible]	[illegible]	[illegible]	[illegible]	[illegible]	[illegible]	[illegible]	[illegible]
[illegible]	[illegible]	[illegible]	[illegible]	[illegible]	[illegible]	[illegible]	[illegible]	[illegible]	[illegible]	[illegible]	[illegible]	[illegible]	[illegible]	[illegible]	[illegible]	[illegible]	[illegible]	[illegible]
[illegible]	[illegible]	[illegible]	[illegible]	[illegible]	[illegible]	[illegible]	[illegible]	[illegible]	[illegible]	[illegible]	[illegible]	[illegible]	[illegible]	[illegible]	[illegible]	[illegible]	[illegible]	[illegible]
[illegible]	[illegible]	[illegible]	[illegible]	[illegible]	[illegible]	[illegible]	[illegible]	[illegible]	[illegible]	[illegible]	[illegible]	[illegible]	[illegible]	[illegible]	[illegible]	[illegible]	[illegible]	[illegible]
[illegible]	[illegible]	[illegible]	[illegible]	[illegible]	[illegible]	[illegible]	[illegible]	[illegible]	[illegible]	[illegible]	[illegible]	[illegible]	[illegible]	[illegible]	[illegible]	[illegible]	[illegible]	[illegible]
[illegible]	[illegible]	[illegible]	[illegible]	[illegible]	[illegible]	[illegible]	[illegible]	[illegible]	[illegible]	[illegible]	[illegible]	[illegible]	[illegible]	[illegible]	[illegible]	[illegible]	[illegible]	[illegible]

TOTAL NUMBER OF DEATHS.—NUMBER of PERSONS who died (1), in INFIRMARIES and GENERAL [illegible] OWN HOMES, &c.; NUMBER of DEATHS from the PRINCIPAL CAUSES; and REGISTRARS' DISTRICTS

SUPERINTENDENT REGISTRARS' DISTRICTS, &c.

SUPERINTENDENT REGISTRARS' DISTRICTS, &c., POOR LAW UNIONS.	Total Number of Deaths.	Number of Persons who Died				Causes of [illegible]											
		[illegible]	[illegible]	[illegible]	[illegible]	[illegible]	[illegible]	[illegible]	[illegible]	[illegible]	[illegible]	[illegible]	[illegible]	[illegible]	[illegible]	[illegible]	[illegible]
[illegible]	[illegible]	[illegible]	[illegible]	[illegible]	[illegible]	[illegible]	[illegible]	[illegible]	[illegible]	[illegible]	[illegible]	[illegible]	[illegible]	[illegible]	[illegible]	[illegible]	[illegible]
[illegible]	[illegible]	[illegible]	[illegible]	[illegible]	[illegible]	[illegible]	[illegible]	[illegible]	[illegible]	[illegible]	[illegible]	[illegible]	[illegible]	[illegible]	[illegible]	[illegible]	[illegible]
[illegible]	[illegible]	[illegible]	[illegible]	[illegible]	[illegible]	[illegible]	[illegible]	[illegible]	[illegible]	[illegible]	[illegible]	[illegible]	[illegible]	[illegible]	[illegible]	[illegible]	[illegible]
[illegible]	[illegible]	[illegible]	[illegible]	[illegible]	[illegible]	[illegible]	[illegible]	[illegible]	[illegible]	[illegible]	[illegible]	[illegible]	[illegible]	[illegible]	[illegible]	[illegible]	[illegible]
[illegible]	[illegible]	[illegible]	[illegible]	[illegible]	[illegible]	[illegible]	[illegible]	[illegible]	[illegible]	[illegible]	[illegible]	[illegible]	[illegible]	[illegible]	[illegible]	[illegible]	[illegible]

and Special Hospitals; (2), in Public Lunatic Asylums; (3), in Workhouses; and (4), at their
Number of Inquests in the Provinces, Counties, and Superintendent
in Ireland in 1891—continued.

Poor Law Unions arranged Alphabetically.

Constitutional Diseases					Local Diseases							Violence				All other Causes	Number of Inquests	Superintendent Registrars' Districts or Poor Law Unions
[illegible]	[illegible]	[illegible]	[illegible]	[illegible]	[illegible]	[illegible]	[illegible]	[illegible]	[illegible]	[illegible]	[illegible]	[illegible]	[illegible]	[illegible]	[illegible]	[illegible]	[illegible]	[illegible]
[illegible]	[illegible]	[illegible]	[illegible]	[illegible]	[illegible]	[illegible]	[illegible]	[illegible]	[illegible]	[illegible]	[illegible]	[illegible]	[illegible]	[illegible]	[illegible]	[illegible]	[illegible]	[illegible]
[illegible]	[illegible]	[illegible]	[illegible]	[illegible]	[illegible]	[illegible]	[illegible]	[illegible]	[illegible]	[illegible]	[illegible]	[illegible]	[illegible]	[illegible]	[illegible]	[illegible]	[illegible]	[illegible]
[illegible]	[illegible]	[illegible]	[illegible]	[illegible]	[illegible]	[illegible]	[illegible]	[illegible]	[illegible]	[illegible]	[illegible]	[illegible]	[illegible]	[illegible]	[illegible]	[illegible]	[illegible]	[illegible]
[illegible]	[illegible]	[illegible]	[illegible]	[illegible]	[illegible]	[illegible]	[illegible]	[illegible]	[illegible]	[illegible]	[illegible]	[illegible]	[illegible]	[illegible]	[illegible]	[illegible]	[illegible]	[illegible]
[illegible]	[illegible]	[illegible]	[illegible]	[illegible]	[illegible]	[illegible]	[illegible]	[illegible]	[illegible]	[illegible]	[illegible]	[illegible]	[illegible]	[illegible]	[illegible]	[illegible]	[illegible]	[illegible]
[illegible]	[illegible]	[illegible]	[illegible]	[illegible]	[illegible]	[illegible]	[illegible]	[illegible]	[illegible]	[illegible]	[illegible]	[illegible]	[illegible]	[illegible]	[illegible]	[illegible]	[illegible]	[illegible]
[illegible]	[illegible]	[illegible]	[illegible]	[illegible]	[illegible]	[illegible]	[illegible]	[illegible]	[illegible]	[illegible]	[illegible]	[illegible]	[illegible]	[illegible]	[illegible]	[illegible]	[illegible]	[illegible]
[illegible]	[illegible]	[illegible]	[illegible]	[illegible]	[illegible]	[illegible]	[illegible]	[illegible]	[illegible]	[illegible]	[illegible]	[illegible]	[illegible]	[illegible]	[illegible]	[illegible]	[illegible]	[illegible]
[illegible]	[illegible]	[illegible]	[illegible]	[illegible]	[illegible]	[illegible]	[illegible]	[illegible]	[illegible]	[illegible]	[illegible]	[illegible]	[illegible]	[illegible]	[illegible]	[illegible]	[illegible]	[illegible]
[illegible]	[illegible]	[illegible]	[illegible]	[illegible]	[illegible]	[illegible]	[illegible]	[illegible]	[illegible]	[illegible]	[illegible]	[illegible]	[illegible]	[illegible]	[illegible]	[illegible]	[illegible]	[illegible]
[illegible]	[illegible]	[illegible]	[illegible]	[illegible]	[illegible]	[illegible]	[illegible]	[illegible]	[illegible]	[illegible]	[illegible]	[illegible]	[illegible]	[illegible]	[illegible]	[illegible]	[illegible]	[illegible]
[illegible]	[illegible]	[illegible]	[illegible]	[illegible]	[illegible]	[illegible]	[illegible]	[illegible]	[illegible]	[illegible]	[illegible]	[illegible]	[illegible]	[illegible]	[illegible]	[illegible]	[illegible]	[illegible]
[illegible]	[illegible]	[illegible]	[illegible]	[illegible]	[illegible]	[illegible]	[illegible]	[illegible]	[illegible]	[illegible]	[illegible]	[illegible]	[illegible]	[illegible]	[illegible]	[illegible]	[illegible]	[illegible]
[illegible]	[illegible]	[illegible]	[illegible]	[illegible]	[illegible]	[illegible]	[illegible]	[illegible]	[illegible]	[illegible]	[illegible]	[illegible]	[illegible]	[illegible]	[illegible]	[illegible]	[illegible]	[illegible]
[illegible]	[illegible]	[illegible]	[illegible]	[illegible]	[illegible]	[illegible]	[illegible]	[illegible]	[illegible]	[illegible]	[illegible]	[illegible]	[illegible]	[illegible]	[illegible]	[illegible]	[illegible]	[illegible]
[illegible]	[illegible]	[illegible]	[illegible]	[illegible]	[illegible]	[illegible]	[illegible]	[illegible]	[illegible]	[illegible]	[illegible]	[illegible]	[illegible]	[illegible]	[illegible]	[illegible]	[illegible]	[illegible]
[illegible]	[illegible]	[illegible]	[illegible]	[illegible]	[illegible]	[illegible]	[illegible]	[illegible]	[illegible]	[illegible]	[illegible]	[illegible]	[illegible]	[illegible]	[illegible]	[illegible]	[illegible]	[illegible]
[illegible]	[illegible]	[illegible]	[illegible]	[illegible]	[illegible]	[illegible]	[illegible]	[illegible]	[illegible]	[illegible]	[illegible]	[illegible]	[illegible]	[illegible]	[illegible]	[illegible]	[illegible]	[illegible]
[illegible]	[illegible]	[illegible]	[illegible]	[illegible]	[illegible]	[illegible]	[illegible]	[illegible]	[illegible]	[illegible]	[illegible]	[illegible]	[illegible]	[illegible]	[illegible]	[illegible]	[illegible]	[illegible]
[illegible]	[illegible]	[illegible]	[illegible]	[illegible]	[illegible]	[illegible]	[illegible]	[illegible]	[illegible]	[illegible]	[illegible]	[illegible]	[illegible]	[illegible]	[illegible]	[illegible]	[illegible]	[illegible]
[illegible]	[illegible]	[illegible]	[illegible]	[illegible]	[illegible]	[illegible]	[illegible]	[illegible]	[illegible]	[illegible]	[illegible]	[illegible]	[illegible]	[illegible]	[illegible]	[illegible]	[illegible]	[illegible]
[illegible]	[illegible]	[illegible]	[illegible]	[illegible]	[illegible]	[illegible]	[illegible]	[illegible]	[illegible]	[illegible]	[illegible]	[illegible]	[illegible]	[illegible]	[illegible]	[illegible]	[illegible]	[illegible]
[illegible]	[illegible]	[illegible]	[illegible]	[illegible]	[illegible]	[illegible]	[illegible]	[illegible]	[illegible]	[illegible]	[illegible]	[illegible]	[illegible]	[illegible]	[illegible]	[illegible]	[illegible]	[illegible]
[illegible]	[illegible]	[illegible]	[illegible]	[illegible]	[illegible]	[illegible]	[illegible]	[illegible]	[illegible]	[illegible]	[illegible]	[illegible]	[illegible]	[illegible]	[illegible]	[illegible]	[illegible]	[illegible]
[illegible]	[illegible]	[illegible]	[illegible]	[illegible]	[illegible]	[illegible]	[illegible]	[illegible]	[illegible]	[illegible]	[illegible]	[illegible]	[illegible]	[illegible]	[illegible]	[illegible]	[illegible]	[illegible]
[illegible]	[illegible]	[illegible]	[illegible]	[illegible]	[illegible]	[illegible]	[illegible]	[illegible]	[illegible]	[illegible]	[illegible]	[illegible]	[illegible]	[illegible]	[illegible]	[illegible]	[illegible]	[illegible]
[illegible]	[illegible]	[illegible]	[illegible]	[illegible]	[illegible]	[illegible]	[illegible]	[illegible]	[illegible]	[illegible]	[illegible]	[illegible]	[illegible]	[illegible]	[illegible]	[illegible]	[illegible]	[illegible]
[illegible]	[illegible]	[illegible]	[illegible]	[illegible]	[illegible]	[illegible]	[illegible]	[illegible]	[illegible]	[illegible]	[illegible]	[illegible]	[illegible]	[illegible]	[illegible]	[illegible]	[illegible]	[illegible]
[illegible]	[illegible]	[illegible]	[illegible]	[illegible]	[illegible]	[illegible]	[illegible]	[illegible]	[illegible]	[illegible]	[illegible]	[illegible]	[illegible]	[illegible]	[illegible]	[illegible]	[illegible]	[illegible]
[illegible]	[illegible]	[illegible]	[illegible]	[illegible]	[illegible]	[illegible]	[illegible]	[illegible]	[illegible]	[illegible]	[illegible]	[illegible]	[illegible]	[illegible]	[illegible]	[illegible]	[illegible]	[illegible]
[illegible]	[illegible]	[illegible]	[illegible]	[illegible]	[illegible]	[illegible]	[illegible]	[illegible]	[illegible]	[illegible]	[illegible]	[illegible]	[illegible]	[illegible]	[illegible]	[illegible]	[illegible]	[illegible]
[illegible]	[illegible]	[illegible]	[illegible]	[illegible]	[illegible]	[illegible]	[illegible]	[illegible]	[illegible]	[illegible]	[illegible]	[illegible]	[illegible]	[illegible]	[illegible]	[illegible]	[illegible]	[illegible]
[illegible]	[illegible]	[illegible]	[illegible]	[illegible]	[illegible]	[illegible]	[illegible]	[illegible]	[illegible]	[illegible]	[illegible]	[illegible]	[illegible]	[illegible]	[illegible]	[illegible]	[illegible]	[illegible]
[illegible]	[illegible]	[illegible]	[illegible]	[illegible]	[illegible]	[illegible]	[illegible]	[illegible]	[illegible]	[illegible]	[illegible]	[illegible]	[illegible]	[illegible]	[illegible]	[illegible]	[illegible]	[illegible]
[illegible]	[illegible]	[illegible]	[illegible]	[illegible]	[illegible]	[illegible]	[illegible]	[illegible]	[illegible]	[illegible]	[illegible]	[illegible]	[illegible]	[illegible]	[illegible]	[illegible]	[illegible]	[illegible]
[illegible]	[illegible]	[illegible]	[illegible]	[illegible]	[illegible]	[illegible]	[illegible]	[illegible]	[illegible]	[illegible]	[illegible]	[illegible]	[illegible]	[illegible]	[illegible]	[illegible]	[illegible]	[illegible]
[illegible]	[illegible]	[illegible]	[illegible]	[illegible]	[illegible]	[illegible]	[illegible]	[illegible]	[illegible]	[illegible]	[illegible]	[illegible]	[illegible]	[illegible]	[illegible]	[illegible]	[illegible]	[illegible]
[illegible]	[illegible]	[illegible]	[illegible]	[illegible]	[illegible]	[illegible]	[illegible]	[illegible]	[illegible]	[illegible]	[illegible]	[illegible]	[illegible]	[illegible]	[illegible]	[illegible]	[illegible]	[illegible]
[illegible]	[illegible]	[illegible]	[illegible]	[illegible]	[illegible]	[illegible]	[illegible]	[illegible]	[illegible]	[illegible]	[illegible]	[illegible]	[illegible]	[illegible]	[illegible]	[illegible]	[illegible]	[illegible]
[illegible]	[illegible]	[illegible]	[illegible]	[illegible]	[illegible]	[illegible]	[illegible]	[illegible]	[illegible]	[illegible]	[illegible]	[illegible]	[illegible]	[illegible]	[illegible]	[illegible]	[illegible]	[illegible]
[illegible]	[illegible]	[illegible]	[illegible]	[illegible]	[illegible]	[illegible]	[illegible]	[illegible]	[illegible]	[illegible]	[illegible]	[illegible]	[illegible]	[illegible]	[illegible]	[illegible]	[illegible]	[illegible]
[illegible]	[illegible]	[illegible]	[illegible]	[illegible]	[illegible]	[illegible]	[illegible]	[illegible]	[illegible]	[illegible]	[illegible]	[illegible]	[illegible]	[illegible]	[illegible]	[illegible]	[illegible]	[illegible]
[illegible]	[illegible]	[illegible]	[illegible]	[illegible]	[illegible]	[illegible]	[illegible]	[illegible]	[illegible]	[illegible]	[illegible]	[illegible]	[illegible]	[illegible]	[illegible]	[illegible]	[illegible]	[illegible]
[illegible]	[illegible]	[illegible]	[illegible]	[illegible]	[illegible]	[illegible]	[illegible]	[illegible]	[illegible]	[illegible]	[illegible]	[illegible]	[illegible]	[illegible]	[illegible]	[illegible]	[illegible]	[illegible]
[illegible]	[illegible]	[illegible]	[illegible]	[illegible]	[illegible]	[illegible]	[illegible]	[illegible]	[illegible]	[illegible]	[illegible]	[illegible]	[illegible]	[illegible]	[illegible]	[illegible]	[illegible]	[illegible]
[illegible]	[illegible]	[illegible]	[illegible]	[illegible]	[illegible]	[illegible]	[illegible]	[illegible]	[illegible]	[illegible]	[illegible]	[illegible]	[illegible]	[illegible]	[illegible]	[illegible]	[illegible]	[illegible]

TOTAL NUMBER OF DEATHS.—NUMBER of PERSONS who died (1), in INFIRMARIES and GENERAL [illegible] OWN HOMES, &c.; NUMBER of DEATHS from the PRINCIPAL CAUSES; and [illegible] REGISTRARS' DISTRICTS

SUPERINTENDENT REGISTRARS' DISTRICTS, OR

[illegible]	[illegible]	[illegible]	[illegible]	[illegible]	[illegible]	[illegible]	[illegible]	[illegible]	[illegible]	[illegible]	[illegible]	[illegible]	[illegible]	[illegible]	[illegible]	[illegible]	[illegible]
[illegible]	[illegible]	.	.	[illegible]	[illegible]	.	.	.	[illegible]	[illegible]	.	.	[illegible]	[illegible]	.	.	[illegible]
[illegible]	[illegible]	.	.	[illegible]	[illegible]	.	.	.	.	[illegible]	.	.	[illegible]	.	[illegible]	[illegible]	[illegible]
[illegible]	[illegible]	.	.	[illegible]	[illegible]	.	.	.	[illegible]	.	.	.	.	.	[illegible]	[illegible]	[illegible]
[illegible]	[illegible]	[illegible]	[illegible]	[illegible]	[illegible]	[illegible]	.	.	.	.	[illegible]	.	[illegible]	.	[illegible]	[illegible]	[illegible]
[illegible]	[illegible]	[illegible]	.	[illegible]	[illegible]	.	.	[illegible]	[illegible]	[illegible]	[illegible]	[illegible]	[illegible]	.	[illegible]	[illegible]	[illegible]
[illegible]	[illegible]	.	.	[illegible]	[illegible]	.	.	.	.	.	.	.	.	.	.	.	[illegible]
[illegible]	[illegible]	.	.	[illegible]	[illegible]	.	.	[illegible]	[illegible]	.	.	.	.	.	[illegible]	[illegible]	[illegible]
[illegible]	[illegible]	.	.	[illegible]	[illegible]	.	[illegible]	[illegible]	[illegible]	[illegible]	.	.	[illegible]	.	[illegible]	[illegible]	[illegible]
[illegible]	[illegible]	.	.	[illegible]	[illegible]	.	.	.	.	.	.	.	.	.	[illegible]	.	.
[illegible]	[illegible]	.	.	[illegible]	[illegible]	.	.	[illegible]	[illegible]	[illegible]	.	.	.	.	[illegible]	[illegible]	.
[illegible]	[illegible]	.	.	[illegible]	[illegible]	.	.	.	[illegible]	[illegible]	[illegible]	[illegible]	[illegible]	.	[illegible]	.	[illegible]
[illegible]	[illegible]	.	.	[illegible]	[illegible]	.	[illegible]	.	[illegible]	[illegible]	[illegible]	[illegible]	[illegible]	.	[illegible]	[illegible]	[illegible]
[illegible]	[illegible]	[illegible]	.	[illegible]	[illegible]	.	[illegible]	.	[illegible]	[illegible]	[illegible]	.	[illegible]	[illegible]	[illegible]	[illegible]	[illegible]
[illegible]	[illegible]	.	.	[illegible]	[illegible]	.	.	.	.	.	[illegible]	[illegible]	.	.	.	[illegible]	[illegible]
[illegible]	[illegible]	.	.	[illegible]	[illegible]	.	.	.	[illegible]	[illegible]	.	[illegible]	[illegible]	.	.	.	[illegible]
[illegible]	[illegible]	.	.	[illegible]	[illegible]	.	.	.	.	[illegible]	.	.	.	.	[illegible]	.	.
[illegible]	[illegible]	[illegible]	.	[illegible]	[illegible]	.	.	[illegible]	[illegible]	.	[illegible]	[illegible]	[illegible]	.	[illegible]	[illegible]	[illegible]
[illegible]	[illegible]	.	.	[illegible]	[illegible]	.	.	[illegible]	[illegible]	.	.	.	[illegible]	.	[illegible]	[illegible]	[illegible]
[illegible]	[illegible]	[illegible]	[illegible]	[illegible]	[illegible]	.	.	[illegible]	[illegible]	[illegible]	.	[illegible]	[illegible]	.	[illegible]	[illegible]	[illegible]
[illegible]	[illegible]	.	.	[illegible]	[illegible]	.	[illegible]	[illegible]	[illegible]	.	[illegible]	[illegible]	.	.	[illegible]	[illegible]	[illegible]
[illegible]	[illegible]	[illegible]	.	[illegible]	[illegible]	.	.	.	.	[illegible]	.	[illegible]	.	.	[illegible]	.	[illegible]
[illegible]	[illegible]	.	.	[illegible]	[illegible]	.	.	.	[illegible]	[illegible]	.	.	[illegible]	.	[illegible]	[illegible]	[illegible]

and SPECIAL HOSPITALS; (2), in PUBLIC LUNATIC ASYLUMS; (3), in WORKHOUSES; and (4), at their
NUMBER of INQUESTS in the PROVINCES, COUNTIES, and SUPERINTENDENT
in IRELAND in 1891—*continued.*

POOR LAW UNIONS ARRANGED ALPHABETICALLY.

DEATHS.																		
[illegible]					[illegible]							[illegible]				All other Causes.	Number of Inquests.	SUPERINTENDENT REGISTRAR'S DISTRICTS or POOR LAW UNIONS.
[illegible]	[illegible]	[illegible]	[illegible]	[illegible]	[illegible]	[illegible]	[illegible]	[illegible]	[illegible]	[illegible]	[illegible]	[illegible]	[illegible]	[illegible]	[illegible]			
[illegible]	[illegible]	[illegible]	[illegible]	[illegible]	[illegible]	[illegible]	[illegible]	[illegible]	[illegible]	[illegible]	[illegible]	[illegible]	[illegible]	[illegible]	[illegible]	[illegible]	[illegible]	[illegible]
[illegible]	[illegible]	[illegible]	[illegible]	[illegible]	[illegible]	[illegible]	[illegible]	[illegible]	[illegible]	[illegible]	[illegible]	[illegible]	[illegible]	[illegible]	[illegible]	[illegible]	[illegible]	[illegible]
[illegible]	[illegible]	[illegible]	[illegible]	[illegible]	[illegible]	[illegible]	[illegible]	[illegible]	[illegible]	[illegible]	[illegible]	[illegible]	[illegible]	[illegible]	[illegible]	[illegible]	[illegible]	[illegible]
[illegible]	[illegible]	[illegible]	[illegible]	[illegible]	[illegible]	[illegible]	[illegible]	[illegible]	[illegible]	[illegible]	[illegible]	[illegible]	[illegible]	[illegible]	[illegible]	[illegible]	[illegible]	[illegible]
[illegible]	[illegible]	[illegible]	[illegible]	[illegible]	[illegible]	[illegible]	[illegible]	[illegible]	[illegible]	[illegible]	[illegible]	[illegible]	[illegible]	[illegible]	[illegible]	[illegible]	[illegible]	[illegible]
[illegible]	[illegible]	[illegible]	[illegible]	[illegible]	[illegible]	[illegible]	[illegible]	[illegible]	[illegible]	[illegible]	[illegible]	[illegible]	[illegible]	[illegible]	[illegible]	[illegible]	[illegible]	[illegible]
[illegible]	[illegible]	[illegible]	[illegible]	[illegible]	[illegible]	[illegible]	[illegible]	[illegible]	[illegible]	[illegible]	[illegible]	[illegible]	[illegible]	[illegible]	[illegible]	[illegible]	[illegible]	[illegible]
[illegible]	[illegible]	[illegible]	[illegible]	[illegible]	[illegible]	[illegible]	[illegible]	[illegible]	[illegible]	[illegible]	[illegible]	[illegible]	[illegible]	[illegible]	[illegible]	[illegible]	[illegible]	[illegible]
[illegible]	[illegible]	[illegible]	[illegible]	[illegible]	[illegible]	[illegible]	[illegible]	[illegible]	[illegible]	[illegible]	[illegible]	[illegible]	[illegible]	[illegible]	[illegible]	[illegible]	[illegible]	[illegible]
[illegible]	[illegible]	[illegible]	[illegible]	[illegible]	[illegible]	[illegible]	[illegible]	[illegible]	[illegible]	[illegible]	[illegible]	[illegible]	[illegible]	[illegible]	[illegible]	[illegible]	[illegible]	[illegible]
[illegible]	[illegible]	[illegible]	[illegible]	[illegible]	[illegible]	[illegible]	[illegible]	[illegible]	[illegible]	[illegible]	[illegible]	[illegible]	[illegible]	[illegible]	[illegible]	[illegible]	[illegible]	[illegible]
[illegible]	[illegible]	[illegible]	[illegible]	[illegible]	[illegible]	[illegible]	[illegible]	[illegible]	[illegible]	[illegible]	[illegible]	[illegible]	[illegible]	[illegible]	[illegible]	[illegible]	[illegible]	[illegible]
[illegible]	[illegible]	[illegible]	[illegible]	[illegible]	[illegible]	[illegible]	[illegible]	[illegible]	[illegible]	[illegible]	[illegible]	[illegible]	[illegible]	[illegible]	[illegible]	[illegible]	[illegible]	[illegible]
[illegible]	[illegible]	[illegible]	[illegible]	[illegible]	[illegible]	[illegible]	[illegible]	[illegible]	[illegible]	[illegible]	[illegible]	[illegible]	[illegible]	[illegible]	[illegible]	[illegible]	[illegible]	[illegible]
[illegible]	[illegible]	[illegible]	[illegible]	[illegible]	[illegible]	[illegible]	[illegible]	[illegible]	[illegible]	[illegible]	[illegible]	[illegible]	[illegible]	[illegible]	[illegible]	[illegible]	[illegible]	[illegible]
[illegible]	[illegible]	[illegible]	[illegible]	[illegible]	[illegible]	[illegible]	[illegible]	[illegible]	[illegible]	[illegible]	[illegible]	[illegible]	[illegible]	[illegible]	[illegible]	[illegible]	[illegible]	[illegible]
[illegible]	[illegible]	[illegible]	[illegible]	[illegible]	[illegible]	[illegible]	[illegible]	[illegible]	[illegible]	[illegible]	[illegible]	[illegible]	[illegible]	[illegible]	[illegible]	[illegible]	[illegible]	[illegible]
[illegible]	[illegible]	[illegible]	[illegible]	[illegible]	[illegible]	[illegible]	[illegible]	[illegible]	[illegible]	[illegible]	[illegible]	[illegible]	[illegible]	[illegible]	[illegible]	[illegible]	[illegible]	[illegible]
[illegible]	[illegible]	[illegible]	[illegible]	[illegible]	[illegible]	[illegible]	[illegible]	[illegible]	[illegible]	[illegible]	[illegible]	[illegible]	[illegible]	[illegible]	[illegible]	[illegible]	[illegible]	[illegible]
[illegible]	[illegible]	[illegible]	[illegible]	[illegible]	[illegible]	[illegible]	[illegible]	[illegible]	[illegible]	[illegible]	[illegible]	[illegible]	[illegible]	[illegible]	[illegible]	[illegible]	[illegible]	[illegible]
[illegible]	[illegible]	[illegible]	[illegible]	[illegible]	[illegible]	[illegible]	[illegible]	[illegible]	[illegible]	[illegible]	[illegible]	[illegible]	[illegible]	[illegible]	[illegible]	[illegible]	[illegible]	[illegible]
[illegible]	[illegible]	[illegible]	[illegible]	[illegible]	[illegible]	[illegible]	[illegible]	[illegible]	[illegible]	[illegible]	[illegible]	[illegible]	[illegible]	[illegible]	[illegible]	[illegible]	[illegible]	[illegible]
[illegible]	[illegible]	[illegible]	[illegible]	[illegible]	[illegible]	[illegible]	[illegible]	[illegible]	[illegible]	[illegible]	[illegible]	[illegible]	[illegible]	[illegible]	[illegible]	[illegible]	[illegible]	[illegible]

POPULATION in 1891; TOTAL NUMBER of DEATHS in the YEAR 1891—NUMBER of PERSONS who died (3), in WORKHOUSES; and (4), at their OWN HOMES, &c.; NUMBER of DEATHS from the and the respective REGISTRARS' DISTRICTS in which the PRINCIPAL PROVINCIAL 1881), are situated; with CORRESPONDING DETAILS for

No.	REGISTRARS' DISTRICTS, &c.	TOWNS [illegible]	Population of Registrars' Districts in 1891.	Total Number of Deaths in 1891.	In Infirmaries and [illegible]	In Public Lunatic Asylums.	In Workhouses and Workhouse Hospitals.	At their Own Homes, &c.	Small-pox.	Measles.	Scarlet Fever.	Typhus.	Whooping-cough.	Diphtheria.	Simple and Ill-defined Fever.	Enteric Fever.	[illegible]
	Province of LEINSTER.																
1	Drogheda, Nos. 1 & 2, and St. Mary's	Drogheda	[illegible]	[illegible]	-	-	[illegible]	[illegible]	-	-	-	[illegible]	-	-	-	[illegible]	-
2	Dublin Registration Area*	Dublin, Pembroke, Rathmines and Rathgar, and Kingstown.	[illegible]	[illegible]	[illegible]	[illegible]	[illegible]	[illegible]	-	[illegible]	[illegible]	[illegible]	[illegible]	[illegible]	[illegible]	[illegible]	[illegible]
3	Dundalk,	Dundalk,	[illegible]	[illegible]	[illegible]	-	[illegible]	[illegible]	-	-	[illegible]	[illegible]	-	-	[illegible]	[illegible]	-
4	Kilkenny, Nos. 1 & 2,	Kilkenny,	[illegible]	[illegible]	[illegible]	[illegible]	[illegible]	[illegible]	-	-	-	[illegible]	[illegible]	[illegible]	[illegible]	[illegible]	-
5	Wexford,	Wexford,	[illegible]	[illegible]	[illegible]	-	[illegible]	[illegible]	-	-	-	-	[illegible]	-	[illegible]	-	-
6	Total of above named Registrars' Districts,		[illegible]	[illegible]	[illegible]	[illegible]	[illegible]	[illegible]	-	[illegible]	[illegible]	[illegible]	[illegible]	[illegible]	[illegible]	[illegible]	[illegible]
7	Remaining portion of Province,		[illegible]	[illegible]	[illegible]	[illegible]	[illegible]	[illegible]	-	[illegible]	[illegible]	[illegible]	[illegible]	[illegible]	[illegible]	[illegible]	[illegible]
8	Total, Leinster,		[illegible]	[illegible]	[illegible]	[illegible]	[illegible]	[illegible]	-	[illegible]	[illegible]	[illegible]	[illegible]	[illegible]	[illegible]	[illegible]	[illegible]
	Province of MUNSTER.																
9	Cork, Nos. 1 to [illegible],	Cork,	[illegible]	[illegible]	[illegible]	[illegible]	[illegible]	[illegible]	-	-	[illegible]	[illegible]	[illegible]	[illegible]	[illegible]	[illegible]	[illegible]
10	Limerick, Nos. 1 to [illegible],	Limerick,	[illegible]	[illegible]	[illegible]	[illegible]	[illegible]	[illegible]	-	-	-	[illegible]	[illegible]	[illegible]	[illegible]	[illegible]	-
11	Waterford, Nos. 1 & 2,	Waterford,	[illegible]	[illegible]	[illegible]	[illegible]	[illegible]	[illegible]	-	-	-	[illegible]	[illegible]	-	-	[illegible]	-
12	Total of above named Registrars' Districts,		[illegible]	[illegible]	[illegible]	[illegible]	[illegible]	[illegible]	-	-	[illegible]	[illegible]	[illegible]	[illegible]	[illegible]	[illegible]	[illegible]
13	Remaining portion of Province,		[illegible]	[illegible]	[illegible]	[illegible]	[illegible]	[illegible]	-	[illegible]	[illegible]	[illegible]	[illegible]	[illegible]	[illegible]	[illegible]	[illegible]
14	Total, Munster,		[illegible]	[illegible]	[illegible]	[illegible]	[illegible]	[illegible]	-	[illegible]	[illegible]	[illegible]	[illegible]	[illegible]	[illegible]	[illegible]	[illegible]
	Province of ULSTER.																
15	Armagh,	Armagh,	[illegible]	[illegible]	[illegible]	[illegible]	[illegible]	[illegible]	-	-	[illegible]	-	[illegible]	-	-	[illegible]	-
16	Belfast, Nos. 1 to [illegible], and [illegible], No. 1.	Belfast,	[illegible]	[illegible]	[illegible]	[illegible]	[illegible]	[illegible]	[illegible]	[illegible]	[illegible]	[illegible]	[illegible]	[illegible]	[illegible]	[illegible]	[illegible]
17	Lisburn,	Lisburn,	[illegible]	[illegible]	[illegible]	-	[illegible]	[illegible]	-	-	[illegible]	-	[illegible]	[illegible]	-	[illegible]	-
18	Londonderry, Nos. 1 & 2, and [illegible]	Londonderry,	[illegible]	[illegible]	[illegible]	[illegible]	[illegible]	[illegible]	-	-	[illegible]	-	-	[illegible]	-	[illegible]	-
19	Lurgan, No. 1,	Lurgan,	[illegible]	[illegible]	-	-	[illegible]	[illegible]	-	-	-	[illegible]	[illegible]	[illegible]	-	[illegible]	-
20	Newry, Nos. 1 & 2,	Newry,	[illegible]	[illegible]	[illegible]	-	[illegible]	[illegible]	-	-	-	-	[illegible]	-	-	-	-
21	Total of above named Registrars' Districts,		[illegible]	[illegible]	[illegible]	[illegible]	[illegible]	[illegible]	[illegible]	[illegible]	[illegible]	[illegible]	[illegible]	[illegible]	[illegible]	[illegible]	[illegible]
22	Remaining portion of Province,		[illegible]	[illegible]	[illegible]	[illegible]	[illegible]	[illegible]	[illegible]	[illegible]	[illegible]	[illegible]	[illegible]	[illegible]	[illegible]	[illegible]	[illegible]
23	Total, Ulster,		[illegible]	[illegible]	[illegible]	[illegible]	[illegible]	[illegible]	[illegible]	[illegible]	[illegible]	[illegible]	[illegible]	[illegible]	[illegible]	[illegible]	[illegible]
	Province of CONNAUGHT.																
24	Galway, Nos. 1 & 2,	Galway,	[illegible]	[illegible]	[illegible]	-	[illegible]	[illegible]	-	[illegible]	-	-	[illegible]	-	-	[illegible]	-
25	Sligo, Nos. 1 and 2,	Sligo,	[illegible]	[illegible]	[illegible]	[illegible]	[illegible]	[illegible]	[illegible]	-	-	-	-	[illegible]	-	[illegible]	-
26	Total of above named Registrars' Districts,		[illegible]	[illegible]	[illegible]	[illegible]	[illegible]	[illegible]	1	1	-	-	[illegible]	[illegible]	-	[illegible]	-
27	Remaining portion of Province,		[illegible]	[illegible]	[illegible]	[illegible]	[illegible]	[illegible]	[illegible]	[illegible]	[illegible]	[illegible]	[illegible]	[illegible]	[illegible]	[illegible]	[illegible]
28	Total, Connaught,		[illegible]	[illegible]	[illegible]	[illegible]	[illegible]	[illegible]	[illegible]	[illegible]	[illegible]	[illegible]	[illegible]	[illegible]	[illegible]	[illegible]	[illegible]
29	Ireland,	All above named Registrars' Districts,	[illegible]	[illegible]	[illegible]	[illegible]	[illegible]	[illegible]	[illegible]	[illegible]	[illegible]	[illegible]	[illegible]	[illegible]	[illegible]	[illegible]	[illegible]
30	Ireland,	All other parts of the Country,	[illegible]	[illegible]	[illegible]	[illegible]	[illegible]	[illegible]	[illegible]	[illegible]	[illegible]	[illegible]	[illegible]	[illegible]	[illegible]	[illegible]	[illegible]
31	Ireland,	Total,	[illegible]	[illegible]	[illegible]	[illegible]	[illegible]	[illegible]	[illegible]	[illegible]	[illegible]	[illegible]	[illegible]	[illegible]	[illegible]	[illegible]	[illegible]

* Comprising the Registrars' Districts in the City of Dublin; the Registrars' Districts of [illegible] and [illegible], No. 1; [illegible] and [illegible], No. 1.

(1), in Infirmaries and General and Special Hospitals; (2), in Public Lunatic Asylums; Principal Causes; and Number of Inquests; in the Dublin Registration District Urban Sanitary Districts (those with a Population of 10,000 or upwards, in the remaining portion of each Province.

Deaths: Strumous			Constitutional Diseases						Local Diseases: Diseases of								Violence				All Causes	Number of Inquests	No.
[illegible]	[illegible]	[illegible]	[illegible]	[illegible]	[illegible]	[illegible]	Phthisis	[illegible]	[illegible]	[illegible]	[illegible]	[illegible]	[illegible]	[illegible]	[illegible]	[illegible]	Accidental	Homicide	Suicide	Execution	[illegible]		
[illegible]	[illegible]	[illegible]	[illegible]	[illegible]	[illegible]	[illegible]	[illegible]	[illegible]	[illegible]	[illegible]	[illegible]	[illegible]	[illegible]	[illegible]	[illegible]	[illegible]	[illegible]	[illegible]	[illegible]	[illegible]	[illegible]	[illegible]	1.
[illegible]	[illegible]	[illegible]	[illegible]	[illegible]	[illegible]	[illegible]	[illegible]	[illegible]	[illegible]	[illegible]	[illegible]	[illegible]	[illegible]	[illegible]	[illegible]	[illegible]	[illegible]	[illegible]	[illegible]	[illegible]	[illegible]	[illegible]	2.
[illegible]	[illegible]	[illegible]	[illegible]	[illegible]	[illegible]	[illegible]	[illegible]	[illegible]	[illegible]	[illegible]	[illegible]	[illegible]	[illegible]	[illegible]	[illegible]	[illegible]	[illegible]	[illegible]	[illegible]	[illegible]	[illegible]	[illegible]	3.
[illegible]	[illegible]	[illegible]	[illegible]	[illegible]	[illegible]	[illegible]	[illegible]	[illegible]	[illegible]	[illegible]	[illegible]	[illegible]	[illegible]	[illegible]	[illegible]	[illegible]	[illegible]	[illegible]	[illegible]	[illegible]	[illegible]	[illegible]	4.
[illegible]	[illegible]	[illegible]	[illegible]	[illegible]	[illegible]	[illegible]	[illegible]	[illegible]	[illegible]	[illegible]	[illegible]	[illegible]	[illegible]	[illegible]	[illegible]	[illegible]	[illegible]	[illegible]	[illegible]	[illegible]	[illegible]	[illegible]	5.
[illegible]	[illegible]	[illegible]	[illegible]	[illegible]	[illegible]	[illegible]	[illegible]	[illegible]	[illegible]	[illegible]	[illegible]	[illegible]	[illegible]	[illegible]	[illegible]	[illegible]	[illegible]	[illegible]	[illegible]	[illegible]	[illegible]	[illegible]	6.
[illegible]	[illegible]	[illegible]	[illegible]	[illegible]	[illegible]	[illegible]	[illegible]	[illegible]	[illegible]	[illegible]	[illegible]	[illegible]	[illegible]	[illegible]	[illegible]	[illegible]	[illegible]	[illegible]	[illegible]	[illegible]	[illegible]	[illegible]	7.
[illegible]	[illegible]	[illegible]	[illegible]	[illegible]	[illegible]	[illegible]	[illegible]	[illegible]	[illegible]	[illegible]	[illegible]	[illegible]	[illegible]	[illegible]	[illegible]	[illegible]	[illegible]	[illegible]	[illegible]	[illegible]	[illegible]	[illegible]	8.
[illegible]	[illegible]	[illegible]	[illegible]	[illegible]	[illegible]	[illegible]	[illegible]	[illegible]	[illegible]	[illegible]	[illegible]	[illegible]	[illegible]	[illegible]	[illegible]	[illegible]	[illegible]	[illegible]	[illegible]	[illegible]	[illegible]	[illegible]	9.
[illegible]	[illegible]	[illegible]	[illegible]	[illegible]	[illegible]	[illegible]	[illegible]	[illegible]	[illegible]	[illegible]	[illegible]	[illegible]	[illegible]	[illegible]	[illegible]	[illegible]	[illegible]	[illegible]	[illegible]	[illegible]	[illegible]	[illegible]	10.
[illegible]	[illegible]	[illegible]	[illegible]	[illegible]	[illegible]	[illegible]	[illegible]	[illegible]	[illegible]	[illegible]	[illegible]	[illegible]	[illegible]	[illegible]	[illegible]	[illegible]	[illegible]	[illegible]	[illegible]	[illegible]	[illegible]	[illegible]	11.
[illegible]	[illegible]	[illegible]	[illegible]	[illegible]	[illegible]	[illegible]	[illegible]	[illegible]	[illegible]	[illegible]	[illegible]	[illegible]	[illegible]	[illegible]	[illegible]	[illegible]	[illegible]	[illegible]	[illegible]	[illegible]	[illegible]	[illegible]	12.
[illegible]	[illegible]	[illegible]	[illegible]	[illegible]	[illegible]	[illegible]	[illegible]	[illegible]	[illegible]	[illegible]	[illegible]	[illegible]	[illegible]	[illegible]	[illegible]	[illegible]	[illegible]	[illegible]	[illegible]	[illegible]	[illegible]	[illegible]	13.
[illegible]	[illegible]	[illegible]	[illegible]	[illegible]	[illegible]	[illegible]	[illegible]	[illegible]	[illegible]	[illegible]	[illegible]	[illegible]	[illegible]	[illegible]	[illegible]	[illegible]	[illegible]	[illegible]	[illegible]	[illegible]	[illegible]	[illegible]	14.
[illegible]	[illegible]	[illegible]	[illegible]	[illegible]	[illegible]	[illegible]	[illegible]	[illegible]	[illegible]	[illegible]	[illegible]	[illegible]	[illegible]	[illegible]	[illegible]	[illegible]	[illegible]	[illegible]	[illegible]	[illegible]	[illegible]	[illegible]	15.
[illegible]	[illegible]	[illegible]	[illegible]	[illegible]	[illegible]	[illegible]	[illegible]	[illegible]	[illegible]	[illegible]	[illegible]	[illegible]	[illegible]	[illegible]	[illegible]	[illegible]	[illegible]	[illegible]	[illegible]	[illegible]	[illegible]	[illegible]	16.
[illegible]	[illegible]	[illegible]	[illegible]	[illegible]	[illegible]	[illegible]	[illegible]	[illegible]	[illegible]	[illegible]	[illegible]	[illegible]	[illegible]	[illegible]	[illegible]	[illegible]	[illegible]	[illegible]	[illegible]	[illegible]	[illegible]	[illegible]	17.
[illegible]	[illegible]	[illegible]	[illegible]	[illegible]	[illegible]	[illegible]	[illegible]	[illegible]	[illegible]	[illegible]	[illegible]	[illegible]	[illegible]	[illegible]	[illegible]	[illegible]	[illegible]	[illegible]	[illegible]	[illegible]	[illegible]	[illegible]	18.
[illegible]	[illegible]	[illegible]	[illegible]	[illegible]	[illegible]	[illegible]	[illegible]	[illegible]	[illegible]	[illegible]	[illegible]	[illegible]	[illegible]	[illegible]	[illegible]	[illegible]	[illegible]	[illegible]	[illegible]	[illegible]	[illegible]	[illegible]	19.
[illegible]	[illegible]	[illegible]	[illegible]	[illegible]	[illegible]	[illegible]	[illegible]	[illegible]	[illegible]	[illegible]	[illegible]	[illegible]	[illegible]	[illegible]	[illegible]	[illegible]	[illegible]	[illegible]	[illegible]	[illegible]	[illegible]	[illegible]	20.
[illegible]	[illegible]	[illegible]	[illegible]	[illegible]	[illegible]	[illegible]	[illegible]	[illegible]	[illegible]	[illegible]	[illegible]	[illegible]	[illegible]	[illegible]	[illegible]	[illegible]	[illegible]	[illegible]	[illegible]	[illegible]	[illegible]	[illegible]	21.
[illegible]	[illegible]	[illegible]	[illegible]	[illegible]	[illegible]	[illegible]	[illegible]	[illegible]	[illegible]	[illegible]	[illegible]	[illegible]	[illegible]	[illegible]	[illegible]	[illegible]	[illegible]	[illegible]	[illegible]	[illegible]	[illegible]	[illegible]	22.
[illegible]	[illegible]	[illegible]	[illegible]	[illegible]	[illegible]	[illegible]	[illegible]	[illegible]	[illegible]	[illegible]	[illegible]	[illegible]	[illegible]	[illegible]	[illegible]	[illegible]	[illegible]	[illegible]	[illegible]	[illegible]	[illegible]	[illegible]	23.
[illegible]	[illegible]	[illegible]	[illegible]	[illegible]	[illegible]	[illegible]	[illegible]	[illegible]	[illegible]	[illegible]	[illegible]	[illegible]	[illegible]	[illegible]	[illegible]	[illegible]	[illegible]	[illegible]	[illegible]	[illegible]	[illegible]	[illegible]	24.
[illegible]	[illegible]	[illegible]	[illegible]	[illegible]	[illegible]	[illegible]	[illegible]	[illegible]	[illegible]	[illegible]	[illegible]	[illegible]	[illegible]	[illegible]	[illegible]	[illegible]	[illegible]	[illegible]	[illegible]	[illegible]	[illegible]	[illegible]	25.
[illegible]	[illegible]	[illegible]	[illegible]	[illegible]	[illegible]	[illegible]	[illegible]	[illegible]	[illegible]	[illegible]	[illegible]	[illegible]	[illegible]	[illegible]	[illegible]	[illegible]	[illegible]	[illegible]	[illegible]	[illegible]	[illegible]	[illegible]	26.
[illegible]	[illegible]	[illegible]	[illegible]	[illegible]	[illegible]	[illegible]	[illegible]	[illegible]	[illegible]	[illegible]	[illegible]	[illegible]	[illegible]	[illegible]	[illegible]	[illegible]	[illegible]	[illegible]	[illegible]	[illegible]	[illegible]	[illegible]	27.
[illegible]	[illegible]	[illegible]	[illegible]	[illegible]	[illegible]	[illegible]	[illegible]	[illegible]	[illegible]	[illegible]	[illegible]	[illegible]	[illegible]	[illegible]	[illegible]	[illegible]	[illegible]	[illegible]	[illegible]	[illegible]	[illegible]	[illegible]	28.
[illegible]	[illegible]	[illegible]	[illegible]	[illegible]	[illegible]	[illegible]	[illegible]	[illegible]	[illegible]	[illegible]	[illegible]	[illegible]	[illegible]	[illegible]	[illegible]	[illegible]	[illegible]	[illegible]	[illegible]	[illegible]	[illegible]	[illegible]	29.
[illegible]	[illegible]	[illegible]	[illegible]	[illegible]	[illegible]	[illegible]	[illegible]	[illegible]	[illegible]	[illegible]	[illegible]	[illegible]	[illegible]	[illegible]	[illegible]	[illegible]	[illegible]	[illegible]	[illegible]	[illegible]	[illegible]	[illegible]	30.
[illegible]	[illegible]	[illegible]	[illegible]	[illegible]	[illegible]	[illegible]	[illegible]	[illegible]	[illegible]	[illegible]	[illegible]	[illegible]	[illegible]	[illegible]	[illegible]	[illegible]	[illegible]	[illegible]	[illegible]	[illegible]	[illegible]	[illegible]	31.

[illegible]

TABLE showing the Monthly and Yearly Rainfall at Dublin during the Twenty-one Years 1871 to 1891, inclusive; with the Means for the Twenty Years 1871 to 1890.

Year.	January.	February.	March.	April.	May.	June.	July.	August.	September.	October.	November.	December.	Yearly Total.
	Inches.	Inches.	Inches.	Inches.	Inches.	Inches.	Inches.	Inches.	Inches.	Inches.	Inches.	Inches.	Inches.
1871,	[illegible]	[illegible]	[illegible]	[illegible]	[illegible]	[illegible]	[illegible]	[illegible]	[illegible]	[illegible]	[illegible]	[illegible]	[illegible]
1872,	[illegible]	[illegible]	[illegible]	[illegible]	[illegible]	[illegible]	[illegible]	[illegible]	[illegible]	[illegible]	[illegible]	[illegible]	[illegible]
1873,	[illegible]	[illegible]	[illegible]	[illegible]	[illegible]	[illegible]	[illegible]	[illegible]	[illegible]	[illegible]	[illegible]	[illegible]	[illegible]
1874,	[illegible]	[illegible]	[illegible]	[illegible]	[illegible]	[illegible]	[illegible]	[illegible]	[illegible]	[illegible]	[illegible]	[illegible]	[illegible]
1875,	[illegible]	[illegible]	[illegible]	[illegible]	[illegible]	[illegible]	[illegible]	[illegible]	[illegible]	[illegible]	[illegible]	[illegible]	[illegible]
1876,	[illegible]	[illegible]	[illegible]	[illegible]	[illegible]	[illegible]	[illegible]	[illegible]	[illegible]	[illegible]	[illegible]	[illegible]	[illegible]
1877,	[illegible]	[illegible]	[illegible]	[illegible]	[illegible]	[illegible]	[illegible]	[illegible]	[illegible]	[illegible]	[illegible]	[illegible]	[illegible]
1878,	[illegible]	[illegible]	[illegible]	[illegible]	[illegible]	[illegible]	[illegible]	[illegible]	[illegible]	[illegible]	[illegible]	[illegible]	[illegible]
1879,	[illegible]	[illegible]	[illegible]	[illegible]	[illegible]	[illegible]	[illegible]	[illegible]	[illegible]	[illegible]	[illegible]	[illegible]	[illegible]
1880,	[illegible]	[illegible]	[illegible]	[illegible]	[illegible]	[illegible]	[illegible]	[illegible]	[illegible]	[illegible]	[illegible]	[illegible]	[illegible]
1881,	[illegible]	[illegible]	[illegible]	[illegible]	[illegible]	[illegible]	[illegible]	[illegible]	[illegible]	[illegible]	[illegible]	[illegible]	[illegible]
1882,	[illegible]	[illegible]	[illegible]	[illegible]	[illegible]	[illegible]	[illegible]	[illegible]	[illegible]	[illegible]	[illegible]	[illegible]	[illegible]
1883,	[illegible]	[illegible]	[illegible]	[illegible]	[illegible]	[illegible]	[illegible]	[illegible]	[illegible]	[illegible]	[illegible]	[illegible]	[illegible]
1884,	[illegible]	[illegible]	[illegible]	[illegible]	[illegible]	[illegible]	[illegible]	[illegible]	[illegible]	[illegible]	[illegible]	[illegible]	[illegible]
1885,	[illegible]	[illegible]	[illegible]	[illegible]	[illegible]	[illegible]	[illegible]	[illegible]	[illegible]	[illegible]	[illegible]	[illegible]	[illegible]
1886,	[illegible]	[illegible]	[illegible]	[illegible]	[illegible]	[illegible]	[illegible]	[illegible]	[illegible]	[illegible]	[illegible]	[illegible]	[illegible]
1887,	[illegible]	[illegible]	[illegible]	[illegible]	[illegible]	[illegible]	[illegible]	[illegible]	[illegible]	[illegible]	[illegible]	[illegible]	[illegible]
1888,	[illegible]	[illegible]	[illegible]	[illegible]	[illegible]	[illegible]	[illegible]	[illegible]	[illegible]	[illegible]	[illegible]	[illegible]	[illegible]
1889,	[illegible]	[illegible]	[illegible]	[illegible]	[illegible]	[illegible]	[illegible]	[illegible]	[illegible]	[illegible]	[illegible]	[illegible]	[illegible]
1890,	[illegible]	[illegible]	[illegible]	[illegible]	[illegible]	[illegible]	[illegible]	[illegible]	[illegible]	[illegible]	[illegible]	[illegible]	[illegible]
Means,	[illegible]	[illegible]	[illegible]	[illegible]	[illegible]	[illegible]	[illegible]	[illegible]	[illegible]	[illegible]	[illegible]	[illegible]	[illegible]
1891,	[illegible]	[illegible]	[illegible]	[illegible]	[illegible]	[illegible]	[illegible]	[illegible]	[illegible]	[illegible]	[illegible]	[illegible]	[illegible]

* February, 1891, was the driest month of the twenty-one years.
† July, [illegible], was the wettest month of the twenty-one years.
‡ December, [illegible], was the month of the heaviest rainfall.
§ Heaviest rainfall in 24 hours—[illegible] inches, on October [illegible], 18[illegible].

TABLE showing the Monthly and Yearly Number of Rainy Days* at Dublin during the Twenty-one Years 1871 to 1891, inclusive; with the Means for the Twenty Years 1871 to 1890.

Year.	January.	February.	March.	April.	May.	June.	July.	August.	September.	October.	November.	December.	Total Rainy Days.
1871,	[illegible]	[illegible]	[illegible]	[illegible]	[illegible]	[illegible]	[illegible]	[illegible]	[illegible]	[illegible]	[illegible]	[illegible]	[illegible]
1872,	[illegible]	[illegible]	[illegible]	[illegible]	[illegible]	[illegible]	[illegible]	[illegible]	[illegible]	[illegible]	[illegible]	[illegible]	[illegible]
1873,	[illegible]	[illegible]	[illegible]	[illegible]	[illegible]	[illegible]	[illegible]	[illegible]	[illegible]	[illegible]	[illegible]	[illegible]	[illegible]
1874,	[illegible]	[illegible]	[illegible]	[illegible]	[illegible]	[illegible]	[illegible]	[illegible]	[illegible]	[illegible]	[illegible]	[illegible]	[illegible]
1875,	[illegible]	[illegible]	[illegible]	[illegible]	[illegible]	[illegible]	[illegible]	[illegible]	[illegible]	[illegible]	[illegible]	[illegible]	[illegible]
1876,	[illegible]	[illegible]	[illegible]	[illegible]	[illegible]	[illegible]	[illegible]	[illegible]	[illegible]	[illegible]	[illegible]	[illegible]	[illegible]
1877,	[illegible]	[illegible]	[illegible]	[illegible]	[illegible]	[illegible]	[illegible]	[illegible]	[illegible]	[illegible]	[illegible]	[illegible]	[illegible]
1878,	[illegible]	[illegible]	[illegible]	[illegible]	[illegible]	[illegible]	[illegible]	[illegible]	[illegible]	[illegible]	[illegible]	[illegible]	[illegible]
1879,	[illegible]	[illegible]	[illegible]	[illegible]	[illegible]	[illegible]	[illegible]	[illegible]	[illegible]	[illegible]	[illegible]	[illegible]	[illegible]
1880,	[illegible]	[illegible]	[illegible]	[illegible]	[illegible]	[illegible]	[illegible]	[illegible]	[illegible]	[illegible]	[illegible]	[illegible]	[illegible]
1881,	[illegible]	[illegible]	[illegible]	[illegible]	[illegible]	[illegible]	[illegible]	[illegible]	[illegible]	[illegible]	[illegible]	[illegible]	[illegible]
1882,	[illegible]	[illegible]	[illegible]	[illegible]	[illegible]	[illegible]	[illegible]	[illegible]	[illegible]	[illegible]	[illegible]	[illegible]	[illegible]
1883,	[illegible]	[illegible]	[illegible]	[illegible]	[illegible]	[illegible]	[illegible]	[illegible]	[illegible]	[illegible]	[illegible]	[illegible]	[illegible]
1884,	[illegible]	[illegible]	[illegible]	[illegible]	[illegible]	[illegible]	[illegible]	[illegible]	[illegible]	[illegible]	[illegible]	[illegible]	[illegible]
1885,	[illegible]	[illegible]	[illegible]	[illegible]	[illegible]	[illegible]	[illegible]	[illegible]	[illegible]	[illegible]	[illegible]	[illegible]	[illegible]
1886,	[illegible]	[illegible]	[illegible]	[illegible]	[illegible]	[illegible]	[illegible]	[illegible]	[illegible]	[illegible]	[illegible]	[illegible]	[illegible]
1887,	[illegible]	[illegible]	[illegible]	[illegible]	[illegible]	[illegible]	[illegible]	[illegible]	[illegible]	[illegible]	[illegible]	[illegible]	[illegible]
1888,	[illegible]	[illegible]	[illegible]	[illegible]	[illegible]	[illegible]	[illegible]	[illegible]	[illegible]	[illegible]	[illegible]	[illegible]	[illegible]
1889,	[illegible]	[illegible]	[illegible]	[illegible]	[illegible]	[illegible]	[illegible]	[illegible]	[illegible]	[illegible]	[illegible]	[illegible]	[illegible]
1890,	[illegible]	[illegible]	[illegible]	[illegible]	[illegible]	[illegible]	[illegible]	[illegible]	[illegible]	[illegible]	[illegible]	[illegible]	[illegible]
Means,	[illegible]	[illegible]	[illegible]	[illegible]	[illegible]	[illegible]	[illegible]	[illegible]	[illegible]	[illegible]	[illegible]	[illegible]	[illegible]
1891,	[illegible]	[illegible]	[illegible]	[illegible]	[illegible]	[illegible]	[illegible]	[illegible]	[illegible]	[illegible]	[illegible]	[illegible]	[illegible]

* i.e. days on which [illegible] [illegible]
† [illegible] [illegible] ‡ [illegible]

TABLE showing the Temperature of the Air in Dublin in 1891, and the Average Temperature for the Twenty Years 1871 to 1890, inclusive, as recorded by Dr. J. W. Moore.

Years.	January.	February.	March.	April.	May.	June.	July.	August.	September.	October.	November.	December.	Year.
	°	°	°	°	°	°	°	°	°	°	°	°	°
1871, ...	[illegible]	[illegible]	[illegible]	[illegible]	[illegible]	[illegible]	[illegible]	[illegible]	[illegible]	[illegible]	[illegible]	[illegible]	[illegible]
1872, ...	41·0	[illegible]	[illegible]	[illegible]	[illegible]	[illegible]	[illegible]	[illegible]	[illegible]	[illegible]	[illegible]	[illegible]	[illegible]
1873, ...	[illegible]	[illegible]	[illegible]	[illegible]	[illegible]	[illegible]	[illegible]	[illegible]	[illegible]	[illegible]	[illegible]	[illegible]	[illegible]
1874, ...	[illegible]	[illegible]	[illegible]	[illegible]	[illegible]	[illegible]	[illegible]	[illegible]	[illegible]	[illegible]	[illegible]	[illegible]	[illegible]
1875, ...	[illegible]	[illegible]	[illegible]	[illegible]	[illegible]	[illegible]	[illegible]	[illegible]	[illegible]	[illegible]	[illegible]	[illegible]	[illegible]
1876, ...	[illegible]	[illegible]	[illegible]	[illegible]	[illegible]	[illegible]	[illegible]	[illegible]	[illegible]	[illegible]	[illegible]	[illegible]	[illegible]
1877, ...	[illegible]	[illegible]	[illegible]	[illegible]	[illegible]	[illegible]	[illegible]	[illegible]	[illegible]	[illegible]	[illegible]	[illegible]	[illegible]
1878, ...	[illegible]	[illegible]	[illegible]	[illegible]	[illegible]	[illegible]	[illegible]	[illegible]	[illegible]	[illegible]	[illegible]	[illegible]	[illegible]
1879, ...	[illegible]	[illegible]	[illegible]	[illegible]	[illegible]	[illegible]	[illegible]	[illegible]	[illegible]	[illegible]	[illegible]	[illegible]	[illegible]
1880, ...	[illegible]	[illegible]	[illegible]	[illegible]	[illegible]	[illegible]	[illegible]	[illegible]	[illegible]	[illegible]	[illegible]	[illegible]	[illegible]
1881, ...	[illegible]	[illegible]	[illegible]	[illegible]	[illegible]	[illegible]	[illegible]	[illegible]	[illegible]	[illegible]	[illegible]	[illegible]	[illegible]
1882, ...	[illegible]	[illegible]	[illegible]	[illegible]	[illegible]	[illegible]	[illegible]	[illegible]	[illegible]	[illegible]	[illegible]	[illegible]	[illegible]
1883, ...	[illegible]	[illegible]	[illegible]	[illegible]	[illegible]	[illegible]	[illegible]	[illegible]	[illegible]	[illegible]	[illegible]	[illegible]	[illegible]
1884, ...	[illegible]	[illegible]	[illegible]	[illegible]	[illegible]	[illegible]	[illegible]	[illegible]	[illegible]	[illegible]	[illegible]	[illegible]	[illegible]
1885, ...	[illegible]	[illegible]	[illegible]	[illegible]	[illegible]	[illegible]	[illegible]	[illegible]	[illegible]	[illegible]	[illegible]	[illegible]	[illegible]
1886, ...	[illegible]	[illegible]	[illegible]	[illegible]	[illegible]	[illegible]	[illegible]	[illegible]	[illegible]	[illegible]	[illegible]	[illegible]	[illegible]
1887, ...	[illegible]	[illegible]	[illegible]	[illegible]	[illegible]	[illegible]	[illegible]	[illegible]	[illegible]	[illegible]	[illegible]	[illegible]	[illegible]
1888, ...	[illegible]	[illegible]	[illegible]	[illegible]	[illegible]	[illegible]	[illegible]	[illegible]	[illegible]	[illegible]	[illegible]	[illegible]	[illegible]
1889, ...	[illegible]	[illegible]	[illegible]	[illegible]	[illegible]	[illegible]	[illegible]	[illegible]	[illegible]	[illegible]	[illegible]	[illegible]	[illegible]
1890, ...	[illegible]	[illegible]	[illegible]	[illegible]	[illegible]	[illegible]	[illegible]	[illegible]	[illegible]	[illegible]	[illegible]	[illegible]	[illegible]
Average, .	[illegible]	[illegible]	[illegible]	[illegible]	[illegible]	[illegible]	[illegible]	[illegible]	[illegible]	[illegible]	[illegible]	[illegible]	[illegible]
1891, ...	[illegible]	[illegible]	[illegible]	[illegible]	[illegible]	[illegible]	[illegible]	[illegible]	[illegible]	[illegible]	[illegible]	[illegible]	[illegible]

POPULATION OF IRELAND (including Army, Navy, and Merchant Seamen on shore and in port) *estimated* to the middle of each of the Years 1801 to 1891, inclusive:—

Middle of the Year.	Estimated Population.			Middle of the Year.	Estimated Population.			Middle of the Year.	Estimated Population.		
	Persons.	Males.	Females.		Persons.	Males.	Females.		Persons.	Males.	Females.
[illegible]	[illegible]	[illegible]	[illegible]	[illegible]	[illegible]	[illegible]	[illegible]	[illegible]	[illegible]	[illegible]	[illegible]
[illegible]	[illegible]	[illegible]	[illegible]	[illegible]	[illegible]	[illegible]	[illegible]	[illegible]	[illegible]	[illegible]	[illegible]
[illegible]	[illegible]	[illegible]	[illegible]	[illegible]	[illegible]	[illegible]	[illegible]	[illegible]	[illegible]	[illegible]	[illegible]
[illegible]	[illegible]	[illegible]	[illegible]	[illegible]	[illegible]	[illegible]	[illegible]	[illegible]	[illegible]	[illegible]	[illegible]
[illegible]	[illegible]	[illegible]	[illegible]	[illegible]	[illegible]	[illegible]	[illegible]	[illegible]	[illegible]	[illegible]	[illegible]
[illegible]	[illegible]	[illegible]	[illegible]	[illegible]	[illegible]	[illegible]	[illegible]	[illegible]	[illegible]	[illegible]	[illegible]
[illegible]	[illegible]	[illegible]	[illegible]	[illegible]	[illegible]	[illegible]	[illegible]	[illegible]	[illegible]	[illegible]	[illegible]
[illegible]	[illegible]	[illegible]	[illegible]	[illegible]	[illegible]	[illegible]	[illegible]	[illegible]	[illegible]	[illegible]	[illegible]
[illegible]	[illegible]	[illegible]	[illegible]	[illegible]	[illegible]	[illegible]	[illegible]	[illegible]	[illegible]	[illegible]	[illegible]
[illegible]	[illegible]	[illegible]	[illegible]	[illegible]	[illegible]	[illegible]	[illegible]	[illegible]	[illegible]	[illegible]	[illegible]
[illegible]	[illegible]	[illegible]	[illegible]	[illegible]	[illegible]	[illegible]	[illegible]	[illegible]	[illegible]	[illegible]	[illegible]
[illegible]	[illegible]	[illegible]	[illegible]	[illegible]	[illegible]	[illegible]	[illegible]	[illegible]	[illegible]	[illegible]	[illegible]
[illegible]	[illegible]	[illegible]	[illegible]	[illegible]	[illegible]	[illegible]	[illegible]	[illegible]	[illegible]	[illegible]	[illegible]
[illegible]	[illegible]	[illegible]	[illegible]	[illegible]	[illegible]	[illegible]	[illegible]	[illegible]	[illegible]	[illegible]	[illegible]
[illegible]	[illegible]	[illegible]	[illegible]	[illegible]	[illegible]	[illegible]	[illegible]	[illegible]	[illegible]	[illegible]	[illegible]
[illegible]	[illegible]	[illegible]	[illegible]	[illegible]	[illegible]	[illegible]	[illegible]	[illegible]	[illegible]	[illegible]	[illegible]
[illegible]	[illegible]	[illegible]	[illegible]	[illegible]	[illegible]	[illegible]	[illegible]	[illegible]	[illegible]	[illegible]	[illegible]
[illegible]	[illegible]	[illegible]	[illegible]	[illegible]	[illegible]	[illegible]	[illegible]	[illegible]	[illegible]	[illegible]	[illegible]
[illegible]	[illegible]	[illegible]	[illegible]	[illegible]	[illegible]	[illegible]	[illegible]	[illegible]	[illegible]	[illegible]	[illegible]
[illegible]	[illegible]	[illegible]	[illegible]	[illegible]	[illegible]	[illegible]	[illegible]	[illegible]	[illegible]	[illegible]	[illegible]
[illegible]	[illegible]	[illegible]	[illegible]	[illegible]	[illegible]	[illegible]	[illegible]	[illegible]	[illegible]	[illegible]	[illegible]
[illegible]	[illegible]	[illegible]	[illegible]	[illegible]	[illegible]	[illegible]	[illegible]	[illegible]	[illegible]	[illegible]	[illegible]
[illegible]	[illegible]	[illegible]	[illegible]	[illegible]	[illegible]	[illegible]	[illegible]	[illegible]	[illegible]	[illegible]	[illegible]
[illegible]	[illegible]	[illegible]	[illegible]	[illegible]	[illegible]	[illegible]	[illegible]	[illegible]	[illegible]	[illegible]	[illegible]
[illegible]	[illegible]	[illegible]	[illegible]	[illegible]	[illegible]	[illegible]	[illegible]	[illegible]	[illegible]	[illegible]	[illegible]
[illegible]	[illegible]	[illegible]	[illegible]	[illegible]	[illegible]	[illegible]	[illegible]	[illegible]	[illegible]	[illegible]	[illegible]
[illegible]	[illegible]	[illegible]	[illegible]	[illegible]	[illegible]	[illegible]	[illegible]	[illegible]	[illegible]	[illegible]	[illegible]
[illegible]	[illegible]	[illegible]	[illegible]	[illegible]	[illegible]	[illegible]	[illegible]	[illegible]	[illegible]	[illegible]	[illegible]
[illegible]	[illegible]	[illegible]	[illegible]	[illegible]	[illegible]	[illegible]	[illegible]	[illegible]	[illegible]	[illegible]	[illegible]
[illegible]	[illegible]	[illegible]	[illegible]	[illegible]	[illegible]	[illegible]	[illegible]				
[illegible]	[illegible]	[illegible]	[illegible]	[illegible]	[illegible]	[illegible]	[illegible]				

NOTE.—[illegible]

AGES of the POPULATION in IRELAND according to the Census Returns of 1861, 1871, 1881, and 1891.

Periods.	Sexes.	Ages—Years.														Total.
		Under 1.	1 and under 5.	5 and under 10.	10 and under 15.	15 and under 20.	20 and under 25.	25 and under 35.	35 and under 45.	45 and under 55.	55 and under 65.	65 and under 75.	75 and under 85.	85 and under 95.	95 and up.	
[illegible]	Males	[illegible]	[illegible]	[illegible]	[illegible]	[illegible]	[illegible]	[illegible]	[illegible]	[illegible]	[illegible]	[illegible]	[illegible]	[illegible]	[illegible]	[illegible]
	Females	[illegible]	[illegible]	[illegible]	[illegible]	[illegible]	[illegible]	[illegible]	[illegible]	[illegible]	[illegible]	[illegible]	[illegible]	[illegible]	[illegible]	[illegible]
	Total	[illegible]	[illegible]	[illegible]	[illegible]	[illegible]	[illegible]	[illegible]	[illegible]	[illegible]	[illegible]	[illegible]	[illegible]	[illegible]	[illegible]	[illegible]
[illegible]	Males	[illegible]	[illegible]	[illegible]	[illegible]	[illegible]	[illegible]	[illegible]	[illegible]	[illegible]	[illegible]	[illegible]	[illegible]	[illegible]	[illegible]	[illegible]
	Females	[illegible]	[illegible]	[illegible]	[illegible]	[illegible]	[illegible]	[illegible]	[illegible]	[illegible]	[illegible]	[illegible]	[illegible]	[illegible]	[illegible]	[illegible]
	Total	[illegible]	[illegible]	[illegible]	[illegible]	[illegible]	[illegible]	[illegible]	[illegible]	[illegible]	[illegible]	[illegible]	[illegible]	[illegible]	[illegible]	[illegible]
[illegible]	Males	[illegible]	[illegible]	[illegible]	[illegible]	[illegible]	[illegible]	[illegible]	[illegible]	[illegible]	[illegible]	[illegible]	[illegible]	[illegible]	[illegible]	[illegible]
	Females	[illegible]	[illegible]	[illegible]	[illegible]	[illegible]	[illegible]	[illegible]	[illegible]	[illegible]	[illegible]	[illegible]	[illegible]	[illegible]	[illegible]	[illegible]
	Total	[illegible]	[illegible]	[illegible]	[illegible]	[illegible]	[illegible]	[illegible]	[illegible]	[illegible]	[illegible]	[illegible]	[illegible]	[illegible]	[illegible]	[illegible]
[illegible]	Males	[illegible]	[illegible]	[illegible]	[illegible]	[illegible]	[illegible]	[illegible]	[illegible]	[illegible]	[illegible]	[illegible]	[illegible]	[illegible]	[illegible]	[illegible]
	Females	[illegible]	[illegible]	[illegible]	[illegible]	[illegible]	[illegible]	[illegible]	[illegible]	[illegible]	[illegible]	[illegible]	[illegible]	[illegible]	[illegible]	[illegible]
	Total	[illegible]	[illegible]	[illegible]	[illegible]	[illegible]	[illegible]	[illegible]	[illegible]	[illegible]	[illegible]	[illegible]	[illegible]	[illegible]	[illegible]	[illegible]

* [illegible]

INDEX TO SUPERINTENDENT REGISTRARS DISTRICTS.

[The following Index furnishes a reference to the *Number* or *Numbers* of each Superintendent Registrar's District in the Tables of Abstracts contained in the Report, in which the numbers run consecutively from 1 to 233.]*

* Thus, the number of Marriages in the [illegible] Superintendent Registrar's District [illegible] by reference to the "Abstract of Marriages" [illegible] Births and Deaths, of Deaths at different ages, &c., will be found by referring to the same Superintendent Registrar's District [illegible] the appropriate Tables.

INDEX TO REGISTRARS' DISTRICTS.

[The Number or Numbers against each Registrar's District in the Third Column refers to the page or pages in which the Total Births, Illegitimate Births, Deaths, &c., in the District during the year are given.]

Cork. No 1.

[illegible]

Registrars' Districts.	Superintendent Registrars' Districts.	Page.	Registrars' Districts.	Superintendent Registrars' Districts.	Page.	Registrars' Districts.	Superintendent Registrars' Districts.	Page.
[illegible]	[illegible]	[illegible]	K.			[illegible]	[illegible]	[illegible]
F.			[illegible]	[illegible]	[illegible]	M.		
[illegible]	[illegible]	[illegible]	[illegible]	[illegible]	[illegible]	[illegible]	[illegible]	[illegible]
G.			[illegible]	[illegible]	[illegible]	N.		
[illegible]	[illegible]	[illegible]	[illegible]	[illegible]	[illegible]	[illegible]	[illegible]	[illegible]
H.			[illegible]	[illegible]	[illegible]	O.		
[illegible]	[illegible]	[illegible]	L.			[illegible]	[illegible]	[illegible]
I.			[illegible]	[illegible]	[illegible]			
[illegible]	[illegible]	[illegible]	[illegible]	[illegible]	[illegible]			
J.			[illegible]	[illegible]	[illegible]			
[illegible]	[illegible]	[illegible]	[illegible]	[illegible]	[illegible]			

Registrars' Districts.	Superintendent Registrars' Districts.	Page.	Registrars' Districts.	Superintendent Registrars' Districts.	Page.	Registrars' Districts.	Superintendent Registrars' Districts.	Page.
[illegible]	[illegible]	[illegible]	[illegible]	[illegible]	[illegible]	[illegible]	[illegible]	[illegible]

APPENDIX.

REPORT on the ADMINISTRATION of the LEGAL WORK of the GENERAL REGISTER OFFICE, DUBLIN for the Financial Year 1891–92.

SIR,—I beg to report that the legal work of your Department during the year 1891–92 was administered as follows:—

During the year, in addition to a large number of cases, in which it was found that no proceedings could be taken against the responsible parties, as the legal time for doing so had elapsed, 434 offences against the Registration Acts were reported by Local Officers, and came under investigation in this department. In many of these the defaulters came forward and complied with the requirements of the law, on becoming aware that proceedings against them were in contemplation.

After careful inquiry into the circumstances and examination of the evidence available, in 164 cases prosecutions were directed against the offenders. In 69 of these the parties were convicted and punished; in 92 cases the proceedings were abandoned, the parties (in most cases) paying the costs of court and complying with the law, and in 3 cases the summonses were dismissed.

The cases dealt with included the following offences:—Neglect to register births; neglect to register deaths; neglect to furnish certificates of marriage; failure of coroner to furnish certificate of inquest; giving false information as to age at death, as to the cause of death, and as to duration of illness previous to death; giving false information as to births, viz., registering illegitimate children as legitimate, and misrepresenting date of birth; omitting to send notification of a burial to the Registrar.

The following are the details in a few of these cases:—

C. P. was prosecuted at the Metropolitan Police Court for wilfully giving false information to the Registrar of South City No. 1 District, as to the age of her child, when registering its death, with the view of obtaining, from certain Societies, moneys in excess of the amount prescribed by the Friendly Societies' Acts. She was convicted, and fined £3 or six weeks' imprisonment.

M. B. was prosecuted at Killinick Petty Sessions for having registered with the Registrar of Broadway District, an illegitimate child as legitimate. She was convicted and fined with costs.

M. D. was prosecuted at Emyvale Petty Sessions, as Caretaker of a Burial Ground, for neglecting to furnish to the Registrar of Glaslough District the notification of a burial required by sec. 17 of the 43 and 44 Vic., cap. 13. She was convicted and fined with costs.

P. M. was prosecuted at Belfast Petty Sessions for neglecting to forward to the Registrar of Belfast No. 6 District a certificate of his marriage, in accordance with sec. 11 of the 26 & 27 Vic., cap. 90. He was convicted and fined with costs.

J. M. was prosecuted at Derrygonnelly Petty Sessions by the Registrar of Ely District for neglecting to register a death in due time. He was convicted and fined with costs.

P. M. and J. G. were prosecuted at Cong Petty Sessions by the Registrar of the District for neglecting to register the births of their children. They were convicted and fined with costs.

Notwithstanding the vigorous measures adopted by the department for the punishment of offenders, several Registrars report that they believe false information is frequently given to them especially in cases of deaths.

The *modus operandi* in one class of offences appears to be as follows: when a member of a family is entered in a Friendly Society or Industrial Assurance Company, the age is frequently given as much below the real age in order to reduce the amount of the premium payable. After a time the person dies, and then the registry is effected so as to suit the statements previously made to the Society or Company.

It sometimes happens, however, that the informant overlooks the fact that the age in the register is to correspond with the age in the policy, and, in order to obtain the money, another nefarious proceeding is then necessary, viz., the making a declaration before a magistrate, altering the age correctly given in the register to an incorrect age, to agree with the age in the policy.

The greatest pains have been taken to obtain evidence in these cases to convict the offenders, but in many of them, I regret to state, for want of documentary proof of age, the case had to be abandoned, though no reasonable doubt existed that the offence had been committed.

The absence of reliable records of birth or baptism in the case of old persons, makes it exceedingly difficult to deal with them. In several cases the age of a deceased person has been successfully proved from a marriage register, giving the age at time of marriage, and in other cases the age inserted or proposed to be inserted in the register has been proved to be impossible from the records of the births or baptisms of the children of the deceased.

The Department is greatly indebted to the Inspector-General of Royal Irish Constabulary and the Commissioner of Metropolitan Police for their kind assistance in investigating these numerous and varied criminal cases.

In addition to the above mentioned, there were a number of cases during the year in which proceedings were taken under the 26 & 27 Vic., cap. 90, before the magistrates at Petty Sessions for corrections in marriage registers, the summonses in these cases being issued at the instance of local Registration Officers.

A sum of £130 was provided in the estimate to meet legal charges. The total cost of the legal service of the Department during the year was £79 8s. 6d., of which sum £11 13s. 4d. was paid for local professional assistance and £16 3s. 0d. for mileage to the Registrars.

I am, Sir,

Your obedient servant,

R. E. Matheson,

Barrister-at-Law.

Thomas W. Grimshaw, Esq., M.D.,

Registrar-General.

Dublin Castle,

3rd January, 1892.

Sir,

I have to acknowledge the receipt of your letter of the 31st ult., forwarding, for submission to His Excellency the Lord Lieutenant, the Annual Report on Marriages, Births, and Deaths in Ireland for the year 1891.

I am, Sir,

Your obedient Servant,

W. S. B. KAYE.

The Registrar-General,

Charlemont House,

Rutland Square.

www.ingramcontent.com/pod-product-compliance
Lightning Source LLC
Chambersburg PA
CBHW030839270326
41928CB00007B/1122
* 9 7 8 3 7 4 2 8 1 1 1 0 3 *